Get the eBook FREE!
(PDF, ePub, Kindle, and liveBook all included)

We believe that once you buy a book from us, you should be able to read it in any format we have available. To get electronic versions of this book at no additional cost to you, purchase and then register this book at the Manning website.

Go to https://www.manning.com/freebook and follow the instructions to complete your pBook registration.

That's it!
Thanks from Manning!

How to Lead in Data Science

How to Lead in Data Science

JIKE CHONG
YUE CATHY CHANG
FOREWORD BY BEN LORICA

MANNING
SHELTER ISLAND

Manning Publications Co.
20 Baldwin Road
PO Box 761
Shelter Island, NY 11964

Development editor:	Karen Miller
Review editor:	Ivan Martinović
Production editor:	Andy Marinkovich
Copy editor:	Christian Berk
Proofreader:	Keri Hales
Typesetter:	Gordan Salinovic
Cover designer:	Marija Tudor

ISBN 9781617298899

Printed in the United States of America

To our parents,
for inspiring us to work hard, dive deep, and give back.

To our readers,
for investing the time to read this book. Together let us accelerate the way
humanity understands and improves our world.

To each other,
for all the debates, encouragement, and support throughout this journey.

brief contents

contents

foreword

Over the past decade, I chaired or co-chaired more than 40 premier data and AI conferences internationally. It has been amazing to witness the evolution and impact of analytics, data science, and machine learning worldwide. Data science continues to be one of the fastest-growing job functions in the industry today. When I was the chief data scientist of O'Reilly Media, study after study we conducted confirmed that companies continue to invest in data infrastructure, data science, and machine learning. We also found the companies that excel in using data science and machine learning were the ones that invested in foundational technologies and used those tools to expand their capabilities gradually, one use case at a time.

While much of what we read about pertains to tools or breakthroughs in models, the reality is that organizational issues pose some of the major bottlenecks within most companies. The critical ingredient is recognizing organizational excellence in people, culture, and structure. If you don't have the right people and organizational structure in place, you will still underperform competitors that do.

As demand for data scientists continues to grow and training programs proliferate, I am frequently asked for advice. Novices ask how they can join the ranks of data scientists, and more experienced data scientists ask for pointers on how they can take their careers to the next level.

Unfortunately, information and advice on how to remain relevant and impactful throughout a data science career are hard to come by. Most of the career-related literature focuses on embarking on the journey—where to study, what skills to learn, and how to interview for and land your first job. There is very little guidance for how employed data scientists can continue to succeed and excel in this career.

How to Lead in Data Science is an essential field guide for data scientists at different stages of their careers as an individual leader, such as a tech lead, staff, principal, or distinguished data scientist, or as a management leader, such as a manager, director, or executive of data science. The book is for data scientists who want to take their careers to the next level. It also provides guidance on tools and techniques in the context of helping data scientists increase their positive impact in business and in society.

I've known the authors, Jike and Cathy, for many years. Together, they bring a diverse set of operating experiences from a broad range of organizations, including public and private companies, as well as consultancy practices. I have seen them teach the material in this book in training courses for data scientists from diverse backgrounds and industries. Their courses are always among the most popular and well received in the conferences I've chaired.

This book is the missing field guide for data scientists looking to advance their careers. Readers at various stages of their careers will find it worthwhile to come back and revisit the book as they grow. It is a book I plan to recommend to data scientists from hereon. I hope it inspires more discussions and literature on this topic. Data scientists and those who work with them will need this book in the years to come!

—BEN LORICA

Ben Lorica is principal writer at GradientFlow.com; co-chair of the NLP Summit and Ray Summit; the former chief data scientist and program chair at O'Reilly Media; the host and organizer of thedataexchange.media podcast; and has been an advisor at many startups and organizations, including Databricks, Anyscale, and Faculty.ai.

preface

As a leader in the practice of data science, you can scale your data, algorithms, and team, but are you scaling you? What is leadership? How are you amplifying your capabilities to produce a more significant impact than what can be achieved as an individual? Are you influencing, nurturing, directing, and inspiring projects and people around you?

These are questions many data science practitioners grapple with as they struggle to advance their careers in this high-growth, fast-evolving field. Most practitioners work in companies with fewer than 10 data scientists, holding broad responsibilities to lead projects, interfacing with cross-functional partners, crafting roadmaps, and influencing executives. Their roles are often not clearly defined and come with unrealistic expectations.

At the same time, there are over 150,000 data scientists in this field worldwide, and that number is growing at 37% per year [1]. Companies are clamoring for leadership talent to lead projects, nurture teams, direct functions, and inspire industries.

Although there are blogs, podcasts, and platforms, such as Meetups and Clubhouse rooms, dedicated to this area, no comprehensive practical field guide has existed to address career evolution in data science . . . until now.

At the urging of friends and colleagues, many of whom we have nurtured from individual contributors to data science leaders, and later, to heads of organizations with as many as 70 data scientists, we authored this book to share what we have learned over the past decade. The insights included in this book come from our own experience founding, growing, and advising data science functions in public and private companies.

We also interviewed dozens of successful data science leaders and highlighted their best practices.

While designing this guide, we were pleased to find that the fundamentals of self-cultivation align with some well-known frameworks. What are the odds that the fundamentals of building skill sets, taking responsibilities, and producing impact in the world have existed for thousands of years? In this book, we recognize leadership stages such as cultivating individual leadership, nurturing a team, directing a function, and inspiring an industry that are based on Confucius's teachings [2]. Within each leadership stage, we discuss the hard skills we call capabilities and soft psychosocial skills we call virtues. Virtues are the necessary character traits that enable practitioners to obtain happiness and well-being, inspired by the Greek philosopher Aristotle [3]. The career stages as well as the capabilities and virtues are illustrated in figure 1.

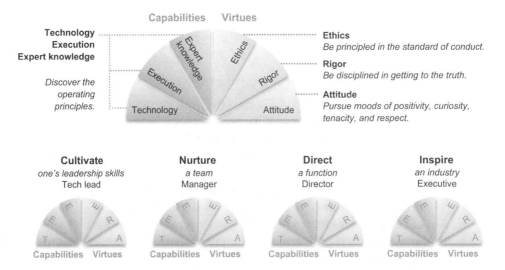

Figure 1   Distinct capabilities and virtues are required in each stage of your career growth.

These time-tested frameworks provide coverage for mapping the specific transformative insights, personal experiences, and industry examples of leading in data science. You can use it to build your leadership confidence by recognizing your strengths, uncovering blind spots, discovering opportunities for new practices, and leveraging your team and your organization to produce a more significant impact.

In this book, we illustrate aspirational goals in data science capabilities and virtues. You can reference these topics to guide your team members' professional development, yet we caution against using them as reasons to hold back promotions. If a team member has demonstrated capabilities and virtues in some areas and potential in others, they could be ready for more responsibilities, and, potentially, a promotion at your company.

The best practices, processes, and advice apply to situations faced by technical leaders in individual contributor roles at the staff, principal, and distinguished data scientist levels as well as people-managing leaders at the manager, director, and executive levels. These are illustrated on this book's inside back cover, as they will make much more sense after you read about them.

To help you recognize situations in which to apply these best practices, processes, and advice, we include seven real-life scenarios faced by data science practitioners, ranging from fresh graduates to experienced executives. In each case, we share a situation, diagnose causes, and propose solutions, so you can reflect on how you might handle these situations when you face them.

We designed this book to be a companion for your career growth for years to come. If you find the book helpful when you encounter challenging situations, please let us know. And remember to share your learnings on social media!

It is a privilege for us to play a part in inspiring you to do the best work of your career and maximizing your potential to make a more significant positive impact in the world with data science!

—JIKE CHONG AND YUE CATHY CHANG

References

[1] "2020 emerging jobs report." LinkedIn. https://business.linkedin.com/content/dam/me/business/en-us/talent-solutions/emerging-jobs-report/Emerging_Jobs_Report_U.S._FINAL.pdf

[2] Da Xue (大学). "The great learning." Chinese Text Project. https://ctext.org/liji/da-xue/ens

[3] Aristotle, *Nicomachean Ethics*. R. Bartlett and S. Collins, Transl. Chicago, IL, USA: University of Chicago Press, 2011.

acknowledgments

First, we would like to thank our parents, Xuetong Zheng, Peiji Chong, Yuexian Hou, and Xiubao Chang, for their support and sacrifices, which gave us the opportunity to pursue an education at Carnegie Mellon University. That opportunity allowed us to enter the world of computer science and engineering, and be partners in projects, life, and this book.

We would like to acknowledge the staff at Manning Publications for guiding us through this process. Thank you especially to our acquisitions editor, Brian Sawyer, for believing in this book early on; our developmental editor, Karen Miller, for her knowledgeable professional perspectives; and Marjan Bace for publishing this book.

Thank you to all those who reviewed the proposal, concepts, and the manuscript at various points and provided invaluable ideas and detailed feedback: Eric Colson, Monica Rogati, Gahl Berkooz, Noahh Gerard, Bruce Lawler, Anjali Samani, Camille Fournier, the late Tom Fawcett, and all the reviewers: Al Krinker, Alex Chittock, Andres Damian Sacco, Brian Cocolicchio, Clemens Baader, Deepak Raghavan, Erin Shelby, Gary Bake, Igor Karp, James Black, Jesús A. Juárez-Guerrero, Krzysztof Jędrzejewski, Marc Paradis, Michael Petrey, Sergio Govoni, Simon Tschöke, Stefano Ongarello, Vishwesh Ravi Shrimali, and Walter Alexander Mata López. Your insightful feedback has greatly clarified our thinking, and in turn, will benefit generations of data science practitioners.

Finally, we would like to thank the many data leaders we have connected with in the context of this book, including Monica Rogati, Eric Colson, Michael Li, Gahl Berkooz, Ben Lorica, Babak Hodjat, Wenjing Zhang, Jeremy Greene, Robin Glinton,

Renjie Li, Jesse Bridgewater, Lingyun Gu, Vikas Sabnani, Yury Markovsky, Pardis Noorzad, Joy Zhang, Datong Chen, Huifang Qin, Doug Gray, Jing Conan Wang, Ling Chen, Rajiv Bhan, Harry Shah, Kelvin Lwin, Chris Geissler, Sean Stauth, Alejandro Herrera, Brad Allen, Colin Higgins, Anjali Samani, and many, many more. Thank you for sharing your wisdom in the practice. Your leadership experiences have informed many of the scenarios in the book and have helped us organize the diverse set of capabilities and virtues in this book. Together we can make a difference in data practitioners' careers in this evolving field of data science!

about this book

How to Lead in Data Science is written by practitioners for practitioners to help you produce a more significant impact as you advance a career in data science. The book is developed as a field guide to highlight the hard capabilities and soft psychosocial virtues for you to cultivate at various leadership levels over a crucial career advancement span of 5 to 15 years.

These capabilities and virtues apply to people-managing leaders as well as technical leaders in individual contributor roles. You can use the capabilities to produce outsized impact with your technical skills, execution capabilities, and industry domain insights. At the same time, you can use the virtues to earn trust and build relationships with customers and colleagues with your principled ethics, rigorous approaches, and powerfully positive attitudes. The book is structured to help you identify your strengths, discover your blind spots, and craft plans to adopt best practices and effective processes. When you continue to refer to this book as you advance in your career at various stages, we consider the book's mission accomplished!

Who should read this book

This book is written for data practitioners with titles such as data scientist, data analyst, data engineer, data strategist, data product manager, machine learning engineer, AI developer, and AI architect, as well as managers, directors, and executives of practitioners with these titles. Many practitioners work in companies with fewer than 10 data scientists, holding broad responsibilities to lead projects, interfacing with cross-functional partners, crafting roadmaps, and influencing executives. Their roles are often not clearly defined and come with unrealistic expectations. This book clarifies their roles and helps to align manager and partner expectations.

Data practitioners can also use this book to locate where they are in their careers, better understand managers' concerns, and clarify what is reasonable to delegate to team members. Executives responsible for data teams, talent acquisition professionals, business function leaders partnering with data science, sales representatives looking to sell to data science leaders, and anybody who works with the data science function can use this book to understand how data scientists think and work. This book can help you build compassion toward the challenges and trade-offs data science practitioners face daily.

How this book is organized

This book is organized as a practical stage-by-stage field guide to your career. Chapter 1 introduces the hard capabilities and soft psychosocial virtues required to be effective in data science. This chapter presents four career stages and highlights seven real-life scenarios faced by data science practitioners. Some of these may be directly relevant to you. Next are parts 1–5, with 1–4 focusing on individual, team, function, and industry leadership stages, and part 5 focusing on how you can apply your analytical rigor to career development.

Part 1 focuses on the role of the data science tech lead, who can use their power of influence to overcome limitations as individuals to produce greater impact by leading teammates to execute projects successfully:

- Chapter 2 discusses the tech lead capabilities of guiding technology choices, making project execution trade-offs, and applying business knowledge and contexts.
- Chapter 3 discusses the tech lead virtues of practicing ethical and rigorous habitual actions with a powerfully positive attitude to influence teammates and partners.

Part 2 focuses on the role of the data science manager or the staff data scientist. Executives depend on them to nurture productive teams and execute business priorities. Team members depend on managers and staff data scientists to empower them to do the best work of their careers:

- Chapter 4 discusses the team leadership capabilities of nurturing the team to deliver results, promoting a portfolio of technical expertise in the team, and increasing the team's potential to capture business opportunities.
- Chapter 5 discusses the team leadership virtues of nurturing team members' habits with data science best practices through coaching, mentoring, and advising.

Part 3 focuses on the role of the data science director, or the principal data scientist, to provide clarity of focus and prioritization of function-level concerns, such as crafting effective roadmaps for producing more significant impact over a longer horizon of time, while avoiding systematic pitfalls:

- Chapter 6 discusses function leadership capabilities, which are demonstrated by architecting roadmaps, championing initiatives, and consistently executing roadmaps for business impact.
- Chapter 7 discusses the function leadership virtues of shaping the culture of the data science function, while recognizing diversity, practicing inclusion, and nurturing belonging within teams.

Part 4 focuses on the role of the data science executive or distinguished data scientist, who is expected to exert influence beyond the company by producing highly valued accomplishments to demonstrate impacts from data science to inspire an industry. In this role, you are expected to operate with a sense of calm confidence that leads to thoughtful and timely planning and actions, with your executive presence centered on bringing out the best in those in your organization:

- Chapter 8 discusses the industry leadership capabilities of driving a company's overall business strategy and articulating its competitiveness within its industry.
- Chapter 9 discusses the industry leadership virtues of demonstrating executive presence and inspiring an industry to responsibly use data to produce business impacts.

Part 5 focuses on applying your analytical rigor to the process of developing your career. This includes the LOOP areas of landscape, organization, opportunity, and practice. We highlight the *why*, *what*, and *how* of data science's increasing importance and speculate on the future by examining evolving trends:

- Chapter 10 discusses the technology landscape for new architectures and practices, maps out organizational structures to navigate, considers four dimensions for evaluating career moves, and shares potential career directions for your next roles.
- Chapter 11 discusses four reasons leadership in data science is increasingly important and summarizes the learning for advancing a career in data science.

Self-assessment and development focus

At the end of each chapter, we provide a one-page checklist of learning points for self-assessment and clarifying your development focus. To best utilize the book, we recommend a four-step process to build your confidence, discover your blind spots, recognize the resources available to you around your organization, and practice your learning:

1 *Finding your strengths*—You can use the *self-assessment* and *development focus* sections at the end of each chapter (chapters 2–9) to recognize your leadership strength areas. This practice provides you with a narrative to help build a trustworthy identity, set examples for others, and communicate career accomplishments.

2   *Identifying your opportunities*—Some areas described in this book may be blind spots for you. These are opportunities in which you can recognize, learn, and adopt new practices. When you practice these new learnings in real-world situations, they can become effective habits and even part of your positive identity.

3   *Leveraging your environment*—In most situations, your role is within a larger organization, where there are resources you can leverage within your team or across functions to amplify your strengths. Understanding who to make requests to, what requests to make, and how to make them are essential leadership skills.

4   *Putting learning into practice*—With clear goals identified in the first three steps, the fourth step is to line up a roadmap and put your learning into practice one concept at a time. As with sprint planning, you can specify a one- to three-week cadence to set goals and schedule a time to check back and evaluate progress.

There can be many concepts to learn and practice at each stage of career development. If you are working on something each week, you will make concrete progress on your career development.

Case studies

In chapter 1, we highlight seven real-life scenarios faced by data science practitioners at various career stages. Some of these may be directly relevant to you and where you are in your career.

Throughout the book, we refer to these seven scenarios and illustrate how the concepts apply. An example is shown in table 1. You can reflect on these scenarios to see if you might be in similar situations, learn from their strengths, and avoid their blind spots. You can also observe whether the support they seek is also available to you.

Table 1   Sample case: How Jennifer can use this book to launch her career

Case	Situation	Useful concepts (section references)
Jennifer *Tech lead*	Jennifer is good at cross-team communication, but her teammates feel micro-managed and are unhappy about a lot of busywork. It turns out that she needs to improve her skills in communicating change and build trust with members of the team.	**Strengths:** • Prioritizing and managing projects (2.2.1) • Leading in incident response (3.3.2) • Taking responsibility for results (3.2.3) **Opportunities:** • Communicating change effectively (3.1.2) • Trusting the team to execute (5.3.2) • Imparting knowledge confidently (3.1.3) **Support requests:** • Nurturing positivity despite failures in the team (3.3.1) • Seeking career coaching from a manager (5.1.1)

Gem insights

There are 101 concepts we call out with a diamond icon throughout the book. These are *gem insights*, which highlight ideas many readers will find helpful. Here is an example.

028

The key difference between intelligence and wisdom is that intelligence is the ability to make good decisions with complete information, while wisdom is the ability to make good decisions with incomplete information.

We hope many of these resonate with you. If so, feel free to share them on social media. When sharing, please include their sequence number to make it easier for others to locate the full context behind the gem insights in this book. A reference to this book would be appreciated.

liveBook discussion forum

Purchase of *How to Lead in Data Science* includes free access to a private web forum run by Manning Publications where you can make comments about the book, ask technical questions, and receive help from the author and from other users. To access the forum, go to https://livebook.manning.com/#!/book/how-to-lead-in-data-science/discussion. You can also learn more about Manning's forums and the rules of conduct at https://livebook.manning.com/#!/discussion.

Manning's commitment to readers is to provide a venue where a meaningful dialogue between individual readers and between readers and the author can take place. It is not a commitment to any specific amount of participation on the part of the author, whose contribution to the forum remains voluntary (and unpaid). Feel free to ask challenging questions to get our attention! The forum and the archives of previous discussions will be accessible from the publisher's website as long as the book is in print.

about the authors

 **DR. JIKE CHONG** is an executive who nurtures teams and crafts cultures to produce billion-dollar business impact. He built and grew multiple high-performing data functions in public and private companies and nurtured dozens of ambitious individual contributor data scientists into leaders; some have gone on to lead teams of more than 70 data scientists.

As a key executive who took Yiren Digital Ltd public on the NYSE, Jike built and led the YRD data team from the ground up, tackled customer churn, and prevented US$30M a year in fraud loss, which is equivalent to the profit from over US$1 billion in extended loans. He also expanded and led the data team as the chief data scientist at Acorns, helping everyday Americans start saving and investing for a more resilient financial future. In addition, Jike advised the Obama administration on using data science to reduce unemployment while serving as the head of data science at Simply Hired; designed and executed a project predicting venture investment risks at Silver Lake; and led the hiring marketplace data science team at LinkedIn, serving a business line with US$4 billion a year in revenue.

Jike designed, developed, and taught a graduate-level Machine Learning for Internet Finance course at Tsinghua University to help prepare more talent for applying machine learning to financial wellness and give back to the community. He also established and co-directed the CUDA Research Center and CUDA Teaching Center at Carnegie Mellon University, where he created and taught a graduate-level course on using highly parallel computing platforms to accelerate key algorithms in machine learning as an adjunct professor and PhD advisor.

Jike received his BS and MS degrees in electrical and computer engineering from Carnegie Mellon University and a PhD in electrical engineering and computer science from the University of California, Berkeley. He has authored 11 patents (six granted, five pending).

 **YUE CATHY CHANG** is an executive recognized for thought leadership and execution in digital transformation. She is passionate about addressing business challenges and often finds herself and her team "parachuting" into situations to tackle challenging and meaningful data needs. Cathy has led teams and functions at blue-chip enterprises as well as startups across financial services and high-tech industries. She is currently an AVP in banking and financial services at an American multinational technology corporation.

Cathy built and ran the financial services and insurance practice at Silicon Valley Data Science before the company's successful conversion to a global consumer technology company. She was the first employee hired by the CEO at venture-funded software startup Rocana (acquired by Splunk). Cathy also worked closely with and represented the CEO of FeedZai to lead the establishment of FeedZai US and transformed the company's focus from general-purpose real-time data analytics to payment processing fraud prevention targeting the financial services sector.

Cathy is a member of the Wall Street Women's Alliance Connect program and a proposal consultant for NASA JPL. She previously co-founded TutumGene, a genome editing technology company aiming to accelerate cures for illnesses, and authored "AI Meets Genomics: Genetics and Genome Editing Revolutionize Medicine" for executive briefings at an O'Reilly AI conference and a data and AI conference to bridge genome editing with data science and AI.

Cathy holds MS and BS degrees in electrical and computer engineering from Carnegie Mellon University, MBA and MS degrees from MIT, and has authored two granted US patents.

about the cover illustration

The figure on the cover of *How to Lead in Data Science* is captioned "Artisanne de Bordeaux," or artisan of Bordeaux. It is selected to celebrate the resourcefulness of data scientists as artisans of quantitative techniques. The illustration is taken from a collection of dress costumes from various countries by Jacques Grasset de Saint-Sauveur (1757–1810), titled *Costumes de Différents Pays,* published in France in 1797. Each illustration is finely drawn and colored by hand. The rich variety of Grasset de Saint-Sauveur's collection reminds us vividly of how culturally apart the world's towns and regions were just 200 years ago. Isolated from each other, people spoke different dialects and languages. In the streets or in the countryside, it was easy to identify where they lived and what their trade or station in life was just by their dress.

The way we dress has changed since then and the diversity by region, so rich at the time, has faded away. It is now hard to tell apart the inhabitants of different continents, let alone different towns, regions, or countries. Perhaps we have traded cultural diversity for a more varied personal life—certainly for a more varied and fast-paced technological life.

At a time when it is hard to tell one computer book from another, Manning celebrates the inventiveness and initiative of the computer business with book covers based on the rich diversity of regional life of two centuries ago, brought back to life by Grasset de Saint-Sauveur's pictures.

What makes a successful data scientist?

This chapter covers

- Learning what is expected of data scientists
- Examining the challenges of a data scientist's career progression

Data science (DS) is driving a quantitative understanding of the world around us. When the technologies to aggregate large quantities of data are paired with inexpensive computing resources, data scientists can discover patterns through analysis and modeling at scales that were not possible just decades earlier. This quantitative understanding of the world through data is being used to predict the future, drive consumer behavior, and make critical business decisions. The scientific process used to improve our understanding of the world allows us to craft solutions based on testable and repeatable results.

Leadership is the ability to amplify your capabilities by influencing, nurturing, directing, and inspiring people around you to produce more significant impact than what can be achieved as an individual. There are opportunities to lead as a technical individual contributor and as a people manager.

001

Leadership is the ability to amplify your capabilities by influencing, nurturing, directing, and inspiring people around you to produce more significant impact than an individual can achieve. There are opportunities to lead as a technical individual contributor and as a people manager.

Building a DS function in a company to produce industry-leading, data-driven innovation is currently within reach for many nimble organizations. However, 95% of the companies with DS teams have teams of fewer than 10 members [1], [2]. Leadership talent who can lead projects, nurture teams, direct functions, and inspire industries are scarce and in high demand. This book lays out many paths for every data scientist to navigate for the next stages of their career. It also shares the expectations of the roles in great DS teams and organizations.

This chapter introduces the historical and current expectations for data scientists, discusses the hard capabilities and soft psychosocial virtues crucial for data scientists, and shares interview and promotion challenges in case studies. It aims to help you contextualize real opportunities and challenges in the workplace. Let's begin!

1.1 *Data scientist expectations*

In 2010, Drew Conway introduced the well-known data science Venn diagram [3] (figure 1.1), which clarified three pillars of skills required for success in the nascent field of DS: math and statistics knowledge, hacking skills, and substantive expertise. The Venn diagram pushed the DS field forward by crystallizing a unique set of skills in an uncommon group of talent who can unleash extraordinary opportunities for nations, businesses, and organizations.

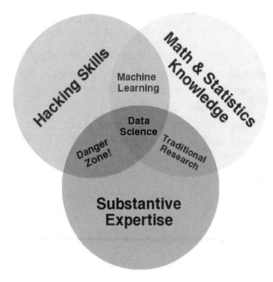

Figure 1.1   Data science Venn diagram from 2010 by Drew Conway

Dr. Conway later founded multiple technology companies, including Datakind, Sum, and Alluvium. Countless blogs and books have since referenced the Venn diagram he introduced. By 2021, over 200,000 DS practitioners worldwide earned the title of *data scientist*. How has the field evolved?

1.1.1 The Venn diagram a decade later

While many of the 2010 original terms and ideas are still valid, there have been updates, debates, and even battles on the topic of the DS Venn diagram; a simple image search of these words would yield scores of variations. The role of a data scientist has significantly expanded since its inception. In 2021, the math and statistical knowledge pillar has broadened to a more general *technology* capability. The technology capability includes tools and frameworks for you to lead projects more effectively. They are used to frame the problem, understand data characteristics, innovate in feature engineering, drive clarity in modeling strategies, and set expectations for success.

The hacking skills pillar has extended to *execution* capabilities and now includes the practices for you to specify projects from vague requirements and prioritize and plan projects while balancing difficult trade-offs, such as speed versus quality, safety versus accountability, and documentation versus progress.

Substantive expertise has expanded to include having *expert knowledge* to clarify project alignment to the organizational vision and mission, account for data source nuances, and navigate structural challenges in the organization to launch projects successfully. While these are the pillars that make a successful data scientist, we find that it is difficult, if not impossible, to locate individuals who are strong in all three dimensions.

For example, a data scientist entering the field of DS with an academic background often has strong capabilities only in the technology dimension. A data scientist with years of experience in the industry can usually pick up execution best practices on the job, including the ability to deploy scalable and maintainable DS solutions. A seasoned DS practitioner with a long tenure in a domain with substantive expert knowledge is rare to find and could be highly valuable to the right employer.

Are these three capabilities, technology, execution, and expert knowledge, sufficient for succeeding in the field of DS today? Let's find out!

1.1.2 What is missing?

As with any practitioners in the field, we had our share of blind spots in building teams. While we diligently assessed candidate capabilities in technology, execution, and expert knowledge, our hiring mishaps showed up when candidates were vetoed in final-round executive interviews or, worse, were hired and then had to be managed out of the team. Many of these failures were summarized as "not a cultural fit." But what does that mean?

What is the *culture* for the DS field that we're looking to "fit"? How is that distinct from an organization's culture or an industry's culture? To analyze these failures, this book expands the interviews, reviews, and promotion criteria of a data scientist to consider not just the *capabilities* but also the *virtues* of a data scientist in pursuing a DS career.

According to the Greek philosopher Aristotle, virtues come from years of practicing being good to benefit oneself as well as society. They are the individual's habitual actions etched into one's character.

Virtues in DS are nurtured. We highlight three dimensions of virtues to nurture into habitual actions that can become pillars in a data scientist's character over time: *ethics, rigor,* and *attitude.*

We have found that when data scientists maintain good practices in these three dimensions, they are more likely to deliver a significant positive impact on their organizations and advance in their careers. On the other hand, when data scientists neglect one or more of these dimensions, they can get into difficult situations in which they must be mentored or, in some cases, that they must be managed out of.

Specifically, we define the three virtues of a data scientist to be:

- *Ethics*—Standards of conduct at work that enable data scientists to avoid unnecessary and self-inflicted breakdowns. There are many aspects of work ethics for data scientists, including data use, project execution, and teamwork.
- *Rigor*—The craftsmanship that generates trust in the results data scientists produce. Rigorous results are repeatable, testable, and discoverable. Rigorous work products can become solid foundations for creating enterprise value.
- *Attitude*—The moods with which a data scientist approaches workplace situations. With positivity and tenacity to work through failures, data scientists should be curious and constructive team players who respect the diverse perspectives in lateral collaborations.

Virtues are meant to be practiced in moderation. Doing too much is just as bad as not doing enough. For example, too much rigor can cause analysis paralysis and indecision. Too little rigor can result in flawed conclusions, leading to adverse outcomes and the loss of trust from executives and business partners.

002

> Virtues are meant to be practiced in moderation. Doing too much is just as bad as not doing enough. For example, too much rigor can cause analysis paralysis and indecision. Too little rigor can result in flawed conclusions, leading to adverse outcomes and loss of trust from executives and business partners.

Putting the virtues of ethics, rigor, and attitude together with the capabilities in technology, execution, and expert knowledge, we have the six fundamental expectation areas for an effective data scientist.

1.1.3 *Understanding ability and motivation: Assessing capabilities and virtues*

With data scientist virtues defined and included in the expectations for success, we have transformed Drew Conway's Venn diagram into a fan with six parts: technology, execution, expert knowledge, ethics, rigor, and attitude—or the *TEE-ERA* fan (figure 1.2). This book is organized to guide you through each of the six dimensions to *TEE* you up to produce more impact at the next level of leadership in the *ERA* of data-driven organizations. We start from individual technical leadership and go on to describe the six dimensions for each level of people leadership for the team, the function, up to the company and industry level in the C-suite.

Capabilities   **Virtues**

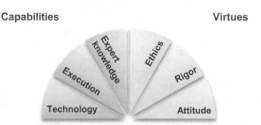

Figure 1.2   The TEE-ERA fan

The *TEE*, in addition to being the acronym of the DS capabilities, also highlights the need for data scientists to be T-shaped talent. The horizontal line in the *T* represents a basic level of capabilities and virtues across the dimensions. The vertical line in the *T* represents depth in at least one dimension of the capabilities and virtues. The *ERA*, in addition to being the acronym of the DS virtues, also highlights the data-driven environment data scientists operate in and the expectations organizations have for them.

A generalist, or a dash-shaped data scientist, with a broad scope of capabilities but no focused specializations can be valuable for an organization, especially in the early days of a new DS team. However, a generalist will find it hard to maintain the respect of a growing DS team unless they develop an identity in at least one area of expertise. Developing depth may be less daunting than you expect, as expert knowledge in a business domain is a highly valued depth dimension that any diligent generalist data scientist can accumulate through their daily work.

A specialist, or an I-shaped data scientist, has in-depth knowledge in one area but incomplete coverage of the capabilities and virtues. A specialist may be able to contribute as a productive member of a large team but will require close management or complementary partnerships with team members as their "crutches" in daily work. A specialist could find it challenging to advance into a leadership position to make or influence more impactful technical or strategic directions.

A data scientist can start as a generalist or a specialist. As you advance in your career, you will find that organizations increasingly value T-shaped talent. These people have a broad set of capabilities and depth of expertise in at least one dimension who can balance technical and business trade-offs, and garner the trust and respect of peers.

TEE-ERA are the capabilities and virtues organizations will increasingly value. As the scope and responsibilities are different for tech leads, managers, directors, and executives, we dedicate chapters to each of these leadership levels. We believe these six dimensions will be essential at each leadership level in the pursuit of an impactful career in DS.

1.2   *Career progression in data science*

According to LinkedIn Talent Insight data, only about 33% of data scientists worked in companies with 30 or more data scientists in 2020 [2]. In large companies, there are often mature processes for interviewing, evaluating, and promoting career growth in DS. These large companies represent only 1% of all companies employing data scientists.

The vast majority (67%) of data scientists work in companies with DS teams of fewer than 30 members, representing 99% of the companies employing data scientists. The career paths for data scientists in this 99% of the companies may not be so clear.

On top of the small sizes of DS teams, companies have organized the DS function in either centralized or distributed structures. The distributed structure further limits potential DS career progression. DS in these distributed teams is often seen as a support function, and data scientists don't have managers with DS expertise to guide their growth.

Even in centralized DS teams, it is often unclear how data scientists can progress in their careers without becoming managers. Figure 1.3 illustrates career progression paths for data scientists on the individual contributor and management career tracks. The main distinctions between career stages are the scope of influence the DS leaders have and the positive impact on their organizations.

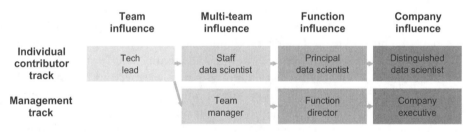

Figure 1.3   Data science leadership career progression paths

This book shares advice, techniques, and quick wins that you can apply to either track. While selected sections, such as section 4.2.1, on building powerful teams under your supervision, apply primarily to the management track, more than 80% of the book also applies to data scientists on the individual contributor track.

As of 2021, very few companies have established a formal DS career track, let alone a DS individual contributor career development track. While the outline of this book will follow the management track, as illustrated in figure 1.4, the majority of this book applies to the individual contributor track as well.

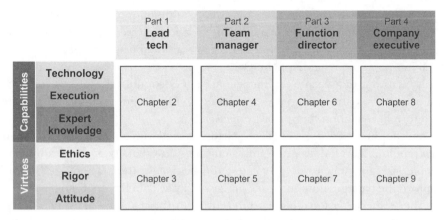

Figure 1.4   The management track laid out in four parts and eight chapters

To help you navigate the material, in section 1.2.1, we present seven real-life scenarios across multiple career stages to illustrate the many career development challenges DS practitioners can face throughout their careers. These scenarios occur in the role, during transitions, in interviews, or around promotion decisions. For each of the scenarios, we provide pointers in section 1.2.2 to the chapters with detailed discussions of what makes a successful DS leader. These scenarios are by no means comprehensive. And many of the DS practitioners' challenges also apply to technical individual contributor leadership roles. Let's take a look at these scenarios!

1.2.1   *Interview and promotion woes*

A data scientist's professional journey can have many different beginnings. Some data scientists come from an analyst background, while others come from software engineering. Still others enter their first DS role after graduating from a master's, doctoral, or professional program.

This book is about leading in DS. We begin our first case with an entry-level data scientist facing interview challenges. We then illustrate challenges faced by tech leads, managers, directors, and executives. Some of the challenges are also experienced by staff and principal and distinguished data scientists pursuing a technical individual contributor leadership career.

Let's examine the scenarios and see how these DS practitioners can improve their situation with techniques discussed in the rest of this book. We reveal the background behind these challenges and action recommendations in section 1.2.2.

CASE 1: ENTERING DS INTERVIEW WOES

Aayana is a graduate student studying computer science at UCLA. Her easygoing nature belies the rigor she gives to her technical work. Since arriving in the US from India 15 months ago, she has already taken several advanced courses in machine learning, worked with two prestigious research groups, and interned at a fast-growing, soon-to-IPO Silicon Valley startup company.

Graduation is coming up in six months. As with many ambitious young professionals, she began interviewing for a full-time position. However, after a couple of interviews, Aayana seemed to have lost her usual confidence and desperately sought help from her mentors. What happened?

It turns out that each DS interview Aayana encountered was quite different. The interview for a natural language processing (NLP) engineering position started with an informal chat about her prior projects.

Another interview, for a FinTech startup, started with a task to write down an entire data pipeline. Aayana was given information on the sparsity of data and the available sample size and was asked to suggest the best algorithm. Then, she was asked to improve the data pipeline to better process the raw data for the final model.

These interviews looked very different from the machine learning course exams she excelled at just weeks earlier. With vastly different starting points for the DS interview processes, she was at a loss about what to expect.

Aayana was confused and frustrated. She did not know whether there was a standard process for DS interviews or if every company and every team would have different hiring criteria.

CASE 2: DATA SCIENTIST PROMOTION CONCERNS

Brian joined Z corporation two years ago as a senior data scientist. He is a capable data scientist with prior work experience at a consulting company and an internet company. Several colleagues who joined around the same time have already been promoted from senior data scientist to tech lead.

Brian has his eye on becoming a technology leader and has set a short-term goal of getting promoted from senior data scientist to tech lead. He brought it up with his manager, Walt, at their recent one-on-one meeting; however, Walt just told him that he is doing all right but needs to deliver more consistently. It is true that Brian has completed the greatest number of projects as a senior data scientist per quarter at Z corporation, though none of those produced spectacular results.

The marketing director whom Brian works with on real-time marketing campaigns almost always wants additional insights after their meetings each week. Brian feels compelled to serve the project stakeholders and provide further insights, which are extra work outside of the original project scope. When this pushed out the start date of a churn prediction project with the customer success department at the end of last quarter, Brian had to rush to complete it. Many other projects Brian has taken on were delayed. Even the ones completed on time compromised quality.

Brian has tried to address the issue by taking the additional work into account in recent project planning cycles. However, when he does that, it just looks like he is not as productive as other teammates or is sandbagging on the schedules and assigning more sprints than necessary for the DS projects he is taking on.

Brian feels trapped in a cycle that goes nowhere. How can he advance his career and become a technology leader at Z corporation?

CASE 3: TECH LEAD CHALLENGES

Jennifer has made two lateral moves and been promoted twice at the company she joined six years ago. Initially joining the company as a business operations analyst, she moved into the business intelligence (BI) function a year later. Three years ago, when the company formed the DS team, she made the leap from BI and turned herself into a data scientist. Jennifer was promoted to senior data scientist a year and a half later; then, three months ago, she was promoted to staff data scientist—also known as a team lead at her company.

While a senior data scientist, Jennifer has already proven to be good at communicating with business partners across the company, including marketing, sales, customer service, and operations. With her knowledge of the business and her tenure at the company, she is also not afraid to push back on project scope creep to deliver her project on time. She is extremely excited to take on new responsibilities as a tech lead.

While the junior DS team members appreciate her mentorship, the more experienced team members feel micromanaged. Team morale has taken a downward dive because people think they are being asked to do a lot of busywork.

Jennifer feels discouraged: "I've been doing all I can to empower the team and am teaching them about best practices. What more can they ask for?" What's happening?

CASE 4: DS MANAGER WOES

As a graduate of a highly selective DS fellowship program, Paul was recruited by and spent three years at a global internet company focused on revenue and retention optimization for a mature product line. He considers himself very fortunate to have worked for an exceptional manager whom he looked up to, and he aspires to be one himself someday.

Six months ago, Paul's opportunity came. His classmate from graduate school, who heads up operations research at a late-stage biotech startup, recruited him to manage the DS team. Paul welcomed the opportunity and was confident that his experience and learning from a much larger company had prepared him well.

Technically strong, Paul also invests significant effort in building relationships with the DS team. In addition to project-related meetings, Paul sets up weekly walks or chats with each of his seven team members, holds weekly office hours to make sure he is available for the team, and hosts a bi-weekly "breakfast with data science" to communicate frequently with project stakeholders and business partners and listen to their needs and keep them informed.

Six months in, Paul feels drained, yet business results are only mixed at best: out of the five main projects his team is on, two are chugging along, two are delayed, and one has changed scope significantly. There are also a few pet projects that haven't even taken off. It seems that Paul's efforts have not paid off as much as he had anticipated. Is he doing the right things? Or is this a case of facing reality after passing the initial honeymoon phase? How can Paul develop into a good manager?

CASE 5: DS MANAGER INTERVIEW ISSUES

Audra is a DS leader at a startup company, managing projects and a team of four data scientists for almost two years. She has always been keen to develop her career. When a management opportunity came up in a larger company in the same industry with the prospect of managing a larger team, she jumped to apply.

She started the interview process quite confidently: she passed the technical test, has a solid industry knowledge base, is likable, and has done well in her current role. However, after three rounds of interviews with the hiring manager, team, and company executives, she did not stand out as the best candidate and ultimately was not extended an offer. As the interviewing company does not provide detailed feedback, her case is assumed to be not a culture fit.

Audra is disappointed and baffled. She thought through how she conveyed her passion for developing her career and what she could have done differently but did not come up with anything significant. And what does "culture fit" mean, anyway? How can she continue to develop herself into a leader in pursuit of an impactful career if there's no feedback?

CASE 6: DATA SCIENCE DIRECTOR CONCERNS

Stephen is an analytics and DS leader with over 15 years of experience in the transportation industry. Eight years ago, he had the initiative to take some machine learning courses from an online education platform and founded the DS practice in his then-company. Stephen joined his current company six years ago and is well respected for his statistics background, excellent working relationship with partners, and long tenure at the company with a broad and deep understanding of the business. He was promoted a year ago to director of DS to manage three DS teams, each having a dedicated internal customer: supply chain, financial planning, and marketing.

It's a big role, and Stephen was able to guide the team to operate consistently on its responsibilities. For example, Stephen oversaw a continuous operational efficiency improvement project for the supply chain group, timely ROI estimation of investments for the financial planning group, and routine customer acquisition and channel optimization projects for marketing. He is also glad to hear from leaders of the supply chain, financial planning, and marketing functions that their needs are being served.

However, something is bothering Stephen. Team morale seems to be low, and each of the teams has seen team members with high growth potential depart for other opportunities in the last year.

Stephen is eager to understand what is happening, so he can at least attempt to turn it around. However, he feels at a loss, as employee feedback surveys only come back with the typical tech debts and work–life balance topics that Stephen doesn't see could be changed any time soon. What else could be happening?

CASE 7: DATA EXECUTIVE CHALLENGES

It has been 10 years since Catherine earned a PhD in computer science. She spent the past six years serving as the head of DS for a public company and a 200-person startup. Her leadership teams at those two companies produced impactful results. Her successes include projects addressing customer awareness and feature adoption and existing market revenue optimization. Last year, she was invited to serve as the chief data scientist for a fast-growing startup.

In less than one year, she established and progressed a clear DS technology roadmap; drove a crisp set of vision, mission, and principles for DS; and captured some impressive business wins for the startup. However, the company was growing fast, and it was hard to scale the DS team in a competitive talent marketplace.

Catherine was recently caught off-guard when Josh, a director managing two managers with a team of a dozen data scientists, indicated his intention to leave. Josh is an early employee at the startup and reported to the CTO before Catherine came on board.

In her conversations with Josh, she assessed that the data scientists are generally happy with her leadership and management style. Still, Josh and at least one other direct report are planning to leave. Catherine is both surprised and puzzled as to why this is happening.

1.2.2 What are (hiring) managers looking for?

You may have seen or even identified with one or more of the cases in section 1.2.1. These cases are derived from real-life scenarios at different stages of a data scientist's career and are intended to represent some of the challenges faced during career progression. This section addresses each case briefly and provides pointers to the sections that dive deeper into solution concepts.

CASE 1: ADDRESSING AAYANA'S ENTERING DS INTERVIEW WOES

Aayana, the UCLA graduate student, lost confidence after experiencing very different interviews for entry-level data scientists at different companies. The interviewers seemed to be focusing on wildly different areas compared to the academic courses she excelled at in school.

It turns out there are six different dimensions to develop skills for to be a successful data scientist, including technology, execution, expert knowledge, ethics, rigor, and attitude. The academic training mainly covers two of these dimensions: technology and rigor.

The assessment of virtues intertwined in the interviews can take conversations into many unfamiliar territories, generating confusion and frustration. The purpose of the interview for the NLP engineering position was to look for the rigor she had in her technical work, which we discuss extensively in section 3.2. The FinTech startup focused on her execution capabilities to complete a DS project across the full DS stack, which we discuss in section 2.2.

Table 1.1 summarizes the situation and the learning from this book. Aayana should first be confident in her solid academic knowledge. She then can identify the blind spots in her understanding of DS to include the six dimensions important for successfully practicing in the field by reading chapter 1. To learn what a highly successful individual contributor would be able to do, read chapters 2 and 3, which have more details.

Table 1.1   Case 1: How Aayana can use this book to launch her career

Case	Situation	Useful concepts
Aayana *New grad*	Aayana has lost some confidence after experiencing very different interviews for entry-level data scientist positions.	**Strengths:** ■ Demonstrating strong academic knowledge **Opportunities:** ■ Understanding the capabilities and virtues of a data scientist better by reading chapters 1–3 **Support requests:** ■ Seeking out alumni and mentors for guidance

Aayana can also leverage her school's alumni network and people in her LinkedIn network for guidance on areas the various companies tend to emphasize. She can then better anticipate and prepare for the various styles of interviews in DS.

CASE 2: ADDRESSING BRIAN'S DATA SCIENTIST PROMOTION CONCERNS

Brian, a technically solid data scientist, feels trapped in a vicious cycle in his pursuit of becoming a leader in DS. He is looking to be promoted to tech lead, but his manager, Walt, sees inconsistent performance across different projects. It turns out he is not comfortable pushing back on project scope creep and managing expectations for success.

Table 1.2 summarizes the situation and outlines the learning Brian can get from the book. First, Brian can build his confidence by recognizing his strengths in framing business problems into diagnostic or predictive DS projects that operate in batch mode or in real-time (see section 2.1.1). He is also proficient in discovering patterns in data with careful data characterization and innovative algorithms (see section 2.1.2). One of Brian's most valuable characteristics is the ability to stay positive despite project failures (see section 3.3.1).

Table 1.2   Case 2: How Brian can use this book to address his promotion concerns

Case	Situation	Useful concepts (section references)
Brian *Senior data scientist*	Brian is technically solid but less comfortable talking to business partners and pushing back on project scope creep.	**Strengths:** ■ Framing the problem (2.1.1) ■ Discovering patterns in data (2.1.2) ■ Staying positive despite failures (3.3.1) **Opportunities:** ■ Specifying and prioritizing projects (2.2.1) ■ Planning and managing projects (2.2.2) ■ Setting expectations for success (2.1.3) **Support requests:** ■ Learning best practices with the team (3.1.3) ■ Getting career coaching from a manager (5.1.1)

Next, he can identify blind spots in his skill set in specifying and prioritizing projects with techniques to manage project scope changes while maintaining relationships (see section 2.2). He can also help set the appropriate level of expectation with business partners for project success (see section 2.1.3). Brian can collaborate with his team-mates, be proactive in sharing and learning best practices with peers (see section 3.1.3), and make specific requests for coaching from Walt, his manager (see section 5.1.1).

Brian can reference the sections from chapters 2 and 3 listed in table 1.2 for more details on his strengths and opportunities. He can also read ahead to chapters 4 and 5 to understand the perspectives and concerns of his manager, Walt, and how to be specific when seeking Walt's coaching, mentorship, or advice.

CASE 3: ADDRESSING JENNIFER'S TECH LEAD CHALLENGES

Jennifer is a strong tech lead who has good cross-team communication skills and is not afraid of pushing back on project scope creep. However, some team members feel micromanaged, and many are stressed out by the busywork she assigns.

Jennifer's manager Kai talked with the team and identified two issues. To keep business partners in sync with project status, Jennifer was checking in with team members two to three times a week. This frequency worked for some team members but annoyed some of the more experienced team members. Kai also observed that when business partners initiated changes to the projects, Jennifer led the team to deliver results. But not all team members understood why the changes were taking place. When Jennifer received this feedback, she was confused. Isn't it a DS tech lead's job to deliver results to business partners?

Table 1.3 summarizes the situation and outlines what Jennifer can learn from the book. First, she can build her confidence by recognizing her strength in prioritizing and managing projects, while clearly communicating expectations with partners (see section 2.2.1). When responding to incidents, she is highly effective in leading the team through in-depth post-mortems with actionable projects to address root causes (see section 3.3.2). She also takes responsibility for business impact when deploying models by being clear on goals and laser-focused on project impacts (see section 3.2.3).

Table 1.3   Case 3: How Jennifer can use this book to address tech lead challenges

Case	Situation	Useful concepts (section references)
Jennifer *Tech lead*	Jennifer is good at cross-team communication, but her teammates feel micro-managed and are unhappy about a lot of busywork. It turns out that she needs to improve her skills in communicating change and build trust with members of the team.	**Strengths:** ▪ Prioritizing and managing projects (2.2.1) ▪ Leading in incident response (3.3.2) ▪ Taking responsibility for results (3.2.3) **Opportunities:** ▪ Communicating change effectively (3.1.2) ▪ Trusting the team to execute (5.3.2) ▪ Imparting knowledge confidently (3.1.3) **Support requests:** ▪ Nurturing positivity despite failures in the team (3.3.1) ▪ Seeking career coaching from a manager (5.1.1)

Next, Jennifer can apply execution, ethics, and rigor techniques to improve the situation. More specifically, she can identify the blind spots in her skill set of trusting teams to execute, so she can ensure project progress without checking in two or three times a week (see section 5.3.2). When business partners initiate changes, Jennifer can better communicate the reason and context of the changes (see section 3.1.2). For more senior members of the team, she can provide opportunities to build identities by encouraging them to share their learning with others (see section 3.1.3).

By coaching her team to recognize their learnings in routine projects and even in failed projects, she can nurture the team to maintain a positive attitude despite adversity (see section 3.3.1). She can also be more specific in seeking coaching from her manager to help her grow as a leader (see section 5.5.1).

Jennifer can reference the sections from chapters 3 and 5 listed in table 1.3 and select one opportunity area to work on every two weeks. She can also schedule checkpoints with herself to self-evaluate her progress and work with her team and manager to practice her capabilities and virtues and become a more successful tech lead.

CASE 4: ADDRESSING PAUL'S DS MANAGER WOES

Paul felt drained after six months on the job as a DS manager, and his efforts had only led to mixed results. In an attempt to build relationships, he accepted too many requests and spread his team too thin. It looked like he had shown little leadership on where to focus.

Table 1.4 summarizes Paul's situation and provides pointers for what he can do next. First, Paul can build his confidence by recognizing his strengths in his technical skills. Specifically, he is skilled in framing DS problems and discovering data patterns (see section 2.1). When faced with difficult trade-offs, Paul is able to strike a balance between speed and quality, safety and accountability, and documentation and process (see section 2.2.3). He is also able to manage consistency between projects with common processes and frameworks (see section 4.1.2).

Table 1.4 Case 4: How Paul can use this book to address DS manager woes

Case	Situation	Useful concepts (section references)
Paul *Manager*	Paul feels drained after six months on the job. He is great at building relationships, took on many requests, and became overwhelmed. When he spreads himself too thin, he doesn't appear to have sufficient leadership to focus the team.	**Strengths:** ■ Framing problems and discovering patterns (2.1.1, 2.1.2) ■ Balancing trade-offs (2.2.3) ■ Managing consistency between projects (4.1.2) **Opportunities:** ■ Planning and prioritization (2.2.1) ■ Broadening knowledge (4.3.1) ■ Managing up to his boss (4.2.3) **Support requests:** ■ Team to take responsibility for impacts (3.2.3) ■ Manager to sponsor/champion projects (6.1.3)

Next, he can identify the blind spots in his skills for planning and prioritization by understanding the motivations behind the requests; assessing the reach, impact, confidence, and effort of the requests; and prioritizing the projects to focus the team on, providing the most significant impact for the business (see section 2.2.1). He can also broaden his domain knowledge (see section 4.3.1) and take care to manage the expectations of his manager (see section 4.2.3).

In working with his team, he can nurture the team members to take on more responsibility by demonstrating business impacts in top business metrics. He will do well to focus on execution velocity by doing proof of concept (PoC) projects and repaying tech debts to remove execution risks (see section 3.2.3).

To reduce partner execution risks, Paul can also request help from his manager, the DS director, to identify and bring on board sponsors and champions within the company for his projects (see section 6.1.3).

Concepts in chapters 2 and 4 discuss many of Paul's strengths and opportunities. He can select one opportunity area to work on every two weeks and schedule checkpoints with himself to self-evaluate his progress. He can also work with his team and manager to practice his capabilities and virtues to become a more successful manager.

Case 5: Addressing Audra's DS manager interview issues

Audra is disappointed and baffled after not getting a job offer for a position that she believes she's highly qualified for. It turns out that, during Audra's interview, at least two interviewers noted that she mostly focused on her own career path and development and did not speak much at all about the team she led. When asked if she had a succession plan for her managerial role, it was clear that she did not have one.

Table 1.5 illustrates Audra's situation and provides pointers for what she can do next. She can recognize her strengths in managing consistency between DS efforts in different teams to minimize the accumulation of tech debts (see section 4.1.2). She is also proficient at clarifying the business context of opportunities based on alignment with the company vision and mission (see section 2.3.1). This way, she can ensure her team's projects are important, useful, and worthwhile. She also has the experience and domain knowledge to make realistic estimates of project ROI based on the reach, effort, and impact of projects for their prioritization (see section 4.3.3).

Next, she can identify the blind spots in her skills. As a manager, one primary responsibility is to empower each team member to do the best work of their career. She can learn to better nurture her team with timely coaching, mentorship, and advice (see section 5.1.1). Another area is working with peer managers to contribute and reciprocate on a broader set of management duties, especially in employment, team operations, and team building (see section 5.1.3). She can also be more sensitive to the differences between the maker's and manager's schedule when scheduling standups and one-on-ones to better tailor them to team members' needs for large blocks of time to focus (see section 5.3.1).

She can encourage her team members to confidently impart knowledge to build a culture of cross-mentoring (see section 3.1.3). She can also seek out mentorship

Table 1.5   Case 5: How Audra can use this book to advance her career

Case	Situation	Useful concepts (section references)
Audra *Manager*	Audra is disappointed and baffled after not getting an offer for a position that she believes she's highly qualified for. It turns out that the hiring manager found she is too focused on building her own career. She did not demonstrate that she is nurturing her team.	**Strengths:** ■ Managing for consistency (4.1.2) ■ Clarifying business context (2.3.1) ■ Assessing ROI for prioritization (4.3.3) **Opportunities:** ■ Coaching, mentoring, and advising (5.1.1) ■ Contributing to broader duties (5.1.3) ■ Managing the maker versus manager schedule (5.3.1) **Support requests:** ■ Team to learn from each other (3.1.3) ■ Manager to help craft a clear career map (6.2.2)

opportunities from her manager to clarify her own career growth path and focus areas (see section 6.2.2).

Concepts in chapters 4 and 5 discuss many of Audra's strengths and opportunities. When Audra can focus on mentoring and growing her team, and be more sensitive to her team's needs, she will have matured into a more successful DS manager.

CASE 6: ADDRESSING STEPHEN'S DS DIRECTOR-LEVEL CONCERNS

Stephen, a well-respected director, notices the morale of the DS team dropping with a few regrettable attritions but is at a loss how to turn that around. It turns out that the teams Stephen is managing are feeling the pains of a lack of a clear technology roadmap.

As the company grows, existing infrastructure and work processes are often strained to support ever-more-demanding business requirements. However, if team members do not see a clear roadmap that will lead them out of the vicious cycle of more frequent breakdowns caused by tech debts, morale will suffer, and they will start to look for alternative teams to join.

Table 1.6 illustrates Stephen's situation and provides pointers for what he can do next. He can recognize his strengths in solving challenges by applying his extensive domain experience to instantiate initial solutions rapidly against urgent issues (see section 6.3.2). He can also represent DS confidently in front of partners by delivering persuasive presentations through storytelling (see section 5.1.2). When communicating complex issues, he can distill them into concise narratives for his team and partners (see section 5.2.3).

Next, he can identify blind spots in his skill set. As a director, he can learn to craft various types of technology roadmaps to communicate with and synchronize his teams and partners and accomplish overall business objectives (see section 6.1.1). He can also coach his team to dive deep in the incident post-mortem process, address tech debts, and ensure the processes and platforms become more robust and mature over time (see section 5.2.2). To help his team members understand their growth potential, Stephen can also build a clear set of opportunities, responsibilities, and success evaluation metrics for their careers (see section 6.2.3).

Table 1.6   Case 6: How Stephen can use this book to address director-level concerns

Case	Situation	Useful concepts (section references)
Stephen *Director*	Stephen was promoted to director last year. He is respected for technique skills, partner relationships, and domain knowledge. He is bothered by low team morale and attrition. It turns out there was a lack of a clear technology roadmap.	**Strengths:** ■ Solving urgent issues rapidly (6.3.2) ■ Representing DS cross-functionality (5.1.2) ■ Driving clarity for complex issues (5.2.3) **Opportunities:** ■ Crafting clear technology roadmaps (6.1.1) ■ Learning effectively from incidents (5.2.2) ■ Building clear career paths (6.2.3) **Support requests:** ■ Team to better manage up (4.2.3) ■ Executive to set DS mission (8.2.1)

Stephen can mentor his team members to more effectively manage up to him by better aligning priorities, timely and accurately reporting progress, and cleanly escalating issues (see section 4.2.3). He can also coordinate with his executives to crystalize the DS mission (see section 8.2.1).

Chapters 5 and 6 discuss many of the strengths and opportunities for Stephen. If he can select one opportunity area to work on every two weeks and schedule checkpoints with himself to self-evaluate his progress, Stephen can make some concrete progress over a few months. He can also use many of the narratives in chapter 4 with his team and the narratives in chapter 8 to manage up to his executive boss.

CASE 7: ADDRESSING CATHERINE'S DATA EXECUTIVE CHALLENGES

Catherine, head of DS, is surprised and puzzled about regrettable attritions by key team leaders in her organization. It turns out the DS organization has not been growing as fast as the rest of the organization, and the DS team is bogged down with more keeping-the-lights-on projects than strategic projects.

While Catherine has been an excellent internal-facing executive, the marketplace for DS talent has become more competitive in recent years. And Catherine has not established a robust external-facing identity or talent brand in the industry to attract talent effectively.

Table 1.7 illustrates Catherine's situation and provides pointers for what she can do next. She can first recognize her strengths in being a visionary subject matter expert who is up-to-date on the specific technologies transforming her industry (see section 8.1.1). She is also effective at infusing DS capabilities into the company's mission and vision, so her teams can have the executive mandate and influence to align priorities with partners in cross-functional collaborations (see section 8.2.1). With the aligned priorities, Catherine is able to deliver results consistently by having a good handle on managing people, processes, and platforms (see section 6.2.1).

Next, Catherine can identify blind spots in her skills. To accelerate the growth of DS teams at her company, she can build a strong talent pool by adopting techniques such as employer branding, content marketing, social recruiting, and interest group

Table 1.7   Case 7: How Catherine can use this book to address executive challenges

Case	Situation	Useful concepts (section references)
Catherine *Executive*	Catherine is the chief data scientist for a growth-stage company. She is well-respected and has crafted clear technology roadmaps. She is surprised and puzzled about regrettable attritions. It turns out hiring was not fast enough, and the team was bogged down with maintenance tasks.	**Strengths:** • Articulating long-term strategy (8.1.1) • Crafting mission and vision (8.2.1) • Delivering consistently (6.2.1) **Opportunities:** • Building a strong talent pool (8.2.2) • Establishing identity in industry (9.3.2) • Differentiating from industry peers (8.3.1) **Support requests:** • Team to drive annual planning (7.2.1) • CEO to support talent brand building (8.2.2)

nurturing (see section 8.2.2). She can also establish a leadership identity for her company via areas such as competitive and attractive product features, robust and efficient technology platforms, and productive and efficient organizational structures (see section 9.3.2). Catherine can also create real value for her company to differentiate its product and services based on products, services, distribution, relationships, reputation, and price (see section 8.3.1).

Catherine can coach her team to take on more responsibilities during annual planning, so she can better allocate her time to focus on building identities external to the company (see section 7.2.1). She can also work with her CEO for more support in building a talent brand for the company (see section 8.2.2).

Chapters 8 and 9 discuss many of Catherine's strengths and opportunities. With a stronger identity in her industry and the DS community, Catherine can attract more talent to her company, so there can be a good balance of keeping-the-lights-on work and new innovative work on the team.

LEADING ACROSS VARIOUS STAGES OF A CAREER

We have discussed seven representative cases along a career path in DS. They are by no means comprehensive but are illustrative of common challenges DS leaders face.

We designed chapters 2 through 9 to help you gain clarity in your career trajectories with clear milestones to produce a more significant impact for your organization. Ultimately, the accomplishments and impact on business will propel your career growth, either within the same team or in different teams.

You may also find it relevant and valuable to introduce this book to managers and colleagues. Managers and colleagues who work with data scientists can adjust their expectations for working with DS practitioners at various levels of leadership.

Companies and organizations differ across industries and sizes. How can we identify the companies and opportunities that would best align with our own leadership strength? In the last part of this book, we introduce the LOOP (landscape, organization, opportunity, and practice), which brings data scientist capabilities and virtues into action in pursuing an impactful career. We conclude the book with a discussion of the why, what, and how of leading in DS and take a peek into the future of the field.

Ready? Let's go!

Summary

- Data scientist expectations have evolved, and there needs to be a different representation to capture the required skills.
- The new expectations include three hard technical capabilities (technology, execution, and expert knowledge) and three soft psychosocial virtues (ethics, rigor, and attitude).
- There are common challenges data scientists encounter in real-world interviews and promotions. We briefly examine what managers and hiring managers are looking for in seven cases, which we will revisit in later chapters.

References

[1] "Global talent trends 2020," LinkedIn. [Online]. Available: https://business.linkedin.com/talent-solutions/recruiting-tips/global-talent-trends-2020

[2] "Thriving as a Data Scientist in the New Twenties," [Online]. Available: https://www.linkedin.com/pulse/thriving-data-scientist-new-roaring-twenties-jike-chong/

[3] D. Conway. "The data science Venn diagram." DrewConway.com. http://drewconway.com/zia/2013/3/26/the-data-science-venn-diagram

Part 1

The tech lead: Cultivating leadership

In your journey toward producing a greater impact in the world with DS, becoming a tech lead and driving project integrity is often the first step. You are discovering your personal limitations as an individual contributor: you can only write so many lines of code and analyze so much data in a day. For some, it can be hard to acknowledge our own finiteness as individual humans. The sooner we realize our own limitations, the more time we have to start practicing what has made human civilizations so powerful, which is our capability to organize and lead.

So what is the *tech lead* role? The tech lead role focuses on leadership and management in technology and projects. This is in contrast to the manager role, which focuses on people and team management.

To enter a tech lead role, the biggest challenge for an individual contributor is the practice of influence. You are expected to lead and mentor a team of data scientists, and work with business and engineering partners, often without any of them reporting to you.

At the same time, a tech lead is at the front line of where all the DS gets done. An organization depends on strong DS tech leads to conduct data-driven projects with a detailed understanding of business needs, data properties, and data nuances. From this position, you can provide detailed feedback to junior data scientists to nurture them technically, and you can provide the earliest feedback and escalation to management when something is going wrong.

Chapters 2 and 3 focus on the capabilities and virtues of a DS tech lead. You will be introduced to the pieces of the TEE-ERA Fan, covering the six dimensions of technology, execution, expert knowledge, ethics, rigor, and attitude.

The chapters illustrate the aspirational goals in each dimension and aim to lay out career paths for DS tech leads. Managers can reference these topics to guide their team members' professional development, but should not use them as reasons to hold back promotions. If a tech lead has demonstrated capabilities and virtues in some topics and potential in others, they could be ready for more responsibilities.

Tech lead is the entry-level individual contributor leadership role. Companies that have established a technical track in DS can have staff, principal, and distinguished data scientist positions with a similar scope of technical influence as managers, directors, and executives—mostly without the people management responsibilities. All right, let's get into the capabilities and virtues of leading projects.

Capabilities
for leading projects

This chapter covers

- Using best practices for pattern discovery and setting expectations for success
- Specifying, prioritizing, and planning projects from vague requirements
- Striking balances between complex technical trade-offs
- Clarifying business contexts and accounting for data nuances
- Navigating structural challenges in organizations

As a tech lead, your team of data scientists looks to you for guidance in technology choices, project execution trade-offs, and business knowledge and contexts. You are entrusted with helping the team cut through the complexities and ambiguities to deliver technical solutions on time with the available resources.

While many general capabilities are required for a data scientist to be effective [1], [2], it is the strategic capabilities that will differentiate you as a tech lead. You are expected to mentor a team of data scientists and work with business and engineering partners, influencing them without any of them reporting to you, to drive projects forward.

003

As a data science tech lead, you are expected to influence without authority by mentoring a team of data scientists and collaborating with business and engineering partners to drive projects forward.

What are these strategic capabilities for a data scientist tech lead? Here are the three topics we will discuss in this chapter:

- *Technology*—The tools and frameworks for you to lead projects more effectively, which are used in framing the problem, understanding data characteristics, innovating in feature engineering, driving clarity in modeling strategies, and setting expectations for success.
- *Execution*—The practices for you to specify projects with vague requirements and prioritize and plan projects, while balancing difficult trade-offs.
- *Expert knowledge*—The domain knowledge for you to clarify project alignment to organizational vision and mission, account for data source nuances, and navigate structural challenges in the organization.

These three topics cover the *TEE* portion in the TEE-ERA fan in figure 2.1 to help you distinguish the tools, practices, and approaches that allow you, the DS lead, to produce more business impact than as an individual data scientist. Let's get right to it!

Capabilities   **Virtues**

Figure 2.1   The *TEE* portion of the TEE-ERA Fan

2.1   *Technology: Tools and skills*

Practicing DS involves translating business needs into quantitative frameworks and optimization techniques, such that we can learn patterns from data and anticipate the future. Setting up a project to learn from data has many challenges involving the following three areas:

1. Framing the problem to maximize business impact
2. Discovering patterns in data:
   - Understanding data characteristics
   - Innovating in feature engineering
   - Clarifying the modeling strategy
3. Setting expectations for success

As a DS tech lead, what tools can you use to gain respect from the team and get the manager's attention when required? Let's look into these three areas one by one.

2.1.1 *Framing the problem to maximize business impact*

Framing the problem can be more important than identifying the data sources. Not all data is readily available when you start. Some data sources may need to be purchased or curated. A powerful framing can inform what data sources are required to achieve the goals you set out to accomplish. Framing the problem can help you be more directed in your search for data.

004

Framing the problem can be more important than identifying the data sources. A powerful framing can inform what data sources are required to achieve the goals you set out to accomplish.

A business challenge can be framed into different scales and scopes of DS projects, resulting in different magnitudes of business impact. A DS tech lead can be acutely aware of the business requirements and can recommend DS solutions that can make an outsized impact on business.

One tool you can use to increase your project's impact is to assess a scenario's analysis type and target definition. Questions to ask yourself include:

- Is the analysis limited to historical data that can be batch processed? Or are there real-time streaming data sources that must be considered?
- Are the results for diagnostic purposes only? Or are the results expected to be predictive?

Remember Brian from case 2 in chapter 1? He was recently introduced to a marketing initiative to drive long-term engagement through the email channel. As the team scopes the project, Brian is asked to provide recommendations from a DS perspective.

Figure 2.2 illustrates the four quadrants created by analysis type (batch versus real-time data) and target definition (diagnostic versus predictive). Using this taxonomy, let's see how Brian can help the team frame the initiative:

- *Hindsight*—One standard DS practice is to run an A/B test with a hold-out set composed of customers who do not see an email marketing campaign. We can run the campaign for a few months and assess whether the lack of a marketing campaign impacts long-term engagement. This kind of hindsight with a long experimentation cycle is *not* efficient in driving improvements in operations.
- *Insight*—Another practice is to produce a real-time dashboard illustrating trends in long-term engagement. We can follow the decays of long-term engagements across user vintages to detect early trends of success or issues. These trends allow the organization to make business decisions in real time with insights from the dashboards.

Figure 2.2   Levels of practice toward intelligence [3]

- *Foresight*—Given historical data, we can also build a model predicting long-term engagement using detectable short-term engagement characteristics, such as open rate, click-through rate (CTR), unsubscribe rate, landing page session length, and session frequency. A prediction model can anticipate long-term effects with short-term observation, so we gain the foresight to adjust our email marketing strategies week-to-week.

- *Intelligence*—Yet more powerful approaches can include real-time analytics on channels such as email to learn the customer segments. We can then prepare sequences of touches on the next best actions (NBAs) to drive long-term engagement for specific segments of users. When we can adapt the content of the next touches based on individual responses in real time, we are beginning to see the intelligence in driving long-term engagements.

By framing the problem with different levels of DS capabilities, the business impact can increase from an A/B test readout to an automated dashboard to agile operations to leading the long-term engagement initiative with intelligence features in the user experience.

The distinctions illustrated in figure 2.2 can help Brian, Jennifer (chapter 1, cases 2 and 3) and you, the tech lead, work with business partners to understand which level would be most appropriate for the resources available, the business impact achievable, and the relative priorities among different projects. The prioritization process for DS projects is discussed in section 2.2. As a tech lead, you can identify the gaps in problem framing and work with your manager and partners to craft strategies and road maps to accomplish the business goals you set out to accomplish.

2.1.2   *Discovering patterns in data*

As a tech lead, there are various dimensions to work with data scientists on your team to ensure the quality of the analysis or prediction, including understanding data characteristics, innovating in feature engineering, and clarifying the modeling strategy.

UNDERSTANDING DATA CHARACTERISTICS

To understand data characteristics, you can articulate four aspects of data with your teammates. As illustrated in figure 2.3, these aspects include the *unit of decisioning, sample size/sparsity/outliers, sample distribution/imbalance,* and *data types.*

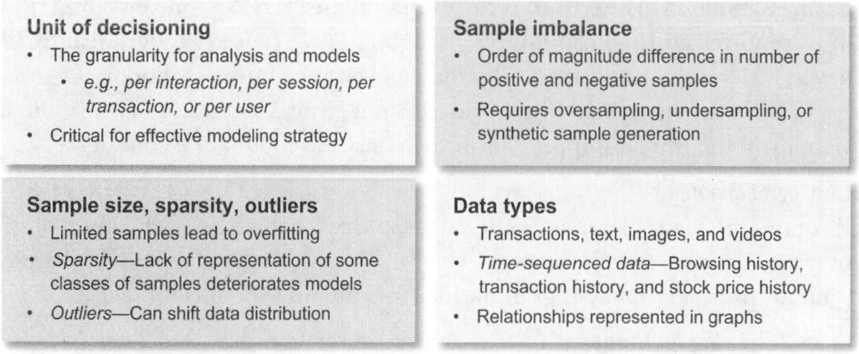

Unit of decisioning
- The granularity for analysis and models
  - *e.g., per interaction, per session, per transaction, or per user*
- Critical for effective modeling strategy

Sample imbalance
- Order of magnitude difference in number of positive and negative samples
- Requires oversampling, undersampling, or synthetic sample generation

Sample size, sparsity, outliers
- Limited samples lead to overfitting
- *Sparsity*—Lack of representation of some classes of samples deteriorates models
- *Outliers*—Can shift data distribution

Data types
- Transactions, text, images, and videos
- *Time-sequenced data*—Browsing history, transaction history, and stock price history
- Relationships represented in graphs

Figure 2.3   Data characteristics to understand for discovering patterns in data

DEFINITION   Imbalance: Order of magnitude differences in the number of positive and negative samples in a data set.

A clear articulation is best illustrated in the context of a real-world scenario: The coronavirus outbreak of 2020 devastated much of commerce around the world. One bright spot was the e-commerce industry, where food, medicine, and pretty much anything can be ordered online and delivered to people's doorsteps, allowing people to avoid potentially risky exposures to communicable diseases in crowded social locations. However, the purchase friction of the thought, "what if I don't like it?" still causes reluctance and missing out on many business opportunities.

One relatively recent innovation that has removed some of this friction is an insurance product called *return-shipping insurance.* On many e-commerce platforms, during online checkout, customers can select a low-cost option, spending $1–$2 to insure their purchase with some return-shipping credit. The insurance premium is rolled into the shopping cart, so no separate payment is necessary. Suppose a customer is not satisfied with the product purchase. In that case, they can just return the product within seven days, and return-shipping credit would be automatically processed within 72 hours without going through any cumbersome claims process at all. This insurance product is hugely popular in e-commerce in China. ZhongAn Online P&C Insurance Co. Ltd. (6060:HK), a pioneer in online-only insurance, has issued more than 5.8 billion insurance policies as of end of 2020, most of which are return-shipping insurance.

DEFINITION   Return-shipping insurance: A low-cost insurance, usually $1–$2, to allow an e-commerce purchase to be returned with the return shipping paid for.

As with any opportunity, there are caveats. Insurance fraud can be rampant in an environment where anyone can register as an online merchant, and anyone can sign up to be an e-commerce customer. When someone can pay $1–2 to get $10–20 of credit over the internet, there is a significant incentive to find schemes to attack the insurance business model. Early trials of return-shipping insurance at one e-commerce company were reported to have claim rates as high as 90%, caused by significantly high fraud levels, which does not make a sustainable insurance business model.

Countering insurance fraud using DS is a critical use case to ensure the long-term viability of the return-shipping insurance business model in e-commerce.

UNIT OF DECISIONING

E-commerce data, like many other data sources, contains a rich range of granularity over time, entity, and interactions. Over the time horizon alone, as a customer is shopping for products, analysis granularities for catching fraud can include:

- The engagement with a product recommendation
- The exploratory actions within a shopping session
- A purchase decision with engagement across multiple sessions
- Multiple purchases with an intent (such as Christmas, the Super Bowl, back-to-school shopping)
- Purchases at a life stage, such as graduation, marriage, or birth of a child

For each transaction, the entities involved include the customer, the merchant, the payment processor, and often the shippers of the physical goods. There is also a rich set of interactions between these entities for each transaction with interaction contexts and patterns across multiple transactions.

> **DEFINITION**   Granularity: The scale or level of detail in a set of data, which can be over dimensions such as time, entity, and interactions.

Choosing the level of granularity to assess return-shipping insurance fraud is crucial for building an effective modeling strategy. However, the choice may not be so obvious, as the fraudulent intent could be coming from one or more of the following parties:

- The customers shopping for products
- The shippers
- A merchant corroborating with customers
- A hacker with access to multiple stolen identities on an e-commerce platform
- Dark web players creating fake merchant/customer identities for sale

In the return-shipping insurance fraud scenario, a common choice is at the granularity of a purchase, where a decision has to be made about whether to offer the return-shipping insurance in the e-commerce checkout process. Depending on the sample size and data sparsity, the unit of decisioning for assessing fraud can also be at the customer level or the merchant level. Information from other levels of granularity can be incorporated as features in the final model.

SAMPLE SIZE, DATA SPARSITY, AND OUTLIERS

Normal business operations can introduce data bias through business expansion, marketing campaigns, or bots/crawlers for a website. These biases can impact data characteristics such as sample size, data sparsity, and outliers.

- *Sample size*—When there are a limited number of samples, the risk for *overfitting* increases. To prevent overfitting, we can limit the complexity of *models* used or increase regularization *term* weights to smooth the models' decision surfaces.
- *Data sparsity*—There may be a lack of representation for some types of data, while the total sample size may be large. For example, for data aggregated for autonomous driving from the front-facing camera, there may be very few samples of the yellow traffic light at intersections just because they appear less often.
- *Outliers*—Points that differ significantly from other observations can shift data distributions significantly. For example, web crawlers that explore all links on a page can shift web behavior data when accidentally included in user behavior analysis.

These data biases are crucial to assess and understand before constructing features. Failure to do so can result in bad business decisions, wasted efforts, and loss of revenue.

> **DEFINITION** Overfitting: A modeling error that occurs when a model is too closely aligned to a limited data set, making predictions not accurate for new data in the same use case.

> **DEFINITION** Complexity of models: The number of features used in a model, or the types of models used to extract linear or nonlinear relationships from data. Complex models are more likely to overfit with limited data.

> **DEFINITION** Regularization term: A term that can tune the model complexity when training machine learning models.

SAMPLE IMBALANCE

Fraud cases are often a small portion of the overall transaction volume. Sample imbalance issues are common when training fraud models. Assessing the degree of imbalance and choosing more robust modeling techniques, such as gradient-boosted trees, are crucial to modeling success. Common techniques to mitigate sample imbalance include random oversampling or undersampling; informed undersampling techniques, such as EasyEnsemble and BalancedCascade [4]; synthetics sampling with data generation, such as SMOTE; and adaptive synthetic sampling, such as Borderline-SMOTE [5].

DATA TYPES

The e-commerce scenario also includes a broad set of data types, including:

- Individual samples, such as articles, images, and videos on merchandise
- Time-sequenced data, such as browsing history, transaction history, and customer service interaction history
- Relationship-based data, such as interactions between customers, merchants, payment processors, and shippers

These data types call for different analysis infrastructures and can offer unique features and perspectives in modeling. For example, relationship-based data, such as interactions between customers, merchants, payment processors, and shippers, can be used to generate knowledge graphs that capture these relationships. A knowledge-graph-based approach has been shown to be effective in highlighting behaviors in organized financial fraud.

DS team members often look to the tech lead, such as Brian and Jennifer from chapter 1, to make a call on the level of confidence for a project's success. You, as a tech lead, can use these articulations of data characteristics to assess project feasibility.

INNOVATIONS IN FEATURE ENGINEERING

Feature engineering allows us to summarize a vast amount of data meaningfully. Simpler models, such as linear regression, rely heavily on feature engineering for summarization. More complex models, such as deep neural networks, can even automate the feature engineering process as part of the model training and use raw signals directly as inputs.

In many use cases, because of the small sample sizes, labeling difficulties, and interpretability and operability considerations, you may opt to use simpler models and engineered features to discover patterns in the scenarios.

Feature engineering can take on many levels of complexity. These levels are illustrated in figure 2.4. You can engineer features from simple statistics, such as counts, sums, averages, extremes, frequencies, differences, ranges, variances, percentiles, and Kurtosis. Or you can infuse domain-specific interpretations, such as business hours in specific time zones for the time of day, or normal or abnormal ranges for health signals. For taxonomy analysis, the features can include seniority levels for job titles, categories of diagnosis in medical records, or categories of purchases for financial transactions. For features one level deeper, one can interpret the portfolio of categories. For financial transactions, this may be a proxy for their income range or even life stage. For data with entities and their relationships, you can use graphs to represent the relationships between entities, their interactions, their connectedness, and the communities the relationships create.

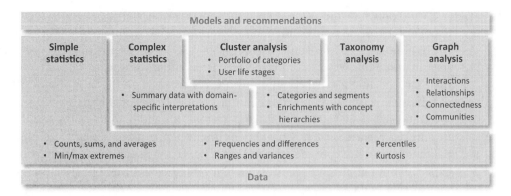

Figure 2.4 **Various types of feature engineering techniques for modeling**

In the e-commerce scenario, the complexity levels of feature engineering for customer data include:

- *Simple statistics*—Average price for goods brought, frequency of purchase
- *Complex statistics*—Weekday/weekend activities, impulse buy or considered purchase
- *Taxonomy-based analysis*—Categories of purchases, diversity of needs
- *Clustering analysis*—The portfolio of categories, customer intent or life stage
- *Graph analysis*—Patterns of interaction with merchants, risks for fraud

Merchants, payment processors, and shippers can have similar complexity levels of features to summarize the rich e-commerce data set's diversity of information.

You can look for these levels of complexities to engineer features from your data. One challenge you may encounter is that there is always limited time and resources to explore a rich data set. How do you prioritize?

You can use your domain expertise to guide prioritization. In our return-shipping insurance fraud mitigation scenario, an experienced fraud investigator can often use clues from a few anomalies in customer or merchant behavior to piece together a potential fraud scheme.

In one scenario, fraud investigators considered merchants with long transaction histories in physical goods more trustworthy than those merchants that sell mainly virtual goods (such as phone cards and gift cards). Historical data validated that fraudsters often look for shortcuts when building transaction history for their merchant accounts so they can be ranked higher in product search results. Virtual goods tend to be an easy way to build transaction history without the trouble of logistics operations. Understanding this domain-specific distinction can prioritize feature development and accelerate time to an accurate anti-fraud model.

While domain expertise is a necessary and valuable starting point to focus feature extraction efforts, it is not sufficient to determine what features should be used.

In another scenario, fraud investigators discovered trends in password recovery security questions, where confirmed fraudsters often use cats or dogs as answers for their favorite animals. We could interpret this discovery as the lack of thoughtfulness of fraudsters setting up their merchant accounts. However, when assessing the trend as a fraud signal, we found that it happens that cats and dogs are most people's favorite animals, regardless of any fraudulent intent. Using it as a signal to alert on potential fraud would increase the false-positive rate. Features engineered based on domain expertise must go through rigorous validation to be confirmed as effective for matching patterns in data.

As a tech lead, your tool kit for feature innovation is not limited to algorithms. Another way to have many features generated quickly is to build a feature assessment platform and gamify feature extraction as a mini-competition. This feature assessment platform can be built on top of a feature store, where features are created and shared by a team of data scientists.

The platform can automatically assess the effectiveness of new features for an ongoing modeling challenge, such as fraud alert accuracy and recall rate. As a team of data scientists works in their respective areas, they often develop particular features for their analysis that could be transferable to a fraud model. With a feature assessment platform, you can invite the whole DS, data engineering, and data analytics teams to contribute to a feature repository. You can regularly reward the top new feature on the leaderboard based on feature effectiveness to promote new submissions. Imagine that as a framework for feature innovation!

CLARIFYING MODELING STRATEGY

The legendary British statistician George Box once wrote, "All models are wrong, but some are useful." If this is the case, where do we start when building any of the, likely, wrong but useful models? First, let's differentiate the *tactic* of what models to build versus the *strategy* of how to start building models.

Many books and blogs address the tactic of what models to build. Popular models include: linear regression, logistic regression, decision tree, SVM, naive Bayes, kNN, k-means, random forest, and gradient boosted algorithms. Open source machine learning packages, such as the Python scikit-learn library, provide tools for exploring what models to build. This is illustrated in figure 2.5.

Adopting an existing model implementation is a DS best practice for all data scientists. Writing a custom version of machine learning is complex and takes significant time to validate. And common optimization techniques have already been developed for most of the situations we encounter in business.

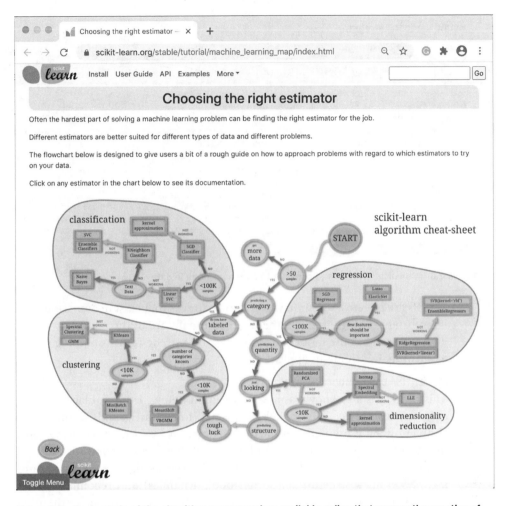

Figure 2.5 An example of the algorithm recommenders available online that answer the question of what models to build

For a DS tech lead, the key differentiation becomes crafting the strategy for how to start building models. While there are many modeling strategies, let's dive into four specific strategies (also illustrated in figure 2.6):

- Momentum-based modeling strategy
- Foundational modeling strategy
- Reflexive modeling strategy
- Hybrid modeling strategies

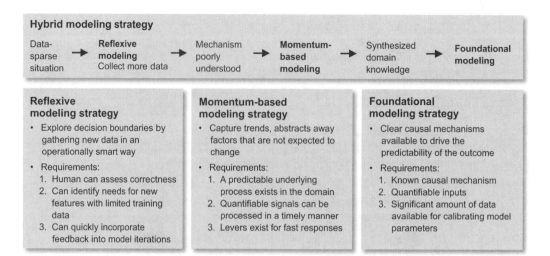

Figure 2.6   Modeling strategies to consider to match patterns in data

Models are effective when they match the patterns that exist in data. Domain expertise is important for forming hypotheses about the nature of the patterns we anticipate.

Let's examine the modeling strategies and use the return-shipping insurance case to illustrate how it might apply.

MOMENTUM-BASED MODELING STRATEGY

This strategy is also known as inertia-based modeling. It is popular in complex multi-agent environments. The model is expected to capture trends in the environments, abstracting away fundamental factors that are not expected to change in a certain time window, to predict what would happen if those trends continue.

Momentum-based modeling is commonly used in high-frequency trading (capturing market microstructure and order book dynamics) and recommendation systems (such as recency, frequency, monetization, or RFM based models), where the human or algorithm decision processes in an environment operate in predictable ways. For this strategy to be successful, three conditions must exist:

- A predictable underlying process exists in the domain
- Quantifiable signals can be timely processed
- Levers exist for fast responses

In anti-fraud models for return-shipping insurance, momentum-based modeling can be used for known fraud mechanisms that cannot be designed out of the products or services. These scenarios include offering insurance for new merchants or products. We can quantify fraud trend signals to watch in these scenarios and activate levers to shut down likely fraudulent transactions before too much damage is done.

FOUNDATIONAL MODELING STRATEGY

This option is often used in scenarios where clear causal mechanisms drive the predictability of the outcome. At an extreme, it can formalize structural modeling in economics where the structure of decision making is fully incorporated in the specification of the model.

Foundational modeling strategy can be used in application areas, such as sales forecasting, infrastructure load prediction, and financial account balance forecasting, where various cyclical patterns drive the outcome. The cyclical patterns could include:

- The time of the day
- The day of the week
- Monthly or semi-monthly rhythms
- Quarter or fiscal year boundaries
- Product launch dates
- Marketing campaign dates
- Regional holidays

The model then uses the training data to assess the relative weights or impacts of various mechanisms to achieve a good precision/recall for the prediction.

In anti-fraud models for return-shipping insurance, foundational modeling can be effective when we have a mature understanding of the common types of known fraud mechanisms and strong *latent variables,* assessing the risks from every kind of known fraud mechanism. For example, we may consider the fraud risk of each transaction from the following categories and assess an overall risk prediction with a foundational model:

- *The customer*—Frequently shopping/returning products
- *The merchant*—With a high return rate
- *The shipper*—Correlating with a high return rate
- *Merchant/customer*—Corroborating fake transactions
- *Merchant/customer/shipper*—Previously hacked identities
- *Fake merchant/customer identities*—incubated by dark web players for sale

Foundational models fail when the latent variables used for known fraud categories no longer capture the fraud mechanisms at hand.

> **DEFINITION** Latent variables: Variables that are not directly observable. In this case, they are the risk components that can be inferred but not directly observed at the time of decision.

REFLEXIVE MODELING STRATEGY

This strategy is also known as the active learning strategy. In many scenarios, it is often challenging to define a boundary for positive and negative cases by looking at data at hand. To improve the models, we need to explore the decision boundaries in an operationally smart approach to gather additional data for training iterations.

Examples of use cases include multiclass classifications, such as job title taxonomies and healthcare provider taxonomies, or fraud detection with active feedback from fraud investigation professionals. In the fraud detection use cases, fraud investigation professionals can assess borderline fraud cases to include in training based on observations that may or may not be included in the feature extraction pipeline yet.

When a return-shipping insurance product is at a nascent stage, a reflexive modeling strategy can be highly effective in aggregating fraud mechanisms. It allows the fraud model to better clarify the separation between the good and the bad and incorporate additional features when necessary. Using additional features and different samples aggregated through a reflexive modeling strategy, we can more quickly arrive at an acceptable operating point to satisfy precision and recall requirements.

HYBRID MODELING STRATEGIES

Depending on the maturity of data set and data infrastructure, the urgency of the task, and the business requirements, the situation often calls for hybrid modeling strategies that combine a selection of the previous strategies.

Let's continue with the return-shipping insurance example. Early in the product development cycle, some obvious fraud schemes might be prevented with product feature design. For example, the service may not be extended to merchants who sell mostly virtual goods. We can start with some simple decision trees encoding business rules with limited distribution while collecting data on potential fraud schemes.

With our limited data set collected, we can start deploying a *reflexive strategy*, iteratively sending borderline cases for fraud investigation professionals to review and label to improve the model's discrimination power. For new merchants or products with the *cold-start modeling challenge*, a *momentum-based strategy* can help quantify fraud trend signals to watch and activate levers to shut down likely fraudulent transactions before too much damage is done. After a period of operations, with significant training data set collected and fraud mechanisms understood, we may move to a *foundational modeling strategy* with an ensemble of sub-models detecting various well-understood fraud schemes to produce latent risk scores.

> **DEFINITION**   Cold-start modeling challenge: Problems where there is a lack of data to train models. Data often have to be collected and labeled to start training models.

Deep domain insights can shape a modeling strategy to address the business challenge at hand. There is no one right answer, as all models are wrong, but some are useful.

Phew! That was a lot of strategies! As a tech lead, all of the strategies are options you can keep in mind when interpreting the business challenge and mentoring data scientist team members on approaches for the modeling problems at hand. Feel free to take a break while these sink in.

2.1.3 *Setting expectations for success*

Setting expectations is important especially in smaller organizations when data scientists are working with senior executives in partner organizations who may have unrealistic expectations after hearing some machine learning use cases from social media or a marketing white paper. When unrealistic expectations are set, even when good insights and models are delivered, partners may not be satisfied. You may recall this is an area Brian, the senior data scientist from Chapter 1, needs to work on.

005 Partners may form unrealistic expectations for data science projects after hearing machine learning use cases from social media or a marketing white paper. When unrealistic expectations are set, even when good insights and models are delivered, partners may not be satisfied.

Success is what we aim for in building DS solutions. How do we define success in a world where "[a]ll models are wrong, but some are useful"? How accurate must a model be to be useful?

At Acorns, Jike and the team developed behavioral nudges to improve people's financial wellness through micro-investing. The team had many great nudges as behavioral recommendations for the customers. The strategic question has been: When would these recommendations be accurate enough and personalized enough for them to be successfully seen as coming from a trusted financial assistant?

What we learned was that success comes down to more than just the *accuracy* of the model but also the *consistency* of the implementation and the *trust* customers have with a data-driven solution.

Depending on the accuracy of the models we can produce, you, as a DS tech lead, should understand your projects' operating context and set realistic expectations with your customers. Figure 2.7 illustrates four levels of confidence for your models that can be evaluated along three dimensions: readiness, riskiness, and reception.

Level 1
Recommendations and ranking
Social media, entertainment, and e-commerce

Level 2
Assistance
Anti-fraud alerts and machine-assisted translation

Level 3
Automation
Data entry, extracting fields out of documents, and reading an MRI for a radiologist

Level 4
Autonomous agents
High-frequency trading agents and self-balancing electrical grid

	Level 1	Level 2	Level 3	Level 4
Readiness Is technology accurate enough?	Mature technologies developed over the past two decades	Matured over the past 10 years; models perform close to, but not yet at human capabilities	Matured in the past 1–2 years; models performing at or better than human capabilities	Selected mature applications in fintech, such as recurring payment recognition
Riskiness What is the downside of being wrong?	Low risk and huge upside	Low risk: human making the final call with greatly increased productivity	Some risks: no human in the loop; must closely monitor and alert for anomalies	High risk: needs significant attention to understand if anything is wrong
Reception Will the market accept it?	Transparent to end user	Transparent to end users; still interacting with human counterparts	Reception requires end-user education and time to achieve acceptance	Trust has to be built; requires a leap of faith for model correctness

Figure 2.7 Levels of confidence for evaluating the success of a model

LEVEL 1: RECOMMENDATIONS AND RANKING

At the recommendations and ranking level, there is a vast set of potential *content* to bring to the attention of the customer with limited attention. The goal is to anticipate what content could be most engaging for a customer.

In an explorational context, the customer's preference is hard to quantify, so the *expectation* is that only some recommendations will be relevant. When it comes to *readiness*, with more deliberate user behavior aggregation, personalization algorithms can segment and target users with some accuracy. There is a huge upside for gaining engagement when we provide relevant recommendations—even a 5% engagement rate could have an outsized business impact in many fields. At the same time, the *riskiness* of a recommendation being wrong is minimal. Personalization is already well accepted in our online experiences to the extent that we may even anticipate it.

Success in recommendations is evaluated by *lift*, which maps to the incremental business impact of using a model. To illustrate lift, an engagement improvement from 4% to 5% would be a 25% lift (as calculated by: 5% / 4% − 1 = 25%).

LEVEL 2: ASSISTANT

At the assistant level, the machine learning models produce results close to human capability, but not quite good enough yet. One example is model-assisted loan fraud detection. The *context* calls for an algorithm to alert human fraud investigators of suspicious loan applications. The *expectation* is for human fraud investigators to assess and decide if a loan application needs to be declined. For *readiness*, a model detecting fraud at the precision of 25% and more than 66% recall would already be *received* as useful for the fraud investigation team. Any greater precision could come at the *risk* of lower recall.

Success is assessed by the increase in human productivity in fraud investigations. *Confidence* is guaranteed by the final human decision in the loop.

LEVEL 3: AUTOMATION

At the automation level, the machine learning models are producing results at human-parity. *Contexts* that operate at this level include data entry (speech recognition), extraction of fields out of documents, and reading of medical images in radiology. The *expectation* is that, while there will be errors, results will be at least as good as what humans can do in a similar situation. These capabilities are often achieved using deep learning algorithms, *readied* by training on a large number of samples at scales beyond what an average human can ever be exposed to. The *risk* of predicting incorrectly could be high in applications such as health care. However, when deployed in scenarios where the automated diagnostic service is used to reach previously unreachable populations, the benefits can outweigh the risks, generating a welcoming *reception*.

Success is the adoption of models that can perform at human accuracy, such that we can significantly increase the reach to serve the previously unreachable populations.

LEVEL 4: AUTONOMOUS AGENTS

At the autonomous agent level, the machine learning models are producing results at superhuman capabilities. We interact with them by:

1 Defining the problem-solving strategy
2 Allowing the models to produce results
3 Taking time to build trust with the capabilities of the autonomous agents

One *context* is high-frequency trading, where trading decisions have to be made in the range of milliseconds to nanoseconds. No human can interpret market signals, synthesize information, and respond at this time granularity. The *expectation* is that the models behind high-frequency trading are correct the majority of the time such that the book of trades can be profitable as a whole. The *readiness* of algorithms is evaluated extensively with backtesting, as being wrong carries the *risk* of serious financial impact. In this case, models are usually tested extensively before being entrusted with large volumes of trades.

Success is when human operators can overcome the leap of faith to trust autonomous agents to correctly operate with the strategies defined to produce the anticipated results.

006

For autonomous agents, success is when human operators can overcome the leap of faith to trust autonomous agents to correctly operate with the strategies defined to produce the anticipated results.

EFFECTIVELY SETTING EXPECTATIONS FOR SUCCESS

With a deeper understanding of the customers and improvements in modeling capabilities, solutions can move up the confidence ladder, from recommendations to assistants to automation to autonomous agents. However, failure occurs when unrealistic expectations are set for the algorithms to achieve. A prime example is with autonomous driving, where the capability of technology is almost as good as a human and can often meet people's expectations at the assistant level. Still, the public is guided to evaluating it at the autonomous agent level. As a society, we are still building trust for autonomous driving to operate in all conditions correctly.

At Acorns, Jike and the team started with building recommendations to help customers save and invest more in the future. Through harvesting the entire company's ingenuity in generating behavioral nudges as recommendations to improve customers' financial wellness, the team created some nudges that generated click-through rates that were an order of magnitude higher than the typical single-digit click-through rate in a standard recommendation. The team also developed an infrastructure to launch and experiment with hundreds of new behavioral nudges each year, which can be used to quickly adapt to new market scenarios and provide timely assistance for the customers in the financial domain. Time will tell if Acorns' highly relevant behavioral nudge recommendations can be successfully perceived as helpful at the financial assistance level from the customer's perspective.

For Brian, the technically solid senior data scientist aspiring to become a tech lead from chapter 1, he can use these four confidence levels as narratives to set expectations when talking to business partners about project scope, so he can better manage his time to deliver high-quality analyses more consistently.

2.2   *Execution: Best practices*

Gartner suggested that more than 85% of DS projects fall short of expectations [6]. Many of the failures are caused not by the lack of technological prowess but by the quality of the execution. There are three major stumbling blocks in project execution:

- Specifying projects from vague requirements and prioritizing them
- Planning and managing a DS project for success
- Striking a balance among hard trade-offs

Many practices to overcome these stumbling blocks are learned on the job, away from academic institutions, fellowship programs, and online courses.

Now, let's buckle down and examine each stumbling block and the practices to overcome them.

2.2.1   *Specifying and prioritizing projects from vague requirements*

Interpreting business needs can be challenging for new DS tech leads. Many of your partners are not yet familiar with all the capabilities DS can bring and provide requests that, at best, may be a suboptimal framing of the problem.

Effective DS tech leads learn to ask *the question behind the question* to take personal accountability for setting DS projects up for success [7].

007

> Effective data science tech leads learn to ask the question behind the question to take personal accountability for setting up data science projects for success.

Let us check in on Brian, the lead data scientist at corporation Z, a social networking company, who was tasked with partnering with marketing and product teams to develop a set of email campaigns aimed at driving long-term user engagement. But does it have to be a set of email campaigns?

In execution, a DS tech lead should be able to first discuss the question behind the question with product and marketing partners: Why are we looking to drive long-term user engagement? What type of user engagement is most valuable for improving enterprise value? What are the return on investment or ROI expectations?

There are various funnel stages for user acquisition, activation, and retention. Depending on the goals of the campaign, driving long-term retention at each stage can reach different goals. Brian can share the trade-offs with partner teams to clarify the goals and expectations for the initiative. Some of the variations to discuss include:

- *Active users*—To improve the user experience for active users of the social networking product, Brian can look at how to make existing interactive features, such as searches for active users, more engaging. This perspective can include features related to search convenience, such as search query auto-complete; engagements with the search results, such as click-through rate; and search relevance, such as dwell time on the search results. When search results are more engaging, users can return to engage with the social network app more often, thus improving long-term engagement.

- *Passive users*—Alternatively, you can improve the personalization recommendations of passive users, who are mainly passively browsing in the social networking product. This leads to projects for collecting personalization hints through the users' browsing activities, such as click-through rate and dwell time, to recognize people's topic preferences. The hypothesis is that by sharing a variety of topics to increase the diversity of content to engage the user's interest and curiosity, you can improve the long-term engagement of passive users.

- *Inactive users*—For many social networks, there are a large number of users who are inactive on the platform. Improving search or recommendation features would not impact them. One way to improve the engagement of inactive users is to reach out to them over email. Projects can take the form of personalizing email subject lines to improve open rate and iterative refinement of email content through click-through analysis. The most powerful form is developing and optimizing a sequence of emails that can lead users through a path of re-engaging with the social network to improve long-term engagement.

- *Prospective users*—Some people are not yet users on a social network, but we can invite these people on to the network. If acquired with relevant intent from effective traffic sources, a significant number of prospective users could become engaged users to drive long-term engagement. Projects involve assessing the conversion of users acquired from various channels, such as search engine marketing (SEM); advertising on specific partner sites; or demand-side platforms for advertising (DSPs). Given an always-limited advertising budget and long user conversion cycles, it can be challenging to optimize user acquisition efficiency to drive long-term engagement over a few months.

For a social networking platform at the growth stage, active users are often the smallest cohort but are contributing the most long-term engagements; passive users have the highest potential to be activated with new features and incentives; inactive users are often the largest in numbers for existing users and are more challenging to bring out of hibernation. Driving long-term engagement from prospective users can be a challenging endeavor because of long conversion cycles.

Working with marketing and product partners to understand the broader strategy can help you, the DS tech lead, take personal responsibility of recommending the technical direction to improve the long-term engagement of the segment of users that will have the most significant business impact. This is asking the question behind the question.

HOW TO PRIORITIZE

With many possible projects for each business initiative, how do you, as a tech lead, prioritize the DS projects? Here are three levels of diligence for DS project prioritization you can reference:

- Innovation and impact
- Priority refinements with RICE
- Prioritize with alignment to data strategy

LEVEL 1: INNOVATION AND IMPACT

Data scientists thrive with innovative and impactful projects. When we evaluate DS projects along innovation and impact axes, the projects that score high on both axes should be prioritized. These projects can provide sound business ROI and motivate some of the best DS work.

There are also routine projects to validate hypotheses with basic DS techniques that provide excellent business impact. These projects should also be prioritized for their business impact and low risk of execution. At the same time, we should be careful not to burn out our DS team members who only get to work on routine tasks.

Some projects are innovative but do not have a path to business impact. They appear as *ivory tower* ideas that create a time sink without much validation of success for what's created. We should avoid these projects until a path to business impact can be identified.

For other projects that may be routine work with a marginal impact on business operations (such as data reporting, for instance), we should deprecate or automate where possible. Make sense?

LEVEL 2: PRIORITY REFINEMENTS WITH RICE

For projects that are impactful to the business, we can refine them further to assess four areas: *reach, impact, confidence,* and *effort,* or RICE for ease of remembering. An initial priority ranking of the projects can be produced using a weighted sum of these factors:

- *Reach*—There are often trade-offs on how specific of a population a DS project can reach. In Brian's case for improving long-term engagement, the prospective user cohort is the largest in population size and a population that we know the least about for targeting and converting. We have the most information and opportunities to target the active user cohort on a social network, but that is also often the smallest cohort of users with more limited reach than the passive, inactive, and prospective user populations.
- *Impact*—The overall business impact is the anticipated lift to key operating metrics for the reachable population. In Brian's case, the lift may be too little in optimizing the user acquisition channels to impact long-term engagement several conversion funnel stages downstream even when it can reach the largest population. Simultaneously, the lift for the active users can be significant, but for a much smaller cohort of users, limiting the overall impact.

- *Confidence*—For a DS project to succeed, there are several operational risks to consider. You can assess the following: What data is available? Of what's available, what is reliable? Of what's reliable, what is statistically significant? Of what's statistically significant, what is predictable? Of what's predictable, what is implementable? Of what's implementable, what is ROI positive? Of what is ROI positive, is there a business partner ready to operationalize it to create business value? To assess the confidence in success, there may be prior projects that have explored the data sources and third-party references that have proven the implementation path or demonstrated ROI for use cases.

008

> You can assess the operational risks for project success by asking: What data is available? Of what's available, what is reliable? Of what's reliable, what is statistically significant? Of what's statistically significant, what is predictable? Of what's predictable, what is implementable? Of what's implementable, what is ROI positive? Of what is ROI positive, is there a business partner ready to operationalize it to create business value?

- *Effort*—The effort to ensure a DS project's success can take significantly longer than the time needed to build a model. The execution process often involves multiple phases of efforts with specific goals to achieve in each phase, such as data proof of concept (PoC), product PoC, and phases of iterative improvements. Items such as documenting learnings, presenting/reviewing with business and engineering partners, and scheduling and reading A/B tests can also be included. The granularity of efforts could be on the order of weeks or sprints required or sometimes estimated with T-shirt sizes, such as small, medium, and large sizes for quick assessments. Keep it simple here.

Using the reach, impact, confidence, and effort scores, we can build a scorecard to provide an absolute prioritization rank to the projects under consideration, while balancing the trade-offs between risk and business impact between projects.

LEVEL 3: PRIORITIZING WITH ALIGNMENT TO DATA STRATEGY

One challenge with many impactful DS projects is that they often span the full stack of technologies, including data source identification, data aggregation, data enrichment, modeling methodologies, evaluation frameworks, and A/B testing. While each project may require too much investment to be prioritized, there may be components in data aggregation and data enrichment that can be shared between projects. Completing one project can offer learning that informs the viability or direction of other related projects.

A data strategy can use relationships between projects to synthesize a roadmap where projects build on each other. Efforts for common components can then be amortized across multiple ambitious projects to improve ROI.

009 A data strategy can use relationships between projects to synthesize a roadmap where projects build on each other. Efforts for common components can then be amortized across multiple ambitious projects to improve ROI.

As a tech lead, you can clarify the data strategy with DS executives and discover opportunities to share overhead across projects to allow high-effort, high-impact DS projects to be prioritized.

Some specific approaches to increase the efficiency of projects through strategic alignment to allow them to be prioritized are discussed in sections 4.1.1 and 4.3.3.

2.2.2 Planning and managing data science projects

There are many ways a project could fail. As the tech lead for a project, your role includes anticipating common risks and either planning to avoid them or allocating time and resources to address the failure modes when they come up.

In *The Art of War*, the ancient teachings by Sun Tzu from the fifth century BC, the first chapter discussed planning. It states that "careful answers to planning questions will determine who will succeed and who will be defeated, even before any troop movements." This also holds true for us today.

There is a broad range of projects in the field of DS. The stereotypical project involving a predictive machine learning model is only one of them. Here are the nine (yes, there are quite a few) most common types, illustrated in figure 2.8.

Compared to other technical or engineering projects, DS projects often involve more partners, face greater uncertainties, and are harder to manage for success.

Figure 2.8   Nine types of data science projects—only one (#5) is modeling-centric

For example, in a simple case of providing personalized recommendation, user demographic information could be coming from user-supplied profile information, prior user transactions may be coming from business operations teams, and past online behavior could be coming from engineering log archives. Just the aggregation and understanding of input data could involve discussions and alignment with three different teams. The availability and consistency of historical data sources for pattern detection and continued availability of data sources as product features evolve are all hidden risks for a DS project.

Each of the nine types of common DS projects has specific project goals and deliverables. They often require different granularity of efforts to complete. Table 2.1 details these goals, deliverables, and resource estimates.

Table 2.1   Nine types of DS projects with goals and deliverables

Project type	Project goal	Project deliverables	Estimated resources
Tracking specification definition	In a data-driven culture, the performance of product features must be tracked. Core metrics and success metrics of the features need to be defined and tracked.	A document specifying what aspects of the product/ feature need to be measured and tracked	1 DS, 1–2 weeks
Monitoring and roll-out	As a feature is launching, we need to interpret early results to detect potential implementation bugs and tracking completeness. With proper tracking in place, we must also monitor A/B tests and the feature success metrics in the context of the core business metrics.	Acceptance of the tracking capabilities and an interpretation of A/B test results with a recommendation for launch	1 DS, 1–2 weeks
Metrics definition and dashboarding	As we operate a product, we have an opportunity to develop metrics to better interpret and track their effectiveness with dashboards to operationalize more business actions.	Metrics defined to guide business operations with dashboards to deliver data in a timely fashion	1–2 DS, 2–4 weeks
Data insights and deep dives	With a deep understanding of products and their metrics, we have an opportunity to discover gaps in product features and make data-informed recommendations about new features.	Report with gaps in product features and specific recommendations on new feature directions to address the gaps	1–2 DS, 2–4 weeks
Modeling and API development	We have an opportunity to use patterns observed in the past to predict the future with certain precision and recall target and deployment path to produce business impact.	Business impact through model deployment and A/B testing, with multiple rounds of improvements	1–3 DS, 8–20 weeks

Table 2.1   Nine types of DS projects with goals and deliverables *(continued)*

Project type	Project goal	Project deliverables	Estimated resources
Data enrichment	We have an opportunity to enrich data sets with extracted or inferred properties or with references to third-party data sources. Enriched properties can simplify metrics construction or model feature engineering.	Enriched data fields with documented accuracy and coverage, designed to improve the efficiency of metrics construction or feature engineering	1–2 DS, 2–4 weeks
Data consistency	Ensure metrics developed across multiple teams are consistent. Inconsistencies erode trust with customers and executives when similar metrics from multiple parts of a product tell different stories.	Multiple teams aligned with a consistent set of metrics, which is deployed and used in customer- and executive-facing use cases	1–3 DS, 8–20 weeks
Infrastructure improvements	Improve DS efficiency by refactoring common workflow or removing tech debts. This includes tools for A/B testing and causal inference. Improvements can free up valuable resources for other projects.	Deployed improvements with demonstrated productivity gain	1–2 DS, 2–4 weeks
Regulatory compliance	Ensure data collection and usage are consistent with local laws and regulations. This often includes compliance with GDPR (general data protection regulation).	Specifications for compliant data infrastructure; documentation for processes that peer data scientists can follow to get legal approval	1–2 DS, 2–4 weeks

As a DS tech lead, there are many common failure modes for you to anticipate. Here are nine:

- Customer of the project is not clearly defined
- Stakeholders are not included in the decision process
- Project goals and impact are not clarified and aligned to company strategy
- Affected partners are not informed
- Value of the project is not clearly defined
- Delivery mechanism is not defined
- Metrics of success are not aligned
- Company strategy changes after project definition
- Data quality is not sufficient for the success of the project

Zeroing in on planning, the purpose of a project plan is to address these failure modes to the best of the team's abilities to avoid wasted efforts. Especially for large and complex projects, a project plan also serves to align understanding with partner teams to coordinate and commit resources toward executing the company strategy.

Here is a sample template of a project plan:

1 Project motivation
   - Background—Customers, challenges, and stakeholders
   - Strategic goal alignment—Company initiative it serves, its impact, and its value
2 Problem definition
   - Outputs and inputs specification
   - Metrics of project success
3 Solution architecture
   - Technology choices
   - Feature engineering and modeling strategy
   - Configurations, tracking, and testing
4 Execution timeline
   - Phases of execution
   - Synchronization cadence
   - A/B test scheduling
5 Risks to anticipate
   - Data and technology risks
   - Organizational alignment risks

That was quite a lot. Now may be a good time for a deep breath before discussing each section's purpose in avoiding common DS project breakdowns.

PROJECT MOTIVATION

For any DS project, you should have a clear customer with a challenge to be resolved. The customer must be able to receive the solution and assess whether the solution has successfully resolved the challenge. The customer of a project can be a business partner responsible for increasing top-line revenue, or it could be the DS team itself looking to improve efficiency.

In larger projects requiring multiple teams, it is essential to clarify the company initiative the project is serving and the scale of the anticipated impact, so your teams can align on the priorities in driving the company initiative.

PROBLEM DEFINITION

A DS project should have a concise *output* that can resolve the customer's challenge. For example, when improving user conversion in a customer acquisition funnel, the output can be a transaction propensity score and a threshold for when to follow up with a user. The follow-up can target users who have been in the conversion funnel for an extended amount of time and consists of reach-outs with an online chatbot or a customer service representative.

In the user conversion improvement case, we can specify the *input* as the sources, fields, and historical window of time for data to be collected for analysis or modeling. They may include profile information, prior user transactions, past online behavior, and current session contexts, such as the device used, time of day, platform (mobile/desktop), or geolocation from an IP address.

The *metrics of project success* can include a baseline conversion rate as the situation presents today and a goal for the project to reach that is both realistic and impactful enough for the investment of resources to be worthwhile.

SOLUTION ARCHITECTURE

The solution architecture section includes an outline of the *technology choices* made for resolving the challenge. This includes the data and modeling platforms, the deployment path, and any coordination required with partner engineering and product teams for product specifications, tracking specifications, and testing specifications.

Making technology dependencies of a project explicit is essential for the project's success. In nascent DS teams, infrastructure risks are common, as some infrastructure components may not have previously been exercised at scale. On the other hand, in mature DS teams, some aging infrastructure may be at risk of being deprecated soon.

For configurations, tracking, and testing of a model-building project, if you are referencing existing engineering processes, the plan should highlight which process will be used and the point of contact in engineering to coordinate with in order to have a successful project outcome.

EXECUTION TIMELINE

The two important components of the execution timeline are phases of execution and synchronization cadence.

Phases of execution

As you undertake a DS project, you may discover many unknowns in the data patterns and business impact. Project direction and methodologies may need to be adjusted in order to adapt to learnings during the execution process.

This situation matches well with conditions under the lean startup methodology. In that methodology, Eric Ries defines the situation as a team developing "a new product or service under conditions of extreme uncertainty." In this situation, Eric highlights the "build, measure, learn" iteration that focuses on a phase-based best practice to develop and learn from the minimum viable product (MVP) [8].

In your effort to develop a data-driven capability, you may choose to create a first phase with the goal to develop a *modeling proof of concept* (PoC) that includes validating the data source, defining input and output formats, engineering a minimal set of features, defining metrics and the measurement of success, and creating a minimum viable model as simple as a decision tree or a linear regression to illustrate modeling feasibility. The purpose is to remove data risks (availability, correctness, and completeness) before aligning with product and engineering on integration specification.

The second phase can be a *product PoC*, where the success criteria and product and engineering specifications are aligned, engineering resources are allocated in sprints, additional input features are developed, models are refined, and A/B tests are scheduled. The validated learning in the second phase is assessing capability/market fit, as observed from A/B test results.

The first product PoC may not generate the desired results. To address the "unknown unknown" at the time of planning, an additional one to three *build, measure, learn* iterations can be planned to learn, align, build, test, and assess a new data-driven capability.

As a tech lead, you may have realized that you are responsible for setting up realistic expectations with partners. The MVP phases and build, measure, learn iterations are essential steps to ensure resources can be allocated efficiently.

Synchronization cadence

A successful project often requires multiple teams to communicate learnings and collaborate toward business impact. Within each of the lean startup iterations, the collaborating parties will need to align on paths forward through design/specification reviews, track progress, and discuss results and learnings.

These communications are best set up as weekly syncs. This creates a project rhythm and keeps the project top of mind for the coordinating teams. Weekly milestones also allow data scientists to break large projects into approachable pieces and facilitate transparency in communicating DS project progress.

RISKS TO ANTICIPATE

There are many sources of technical risks that can derail a DS project and prevent it from achieving the return on investment it promises, including:

- *New data source*—Data availability, correctness, and completeness may be at risk.
- *Partner re-org*—Disruption of prior alignment with partners; re-alignment is required.
- *New data-driven feature*—Tracking bugs, data pipeline issues, population drifts from product feature updates, and integration issues must be discovered and resolved.
- *Existing product*—Feature upgrades can change the meaning of metrics and signals.
- *Solution architecture dependencies*—Technology platform updates can disrupt the operations of DS capabilities.

This list can serve as a checklist as you align with partners in the project plan review and between project phases, so common breakdowns can be anticipated and mitigated. A more comprehensive set of risks are discussed from a project management perspective in section 7.1.1.

Before you get concerned about this project plan looking extensive and time-consuming, know that it does not have to be. Three to five bullet points for each subsection can go a long way in reducing the risk of failure and increasing your project's likelihood of success.

PROJECT MANAGEMENT: WATERFALL OR SCRUM?

DS projects have distinct characteristics that are different from typical software engineering projects. Three top ones drive many project management considerations:

- *Project team size*—Involves 1–2 data scientists, compared with 3–10 engineers.
- *Project uncertainty*—Data-dependent risks exist on top of engineering risks.
- *Project value*—Demonstrated through A/B tests, feature completion is not enough.

Compared to the software development scenario, the smaller team size calls for project management techniques with lower coordination overhead. The increased uncertainty calls for more diligence in architecting for flexibility and more agile processes to adapt and pivot in implementation directions with new learning. The larger scope for demonstrating project value is often beyond a typical software planning process of delivering to acceptance criteria in the specification, which requires more diligence in planning.

If you already have a preference, try putting on your neutral hat for a minute. Between waterfall and scrums project management processes, which should you adopt?

Waterfall project management is a process where project activities are broken down into linear sequential phases. The phases include requirements, design, implementation, verification, and maintenance. The process is top-heavy. It calls for 20–40% of time spent in requirement gathering and design, 30–40% in implementation, and the rest in verification. Because project progress flows mainly in one downward direction, it is named *waterfall*.

Scrum is an agile process developed for managing complex knowledge work with an emphasis on software development. It is most helpful in discovering and adapting to the unknown unknowns that emerge in projects. Work happens in timeboxed iterations, or *sprints*, that are 1–4 weeks long, and then progress is synced in 10–15-minute timeboxed daily meetings, or *daily scrums*. Many teams choose 2 weeks as the length of sprints.

There have been significant discussions in the field on the best approach for DS project management. A successful DS team can draw on both waterfall and scrums processes for different types of DS projects. So, if you had said, "it depends," then you would have been right!

Table 2.1 illustrates the different types of DS projects with different complexities:

- *Small projects* require one data scientist 1–2 weeks to accomplish. Such projects include tracking specification definition and monitoring and rollout, which often have fewer uncertainties and can be managed within one sprint of the *scrum* process.
- *Mid-sized projects* require one or two data scientists 2–4 weeks to complete. Such projects include metrics definition and dashboarding, data insights and deep dives, data enrichment, infrastructure improvements, and regulatory items.

These projects can involve significant communication and coordination with business and technology partners. Planning helps lay out the phases of execution and cadence of synchronization to adapt to shifting requirements, as the collaborating data scientist and partners take new learning into account toward a clear problem definition. The project's actual length may stretch over more than two sprints as business and technology partners may need time to assess updates and provide feedback.

- *Large projects*, such as modeling, API development, and data consistency, usually require one to three data scientists to collaborate over 4–10 sprints. These projects involve not just the technical solution but also project deployments to drive business impact. Planning is essential to make sure key project risks are removed early. Scrums can be crucial to keep all team members, including data scientists, product and engineering partners, and business stakeholders in sync throughout the project.

To summarize, smaller DS projects with clear definitions can be well-suited for the scrum process with minimal planning overhead. More extensive DS projects with many failure modes often require a planning and alignment process. Project phases are defined to take advantage of scrum processes that can adjust to the specific learning from phase to phase.

2.2.3 *Striking a balance between trade-offs*

As a DS tech lead, effective execution of DS projects with the team requires many trade-offs to be balanced between speed and quality, safety and accountability, and documentation and progress.

BALANCING SPEED AND QUALITY

As a manager of projects, a tech lead must understand when to quickly empower a business partner to make a timely business decision and when to practice the art of craftsmanship. In this situation, understanding the granularity of business decisions is vital. Yes, there is both art and science in this balancing act.

Guiding toward speed

A business decision at the *go or no-go* granularity can be guided toward speed. For example, data scientists are making recommendations on potential product improvements in data insight and deep-dive projects. A typical deliverable may suggest dozens of enhancements with the top three to five recommendations prioritized. While the data insights and deep dives should have sound methodologies, the reach and impact of the recommendations may differ by an order of magnitude. The estimates for reach and impact for top recommendations can emphasize speed, as they govern *go or no-go* decisions. If many top recommendations have similar reach and impact, in the rare case, estimates can always be refined.

Guiding toward quality

When incremental improvements can result in significant business impact, quality becomes important to emphasize. An example is in infrastructure improvement projects for tackling tech debt. Section 2.2.2 discussed a phase-based approach of using modeling PoC and product PoC to remove project risk for a faster project go or no-go decision. This approach can accumulate tech debts, resulting in manually operating automatable reports and analyses, or frequent data processing/modeling job failures becoming a heavy burden for data scientists to bring models back online. Tech debt is a tool that, when used properly, can actually improve the overall efficiency. The key is to pay down the tech debts in a timely manner.

010

When balancing speed and quality, a tech lead must understand when to quickly empower a business partner to make a timely business decision and when to practice the art of craftsmanship.

As a tech lead, while you are looking to improve the overall productivity of the team by developing projects to remove the tech debts that slow them down, a common challenge is that team members often want to work on new features, and team managers have a constant stream of requests from business partners.

Influencing the team to improve quality and pay down tech debt is never easy and often requires personalized narratives to motivate the team. Some team members can be motivated by how removing tech debt can increase project iteration speed. Others can be motivated by projects to re-architect and build a more reliable modeling infrastructure. To influence up, tackling tech debt can be an investment in reducing operational overhead, so there can be more capacity to take on business partner requests in the future. The exact narrative to use requires careful listening during your one-on-ones with teammates and manager, communicating the challenges and obstacles in team productivity and calibrating your narratives to best influence them toward quality.

BALANCING SAFETY AND ACCOUNTABILITY

Regardless of how carefully we have planned and executed our DS projects, they may still fail due to unknown risks. This is often inevitable when working with new systems affected by new teams, processes, and platforms. To fail is human. What's important is how we learn from the failures.

This learning process could be called a post-mortem, learning review, after-action review, or incident review in different organizations. A post-mortem process instills a culture of learning, so the team identifies opportunities for improvement that otherwise would be lost.

It is human nature to find and assign blame, but that is often counterproductive. To learn from our past, we first need an accurate account. What happened? What effect was observed? What was expected? And what assumptions were made? Suppose data scientists or business partners believe they would be punished. In that case, they may not be open to sharing the true nature of the mechanism, pathology, and operation of the failure, and the team will not learn from the failure. John Allspaw wrote an excellent blog on this topic [9].

Data scientists must feel safe to accurately share the situation to begin an effective post-mortem process. But how do we balance this with accountability?

Rather than punishing our team members, we can give them accountability by providing them with authority to improve the process or platform involved in the failure. This can start by empowering them to give detailed accounts of their contributions to failures. We then allow those who made mistakes to become experts on educating the rest of the organization on how not to make those mistakes in the future. Yes, we know this is easier said than done.

How would we operationalize an effective DS post-mortem? Table 2.2 illustrates two types of DS failures to learn from, including failures to deploy and failures in operation.

Table 2.2 Five-step post-mortem process for failure to deploy and failure in operation

Five-step post-mortem	Failure to deploy Failure to launch on spec and on time	Failure in operation Failure to produce correct results on time
1 Brief summary	Include the context of the issue, highlighting the situation, the impact, and whether the situation is fixable.	Include the context of the incident, highlighting the incident type, length, impact, and fix.
2 Detailed timeline	Include an account of the sequence of events leading up to the issue.	
3 Root cause	Identify the root cause with the "five whys" methodology to discover the deeper reason of how the incident occurred, such as how spec drifted or how partner priorities changed.	Identify root cause with the "five whys" methodology to discover the deeper reason of how the incident occurred, such as lack of testing or human error because of lack of automation.
4 Resolution and recovery	Include potential paths and timeline to mitigate the specific issue. Include the choices and rationales behind the fix for specific incidents.	
5 Action to mitigate future risks	Work through the path and timeline to address the root causes in order to systematically prevent the type of issue from happening again without hurting team agility.	

We have found that it works best when the post-mortem documentation is conducted in a timely manner, within two to three days of the incident, while the details are fresh in the team members' minds. This way, those in the organization can also learn the most from past mistakes.

In responding to incidents, a mood of curiosity and collaboration with partners and teammates is important in acknowledging, triaging, escalating, prioritizing, communicating, resolving, and learning from them. These attitudes are addressed in section 3.3.2.

To rally the team to do a timely and rigorous post-mortem, you can leverage your manager by coordinating with them to drive team and partner participation and prioritization in scheduling. Section 5.2.2 describes the rigor required for a DS manager to coordinate with you in driving in a post-mortem process.

With coordination between you and your manager, you can work toward setting up a culture of institutionalized learning in your organization. We address this more in section 5.3.3, where the skill focus is on the people manager.

BALANCING DOCUMENTATION AND PROGRESS

Documentation is a hard topic for DS, as it is often seen as competing with making progress on additional projects. Many question how useful it really is for one or more of the following reasons:

- *Small teams*—Most DS projects are performed by teams of one to three data scientists with good communication between team members.
- *New teams*—Many DS teams are new and have not experienced project handoffs where documentation becomes essential.
- *Technical decisions*—Many DS decisions are highly technical and are made within the team without extensive reviews from business partners.
- *Who's got the time*—There is a significant demand on the team to tackle new projects rather than documenting existing work.
- *No obvious location*—Many tools (ad hoc queries, spreadsheets, slides, scripts) are used, and there is no single obvious place to document both the code and data.

With a growing team, and without sufficient documentation, onboarding new team members can become highly inefficient. You may have observed team members getting stuck over similar challenges for days, while best practices already exist in the team.

The purpose of documentation in DS is to institutionalize hard-learned knowledge in a project about the data, the process, as well as the technical and business decisions made along the way. The primary audience of the documentation is your future self and a new teammate joining the team to continue the good work you have started.

So what constitutes good documentation? Good documentation doesn't have to be long and nuanced [10], but it does have to have the following three properties: reproducibility, transferability, and discoverability.

011

> Good documentation doesn't have to be long and nuanced, but it does have to have three properties: reproducibility, transferability, and discoverability.

Reproducibility

A DS project is well-documented to be reproducible when one can obtain consistent results using the same input data, processing steps, methods, code, and conditions of analysis. When a piece of work is reproducible, it increases the confidence your customers have in the results.

Reproducibility may sound simple, but it is full of caveats. For example, input data for analyses are often aggregated from data warehouses, where new data is appended on a daily basis. Historical data may change when new users sign up for a service and when we aggregate historical transactions from third-party sources for them. To make the analyses reproducible, the query documentation needs to include not just the data observation time window but also the data aggregation time window. To be exact, if you are analyzing financial transactions observed for the month of December, you also need to specify a transaction aggregation cut-off date, such as January 5, as some transactions may post later than your cut-off date.

Another example is the use of modeling methodologies that require certain randomness, such as cross-validation sample selection, random forest classification, and gradient boosting regression. To be reproducible, the packages and random seeds must be documented.

These details for reproducibility are crucial when we return to the project in the next iteration of refinement to compare new results with the reproduced previous results.

Transferability

Transferability describes the process of applying the learning from one context to another. It is established by providing readers of the documentation with contexts of the DS project, so the reader can qualify whether the learning is applicable in an alternative context. The degree of transferability is an assessment by the reader.

Good documentation for transferability contains the business context in which the project was constituted and the assumptions were made and validated, focusing on the methodologies used. If there is an underlying market mechanism or fundamental human behavior discovered in the analysis, it should be highlighted as well. In short, these contexts and fundamental discoveries provide outsized long-term impact for the organization far beyond a particular DS project itself.

Discoverability

The documentation for a DS project is discoverable when it can appear in relevant search results for team members at a later point in time. There are many tools available for collaborative documentation; all of these tools have their highlights and inefficiencies.

Wikis are highly effective for incorporating multi-faceted content in a collaborative manner. Authorship and versioning are standard features, and the search function comes with the content management system. It is also accessible across platforms and integrates access control for pages that are intended for a limited audience. However, tables and graphs are less easily incorporated, and spreadsheet functions are not as well supported as in other platforms such as Google Sheets.

Google Docs/Sheets and alternatives are also great choices, with authorship, versioning, and search functions come as standard. Google Sheets has quite comprehensive functionality for normal spreadsheet operations, such as sorting, pivoting, and graphing. However, it does not connect directly to data warehouse data sources to pull in fresh data.

Scripting notebooks are great choices for documenting data, code, figures, and contexts. However, the search functions in the current generation of notebooks, such as Jupyter Notebooks and Databricks Notebooks, are weak, and integrations with versioning and repositories are not yet as automated as with Google Docs or wikis.

The current best practice for discoverability is to use wikis or Google Docs as the main document location, recording the contexts and business decisions, and linking scripting notebooks, spreadsheets, and production code check-ins to complete the documentation.

2.3　*Expert knowledge: Deep domain understanding*

Expert knowledge is the domain-specific insights that can be acquired through years of practicing DS in a domain. These insights include business opportunities, data source limitations, and organizational structure challenges that can expand or reduce DS projects' impacts in a domain.

How can you guide the technical direction of critical projects to align with business goals? How do you crystalize your project plan narratives for fast project approval by your manager? What are some fundamental data source limitations your team should look out for? How do you tread a path through organizational constraints to drive project success? As a DS tech lead, being observant of these distinctions and learning to work with these opportunities, limitations, and challenges can help you lead projects to success.

This section focuses on improving project success through the rigorous application of expert knowledge. You can infuse expert knowledge into the projects with a *CAN* process:

- *Clarify* the business context of opportunities or risks
- *Account* for domain data source nuances
- *Navigate* organizational structures in an industry

In the *clarify* section, we discuss the use of organizational vision and mission to help clarify your project's technical direction and craft a five-point narrative to help crystalize your thinking and align with your manager on the direction of your project. In the *account* section, we provide three examples of data limitations across different industries to highlight the value of expert knowledge to anticipate and mitigate pitfalls in projects. In the *navigate* section, we provide a framework for interpreting the maturity of the DS infrastructure in your organization and adapting your DS solutions to the acceptable industry norms to pave the path for a smooth deployment toward producing impact.

2.3.1 Clarifying business context of opportunities

As a tech lead, your team depends on you for technical direction that align with the business context. Before executing a project, do you and the project team understand how the DS project is strategically positioned in the organization? Is it a product or a feature? What hypothesis are you looking to validate?

Clarifying the business context for your project team involves first interpreting the organizational vision and mission. *Vision* is the desired future position of an organization. It is the dream, a team's true north, with the primary objective of inspiring and creating a shared sense of purpose throughout the company. *Mission* defines a company's business, its objectives, and its approach to reach those objectives. It is the overarching objective of the organization that should be measurable, achievable, and ideally inspirational. It should not be used synonymously with a vision statement.

012

Clarifying the business context for your project team involves first interpreting the organizational vision and mission. Vision is the desired future position of an organization. Mission defines a company's business, its objectives, and its approach to reach those objectives.

Vision and mission together guide companies when they grow beyond 100–200 employees. Above this size, the company's focus and decision-making process as intended by the executive team can be obscured, as it propagates through one or two management layers. Section 8.2.1 discusses how an executive leading DS can induce DS capabilities in the vision and mission of a company.

As a DS tech lead, you should be sensitive to the way the vision and mission are defined and check current projects for consistency, so your work and the team's work can stay aligned with the direction intended by the executive team. Specifically, projects should be:

- Important, such that if not done, they would have a negative consequence for the company
- Useful, such that they progress the company along with its mission
- Worthwhile, such that they produce good ROI at low risk

Let's look at a few examples:

- *LinkedIn*—LinkedIn's vision is to create economic opportunity for every member of the global workforce. Its mission is to connect the world's professionals to make them more productive and successful.

  LinkedIn DS projects include improving the efficiency for members to be matched to jobs that can further their careers, and help sales professionals become more productive in identifying critical decision-makers in companies to prospect for potential sales opportunities. These projects align well with creating economic opportunities and making members more productive.

- *OkCupid*—OkCupid's mission is to serve the most fundamental and transformative human need—to find love and happiness through meaningful relationships with deep social connections.

  In 2014, OkCupid published results from a series of A/B tests. In one test, OkCupid enrolled pairs of customers whom the algorithm deemed to be 30%, 60%, and 90% matches. For each of those groups, OkCupid told a third of them they were 30% matches, a third of them that they were 60% matches, and a third of them that they were 90% matches. This way, two-thirds of the population were intentionally shown an inaccurate matching percentage.

  While this is a typical experiment setup in DS with technical merit, used to assess a matching score's effectiveness, many people, especially ones who have gone through complicated relationships, may feel strongly about the experiment's intentionally deceptive nature. Section 3.1 discusses the ethical challenges in this kind of research in more depth.

  As a DS tech lead, when you examine this project in the context of the company's mission, would you find the alignment? Would this kind of deceptive power-of-suggestion experiment align with the mission to serve the human need "to find love and happiness through meaningful relationships with deep social connections"?

This is the kind of situation when you, as a tech lead, get to step up and apply your expert domain knowledge on projects' alignment with the company's vision and mission.

2.3.2 *Accounting for domain data source nuances*

There exist many domain-specific biases, inaccuracies, and areas of incompleteness in data sources used across different industries. They often show up unexpectedly for less-experienced data scientists, throwing off project milestones and, at times, causing complete failures of essential projects.

As an experienced DS tech lead, you have the responsibility to account for data source nuances and anticipate, recognize, and mitigate data biases, inaccuracies, and areas of incompleteness on the road to achieving project success.

013

Domain data source nuances often show up unexpectedly and can throw off project milestones or cause complete project failures. As a tech lead, you have the responsibility to anticipate, recognize, and mitigate data biases, inaccuracies, and areas of incompleteness to achieve project success.

A bias is a systematic difference between the data collected and the populations represented. An inaccurate piece of data is one that misrepresents the fact in some ways. An incomplete piece of data is one that is not completely collected.

These fundamental data limitations, which often emerge from the standard approaches with which data is collected and processed, are the expert knowledge that is so valuable for reducing project failure rates.

Let's examine the data source nuances through three case studies:

- Web sessions
- Geolocation
- Financial transactions

CASE 1: WEB SESSIONS

When users interact with a website, the interactions are recorded to analyze and understand user behavior, which can be used to improve personalization on future visits:

- *Assumption*—Some user states are stored by each web client in a distributed fashion and some on the server centrally. The client-side states are stored in HTTP cookies in browsers to maintain states within web sessions and across web sessions.
- *Definition nuances*—A web session is defined as a sequence of interactions between a client and a server, followed by periods of inactivity, without an explicit endpoint. An endpoint is not explicit because users can end their interactions at any time. They could be distracted or have lost interest and went on to work on something else.

What are some fundamental data limitations that cause biases, inaccuracies, and incompleteness in the web session data?

- *Biases*—For websites with frequently updating content, robot crawlers, which are programs automatically checking for updates on websites, may account for more than 90% of the interactions on a website. Websites welcome robot crawlers, especially the ones from search engines, as they get web content to show up in searches. For an analysis of human behavior on websites to be meaningful, automatic robot crawlers must be filtered out to remove the influence of their behavior, which tends to explore all elements on a web page rather than only the interesting or relevant ones for a human.
- *Inaccuracies*—A web page, at times, may have bugs in its implementation that pollute the client-side states that are stored in HTTP cookies. Even after the bugs are fixed, those polluted client-side states may not be recoverable. If the users with polluted cookie states do not revisit the web page, the polluted cookies will not have an opportunity to be reset. Bugs that pollute cookie states can produce long-lasting effects on later analyses involving the user state. We must be aware of any historical client-side bugs when analyzing user states and account for them in our analysis or modeling.
- *Incompleteness*—There can always be missing data when collected online because of the best-effort delivery mechanism of web traffic. Also, users can always clear cookies for privacy reasons, which results in a loss of interaction histories stored on the client. To assess the degree of data loss from web traffic due to its best-effort delivery mechanism, client-side states can be used to track how many

actions have been shared with the server, and each action can be sent with a sequence number. This technique has been successfully used within the transfer control protocol (TCP) to track client–server connections. In this case, we use the sequence numbers only for assessing the reliability of analytical data collection, and we are not requiring data transfer completeness, which may create performance bottlenecks in the user experience.

These examples of expert domain knowledge in web session data are common biases, inaccuracies, and areas of incompleteness that must be accounted for in web session analysis. In large DS organizations, the consistency with which different tech leads choose to handle these data nuances can impact the consistency of metrics and modeling results from different teams.

As a DS tech lead, you will find it beneficial to be aware of these common biases, inaccuracies, and areas of incompleteness in your projects, so you can produce consistent analysis results that business partners can trust. It is a lot, but you will find that understanding and managing these better is well worth it.

CASE 2: GEOLOCATION

To provide location-based personalized services, such as driving directions or restaurant recommendations, or to understand interaction context, such as in the office, on vacation, or at home, we need to understand the geolocation of the user:

- *Assumption*—Geolocation data is often collected from mobile devices. There are multiple approaches to getting location information, including through the built-in GPS on the mobile device, the IP address from which the requests are coming, cell tower triangulation, or with WiFi hotspot or beacon strengths nearby.
- *Definition nuances*—There are nuances in interpreting the location data collected. The Earth is an ellipsoid and ablated, or fatter at the equator. The system used by GPS is WGS84. WGS84 differs slightly from Google Maps and Bing Maps, which take a more straightforward approach and assume the Earth is a sphere. The maps' app coordinates, when matched to local maps, can be off by as much as 20 km if not calibrated, due to the difference in the assumption of the Earth's shape. Countries sometimes add obfuscations for national security reasons or personal privacy purposes, and we need to be aware of such nuances when interpreting geolocation data.

What are some fundamental data limitations that cause biases, inaccuracies, and incompleteness in geolocation data?

- *Biases*—Often, for privacy reasons, geolocation data is collected from mobile devices only when an app is in use, so the geolocation collected is correlated with app usage patterns. Some apps are used only at work or home; others are used while traveling. The geolocation collected will be a biased subset of all the places a mobile device has been to for different apps.
- *Inaccuracies*—The four sources of geolocation information have different systematic errors: 1) GPS location may be susceptible to signal interference in

metropolitan areas with high-rise buildings, tunnels, or mountainous regions; 2) the use of IP addresses for the source of geolocation collection is susceptible to people using VPNs or proxies that modify the IP address from which the request is coming; 3) cell tower triangulation is susceptible to tower database freshness; 4) WiFi triangulations are susceptible to signal availability. For example, there may be a lack of WiFi in remote areas, and non-stationary mobile hotspots may add noise to the interpretation.

- *Incompleteness*—A device may not be connected to the internet at the time of app usage, such as when a user is on a remote hike or when traveling abroad with a gap in data services. GPS data collected by apps may not be transferred back to the server promptly. Even when they are transmitted, the geolocation time series may not be completely stored and forwarded.

When drawing conclusions from geolocation data, these data nuances must be accounted for to provide differentiated services for your customers. Also, fraudsters may use these gaps in technology to spoof services into providing promotions or loans to otherwise ineligible customers.

As a DS tech lead, knowledge of these types of geolocation data nuances can help you assess projects' riskiness to better prioritize and plan the projects critical to your organization's success.

CASE 3: FINANCIAL TRANSACTIONS

Many financial wellness apps are looking to gain a comprehensive picture of a user's financial transactions across accounts in multiple institutions to provide better personalized financial recommendations.

- *Assumption*—Users have authorized data aggregations from multiple financial institutions by providing usernames and passwords to authenticate with the various institutions.
- *Definition nuances*—Depending on business relationships and technology integration, data accuracy, completeness, and timeliness can vary significantly.

What are some fundamental data limitations that cause biases, inaccuracies, and incompleteness in financial transaction data?

- *Biases*—There are two critical sources of biases: reach and timing. The reach bias is caused by the partial view of a user's financial situation for a particular financial wellness app, as a user may hold accounts at a variety of financial institutions. While data can be aggregated from other financial institutions through data aggregation services, and the top 12 financial institutions cover 80% of the bank accounts, there is a long tail of over 10,000 financial institutions in the US alone. It can be a continuous challenge to reliably aggregate transactions for all users from all financial institutions.

  The timing bias is caused by the aggregation frequency across different financial institutions. Aggregated transactions can be 1–5 days old. For example, when a credit card is swiped, a bank may be able to see the transaction right away, but the aggregators may not see those transactions for 1–2 days. Financial wellness companies that depend on the aggregators may not see those transactions for another 1–2 days. The uncertainty in the data delay across the aggregation process creates biases in timing.

- *Inaccuracies*—Inaccuracies can come from two sources: timing and user behavior. The timing inaccuracy is caused by industry norms in the timing between pending and settled transactions. For example, when a customer pays for a meal with a credit card on a Saturday night, the credit card may have a pending transaction. When the customer adds the gratuity, there's a reconciliation process, where the restaurant may post the final amount a day or two later.

  The user-behavior-triggered inaccuracies are caused by account transaction reconciliations between account connections. When a user accesses their financial accounts infrequently, they may forget their credentials and need to reset passwords. Each time the password is reset, the transaction aggregation binding on the account breaks, and the connection needs to be reestablished. When the transaction aggregator reloads the transactions, some transactions of the same amount on the same day could be duplicated or unduplicated incorrectly, causing inaccuracies.

- *Incompleteness*—There are at least two sources of data incompleteness: access and connection. The incompleteness of transactions caused by access comes from the fact that not all accounts from a user are linked at all times. Some accounts have been accessible at some point, but when users update their passwords without informing the financial wellness app, the account connection will break, causing aggregated transactions to be incomplete.

  The incompleteness of transactions caused by connection comes from the different types of links used in data aggregation. Data aggregators have tiers of connections with the financial institutions they are aggregating data from. There could be a tight point-to-point integration with a financial institution, connections through a standard API, or connections from crawling the financial accounts' web pages. The primary data fields, such as transaction date, description, and amounts, are usually available. However, transaction details such as unique transaction ID, merchant location data, and merchant categorization code (MCC) labels may not be available in the less-integrated data connections. This means the aggregated transactions may not be well labeled, such that there can be transactions between accounts that are not properly matched, causing misinterpretations of a user's cash flow.

These biases, inaccuracies, and incompleteness are expert knowledge that allows you to anticipate many complications of DS projects in the financial domain. As a DS tech lead, knowledge of these types of financial transaction complications can help you prioritize and make realistic project plans toward making impact on the business.

This section demonstrated the depth of expert knowledge, using the domains of web sessions, geolocation data, and financial transaction data as examples. The biases, inaccuracies, and areas of incompleteness described here may have implications for understanding other data transmitted through best-effort means, other data collected from multiple technologies, and other aggregation of data from different institutions.

As DS tech leads, you can take care of domain concerns by

- Recognizing data nuances as expert knowledge in your domain
- Respecting teammates with expert knowledge to fill the team's knowledge gaps
- Being sensitive to building this expert knowledge as a source of enterprise value
- Openly sharing expert knowledge with other DS teams as well as business partners to better prioritize and plan projects that can provide a more significant business impact

2.3.3 *Navigating organizational structure*

Organizational structure is another source of uncertainty in the path toward project success. Navigating this domain involves two skills: internally assessing the DS organization's capabilities and maturity, and externally navigating the business partners' organization structure outside the DS organization.

Internally, the DS organization's maturity is highly dependent on data technology platform capabilities. These capabilities can determine how fast a project team can move to execute projects successfully. DS is also a team sport. External to the DS organization, the business partners' organization structure determines how well the goals of the DS projects align with the mandates of business partners.

Let's examine the navigation of the organizational structure, both internal and external to the DS function, in this section.

ASSESSING THE MATURITY OF DS ORGANIZATION

The maturity of a DS organization is measured by the velocity with which it can produce impact. Taking the modeling capabilities of a DS team as an example, figure 2.9

Data science modeling focused maturity stages

AD HOC	FUNCTIONAL	INTEGRATED	GOVERNANCE	CULTURAL
Focuses on PoC of potential use cases, starting with data sourcing and cleansing	Identifies use cases; successfully launches a few projects; ad hoc integration with business flows	Focuses on integrating into wider business flows, launches many successful projects; selected enterprise software for DS	Focuses on strong middleware architecture with intelligence capabilities that nimbly combines into a new product offering	Predictive use cases are explored in every business line and function; high value use cases regularly discovered and implemented
Some promising early results	Challenging to operationalize	Use of A/B testing at multiple levels	A/B testing and ramp for every feature	Seamless integration with analytics and data engineering

Figure 2.9 Maturity of a data science organization

illustrates five levels of maturity for infusing intelligence into business functions and user experiences to generate business results and make strategic impact:

- *Ad hoc*—Opportunities for predictive capabilities are just being prototyped; there is no data infrastructure, so projects have to start from data sourcing and cleansing. Productivity is low, as much coordination is required to implement and deploy models in the product.
- *Functional*—A few use cases have been successfully launched with positive results. There are still challenges with the solution's reliability and efficiency in coordinating with business partners and launching new capabilities.
- *Integrated*—There is an efficient process for coordinating with business partners in launching new predictive capabilities. Predictive capabilities are being deployed into a wide range of business functions and user experiences. A/B testing methodology is being used at multiple levels of products, including frontend UI and backend algorithms.
- *Governance*—Predictive models are automatically calibrated, and inputs are being actively monitored for data drifts. Predictive capabilities are consolidated into middleware to serve a great range of product scenarios nimbly. A/B test is being applied to every product change.
- *Cultural*—Every business line and function is capturing opportunities in DS. Partner teams are regularly articulating and collaborating on new high-impact use cases. New capabilities seamlessly integrate with analytics and data engineering aspects of DS.

As a DS tech lead, you can calibrate the current maturity of your DS organization. It can help you anticipate the potential roadblocks a DS project may encounter on its path to success. To navigate around these potential roadblocks, you can identify specific data sources, data processing pipelines, or deploy environments that may be more mature than others to build a DS solution to accelerate the production of impact.

NAVIGATING BUSINESS PARTNER ORGANIZATION STRUCTURE

When establishing DS projects in traditional industries, perfectly reasonable DS projects can run into deployment challenges within existing business organizational structures. Understanding how business partners operate in traditional industries can be crucial for improving DS project success.

This organizational expert knowledge can be elaborated in four parts:

1. Understanding the traditional industries landscape
2. Specifying the business opportunities presented by DS
3. Highlighting the organization challenges for DS to produce business impact
4. Presenting alternative paths for project success

Traditional industries have pain points that exist independently of DS concerns. Understanding the intricacies of these pain points within the industry landscape allows you to better align with business partners. The business opportunity presented by DS specifies the path that DS enables to resolve the industry pain point and illustrates the DS impact on the business and the industry.

The organization structure challenge highlights the entrenched organizational bottlenecks in the traditional industry that cannot be quickly solved through one or two projects.

The alternate path for project success accounts for the organization structure challenge and offers a different path to overcome the entrenched organizational bottleneck. To illustrate how this can be done, let's take a look at a case study of applying DS in consumer lending in the financial industry:

- *Traditional industries landscape*—Credit is a financial tool that can boost a country's economy. Just like dining in restaurants, where you can eat first and pay after the meal, credit allows people to consume first and pay later. The effectiveness of credit in boosting economies depends on the ability to extend credit only to those who can repay. However, many countries in Southeast Asia, South America, and Africa do not yet have mature financial systems and cannot reliably assess creditworthiness for much of their population. This need for ways to reliably evaluate creditworthiness is something DS can help with.

- *Business opportunity*—In many countries that do not yet have sophisticated financial systems, smartphone use has already become ubiquitous. Smartphone usage can provide signals for assessing a person's creditworthiness. A lending app can use data that resides on a smartphone to predict a person's creditworthiness for individuals with little credit history.

  Fraud is rampant in lending. A fully repaid personal loan with a 15–36% interest rate usually generates a profit equivalent to 3% of the loan amount. If a loan is fraudulent, the lender loses 100% of the loan amount. Organized fraud can quickly take a lender out of business. Since repayment commonly occurs monthly, the first payment is typically 30 days after the loan is released. Fraud may not be detected until months after the loan is issued. DS can sift through tens of thousands of features collected from smartphone usage patterns to effectively predict the likelihood of fraud and credit risks from a loan applicant.

- *Organization structure challenge*—In traditional consumer lending businesses, credit risk and loan operating teams can be separate by design. This organizational structure is set up to prevent operating pressures to increase loan volume from lowering lending standards. Lowering lending standards can result in a short-term boost in loan volume but cause long-term financial losses, as an excess percentage of lower-quality loans starts to become delinquent.

  The DS teams in the traditional banking industry are often built on the operating side of the business, as many applications of DS apply to marketing, sales, customer service, and loan collection teams. By collaborating with the various functions, many signals can be collected for interpreting mobile data to assess potentially risky behavior for credit and fraud risks. However, the credit risk team is not structured to have extensive collaboration with the operating teams.

- *Alternate path for project success*—In one consumer lending business, significant business benefits are anticipated from transferring DS knowledge from operations to the risk functions. A path is set up to first collaborate with the fraud investigation teams, where the needs are more operational in nature. Projects were scoped to identify likely fraudulent cases to prioritize in fraud investigations.

    Over 30 weeks of cross-functional deep-dives were conducted through a tight weekly feedback loop between DS and fraud investigation teams. As a result, over 100 highly effective features were discovered among tens of thousands of features experimented on. The improvements in fraud prevention helped save a company more than $30 million per year in fraud losses [11].

    While the credit risk and operating sides of the consumer lending company stayed separate, the DS team was able to maintain a pool of more than 100 highly effective features, allowing the risk team to selectively use a subset of these features for their credit risk models.

Organizational expert knowledge, like the knowledge illustrated for the financial industry above, can be crucial for recognizing partnership risks and solution deployment risks for otherwise perfectly reasonable DS projects. Being able to navigate around these organization structure challenges when leading DS projects in traditional industries can be an invaluable capability for a DS tech lead.

2.4   Self-assessment and development focus

Congratulations on working through the capabilities section for becoming an effective tech lead! This is a major undertaking in your journey to produce more significant impact for your organization with DS!

The purpose of the tech lead capabilities self-assessment is to help you internalize and practice the concepts by:

- Understanding your interests and leadership strengths
- Practicing one to two areas with the choose, practice, and review (CPR) process
- Developing a prioritize-practice-and-perform plan to go through more CPRs

Once you start doing this, you will have courageously taken the steps to acknowledge your own finitude as individual human beings to discover personal limitations, recognize strengths, and gain some clarity for the paths forward.

2.4.1   Understanding your interests and leadership strengths

Table 2.3 summarizes the capability areas discussed in this chapter. The rightmost column is available for you to check off the areas you currently feel comfortable with quickly. There is no judgment, no right or wrong, nor are there any specific patterns to follow. Feel free to leave any or all rows blank.

If you are already aware of some of these aspects, this is a great way to build a narrative around your existing leadership strengths. If some aspects are not yet familiar, this is the opportunity for you to assess whether they can be of help in your daily work, starting today!

Table 2.3 Self-assessment areas for capabilities for the DS tech lead

	Capability areas/self-assessment		?
Technology	*Framing* the problem to maximize business impact	Assessing opportunities and impact when using DS to produce hindsight, insight, foresight, or intelligence	
	Discovering patterns in data	Vigilance in understanding data characteristics, such as unit of decisioning, sample size, sparsity, outliers, sample distribution/imbalance, and data types	
		Innovation in feature engineering in flexibly using simple and complex statistics, taxonomy-based analysis, clustering analysis, and graph analysis	
		The clarity in modeling strategy with momentum-based, foundational, reflexive, or hybrid strategies	
	Setting expectations for success	Using four levels of confidence to set success expectations for the capability of a model in recommendation and ranking, assistance, automation, and autonomous agents	
Execution	*Specifying* and *prioritizing* projects from vague requirements	Asking the question behind the question to take personal responsibilities for getting business results	
		Prioritizing DS projects by assessing three levels of details: innovation and impact; assessing reach, impact, confidence, and effort (RICE); and alignments to data strategies	
	Planning and *managing* a DS project	Interpreting project types, while specifying project goals, deliverables, and estimated resources	
		Planning a project across five areas of concerns: project motivation, problem definition, solution architecture, execution timeline, and risk to anticipate	
		Project management: leverage the best of waterfall and scrum techniques based on project team size and degree of uncertainty	
	Striking a balance between trade-offs	Balancing speed and quality, safety and accountability, and documentation and progress	

Table 2.3   Self-assessment areas for capabilities for the DS tech lead *(continued)*

Capability areas/self-assessment		?
Expert knowledge	*Clarifying* the business context of opportunities	Understand organizational vision and mission, and check for project alignment	
	Accounting for domain data source nuances	Account for assumptions, definition nuances, biases, inaccuracies, and incompleteness in domain	
	Navigating organizational structure	Internally: assess the maturity of the DS organization Externally: understand the industries landscape, specify business opportunities, highlight organizational challenges, and present alternative paths for project success	

2.4.2   *Practicing with the CPR process*

With your leadership strength and potential development area identified, you can experiment with a simple choose, practice, and review (CPR) process with two-week check-ins:

- *Choose*—Select one to two items from the table to work on. As an example, you may choose to first better understand your organization's vision and mission for more expert knowledge.
- *Practice*—For each project you are involved in, practice the skill you have chosen to work on. If you have chosen to better understand the company vision and mission, you may want to review them on your company's website, clarify the technical direction of your projects, and find examples where projects align well or do not align well with the vision and mission.
- *Review*—Set up a meeting with yourself in two weeks to check in and come back to this section of the book to assess whether you have now gained a better understanding or command of the skill. You can choose to take another sprint to further develop the skill or move on to the next CPR cycle.

For your self-review, you can use a project-based skill improvement template to help you structure your actions over the two weeks:

- *Skill/task*—Select a skill or task you have chosen to work on.
- *Date*—Select a date in the two-week period when you can apply the skill.
- *People*—Write down the names of the people with whom you can apply the skill, or write *self*.
- *Place*—Select the location or occasion at which you can apply the skill (for example, a one-on-one with a manager or a team huddle on next steps for project X).
- *Review result*—How did you do compared to before? The same, better, or worse?

By holding yourself accountable for these steps in a self-review, you can start to exercise your strengths and shed light on any blind spots in your tech lead capabilities.

2.4.3 *Developing a prioritize, practice, and perform plan*

After working through a few CPR cycles, you should gain insights into how you work with the elements of technology leadership capabilities. To form a self-improvement habit, be aware of the best practices you are using and also for those being used in other teams. If you find yourself enthusiastically working on integrating these best practices into your own daily work, we recommend that you put together a prioritize, practice, and perform plan.

The prioritize-practice-perform plan is a set of CPR cycles for building a self-improvement plan to become a more self-aware, powerful, and considerate tech lead in DS over a few quarters. You can use each CPR self-review to demonstrate your progress.

In working on the CPR cycles, many data scientists have also found peer support in working with another DS partner to keep each other accountable. Competency in a skill takes time to build. Have empathy with yourself and your partner in peer support as you improve your competencies. You can observe your progress over four levels:

1 *Unconsciously incompetent*—Happily unaware that you don't have some skills
2 *Consciously incompetent*—Aware that you lack some skills you can't practice yet
3 *Consciously competent*—Great efforts in practicing skills, can self-assess success
4 *Unconsciously competent*—Best practices become habit, can use them effortlessly

As you become competent in these skill sets as a tech lead, you are in a position to produce more significant business impact. Next, you can qualify your interest for pursuing a more technical or more managerial path.

If you are pursuing a more technical path, check out sections 4.1 and 4.3 for technical-staff-level milestones, and sections 6.1 and 6.3 for principal-staff-level milestones. If you are pursuing a more managerial path with team leadership opportunities, you can follow the progressions of this book in later chapters, with chapters 4 and 5 discussing DS team leadership, chapters 6 and 7 discussing DS function leadership, and chapters 8 and 9 discussing company leadership.

2.4.4 *Note for DS tech lead managers*

If you are using the technology, execution, and expert knowledge to evaluate team members, the topics discussed in this book are aspirational expectations in each area. They are best used to coach tech leads to do the best work of their careers and are not meant to be blocks to hold back promotions. In fact, if a DS tech lead has demonstrated capabilities and virtues in some of these areas, they could be excellent candidates to be given the challenge of people management.

Summary

- *Technologies* are tools and best practices you can use to frame business problems, discover patterns in data, and set expectations for success.
  - In framing business problems, strive to produce a more significant impact by not only providing hindsight, insight, and foresight for business decisions but also by driving customer actions with predictive intelligence capabilities.
  - In discovering patterns in data, use vigilance in correctly understanding data characteristics, innovate with partners in feature engineering, and provide clarity in modeling strategies that are coherent with fundamental mechanisms of the domain.
  - Given the available model accuracy, communicate the right level of confidence with customers to set expectations for success.
- *Execution* is what must be practiced toward project success in specifying projects from vague requirements; prioritizing, planning, and managing projects; and striking a balance between hard trade-offs.
  - In specifying projects, avoid being task-oriented, and ask the question behind the question in order to take personal responsibility to produce the best business results in projects.
  - In prioritizing, planning, and managing projects, assess projects in terms of reach, impact, confidence, and effort (RICE) and alignment to data strategies; address common project failure modes with a simple and concise project plan; and leverage waterfall or scrum techniques, depending on your project, to manage your projects.
  - In balancing hard trade-offs between speed and quality, safety and accountability, and documentation and progress, improve the long-term productivity of the team.
- *Expert knowledge* is the domain-specific insights that can be acquired through years of practicing DS and can show up in the clarity of recognizing the business context, accounting for domain data source nuances, and navigating organizational structures.
  - In recognizing business context, check for project alignment with the vision and mission of your organization.
  - In accounting for domain-specific nuances, knowledge on data source assumptions, definitions, biases, inaccuracies, and incompleteness can help avoid costly failures.
  - In navigating organizational structure, you can assess the team maturity internal to the DS organization and uncover team structure challenges external to the DS function to find alternative paths to launch successful projects.

References

[1] E. Robinson and J. Nolis, *Build a Career in Data Science.* Shelter Island, NY: Manning Publications, 2020.

[2] B. Godsey, *Think Like a Data Scientist.* Shelter Island, NY: Manning Publications, 2017.

[3] V. A. Ganesan, 2013.

[4] H. He and E. A. Garcia, "Learning from imbalanced data," *IEEE Transactions on Knowledge and Data Engineering*, 2009.

[5] N. V. Chawla, "SMOTE: Synthetic minority over-sampling technique," *Journal of Artificial Intelligence Research*, 2002.

[6] M. Asay. "85% of big data projects fail, but your developers can help yours succeed." TechRepublic.https://www.techrepublic.com/article/85-of-big-data-projects-fail-but-your-developers-can-help-yours-succeed/

[7] J. G. Miller, *QBQ! The question behind the question: Practicing personal accountability at work and in life*, TarcherPerigee, 2004.

[8] E. Ries, *The Lean Startup.* New York, NY: Crown Publishing Group, 2001.

[9] J. Allspaw. "Blameless postmortems and a just culture." Code as Craft. https://codeascraft.com/2012/05/22/blameless-postmortems/

[10] Mark D. Wilkinson et al. "The FAIR Guiding Principles for scientific data management and stewardship," *Sci Data*. 2016; 3: 160018. Published online 2016 Mar 15. doi: 10.1038/sdata.2016.18.

[11] J. Chong, "Deploying AI in Mobile-first Customer-facing Financial Products: A Tale of Two Cycles," [Online]. Available: https://www.youtube.com/watch?v=_GNikKSOBwM

Virtues for leading projects

3

This chapter covers

- Operating in the customers' best interest as the standard of professional conduct in DS
- Adapting to business priorities and confidently imparting knowledge
- Practicing the fundamentals of scientific rigor
- Monitoring for anomalies and taking responsibility for creating enterprise value
- Maintaining a positive attitude with tenacity, curiosity, and collaboration

In leadership, virtues are often emphasized over capabilities. While we can round off gaps in capabilities with the right combination of talent on a team, gaps in virtues can cause a project to fail or, worse, negatively impact the business. The Greek philosopher Aristotle explained virtues as the individual's habitual actions etched into one's character, which come from years of practicing being good to benefit oneself and society. They are what others can trust you to do when no one is looking.

As a tech lead, practicing *ethical* and *rigorous* habitual actions with a positive *attitude* is crucial to forming your character to succeed as a DS leader. When you maintain acceptable practices in these three dimensions, you are more likely to deliver a significant impact on your organization and advance in your career. We have also observed that when data scientists neglect one or more of these dimensions, they can get into difficult situations they must be mentored through or, in some cases, be managed out of.

What do we mean by *ethics, rigor,* and *attitude* here?

- *Ethics*—Standards of conduct at work that enable you to avoid unnecessary and self-inflicted breakdowns. There are many aspects of work ethics for data scientists, including data use, project execution, and teamwork.
- *Rigor*—The craftsmanship that generates trust in the results data scientists produce. Rigorous results are repeatable, testable, and discoverable. And rigorous work products can become solid foundations for creating enterprise value.
- *Attitude*—The moods with which you approach workplace situations. With positivity and tenacity to work through failures, data scientists should be curious and collaborative team players. We should also respect the diverse perspectives in lateral collaborations.

Virtues are meant to be practiced in moderation. Doing too much can be just as bad as not doing enough. For example, too much rigor can cause analysis paralysis and indecision. Too little rigor can result in flawed conclusions, which may lead to adverse outcomes and loss of trust from executives and business partners. You may have seen examples in one or both extremes. Let's dive into each of these dimensions in more detail.

3.1 Ethical standards of conduct

As a data scientist or practitioner, you have access to a vast amount of data to serve your customers. The data may impact how the financial market assesses a company's enterprise value or may be personally sensitive with reference to users' financial situations, health conditions, or geographic locations. How we work with the data that is entrusted to us, especially when no one is looking, is a demonstration of our ethical standards.

We define ethics in DS as this field's standard of professional conduct. These ethics are intended to be practical rather than theoretical. For a DS tech lead, we discuss three areas of professional conduct:

- Leading projects that operate in customers' best interest
- Adapting to business priorities in a dynamic market environment
- Imparting knowledge to team members confidently

We recommend these practices for you to avoid unnecessary, self-inflicted breakdowns. For Jennifer (from chapter 1, case 3), whose teammates feel micromanaged and are unhappy about busywork, improving her skills in communicating changes would help her build trust with her team. These practices can also open up opportunities for a positive, agile, and productive work environment.

3.1.1   *Operating in the customers' best interest*

Data practitioners often have access to and work with sensitive data. For example, in the ridesharing industry, data scientists may have access to riders' detailed transaction records, including riders' daily routines, visits to hospitals, or other weekend adventures. In the online dating industry, data scientists build potentially life-changing couple-matching algorithms and run emotionally impactful A/B tests.

Being ethical here has two aspects:

- Asking questions with sensitivity and empathy to customers' well-being and not asking questions that one would not want to be asked about oneself [1]
- Running experiments with sensitivity and empathy to customers' well-being and not experiments that would negatively impact customers' emotional well-being

INSENSITIVE USE OF DS

An example of questionable ethics on insensitive use of DS is the infamous 2012 "Uberdata: The Ride of Glory" blog [2]. An Uber employee inferred potential one-night stands by analyzing passenger rides to an unfamiliar location between 10 p.m. and 4 a.m. on a Friday or Saturday, then taking a second ride within 1/10th of a mile of the drop-off location four to six hours later. While the analysis was sound and rigorous from a DS perspective, and the results were in aggregate with no personal information released, the topic was selected in bad taste and eroded trust with riders.

The "Ride of Glory" analysis produced significant social backlash for Uber as a company. The fact that this type of analysis was produced, socialized, and published indicates a culture, in 2012, that tolerated insensitivity on the questions being asked in the ridership behavior analyses.

As a tech lead, you are the first line of defense guarding a company against unethical DS practices. An internal ethical compass can help you call off an analysis direction that could be seen as insensitive to the customer's well-being.

014

> The tech lead is the first line of defense guarding a company against unethical data science practices. An internal ethical compass can help you call off an analysis direction that could be seen as insensitive to the customer's well-being.

One technique used to evaluate whether something could be seen as insensitive to customers is to apply the so-called *New York Times* rule, or major newspaper rule. It is a commonsense rule of ethical conduct that you should not do anything in public or private that you would mind having reported on the front page of a major newspaper.

Suppose the author of the "Ride of Glory" blog used the *New York Times* rule to assess the appropriateness before conducting the analysis. In that case, they might have recognized the highly controversial nature of the topic and potential backlash, and acted differently.

Some analyses and experiments can pass the *New York Times* rule even when they may hurt user experience in the short term but benefit user experience in the long term. Examples include experimenting with more or fewer ads on a web page to increase the profitability of the business to better serve future customers, or assessing the effect of web page loading delays on web page engagement to justify engineering investment by intentionally slowing down some web page loads.

IMPACT ON CUSTOMERS' EMOTIONAL WELL-BEING

An example of DS profoundly impacting customers' emotional well-being is a series of 2014 A/B test results OkCupid published in blog format [3]. The experiment enrolled pairs of customers who the algorithm said were 30%, 60%, or 90% matches. For each group, the app told a third of them that they were 30% matches, a third of them that they were 60% matches, and a third of them were 90% matches. This way, two-thirds of the population were intentionally shown a matching percentage that was not accurate. This type of experiment has technical merits but can also negatively impact customers' emotional well-being.

How can you assess when a DS use case may have crossed the ethics line? Three principles from ethics research can help us evaluate a challenging situation [4], [5]:

- *Respect for persons*—Treat customers with respect. Provide transparency, truthfulness, and voluntariness (choice and consent) when conducting experiments.
- *Beneficence*—Protect people from harm, and minimize risks and maximize benefits.
- *Justice*—Ensure that participants are not exploited and there is a fair balance of risks and benefits.

Are we making too big a deal? After all, is changing a displayed guesstimate of a score on a screen going to cause significant psychological harm?

The OkCupid match score exercise crosses the line from trying out new features to an experiment of deception or power-of-suggestion experiment that focuses on behavioral experimentation on relationships between people. Think about the emotional trauma of those who thought they had finally found the love of their lives on the platform, as suggested by the match score, only to have wasted precious time within the prime years of their lives to find a life companion. Would you like those experiments to be unknowingly done to you? Deceptive experiments raise many questions about whether the users are respected.

The data scientist who conducted the experiment might have had the best intention to prove that the OkCupid match score has merit and can be trusted by its customers. However, the implication that the experiment took place without transparency and voluntariness actually could hurt customer trust. In the future, customers would not know when they might be subjected to another test and would likely not trust the scores anymore. As the saying goes: "Fool me once, shame on you. Fool me twice, shame on me."

3.1.2 Adapting to business priorities in dynamic business environments

Business priorities can change quickly. As a DS tech lead, what would you do when the project you are managing is put on hold, and the team is asked to focus on some-thing else?

Fundamentally, team members' responsibility to the organization is to execute the business's priorities. Many types of DS projects can take 8–20 weeks (as shown in table

2.1 in section 2.2), and when the business needs the team to work on something more urgent before these large projects can complete, tech leads must help team members and partners adapt to the change.

There are four concerns for a tech lead to manage project changes:

- Discern the changes that require attention.
- Understand the reasons behind a change.
- Communicate with team members and stakeholders.
- Document current progress and move on.

Figure 3.1 illustrates these four concerns, and the following section takes you through them one by one.

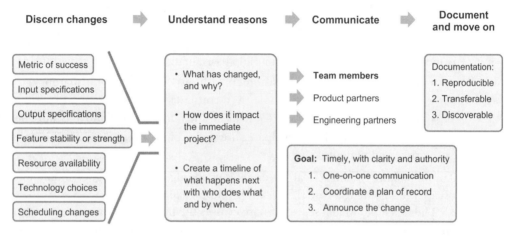

Figure 3.1 **Four steps in communicating changes effectively to a team and stakeholders**

DISCERNING THE CHANGES THAT REQUIRE ATTENTION

Things inevitably change during a DS project. As a tech lead, it is crucial to keep your team and partners informed proactively of any changes. Partners often have project dependencies on the milestones to be delivered, as described in the project plan, which you might not have realized they are sensitive to.

Who should be included in the communication? The answer is all partners in the project stakeholder list of the project plan. You can find it in the project motivation background section, as elaborated on in section 2.2.

How about some examples of these changes?

- *Metrics of success*—When a project's motivation changes, it may not impact the DS portion of the project, but it may affect the engineering portion. For example, when a success metric shifts from short-term to long-term engagement, the DS work of predicting the next best action may remain the same. However, the frequency of computing the metrics may change and warrant a different level of engineering complexity.

- *Input specifications*—Input specifications in data type, data format, and update frequency may change because of documentation errors or partner upgrades; some are planned, and others are unplanned. It's important to share the changes with all partners, as certain changes may have severe implications on user experience, privacy, and compliance.

- *Output specifications*—Output specifications in data type, format, expected accuracy, or update frequency may change because of unexpected limitations in feature extraction, modeling environment, or changes in requirements. This type of change would have obvious implications on downstream services that depend on the output and should be communicated in a timely manner.

- *Technology choices*—Technology choices can change because of system limitations, updates, or changes in resource availability. These may have unexpected implications on the output specification, so they must be communicated.

- *Feature stability or strength*—Although feature stability or strength changes detected are modeling details, they may be symptoms for system issues or market trends that warrant a close look by a broader team, which should be communicated promptly.

- *Resource availability*—When resource availability changes, informing partner teams in a timely manner can help them adjust schedules to accommodate or help escalate and reinstate resources if they were taken away.

- *Scheduling changes*—When scheduling on the team changes because of internal conflicts or delays, or because of external dependency changes, informing partner teams in a timely manner can help them adjust schedules or escalate to reassess priorities to get projects back on track.

In all of these situations, timely communication with the team and partners is essential to build and maintain trust, while helping projects stay on track as much as possible. Priorities can change for many reasons: a change in management occurred, a related project was accelerated or delayed, or the business environment changed because of disruption from technology, policy, the economy, or natural disasters.

Remember Jennifer from chapter 1, the tech lead who's good at communicating with business partners across the company and not afraid to push back on project scope creep to deliver her project on time? Let's keep her in mind as we examine the next three steps on how she can better communicate changes within her own team.

Understanding the reasons behind a change

Understanding the reason behind the change may not be easy. If there has been a change in management, it is crucial to learn about the new manager's style and previous experiences. Talk to your new manager, as well as people who have worked with them before, to gather as much information as possible. This action is an overhead that you, as the tech lead, can take on, so you can better anticipate the set of new demands that will be coming your way.

If acceleration or delays in related projects cause the change, it is important to understand the root cause as well as the impact beyond the specific projects you are leading. This can help you understand any secondary impact, such as A/B testing schedule contention, as you plan the new priority.

Suppose the change is caused by changes in the business environment, such as disruptions from technology innovations, government policy changes, the expansion or recession of the economy, or special circumstances caused by natural disasters. It is then an opportunity to broaden your horizons and understand how the organization responds to the situation, as well as what the next few steps may be to help team members anticipate what would come next.

Sometimes, it may make sense just to complete the current project. This is a conversation with your manager that can be worthwhile to ensure the decision is in the organization's best interest. When a business decision is made, however, you need to follow through and execute it.

The team members on your project are looking to you for what to do next. With an understanding of the situation, you should coordinate with your manager to clearly articulate the changes to team members.

Clear communication includes the following:

- What has changed, and why?
- How does it impact the immediate project?
- A timeline of what happens next should be included with who does what and by when.

Communicating to team members and stakeholders

During times of change, team members depend on the tech leads to bring certainty and clarity to potentially chaotic situations. This communication needs to happen quickly, as the information travels fast with today's instant messaging channels, and misinformation (and sometimes rumors) from alternate channels can undermine trust with team members. In addition to your team members, it is essential to inform all stakeholders of any changes, including product and engineering partners, who may not be aware of the implications of the changes.

In determining what happens next, you can start with a quick evaluation of whether all the necessary resources are available for handling the new priorities. Your manager will appreciate you identifying potential roadblocks for the new direction, so that the team has a feasible work plan going forward that you and your manager have committed to.

If we are communicating changes, here are some best practices to keep in mind. The goals for effective communication of changes are to communicate in a timely, clear, and authoritative manner. One powerful way is to start with one-on-one communication, coordinate a plan of record, announce the aligned plan of record, and solicit any questions or comments before moving forward:

- *One-on-one communication*—Direct and personal "heads-up" communication with the product partners, engineering partners, and other partners can build trust, provide a private forum for candid feedback and safe brainstorming of solutions, and allow time for partners to prepare to communicate to their team. For small changes, this can be as simple as a message on the company business communication platform—be it Slack, Teams, or another service.
- *Coordinate a plan of record*—If any adjustments or escalations are required, the parties can align on a plan of record, so when the change is announced, it does not leave the broader team confused about what's next.
- *Announce the change*—Announcing a change with a plan of record for a path forward provides a sense of certainty for the broader team, so problems can be presented with a solution plan in place. The heads-up also helps partner leads build trust and authority with their teams. Being open to questions or comments can help you understand any remaining unaddressed areas.

This process may appear cumbersome, but, over time, it can help build trust between business partners and help you, the DS tech lead, build authority with the team, allowing the change announcement to be clear and solution-driven.

Documenting and moving on

When documenting the current project, you can refer to the project plan structure in section 2.2.2 and state clearly what stage of the project you are stopping on. It is essential to document the solution architecture, the current learning, and the risks that were removed through the work done so far.

If there is partially developed code, it is crucial to make sure that the comments reflect what is done so far, with high-level placeholders for the modules that remain to be developed. One of the most painful experiences when picking up a half-developed project later is when documentation such as comments and code don't match.

So what constitutes good documentation? As discussed in section 2.2.3, good documentation doesn't have to be long and nuanced, but it does have to satisfy the following three conditions:

- *Reproducible*—Able to obtain consistent results using the same input data, processing steps, methods, code, and conditions of analysis
- *Transferable*—Able to apply the learning in multiple contexts
- *Discoverable*—Able to appear in relevant search results for team members at a later point in time

With a clear set of documentation of the progress thus far, you can update any tickets and be well positioned to tackle the team's new priorities.

As for Jennifer from chapter 1, now with a better understanding of the three steps she can use to better communicate to her own team, she may: 1) ask the questions behind the questions from business partners when they initiate changes to projects; 2) communicate the change and its context with clarity and authority in a timely manner; and 3) document current work and move on. With these practices, both Jennifer and her teammates can have a much-improved experience.

3.1.3   *Imparting knowledge confidently*

There is significant learning generated in pursuing a DS project beyond the deliverables for its customers. For example, learning can come from the *data sources* examined, the *tools* used, the *assumptions* made, and the *methodologies* developed, as illustrated in figure 3.2.

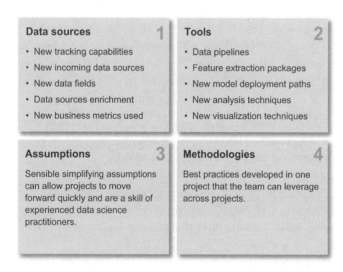

Data sources   1

- New tracking capabilities
- New incoming data sources
- New data fields
- Data sources enrichment
- New business metrics used

Tools   2

- Data pipelines
- Feature extraction packages
- New model deployment paths
- New analysis techniques
- New visualization techniques

Assumptions   3

Sensible simplifying assumptions can allow projects to move forward quickly and are a skill of experienced data science practitioners.

Methodologies   4

Best practices developed in one project that the team can leverage across projects.

Figure 3.2   **Four types of knowledge to share, regardless of project success or failure**

As a DS tech lead, your ethics, or standard of professional conduct, include ensuring the learnings are captured and disseminated as much as possible to your team members, so the team's experience and expertise can accumulate and grow over time.

015

As a tech lead, you are responsible for ensuring the learnings from the team are captured and disseminated as much as possible, so the team's experience and expertise can accumulate and grow over time.

That's easier said than done, you might say, as so much of the learning happens in a data scientist's everyday work. Sometimes, data scientists may even feel embarrassed to share details of simplification and assumptions with peers. In the daily wrangling with data and algorithms, the code and analysis may also include quick trials and errors that may look messy at times. When it comes to sharing, data scientists are often more willing to share the results than the steps they took toward the results.

How do we encourage a more open culture of sharing among team members? What might some of these learnings look like?

DATA SOURCES

Many DS projects are defining new tracking capabilities to produce new data sources, exploring new incoming data sources, examining new data fields in existing data sources, enriching data sources with third-party data, or creating new metrics with existing data sources.

In defining *new tracking capabilities* to produce new data sources, you answer important questions, such as what are the opportunities the new tracking provides? What are some limitations that existing tracking capabilities have and that new tracking capabilities will solve? What is the timeline of implementation? What projects will the latest tracking data likely benefit? Are there earlier versions of tracking capabilities that will be deprecated when new ones come online? What projects may need to update their data sources? These learnings are important to share with DS peers and are often neglected when only the deliverables are presented to the product and engineering business partners.

In exploring *new incoming data sources*, the data source availability, correctness, completeness, and consistency are aspects that other DS team members looking to use the data source will be interested in learning about. These simple metrics can be time-consuming to assess, and any infrastructure for monitoring or assessing them can significantly accelerate future DS projects.

In examining *new data fields* in existing data sources, data distribution, and internal consistency with other existing fields are important learnings. Any consistency issues with other data fields within the same data source or across data sources are especially important to share, as data consistency issues are hard to discover and resolve across product organizations.

In one real-world incident in a large organization, a tracking issue manifested as an inconsistent metric and was left unresolved for over a year; when fixed, the tracking issue was estimated to have resulted in tens of millions of dollars of unbilled revenue. There can be great value in diligently assessing the impact of data inconsistencies when they are detected.

In *enriching data sources* with third-party data, there is an opportunity to benchmark data sources with external references. For example, if you are annotating users coming to a website with age estimates, this data could be used to benchmark against government statistics for population demographics of a particular region. Benchmarking can also be performed against marketing surveys or industry analyst reports. Such information can help the team better understand the population biases of your products or services and contribute to assessing alternative marketing channels.

When *creating new metrics* with existing data sources, you are crafting summary indicators that can better address business concerns and guide business operations. One example of a summarizing indicator is the conversion ratio in customer acquisition. While the metrics can be as simple as a ratio between two numbers, there are many design decisions to consider to make them meaningful. How do you choose the specific conversion stage that can balance between the clarity of conversion intent, the accuracy of predicting short-term or long-term revenue, the length of the observation window for conversion, and the number of observations required? All these aspects must be selected with analyses and domain insights. These learnings are essential to share among DS team members.

TOOLS USED

A DS project may touch on many tools. These may include real-time data pipelines, feature extraction packages, new model deployment paths, or new analysis techniques.

Real-time *data pipelines* can bring unique challenges to feature extraction, as many feature engineering routines are performed on batches of historical data. Some standard architectures and techniques can be used in real-time data pipelines, such as Lambda architectures and incremental processing. Any experiences in working with the limitations and opportunities of real-time data pipelines are valuable to share with peer data scientists.

Feature extraction packages can vary from the standard NLP packages to graph databases and algorithms to deep learning packages for vector embeddings. When novel features are being explored, the nuances of working with these tools can accelerate the learning curve of peer data scientists looking to use the same tools in future projects.

New model deployment paths are crucial for DS to demonstrate business value. It is also the component that requires the most coordination with business partners. Any changes in the tools and practices used for feature ramp, A/B tests, and tracking are essential to share with the team, along with the final results.

If a *new analysis technique* is being used to answer critical questions about the business, you may also want to share that with the team. For example, for the analyses where we can't do A/B tests, observational causal inference based on historical data is a popular approach. Best practices and templates for working with various observational causal inference techniques are great topics to share with the team.

New visualization techniques can allow critical information to be communicated more succinctly. For example, illustrations of cohort revenue contribution can highlight the value of different vintages of customers as they go through the customer life cycle, which can inspire visualizations across marketing channels or over geographical regions.

ASSUMPTIONS MADE

Even simple-looking DS projects can have complexities that require crude assumptions to produce results. For example, to derive a set of business rules to detect anomalies in customer acquisition channels, many assumptions need to be made. How long should the observation window of the customer acquisition channels be? How long should the conversion time windows between user acquisition and user activation be? What are the user behaviors patterns over the time of the day, days of the week, and weeks of the month? And do bank business days and national holidays affect conversion? On top of these assumptions, demographic shifts, the acquisition flow updates, and advertising message tweaks could all influence the detection of anomalies across customer acquisition channels.

For many data scientists, exposing simplifying assumptions in an initial version of a project may feel embarrassing and not rigorous. As tech leads, we should all have the humility and understanding that assumptions are necessary and essential to prioritize our time on our analysis's most important and sensitive factors. Being able to make sensible assumptions quickly is a key capability for executive decision-making, especially when information for decision-making is incomplete. When team members make appropriate assumptions, make sure to point them out and compliment them. When inappropriate assumptions are made, guide gently, and try not to criticize.

What's even more powerful is to build institutional knowledge by understanding the sensitivity of conclusions to the assumptions made. For example, if you can show that the conclusion stays the same with half or double the observation time window, you can significantly accelerate the velocity of innovation by running twice as many experiments in the same time period.

When you drive the explicit sharing of the assumptions made, the team can understand the limitations of the conclusion and areas to validate when more time and more resources can be dedicated to investigate a particular direction.

METHODOLOGIES DEVELOPED

As you work on DS projects, you may develop methodologies and best practices that the team can leverage in future projects. For example, DS teams are often involved in validating new features with A/B tests. In guiding features through A/B tests, a feature may be launched to 1% of users first, then 10%, 50%, and 100% as the team gains more confidence in the new feature's effectiveness. You may ask: How can I make ramp decisions that can balance speed, quality, and risk considerations? Well, this is the kind of methodology that can benefit the broader team when you share the best practices you have worked out [6].

As for Jennifer, the tech lead from chapter 1, she can provide opportunities for building identities by encouraging senior members of her team to share their learning with others. This can be a great way to highlight aspects of projects that can generate enterprise value. Sharing the data sources examined, the tools used, the assumptions made, or the methodologies developed can allow he benefits of best practices to quickly scale from an individual level to a team level, and makes up an important part of a tech lead's value for the company.

3.2 *Rigor cultivation, higher standards*

Trust is precious to build for all DS work. Much of the trust in data and modeling comes from the rigor with which data scientists treat the subject. Partners expect your work to be scientifically rigorous, and the responsibility of holding up that bar of rigor is in your hands.

Rigor manifests in the way you work with technology, execution, and expert knowledge:

- *Technology*—The foundation of scientific methodology, on which DS stands.
- *Execution*—Rigor in deploying and maintaining data platforms and systems.
- *Expert knowledge*—Responsibilities you take on to create enterprise value.

Yes, these are the capabilities examined in chapter 2, as rigor manifests in the same way you work with capabilities. Now, let's explore these in the context of rigor one at a time.

3.2.1 Getting clarity on the fundamentals of scientific rigor

DS rigor borrows from the scientific rigor mechanisms [7], which occur in four stages: project design and review, executing experiments, peer review before publication, and published results. As a DS tech lead, you can use this rigor mechanism as a tool or technology for nurturing DS projects across all their equivalent stages:

1 *Project design and review*—The purpose is to ensure resources are dedicated to the most promising endeavors in the most efficient manner. Section 2.2 described this process of prioritizing, crafting, and aligning DS projects with customers and business partners.

 For many data practitioners with advanced degrees, the DS project plan can be considered as the scientific proposal. The review process is an early feedback mechanism for increasing the success rate of high-potential projects.

2 *Executing experiments*—This is the core of the scientific method of crafting a controlled experiment with a clear hypothesis, testing it, and iterating until impactful learning can be validated. This is the solution architecting, analysis, model building, and A/B testing of the DS hypothesis. This stage is not directly scrutinized by peers. Both scientific and ethical rigor are driven by you, the DS tech lead.

3 *Peer review before publication*—The purpose of the small-audience peer review is to catch issues early on, according to the five principles of scientific rigor [8]: redundant experimental design, sound statistical analysis, recognition of error, avoidance of logical fallacies, and intellectual honesty.

 An internal project review is also an opportunity to share the learnings from the data sources examined, the tools used, the assumptions made, and the methodologies developed. Section 3.1.3 discusses these in more detail.

4 *Published results*—The purpose of publishing results is to allow learning to be discoverable and transferable, such that it can be reproduced and built upon by others. This corresponds to communicating insights to drive business strategies and roadmaps or launching predictive capabilities in products to drive intelligent user experience in DS.

Between 2010 and 2020, many practitioners came into DS with advanced scientific degrees from adjacent fields. These research experiences provided the field with extensive background for scientific rigor.

In recent years, many undergraduate and course-based master's programs for DS have become effective in teaching the technology and execution tactics in DS. However, the rigor of the scientific methods is less frequently taught. Some may argue that rigor needs to be practiced rather than taught.

016

> The rigor of the scientific methods is less frequently taught. Some may argue that rigor needs to be practiced rather than taught.

You should be sensitive to these background differences and gently guide data scientists in the five scientific rigor principles when the background is missing. This way, you can uphold the following five standards of rigor in data scientist projects to maintain customer and partner trust in your projects:

- Redundancy in experimental design
- Sound statistical analysis
- Recognizing error
- Avoiding logical traps
- Intellectual honesty

How do the five principles of scientific rigor apply to the field of DS? Let's take a look.

REDUNDANCY IN EXPERIMENTAL DESIGN

Good experimental design involves defining clear hypotheses before the experiments are built and conducted [9]. The results should be validated with controlled online experiments where two randomly selected sample populations are presented with different experiences, and the only difference is the feature under test. The randomization is to ensure that both samples can be representative of the total population.

The experimental setup should be flexible enough to be repeated and analyzed over various dimensions. This means across different time horizons, in different geographical regions, targeting different operating platforms, and more. What we want is for the setup to provide the replication, generalization, and sensitivity checks for trustworthy results.

For example, one test in 2012, shown in figure 3.3, changed the way the Microsoft Bing search engine displayed ads and improved revenue by 12%. This change translated to over $100M a year of additional revenue in the US alone, without hurting key user-experience metrics. More than 10,000 experiments take place on Bing each year, but simple features resulting in such a significant improvement are rare. The experiment was *replicated* multiple times over a long period to increase the redundancy and the trustworthiness of the result, and the result was eventually validated.

While controlled experiments can tell us the business impact we can anticipate from a new feature with some statistical power, they do not explain the underlying mechanisms that cause the differences in outcomes. The underlying mechanisms have to be interpreted by the tech lead in partnership with product and engineering teams. The interpretations can lead to new hypotheses in designing experiments to validate and amplify the discovered benefits.

New hypotheses can be related to the *generalization* of previous results. Experimental confirmation of these predictions provides added assurance that the original findings

Figure 3.3   A controlled experiment on Microsoft Bing search engine, where part of the description was promoted to result title, leading to a 12% revenue increase [9]

are valid. Extending the earlier Bing example, that learning led to further refinements of bringing context into the title section of a result in the ads section.

To further improve the rigor of the learning, perturbations of the setup can be tested to understand the *sensitivity* of the results to other system environment variables, such as font colors, algorithm relevance, and page loading time.

SOUND STATISTICAL ANALYSIS

While a prerequisite of being a data scientist is having a good command of probabilities and statistics, the skills and best practices may not be equally applied in all aspects of the work. Data scientists are often careful in examining the statistical properties of input data. Still, when it comes to using t-test to decide when experiments are showing statistically significant results in the launch process, we need to note many nuances.

For example, using a two-sample t-test assumes that the underlying variable is normally distributed. The central limit theorem may need to be invoked to apply t-tests on subsampled means, as the subsampled mean follows a normal distribution.

All right, two down, three more principles of scientific rigor to go! Now may be a good time for a quick breather if needed.

RECOGNIZING ERROR

Measurements are sampled from the world around us, and they all have measurement errors. There are two components to errors: systematic and random errors. Systematic errors are also called *biases*. They can be caused by a platform bug, a flawed experiment design, or an unrepresentative sample, such as the population in one region with specific demographic characteristics that are different from the overall population demographics.

Random errors can come from the sampling process in experiments. In a controlled online experiment, we can compute the size of random errors as the power of a test setup. That power is the probability of detecting a difference between variants, conditioned on the fact that there is a difference [9]. It is the likelihood of rejecting the null hypothesis when there is no difference between test and control. The industry standard is to achieve 80–95% power in our tests. A rigorous tech lead will be aware of the sources of systematic and random errors in an exploration process and help the team assess when a result is trustworthy or not.

AVOIDING LOGICAL TRAPS

There are many logical traps and fallacies in experimental science, especially in the interpretation of results. Over 175 cognitive biases have been documented [10]. Let's discuss the three most common logical traps in DS: confirmation bias, denying the antecedent, and base rate fallacy.

Confirmation bias happens with the direct influence of desire on beliefs. When people would like an idea or concept to be true, they end up believing it to be true. This is often motivated by wishful thinking. Individuals with confirmation bias tend to stop gathering information when the evidence gathered so far confirms the belief they would like to be true.

An excellent way to get around confirmation bias is to rigorously pose null hypotheses and use the experimental evidence to disprove each null hypothesis. We will then be looking for enough evidence gathered in an experiment to reject the null hypothesis with a threshold (usually 95%) of confidence.

Denying the antecedent happens when we confuse the if–then relationship with the if-and-only-if–then (iff–then) relationship. A typical illustration of a false conclusion is: Any person who is running must be alive. A sleeping person is not running. Therefore, all sleeping people are dead. Umm, what?

This illustration may seem obvious, but when we are not careful, we could just as quickly conclude: A personalization algorithm that includes location information gets good engagement. A particular algorithm does not include location information. Therefore, this algorithm will get bad engagement. This conclusion is flawed and does not follow logically from the previous statements.

Base-rate fallacy happens when we have a high accuracy classification algorithm deployed on a population with a low incident rate. It is caused by the inherent difficulty of the untrained human brain to deal with probabilities and likelihood.

Let's use one example with real data from the medical field. A rapid influenza diagnostic test (RIDT) for the influenza virus can have a 70% sensitivity and a specificity of 95% [11]. If 1 in 100 students gets infected with the influenza virus in a university with 10,000 students, and all students receive a test, what would be the test's observed accuracy?

Intuition may lead one to give a number between 70% and 95%. If you did the calculations, as illustrated in table 3.1, the test's perceived accuracy, which is the number of students infected among the ones who tested positive, would come out to be 70 / 565 = 12.4%. This is why these tests are not recommended for everyone and are prescribed only to populations with symptoms or with a high risk of getting infected.

These three common fallacies are often detected in the project design reviews and in reviews for the findings and recommendations at the end. In evaluating intermediate results and iterating on experiments, you, as a rigorous tech lead, must be aware of these logical traps that come naturally to humans and help the team navigate around them.

Table 3.1   Illustration of base-rate fallacy with the rapid influenza diagnostic test

	Infected	Uninfected	Total	Observed accuracy
Test positive	70	495	565	
Test negative	30	9,405	9,435	70 / 565 = 12.4%
Total	100	9,900	10,000	
Note	*70% sensitivity*	*95% specificity*		

INTELLECTUAL HONESTY

Intellectual honesty is a mindset in scientific rigor. It is the acknowledgment of nagging details that do not fit with one's hypothesis. These nagging details are often the first steps to a new understanding and a better hypothesis. Intellectual honesty also includes the acknowledgment of earlier work and the process of reconciling one's observations with those made by others.

For a DS tech lead, the rigor in intellectual honesty includes ensuring observations that do not align with the hypothesis are also shared, credits are given to all collaborators, and references on earlier work are cited.

As illustrated by these five principles, *scientific rigor* is multifaceted. Among the five principles, no single principle can define rigor alone. As the authors of "Rigorous Science: A How-To Guide" put it [8]: "Even the most careful experimental approach is not rigorous if the interpretation relies on a logical fallacy or is intellectually dishonest." On the other hand, the principles of rigor can be synergistic. For example, a logical approach and the awareness of error can lead to greater purposeful redundancy in experimental design.

017

"Even the most careful experimental approach is not rigorous if the interpretation relies on a logical fallacy or is intellectually dishonest." —Casadevall and Fang

As DS tech lead, the responsibility rests on you to uphold all five principles for projects and results to be considered rigorous.

3.2.2   *Monitoring for anomalies in data and in deployment*

William Anthony Twyman coined Twyman's Law, which states: "Any piece of data or evidence that looks interesting or unusual is probably wrong!" When we see an unusually good result, the inclination is to build a narrative around it. When we encounter an unusually bad result, we tend to dismiss it as some limitation of the experiment framing. However, most of the time, extreme results are caused by implementation issues due to logging errors or computation logic bugs. To facilitate the understanding of unusual or extreme results, we need to be able to validate the tracking capabilities as well as detect and diagnose these results at the code level and the data level.

VALIDATING TRACKING CAPABILITIES

To be rigorous in tracking, it is not enough to check for the tracking events' availability. Its correctness and completeness also need to be tested.

Correctness may fail if the data appears in the wrong format; is missing important information, such as a time zone label for timestamps; has excessive null entries; or has different types of null values, such as *null* versus *none* versus empty string, to represent missing values.

Completeness may fail if not all signals are captured reliably. This may happen because the inherent best-effort delivery mechanism of the internet causes some browsers to suppress certain types of requests, or the code may contain implementation errors. Incompleteness in logs can be detected by sending messages with sequence numbers from the client side. This is a well-known technique used in the TCP protocol in networking. By looking at the completeness of the sequence numbers received at the recipient, you can estimate the channel's reliability.

RIGOR AT THE CODE LEVEL

With effective tracking in place, defensive code techniques, such as assertions, cross-checks, and cross-validations, can help you increase rigor at the code level when performing analysis or building models.

An *assertion* is a Boolean expression at a specific point in a program, which will always be true unless there is a bug in the program. The execution of a program stops when an assertion is not satisfied. This way, correctness issues can be detected as soon as they happen and before they propagate to a later part of the analysis. The downside of this technique is that when an assertion fires by mistake, it can disrupt the execution pipeline. For this reason, assertions should be reserved for logically incorrect outputs, such as non-empty outputs, or cases when the number of rows in the output should, but doesn't, match the number of rows in the input.

Cross-checks use the redundancy principle discussed in scientific rigor to come to a result from different analysis angles. The common angles are top-down, where an estimate is produced as part of the whole, and bottom-up, when an estimate is produced as a summation of the contributing parts. Cross-checks can quickly uncover issues with missing data or uncategorized data that can fall out of the analysis scope.

Cross-validations maintain the same methodology or computation and select multiple random samples of the available data to see if the method or computation are robust enough to arrive at the same conclusion. A cross-validation can quickly detect if an interesting result was an artifact of an unusual sampling of data.

RIGOR AT THE DATA LEVEL

Rigor at the data level is vital in DS, as after an analysis or a model is deployed, the model's operating environment may change. There are two main scenarios in which this can happen:

- The distribution of the data changed.
- The meaning of features changed.

The change in data distribution is also known as the *covariate shift*. When the training and test inputs follow different distributions, the underlying functional relationship stays the same. Some examples include:

- A credit card approval algorithm, trained on data from one advertising channel, can be applied to applicants from a new advertising channel with a different mix of customers.
- A life insurance model predicting life expectancy can be built with very few samples of people who smoke in the training set, but many more individuals may be smokers in practice.

The change in the meaning of features is also known as *concept drift*. In concept drift, the relationship between input and output has changed, where the input required to produce the same meaning in the output is changing. Some examples include:

- When the economy goes through boom or bust cycles, borrowers' ability to repay also moves up and down with their job security.
- With breakthrough medical advances, the life expectancy of people with certain preexisting conditions may be extended, and the requirement to qualify for certain life insurance rates may change, as some medical conditions are no longer as fatal.

How do you detect these changes? You can monitor the accuracy of models by measuring the difference between the predictions produced by a model and the observed outcomes. However, as illustrated in the previous credit card and life insurance examples, you may need to wait months, years, or even decades to see if the observations will match the prediction. As an alternative approach, you can detect anomalies in the output or monitor the shifts in the input variables to catch the changes early.

Anomalies in the output can manifest as an excessive number of values being detected in some dimensions. There could be a disproportionate number of credit cards approved or rejected for a region, an income level, or a particular age group over a time window. These dimensions can be monitored as time series and historical trends, and can be used to set sensitivities for alerts and to reduce false positives for reporting anomalous output.

You can also detect shifts in input distributions with a variety of distribution divergence estimates, one of which is the *population stability index* (PSI), which is a form of Kullback-Liebler (KL) divergence. PSI measures how much a variable has changed in distribution over two points in time. The two points in time can be over consecutive days, which detects sudden changes. They can also be between a long-term baseline and the current inputs, which detects slow shifts over time that may not show up across consecutive days. The long-term baseline is usually set at the time of the most recent model launch, and any drift detected provides an indicator of the trustworthiness of the model output.

PSI is widely used to monitor changes in an incoming population's characteristics and diagnose potential issues in model performance. It is formulated for discrete variables. We can convert continuous variables into discrete variables by sorting the samples on the continuous range and bucketing them into discrete chunks. As an example, figure 3.4 illustrates how a continuous score range can be discretized into discrete score ranges. To account for potential changes in the unlabeled or unscored population, there is usually also a null bucket included in the calculation.

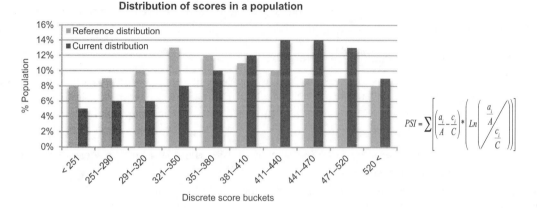

Figure 3.4   Population stability index (PSI) illustrated in a score distribution

Specifically, PSI looks at the data distribution at two points in time: *A* and *C* and computes the contribution of samples of a particular bucket *i* as a_i/A and c_i/C and computes the difference, weighted by $ln((a_i/A)/(c_i/C))$.

As the calculation always looks at the percent contribution of the data's buckets, PSI's magnitude has some meaning. The rule of thumb for interpreting the PSI value is summarized in table 3.2. When you detect shifts and drifts in the input and output, you should perform further diagnoses to check whether individual samples are being predicted as expected.

Table 3.2   Interpretations for PSI values

PSI value	Interpretation
< 0.1	Slight change
0.1–0.2	Minor change
> 0.2	Major change

If each sample is still being predicted correctly, and only the distributions of samples changed, this would be a case of covariance shift. We can try importance reweighting to up-weight training instances that are similar to test samples. This attempts to shift the training sample set to look like it is sampled from the test sample set.

Suppose samples are no longer being predicted correctly, and the cause is drifts in the meaning of some input variables. In that case, we must first try to understand if there is a reason for the divergence. In a real-world scenario, a bug caused two features to be swapped, leading to drifting feature values. If the divergence is not a fixable bug, you can consider removing the variables that differ significantly between training and deployment from the data set. As an example, a common threshold in financial risk management is that any variable with PSI greater than 0.2 is considered a major shift and will be removed from a model.

3.2.3 *Taking responsibility for enterprise value*

Rigor to produce business impact is just as important as the technical aspects discussed in sections 3.2.1 and 3.2.2. As data scientists, we are responsible for generating enterprise value for our business. But what does generating enterprise value mean? Let's highlight three aspects:

- *Maintaining clarity on goals*—Move business metrics with projects, using the simplest methods first.
- *Focusing on velocity*—Succeed quickly by failing fast.
- *Communicating the impact*—Listen, engage, and lead.

MAINTAINING CLARITY ON GOALS

Each well-defined DS project serves a business purpose. While there may be multiple ways to achieve the business purpose, the tech lead can evaluate whether the DS project plan's solution is the simplest method possible to achieve the business purpose.

What are the business purposes for DS projects? Section 2.2.2 listed the nine most common DS types, which can be organized into three categories:

- *Category 1*—Empowering launches
  - Tracking specification definition
  - Monitoring and rollout
- *Category 2*—Optimizing with business insights
  - Metrics definition and dashboarding
  - Data insights and deep dives
- *Category 3*—Solidifying foundations
  - Modeling and API development
  - Data enrichment
  - Data consistency
  - Infrastructure improvements
  - Regulatory items

Category 1 projects unblock business progress and provide the data foundation for products and programs to be tracked and monitored with immediate strategic returns. Returns for business include clarifying key business metrics to move for a new feature or process and identifying hard-to-find bugs in product or process rollouts.

Category 2 projects drive direct business impact by optimizing the incremental operational gains and recommendations for features or processes that can provide step-function improvements. Returns for the business are realized when recommendations are adopted in products or operational processes. Returns on time and efforts invested can be measured in percentage improvements in revenue, profit, or cost savings.

Category 3 projects drive strategic productivity and availability gains over the long term. Returns can manifest in personnel/weeks saved, new projects enabled, and new market opportunities unlocked.

While defining the business purpose is essential for clarifying the goals, a DS tech lead also needs to be rigorous in keeping the solution as simple as possible. Methods that don't involve complex algorithms may be just as effective in accomplishing the business purpose.

At LinkedIn, one of the most prized values in engineering and DS is craftsmanship, where one component is how a technology practitioner deals with complexity. Specifically, the *complexity* is not the complexity you can incorporate but the complexity you can remove to provide the most straightforward system that accomplishes business purposes. You can refer to the case study in the following sidebar to see how complexities are removed to accomplish the business goal. To briefly summarize, DS tech leads need to be rigorous in clarifying how project goals can move business metrics and identifying ways to simplify the approach as much as possible in reaching a business goal.

Case study: North star metrics for an organization

How do you build a metric that can guide an organization with hundreds of employees to align and work toward a single direction? In specifying a north star metric to guide the LinkedIn Talent Solutions product line, a product line that generates billions of dollars of revenue for LinkedIn each year, we need a metric that is simple to understand for stakeholders internal and external to LinkedIn. LinkedIn Talent Solutions looks to build the world's definitive hiring marketplace to help talent get the best opportunities, and help employers hire the best talent.

By following the business revenue, which comes mostly from employers using LinkedIn as a talent-sourcing tool, one success metric can be based on the number of candidates reached. Optimizing this metric may cause candidates to feel spammed when employers reach out to as many candidates as possible.

If you are instead looking to increase engagement on the platform, job applications could be used as a success metric. However, optimizing it may cause an excessive number of applications to pile up for each job opening, which would not be a good experience for either the candidates or employers.

A data scientist may suggest a hybrid metric that is a weighted combination of the previously mentioned metrics. However, it would be far too complicated for team members to understand.

(continued)

The team eventually arrived at a metric called *confirmed hire*. Confirmed hire is the number of members LinkedIn services assisted during their most recent job search process. The metric elegantly combines the success factors from employers and job seekers. When optimized, it can increase the satisfaction of both sides of the talent marketplace.

Confirmed hire was considered simple enough to become part of LinkedIn's press kit. It is used to drive both internal and external conversations and allows members and employers to experience LinkedIn's progress in building a better product year after year.

FOCUSING ON VELOCITY

DS project velocity comes from two perspectives: speed to solution and low friction to incremental improvements. Speed to solution requires us to remove risks and build confidence that the organization is moving in the right direction. Low friction to incremental improvements requires strategic choices and timely resolution of technical debts such that there is a firm foundational architecture for iterative innovation.

In this section, we discuss proof of concept as a fast path to the initial solution. We discuss the various forms of technical debt and their resolution to reduce friction to further iterative innovation.

Proof of concept

One common misconception about proof of concept (PoC) is that we should pursue a quick and simple version of a project and build on it. Teams often choose to create the pieces they understand first, leaving the uncertain parts to the end.

The real purpose of a PoC is to explore the feasibility of the portion of a project with the highest risk of failure. It is an attempt to emphasize the project component with the most heightened uncertainty and simplify the rest. Should the project fail as architected initially, we can find an alternative path to make the project work. Eric Ries, in *The Lean Startup*, calls the process of potentially finding an alternative path "the pivot," and defines it as "a change in strategy without a change in vision" [12].

In section 2.2.2, we listed five top risk factors common for DS analytics and modeling projects:

- *New data source*—Data availability, correctness, and completeness may be at risk.
- *Partner reorganization*—Prior alignment with partners is disrupted; realignment is required.
- *New data-driven feature*—Tracking bugs, data pipeline issues, population drifts from product feature updates, and integration issues must be discovered and resolved.

- *Existing product*—Feature upgrades can change the meanings of metrics and signals.
- *Solution architecture dependencies*—Technology platform updates can disrupt the operations of DS capabilities.

In different projects, the susceptibility to these risk factors may be different, so the emphasis in the PoC will be different. However, there are some common patterns.

Building a new product or feature

When building a new product or feature that customers are unfamiliar with, the top risk area is product market fit. The goal is to create the simplest technical solution possible to see whether the user experience is acceptable to our customers. Places that you may choose to trade off in simplifying the PoC are process steps that may stay manual instead of being automated and model accuracy or coverage that may not be as high as one could get to.

These trade-offs have consequences. Keeping process steps manual accumulates tech debts, which we will address later in this section. However, the alternative would be automating something that will be thrown away if we discover a mismatch in product/feature-to-market fit. At the same time, when a model with low accuracy or coverage is used, there is also the concern that it may impact the very user experience you would like to test.

There are techniques you can reference to tackle these challenging trade-offs. If the product-to-market fit can be tested with a smaller, invitation-only group of customers, you can work with product partners to reduce project scope to focus on a subset of all potential features. This way, you can make sure the subset of features can be good enough for proving product-to-market fit.

Improving on an existing product or feature

For an existing product or feature, the product/feature-to-market fit may already be resolved. If the product or feature needs to scale to accommodate more users, one risk area is often the feasibility of a new technology platform. In project planning, you may have evaluated the technology feature set availability and have confirmed that the necessary capabilities are available in the documentation. However, feature availability has many levels, and documentation can be outdated.

A technology platform feature may be planned, completed, available, or robust. If it is just planned, it may only exist as an item in the backlog of features to come. Any prioritization change or personnel change could change its launch time. If a feature is completed, it may have just finished being implemented and not have gone through testing. A few users may have used it if it is available, but a consistent, expected level of service for your product or feature improvement may not be dependable. Only when a technology platform is robust can you expect a smooth migration to improve your product or feature.

Does that mean you cannot undertake a product or feature improvement project when there is no proof (yet) that a target technology platform is robust in your application area? Of course, you can. You just need to incorporate additional time in doing a PoC to test the technology platform for your product, so if the technology platform needs to be tweaked, there is time to iterate or pivot to plan B.

Suppose you are upgrading the technology platform for an existing product or feature. In that case, a PoC can focus on the platform's scalability aspects while reducing the number of features that require testing. This way, the platform can be load-stress tested with only one or two functions to validate the viability of the new technology platform.

You may feel that planning for a PoC is slowing down the development process. The alternative could be worse. When project risks are not removed early in a project, they can come back with a vengeance during the project integration phase or during product or feature launches. They can manifest as hard-to-recover failures like technology incompatibilities.

As the tech lead, your responsibility is to rigorously organize project plan reviews to anticipate as many areas of risks as possible, plan the necessary PoC milestones, and make the trade-offs of what milestones need to be emphasized early and what can be simplified.

We have discussed accelerating the speed to solution. Let's now take a look at reducing the friction to incremental improvements by addressing technical debts.

Technical debt

First coined by Ward Cunningham in 1992, *technical debt* describes the long-term costs incurred by moving quickly in software engineering. In developing nimble PoCs to remove project risks and quickly iterate on features, a company naturally takes on technical debt. Not all tech debts are bad, as they allow for nimble experimentation to remove product or process risks. However, all debts need to be serviced. When debts are not serviced, they can slow down the velocity of producing new capabilities.

018

Not all tech debts are bad, as they allow for nimble experimentation to remove product or process risks. However, all debts need to be serviced. When debts are not serviced, they can slow down the velocity of producing new capabilities.

Table 3.3 lists 13 distinct types of common technical debts in software engineering [13] that can be serviced by refactoring code or models, improving testing, deleting dead code, reducing dependencies, tightening APIs, and improving documentation.

Since many of the DS insights and deliverables are implemented through software, all software technical debts can manifest themselves in DS. On top of that, DS and machine learning (ML) have their own set of tech debts, as these techniques are most useful when you cannot express the desired behavior in simple software logic.

Table 3.3 Common technical debt types and definitions identified in software engineering

Debt type	Definition
Architecture debt	Problems encountered in project architecture, such as violation of modularity, which affects architectural requirements (e.g., performance, robustness, etc.) and cannot be paid with simple interventions in the code.
Build debt	Issues that make builds harder and are more time- or processing-consuming.
Code debt	Problems found in the source code, which can negatively affect the legibility of the code, making it more difficult to maintain.
Defect debt	Known software defects identified by testing activities or by the user, but due to competing priorities and limited resources, fixes have to be deferred. An accumulation of defects can make the debt more difficult to repay later.
Design debt	Source code that violated the principles of good object-oriented design.
Documentation debt	Missing, inadequate, or incomplete documentation of any type for code that currently works correctly in the system but fails to meet documentation criteria.
Infrastructure debt	Infrastructure issues that delay or hinder development activities. Examples include delaying an upgrade or an infrastructure fix.
People debt	People issues that can delay or hinder some development activities, such as expertise concentrated in too few people or delayed training and/or hiring.
Process debt	Inefficient or outdated processes that may no longer be appropriate.
Requirement debt	Trade-offs made with only partially implemented requirements. They are often not available for all cases or don't fully satisfy all the non-functional requirements, such as security or performance.
Service debt	Substituting private servers with cloud services could be driven by business or technical objectives. Cloud services and resources still need to be managed for accessibility and reliability requirements, which can be tech debts to serve.
Test automation debt	The work involved in automating tests of previously developed functionality to support continuous integration and faster development cycles.
Test debt	Issues found in testing activities, which can affect the quality of testing, such as planned tests that were not performed or low code coverage in the test suite.

Patterns learned from data are crystalized in algorithm parameters, which become part of the logic that produces the output. The data sets used in analysis and model training are not only the input but also part of the deliverable.

With our understanding of the software engineering technical debts, let's shift gears and focus on DS-specific technical debts. In this new scenario, the potential to take on technical debts increases significantly. As a DS tech lead, you should be aware of at least five top technical debt categories in ML systems, as discussed by Scully et al. [14]:

- Model boundaries
- Data dependencies
- Feedback loops
- Configuration debt
- Environment adaptation

Model boundaries

Technical debts from ML models mainly follow the *CARE entanglement principle*: "Change Anything, Retrain Everything." If any input features, hyperparameters, learning settings, sampling methods, or convergence thresholds change, the model will need to be retrained. The cascade of models that depend on a model's output may also need to be retrained. The retraining cascades become technical debts that must be served, and any undeclared data/model/customer dependencies can cause issues like landmines waiting to explode. Correction cascades and undeclared customers can disrupt DS velocity when changes in the chain of dependencies affect all downstream models' accuracy. This can create improvement deadlock, as any incremental improvement upstream carries the cost of reevaluating or retraining all downstream models.

Mitigation strategies include isolating large models into smaller models' ensembles, so latent variables can be trained and calibrated separately. When submodel features are updated, the submodels can be recalibrated to produce consistent latent variables, so the overall ensembles don't need to be retrained. This makes detecting change and automating the calibration process key to countering entanglement. For correction cascades, we can upgrade an existing model to include the corrections directly as a special case or accept the cost and build a separate model. For undeclared consumers, systems can be designed to guard against this case with access restrictions or strict service-level agreements (SLAs). Table 3.4 elaborates on the three types of model boundary technical debts and their mitigation strategies.

019

One technical debt of operating machine learning models follows the CARE entanglement principle: "Change Anything, Retrain Everything." Mitigation strategies include isolating large models into smaller models' ensembles, so latent variables can be trained and calibrated separately.

Data dependencies

This debt can be costly when maintaining complex models that use multifaceted data sources. Any data sources could fail, and failures are often hard to detect. While software code dependencies can be detected through static analysis by compilers and linkers, data dependencies lack standard tools and practices to detect automatically. Large systems often have dependencies that are maintained through institutional knowledge passed down from person to person, which is a lossy process that is costly to maintain over time. The worse news is that data dependencies are easy to accumulate

Table 3.4 Model boundary technical debts in ML systems

Debt categories	Description	Mitigation strategy
Model boundaries— Entanglement, correction cascades, undeclared consumers	*Entanglement*—Machine learning systems mix signals together, entangling them and making isolation of improvements impossible. When a feature is added or removed, the whole model needs to be retrained. This is the CARE principle: "Change Anything, Retrain Everything." CARE applies not only to input signals but also to hyperparameters, learning settings, sampling methods, convergence thresholds, data selection, and essentially every other possible tweak.	*Entanglement*—Isolate models and serve ensembles or focus on detecting changes and automate the retraining process.
	Correction cascades—Given a set of existing models, there are often situations where a solution for a slightly different problem is required. It can be tempting to learn a new model using the output of an existing model as input and learn a small correction as a fast way to solve the problem. However, a correction cascade can create an improvement deadlock, as improving the accuracy of any individual component actually leads to system-level detriments.	*Correction cascades*— Upgrade an existing model to include the corrections directly as a special case, or accept the cost of creating a separate model.
	Undeclared consumers—Output of a ML model is often made widely accessible without access control. Consumers of the results are often silently using the output as an input without the knowledge of the model owner. Undeclared consumers are expensive at best and dangerous at worst because they create a hidden tight coupling of a model to other parts of the stack. This tight coupling can radically increase the cost and difficulty of making any changes at all even if they are improvements.	*Undeclared consumers*— Systems can be designed to guard against this case with access restrictions or strict SLAs.

and difficult to untangle, and many of them carry significant maintenance costs but contribute marginally to result in improvements.

To mitigate technical debts related to unstable data dependencies, input signals should be versioned so their changes do not go unnoticed. Versioning input also carries the cost of potential staleness of input; over some period of feature migration, there is the cost of maintaining multiple versions of the same signal. For underutilized data dependencies, such as features that may provide only marginal model improvements, they can be detected via exhaustive leave-one-feature-out evaluations. These evaluations can be run regularly to identify and remove unnecessary features. As for the lack of static analysis, we can annotate data sources and features, so checks for dependency, migration, and deletion can be automated and much safer. Table 3.5 elaborates on the three types of data dependency technical debts and their mitigation strategies.

Table 3.5   Data dependency technical debts in ML systems

Debt categories	Description	Mitigation strategy
Data dependencies—Unstable, underutilized, lack of static analysis	*Unstable data dependencies*—To make progress quickly, it is often convenient to consume signals as input features that are produced by other systems. However, some input signals can be unstable when changes from upstream data happen implicitly (i.e., as data characteristics change) or explicitly (i.e., when different teams own the data). This is dangerous because even improvements to input signals may have arbitrary detrimental effects in the consuming system that are costly to diagnose and address.	*Unstable data dependencies*—Input signals should be versioned, although it carries the cost of potential staleness and maintaining multiple versions of the same signal over time.
	Underutilized data dependencies—Some input signals provide little incremental modeling benefits but carry outsized system maintenance costs. They can make a machine learning (ML) system unnecessarily vulnerable to change when they could be removed with no detriment. The mechanisms to look out for include: ■ *Legacy features*—Old features are made redundant by better new features but go undetected. ■ *Bundled features*—A beneficial group of features is added to the model together, including features that add little or no value. ■ *ϱ-Features*—To drive accuracy, features are included even when accuracy gain is small, while complexity overhead is high. ■ *Correlated features*—Two features are strongly correlated, but one is more directly causal. ML methods may credit the two features equally or even pick the non-causal one.	*Underutilized data dependencies*—These can be detected via exhaustive leave-one-feature-out evaluations. These could be run regularly to identify and remove unnecessary features.
	Lack of static analysis for data dependencies—Data sources and features are not annotated, which makes it challenging to perform static analysis of data dependencies, error checking, tracking down consumers, and enforcing migration and updates.	*Lack of static analysis*—Annotate data sources and features, so checks for dependency, migration, and deletion can be much safer.

Feedback loops

Live ML systems can often influence their own behavior as they are updated over time. This leads to a form of analysis debt, where it can be hard to anticipate the behavior of a given model before it is released. These feedback loops can take different forms—some are more obvious and direct, while others may involve completely disjointed systems, as they influence end customer interactions. They can be costly to monitor, detect, and address, especially if they occur gradually over time. To anticipate the cost of direct and hidden feedback loops, we need to be aware of their existence and use multi-armed bandit algorithms or a holdback set to isolate influence by a given model. Table 3.6 elaborates on the two types of feedback loop technical debts and their mitigation strategies.

Table 3.6 Feedback loop technical debts in ML systems

Debt categories	Description	Mitigation strategy
Feedback loops— Direct and hidden loops	*Direct feedback loops*—A model may directly influence the selection of its own future training data. An example is the relevance algorithm for a search engine, where items initially considered to be most popular are listed at the top of the search results and will get the most attention and click-through rate.	*Direct feedback loops*—Multi-armed bandit algorithms or a holdback set can isolate influence by a given model.
	Hidden feedback loops—Two completely disjointed systems may influence each other indirectly through the world. For example, if two systems independently determine the look of a web page, with one selecting products to show and another selecting related reviews, improving one system may lead to changes in behavior in the other. Improvements or bugs in one may influence the performance of the other.	*Hidden feedback loops*—Be aware of the potential feedback loops, and experiment as a whole system.

Configuration debt

Configurations of modeling systems include feature sets used, data time windows, algorithm-specific learning settings, cluster settings, and verification methods. They often come as an afterthought in system design after feature selection, model selection, and model tuning. Each configuration line has the potential for mistakes. These mistakes can be costly, leading to serious loss of time, waste of computing resources, or production issues.

Sculley and colleagues articulated a few principles for good configuration systems to avoid excessive configuration debt:

- Easy to specify a small change
- Hard to make manual errors or omissions
- Easy to visualize configuration differences between two models
- Easy to automatically assert and verify
- Possible to detect redundant settings
- Easy for code review and repository check-in

Environment adaptation

Machine learning systems often interact directly with their environment in the real world. The real world is rarely stable. In ML systems, it is often necessary to pick a decision threshold for a given model to perform some action, such as predicting true or false or marking an email as spam or non-spam. However, when thresholds are manually set, over time, the threshold may not be valid because of feature drift, and manually updating many thresholds across many models is time consuming and error-prone.

To address the calibration of fixed thresholds in dynamic ML systems, we can learn thresholds via evaluation on holdout data, or we can calibrate them against down-funnel metrics. Table 3.7 elaborates on the configuration debt and environment adaptation technical debts and their mitigation strategies.

Table 3.7   Configuration debt and environment adaptation technical debts

Debt categories	Description	Mitigation strategy
Configuration debt	*Configuration debt*—A large analytics or modeling system can have a range of configurable options. Examples include feature sets used, data time window, algorithm-specific learning settings, potential pre- or post-processing, cluster settings, and verification methods. Configurations may be an afterthought and not considered important. Each configuration line has the potential for mistakes, and mistakes can be costly, leading to serious loss of time, waste of computing resources, or production issues.	Configuration best practices include: • Easy to specify a small change • Hard to make manual errors or omissions • Easy to visualize configuration differences between two models • Easy to automatically assert and verify • Possible to detect redundant settings • Easy for code review and repository check-in
Environment adaptation	*Fixed thresholds in dynamic systems*—It is often necessary to pick a decision threshold for a given model to perform some action, such as predicting true or false or marking an email as spam or not spam. However, when thresholds are manually set, over time, the threshold may become invalid because of feature drift, and manually updating many thresholds across many models is time-consuming and error-prone.	*Fixed thresholds in dynamic systems*—Thresholds can be learned via evaluation on holdout data or calibrated against down-funnel metrics.

In summary, paying down technical debt means that the goal is not to add new functionality but to enable future improvements, reduce errors, and improve maintainability. They can be paid down by refactoring code, improving unit tests, deleting dead code, reducing dependencies, tightening APIs, and improving documentation. Deferring such payments can result in compounding costs, causing greater failures down the road.

A DS tech lead should recognize when a project is taking on technical debts and plan to service them later. You need to help the team be aware of their technical decisions' long-term impact and help your managers understand any resources allocated to mitigate technical debts.

COMMUNICATING THE IMPACT

Rigor for a tech lead extends beyond the technical aspect. You also have the responsibility to interpret company initiatives, recommend project plans, and communicate the impact of the DS work to the project team, the manager, the business partners, and other tech leads across teams.

A successful tech lead reads carefully, writes well, and can get up in front of a group and speak [15]. What does that look like when communicating with different stakeholders?

To the team

As a tech lead, you are expected to listen to all the technical concerns in the projects, synthesize the challenges, and make technical recommendations where required. While there may be many technician details, you should understand the project's complexity and merit to represent the team at related technical review meetings and share relevant information with the team. The team also depends on you to communicate the business impact of the projects to motivate them.

To the manager

You are expected to regularly summarize the progress of ongoing projects, write or lead the writing of design documents, and lead the reviews of incidents and post-mortems when they happen. Your manager also depends on you to listen for key company initiatives, provide feedback on any technical challenges in driving these initiatives, and work with them to align team priorities in the planning process.

To business partners

You are expected to speak in universal terms that everyone understands and be a trusted advisor to business partners by explaining the technical basics in a non-condescending way. Your business partners depend on you to have good communication habits and lead by example. This is especially important in translating business needs into technical specifications and exploring trade-offs with business partners. You can also choose to bring team members into these partner conversations to help develop them and build deeper collaborative relationships with business partners.

To technical peers in other teams

You can document the learnings from projects that either succeeded or failed, so the organization can build institutional knowledge on data sources, tools used, assumptions made, and technologies developed. The organization depends on you to continually learn from other technical peers to bring best practices into the team and help the team navigate known technology or methodology issues.

With these communication skills, you are responsible for generating enterprise value when working with the project team, manager, business partners, and other tech leads across teams.

Before we conclude section 3.2 on rigor, let's revisit Brian, the technically-sound tech lead from chapter 1 who is not comfortable speaking with business partners. He often takes on additional work, as he feels compelled to devote time to partners' asks. Brian's project delays and quality compromises are partly an execution issue (section 2.2), while his rushed results may show up as a lack of rigor in his work.

3.3   Attitude of positivity

DS is a field with high failure rates. It is common to expect 70% of the experiments not to show positive results [16]. In well-optimized domains like Bing, Google, and Netflix, success happens about 10–20% of the time [17], [18]. It takes an immense amount of curiosity and tenacity to stay upbeat and focused on staying the course to deliver project wins.

How do we maintain positivity in the midst of adversity, celebrate the successes, and learn from the failures, while building trust with partners to execute toward the major business wins? There are three aspects to emphasize:

- Positivity and tenacity to work through failures
- Curiosity and collaboration in responding to incidents
- Respecting diverse perspectives in lateral collaborations

Let's look at these one by one.

3.3.1   Exhibiting positivity and tenacity to work through failures

You may have come across idealized stories like this: a data wizard hacks together a solution using off-the-shelf ML algorithms and, in a few days or weeks, saves an organization millions of dollars a year! Well, the reality is very different from the hype in the media.

What does reality look like? Winston Churchill once said, "Success consists of going from failure to failure without loss of enthusiasm."

The idealized DS wins are but one of nine different types of projects you can take on. As shown in the following list, only two of the nine types of projects introduced in section 2.2 have direct DS-driven business impact. The purpose of most DS projects is building tracking and data foundations, servicing technical debts, and/or supporting daily business operations:

- Tracking specification definition
- Monitoring and rollout
- Metrics definition and dashboarding
- Data insights and deep dives => *direct DS-driven business impact*
- Modeling and API development => *direct DS-driven business impact*
- Data enrichment
- Data consistency
- Infrastructure improvements
- Regulatory items

Of the two project types with direct DS-driven business impact, data insights and deep dives is the project type that recommends new features or processes. Only modeling and API development type projects produce new predictive capabilities. Even with the best technical capabilities, not all attempts will arrive at successful outcomes. Only 10–30%

of features considered promising enough to be resourced and implemented eventually attain business success.

While these are grim statistics that tech leads need to work with when managing stakeholder expectations, each project, even those that failed to achieve desired business results, can reveal learning that drives enterprise value. Throughout a DS project, the learning includes the data sources explored, tools used, assumptions made, and methodologies developed. These opportunities are described in detail in section 3.1.3.

Being a tech lead who manages DS projects can be challenging. When the team is performing well and enjoying their work, it can feel incredibly rewarding for you. When deadlines are looming, or when technical debts become overwhelming, the situation can feel quite stressful. Leading applies not only to the technical area but also to the virtues and attitude required to facilitate a productive work environment.

One technique for motivating the team and building trust with partners as the tech lead is to communicate any institutional learning from successful and failed projects promptly and regularly. These crystallized learnings can help individual team members stay motivated in their projects by recognizing their impact on the business and help your business partners and executives see the progress toward bigger wins down the road. You must embody tenacity and enthusiasm as a tech lead, so you can lead teams through the difficult times many projects will inevitably go through.

3.3.2 *Being curious and collaborative in responding to incidents*

An *incident* is defined as an outage or significant degradation of a business service. In a fast-moving business and technology environment, incidents are quite inevitable. The potential negative impact of incidents tends to increase as the number of customers grows. The team can come under significant pressure when something breaks unexpectedly. It is crucial for you, the tech lead, to maintain a safe and respectful atmosphere in these stressful situations.

In a mature engineering environment, incidents are managed by acknowledging the incident with the business; triaging; escalating; prioritizing; communicating with management; and resolving and learning from the incident. Such a process provides organization-level visibility of all scheduled changes and unexpected outages. The process can also mitigate risk to planned interruptions of service, and reduces preventable incidents caused by ad hoc changes.

Incident management can be delicate. Significant customer relationships and business revenue could be on the line. *War rooms* are where colleagues from different functions gather together to return the business to operational as quickly as possible, and to diagnose and learn from the root cause. As the tech lead, your role of balancing pressure and reducing stress through the incident-handling process is crucial. Let's look at how attitude plays a vital role in each stage of the process, as illustrated in figure 3.5.

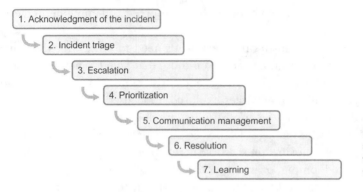

Figure 3.5   The seven-step incident management flow for organization-level visibility

- *Acknowledgment of the incident to the business*—Anomalies may be detected through internal monitoring, partner notifications, or user reporting. In most mature engineering organizations, a site reliability engineer on call will log the issue. As a tech lead, you will be immediately notified if it involves or impacts a DS-related system. In this situation, your timely response can build significant trust in cross-functional collaboration, regardless of whether DS models or services caused the incident.

  The attitude of appreciating an on-call engineer's awareness of the value DS can bring to the incident resolution process is critical. This is not a time to be suspicious of potential finger-pointing. Everyone should focus on triaging and potential escalations.

- *Incident triage*—The primary purpose of triaging is to decide whether the incident needs to be escalated to senior executives to coordinate potential external communication. DS insights can be crucial for estimating the number of impacted customers or partners, the potential for regulatory scrutiny, the potential scope of critical data losses, and potential critical security issues.

  As the tech lead, you need to maintain a curious, objective, and non-judgmental attitude, while not shying away from a realistic negative assessment of the situation throughout the incident triage process.

- *Escalation*—If the incident is determined to be severe enough in impact, it will be escalated to senior executives. The DS tech lead's role is to confirm and cross-check whether the impact merits external communication to customers or partners.

  Your attitude at this time should be respectful of all stakeholders' needs and may include promptly providing as accurate an estimate of impact as possible. If the incident is below the severity threshold, the incident is often handled by the on-call team with related resources pulled in as necessary.

- *Prioritization*—While all incidents should be examined, not all are important enough to warrant dropping everything to address them immediately. Different organizations with different customer or partner commitments may define severity thresholds differently. Likely, there are those that require immediate all-hands-on-deck war room situations, those that can be handled by respective teams within the same business day, those that can be handled within the same sprint, those that can be placed on the backlog for the next sprint, and those that can be placed on next quarter's roadmap.

Here, you should maintain empathy in helping relevant stakeholders understand these severity levels and cooperate with any requests from on-call engineers handling the incident.

- *Communication management*—After triage and prioritization, if the incident is DS-related, you should resolutely drive the discovery of the root cause, develop a path to resolution, and execute a timely resolution according to the determined priority. In this process, it is important to document and communicate regularly. Depending on the severity of the incident, the communication cadence could be multiple times a day for the most severe incidents and daily or weekly for less critical incidents.

  When highlighting the observations and learning, you should maintain objectivity in your role, while highlighting the process and not pointing fingers at any particular person. The goal is to focus the teams on resolution and not on blame, especially when communicating to a broad audience.

- *Resolution*—The resolution can look very different, depending on the nature of the incident. For you, an attitude of humility goes a long way. You can achieve this attitude by being inclusive in informing and consulting the stakeholders on the resolution. Failing to inform and consult the stakeholders may create additional problems.

- *Learning*—The learning from an incident can be crystallized in an incident post-mortem. The post-mortem usually summarizes the incident resolution process and informs process improvements that can mitigate future risks, while promoting best practices that have worked well in handling the incident.

As introduced in section 2.2.3, a DS incident post-mortem may include five sections (table 3.8).

Table 3.8   Post-mortem content in five sections

Section	Content
Brief summary	Describe the incident's context and highlight the incident type, length, impact, escalations, and fixes.
Detailed timeline	Account for the events leading up to the incident and the response actions taken.
Root cause	Identify the root cause with the five whys methodology to discover the deeper reason the incident occurred.
Resolution and recovery	Include the choices and rationales behind the fix and the particular mitigation steps being taken with the stakeholders informed and consulted.
Actions to mitigate future risks	Address the root causes to prevent the incident from happening again, systematically while not hurting agility.

The *brief summary* should include the incident's context, type, length, impact, escalations, and fixes. Any escalations will be important to highlight to inform potential process improvements on minimizing unnecessary escalations or disruptions to the business's normal course. The *detailed timeline* should include an accounting of the events leading up to the incident and the response actions taken. Diligence here can help train new team members via simulations of how incidents evolve and in justifying investment in shortening incidence response times. The *root cause* should be identified with the five whys methodology to discover the deeper reason the incident occurred, such as lack of testing or human error because of a lack of automation.

Five whys is an iterative interrogative methodology used to explore the cause-and-effect relationships underlying a particular incident. The technique's primary goal is to determine the root cause of an incident by repeating the question "Why?" Each answer forms the basis of the next question.

Five is symbolic of a handful of iterations. For incidents of different complexity, it could usually take three to eight iterations to get to more in-depth insight as to how best to mitigate a class of future risks more systematically. The depth of the insight depends on the involved people's knowledge and persistence; it is essential to engage experienced representatives of all stakeholders' discussions.

You can leverage your manager, who is ultimately responsible for the team, to learn from past incidents rigorously. This process will be discussed in detail in section 5.2.2.

Resolution and recovery should include the choices and rationales behind the fix for the specific incident and the particular mitigation steps being taken, with the stakeholders informed and consulted. This is the time to build or rebuild trust among partner teams. When you successfully use a specific backup system or rollback feature to reduce response time for unexpected failures, take the opportunity to celebrate!

The *actions to mitigate future risks* work through the path and timeline to address the root causes and prevent the incident from happening again systematically. There should be concrete tickets with priorities and sizing placed on the backlog. Your attitude at this stage may be one of ambition toward the opportunities ahead to prevent similar issues from happening again.

As DS tech lead, a strategic and focused attitude is crucial in the incident life cycle's learning phase. You can take leadership in being strategic and seeing the larger picture in driving the mitigation of a class of future risks rather than applying a hasty solution for the incident at hand. It is also your responsibility to hold stakeholders accountable for delivering the planned mitigations before similar incidents happen again.

3.3.3   *Respecting diverse perspectives in lateral collaborations*

DS is often described as a team sport that requires coordination and collaboration between product, engineering, business functions, and DS to generate business value. How does it work in practice?

Businesses survive and flourish by optimizing three areas: increasing revenue, reducing cost, and improving profitability/efficiency. To provide business impact, data scientists need to work with business functions to implement DS recommendations that affect revenue, cost, or profitability/efficiency. Similar to a team sport, strong collaboration and coordination with other business functions are critical for the success of DS initiatives.

020

> To produce business impact, data scientists need to work with business functions to implement data science recommendations that affect revenue, cost, or profitability/efficiency. Strong respect for and strong coordination with business functions are critical for the success of data science initiatives.

In these collaborations, team members from different functions bring distinct perspectives. You are responsible for representing the rigor of DS perspective and for learning and synthesizing the views of the other functions. What could be some different perspectives?

BEING RESPECTFUL OF MULTIPLE PERSPECTIVES AND CONCERNS

Let's take a look at a case study. The finance department of an enterprise software company has proposed a project to better predict future revenue. The project would use historical and current sales pipeline data in the customer relationship management (CRM) system to assess future expected income. The finance department would like to use a diverse feature set to build a prediction algorithm that is as accurate as possible. From the stakeholder perspective, the sales executive would like to have as simple a model as possible, with a deep understanding of each factor's sensitivities. Sales strategies can then be adjusted, and sales compensation plans can be reformulated to better motivate sales professionals.

DS practitioners may feel uneasy in this case, as sales strategy and compensation adjustments are nightmare situations for the predictability of a revenue model. They mean that past trends may no longer be predictive of future sales. They can be detrimental and counterproductive toward producing an accurate prediction of revenue, which is the project's success metric from the finance department's perspective! How could these disparate, but seemingly reasonable, finance, DS, and sales perspectives be aligned?

A locally optimal solution would be to build a sophisticated revenue prediction model with no clear path to sales function optimization such that the finance department project will succeed. However, when the sales strategy and compensation plan change, the predictions may no longer be relevant. A global alignment would be to work with the sales executive to investigate the sensitivity of sales performance concerning different factors, improve sales strategy, reformulate sales compensation, and use the DS model to anticipate as much as possible what future revenue would look like.

The global alignment may look more troublesome and less appealing from the perspective of efficiently completing a project. However, from an enterprise perspective, sales strategies and sales compensation will be adjusted from time to time. It is better to be part of that process than to build a model based on historical data and then have the model be out of date in a quarter or two. As a DS tech lead, you should be aware of these disparate perspectives and realize that alignment does not mean persuading others of the technology perspective but listening to others' perspectives and aligning on a globally optimal solution.

ALIGNMENT AND PROGRESS TOWARD A JOINT VISION

Another example that illustrates collaboration and respect of partner concerns involves providing mission-critical features for credit and fraud risk models in a financial services company. Part of the solution is to have an open, anonymized data platform for the teams to experiment with, in order to create novel, effective features.

When reviewing it with the credit risk department, there were strong pushbacks. Why would anyone be against open innovation? Who is right, and who is wrong?

It turns out that traditional credit risk models were scorecards with only a dozen closely guarded variables. The concern is that if the most useful variables used were leaked, fraudsters could find ways to game the scorecards' logic, get their fraudulent applications approved, and cause significant financial losses for the fintech company.

Such hidden social feedback loops are common in the lending industry, and they are not apparent to many data practitioners new to the domain. Would you give up on the speed of innovation and turn away the capability to provide significant opportunities to improve credit risk scoring and fraud risk scoring potential?

Fortunately, there are solutions. In this case, the teams eventually aligned on a solution architecture where feature selection secrecy was addressed. A pool of 100+ of the most useful features was maintained on the open innovation platform. The credit risk team then selected a subset of the features to be used in production without sharing which features are the most effective at any particular point in time. This step incurred additional operating costs due to maintaining a large pool of features, but retained the security of features through obscurity and provided robustness in the system—in other words, if/when one feature was compromised, the credit risk team had many other features to fall back on.

Such accommodations of domain-specific concerns are common in a tech lead's attempts to communicate and align on paths forward in DS projects. In the end, it is not about who is right and who is wrong. The truth lies somewhere in between. As DS practitioners, we must humbly approach our partners with respect and play the team sport to succeed together.

3.4   *Self-assessment and development focus*

Congratulations on working through the virtues section for becoming an effective tech lead! We hope you can practice these virtues to produce more significant results for your organization with DS!

To some, this section may be challenging because it involves acknowledging their own finiteness as individual human beings. It is here for you to discover personal limitations, recognize strengths, and gain clarity on the paths forward. This self-assessment aims to help you internalize and practice the tech lead virtues by:

- Understanding your interests and leadership strengths

- Practicing one to two areas with the choose, practice, and review process (CPR)
- Self-coaching with the GROW model and developing a prioritize, practice, and perform plan to go through more CPRs

In addition to the assessment and development approaches presented in section 2.4, we introduce the self-coaching GROW model in this section. For self-assessment and development of virtues, we advise using a combination of the GROW and the prioritize, practice, and perform approaches.

3.4.1 Understanding your interests and leadership strengths

Table 3.9 summarizes the virtues areas needed. The column on the right is for you to check off the areas you currently feel comfortable with quickly. As before, any and all rows can be left blank. You can make your individual assessments; there is no judgment, there are no right or wrong answers, and there are no specific patterns to follow.

Table 3.9   DS tech lead virtue self-assessment

Capability areas\self-assessment			?
Ethics	*Operating* in customers' best interest	Avoiding insensitive use of DS, being aware of project impact on customers' emotional well-being	
	Adapting to dynamic business environments	Being sensitive to all changes that need to be communicated	
		Understanding the reasons for changing priorities, communicating changes to team members, documenting and moving on	
	Imparting knowledge confidently	Openly sharing learnings from the data sources examined, the tools used, the assumptions made, and the methodologies developed	
Rigor	*Getting clarity* on the foundations of scientific rigor	Practicing the five principles of scientific rigor: ■ Redundancy in experimental design ■ Sound statistical analysis ■ Recognition of error ■ Avoidance of logical traps ■ Intellectual honesty	
	Monitoring for anomalies in deployment and in data	Facilitating the understanding of unusual or extreme results, validating tracking capabilities, and detecting and diagnosing these results at the code and data levels	
	Taking responsibility for enterprise value	Moving business metrics with the simplest method	
		Focusing on execution velocity by balancing the building of new capabilities through proof of concept and taking care of tech debts	
		Communicating the impact of the DS work to the project team, manager, business partners, and other tech leads across teams	

Table 3.9   DS tech lead virtue self-assessment *(continued)*

Capability areas\self-assessment		?
Attitude	*Maintaining* positivity and tenacity while working through failures	Focusing on communicating institutional learnings promptly, regularly motivating the team, and building trust with partners	
	Responding to incidents with curiosity and collaboration	Maintaining an attitude of respect, appreciation, objectivity, and non-judgment to create a safe environment for team members and partners to collaborate on preventing similar incidents from happening again	
	Respecting diverse perspectives in lateral collaborations	Being respectful of multiple perspectives and concerns	
		Aligning and progressing toward a joint vision	

3.4.2 Practicing with the CPR process

Similar to the tech lead capability assessment in section 2.4, you can experiment with a simple CPR process with two-week check-ins. For your self-review, you can use the project-based skill improvement template to help you structure your actions over the two weeks:

- *Skill/task*—Select a virtue you have chosen to work on.
- *Date*—Select a date in the two-week period when you can apply the virtue.
- *People*—Write down the names of the people with whom you can apply the virtue, or write *self.*
- *Place*—Select the location or occasion at which you can apply the virtue (for example, a one-on-one with a manager or a team huddle on next steps for project X).
- *Review result*—How did you do compared to before? The same, better, or worse?

By holding yourself accountable for these steps in a self-review, you can start to exercise your strengths and shed light on any blind spots in your tech lead virtues.

3.4.3 Self-coaching with the GROW model

After working through a few CPR cycles, you should gain insights into how you work with the elements of tech lead virtues. To form a self-improvement habit, be aware of the best practices you are using and also for those being used in other teams. If you find yourself enthusiastically working on integrating these best practices into your own daily work, it is a good time to look into self-coaching with the GROW model.

The *GROW model* [19] stands for *goal, reality, obstacles or options,* and *will or way forward.* It can be an effective tool for self-coaching. To keep it light, we suggest asking yourself three questions for each part of G-R-O-W, as illustrated in table 3.10.

As an example, if you decided to focus on the *goal* of improving rigor by taking more responsibility for driving enterprise value within a timeline of three months, your specific goal could be that your team can address the top business initiatives that your business partners care about with more velocity and less tech debts.

Table 3.10 Sample GROW questions

Goal	1 What goal are you looking to achieve? 2 When would you like to achieve it? 3 What would it mean if you achieved your goal?
Reality	1 What action(s) have you taken so far? 2 What is moving you toward your goal? 3 What is getting in the way?
Obstacles/ options	1 What different kinds of options do you have to achieve your goal? 2 What else could you do? 3 What are the advantages and disadvantages of each option?
Will/way forward	1 Which options will you choose to act on? 2 When are you going to start each action? 3 What will you commit to doing? (Note: There is also an option to do nothing and review at a later date.)

Next, let us check in on *reality*: What action(s) have you taken so far? Have you examined the business purposes for your DS projects (section 3.2.3)? What is the metric you are moving to produce enterprise value? What is getting in the way?

As you examine the *obstacles/options*, have you looked into the tech debts that need to be paid to gain velocity to move the metric to produce the enterprise value for the top business initiatives? What are the different options? Do any new ones emerge after reading section 3.2.3? What are the pros and cons of each option?

Finally, let us look at the *will/way forward*. What option will you choose? When will you start each action, and what will you commit to doing? Identifying the top business initiative could be the first step. Then you can schedule a review in two weeks to take the next step.

With the GROW questions addressed, you may find putting together a prioritize, practice, and perform plan useful in the context of GROW. You can observe your progress to practice these virtues over four levels:

1 *Unconsciously incompetent*—Happily unaware that you don't have some skills
2 *Consciously incompetent*—Aware that you lack some skills you can't practice yet
3 *Consciously competent*—Great efforts in practicing skills, can self-assess success
4 *Unconsciously competent*—Best practices become habit, can use them effortlessly

As you become competent in these virtues as a tech lead, you are in a position to generate more trust and avoid more breakdowns in projects.

Now you can qualify your interest in pursuing a more technical or more managerial path. If you are pursuing a more technical path, check out chapter 5 for technical staff-level milestones and chapter 7 for principal staff-level milestones. Suppose you are pursuing a more managerial path with team leadership opportunities. In that case, you can follow the progressions of this book for later chapters, with chapters 4 and 5 discussing DS team leadership, chapters 6 and 7 discussing DS function leadership, and chapters 8 and 9 discussing company leadership.

3.4.4   *Note for DS tech lead managers*

If you are using the ethics, rigor, and attitude topics discussed in this book to evaluate team members, please note that they are are aspirational expectations. They are best used to coach tech leads to do the best work of their careers and are not meant to be roadblocks to hold back promotions. In fact, if a DS tech lead has demonstrated skills in some of these areas, they could be excellent candidates to be given the challenge of more responsibilities.

Summary

- *Ethics* is the standard of conduct at work that enables data scientists to avoid unnecessary and self-inflicted breakdowns.
  - To operate in customers' best interest, avoid insensitive use of DS by applying the *New York Times* rule and staying vigilant of your project's impact on customers' emotional well-being.
  - To adapt to changing priorities, be sensitive and over-communicate changes to teams, management, and partners. Always understand the reasons for the changes and lead the team to move on.
  - To drive the sharing of institutional knowledge, promote discussions of the data sources examined, the tools used, the assumptions made, and the methodologies developed during projects.
- *Rigor* is the craftsmanship that generates trust in the repeatable, testable, and discoverable results data scientists produce. Rigorous work products can become solid foundations for creating enterprise value.
  - To practice scientific rigor, you can work with these five principles: redundancy in experimental design, sound statistical analysis, recognition of error, avoidance of logical traps, and intellectual honesty.
  - To take responsibility for data and model deployments, you can validate product feature tracking capabilities and facilitate outlier understanding to detect and diagnose issues at both the code and data levels.
  - To take responsibility for driving enterprise value, move business metrics with the simplest method, focus on execution velocity by taking care of tech debts, and broadly communicate impact of the DS work to generate trust.
- *Attitude* is the mood with which a data scientist approaches workplace situations. With positivity and tenacity to work through failures, data scientists are curious and collaborative team players who respect partners' diverse perspectives.
  - To work through failures on the path to success, you can promote positivity and tenacity by focusing on communicating institutional learnings in a prompt and regular fashion to motivate teams and build trust.
  - Create a safe environment to respond to incidents and lead the team to be curious, respectful, appreciative, objective, and non-judgmental, so team members and partners can collaborate on preventing similar incidents from happening again.

– To succeed in DS as a team sport, be respectful of multiple perspectives across different stakeholders in a project, and work to align and progress toward a joint vision in lateral collaborations.

References

[1] Kelvin Lwin, "AI, Empathy, and Ethics," AISV.806, UC Santa Cruz Silicon Valley Extension. Also available on Coursera. https://coursera.org/learn/ai-empathy-ethics

[2] "Uberdata: The ride of glory," March 26, 2012. https://rideofglory.wordpress.com

[3] "We experiment on human beings!" July 28, 2014. https://www.gwern.net/docs/psychology/okcupid/weexperimentonhumanbeings.html

[4] "Nuremberg code," 1947. https://history.nih.gov/display/history/Nuremberg+Code

[5] "National research act of 1974," 1974. https://www.imarcresearch.com/blog/the-national-research-act-1974

[6] X. Ya et al., "SQR: Balancing speed, quality and risk in online experiments," *KDD*, 2018.

[7] L. J. Hofseth, "Getting rigorous with scientific rigor," *Carcinogenesis*, vol. 39, no. 1, pp. 21–25, Jan. 2018, doi: 10.1093/carcin/bgx085.

[8] A. Casadevall and F. C. Fang, "Rigorous science: A how-to guide," *mBio*, vol. 7, no. 6, Nov. 2016, doi:10.1128/mBio.01902-16.

[9] R. Kohavi et al., *Trustworthy Online Controlled Experiments: A Practical Guide to A/B Testing.* Cambridge, UK: Cambridge University Press, 2020.

[10] B. Benson, "Cognitive bias cheat sheet: 175 cognitive biases organized into 20 unique biased mental strategies in four groups," https://medium.com/better-humans/cognitive-bias-cheat-sheet-55a472476b18

[11] CDC, RIDT, "Rapid influenza diagnostic tests," https://www.cdc.gov/flu/professionals/diagnosis/clinician_guidance_ridt.htm

[12] E. Ries, *The Lean Startup.* New York City, NY, USA: Crown Business, 2011.

[13] N. Alves et al., "Towards an ontology of terms on technical debt," presented at the *6th IEEE Int. Workshop on Managing Tech. Debt*, Victoria, BC, Canada, Sep. 30, 2014, pp. 1–7, doi: 10.1109/MTD.2014.9.

[14] D. Scully et al., "Hidden technical debt in machine learning systems," presented at the *28th Int. Conf. on Neural Information Processing Systems*, Cambridge, MA, USA, Dec. 7–12, 2015, pp. 2503–2511, doi: 10.5555/2969442.2969519. [Online]. Available: https://papers.nips.cc/paper/5656-hidden-technical-debt-in-machine-learning-systems.pdf

[15] C. Fournier, *The Manager's Path: A Guide for Tech Leaders Navigating Growth & Change.* Newton, MA, USA: O'Reilly Media, 2017.

[16] R. Kohavi, T. Crook, and R. Longbotham, "Online Experimentation at Microsoft," Third Workshop on Data Mining Case Studies and Practice Prize, September, 2009. https://exp-platform.com/Documents/ExP_DMCaseStudies.pdf

[17] J. Manzi, *Uncontrolled: The Surprising Payoff of Trial-and-Error for Business, Politics, and Society.* New York, NY, USA: Basic Books, 2012.

[18] M. Moran, *Do It Wrong Quickly: How the Web Changes the Old Marketing Rules*, Indianapolis, IN, USA: IBM Press, 2007.

[19] "The GROW model of coaching and mentoring: A simple process for developing your people," MindTools. https://www.mindtools.com/pages/article/newLDR_89.htm

Part 2

The manager: Nurturing a team

With demonstrated capabilities and virtues to manage technical projects, you may be ready to take on the responsibility of managing team members or managing broader scopes of technical projects as a staff data scientist. As a people manager or a staff data scientist, your organization relies on you to empower your DS team to be as productive as possible across many projects. Your team members depend on you to empower them to do the best work of their careers. How can you meet and exceed such high expectations?

With broader scope comes greater responsibility. Your responsibilities do not stop at managing people. The *purpose* of managing a team is to supervise the building of technical capabilities. The *approach* is to build a capable professional team through hiring, coaching, and performance managing data scientists. The team will look to their manager and staff data scientists as role models for domain expertise and technical insights. We discuss the purpose and the many approaches in chapter 4.

To produce positive impact with DS, you can nurture the DS virtues, described previously in chapter 3, in ethics, rigor, and attitude within the team, as well as practice additional people management virtues, which we address in chapter 5.

Successful DS managers are passionate about the field of DS. They take on more responsibilities for opportunities to produce a more significant impact. The people management part is a means to an end for greater impact.

Eric Colson, former chief algorithms officer of Stitch Fix and ex-DS executive at Netflix and Yahoo, once wrote, "In my experience, many of the best DS leaders approach management with ambivalence. They love scripting, coding, analyzing, storytelling, framing, and so on, and are reluctant to give it up. But, in the end, they love impact more" [1].

The management track is not the only way for a data practitioner to advance. Many DS organizations offer a technical track with growing functional responsibilities to lead projects and influence business decisions. If you choose a career on the technical path, you can reference sections 4.1 and 4.3 for technical staff-level milestones and sections 6.1 and 6.3 for principal staff-level milestones.

If you have set your eyes on eventually becoming a data executive, the path to become a manager, which we will describe in detail in chapters 4 and 5, can allow you to practice the capabilities and virtues essential for a successful executive. Let's begin!

Reference

[1] E. Colson. "How do I move from data scientist to DS management?" Quora. https://qr.ae/pNFfix

Capabilities
for leading people

4

This chapter covers

- Delegating projects while ensuring result consistency across projects
- Making buy-versus-build recommendations
- Building powerful teams and influencing partners to increase their impact
- Managing up to your manager
- Broadening and deepening your business understanding

As a DS manager, your primary responsibility is to nurture your team to produce business impact. Your capabilities are reflected in your ability to deliver results, promote a portfolio of technical expertise in your team, and increase your team's potential to capture additional opportunities. Many of these responsibilities also apply to a staff data scientist.

The primary technology for a DS manager is the delegation process. Effective delegation maximizes the productivity of the team. As a manager or staff data scientist, you can also manage consistency across models and projects and make recommendations for build-versus-buy decisions to improve team productivity. We discuss these technology concerns in section 4.1.

To have a powerful team to delegate to, you can build and nurture a team of talent under your supervision. As manager or staff data scientist, influencing partner teams and coordinating on producing more impact together can help your team members be more successful. Aligning your team's effort with senior executives' goals and managing up is also crucial for the successful execution of company initiatives. We discuss these in section 4.2.

To better anticipate the needs of executives and partners, DS knowledge alone is not enough. Expert knowledge in the business domain can help you understand fundamental opportunities. This knowledge can also help you better determine your team's priorities when critical metrics are missing while assessing ROI.

With the aid of these team management tools and practices, you are well on your way to becoming a capable DS manager. Let's dive in!

4.1   *Technology: Tools and skills*

As a DS manager, you are responsible for delegating projects to team members. What does clear delegation look like? How do you balance the need to deliver with the need to assign stretch assignments to help team members grow? As a manager or staff data scientist, how do you ensure consistency across different projects? How do you determine when to build capabilities in-house and when to buy products or services externally? These are essential questions with tools that have been honed over decades of technology leadership experiences.

Delegating takes work. Section 4.1.1 describes a set of tools you, as a manager, can use to diagnose your delegation techniques. You also have responsibilities beyond the delegating process to ensure the projects' success. When projects come with different risks and rewards, prioritization decisions as a manager can look different than those of a tech lead.

When projects are delegated, as a manager or staff data scientist, the consistency of results across multiple projects can be challenging to guarantee without the appearance of micromanaging. Section 4.1.2 provides guidance for aligning tools and practices while maintaining the execution velocity of the team.

There is always a limit to the capabilities of a particular team. To further increase the team's velocity, you can make buy-versus-build recommendations to bring in third-party solutions. We discuss making recommendations for build-versus-buy decisions with careful assessments of strategy, cost, and risks in section 4.1.3. Here we go with the technology considerations!

4.1.1   *Delegating projects effectively*

As a DS manager, delegation is critical. Many first-time managers find the prospect of not doing the project themselves daunting. As data scientists, we are trained to be skeptical about our results. "Any piece of data or evidence that looks interesting or unusual is probably wrong!" is Twyman's law [1], and many of us have had it seared into our brain through years of experience. This skepticism makes it even harder to delegate a project to a team member.

This anxiety is natural. To be responsible for the final result, many first-time DS managers exhibit the following actions even after delegating a project to a member of the team:

- Attending all stand-ups and meetings for all projects
- Asking the broader team directly about blocks rather than the project lead
- Scrutinizing project lead decisions and overruling some of them

Recognize any of these? These are common signs of micromanaging. Many of us have come across these in one form or another. The key is learning how we can avoid them.

021 Two key concepts for new managers: avoid micromanaging and use delegation to nurture your team members' careers.

Good delegation takes effort and starts with proper planning and attention to detail. Here are seven areas you can craft and communicate in a clear delegation:

- *Goal*—Communicate what you would like to get done, preferably following the SMART goal framework [2], where the goal is crafted to be specific, measurable, achievable, relevant, and time-bound. The clearer your goal is, the easier it will be to review later.
- *Context*—Communicate why the project matters. Context is an important aspect of driving motivation for the delegated project because it can aid your team members in understanding the purpose and impact of the project and how you or business partners will use it later.
- *Definition of success*—Clarifying the metrics of success is essential for evaluating performance afterward. Often, the root cause for employees not performing to expectations comes down to a manager providing only a vague success metric. Managers can't expect team members to read our minds on what looks good. A framework of "this, not that" can work well by including concrete positive and negative examples.
- *Boundaries*—Some motivated team members can be creative in seeking out resources to get projects done. A manager needs to clarify the ground rules or the scope of authorities granted to a team member at delegation time. This includes what resources are available, who could be involved, who should not be bothered, and which and when decisions should be escalated.
- *Confirm the understanding*—After defining the goal, context, metrics of success, and boundaries, you should confirm understanding. One useful approach is to ask what the team members need to get started. This approach allows the team

member to articulate in their words what they understood from the delegation process.

- *Align on the next steps*—This sets up expectations for the project milestones and how often there will be check-ins. It is critical to attain a shared understanding up-front, so check-ins are not perceived to be micromanaging.
- *Review the project*—The concluding move for delegation is to conduct the check-ins at the agreed-upon time to evaluate milestones against their success criteria. When you don't do this promptly, team members will not know how seriously to take the milestones and check-ins in the future. Be sure to set a precedent right away, and stick to what you say.

As you can see, delegation takes work—a lot of work. So how should we decide what to delegate?

TYPES OF PROJECTS TO PRIORITIZE IN DELEGATION

One tool you can use is the priority matrix (PMAT) [3] developed by Daniel Shapero, illustrated in figure 4.1. When a project is likely to succeed, and the return is significant, it is called a *home run*. When a project is expected to succeed, and the return is small, it is a *small win*. When a project has many risks, but the return can be large, it is a *big bet*. And projects that are high risk with a low return are often seen as *junk projects*.

	High	Big bets	Home run
Size of the prize			
	Low	Junk	Small wins
		Low	High
		Probability of success	

Figure 4.1   The priority matrix (PMAT) for project delegation

As a DS manager, which kind of projects would you take on yourself, and which ones would you delegate? For many first-time managers, the answer is to focus on the home runs and the big bets. It is instinctive for ambitious data scientists to prioritize projects with large payoffs! Many may choose to take on the responsibility to deliver the home runs personally and delegate the big bets and small wins as team members' capabilities allow. Reasonable, right?

However, there is an alternative perspective that can be more effective in maximizing the output of the team. This perspective starts by asking, "Will my team members also be able to complete projects with a high probability of success?"

If the answer is yes, then the project can be delegated effectively. If you would like to grow your team, you can give the home-run projects to your star team members to help them build confidence and a portfolio of success toward their next promotion.

This action can help develop their sense of accomplishment and loyalty to the team and you.

Projects that are small wins with a high probability of success are great to delegate to junior team members. There are two reasons for this delegation choice. First, you are taking care of the team members, as small-win projects help junior team members build a track record toward becoming the next wave of star players. Secondly, you are taking care of the company: in the unlikely case that junior team members stumble, the team's overall wins are less affected.

Delegating a project does not mean you should dump it and forget about it. You, the manager, should absolutely check in at the agreed-upon milestones to make sure the project is on track.

What should you, as a manager, take on for yourself? The recommendation is one big bet project and all the junk projects. Say what? Taking on one big bet project is relatively easy to understand. You can prioritize the project with the most significant return, and you can demonstrate leadership by taking on the most risk for project success. You should also be careful not to take on too many big bet projects, as the uncertainties inherent with them often require significant attention and could be overwhelming for anyone.

All right, but why should *you* take on the junk projects? If the junk projects are to be delegated, you may have a hard time specifying their goals or justifying their impact, and your team members would have no choice but to execute on them. You are the best person on the team to decide whether a junk project can be canceled or redefined. If you can remove commitments to junk projects and redefine them to reduce risks or increase their payoffs, it can simplify the team's commitments and increase the team's efficiency. Make sense?

022

In delegation, you can give the home-run projects to your star team members to help them build confidence and a portfolio of success. For junk projects, you are the best person to decide if they can be canceled or redefined.

4.1.2 Managing for consistency across models and projects

As a manager or staff data scientist, you may have seen this scenario play out in teams you are involved in: the DS team has been successfully working through proof of concept projects and quick wins, but gradually, progress slows to a crawl. When you investigate the causes, you may find that innovation in one part of the system has been repeatedly implemented in other parts of the system from scratch, often with slight variations. The different deployment variants produce incoherent insights, confuse business decision-makers, and compromise trust in DS results. This scenario usually occurs as innovations in other parts of the systems are introduced with different methodologies by data scientists with varied domain expertise. This way, a team can end up maintaining 10 incoherent solutions across 5 separate business use cases. Yikes!

Such a scenario is commonly discovered when diligent DS managers take the initiative in looking into the junk quadrant of the PMAT in figure 4.1.

Remember Audra, the data science manager from chapter 1, case 5? She is strong in managing consistency between DS efforts in different teams to minimize the accumulation of tech debts, and you can be too! These are the signs of accumulating tech debts in DS, and there are significant projects you can develop to increase your team's velocity. Here are some questions you may want to explore, which are also summarized in figure 4.2:

- Do you have a consistent A/B testing framework to assess different types of incremental improvements quickly?
- Do you have an easy-to-maintain dashboarding and reporting infrastructure?
- Do you have a shared data-enrichment platform such that improvements can be quickly assessed and deployed to production models?
- Do you have standard metrics pipelines, such that new metrics can be quickly deployed to different product lines?

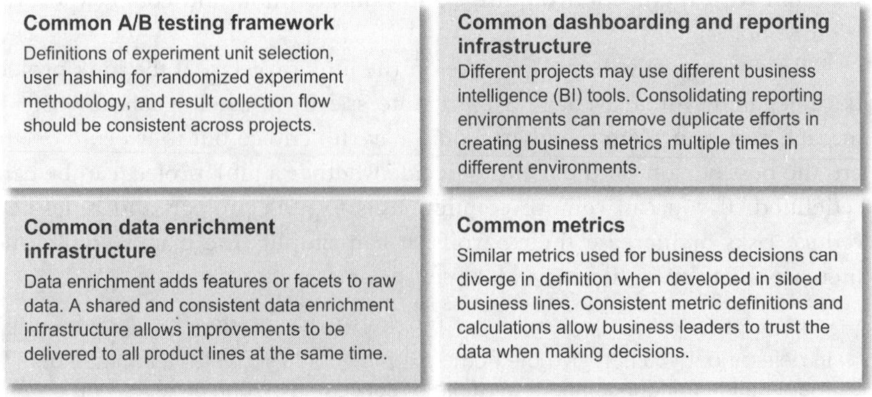

Common A/B testing framework

Definitions of experiment unit selection, user hashing for randomized experiment methodology, and result collection flow should be consistent across projects.

Common dashboarding and reporting infrastructure

Different projects may use different business intelligence (BI) tools. Consolidating reporting environments can remove duplicate efforts in creating business metrics multiple times in different environments.

Common data enrichment infrastructure

Data enrichment adds features or facets to raw data. A shared and consistent data enrichment infrastructure allows improvements to be delivered to all product lines at the same time.

Common metrics

Similar metrics used for business decisions can diverge in definition when developed in siloed business lines. Consistent metric definitions and calculations allow business leaders to trust the data when making decisions.

Figure 4.2   Four areas to manage for consistency across multiple projects

COMMON A/B TESTING FRAMEWORK

In the early stage of a company's data-driven journey, it can be important to launch the initial versions of features with only crude measurements to guide product/market fit decisions. Over time, there may be multiple projects requiring different levels of A/B tests. For example, for a common newsfeed feature in an app, you may conduct experiments on the user interface with fonts and colors. There can also be experiments at the API level with a different selection of content for a specific user type. There can also be experiments on the user segmentation level with varying hypotheses of next best action for different user types. For the fastest path to launch, the UI layer may use off-the-shelf capabilities, while the user segmentation level may have some in-house experimentation capabilities.

At some point, you may want innovations in user cohorts, selection, and feature soft launches to coordinate across experimenting layers, and the experimentation capabilities may need to be implemented across all levels of systems. You will need to consider an off-the-shelf solution or evolve an in-house solution to support these capabilities. In general, modern off-the-shelf online experimentation platforms have most of the experimentation capabilities a startup needs to get off the ground. The challenge lies in reporting the results and the latency of the extra third-party calls for latency-sensitive user experiences. We will discuss the build-versus-buy trade-offs and recommendations as the next topic in this section.

Having a standard A/B testing framework allows a DS manager to produce assessments of its capabilities in a timely manner and make prioritization trade-offs for impact and efforts across multiple experimenting layers. If you decide to build an A/B test capability in house, any improvements in experimentation unit selection, orthogonal experiment rehashing, and result interpretation should be shared by all the experiment layers without reimplementation. For more details on building or evaluating experimentation platforms, a great resource is *Trustworthy Online Controlled Experiments: A Practical Guide to A/B Testing* by Kohavi et al. [4].

COMMON DASHBOARDING AND REPORTING INFRASTRUCTURE

In the early stages of development, reports are usually built with ad hoc data-processing pipelines. Results are shared via email on a custom-built web dashboard using Google Charts/R Shiny, over SMS, or over Slack. Eventually, some data pipelines may be mapped to more sophisticated BI tools, such as Tableau, Looker, Domo, GoodData, Birst, and others, while other dashboards may be used in the experimentation platforms.

When we develop new metrics and metrics pipelines to assess the business in one area, we would like to reuse these efforts as much as possible in other business areas. Disparate reporting environments may mean duplicated efforts in re-creating metrics multiple times in different reporting pipelines. A common dashboarding and reporting infrastructure can help reduce junk work in re-creating the same metric in different data processing pipelines.

COMMON DATA-ENRICHMENT INFRASTRUCTURE

Data enrichment is the process of adding features or facets to refine and enhance raw data through techniques such as segmentation, categorization, or matching to third-party data. Disparate projects using raw data may each develop similar data-enrichment processes over time.

For example, when a DS team supports multiple product lines, each product line can demand its own data-enrichment capabilities for its purchase propensity models based on different customer segmentation in location and budget. Improvements from one pipeline may require significant work to be duplicated and validated in other pipelines, introducing junk work in the process.

A shared and consistent data-enrichment infrastructure can allow improvements to be delivered to all product lines at the same time. Please note that upgrading a data-enrichment capability across models and reporting infrastructures can still be involved. Model boundary entanglement, as discussed in section 3.2.3, can mean that models dependent on a shared data-enrichment process will require retraining to leverage the full benefits of the data-enrichment improvements. What is saved with a shared data-enrichment infrastructure is the implementation effort, not the deployment effort.

COMMON METRICS

Challenges from disparate metrics pipelines are sometimes the hardest to grok. They occur when different business lines have evolved similar metrics over time to make business decisions or produce customer-facing reporting features in the product.

When similar metrics diverge in implementation across different product lines, business decisions may become inconsistent across business lines. Customers may see different numbers across different interfaces, reducing trust in the product and casting doubt on its data integrity.

The cause for different definitions can come from the various choices of raw data source (e.g., before or after filtering for bots or anomalies), the different observation windows (e.g., calendar-monthly active users versus rolling 30-day active users), or distinct interpretations of company granularity (e.g., including or excluding known ownership and subsidiary hierarchies). As a DS manager, resolving technical debts from disparities in metrics to produce standard metrics can facilitate faster business decisions and reduce customer confusion.

To summarize, with a broader view across multiple projects, a DS manager has more opportunities to look for synergies across these projects and diagnose challenges that cannot be observed at a single-project level. As a team leader, you can also work with peer DS teams to coordinate on efforts in tackling technical debts and reducing the amount of junk or inefficient projects in the DS function.

4.1.3 *Making build-versus-buy recommendations*

To drive impact, DS teams often have to integrate a variety of capabilities. These capabilities include data sourcing, data aggregation, data validation, data enrichment, data warehousing, data wrangling, modeling, dashboarding, A/B testing, anomaly detection, incident alerting, and more. Many of these components are missing in the early stages of a DS team's growth.

You, the DS manager or the staff data scientist, are closest to the team's needs in moving projects forward and have a responsibility to assess the situation and recommend whether the team should build or buy a solution to move projects forward. The ultimate decision in these cases will be made by senior DS leadership with approval by finance and operating executives. How do you think about a buy-versus-build recommendation, so you can make a well-articulated proposal?

One bit of advice is not to overthink it. If a particular data set costs a few hundred dollars and can immediately accelerate a project by a week, it is a no-brainer buy decision. Many VP-level positions can approve small budgets with minimal documentation. An email chain and receipts will often suffice. If the decision involves thousands of dollars, and the cost can increase with usage levels, then it is worthwhile to investigate three aspects more thoroughly: strategy, cost, and risk. Let's look at these one by one.

STRATEGY

There are three strategy questions to examine when considering whether to build a capability in-house versus buying externally:

- Is the capability core to the competitive business advantage of the company?
- Are external solutions mature, commoditized, and flexible for customization?
- Can buying help launch the core products faster?

First, let's assess whether the capability under consideration is core to your company's business competitive advantage. A key question is: if the capability is developed in-house, can it be a best-of-breed solution so desirable that others may be willing to pay for it?

There are no right or wrong considerations, and a company may have different concerns at different times. For example, Google considered web search relevance to be its core business competitive advantage. In contrast, for several years, Yahoo considered it a marginal service and purchased it as a technology solution. For a fintech business, understanding customer financial transaction categories can be regarded as core to its competitive business advantage or considered a data-enrichment capability that can be purchased.

If the capability is considered marginal, we need to assess whether a solution is available to buy. The maturity of the external solution can be evaluated in the completeness of the required features, the number of deployed cases, the iterations the solution has evolved through, and its customization flexibility.

The completeness of the required features can help us assess whether the available capabilities will satisfy our core needs. We can examine whether the capability and deployment process was exercised well enough that most bugs were ironed out from the number of deployed cases. The iterations that the solution evolved through can illustrate whether domain best practices were incorporated into the solution over time. And the flexibility for customization leaves room for unexpected features that we may realize we need later.

One unspoken belief that should be examined is whether buying a solution will lead to a faster time to market. In a world with many software-as-a-service offerings, it may seem that all you need is to create an account at an online portal, and you will immediately gain access to a whole set of new capabilities. The reality of integrating a third-party data processing capability is not so straightforward.

For example, to best use a third-party A/B testing platform, we need first to upload or stream all data relevant to user segmentation to select users for experiments. Next, we need to upload or stream all down-funnel events to the A/B testing framework for the platform to compute core evaluation criteria to evaluate success.

Some of these data may need to be desensitized or anonymized before transmitting to third-party platforms. And if the platform has gaps in supporting complex business logic for user selection, additional adaptor logic needs to be developed. On the one hand, this glue logic may still be faster than developing a full-fledged A/B testing framework in-house. On the other hand, it may be faster to have a simple A/B test setup as a stop-gap solution for the first few features before a full A/B test infrastructure can be put in place, especially in an early-stage startup.

COST

The cost evaluation of buy-versus-build decisions is often the focal point of the discussions. For a buy option, the cost can be significantly higher than the amount paid to the third-party. Other than the invoice price, the integration cost in engineering resources and the maintenance cost of ongoing data channels to and from the third-party vendor are critical components to estimate. Depending on the third-party vendor's business model, you may also need to consider how the cost will scale as your business grows.

For a build option, the total cost of ownership includes not just the engineering cost but also the design, test, verification, and maintenance cost. Other than these direct costs for building a solution, there is also the research of industry best practices, user feedback and iterations, and the team's management overhead to be accounted for. Most importantly, what is the opportunity cost? Should the team be spending time on this build or looking at other projects with higher ROI?

One common challenge with the build option is the scope of the target audience. Data scientists often build internal systems for an internal audience with limited scalability and high operating costs in deployment. Third-party solutions often offer better user interfaces that allow many tasks to be self-serviced by data analysts and product managers with no DS support. When comparing costs for operating the solutions, we should take these differences into account.

RISKS

When assessing risks in buy-versus-build options, the fact is that an existing solution you can buy is available today, and the solution to build does not yet exist. There are inherent risks in estimating the cost, feasibility, and capability of something that does not yet exist. Also, until you have used a solution in a particular context, the gaps in features and best practices may not be completely known.

For a buy option, capabilities are more than what's in a spec sheet. To properly evaluate risk, we must also understand the commoditization of the solution, as demonstrated with multiple competing satisfactory offerings, and the maturity of the solutions to buy, as demonstrated in service-level agreements (SLAs) of the capabilities and the support experience for incidents and outages.

For the build option, other than the technology and scheduling risks, we also need to assess whether the expertise to build is available in the team. If yes, would the talent with the expertise like to work on the *build* project? If talent is not available, how difficult would it be and how long would it take to hire the right talent?

The DS manager or the staff data scientist is in the best position to understand the situation, collect information, estimate cost, and assess risks to make the buy-versus-build recommendations to senior management. The recommendation is not a decision.

The analysis behind the recommendation is what's most useful for executives to work toward a decision. Depending on the complexity of the task, how strategic it is toward core competitiveness, the urgency of needs, and the relative cost of buy-versus-build options, the final buy-versus-build decision often involves a sequence of actions. For example, a capability acquisition strategy may include build-now, buy-later or buy-now, build-later sequences of milestones.

These are quite a lot of considerations on three seemingly straightforward words: strategy, cost, and risk. For a more detailed analysis of the buy-versus-build decision, the paper "Factors Affecting the Buy vs. Build Decision in Large Australian Organizations" [5] can be a great reference. Now may be a great time to take a quick break, as we will be diving into execution next!

4.2 Execution: Best practices

As a DS manager, you create value through the execution of your team and the teams you influence. If technology is what can be learned, execution is what must be practiced. Let's look at the execution capabilities in three parts:

- Building powerful teams under your supervision
- Influencing partner teams to increase your impact
- Managing up to your manager

For a manager, building a team is an exciting endeavor. In non-people-management roles, you are assigned to work with whomever is on the team. As a manager, you decide who you would like to invite onto your team and who you would like to manage out. Team building is discussed in section 4.2.1.

Many, including DJ Patil, former chief data scientist of the US Office of Science and Technology Policy, emphasize that DS is a team sport. For a manager and a staff data scientist alike, influencing adjacent functions on executing data-driven methodologies and strategies can greatly improve the impact of your team. The practice of influence is discussed in section 4.2.2.

And most importantly, your outputs must be aligned with your manager's goals for your team. You are expected to fulfill three fundamental responsibilities: align on priorities, produce progress reports, and escalate issues. This way, your manager can be informed about your priorities and your progress, and can help you resolve challenging situations when required. The techniques for managing up are discussed in section 4.2.3.

023

> If technology is what can be learned, execution is what must be practiced.

4.2.1 Building powerful teams under your supervision

Building a team involves inviting a group of individuals into your organization. Building a powerful team involves nurturing your team members to produce a greater impact than what they can do as a group of individuals.

There are seven areas of concern you can work on to be successful in your management role. They are summarized in figure 4.3.

Figure 4.3   **Seven areas of concern for building powerful teams under your supervision**

HIRING NEW TEAM MEMBERS

When hiring, you can evaluate DS candidates on their capabilities and virtues, as discussed in chapters 2 and 3. The capabilities include experience and accomplishments in technology, execution, and expert knowledge. The virtues include ethics, rigor, and attitude.

Hiring itself can be compared to a predictive algorithm. You are using short-term interactions with candidates to predict their long-term success in your team. After interviewing hundreds of candidates, here are three heuristics and methodologies that can help you get a firm start:

- *Understand the risk of failure*—If hiring an intern, the risk of a wrong hire is low; the talent pool is large, and technical skills are mostly undifferentiated. Value your recruiter's time and aggressively screen in early stages, using techniques such as take-home questions. Select for high-potential candidates after they pass a certain technical bar and allow them to prove themselves on the job. If you are hiring a tech lead and expect that their actions will influence a team's technical direction, the downside of a wrong hire is high, and the talent pool is limited. Develop a rigorous interview panel with multiple rounds to protect the interviewers' time, and expect to interview 10–50 candidates across multiple rounds before finding a fit. You can seek executive and partner support in setting up a robust hiring process, which is discussed in more detail in section 6.2.2.
- *Select the most critical attributes to interview for*—At different stages of a team's growth, you may want to focus on specific attributes. For example, the first hires may be generalists who can work with diverse stakeholders, and the later hires

can be specialists to complete the team's skill set. The TEE-ERA fan can also provide a starting point for assessing generalists versus specialists. Entry-level roles may emphasize technology competencies, scientific rigor, and positivity in attitude, while a tech lead role may emphasize project execution, expert knowledge, and professional ethics.

- *Collect broad input*—DS is a team sport. For roles that will frequently be interacting with business partners, it is critical to set up an interview panel that includes those partners in products, marketing, and others. A panel-based interview process allows the candidate to understand the partnership context of the role better. It also enables the partners to express with whom they would like to work.

As a hiring manager, the panel helps illuminate any blind spot you may have. You should solicit detailed responses from your panelists and discuss any concerns they may have about the candidates. Although the hiring manager makes the final hiring decision, there should be a consensus after the discussion to hire or to reject. These discussions are great opportunities for the panel to learn how best to evaluate future candidates. In the unlikely event of significant differences in opinions, the risk of failure (the first point in this list) can be used to guide the decision. For example, if there is a high risk of failure, when there is a firm no-hire opinion in the interview panel, we recommend rejecting the candidate. Let's continue the predictive algorithm analogy, shall we?

Understanding the risk of failure allows you to select an operating point with an acceptable level of false positives and false negatives. Selecting critical interview attributes is like feature engineering. Collecting broad input is like building an ensemble of models toward a more informed hiring decision.

When you are a hiring manager, there is often an awe factor from new members you have personally invited onto your team. Awe is a combination of admiration and fear—not the kind of emotion experienced in the presence of danger but more of the trepidation associated with the unfamiliar.

Through the interview process, candidates often choose to join a group because they value the opportunity you are giving them as a manager. There can also be the fear that you have the power to take that opportunity away. This awe factor can be a useful starting point for building trusting manager-to-team member relationships.

INHERITED TEAM MEMBERS

If you were promoted to a manager, and your ex-peers now report to you, congratulations! In working with your teammates, you may already be familiar with their work, capabilities, and gaps. This background allows you to know when to trust your team members. However, you, as a manager, still need to earn trust in supporting them and helping them with their career development.

If you were hired to manage an existing team, you have been entrusted with producing a significant impact on your team members' careers and with producing a significant impact on the company. The top priority is to get to know your team members and let your team members know more about you. What you share and learn in the first few meetings will be crucial for successful relationships later on.

Here is a list of topics you may want to discuss in the first few interactions after inheriting a team:

- *Share what you stand for.* Help the team understand any guiding principles you work with for DS leadership. Some examples include:
  - Seeking deep understanding through data to make product experiences delightfully natural
  - Owning the intelligence roadmap and building systems with robustness and efficiency
  - Operating with collaboration and openness, while using data ethically, with sensitivity and empathy to customers' well-being.
- *Explain how you want the team to work.* For example, you may expect the team to work with specific work ethics, professional rigor, and a positive attitude.

  Chapter 3 lists some points for your consideration, including: ethics for responsibly operating in customers' best interest, adapting to business priorities in dynamic environments, and confidently imparting knowledge with team members; rigor in the scientific methods, monitoring for anomalies, and taking responsibilities for enterprise value; and positive attitude for the tenacity to work through failures, curiosity and collaboration in responding to incidents, and respecting diverse perspectives in lateral collaborations.
- *Clarify goals.* As a new manager, you often start by first executing on existing goals for the organization you inherited. Be prepared to communicate how the team's goals are aligned with the company's mission, and be clear about what goes into your decision-making and how you'll evaluate the team's progress.

GETTING TO KNOW YOUR TEAM MEMBERS

Be it newly hired or inherited team members, building trust and rapport at the beginning will allow you to help your team members through the highs and lows of the team's journey. In your first few one-on-ones with your team member, there are some standard topics you may want discuss:

- What is most important to you in one-on-ones?

  Some would like to discuss the most important topics of the week by going through a to-do list, others prefer to have a coaching session by bringing scenarios to discuss, and some like to receive a progress report to receive feedback. Regardless of the specific format, the goal is to understand what each team member values and have an effective format that both you and the team member feel comfortable with.
- What are your 5- to 10-year career goals? What are the immediate milestones we can work on together to help you make progress toward those goals?

  Junior team members may not yet be clear about these goals or may have generic goals, such as being promoted in 24 months. Senior team members may have a more defined goal of becoming a senior manager, becoming an executive, or starting their own company. Helping team members gain clarity in their long-term goals establishes a path for coaching them and highlighting the relevance of their current projects to aspects that build their experience toward their long-term goals.

- What do you need from your manager, your peers, and your partners?

    Depending on the team member's skills in managing up, you may or may not receive a clear request of who would like to do what by when. Any response you receive here can be an excellent starting point to discover potential deeper issues that require your attention.

Other than these standard questions, some additional items can help a first-time manager navigate the world of people management. Lara Hogan, in her blog post "Questions for Our First One-on-One," [6] also suggests the following:

- What makes you grumpy? How will I know when you're cranky? How can I help you when you're grumpy?

    Whether it be children at home or fasting for religious or health reasons, knowing this can be invaluable when seeking understanding and empathy in difficult times for the team member.

- How do you like feedback? Through email or in person; in one-on-ones or as it happens?

    Some team members prefer to have feedback in writing, so they can think and respond, while others would like more context and have a better understanding of feedback as it happens.

- Do you prefer to receive recognition in public or in private?

    In some cultures, people don't like to be praised in public. It is best to understand this to avoid putting team members in uncomfortable situations unintentionally.

- What's your favorite way to treat yourself?

    It might be good to keep this in mind because there could always be a time when you would like to thank a team member in a personally meaningful way.

Now you have a toolbox for assembling a group of talent in one organization and getting to know them through one-on-ones. If team members all perform well as individuals, what more can you ask? Let's discuss getting your group of data scientists to perform well as a team.

TEAM BUILDING

Successful DS practitioners are great with challenges in the quantitative domains. However, team management often requires high emotional intelligence that may not come naturally to many data scientists. Even if the DS manager has excellent emotional intelligence skills, helping team members connect as a team may be challenging.

Fortunately, there are many tools available to help quantify team member capabilities in an empowering format. One of which is the Clifton StrengthsFinder [7].

Like the Myers Briggs Type Indicator [8] and Erin Meyer's CultureMap [9], Clifton StrengthsFinder is a psychological assessment that asks participants to answer a series of adaptive questions to assess their psychological properties. Unlike many psychological assessments, the output of Clifton StrengthsFinder is a list of top leadership strengths for an individual, rather than a set of mental properties that one has to interpret for specific situations.

A fundamental observation by Don Clifton, the American psychologist and chairman of Gallup, Inc., is that when people blindly follow their leadership role models, they often fail. An individual may have different leadership strengths than their role models. How can people recognize their own leadership style based on their leadership strengths?

The Clifton StrengthsFinder highlights your top 5 leadership strengths from the 35 leadership strengths identified from studying highly successful leaders. You can leverage your top five leadership strengths to form your leadership style to succeed. Each leadership strength comes with its balcony, where the strength is used successfully and appreciated by peers, and its basement, where the strength may be misused or taken to an extreme to cause negative responses.

For example, the achiever strength can have balcony properties, such as tirelessness, a strong work ethic, leading by example, and being a go-getter. The achiever strength's basement properties include being unbalanced, being a brown-noser, being overcommitted, not being able to say no, and being too concentrated on work.

Such a system can be used at four levels to help a group of quantitatively-minded data scientists better collaborate as a team:

- *Level 1: Individual understanding*—Figure 4.4 shows the result of the Clifton StrengthsFinder for a team of seven data scientists. Each individual's top five strengths are represented on each column of the table. Using this result, each data scientist can look up the balcony and basement properties of their strengths and reflect and calibrate their actions when working with colleagues. Their strengths can manifest positively via teamwork.

- *Level 2: Team understanding*—The team can also look at their collective strengths. In this example, the DS team is stronger in strategic thinking and execution with relatively weaker relationship-building and influencing strengths. This bias is typical for DS teams in more straightforward organizations. Influencing and relationship-building strengths tend to become more critical in larger companies, where team success depends on an acute sensitivity to organizational dynamics. A DS team can follow strength areas' overall coverage to emphasize projects and commitments that fit the team's collective strengths.

- *Level 3: Collaborative engagements*—Through the individual introspections in level 1, team members can discuss their strengths' balcony and basement properties with teammates. Topics can include: what interactions bring out the best of me, what happens when you get the worst of me, what can you count on me for, and what do I need from you. These discussions take no more than 10 minutes between each pair of team members, but the specific strengths highlighted by the Clifton StrengthsFinder can quickly illuminate future potential collaboration opportunities.

Team members and their top 5 strengths (ranked 1–5)			Aadi	Bruno	Christian	Dali	Eunjung	Fatima	George
Executing	Leaders with dominant strength in the executing domain know how to make things happen. When you need someone to implement a solution, these are the people who will work tirelessly to get it done. Leaders with a strength to execute have the ability to "catch" an idea and make it a reality.	Achiever	5		1			3	
		Arranger						5	
		Belief							
		Consistency							
		Deliberative					2		
		Discipline							
		Focus							
		Responsibility	2						
		Restorative							1
Influencing	Those who lead by influencing help their team reach a much broader audience. People with strength in this domain are always selling the team's ideas inside and outside the organization. When you need someone to take charge and speak up to make sure your group is heard, look to someone with the strength to influence.	Activator							
		Command							
		Communication							
		Competition					4		
		Maximizer							
		Self-assurance							
		Significance							
		Woo							
Relationship building	Those who lead through relationship building are the essential glue that holds a team together. Without these strengths on a team, in many cases, the group is simply a composite of individuals. In contrast, leaders with exceptional relationship building strength have the unique ability to create groups and organizations that are much greater than the sum of their parts.	Adaptability							
		Connectedness							
		Developer							
		Empathy							
		Harmony							
		Includer				3			
		Individualization					5		
		Positivity						4	
		Relator		5			3		3
Strategic thinking	Leaders with great strategic thinking strengths are the ones who keep us all focused on what could be. They are constantly absorbing and analyzing information and helping the team make better decisions. People with strength in this domain continually stretch our thinking about the future.	Analytical	3	3		3	4		2
		Context					5		
		Futuristic	4			4			
		Ideation				1			4
		Input			1				
		Intellect			2		1		
		Learner	1	4	5	2		2	5
		Strategic			2			1	

Figure 4.4   Sample output of the Clifton StrengthsFinder test

- *Level 4: Team leadership*—As the individual and team strengths are understood, team members with rare strengths can have the opportunity to provide office hours to advise teammates. Areas of advice may include how they might handle various situations, such as influencing through storytelling with data or relationship building with business partners in challenging situations. This peer-help mechanism allows team members to establish leadership identities for their career growth and helps them raise the proficiency of many areas of leadership strengths.

The Clifton StrengthsFinder is just one of many quantitative tools you can use to build your team with positive psychology. The goal is to help the team identify its collective strengths and help each teammate do the best work of their career to contribute to the organization's vision and mission. While building your team can be fun and rewarding, no process is complete without reviews. Yes, that means performance reviews.

PERFORMANCE REVIEWS

As a manager, you are responsible for helping team members do the best work of their careers. The performance review is one of many feedback mechanisms to guide DS team members to perform at their best. Team members are only human, and they have good days and bad days on their projects. When do you provide feedback? What feedback would you look to provide?

First of all, continuous feedback always beats the once-a-quarter or once-a-year cycles, mainly for two reasons:

- Fresh and timely feedback on a recent positive or negative situation provides a more nuanced context to learn from. If feedback is for an event that happened months ago, only a generalized context and recommendation could be conveyed.
- Fresh and timely feedback can trigger actions that further boost positive behavior or quickly dampen negative behavior, so the team member can improve faster.

One thing to avoid is to deliver only negative feedback. This could produce the perception that all continuous feedback is negative feedback. We discuss how best to build a positive attitude toward continuous feedback in detail in section 5.3.2.

Other than continuous feedback, organizations also have quarterly or annual formal performance reviews. These processes are often put in place to synchronize the assessment of promotion and the performance management processes.

These reviews can carry significant weight on team members' career growth. As a DS manager, you should take them seriously and consider the following three actions:

- *Take the time to write feedback.* The TEE-ERA fan can help provide specific DS dimensions in technology, execution, expert knowledge, ethics, rigor, and attitude. Make sure to highlight the areas to start, stop, and continue toward reaching team members' next career milestone.
- *Draw from team members' strengths.* The Clifton StrengthsFinder results can be used to comment on how team members' strengths have exhibited their balcony and basement properties and how they can channel their strengths to improve their performance.
- *Maintain a balance of past observations and future expectations.* Managers sometimes fall into the trap of elaborating on top performers' accomplishments and providing limited input for future improvements, minimizing negative feedback for underperformers and elaborating on future development areas. To help

data scientists do the best work of their careers, maintaining a balanced performance review is critical. The career path described in this book can provide material to help you map out the path for top performers. The requirements for TEE-ERA can help you highlight more rigorous expectations for your team members to perform well.

HANDLING QUITS

Sometimes, a highly valued and esteemed team member decides to quit—not for more pay or better perks at another organization, but because they feel their work is not appreciated. This situation is common in a field where companies are competing for top talent. You and your organization do not want to lose them, yet their decision may indicate that you have neglected parts of your job as a manager.

Andy Grove, in *High Output Management* [10], describes such a scenario. The quitting news is often delivered as a surprise and at the most inconvenient time. Andy vividly describes the situation and coaches managers on a technique that maximizes your chance to retain the quitting team member:

- *Drop what you are doing*—Sit them down and ask them why they are quitting. The risk of losing an esteemed team member should be a higher priority than many other tasks.
- *Let them talk*—The team member likely has rehearsed their speech countless times. Don't argue about anything with them.
- *Ask more questions*—After the prepared speech, the real reasons may come out. Don't argue; don't lecture; don't panic.

Demonstrate through your actions that they are important to you and the organization. You, in turn, become the project manager for driving the solution. Involve your manager, HR, and any other support source you might have to help you save the employee, even if it involves allowing them to report to a fellow manager. If this is a highly valued employee worth saving, your fellow manager will appreciate it and potentially return the favor later.

The quitting team member will likely appreciate that you have addressed their real reason for quitting with a solution. However, there may be a lingering sentiment that they may be seen as having forced you into the new situation.

To keep the team member, you will need to make them feel comfortable to stay and convince them that they did not "blackmail" you into doing anything that you would not have done otherwise. They just made you aware of some gaps in your responsibilities that should have been addressed before.

Managers are only human; we all have blind spots and make mistakes. However, turning around this type of situation has implications beyond just the quitting team member. When a well-respected top performer quits, it can hurt the entire team's morale and organizational loyalty.

MANAGING UNDERPERFORMERS

One area DS managers can spend a significant amount of time on is managing under-performers. With limited time and immense responsibilities to increase team impact, the opportunity cost of managing underperformers is enormous. How do you assess whether an underperformer can be turned around quickly or is a lost cause?

One diagnosis to be made is whether the underperformer has an ability issue, a motivational issue, or both. Ability issues occur when a team member has gaps in their training to perform a project. Motivation issues arise when a team member is unwilling to complete or is distracted from a project.

Suppose the team member has an ability issue but is motivated. In that case, this may have been a blind spot in the manager's understanding of the team member's capabilities when assigning the project. It is an opportunity for the team member to be mentored by another team member with expertise in the capability. The project may take longer to complete, but it can be a growth opportunity for both the mentor and mentee. Most of the time, the motivated underperforming team member can quickly get up to speed. If the gap is too large to close, the underperformer may have to be managed out.

A common misperception is that motivational issues are easier to resolve. Although you may be able to resolve some motivational issues caused by workplace situations, many motivational issues have roots outside of work. Some empathy and patience from you can help nudge the underperforming team member to resolve the issues outside of work independently. You should limit how much time you spend on the underperforming team member, as your time could be better spent on growing your top performers. If issues persist, the underperformer will have to be managed out.

If the underperforming team member has both an ability issue and a motivational issue, focus on solving the motivation issue first. When motivation is low, any effort to bridge the ability gap will not be as efficient. You may need to examine the hiring process to better understand how to avoid such situations in the future.

In the diagnostic process, be sure to document your findings and follow any HR recommendations and procedures. One standard process is to document what you and the team member agreed to work on improving in a performance improvement plan. This process is a set of clearly defined objectives that the team member must achieve within a fixed period. Be sure to have frequent check-ins, and document a shared understanding of whether the situation is improving. When things improve, the process can be a significant learning experience for the team member. What happens more often is that the gap is simply too large to close. The HR process will have ensured there is mutual respect, and the company is legally protected.

BRINGING THE CONCEPTS TOGETHER

Building your team involves hiring new team members and inheriting existing team members. When hiring new team members, calibrate the rigor of the interviews with the seniority of the role, select the most critical attributes to interview for, and collect broad input to get a full picture of the candidate. When inheriting existing team members, build rapport by proactively sharing what you stand for, explain how you want the team to work, and clarify goals you will be evaluating the team's progress on.

You may want to set up regular one-on-ones and understand your team members' long-term career goals when getting to know them. To get to know your team and help them get to know each other, you can use a psychological assessment to quantify their psychological strengths during team building. The Clifton StrengthsFinder can be used for individual understanding, team understanding, collaborative engagement, and team leadership.

In delivering feedback, frequent and timely feedback is more effective than quarterly or yearly performance reviews in reinforcing or dampening behaviors. Balancing positive and negative feedback can avoid the perception that all continuous feedback is negative. In formal performance reviews, take the time to write the feedback, draw from the team members' strengths, and maintain a balance of past observations and future expectations.

If a valued team member indicates they want to quit or resign, drop what you are doing, let them talk, and ask only clarifying questions to find the real reason. Work with your manager and HR on a solution, and make them feel comfortable to stay on without the stigma of having forced you into a situation.

To manage underperformers, diagnose for motivational and ability causes. While ability causes can be addressed with mentorship, you can only address motivational causes from workplace situations. When there are both motivation and ability causes for underperforming, you may want to solve the motivational causes first.

That was a lot of dense information on the somewhat heavy topic of handling teammates who have quit and managing underperformers. Now may be a good time for a breather before we switch gears and talk about expanding your influence outside of your immediate team.

4.2.2 *Influencing partner teams to increase impact*

As a DS manager or a staff data scientist, your impact reaches beyond your team. You also have the capability and responsibility to influence and improve the partner teams' operations, including product, engineering, and business functions, in order to generate value for the organization. You have two levels of influence to propagate: as an individual and as a team.

INFLUENCING AS AN INDIVIDUAL

As an individual, there are rigorous recommendations you can provide through your frequent communication with business partners to deeply understand their challenges—not just on the projects but also on the day-to-day processes—that can significantly improve partner team productivity. Let's look at an example that demonstrates individual influence.

Launching a feature is often not a smooth process. An experienced DS practitioner may have seen this situation play out in one variant or another: after the engineering partner team spends weeks architecting, developing, testing, integrating, and releasing a feature, the user experience looks as expected, but the data collected looks off. A few weeks later, when you are invited to review some difficult-to-interpret A/B test results, you discover incomplete tracking events, biased sample sizes between the treatment and control, bugs in the data pipeline, and missing metrics on the operating dashboard. These issues trigger another round of engineering bug fixes, testing, integration, and release before another attempt to validate the product hypothesis.

You can help engineering teams recognize issues more quickly by defining a methodology to quickly validate tracking capabilities after feature launches. The method should test whether:

- *Events are firing according to the tracking specifications.* As discussed in Section 3.2.2, this rigor includes the validation for availability, correctness, and completeness. Availability is the presence of the tracking signal. Correctness is the satisfaction of the data format specification. Completeness means that events are collected without losses.
- *Data is processing through the metrics pipelines and appearing on the result dashboards.* There may be numerous metrics, such as click-through rates and session length, that involve a degree of aggregation or processing. Incoming event signals often have to be annotated appropriately and placed in specific locations to be picked up by the metrics pipelines.
- *Users are being selected according to the experimentation specifications.* Bugs can cause too many or too few users to be selected in the experiment. For example, bot-filter issues can allow too many crawlers into an online experiment, preventing the effective learning of human user behavior insights. Bugs in the experimental setup can also allow too few users into a test, such that there will unlikely be enough data collected over a reasonable experimentation time window. Other bugs can bias the users' selection into treatment or control, breaking the statistically random user selection assumption and causing the resulting measurements to be invalid.

Such tracking methodology can be documented to influence engineering partner teams to adopt data best practices by performing self-checks during the integration test of a feature and the first day of launch. The documented best practices can tighten the feedback loop for bug discovery. Further, these kinds of methodology documents can also be provided to product teams and business vertical teams to ramp features and read A/B tests. Authoring, sharing, and evangelizing data-driven best practices demonstrate the influence you can have on increasing the organization's overall efficiency and output.

INFLUENCING AS A TEAM

As a DS team, you can have a much broader scope of influence on your peer DS teams and business partner teams. In level 4 of your team-building exercises, illustrated in section 4.2.1, you may have observed some team members excelling in specific areas in DS.

You can empower these team members with unique strengths to advise teammates and broaden their influence on a diverse set of peer teams. Topics can include statistical modeling, storytelling with data, natural language processing in feature engineering, and causal inference. How can you effectively facilitate the sharing of these skills and knowledge?

If you just announce to peers and partners they can seek help from a team member with a unique and valuable skill set and knowledge, the team member may quickly be bombarded with work-interrupting inquiries and won't be able to focus on their own work. In other words, the team member could become a victim of their expertise. One technique to mitigate ad hoc disruptions, protect your team member's productivity, and empower them to establish their influence is to institute office hours.

024

A team member with a unique and valuable skill set can quickly be bombarded with work-interrupting inquiries and won't be able to focus on their own work. They could become a victim of their expertise. One technique to try: institute office hours.

An effective starting point for setting up efficient office hours can involve four components, as illustrated in figure 4.5 and the following list:

- *Determine the purpose*—We can determine the intended audience of the office hours with a clear purpose. Here are a few examples of purpose statements:
  - Modeling office hours empower peer data scientists to use the most appropriate modeling technologies for the project at hand and increase the rigor in the modeling process.
  - Data access office hours enable business partners to independently pull data with simple queries, select the best data sources to use, and create dashboards to track business metrics.
  - Storytelling office hours help peer data scientists turn their analyses into impact and build their brand as powerful communicators.
- *Define a format*—Setting aside one or two fixed 30-minute slots every week can minimize disruptions to the team member running the office hours. A recurring

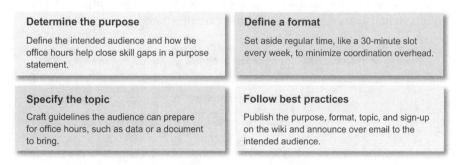

Determine the purpose

Define the intended audience and how the office hours help close skill gaps in a purpose statement.

Define a format

Set aside regular time, like a 30-minute slot every week, to minimize coordination overhead.

Specify the topic

Craft guidelines the audience can prepare for office hours, such as data or a document to bring.

Follow best practices

Publish the purpose, format, topic, and sign-up on the wiki and announce over email to the intended audience.

Figure 4.5   Four components to setting up effective office hours

time can also provide some certainty to the office-hour audience that the team member with valuable skills and knowledge can be available with minimal coordination when help is required.

- *Specify the topic*—To make the best of a 30-minute session, a set of guidelines could help the audience prepare for such a session. For a modeling office hour, a project plan with initial modeling challenges or initial results can help set up the context for providing feedback. For a storytelling office hour, an initial version of a presentation with a clearly defined target customer can help focus the session on improving the DS's results delivery.
- *Follow best practices*—To run a successful office hour, you may want to publish the purpose, format, and topic on a wiki and make an announcement over email to your intended audience. A shared sign-up sheet can also minimize coordination overhead with the audience. If there are no sign-ups for a particular week, you can cancel the session the evening before to discourage unprepared ad hoc attendance.

As data scientists, we should be data-driven in continuously improving best practices for running an office hour. Be sure to collect feedback and testimonies after the session. Good testimonies can also highlight the impact and influence your team is having and motivate and recruit more data scientist peers to become coaches to scale office hours further.

Office hours are just one of many ways to expand your team's influence in the organization. Other methods include setting up weekly seminars to share learnings from key projects with peer DS teams, or craft training sessions for business partners to better self-serve simple data questions with data tools. All of these actions can extend your team's positive influence and impact on the rest of the organization.

4.2.3   *Managing up to your manager*

If you are a DS manager, you represent the organization to the team, and you represent the team to the organization. If you are a staff data scientist, you represent the interest of significant DS initiatives in the company. In reporting to your manager, who may be a senior manager, director, or another senior employee, there are three fundamental areas you can fulfill, which are illustrated in figure 4.6.

Figure 4.6   Three areas for managing up to your manager

ALIGNING PRIORITIES

For a group of people to execute together as a company, everyone must perform their part of the company's plan. Priorities must be aligned between you and your manager during regular planning cycles and when ad hoc changes emerge.

During regular planning cycles, your responsibility is to interpret high-level initiatives from your manager and refine them into a set of projects and specifications for your team to execute. This alignment process first involves clarifying your understanding of your manager's high-level initiatives. This is best done in written form, based on a firm grasp of the strategic growth direction and aligned with the company's vision and mission. In typical business environments, the high-level initiative should not change frequently, and this alignment often only takes place once a quarter.

While projects are prioritized to progress toward the high-level initiatives, many assumptions have to be made in the prioritization process. Data scientists and their tech leads use their best judgment on project innovation and impact; the project's reach, impact, confidence, and effort; and they evaluate strategic alignment with the longer-term data strategy. We describe these techniques in section 2.2.1.

In aligning with your manager during the regular planning cycles, you seek their feedback on the portfolio of projects for delivering the high-level initiatives and validating the assumptions made in the prioritization process. Success means their feedback is promptly accounted for with a plan that your manager can sign off on.

There are also ad hoc changes that can emerge when the conditions of the operating environment change. These are times when your manager may bring forth changes in priorities for you to implement with your team.

In managing up, if you feel that the changes in priorities are making it impossible for your team to deliver, speaking frankly about the trade-offs with your manager can minimize surprises later when milestones on existing commitments are missed because of priority changes. Facts and figures to support these trade-offs are essential to bring to your manager, so they can make decisions on how to move forward.

REPORTING PROGRESS

During the execution of plans, progress reporting is vital for communication with your manager. Progress reporting involves more than sharing current milestones. It should include any critical learnings along the way and the implications of the learnings toward meeting future milestones.

With the team's productivity in mind, progress reporting should include learnings such as the data sources explored, the productivity tools used, the assumptions made, and the methodologies developed. Section 3.1.3 described each of these learnings in the context of sharing with the rest of the team.

When managing up, sharing your team's learnings allows your manager to learn about your work, build trust in your management capabilities, and provide feedback. Your manager may be aware of other teams' learnings to help accelerate your progress. They may also help escalate issues, provide additional context for assumptions made, and amplify your best practices more broadly to other teams.

025

In managing up, you are expected to align priorities, report progress, and escalate issues. Progress reporting is more than sharing milestones. It can include critical learnings and their future implications to build trust in your management capabilities. It can also provide your manager an opportunity to share other teams' learnings to accelerate your progress.

Another part of managing up is to share updates on the likelihood of completing ongoing commitments, given your learning so far. Were there additional risks discovered from data source explorations? Were there pieces of the projects that can be accelerated with the use of productivity tools? Were there bugs in productivity tools that required work-arounds and will cause further delays? Were there assumptions that would need to be revisited?

These assessments will help your manager manage expectations with business partners for possible delays. They can also allow your manager to provide alternative solutions or support to help get projects back on track. Your manager can also take these learnings to perform a likelihood-of-success assessment on projects in other teams that may benefit from the same best practices or encounter the same challenges.

ESCALATING ISSUES

Even with the best intentions, challenges and differences can emerge when collaborating with partners facing different constraints. When project success is at risk, the situation may need to be escalated. Let's discuss the *clean escalation* of an issue while building a trusting working relationship with partners.

Before escalating, the teams should first recognize the misalignment and the negative impact of non-resolution. Sometimes, the effect may be small enough that some delay in project delivery is the least disruptive trade-off for all parties involved. When a misalignment has a significant negative impact on the outcome, it's essential to identify the stakeholders affected and first collaborate on identifying possible solutions to see if the challenge can be resolved between the stakeholders. When you can resolve the differences, the situation becomes one of progress reporting, involving identifying a challenge and resourcefully resolving it with learnings to share.

When the differences cannot be resolved, you can manage the escalation process up the reporting chain. Escalation implies that you have exhausted all options within your execution capabilities. You should then bring the issue to your manager along with other stakeholders, highlighting the misalignment, the significant negative impact of non-resolution, the alternative solutions already explored, and the trade-offs that cannot be resolved without the manager's support.

A precise description of the misalignment allows your manager to grasp the full context of the issue quickly. The negative impact's significance allows your manager to appropriately prioritize resolving this issue among all the other issues they are working with. The alternative solutions already explored allow them to focus on what has yet to be tried with the broader set of resources, resolving, deferring, or escalating the issue up the reporting chain. By aligning on priorities, reporting on progress, and escalating issues, you can start building a trusting working relationship with your manager to execute DS projects.

Remember, as a first-line DS manager or staff data scientist, you should be confident in sharing your perspective. You are closer to the data scientists and the projects. You should have a better read on the team's implementation capabilities than anyone else in the organization, including your manager. With this knowledge, you are responsible for managing your manager's expectations of what is possible to bring out your team's full potential.

To bring it together

To bring it together, in managing up, you are expected to fulfill three fundamental responsibilities: align priorities, report progress, and escalate issues. When aligning priorities, prepare to accurately translate your manager's high-level initiatives into prioritized projects for the team and present them to your manager for feedback. When reporting on progress, share the learnings and their implications on the outlook of meeting future milestones. When escalating issues, ensure that the matter can lead to a significant enough negative impact. If possible, highlight the misalignment, the significant negative impact of non-resolution, the alternative solutions already explored, and the trade-offs that cannot be resolved without the manager's support. This way, your manager can have the full context of resolving, deferring, or continuing to escalate the issue up the reporting chain.

Paul (from chapter 1, case 4), who felt drained after six months on the job as a DS manager, can use these techniques to manage up to his boss. He can align priorities with his boss to clarify where he should invest more time and team resources, and he can escalate requests from partners he cannot satisfy to prevent his team from being spread too thin on too many projects.

4.3 Expert knowledge: Deep domain understanding

Paul from chapter 1 took on many requests, and he felt overwhelmed and drained. He only had mixed results and came across as showing little leadership on where to focus.

Your team looks to you to connect their day-to-day work to the big picture. It is your responsibility to identify strategic and tactical opportunities with expert domain knowledge and turn them into team goals and priorities. This section provides the tools for Paul, and managers in similar situations, to gain the domain knowledge to effectively assess, anticipate, and prioritize requests from the team and business partners. With these tools, Paul (and you!) can then provide the leadership that the teams seek and boost the teams' morale.

How do you do it successfully? Three elements are essential:

- Broadening knowledge in multiple technical and business domains
- Recognizing the fundamental domain opportunities
- Assessing the ROI of projects despite missing data

To help connect DS capabilities to business needs, broadening domain knowledge is essential for serving a broad range of business partners, such as finance, marketing, product, and customer service. It will be beneficial to use different key performance indicators (KPIs) and optimization techniques to drive business impact.

While serving specific business needs, there are also fundamental data opportunities that only someone with deep DS expertise can realize. You are responsible for proposing and executing the ideas that can materially affect revenue, cost, or profit immediately or over time.

When proposing new DS projects, the priority is often on the project with the highest business impact. However, critical parameters to assess business impact are frequently missing. Business leaders regularly make decisions with missing data. We can learn from them to leverage expert domain knowledge to make the best estimate possible for these crucial parameters. We can then use our analytical strengths to assess the outcomes' sensitivity to a wide range of estimates for more confidence in our assessment of a project's impact.

4.3.1   *Broadening knowledge to multiple technical and business domains*

Many first-time managers and staff data scientists are savvy and confident when interacting with other data scientists. When meeting with business partners, however, the discussions can become awkward quickly. Topics may seem to be coming from unfamiliar angles, and first-time managers and staff data scientists can find it challenging to think on their feet and respond with confidence.

If this has happened to you, don't worry; you are not alone. The awkwardness usually comes from a limited understanding of the business partners' fundamental concerns and the real intent of their questions and requests. By broadening your understanding of these fundamental business concerns, you can anticipate and prepare for their questions and requests.

026

First-time managers and staff data scientists may feel awkward when talking to business partners. This can be caused by a limited understanding of the business partners' fundamental concerns and the real intent of their questions and requests. Try to broaden your understanding.

In organizations, especially the fast-moving ones, each business function is under tremendous pressure to deliver its objectives. Table 4.1 illustrates some fundamental concerns and KPIs for various business functions.

As you can see in table 4.1, various business functions' fundamental concerns differ significantly. At any point in time, a business partner could be focusing on validating or optimizing a particular subset of KPIs.

As a DS manager or staff data scientist, it is essential to learn the company revenue sources and how they might be at risk. You can do this by studying public- and private-facing documentation and making an effort to know your business partners personally.

Table 4.1   Fundamental concerns of various business functions and sample KPIs

Business functions	Fundamental concerns addressed	Sample key performance indicators
Marketing	Find customers with narratives that produce dissatisfaction with the status quo and offer help	▪ *Brand recall*—Awareness of brand ▪ *Net promoter score (NPS)*—Propensity to evangelize the brand ▪ *Customer Acquisition Cost (CAC)*—Cost of acquiring a customer
Sales	Produce transactions with willing customers to bring in revenue	▪ *Opportunity-to-win ratio*—Percent of qualified leads resulting in a deal close ▪ *Sales cycle length*—Time from lead to close (B2B) ▪ *Gross merchandise value (GMV)*—Total merchandise transacted (in dollars)
Distribution	Optimize logistics for cooperation and coordination in transactions	▪ *Delivery time*—Time from order placement to delivery ▪ *Transportation costs*—All expenses from order placement to delivery ▪ *Inventory turnover*—Number of times your entire inventory is sold
Product	Deliver satisfaction to meet customers' expectations	▪ *Conversion ratio*—Ratio of users who go from one stage to the next ▪ *Customer churn*—Ratio of customers who left after a period of time ▪ *Virality*—Speed at which a product spreads from one user to another
Finance	Maintain financial viability while optimizing enterprise value and cash flow	▪ *Gross margin*—Total sales revenue minus the cost of goods sold ▪ *Average revenue per user (ARPU)*—Total revenue / # of users ▪ *Lifetime value (LTV)*—Future net profit throughout a relationship
Customer Service	Produce customer trust to maintain the willingness for further transactions	▪ *CSAT score*—Customer satisfaction score through surveys ▪ *First response time*—Time between support ticket and initial response ▪ *Average resolution time (ART)*—Time taken to resolution

Sometimes the most challenging hurdle to get over is the willingness to ask "dumb" questions. When you feel more confident, find smarter folks and ask more dumb questions. Very quickly, after a few of these sessions in each of the business functions you work with, you will be able to anticipate common problems to address.

On top of a broad business understanding, the "expert" part of expert knowledge also requires you to follow the business domain's rigor. Here are three examples of common confusion in connecting DS capabilities to business needs:

- Month-over-month (MoM) growth
- Gross merchandise value (GMV) versus revenue
- Customer acquisition cost (CAC)

MONTH-OVER-MONTH GROWTH

MoM is often measured as the simple average of monthly growth rates. However, the purpose of measuring this metric is usually to use historical data to anticipate the effects of future growth. As organizations grow and product features mature, the growth is often predicated on the compounding of the current business size. To be exact, compounded monthly growth rate (CMGR) can be a more meaningful metric for MoM growth.

The CMGR is calculated using the following formula: $[\text{CMGR} = (\text{latest month}/\text{first month})^{(1/\#\text{ of months})} - 1]$. It will be smaller than the simple average in a growing business. It is also what prospective venture investors will use to benchmark across companies.

GROSS MERCHANDISE VALUE VS. REVENUE

GMV is the total sales dollar volume of merchandise transacting through a marketplace in a specific period. It is what consumers spend, and it is a meaningful measure of the size of the market. However, it is not the revenue for the marketplace.

Revenue is the portion of GMV that the marketplace earns, consisting of the various fees that the marketplace collects to provide its services, ad revenues, and sponsorship revenues. Depending on the services a marketplace provides, revenues may include return handling fees, shipping and handling fees, customer service fees, and payment processing fees.

CUSTOMER ACQUISITION COST

The cost of acquiring customers can make or break a business model. It is often a closely watched metric in business operations for startups and mature companies alike. While one can simply define it as the full cost of acquiring users stated on a per-user basis, the interpretation and calculation come in many variants.

Rigorously speaking, CAC is the spending required to acquire the next incremental user. In the numerator, the full cost should include all the referral fees, credits, and discounts. The number of users acquired should include only those attributed to paid channels and should not be blended with organic traffic in the denominator. This definition is used because the paid marketing channels provide the most direct levers moveable with additional marketing spend.

However, one may argue that some impact of paid marketing may not be accurately attributed to acquired users. Properly designed split-geo tests can help assess whether a portion of the organic traffic should be attributed to paid campaigns.

In some situations, a blended view of CAC that includes paid and organic traffic can also be informative as a reporting metric. It can be used to monitor CAC with respect to customer LTV. A CAC that is lower than LTV can confirm that customer acquisition spend is in line with the business strategy at a particular stage of a company's growth.

These three business metrics (MoM growth, GMV revenue, and CAC) are part of the vocabulary of your business partners. They illustrate that business metrics should not be taken at face value. It is your responsibility to also understand why you are using them and how they could be properly computed to guide future business decisions.

You can check out the blog post "16 Startup Metrics" from the venture capital firm Andreessen Horowitz for more business metrics discussions [11]. In collaborations on DS projects with the goal of making business impact, only when we speak our business partners' languages can we gain their trust and respect.

To bring it together, you are responsible for identifying strategic and tactical opportunities to define team goals and priorities and connecting DS capabilities to business needs. You can understand the fundamental concerns being addressed in different business functions, including marketing, sales, distribution, product, finance, customer service, and the KPIs important to them. Among them, the nuances of the KPIs connecting the company's business model to revenue, such as MoM growth, GMV, and CAC, are especially important to clarify and align.

4.3.2 Understanding the fundamental domain opportunities

As a manager or staff data scientist, the team looks up to you to connect DS capabilities to company priorities. Your responsibilities require you to think beyond the business partners' requests and discover fundamental data opportunities that only someone with deep DS expertise can recognize. You are responsible for proposing and executing ideas with material revenue impact and data strategies with long-term business impact. One process to accomplish this involves the creation of impactful ideas with expert knowledge through the benchmarking, interpretation, and generation (B.I.G.) approach:

- *Benchmarking*—Benchmarking aims to understand the domain contexts beyond a company's internal business perspectives. Existing internal data may contain biases and limitations of the existing business. Benchmarking with external sources allows DS to be a partner in framing the business context.

  Reference benchmark data sets can come from governments or companies. Government sources include federal agencies such as the Bureau of Labor Statistics, the Census Bureau, and public records from states and cities. Private-sector data can come from Google Trends for online traffic, Dun and Bradstreet for company entity data, or LinkedIn for talent data and professional connections.

- *Interpretation*—This is the understanding of the implications of the benchmark statistics for your customer segments. It can inform the quantitative grounding for your prioritization decisions and focus your team on projects with the most impact.

- *Generation*—When new opportunities are generated with benchmarked business context and prioritized with quantitative grounding, you are more likely to discover the fundamental opportunities that can produce outsized impact.

While you can build expert knowledge in the benchmarking and interpretation steps yourself, the generation step usually works well in a team setting. Let's examine an example of the B.I.G. approach, used to drive smartphone users' everyday financial wellness, within a consumer-facing financial services company.

027

As a manager or a staff data scientist, you are responsible for thinking beyond the business partners' requests to discover fundamental data opportunities that only someone with deep data science expertise can recognize. Try the B.I.G. approach: benchmark, interpret, generate.

DOMAIN BACKGROUND

Financial wellness is defined as the effective management of one's financial life. Whether one's income is $20K or $200K a year, financial wellness is associated with living within one's means, while saving and investing for an emergency and retirement. However, with so many sources enticing us to spend and consume, almost 40% of American adults wouldn't be able to cover a $400 emergency with cash, savings, or a credit card charge that they could quickly pay off, according to the Federal Reserve's 2018 report on the economic well-being of US households released in 2019 [12].

Many financial wellness companies are providing mobile app-based solutions to nudge users to save more for retirement. They allow users to link their credit card and debit card accounts and use the aggregated transaction data to provide savings and investment services. Some also offer debit cards and checking accounts with features to lower users' exposure to bank fees for their everyday transactions. With a wealth of data aggregated by serving millions of users, financial wellness companies have a plethora of opportunities to personalize their nudges to help users build habits of saving and investing for their financial future.

Building good financial habits for users can profoundly benefit both users and financial wellness companies. A habit of investing just $2 a day starting at birth can accumulate a nest egg of more than $1 million when retiring at the age of 68 (calculated as a $730 investment per year over 68 years, assuming 7% average expected annual returns).

For companies promoting financial wellness, more users with savings habits built on a financial platform can reduce user churn, which increases the LTV of users' and companies' enterprise value.

BENCHMARKING

Benchmarking with government data, the median income of a working American adult is $52,000 per year. After taxes and FICA, that translates to about $3,600 of take-home income a month. According to the US Bureau of Labor Statistics Consumer Expenditure Survey [13], median monthly spending is broken down by the following categories for someone with a median income:

- *Income*—~$3,600 coming into a bank account each month
- *Shelter*—~$1,300 for rent, utilities, furniture, and supplies
- *Essential expenses*—~$1,600 for transportation, food, and healthcare
- *Discretionary expenses*—~$700 for entertainment, apparel, education, etc.

INTERPRETATION

Interpreting consumer expenditure categories is crucial for developing expert knowledge. The four consumer expenditure categories are

- *Income*—These are the most significant financial events each month. Users feel the richest right after they are paid and are more open to setting aside savings for emergencies and retirement.
- *Shelter*—These are fixed expenses that are difficult to change and painful to see going out of one's account each month.
- *Essential expenses*—These are relatively consistent expenses each month with plenty of opportunities for optimization.
- *Discretionary expenses*—These expenses are possible to cut, but they come with high emotional costs. Imagine forgoing the weekly night out at the movies with friends only to save $50 a month toward a goal far into the future. Few would go for that.

When developing nudges to encourage users to build saving and investing habits, personalization of messages can boost response rates from the low single digits to more than 10× that response rate. The challenge is to create many highly personalized messages efficiently to reach a broad enough audience to make the ROI worthwhile.

How can this be accomplished? The key is in the systematic understanding of the transaction contexts between the customers and merchants.

GENERATION

With the benchmarking and interpretations clarified, the generation step can benefit from team brainstorming. The team can work together to develop all sorts of nudges to be tested with real users:

- *Income*—By detecting and recognizing users' paychecks arriving in their account, we can nudge them to contribute toward their long-term financial health at a time when they feel the richest.
- *Shelter*—While it can be hard to nudge people to save and invest for their retirement directly, rent or mortgage payments can be effective training nudges to set aside cash for short-term payments, allowing users to build good financial habits and disciplines.
- *Essential expenses*—Optimization hacks for essential expenses include suggesting meal kit deliveries if food expenses are high and usually from high-end grocery stores. Meal kits are a good alternative with high-quality ingredients and just the right proportions to minimize waste. Investing in a warehouse store membership can also be a hack to reduce expenses if food expenses from everyday grocery stores are high, indicating a large family. Any expenses reduced in this category could be recommended to be saved and invested.
- *Discretionary expenses*—One concept that has gained significant traction over the past few years is *temptation bundling*. Coined by behavioral psychologist Katherine Milkman and colleagues in a 2014 study [14], it involves bundling an *instant gratification* source with a less fun, but *should-do activity*.

As an example of temptation bundling, a weekly night out at the movies can provide instant gratification, while saving for one's financial future can be the should-do activity. When instant gratification spends are detected, they can be used to nudge users to match their specific transaction with a contribution to their own financial future. This kind of nudge has been shown to be highly effective, and the resulting engagement was more than 10 times higher than a generic marketing nudge.

In this illustration of the three-step process of benchmarking, interpretation, and generation for driving financial wellness, we demonstrated how expert knowledge could be built through quantitative benchmarking of the business context, interpreting their implications, and generating ideas with your team. The benchmarking step uses external data from the government or private sectors to understand the domain contexts beyond internal business perspectives. The interpreting step seeks to understand the implications of these statistics for your customer segments. The generating step leverages your team to create a diverse set of ideas for outsized business impact. Using the B.I.G. approach, you can generate new expert knowledge unique to your team's DS capabilities and business strategy.

4.3.3   *Assessing ROI for prioritization, despite missing data*

As a DS manager or staff data scientist, assessing project prioritization involves calculating the ROI to determine whether the project is worthwhile to pursue. What do we do when components of the ROI calculation are missing?

This scenario happens often, as components of data that go into an ROI calculation can take time to manifest. For example, the churn component of LTV for subscription customers can take months to reveal. The delinquency rates for borrowers to estimate profit margins of financial loans can take quarters to uncover.

Missing input is challenging, especially for data scientists, as the intelligent systems we have created require complete input for predicting the output. When inputs are missing, our first instinct is to get to work figuring out what the input should be. In contrast, business professionals, especially executives, are frequently forced to make business decisions in situations with missing information.

This is the key difference between *intelligence* and *wisdom*. Intelligence is the ability to make good decisions with complete information, while wisdom is the ability to make good decisions with incomplete information. How do we apply wisdom in producing ROI calculations with missing information?

028

> The key difference between intelligence and wisdom is that intelligence is the ability to make good decisions with complete information, while wisdom is the ability to make good decisions with incomplete information.

First of all, ROI is just one of many factors used for prioritizing projects. ROI is usually computed as (reach * impact / effort). Other factors to consider for prioritization include project innovativeness, the confidence of success, and alignment with data strategies, as discussed in section 2.2.1. In many cases, as long as the order of magnitude of ROI is correct, it will be informative enough to stack rank the projects for go or no-go decisions.

To get a quick estimate of ROI, let's look at the three components: reach, impact, and effort.

REACH

As introduced in section 2.2.2, project plans include a description of a project's customers. This description can be used to assess the potential reach of a project. In fast-growing companies, the uncertainty is often in estimating the forward-looking reach when the project is complete. When in doubt about what numbers to use for reach, you can seek advice from your organization's product or finance leaders, who usually have these projections as part of the enterprise roadmap.

IMPACT

This is the expected lift or improvement for the target customers provided by a project. The magnitude can be higher for a narrowly defined audience or more diluted for a broader audience with greater leverage. It is hard to estimate how much improvement is achievable before the project is complete. Experience from a similar project in a comparable context could help.

In the absence of experience from a similar project, you can reverse your focus to the magnitude of improvement required to make a project worthwhile. Given the leverage provided by the customer reach, would 1% lift provide a compelling ROI? What if the lift is 10% or 50%? With this perspective, we can evaluate whether the impact required to make the project worthwhile is realistic for the solution proposed.

For example, in the early stages of product development, a 10–20% improvement is expected, as the baseline implementation has a lot of room for improvement. In a relatively mature product that has gone through years of iterative refinements, a 1–2% improvement could be significant!

EFFORT

Effort can be estimated in engineering weeks or data scientist weeks required to launch and iterate on a solution. When a team or team member has undertaken similar projects in comparable organizations in the past, an estimate can be relatively straightforward. If this is the first time such a DS project is being planned in an organization, breaking the project down to milestones and estimating each milestone as large, medium, or small could help provide a rough overall estimate.

After estimating the ROI by analyzing the reach, impact, and effort of a project, you can note the components that were estimated with low confidence and check the sensitivity of your overall project prioritization when the uncertain estimate is off by 10% or 30%. Most of the time, there is a cluster of projects with outsized ROI that are excellent prioritization choices. If there are close contenders, you can always include the error bars from your sensitivity analysis toward more nuanced prioritization considerations.

Table 4.2 provides ROI estimates for a sample portfolio of projects at a fintech startup for illustrative purposes. By estimating the reach, impact, and effort with uncertainties, you can observe the sensitivity of ROI to these uncertainties in the estimates.

Table 4.2   DS projects and their ROI ranges

Project	Reach	Impact	Upside	Effort (weeks)	Uncertainty	ROI ($/week)
Personalized nudge campaign to save more	500K users through 10 campaigns	30% lift to engagement; 8% more retention; $50/user LTV	$2M	10 wks to build; 3 wks to maintain	Retention increase can be 5%–10%	7.7×; $154K/week ($96K–$192K)
User upsell of premium service	3M users	1.5% to 3%; $50/user upsell to $200/user revenue	$6.75M	30 wks to build; 20 wks to maintain	Build effort can be 25 to 38 wks	6.75×; $135K/week ($116K–$150K)
User activation improvements for feature X	400K users	20% lift; 25% to 30% conversion; $45/user revenue	$900K	8 wks for 3 rounds of testing	Revenue could be $30–50/user	5.6×; $113K/week ($75K–$125K)
Weekly email campaign open rate optimization	1.3M users; 52 weekly emails/year	8% lift in open rate; 23% CTR for opened email, at $0.1/click	$124K	2 wks for optimization	Build effort may take 2 to 4 wks	3×; $62K/week ($31K–$62K)
Personalization improvement for partner promo	1M users	10% lift on 250k/month promotion revenue	$300K	6 wks for an improved algorithm	Build effort may take 5 to 8 wks	2.5×; $50K/week ($37K–$60K)
Customer education optimization	500K users	1.5% increase in converting to paid users at $50/user	$375K	10 wks to build; 3 wks to maintain	Impact could be in the 1–2% range	1.5×; $29K/week ($20K–$40K)

ROI is the ratio of monetary return over investment. To assess an investment's dollar value, the rule of thumb used here is $20,000 per experienced data scientist's week of work. This amount includes the infrastructure engineering and data engineering support, product management, project management, and people management overheads. It is commonly used in consultancy firms and startups for project cost estimations.

How might this differ for DS organizations of various maturities? Section 2.3.3 discussed five levels of DS practice maturity for organizations in learning, emerging, functional, integrated, and cultural stages. In the learning and emerging stages, organizations do not have the capability to productionize DS projects. We focus on the functional to cultural stages in this discussion.

As data organizations become more mature, the same project can use better DS infrastructure and be accomplished in a shorter amount of time. However, the overhead amount for tool support for each week of DS work may not decrease. $20,000 per week can be a fair estimate for DS projects across functional, integrated, and cultural stages. That said, the overall productivity of DS organizations increases as they mature. The same project in mature DS organizations can be completed in fewer weeks and with better tools, achieving a higher ROI.

To decide what amount of ROI makes a DS project worthwhile, we first have to make sure the return is aligned with the north star metrics that the organization is looking to move. Then, it will be essential to consider the opportunity cost of funding DS projects versus building other product features from a financial perspective. The rule of thumb is that projects with 5–10× fully loaded ROI are worth investing in. In our example in table 4.2, there is a cluster of projects with 5.6–7.7× ROI, and the rest have 1.5–3× ROI. The three projects with top ROI pass the bar. The rest of the projects might still make sense at a later time when better infrastructures become available to reduce the efforts required, or the audience has increased to provide better leverage for revenue with the same technical improvement.

By illustrating the uncertainty with sensitivity ranges of ROI, you can continue to drive prioritization and partner/executive buy-in for projects, even in situations with missing data. With expert knowledge referenced from past projects, these uncertainty ranges can be reduced for more accurate ROI estimates toward better prioritizations.

4.4 Self-assessment and development focus

Congratulations on working through the chapter on manager capabilities! This is an important milestone for becoming a people manager or staff data scientist with influence over multiple teams!

The purpose of the capabilities self-assessment is to help you internalize and practice the concepts by:

- Understanding your interests and leadership strengths
- Practicing one to two areas with the choose, practice, and review (CPR) process
- Developing a prioritize-practice-perform plan to go through more CPRs

Once you start doing this, you will have courageously taken the steps to delegate responsibilities, nurture powerful teams, and enrich your domain knowledge, while gaining clarity of the paths forward.

4.4.1 Understanding your interests and leadership strengths

Table 4.3 summarizes the capability areas discussed in this chapter. The rightmost column is available for you to check off the areas you currently feel comfortable with quickly. There is no judgment, no right or wrong, nor are there any specific patterns to follow. Feel free to leave any or all rows blank.

If you are already aware of some of these aspects, this is a great way to build a narrative around your existing leadership strengths. If some aspects are not yet familiar, this is the opportunity for you to assess whether they can be of help in your daily work, starting today!

Table 4.3   Self-assessment areas for capabilities of managers and staff data scientists

Capability areas/self-assessment (italic items primarily apply to managers)		?
Technology	*Delegating projects effectively*	*Delegating projects with succinct requirements*	
		Prioritizing home runs and small wins when delegating	
	Managing for consistency across multiple projects	Managing common A/B test methodologies	
		Managing dashboard and reporting infrastructures	
		Managing data-enrichment capabilities	
		Managing shared business metrics	
	Making buy-versus-build recommendations	Assessing strategy, cost, and risk of buy and build options to accelerate team velocity	
Execution	*Building powerful teams under your supervision*	*Hiring new team members: appropriately invest time*	
		Inheriting team members: share your management style	
		Getting to know your team members through one-on-ones	
		Building teams: Creating trust with quantitative assessments	
		Reviewing performance: timely with a mix of positive and negative	
		Managing underperformers and handle quitting teammates	
	Influencing partner teams to increase impact	Individual influence: Enforcing and spreading best practices	
		Team influence: Building expert identity, facilitating sharing	
	Managing up to your manager	Aligning on priorities in planning and for ad hoc changes	
		Reporting on progress: Including data sources explored, productivity tools used, assumptions made, and methodologies developed	
		Escalating issues: Escalating confidently, together with third parties, and suggesting solutions where possible	
Expert knowledge	Broadening knowledge to multiple technical and business domains	Getting familiar with KPIs in domains including marketing, sales, distribution, product, finance, and customer service	
	Understanding the fundamental domain opportunities	Benchmarking with external data for domain insights	
		Interpreting: Understanding the implications for your segment to ground decisions and focusing your team	
		Generating new opportunities based on problem contexts	
	Assessing ROI for prioritization despite missing data	Understanding the difference between intelligence and wisdom	
		Using reach, impact, and effort ranges to assess ROI sensitivity and gaining more confidence in decisions	

4.4.2 *Practicing with the CPR process*

Like the tech lead capability assessment in section 2.4, you can experiment with a simple CPR process with two-week check-ins. For your self-review, you can use the project-based skill improvement template to help you structure your actions over the two weeks:

- *Skill/task*—Select a capability to work on.
- *Date*—Select a date in the two-week period when you can apply the capability.
- *People*—Write down the names of the people with whom you can apply the capability, or write *self*.
- *Place*—Select the location or occasion at which you can apply the capability (for example, a one-on-one with a team member or an alignment meeting with your engineering partner).
- *Review result*—How did you do compared to before? The same, better, or worse?

By holding yourself accountable for these steps in a self-review, you can start to exercise your strength and shed light on any blind spots in the manager and staff data scientist capabilities.

Summary

- *Technologies* for managers and staff data scientists include tools and practices to delegate projects, manage for result consistency, and recommend buy-versus-build decisions.
  - When delegating projects, you can start with six areas of succinct requirements and prioritize based on the risks and reward, starting with home runs and small wins.
  - When managing for consistency, work with shared A/B test methodologies, dashboard and reporting infrastructures, data-enrichment capabilities, and business metrics.
  - In buy-versus-build recommendations, assess strategy, cost, and risk concerns to accelerate team velocity.
- *Execution* is effective when you can build a team and capabilities for the long term, influence partners to amplify impact, and manage up to your manager.
  - When building a team, use best practices to build and nurture teams of new and existing members, use quantitative assessments, conduct performance reviews, manage underperformers, and handle quitting team members.
  - When influencing partners, you can use individual influence by authoring processes or use team influence by building expert identities and facilitating knowledge sharing.
  - When managing up, you can proactively align on priorities, report on progress while sharing learnings, and cleanly escalate issues while suggesting solutions where possible.

- *Expert knowledge* can improve your effectiveness when you broaden your knowledge to multiple business domains, understand the fundamental domain opportunities, and can assess ROI for prioritization despite missing data.
  - When expanding knowledge, you can get familiar with KPIs in marketing, sales, distribution, product, finance, and customer service.
  - When understanding the fundamental domain opportunities, you can benchmark with external data, interpret the implications, and then generate new opportunities.
  - When assessing ROI despite missing data, you can create reach, impact, and effort estimates with domain knowledge, then perform sensitivity analysis to increase confidence in your decisions quantitatively.

References

[1] A. S. C. Ehrenberg and W. A. Twyman, "On measuring television audiences," *Journal of the Royal Statistical Society, series A (general)*, vol. 130, no. 1, pp. 1–60, 1967, doi: 10.2307/2344037.

[2] G. T. Doran, "There's a S.M.A.R.T. way to write management's goals and objectives," *Management Review*, vol. 70, no. 11, pp. 35–36, 1981.

[3] D. Shapero, "How to manage projects: Double down, delegate, or destroy." LinkedIn. https://www.linkedin.com/pulse/20130114082551-314058-double-down-delegate-or-destroy/

[4] R. Kohavi, *Trustworthy Online Controlled Experiments: A Practical Guide to A/B Testing*. Cambridge, UK: Cambridge University Press, 2020.

[5] P. Hung and G. Low, "Factors affecting the buy vs, build decision in large Australian organisations," *Journal of Information Technology*, vol. 23, pp. 118–131, 2008, doi: 10.1057/palgrave.jit.2000098.

[6] L. Hogan. "Questions for our first 1:1." Laura Hogan. https://larahogan.me/blog/first-one-on-one-questions/

[7] T. Gallup and B. Conchie, *Strengths Based Leadership: Great Leaders, Teams, and Why People Follow*. Washington, DC, USA: Gallup Press, 2008.

[8] N. L. Quenk, *Essentials of Myers-Briggs Type Indicator Assessment*. New York, NY, USA: Wiley, 2009.

[9] E. Meyer, *The Culture Map: Breaking Through the Invisible Boundaries of Global Business*. New York, NY, USA: PublicAffairs, 2014.

[10] A. Grove, *High Output Management*. New York, NY, USA: Random House, 1983.

[11] J. Jordan et al, "16 startup metrics." Andreessen Horowitz. https://a16z.com/2015/08/21/16-metrics/

[12] "Report on the economic well-being of U.S. households in 2018," Federal Reserve. [Online]. Available: https://www.federalreserve.gov/publications/files/2018-report-economic-well-being-us-households-201905.pdf

[13] "Consumer expenditure survey," Bureau of Labor Statistics. [Online]. Available: https://www.bls.gov/cex

[14] Katherine L. Milkman, Julia A. Minson, and Kevin G. M. Volpp, "Holding the Hunger Games Hostage at the Gym: An Evaluation of Temptation Bundling," Manage Sci. 2014 Feb; 60(2): 283–299. https://www.ncbi.nlm.nih.gov/pmc/articles/PMC4381662/

Virtues for leading people

This chapter covers

- Growing the team with coaching, mentoring, and advising
- Representing the team confidently and contributing to broader management duties
- Observing and mitigating system anti-patterns and learning from incidents
- Driving clarity by distilling complex issues into concise narratives
- Managing the maker's schedule versus the manager's schedule

As a manager or staff data scientist, you have the responsibility to practice effective DS and nurture your team members' habits with DS best practices. These virtues are the habitual actions that are etched into your character as a DS practitioner.

Ethics are the standards of conduct at work that enable data scientists to avoid unnecessary and self-inflicted breakdowns. For DS managers and staff data scientists, this involves nurturing the team with coaching, mentoring, advising, confidently representing DS in cross-functional discussions, and constructively contributing reviews for systems touching DS.

Rigor is the craftsmanship and diligence with which we approach DS. This involves thinking bigger by taking the lead in maintaining reliable results, thinking deeper to diagnose effectively, triaging, learning from incidents, and simplifying complex issues by distilling them into concise explanations for partners.

Attitude is the mood of positivity with which we approach DS. Maintaining a positive attitude involves handling personal mindset adjustments from a maker's schedule to a manager's schedule, fostering the trust of direct reports in execution, and nurturing the organization for a culture of learning and sharing.

When you are nurturing your team, you are, in effect, determining your team's culture. How you choose to practice strong ethics, diligence in rigor, and a positive attitude determines your team's long-term effectiveness.

5.1   Ethical standards of conduct

To lead is to serve. As a manager or a staff data scientist, you have the responsibility to nurture your immediate team to produce the best work of their lives. At the same time, you are representing your team in cross-functional interactions. As a part of the management team, you are also called upon to contribute to the broader organization's critical business decisions.

Your ethics are the standards of conduct for serving the various teams you are part of. This section discusses three specific aspects of professional conduct:

- Growing the team through coaching, mentoring, and advising
- Representing DS confidently in cross-functional discussions
- Contributing to and reciprocating broader management duties

These distinctions and practices are essential when serving teams to avoid unnecessary, self-inflicted breakdowns, and to open up opportunities for a positive, agile, and productive work environment.

5.1.1   Growing the team with coaching, mentoring, and advising

Growing a DS team is not just about hiring more data scientists. Increasing the capacity of your existing team members can also produce greater impact for your organization. Nurturing the capabilities of your current team members takes time.

Remember Audra from case 5 in chapter 1? She was disappointed and baffled after not getting an offer from a position she believed she was highly qualified for. Audra had focused a lot on her own career path and development, but she did not focus as much on her team.

One responsibility of a manager is empowering team members to do the best work of their careers; the other responsibility is taking care of the team and the company whenever possible. This section can provide Audra with a set of tools to help her fulfill her responsibilities, create mutually beneficial professional networks, and build some lifelong friendships.

029

One responsibility of a manager is to empower team members to do the best work of their careers; the other responsibility is taking care of the team and the company whenever possible.

As a manager or staff data scientist, one challenge of nurturing team members to increase the team's impact is that there is no single effective approach. A more detailed nurturing style may be useful for junior team members, while the same style would make some senior members feel micromanaged. Some senior team members may prefer a more hands-off approach, while the same process may leave some junior members feeling neglected.

If every team member is at a different stage in their professional careers, does that mean they each require a different nurturing style? That would be pretty overwhelming, even for managers with small teams. Fortunately, as you begin managing more team members, patterns emerge.

Let's discern three types of approaches to take care of team members and their career development concerns: coaching, mentoring, and advising. These approaches are illustrated in figure 5.1.

Distinctions	Coaching Unlocking a team member's potential to maximize their performance	Mentoring Imparting wisdom and sharing knowledge with a less-experienced colleague	Advising Providing information and direction
How much of yourself are you bringing to the relationship?	* Only observe and provide feedback for the team member's self-discovery and growth.	*** Share your past experiences to help team members build skills.	***** Provide information and direction to solve team members' challenges.
How much prior expertise do you need for the challenges at hand?	* No previous experience in the challenge at hand required.	*** Some related prior experience is required to highlight blind spots on the paths to success.	***** Direct experience is required to give specific feedback about a team member's specific challenge.
What does success look like?	Provide support and accountability.	Endorse mentee's vision of their ideal self and be a guide to develop missing capabilities and virtues.	Help the team member understand the complexity of a specific problem and make more informed decisions.
What is the long-term impact?	***** The team member can learn to independently resolve issues through self-growth.	*** The team member can learn to solve similar issues with the skills built.	* The team member relies on further support to solve similar issues.

Figure 5.1 Growing the team through coaching, mentoring, and advising

COACHING

Coaching is the process of unlocking a team member's potential to maximize their performance. It is a custom-tailored developmental process in a formal one-on-one setting. A coach observes and provides feedback with a focus on the process of asking questions. Through these questions, a good coach facilitates a team member to clarify goals, focus on what needs to be done, and discover the best strategies for achieving those goals.

To coach, you will first need to create a safe, judgment-free space for a team member to go on a process of self-discovery and growth. You should demonstrate genuine care for your team member's well-being and be sensitive to their potential fear of failure.

To coach effectively, a coach must first actively listen to what the team member is saying and not saying, distinguish emotions through tone of voice and body language, and reflect back and summarize any observations. When in doubt, the coach can use open-ended questions to cultivate greater clarity in the situation. You know you have succeeded when your team member claims, "Yes! I could not have said it better!"

To be a great coach, you should deeply understand the situation and guide your team member to identify SMART goals that are specific, measurable, attainable, relevant, and time bound, as well as to design new actions to attain the desired results. The team member is ultimately responsible for their own actions and results. You are there to provide support and accountability.

MENTORING

Mentoring is the process of imparting wisdom and sharing knowledge with a less-experienced colleague. For mentoring to work well, you need to start with an authentic relationship and break away from the typical manager–employee structure to focus on the team member's career growth. In some sense, mentoring as a staff data scientist can be a more natural nurturing relationship.

For mentoring to work effectively, topics should expand beyond coaching for goals, focus, process, and strategy to include mastery of the capabilities and practice of the virtues described in this book. While mentorship for capabilities can immediately benefit execution, mentorship in virtues can have a lasting impact on your team member's character.

To be a great mentor, you should listen to your team member's vision of their ideal self and accept it by consistently endorsing their vision. Often, their vision is beyond the scope of your team. Value the time you have with your ambitious team members, and do what you can to help engage them in projects aligned with their ideal self where possible. You will likely earn their trust and dedication, and help them produce their best work through the highs and lows of your projects.

ADVISING

Advising is the process of providing information and direction. As an advisor, you have direct experience and deep knowledge in helping your team members achieve their goals. You offer value by giving specific feedback about specific questions.

For advising to work well, you must be aware of your team members' strengths and weaknesses, and position them in projects that highlight their strengths and help them deal with their weaknesses. Section 4.2.1 discussed psychological assessments, such as the Clifton StrengthsFinder, that can quantify team members' strengths.

To advise effectively, you must first assess whether you have the expertise and experience to help. In case you don't, either resort to coaching or identify other potential sources of guidance to recommend. If you have the expertise, practice active listening, and suspend judgment until you have a complete picture of the problem. With an understanding of the problem, you can guide your team member to generate viable choices. Rationales, personal experiences, and the principles behind your recommendations can make your advice more powerful and easier to remember and adopt. Part of your guidance should be ensuring that team members evaluate options before jumping too quickly to a solution. It should be clear that the decision and consequences are the responsibility of the team member.

To be a great advisor, you can always be looking to provide a deeper understanding of complex issues to help your team member make more informed decisions. The advice involves introducing them to previously unexamined alternatives and expanding their repertoire of action steps. Other than the specific decisions and actions, your advice can also reduce the anxiety and confusion team members often feel when facing difficult or uncertain situations and instill calm and confidence to create space for more thoughtful planning and actions.

WHEN TO USE EACH APPROACH?

The coaching, mentoring, and advising approaches have many similarities. To perform any of them well, you will need to start with a safe, authentic, and mutually respectful relationship with your team member.

There are three key differences between coaching, mentoring, and advising:

- *How much of yourself are you bringing into the relationship?* Coaching focuses on observing and providing feedback for your team member's self-discovery and growth. Mentoring focuses on sharing your past experiences to help team members build skills. Advising focuses on how you can provide information and direction to solve a team member's challenges.
- *How much prior expertise do you need for challenges at hand?* For coaching, you don't need previous experience in the challenge at hand. Experience in the general process is often enough to be able to ask intelligent questions to cultivate greater clarity for your team member's situation. For mentoring, you need some related prior experience to highlight your team member's blind spots and help them avoid pitfalls on the path to success. For advising, you need direct experience to give specific feedback about a team member's specific challenge.
- *What does success look like?* When coaching, you are there to provide support and accountability. When mentoring, you are there to endorse your team member's vision of their ideal self and to guide them to develop missing capabilities and

virtues on their road to becoming an effective data scientist. When advising, you help your team member understand the complexity of a specific problem at hand to make more-informed decisions. You also aim to reduce anxiety and confusion and instill calm and confidence, so your team members can take more effective actions.

As we clarify these fundamental differences, you can begin to see how to distinguish coaching, mentoring, and advising situations.

For senior team members working on innovative projects with a high likelihood of success, coaching is enough to provide feedback and build confidence and experience through self-discovery and growth. When senior team members take on challenging projects with increased risks of failure, mentoring may help. You can use your experience to highlight potential blind spots and project pitfalls and guide team members to develop the critical skills required for success. When junior team members work through specific challenges where you have expert knowledge of directions and best practices, you can advise them, so they can better understand the problem's complexity and make more informed decisions.

You can flexibly switch among these three modes of nurturing to grow your team members and produce a greater impact on the organization. When applied appropriately, your efforts can empower your team members to perform the best work of their careers.

Audra from chapter 1 was too focused on building her own career and did not demonstrate that she was nurturing her team. She can use the coaching, mentoring, and advising techniques discussed here to empower her team members to do the best work of their careers.

5.1.2 *Representing the team confidently in cross-functional discussions*

As a DS manager or a staff data scientist, business partners are looking to you to gain confidence in the DS progress in cross-functional projects. When you speak on behalf of the team on the DS perspective, the questions that are likely in the back of your business partners' minds include

- Can we trust this person?
- Can we believe what we are hearing?
- Does this person have the background knowledge for this subject?

You may have seen some drafts of junior data scientists' presentations. In an attempt to be rigorous, they often start with 10 minutes of experiment setup and caveats, followed by an initial result, and ending with many technical uncertainties in the analysis. Such a presentation opens up more questions than answers, leaves the audience feeling more confused than before, and does not generate much trust with the cross-functional business partners.

DS results are hard to present, as there are many uncertainties and caveats in any one analysis. However, the responsibility of data scientists is to answer questions and not to cause confusion. How can you help bridge this gap?

There are two approaches borrowed from the product management discipline that can help in complementary ways. First, your analysis can practice "strong opinions, weakly held." Second, you can use storytelling to frame persuasive narratives and presentations. Figure 5.2 illustrates the challenges and the approaches to mitigate them.

Partner concerns:
- Can we trust this person?
- Can we believe what we are hearing?
- Does this person have the background knowledge for this subject?

Strong opinions, weakly held	**Persuasive presentations through storytelling**
• Seek collaboration early to gain the collective wisdom • Overcome common biases • Have a working decision ready	• Understand your audience • Deliver actionable recommendations • Craft a clear structure

Figure 5.2　Challenges and approaches for representing your team

STRONG OPINIONS, WEAKLY HELD

When business partners seek out the DS perspective, they are looking for a quantitatively driven view of the business decisions at hand. How can you focus the team's effort on answering the business questions, using limited time and resources?

The practice of *strong opinions, weakly held* [1] may help. This practice calls on your intuition to guide you to a quick first conclusion. However imperfect this first conclusion can be, this is the strong opinion. You can then look for quantitative evidence to prove yourself wrong, which is why the opinion is weakly held.

This practice is beneficial for DS organizations where the virtue of rigor is taken to an extreme such that the organization becomes decision-paralyzed. The concept provides a much-needed bias for action for the team to continue to operate, while further analysis seeks to provide counterexamples.

Specifically, the concept has three main benefits:

- Seeking collaboration early to gain collective wisdom
- Overcoming common biases
- Having a working decision

Seeking collaboration early to gain collective wisdom

While many DS projects have a review at the end, there is often little time to make major changes without schedule impact. The push to have a strong opinion at the beginning of a project forces you to have a clear hypothesis to guide the progress toward more detailed iterations. In product, this can be a way to move a key success metric. In DS projects, this can be the cause of churn and ways to improve retention. The team can then have more opportunities to suggest disconfirming evidence and introduce additional ideas, intuitions, and perspectives to iteratively strengthen the weakly held opinion.

Overcoming common biases

Section 3.2.1 discussed three common cognitive biases, including confirmation bias, denying the antecedent, and base-rate fallacy, which are among 175 bias categories listed by Buster Benson [2]. By seeking disconfirming evidence, you can counter confirmation bias. In contrast, people tend to only look for evidence confirming their opinions, leading to confirmation bias. As you discover different perspectives in the process, you can overcome selection bias by selecting statistically significant results, rather than only positive anecdotal examples. You can also counter optimism bias by planning for the likely scenario, rather than the unrealistically optimistic best-case scenario.

Having a working decision

When the strong opinion is formed, you can keep an operational decision based on the best available data. This working decision is one you can fall back on if priorities change or when a decision is required earlier than expected.

The strong opinions, weakly held approach is fundamental and can quickly drive clarity toward business decisions. Effectively communicating your recommendation is the next step in successfully instilling confidence when representing DS in cross-functional discussions.

PERSUASIVE NARRATIVES AND PRESENTATIONS THROUGH STORYTELLING

To successfully convey the insights and generate trust when presenting DS results, you must first understand your audience, have specific recommendations, and produce narratives that have an easy-to-follow structure.

Understanding your audience

Different audiences come with different prior experiences. A presentation for an engineering partner will need to address different concerns than a presentation for the product or sales organization. An engineering partner may be concerned with your component's reliability, the performance impact on existing user experience service level agreements (SLAs), ease of maintenance, and ease of testing. A product organization is likely more concerned about the A/B test, the release process, and how a new feature will impact product conversion and customer churn. A sales organization may be more concerned about how a new product feature might affect the opportunity-to-win ratio, the sales cycle, and sales team compensation.

Given the differences in the target audiences, you can coach your team members to ask the following questions before presenting the results:

- Who are my audiences?
- What are their fundamental concerns? What is the context of the project?
- What evidence do they need to believe in the results?

Delivering Actionable Recommendations

Business partners have limited attention. Lead with your recommendation on how to proceed with clear, data-driven evidence to support it. You can also present multiple options you may have considered in the *strong opinions, weakly held* exploration process and highlight the trade-offs between the different options.

030

> In delivering actionable recommendations, lead with your recommendation on how to proceed with clear, data-driven evidence to support it.

Questions for coaching your team members include

- What is the main message or recommendation you are trying to get across?
- Why is this the best choice for the greater organization?
- What are the different options, and why is this recommendation the preferred option?

Crafting a clear structure

With the main recommendation identified, your analysis should have examined potentially disconfirming evidence and produced enough confidence to support the recommendation. The remaining work is to tell the story in a compelling way.

In telling the story, less is often more. To highlight the key recommendation, include only the main points that support the recommendation, and keep any information that is not directly relevant to the story in the appendix. This is different from confirmation bias and providing cherry-picked results where conflicting evidence is removed. If there is contradictory evidence, we should stop crafting the presentation and go back to forming a different hypothesis that is consistent with the available evidence.

Questions for coaching your team members to crafting a clear presentation include

- What is the impact of this recommendation?
- What is the primary recommendation?
- What is the set of evidence that supports the recommendation?

You can find more discussions on the rigor of the presentation format in section 5.2.3.

To summarize, the strong opinions, weakly held approach can focus the team's effort on growing confidence in the best current hypothesis by collecting disconfirming evidence to counter confirmation bias. Once you are confident enough about the result, you can use storytelling techniques to communicate to your customers through a deep understanding of the audiences, actionable recommendations, and well-crafted persuasive narratives to guide and generate trust with cross-functional business partners.

5.1.3   *Contributing to and reciprocating on broader management duties*

As a member of an organization's management team, you can be called upon to contribute to the broader organizational duties. These may include people-related leadership matters as well as technology-related matters. When you have ambitions to take on greater responsibilities and produce a more significant impact, these duties will shed light on a broad range of concerns across various parts of the organization and provide a fertile training ground to practice leadership.

031

> When you have ambitions to take on greater responsibilities and produce a more significant impact, contributing to and reciprocating broader management duties will shed light on a broad range of concerns across various parts of the organization and provide a fertile training ground to practice leadership.

Figure 5.3 illustrates a list of responsibilities for a manager. It may look overwhelming, especially if you have recently been promoted into a team leadership role and have not been formally trained to be a manager. While this book can guide you in DS management, there may be cultural nuances within your particular organization that require specific approaches to handle management responsibilities.

Employment
- Recruiting and hiring
- Compensation
- Retaining employees
- Assisting with immigration cases
- Onboarding and integration
- Handling transitions associated with exiting employees

Team operations
- Having weekly one-on-one meetings
- Coaching/mentoring
- Training and development of team
- Motivation and morale
- Rewards and recognition
- Performance management/reviews
- Calibrating talent
- Disciplinary actions

Team building
- Leading team meetings
- EVS action planning
- Organizing and attending offsites and summits
- Fostering an inclusive and diverse environment

Planning
- Setting direction/defining success
- Achieving results
- Assigning and delegating work
- Workforce planning

Communications
- Addressing team conflicts
- Processing change management
- Organization change management

Resource management
- Budgeting/cost control
- Planning and prioritization
- Allocating resources
- Legal compliance

Career development
- Self development as a manager
- Succession planning

Figure 5.3   Broader duties to contribute to as a data science manager

Just as you can provide coaching, mentoring, and advising to your team members, you can also seek out coaches, mentors, and advisors to help you develop a deeper understanding of leadership responsibilities, so you can practice these responsibilities when situations call for them.

While you can seek mentorship from your manager, they don't have to be your only mentor. Many management challenges are common across technical teams. You can look for other well-run teams in your company or industry and seek mentorship or advice from their managers.

While the fulfillment of many of your management responsibilities, such as hiring, promotions, and project reviews, will require support from partner organizations, you are also expected to reciprocate by supporting your peer organizations. Here is a list of mutually beneficial opportunities to make yourself available and build closer relationships with partner teams:

- Interviewing candidates for partner teams
- Providing promotion recommendations for partner team members
- Reviewing product roadmaps
- Reviewing infrastructure roadmaps
- Reviewing business operations

Interviewing candidates

From time to time, a business partner will seek your help in evaluating whether a candidate can be successful as a collaborator between your teams. This is your opportunity to meet a potential colleague early and provide feedback to your business partner.

In this situation, verify your business partner's expectations for feedback before the interview, and understand what areas you should explore. These interviews are also an opportunity for the candidate to meet their future cross-functional partners. Be courteous and respectful as you would be with a business partner, while probing for the boundaries of the candidate's knowledge and experience working with DS.

Sometimes, you may be tapped to provide candid feedback on your business partner's hiring decision. At other times, you may be urged to ask some light questions and focus on selling the candidate on joining the company. Remember, you are doing these interviews for your partners, and you should, first and foremost, respect their preferences.

Promotion recommendations

Just like the way you have put in effort to grow the capabilities and virtues of your team members, your partner teams are also looking to develop their team members. As you are working with partner teams, observe areas where the collaborations went well and areas that have room for improvement. When business partners are looking to promote a partner team member you have worked with, you should have evidence of positive experience and development areas readily available.

If you observe a partner team member performing above and beyond in your collaborations, don't wait for promotion season. Be sure to call it out in a timely manner and thank them, while also letting their manager know. This is one of the most powerful ways to build relationships and is often neglected or delayed when work gets busy.

Product roadmap review

It can take months or quarters to gather training data, prepare data pipelines, build models, and test impact for many DS capabilities. Understanding the milestones for products and features on the product roadmap allows you to anticipate the product's future needs. The review process enables you to provide feedback on whether the product timelines are feasible and whether expectations for initial versions of algorithms are realistic.

In product roadmap reviews, you can also help product business partners clarify core metrics of success, understand potential challenges in measurements, prepare supporting diagnostic metrics, and craft engineering specifications to reliably capture metrics.

Infrastructure roadmap review

Infrastructure roadmap reviews are crucial opportunities to learn about and anticipate upcoming infrastructure updates. DS is often called upon to provide perspectives and feedback for infrastructure decisions.

In many DS organizations, predictive models are created using features processed through data pipelines that depend on specific data sources. Any updates to the underlying infrastructure roadmap can be disruptive and cost valuable cycles to migrate data pipelines and recalibrate/retrain models. At the same time, infrastructures have to be updated over time to meet the needs of newer, more responsive product features.

You can provide feedback on the impact of the infrastructure updates on the DS processes and services. There are also opportunities to help the infrastructure partner team understand current bottlenecks and develop additional features to empower your work to be more impactful for the organization.

Business operations review

In a data-driven approach for operations, DS managers are often invited to weekly or biweekly business operations reviews. These are great opportunities for you to keep a pulse on the business areas in which you would like to make an impact. If any business updates impact your team's work, you can inform your team members and escalate issues to your manager where required.

These reviews also allow you to discover additional opportunities where DS may be of help. You can shift DS priorities to drive the impact to where the business requires. Based on your understanding of the product roadmap and infrastructure roadmap, you can also surface any upcoming resource conflicts, so business partners are not surprised when projects need more time to complete.

DS is a team sport. Teamwork at the management level is broader than technical project collaborations; it also extends to collaboration and reciprocation of management responsibilities across teams. The opportunities include collaborating and reciprocating in interviewing candidates; recommending team members for promotions; and reviewing product roadmaps, infrastructure roadmaps, and business operations.

These are a few examples of trust building with business partners—a standard of conduct of an effective DS manager.

For Audra from chapter 1, who was too focused on building her own career, reciprocating on broader management duties can help her build a cross-functional support system at work, and help her be less self-centered and more focused on the broader team's success.

That was a bit of serious talk on ethical standards of conduct. Now may be a good time to reflect on how this is different or similar to the ethical standards of conduct for a DS tech lead … or take a break.

5.2 Rigor nurturing, higher standards

Rigor is the continuous pursuit of higher standards. Section 3.2 extensively discussed the data scientist's standard of scientific rigor, diligence in monitoring anomalies, and responsibility for generating enterprise value. While these areas continue to be essential, DS managers and staff data scientists must strive to go beyond these standards to seek broader and deeper levels of rigor.

This section discusses three aspects of practices for coaching a DS team:

- Leading with a goal of maintaining trustworthy results
- Learning effectively from incidents
- Driving clarity by distilling complex issues into concise narratives

We look to build a more expansive perspective to anticipate potential challenges in DS solutions for maintaining trustworthy results, dive deeper into incidents to learn from failures, and provide clarity for partners by simplifying many inherent complexities in DS.

5.2.1 Observing and mitigating anti-patterns in ML and DS systems

To produce continued impact, a DS team must create innovative solutions to capture the business potential in available or potentially available data resources. The team also needs to maintain existing solutions such that past investments in DS continue to pay dividends over time.

While you can rely on your tech leads to articulate technical trade-offs in executing specific projects, you are responsible for observing and detecting any DS anti-patterns showing up across projects and mitigating them before they cause widespread disruptions to projects.

032

Team managers and staff data scientists are responsible for observing and detecting any data science anti-patterns showing up across projects and mitigating them before they cause widespread disruptions to projects.

Anti-patterns are undesirable DS practices that increase the risk of failure. Like a chess master can observe a chessboard and articulate which side may be winning, a DS manager or a staff data scientist should be able to observe and detect anti-patterns in their projects before the projects begin to fail.

There are many common anti-patterns in DS and machine learning systems. We highlight six that were discussed in the 2015 NIPS paper "Hidden Technical Debt in Machine Learning Systems" [3]:

- Glue code
- Pipeline jungle
- Dead experimental code path
- Under-documented data fields
- Excessive use of multiple languages
- Dependency on prototyping environment

GLUE CODE

Machine learning algorithms can be computationally intensive and complex to tune. Fortunately, there are preoptimized machine learning library components we can use off the shelf. Many of them are even available as downloadable open-source components.

However, each of these components has been designed for specific usage scenarios that require input and output to be of specific formats, accessible in specific languages, and through specific batch or streaming connectors. To take advantage of these library components, a significant amount of glue code is often implemented to connect your specific use case to the existing library components.

As figure 5.4 illustrates, many real-world systems deployed to production consist of a large amount of code for data collection, data verification, feature extraction, machine resource management, analytics tools, process management tools serving infrastructure, configuration, and monitoring. In contrast, only a small fraction of the code base is the machine learning (ML) system.

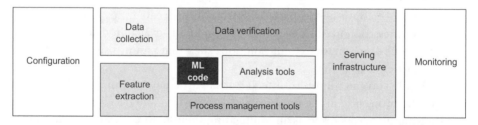

Figure 5.4   Only a fraction of ML systems are composed of ML code [3]

Maintaining large amounts of glue code can be costly over the lifetime of a system when the usage scenario has been overfitted into the particularities of one algorithm implementation. Prediction performance could degrade when domain-specific properties are tweaked to match the algorithm's implementation requirements. An example is when continuous target variables must be discretized to use a classification-based machine learning infrastructure. Improvements from using an alternative algorithm implementation with different input and output formats become difficult. Challenges can come from the test and deployment infrastructure in the significantly rewired glue logic.

One strategy to mitigate the glue code anti-pattern is to wrap specific algorithm implementations with an API that can work with multiple alternative algorithm implementations. In the Python machine learning ecosystem, ScikitLearn [4] has done this well, allowing hundreds of algorithm implementations to share a small subset of input and output connectors. This level of abstraction is especially important if you intend to use an in-house implementation and look to migrate to external implementations in the future or vice versa.

PIPELINE JUNGLES

To democratize access to data, centralized data repositories are often shared with various teams. The shared repositories can include raw data and prepared summary data for business reporting and model building.

Initially, this can maximize collaboration and reuse in an environment with always-constrained resources. As the number of contributors increases, the lineage of producer–consumer relationships can get complicated fast. It is not uncommon to have data preparation pipelines that are four to five layers deep, and a final union table may aggregate information from hundreds of raw data sources and tens of data preparation steps.

When a particular set of summary data is selected as executive-facing operations metrics, or when it is selected as an input feature that goes into a machine learning model being deployed to production, the reliability of the summary data becomes crucial. Unfortunately, when any of the hundreds of raw data sources or any of the tens of data preparation steps in the four to five layers of pipelines break, the final output cannot be produced.

The logical dependencies are further complicated by the scheduling of different processing steps, as when computation resources are adjusted for upstream steps, downstream steps may miss SLA or use stale data for their calculation. Deploying new pipelines now requires expensive end-to-end integration tests. Detecting and recovering from failures becomes difficult and costly. While it is not practical to scrap an existing pipeline jungle and rebuild the data preparation pipelines from scratch, you can introduce people, platforms, and practices to mitigate this challenge.

For the people component, the collaboration between data scientists and model deployment engineers is key. When data scientists prototype models without regard to data lineage and processing reliability and deliver black box models to model deployment engineers, there is no opportunity to consider trade-offs in reliability and model performance. When data scientists and model deployment engineers work together, you can make many trade-offs. For example, you can choose whether to use a downstream data field for better reuse of effort, or use an upstream data source for less dependency on other data processing steps.

For the platform component, there are numerous tools, such as Colibra Lineage [5] available to map data lineage through the scripts and queries that produce intermediate results. Workflow management tools, such as Apache Airflow [6] can also track the scheduling, completion time, and completion rates of existing data pipelines. These data can be used to tune the scheduling and maximize the completion rate of existing pipelines.

When building models or doing analyses, there needs to be a process to find required data from the earliest point in the data processing pipeline. This is to keep the pipeline jungle from becoming deeper and more unmanageable over time. Also, the reliability of earlier layers of the data processing pipeline needs to be as robust as possible, as outages in earlier layers can cause a broader negative impact on downstream processing steps. Time should be allocated for refactoring the data processing steps to squash processing layers where possible.

DEAD EXPERIMENTAL CODE PATHS

The controlled experiment methodology uses conditional branches within the production code to send a limited portion of users or executions down an alternative code path to test new features with reduced risks. While some of these experiments lead to positive results and become part of the main production code path, many have negative or insignificant results and are tested once, then abandoned.

While the cost of each individual change may be low, when an organization performs hundreds to thousands of experiments a year, the accumulated abandoned code paths can become overwhelming. Especially when there is churn in the engineering team, the numerous conditional branches for alternative code paths can be hard to understand, maintain, and may become a significant liability.

In 2012, Knight Capital's trading system lost $440 million in 30 minutes [7], [8]. The root cause was diagnosed as unexpected behavior from obsolete experimental code paths that remained in the code base for almost 10 years, reactivated by a reused flag. To mitigate this type of issue, you can periodically declare experiments to be deprecated and work with the engineering team to rip out and clean up dead code branches.

UNDER-DOCUMENTED DATA FIELDS

Data fields in tables have limited types, such as integer, floating-point real numbers, or text. For a centralized data repository to work well, each field must be documented carefully to provide confidence in reuse.

Good documentation should include details such as whether an integer field encodes a count, a unique identifier, or categorical data. A floating-point real number field should specify whether it represents a dollar amount, a ratio, a multiplier, a decision threshold, or some other value. A text field should specify whether it is a unique identifier, categorical field, free form description, or has some different meaning.

A great description should also include any invariant for the field, including expectations for missing values (empty versus null), expected ranges, expected values, and expected formats. For example, is a field a cross-referencing key, such that there should not be an empty or null value? If a floating-point value is a percentage, should it always be between zero and one? For a categorical field, what are the valid values it can take? For a text field representing a serial number or classification code, is there a particular format such as the number of digits or characters in a sequence that the field should satisfy?

Invariant checks enabled by great documentation can automatically detect errors in data pipelines early. They can be invaluable for catching errors from unintended side effects.

EXCESSIVE USE OF MULTIPLE LANGUAGES

There are numerous programming and data querying languages in the field of DS that come with outstanding readily available packages for statistical analysis, natural language processing (NLP), and graph processing. Each language tends to be good for some purposes but not for others.

For example, R has great statistical analysis packages but is not as efficient for NLP or massively parallel processing (MPP). Python is great for machine learning and NLP but not as good for parallel processing or graph processing. Spark is great for MPP and machine learning but does not have as many statistical analysis packages as R. Cypher and APOC are great for graph queries and graph algorithms but not suitable for detailed NLP or statistical analysis.

Many DS projects and systems end up using a combination of multiple languages. Web-based notebook systems, such as the Jupyter notebook or the Databricks notebook, empower data scientists to use multiple languages in the same notebook. Although you can take advantage of the most suitable analytical and machine learning tools available, maintenance often becomes a challenge. Any successive owner of these deployed projects and systems would have to be familiar with all the languages to make iterative improvements, which can increase the cost and difficulty of ownership transfers significantly. As the DS manager or the staff data scientist, it is your responsibility to make the trade-offs of limiting language usage or organizing training to ensure there is no single point of failure for critical projects when team member transitions happen.

DEPENDENCY ON PROTOTYPING ENVIRONMENT

Section 3.2.3 discussed the benefit of prototyping to explore the feasibility of the portion of a project with the highest risk of failure, so if the project as architected will fail, you can find out and pivot as early as possible. The environment you use to prototype a new product or feature may use real production data with shortcuts or manual steps simulating what the eventual automated systems will look like.

However, if features go to production based on models in the prototyping environment, it is a symptom of accumulating tech debts, an anti-pattern to be concerned about. Reliance on a prototyping environment could be an indication of a production environment that is too burdensome to deploy to. Prototyping environments are often less robust, and maintaining prototypes in them can quickly use up your precious resources and limit the team's impact on the organization.

Common solutions include clearly tracking the states of features and being acutely aware of the number of features operating in a prototyping environment. Specify projects with features that should be deployed into the production environment and clearly indicate the negative consequences of not doing so, then work with executives to prioritize these projects.

In summary, we discussed six DS anti-patterns for you to watch out for in the interest of the team's long-term productivity, including glue code, pipeline jungle, dead experimental code path, under-documented data fields, excessive use of multiple languages, and dependencies on prototyping environment. These anti-patterns often creep in naturally, despite our best intentions at the various stages of a DS team's maturing trajectory. The team is relying on you, the team manager or staff data scientist, to step up and set the expectations to balance short-term efficiency and long-term team productivity in everyday project decisions.

5.2.2 *Learning effectively from incidents*

As a DS manager or staff data scientist, it is your responsibility to ensure that the team rigorously learns from past incidents. It would be a failure of management if the same root cause triggers multiple breakdowns over time without any efforts in place to improve the situation. Coaching your team to dive deep in the post-mortem process is one place you can demonstrate your leadership.

Ineffective learning from incidents can affect team morale. As we saw from Stephen's case (from chapter 1, case 6), the failure to craft roadmaps to prevent more tech-debt-related breakdowns can result in regrettable attrition of your best team members.

033

Ineffective learning from incidents can affect team morale, and the failure to craft roadmaps to prevent more tech-debt-related breakdowns can result in regrettable attrition of your best team members.

In section 2.2.3, we introduced tech lead execution challenges in handling incidents, where team members' feelings of safety and accountability must be balanced. We concluded that a five-step structure can be used to summarize the learnings for current and future members of the team. We can use the five-whys [9] process in step 3 to identify the root cause:

1 Brief summary
2 Detailed timeline
3 Root cause—using the five-whys process
   - Gather a team and develop the problem statement
   - Ask the first why of the team: why is this or that problem taking place?
   - Ask four more successive whys, and follow up on all plausible answers
   - Among all plausible answers, look for systemic causes of the problem
   - Develop corrective actions to remove the root cause from the system

4 Resolution and recovery

5 Actions to mitigate future risks

The purpose of the post-mortem process is to learn from past mistakes and prevent a class of future breakdowns with the same root cause from occurring again. The five-whys technique was first developed by Sakichi Toyoda and used at Toyota for improving the manufacturing process. It has found application in operations across a diverse set of industries, including the Kaizen process, lean manufacturing, and the Six Sigma process.

While the specifics of the post-mortem process should be delegated to your tech lead, your support in the root cause analysis (step 3) is key in institutionalizing the learning. The following types of specific support are most important for root cause analysis:

- *Participation*—Ensure all DS and partner team members with involvement in the incident are present. We need first-hand information from those who experienced the incident and knew the visible and not easily visible parts of the problem.
- *Scheduling*—Clear schedules, so the post-mortem can be done within two to three days of the incident. It is important to document learning while memory is fresh and people have not context-switched their mindset to other projects.
- *Coaching*—Guide tech leads to avoid common pitfalls in the five-whys process, and make sure the depth of the issues is fully appreciated.

Let's go through an example with some depth in investigating the root cause of one data pipeline failure. In this example, some logs failed, and an important company-wide metric was not produced for a segment of users for a week:

- *Why* did the data pipeline break?

  Cause—A new feature launch caused major tracking disruption.
- *Why* did the new feature launch cause major tracking disruption?

  Cause—The feature launch did not go through the ramp process to launch to 1%, 10%, 50%, then 100% of users iteratively to reduce feature risks. Instead, the feature was launched to 100% of users directly.
- *Why* did the feature launch skip the ramp process?

  Cause—A tight launch schedule left no time for feature ramp.
- *Why* did the launch schedule leave no time for feature ramp?

  Cause—The new product manager was not trained on allocating time for launch best practices at the company.
- *Why* was the new product manager not trained on best practices for launch?

  Cause—The company is growing quickly, and we do not yet have a rigorous onboarding training for data-driven launches for new product managers.

In this example, the root cause came back to something we can act on as data scientists to prevent a whole class of issues from recurring. It is a gap we may not have been aware of before. The DS team can take the lead in the partner team onboarding process to explain the data-driven product launch process to new product managers.

Not all root cause analysis will require five levels of whys, and some may need more levels to get to the root cause. The five-whys process refers to a figurative depth that is deeper than one or two layers.

What are some common pitfalls in the five-whys process for you to coach the team through? Let's look at three in detail:

- Stopping investigations at symptoms—not root causes
- Causes diagnosed are not necessary or sufficient to cause breakdowns
- Causes assessed are not the process but the people

STOPPING INVESTIGATIONS AT SYMPTOMS—NOT ROOT CAUSES

In the above example, if we stop the line of inquiries at the second why, not following the ramp process would have been a symptom of a tight launch schedule that did not allow the team to follow the launch best practices. It is plausible for others to step in and inquire about the lack of adherence to the launch best practice. However, a launch is guided by the launch schedule, and there can be good reasons to skip the ramp process for extremely urgent and high-confidence hotfixes. We have to diagnose to find that it's not the case in this incident.

A root cause is often a broken process, an alterable behavior, or a process that does not yet exist. Don't stop investigations at symptoms, such as not having enough time or investments, which are often issues outside your immediate control. If we continue to ask why, we can get to some real process improvement within your control that is beneficial for all parties involved.

CAUSES DIAGNOSED ARE NOT NECESSARY OR SUFFICIENT TO CAUSE BREAKDOWNS

In dissecting the causes of an incident, some are necessary but not sufficient, while others are sufficient but not necessary. In the previous example, one cause for the third level why—"Why did the feature launch skip the ramp process?"—may be the lack of a convenient UI in the platform for setting up a ramp process. This would be a necessary but not sufficient cause, as a good UI is necessary, but a product manager still needs to know to use the platform to avoid this incident.

An alternative cause is that the launch platform does not force all feature launches to go through a launch ramp process. This would be a sufficient but not necessary cause, as we may want to launch hotfixes in well-articulated emergencies without going through a ramp process. As long as product managers know when to use a launch ramp process and have tools and training available to them, there should be necessary and sufficient conditions to avoid this type of incident in the future.

CAUSES ASSESSED ARE NOT THE PROCESS BUT THE PEOPLE

The five-whys process should foster an atmosphere of trust and sincerity in the team. We should give the benefit of the doubt and assume team members' best intentions in the process, and develop processes that can help team members do the best work of their career with us together.

In this spirit, we should not use vague causes such as human error or worker's inattention, or, worse, place all blame on a team member. Try to make answers more precise. For example, answers like "a plan left no time for a ramp process," or "someone was not trained on an existing process" point to specific issues. These more precise answers can be modified and improved, such that concrete steps can be made toward preventing similar types of incidents from happening again.

In summary, rigorous learning from past incidents requires timely deep root cause analysis. As a DS manager or a staff data scientist, you are responsible for participating in post-mortems, prioritizing their scheduling, and coaching your team and partner teams through common pitfalls. These common pitfalls include stopping investigations too early at symptoms and not root causes, diagnosing causes that are not necessary or sufficient for breakdowns, and assessing how causes are not about processes but about people.

Your rigorous efforts will pay off in the form of an increasingly robust and data-driven execution environment, such that your team and partner teams will have fewer breakdowns and have more time to address strategic efforts toward producing greater business impact. Learning effectively from incidents is one practice that Stephen (from chapter 1, case 6) can adopt to address his team morale and build his own leadership identity.

5.2.3 *Driving clarity by distilling complex issues into concise narratives*

In your work, you may face many complexities in technical and business situations. You are given the responsibility to manage a team because of your ability to comprehend significant complexity. But others may not be as skilled in handling complexity. Now is the time to hone your craft at simplifying the complexities you encounter in your work.

Rigor is often confused with providing details. There is an old saying, "I asked him what time it was, and he taught me how to build a watch." When we are passionate about our work, we frequently fall into this trap. A long explanation could appear to make you look smart, but it may not help you produce more impact.

As Harry Shah, a senior staff data scientist at LinkedIn, describes it: "Your impact on the organization does not come from how much complexity you create, but how much complexity you can simplify in an already complex environment. As you grow in your career [as an individual contributor or team leader], the complexity of the problems scales up, but your solutions should not. Elegant and simpler solutions are always the best."

034

"Your impact on the organization does not come from how much complexity you create, but how much complexity you can simplify in an already complex environment. As you grow in your career [as an individual contributor or team leader], the complexity of the problems scales up, your solutions should not. Elegant and simpler solutions are always the best."—Harry Shah

There are at least three areas in which you can strive for simplicity: definitions, algorithms, and presentations. They are illustrated in figure 5.5.

Simplicity in definitions	Simplicity in algorithms	Simplicity in presentations
• Build trust across organizations by crafting 15-second descriptions of complex concepts • Avoid being perceived as condescending to those unfamiliar with complexities	• A simpler model is easier to explain and understand, and it costs less to deploy and maintain • Guide team toward the simplest algorithms and methods possible with acceptable performance	• Crystallize a storyline to bring the audience with you • Declare your goal on the title slide, have no more than three key ideas, and consistently highlight key narratives on each slide's title

Figure 5.5   Three areas to distill complex issues into concise narratives

SIMPLICITY IN DEFINITIONS

One way to demonstrate rigor through simplicity is to start crafting 15-second descriptions of complex concepts for someone with little background in your domain. The purpose is to provide a shared understanding and generate trust with your business partners with whom you can then build alignment for the next steps.

For example, explaining area under the curve (AUC) could be as simple as, "a metric that shows how good a predictive model is to business partners." A success metric in social networks, such as explicit user relationships, could be explained as, "if user A adds user B, and user B confirms, we call it an explicit user relationship." If you can't explain a concept in 15 seconds or less, it's likely that you either don't know it well enough or you are not explaining it well.

One area to coach your team on is avoiding being perceived as condescending to those unfamiliar with certain complexities of a DS project. You may have heard some data scientists responding to business partners' inquiries with, "It's pretty complicated. Don't worry about what you wouldn't understand—I have it covered." They may also respond to DS peers with, "Just read the code!" or "It's all documented in my Jira ticket comments."

Such comments can leave peers and business partners in the dark on pieces of the system they don't understand. That feeling can translate to fear and suspicion in the critical systems the company depends on for important customer experiences.

Alternatively, when definitions are crystallized and simplified and capture the intent and purpose of complex concepts in DS, peers, partners, and other managers will be grateful. These efforts in simplified definitions go a long way in building trust across organizations.

SIMPLICITY IN ALGORITHMS

Rigor in managing DS projects involves guiding the team toward the simplest algorithms and methods possible to understand historical patterns in data and to anticipate future trends. When given the choice between two system implementations that have orders of magnitude of difference in complexity and comparable outcomes, the rational choice is to select the simpler algorithm. For example, when choosing between a simple linear model and an ensemble model with many submodels that both achieve a similar model outcome, the simpler linear model should be a better choice.

A simpler model is a more concise quantitative narrative of historical patterns and is easier to explain and understand. It also requires fewer data samples to train. As described in section 3.2.2, data drifts are easier to detect in simpler models as well, as there would be fewer input parameters to track. From a total-cost-of-ownership perspective, a simpler model costs less to deploy and maintain. When team members move on from one project to the next, there is also less burden for handoffs.

With these considerations in mind, it would not be surprising to see that the grand prize-winning solution of the famous million-dollar Netflix Prize challenge was never deployed. The winning solution was an overly-elaborate ensemble model. Per Netflix's own technology blog [10], "the additional accuracy gains that we measured did not seem to justify the engineering effort needed to bring them into a production environment."

SIMPLICITY IN PRESENTATIONS

Rigor in presentation means taking the time to crystallize a storyline to bring the audience with you on the journey. It is not about putting all the information in a slide deck but about accomplishing the goal you set out to present.

The goal of the presentation can be communicating a process, aligning on paths forward, or reviewing new insights and findings. You can declare this goal on the title slide to set up a shared purpose for the presentation. The presentation then becomes a journey on which you bring you audience to achieve a shared purpose. This way, your relationship with your audience shifts from a presenter and listeners to co-creators in accomplishing the shared goal.

For the content of the presentation, we discussed understanding the audience, delivering actionable recommendations, and crafting a clear structure as part of section 5.1.2, where we elaborated on the storytelling process. This section focuses on the clarity of the format.

For a memorable presentation, you should simplify it to have no more than three key ideas you want the audience to take away. More ideas could be incorporated but only as supporting evidence for one of the key ideas. Each key idea can be illustrated with any negative consequences when it is not addressed to highlight the importance of spending time with your audience together on resolving it. You can find more tips and samples for presenting key ideas at IdRatherBeWriting.com [11].

Going into the rigor of the presentation details, the title of each slide should summarize the main takeaway of the slide. The sequence of slide titles should outline your story from start to finish. Table 5.1 shows an example of a presentation for aligning stakeholders on a new propensity score for user conversion.

As illustrated in table 5.1, a crystallized goal and outline can focus a presentation and bring out the key narrative for a partner at a glance. A clear goal is presented on

Table 5.1   Side-by-side comparison of a typical presentation goal and outline vs. a crystallized goal and outline

A typical outline	A crystallized outline

Title: Propensity Score 2.0
 	
Goal: Present the latest insights and align on next steps
Slide titles:
▪ Propensity score impact
▪ Propensity score ver 1.0
▪ Ver 2.0 differences
▪ Ver 2.0 advantages
▪ Ver 2.0 performance
▪ Model architecture details
▪ Model performance details
▪ Model performance stability
▪ Application #1
▪ Application #2
▪ Next steps
	Title: Propensity Score 2.0
	
	Goal: This meeting would be successful if we align on the new proposed framework and timeline for the availability of the metric.
	Slide titles:
	▪ *Propensity score*—Assessment of conversion intent. Accurate assessment is foundational to our success with broad impact.
	  – Ver 1.0 anchors on past activities with lightweight intent signals.
	  – Ver 2.0 incorporates both explicit intent and broader signals to predict future intent.
	  – Ver 2.0 also better differentiates use cases.
	  – Ver 2.0 segments predict intent accurately. Future one-week engagement correlates well with segments.
	▪ *Identifying the look-alike*—Built a model to capture patterns to predict future 1-week engagement.
	  – The look-alike model successfully predicts future engagement with 2% average error rate.
	  – Look-alike segments are stable week over week with 80% of look-alike segments remaining in the same segment after four weeks.
	▪ *Application #1*—Upside to increase 5% conversion through better targeting and efficiency.
	▪ *Application #2*—80% of the predicted high propensity users are WAU in future 1-week.
	▪ *Next steps*—Deploy ver 2.0 in production and test on application #1, the user targeting use case.

the title slide to orient the audience to the purpose of the presentation. The three main topics of the sample presentation are: advantages of the new score, underlying algorithm capabilities, and simulated impacts to applications. The presentation closes with a discussion on next steps. When these techniques are used consistently, your team can powerfully rally business partners and executives on an effective path for producing impact.

As mentioned before, your impact on the organization does not come from how much complexity you create but how much complexity you simplify in an already complex environment. Rigor can be found in simplifying definitions, algorithms, and presentations, and distilling complex issues into concise narratives for peers, business partners, and executives.

5.3   *Attitude of positivity*

Taking on a people management role can be a big transition for any data scientist. As a data scientist, you have built up the tenacity to work through failures, stayed curious and collaborative in responding to incidents, and nurtured mutual respect with business partners. Adding in management responsibilities can feel disruptive for someone familiar with an individual contributor type of work schedule. Further, you are not only responsible for your own positivity at work, but also the positivity of your team as well as the organization's positivity in times of crisis.

This section discusses three specific aspects of attitude a DS manager should manage:

- Managing the maker's schedule versus the manager's schedule
- Trusting team members to execute
- Fostering a culture of institutionalized learning

Maintaining a positive attitude is essential for building a productive work environment in which your DS team can provide the most impact for the organization.

5.3.1 *Managing the maker's schedule versus the manager's schedule*

As a manager, your team members, your business partners, your manager, and other executives all demand your time and attention. Your days are often divided into 30-minute slots, and you are rushing from meeting to meeting all day long. At the end of many weeks, you may feel drained, with little time to reflect and focus on your projects and produce accomplishments you would like to call your own.

If you feel this way, you are not alone. In DS, transitioning from an individual contributor role to management can be hard and overwhelming. Understanding the difference between a maker's schedule and a manager's schedule may help you adjust to your new situation. The concepts of a maker's schedule versus a manager's schedule [12] were first popularized by Paul Graham, the legendary co-founder of the Y Combinator startup accelerator in 2009.

Paul wrote, "Most powerful people are on the manager's schedule. It's the schedule of command. But there's another way of using time that's common among people who make things, like programmers and writers. They generally prefer to use time in units of half a day at least. You can't write or program well in units of an hour. That's barely enough time to get started."

035

"Most powerful people are on the manager's schedule. It's the schedule of command. But there's another way of using time that's common among people who make things, like programmers and writers. They generally prefer to use time in units of half a day at least. You can't write or program well in units of an hour. That's barely enough time to get started." — Paul Graham, co-founder of Y Combinator

MAKER'S SCHEDULE AND FLOW

We all have experienced productive full days of data analysis and coding in the maker's schedule as data scientists. When we work on a project, it takes time to internalize business requirements, get a mental image of the problem space, collect and interpret the available data, and strategize the project architecture and next steps to execute. It may take 30 minutes to two hours of focused effort to get into the *flow*, which is a psychologically recognized state of mind characterized by a feeling of energized focus, full involvement, and enjoyment in the process of the activity.

What happens when there's a meeting scheduled in the middle of that? Paul Graham compares a meeting to an executing software program throwing an exception: "It doesn't merely cause you to switch from one task to another; it changes the mode in which you work. A meeting commonly blows at least half a day by breaking up a morning or afternoon. But in addition, there's sometimes a cascading effect. If I know the afternoon is going to be broken up, I'm less likely to start something ambitious in the morning."

When managing a team, you are responsible for protecting the output capacity of your team. One important aspect is to create an environment for your team members to get into the flow. Figure 5.6 illustrates six specific situations you can keep an eye on for your team and yourself.

Stand-up scheduling 1	One-on-one scheduling 2	Meeting-free (half) days 3
• A daily stand-up is an opportunity for the team to be informed, connected, and calibrated. • Choose a time of day to huddle for 5–10 minutes without breaking the team's flow (e.g., before lunch).	• A weekly one-on-one is a big deal for your team members, so don't cancel at the last minute when conflicts arise. • Respect your team members' maker's schedule and try to reschedule 24 hours in advance.	• Institute days of the week for team members to have flow time. • Support and coordinate with partners to block the time to increase the team's productivity, self-esteem, and performance.

Offsites for brainstorming 4	Self-serve infrastructure 5	On-call process 6
• Create flow time for a dedicated team to focus on tackling important challenges together. • Build relationships to foster deep discussions, lasting 3+ hours (with preparation beforehand).	• Technology solutions, training, and documentation can empower partners to self-serve some requests. • You can focus on training partners and making more strategic requests.	• Team members can rotate on protecting each other's flow by solving ad hoc requests for the team that cannot be self-served. • The on-call process also provides members a broader understanding of others' work.

Figure 5.6   Six techniques to protect your team's flow

STAND-UP SCHEDULING

In the agile software development process, the daily stand-up is an opportunity for the team to be informed, connected, and calibrated on ongoing projects. For DS teams that have adopted the agile software development process, one challenge is choosing a time of day for the team to huddle for 5–10 minutes without breaking their flow.

Some teams choose to do it first thing in the morning, at 9:30 a.m. or 10:00 a.m., before most team members start the day. However, as your team grows, some members may have schedules that start the workday much earlier. A stand-up at 9:30 a.m. or 10:00 a.m. breaks the morning in two. Forcing everyone to start the workday earlier is not practical for many engineering schedules. Scheduling the stand-up at the end of the workday is an option, but some team members may have family obligations, such as picking up kids from school, while others prefer to work continuously through to a late dinner.

We found scheduling the 5–10 minute stand-up between 11:30 a.m. and noon, before lunch, can be a compromise. All team members are present in the middle of the day, and lunch is a natural break for most. As a side feature, eagerness to go to lunch can keep stand-ups short and concise. The only conflict is when team members have an occasional lunch appointment, which can be managed on a case-by-case basis.

ONE-ON-ONE SCHEDULING

You may have experienced it. Your manager scheduled a one-on-one with you, and at the last minute, they canceled it. You spent the morning thinking about the meeting in the back of your mind while working, and now your focus for the entire day has been affected for nothing.

From the manager's perspective, there are many demands on their time. When team discussions unexpectedly drag on or executives ask for something urgent, out of all the meetings on the calendar, one-on-ones seem to be the least disruptive to push off to another day.

To respect your team members' maker's schedule, and allowing time for them to get into the flow, try to make the one-on-ones as scheduled. If that isn't possible, make every effort to reschedule at least 24 hours in advance, especially if it is something you can anticipate, such as delivering reviews and roadmaps for executives at the end of a quarter. For team discussions before team member one-on-ones, try to anticipate the amount of discussion required, and schedule accordingly. You can always complete a meeting early and return some time back to the attendees. When you sincerely respect your team members' flow, even in the scheduling of one-on-ones, your team members will notice and appreciate your actions.

MEETING-FREE DAYS (OR HALF DAYS)

Some DS teams have instituted days of the week for team members to have flow time. Depending on the team member, it could be Wednesday afternoons, Thursday mornings, a Friday, or some other time.

As long as your team members can be flexible and coordinate with the rest of the team to schedule any necessary synchronizations, you can empower them by communicating with business partners the reasons to protect blocks of team members' time for flow. You will be rewarded with improved productivity, self-esteem, and performance of your team.

This technique can be used not just for the team but also for yourself. You can reserve half a day each week for more focused strategic thinking. This may be some alone time or brainstorming time with a few members of the team on a strategic topic. The goal is to channel your focused energy toward important decisions that can drive significant impact.

OFFSITES FOR BRAINSTORMING

Sometimes, the distractions of the office do not allow a dedicated team enough focus to get into the flow to tackle some important challenges together. As the challenges vary, some can be tackled by a team of data scientists, while others require an interdisciplinary team with professionals from engineering, product, and user experience.

Offsites, or extended meetings away from the office, are a good way to get a block of time to work on the challenge and allow the team to get into the flow together. They often involve three or more hours together with preparations beforehand and time set aside to build relationships, while diving into a significant amount of detail. These goals usually will not fit into a typical 30-to-60-minute time format.

Offsites are not to be confused with team-building events, where the main focus is relationship-building rather than solving a particular challenge together. Offsites also do not mean having to travel far. Even a restaurant next door to the office with a private room could be an option to free the team from the many distractions in the office and focus on getting into the flow to resolve some important challenges.

SELF-SERVE INFRASTRUCTURE

While there are organizational approaches, such as stand-up scheduling, one-on-one scheduling, meeting-free days, and offsites to help team members get into the flow, we can also use technological solutions to reduce incoming distractions for the team. When you analyze incoming inquiries for your team, there may be subsets of inquiries that could be self-served with the right data infrastructure and access. Investing in providing self-serve infrastructure, along with the necessary training and documentation to reliably access data, can empower partners to get more timely access to data and create the space for your team members to focus on more challenging and not easily automated questions.

As companies grow, self-serve infrastructures will be increasingly important to allow your nimble team of data scientists to produce outsized impact. To be successful at it, make sure to follow product development best practices when creating self-serve infrastructures, as they are internally-facing data products.

ON-CALL PROCESS

Many ad hoc incoming inquiries for your team may not be solved by self-service methods. When individual team members are fielding ad hoc inquiries, it can be frustrating for all parties involved. Team members' flows are constantly interrupted. There are no clear mechanisms to track these ad hoc inquiries, and there is little chance for you, the manager, to defend the team from the distractions. In the end, the organization will suffer from unexpected delays in DS projects, and your team members may be forced to work overtime to get projects back on track.

Alternatively, you can request that all inquiries come to you first to centralize the process, but then you become the bottleneck in the process, and reviewing inquiries can quickly suck up all your time, even when there are many other demands. How can we resolve this issue?

One way to field ad hoc inquiries for a DS team is to institute an on-call process. For team sizes of 5–15 data scientists, team members can rotate to be the dedicated on-call person fielding ad hoc requests each week. The on-call process becomes a line of defense to make room for the rest of the team to have as much flow time as possible. This also centralizes the ad hoc requests, so new opportunities for self-service infrastructures can emerge, and distributes the triaging workload, so you don't become the bottleneck in the process.

While the on-call team member can prioritize inquiries, resolving them sometimes calls for domain context and expertise that resides with another team member. Having a data scientist translate partner requests and execute the resolution under the guidance of other DS team members with context and expertise has three main benefits:

- The on-call team member can filter and qualify the inquiries by their urgency and impact objectively for the team.
- For the DS team member not on call for the week, guiding another data scientist to resolving an inquiry can be less disruptive and more efficient.
- Over time, your team members can build up institutional knowledge of not just their own work but also what each team member is working on. Best ideas and practices can propagate from project to project. Data nuances across different product lines can be learned by multiple team members. This way, when one data scientist is on vacation or leaves the team, their domain knowledge is still available in the team.

Given these advantages, an on-call process can be highly effective in protecting your team members' focus and flow and retain more institutional knowledge within the team.

In summary, understanding and protecting the maker's schedule can empower your team members to better focus and get into the flow. You may also find other positive attitudes emerge, such as improved concentration, self-esteem, and performance. In the short term, positive attitudes can be good for the team's productivity. In the long term, this can improve team members' retention and help accelerate their progress toward their respective career goals. As for Audra from chapter 1, being mindful of the manager's and the maker's schedule is a great way to demonstrate that she cares for her team and its productivity.

5.3.2 *Trusting the team members to execute*

As a DS manager, you are no longer making the detailed technical decisions in your team's projects, yet you are responsible for their outcomes. If this feels uncomfortable, you are not alone. Many first-time managers feel this way, which is a common cause of micromanagement. For experienced managers, this feeling points to a deeper issue of trust. Given the situation at hand, do you trust your team members to make the best technical decisions available?

Some managers choose to be hands-off—dump a project in a team member's lap, and leave them alone to work through it—which often creates more risk in the execution outcome than necessary from the organization's perspective. Is this amount of prudence appropriate? Trust in team members requires time to build. The trust-building process has best practices that can reduce the time it takes for you to gain your team member's trust and for you to trust them.

Dr. Ken Blanchard and Dr. Spencer Johnson describe one set of best practices in their book, *The New One Minute Manager* [13]. It starts with setting goals and goes into specific techniques for providing timely positive and negative feedback toward building trust between a manager and a team member. This is illustrated in figure 5.7.

Setting goals	Positive feedback	Negative feedback
• Aligning on end results to avoid micromanaging the specifics • Focusing on building trust, so goal setting and tracking are accomplished autonomously	• Noticing when team members are doing things right or approximately right to build trust • Providing specific, timely, and impactful praise that reinforces good performance and confidence	• Building trust by being specific about what went wrong, while reaffirming the value you place in the person • Redirecting negative situations into motivation and support

Figure 5.7   **Three steps to trusting your team members**

SETTING GOALS

- *Purpose*—The purpose of setting goals is to align on the end results and avoid micromanagement of specific decisions when completing a project or fulfilling a set of responsibilities. The process should focus on building trust, such that goal setting can be accomplished as autonomously as possible by team members.
- *Practice*—The practice involves spending time with your team members at the beginning of a new task or responsibility through four techniques:
  - Work with a team member to set up the goals and understand what good performance looks like.
  - Have the team member write out each goal, with the delivery date, on a single sheet of paper.
  - Ask the team member to review alignment to the most important goals every day and assess progress toward the delivery date.
  - If work does not match the goals, encourage the team member to adjust their focus toward their goals.
- *Benefit*—Working side by side with team members to develop goals can encourage team member ownership for the goals and performance standards. Keeping the most important goals on one page allows the goals to be reviewed every day. Team members can self-adjust when their effort deviates from the goals or when progress diverges from the delivery date. In effect, this encourages team members to be more autonomous and empowers them to self-manage their progress.

- *Guidance*—How do we set these goals? There are three steps to guide a team member to crystallize results-oriented goals.
  - What are people doing, or not doing, that is causing the problem?
  - What would you like to see happen?
  - What are you going to do about it?

A team member should describe the problem and what they would like to see happen. If they are not clear about what they would like to see happen, there is not yet a problem—it is just a grievance. A problem is the gap between observation and expectation.

036

> If a team member is not clear about what they would like to see happen, there is not yet a problem—it is just a grievance. A problem is the gap between observation and expectation.

When a team member identifies a problem, a solution is a sequence of steps they can suggest to bridge the gap between observation and expectation. A results-oriented goal is a one-page description of the solution that can be reviewed regularly to aid in achieving it by the delivery date.

Not all goals need to go through this process. Three to five top goals can usually cover 80% of your important results. Let's look at some examples. When building a forecast model, one goal could be to assess whether inputs to the forecast model are stable and robust. When there are data quality issues or inherent data biases, data needs to be characterized and taken into account in model construction.

Another goal could be launching the model, which involves specifying how long the model needs to be tested in shadow mode (with the model running and business partners monitoring but not yet making decisions based on the result) before partners trust it. What is the performance metric (root mean square error [RMSE], dollar amount optimized, or value at risk [VaR]) for building trust? You know you have succeeded in the practice of goal setting when your team members can ask themselves qualifying questions and come to you with well-crafted one-page goals to review.

POSITIVE FEEDBACK

- *Purpose*—The purpose of positive feedback is to build trust by noticing when team members are doing things right or approximately right. This encourages the team to continue to do what works well. It is also a way for the team to learn to anticipate both positive and negative feedback when the majority of managerial feedback tends to be negative.
- *Practice*—How do you make your positive feedback more impactful? *The New One Minute Manager* [13] introduces six steps:
  - Praise people as soon as possible.
  - Be specific about what they did right.

- Tell team members about their impact—how good you feel about it and how it helps.
- Pause for a moment for the praise to sink in (a pause of five to seven seconds will do).
- Encourage the team member to do more of the same.
- Make it clear you have confidence in the team member and support their success.

- *Benefit*—Providing specific positive feedback early on helps team members understand exactly what aspect of their excellent work they should keep up. It also trains your team members to recognize when they are doing something right, so they can feel good about what they have done well, even when you are not around to give praise.
- *Guidance*—Recognizing good work to provide positive feedback does not have to involve peeking over team members' shoulders. It can come from their progress report, the results they generated, or processes they have set up, as well as from feedback you receive from partners.

When a team member starts a new project or responsibility, your consistent positive feedback will be important, especially when some other projects that are not going as well may affect your mood as a manager.

When new members start on the team, it may be hard for them to do something exactly right the first time. Even when they have gotten it approximately right, it can be a good opportunity to praise their effort and encourage them to get it exactly right the next time.

You know you have succeeded in the practice of timely and specific positive feedback when you see your team member grow into a group of more confident and effective data scientists over time. You have really succeeded when team members learn to give themselves and each other praise and can keep themselves motivated even when you are not around.

NEGATIVE FEEDBACK

- *Purpose*—The purpose of negative feedback is to build trust by being specific about what went wrong with a team member, while reaffirming the value you place in the team member. It redirects the negative situations into motivation and support for team members to help them get back on track.
- *Practice*—How do you make your negative feedback more impactful? *The New One Minute Manager* [13] introduces seven steps:
  - Redirect people as soon as possible.
  - Confirm the facts first, and review the specific mistakes together.
  - Share how you feel about the mistake and its broader impact.
  - Pause for a moment to allow time for the feedback to sink in.

- Share that they are better than their mistakes, and you think well of them as a person.
- Remind them that you have confidence and trust in them and support their success.
- Realize that when the redirect is over, it's over.

- *Benefit*—Providing negative feedback in small doses early is less overwhelming to the team member. Being specific allows you to pinpoint and rid the bad behavior and keep the good person. Sharing how you feel, describing the broader impact, and pausing afterward provide the team member with an opportunity to feel the responsibility of the mistake and its impact on the organization. Reaffirming the team member's capability allows you to build trust with them and allows them to feel confident as a person, so they can grow in professional maturity and prevent similar mistakes from happening in the future.

- *Guidance*—If the mistake is a result of goals not being set clearly, you, as the manager, should take responsibility for the mistake and clarify the goal. For steps one to four of the practice, the focus is on the mistake. Your ability to be specific about what went wrong will build trust by allowing the team member to feel that you are on top of things. Focusing on the bad behavior rather than the person reduces the chance that the team member will feel they are under attack, become defensive, and, ultimately, not learn from the mistake. Steps five to seven are focused on building confidence in team members and helping the team get better results. Reaffirming your trust in the team member can not only help them feel better, but it can also help put yourself in a more trusting mood when interacting with others.

If you have to provide multiple pieces of negative feedback on the same type of mistake for a team member, the nature of the mistakes may shift from an ability problem to a motivational problem. At some point, you will need to evaluate the cost of the mistakes to the organization and whether you can afford to keep such a person on the team.

In summary, the ultimate objective for setting goals together and providing specific and timely positive and negative feedback is to show people how to manage themselves and help the team succeed when you are not around. The key underpinning for the concept introduced in *The New One Minute Manager* [13] is that we are not just our behavior, we are the person managing our behavior. We can be tough on poor performance but not on the person. This way, you can maintain an attitude of positivity in the team, while trusting the team members to execute.

For Jennifer (from chapter 1, case 3), the tech lead whose team felt micromanaged, these techniques for setting goals and providing positive and negative feedback can be helpful to establish a mutually agreed upon cadence for checking in on projects and to build trust with team members.

5.3.3   *Creating a culture of institutionalized learning*

As your organization grows, institutionalizing learning becomes important. Data scientists collaborate cross-functionally with the product, engineering, and operations teams, and many pitfalls exist on the path toward business impact. If learnings are not institutionalized, the same type of breakdowns can occur repeatedly across teams and functions, significantly lowering project success rate.

In section 2.2.3, we discussed striking a balance in speed and quality for a tech lead in their execution. In section 3.3.2, we discussed how tech leads should maintain the team's mood of curiosity and collaboration when responding to incidents. And in section 5.2.2, we discussed the rigor to which DS managers and staff data scientists should hold the team to dive deep into the root cause of the post-mortem process.

As a DS manager or staff data scientist, you also have the responsibility to nurture a culture of learning institutionalization. The human nervous system learns through the three fundamental processes [14] illustrated in figure 5.8: reciprocation, recurrence, and recursion. Let's go into them one by one.

Reciprocation	Recurrence	Recursion
• An exchange of interpretations to deepen strategic knowledge • Use post-mortem meetings to dive deep into the root causes to prevent similar mistakes from happening again.	• Periodic and frequent practice of strategic knowledge • Regularly review documented post-mortems as business cases for fragilities in infrastructure and good incident mitigation practices.	• Deepen the understanding, and design more powerful solutions • As infrastructures improve, new practices can be invented to mitigate or even prevent some types of incidents from happening.

Figure 5.8   Three processes for building a culture of institutionalized learning

037

To produce a culture of institutionalized learning, you can work with the three fundamental learning processes of the human nervous system: reciprocation, recurrence, and recursion.

RECIPROCATION

To establish reciprocation, the discussion in each post-mortem session are guided toward the prevention of a similar incident from happening again. It is not about assigning blame to a person. The solution should involve a systematic improvement that eliminates situations that allows the root cause to occur—not excluding a "bad apple" from the team.

Suppose an incident involved an important model producing unreliable predictions, and it was found that a product feature launch broke a model data source. Processes must be put in place as part of the system to prevent the situation, in this case the problematic feature launches, from happening again.

One solution may involve documenting and communicating critical data sources for all models in production. It is the model owner's responsibility to discuss data sources with product owners, review the product roadmap to discover any potential upcoming disruptions through feature revamp, and inform the product owners of any sensitivities of the final model to the data produced by their features. Such solutions can only be successful through reciprocal coordination and understanding with partner teams that share the common goals of greater business impact.

RECURRENCE

In a fast-growing organization, it is not enough to document post-mortems for incidents and archive them. They need to be reviewed regularly. Well-written post-mortems are like business cases. They highlight the common fragilities in the current infrastructure, exhibit existing incident mitigation practices, and outline roadmaps for process and infrastructure improvements to come.

Powerful organizations, such as Google, employ site reliability engineering practices [15], such as reviewing an exemplary post-mortem each month as part of a newsletter. When your organization does not have many incident post-mortems, sharing once a quarter could also work. The purpose of this practice is threefold:

- It is an opportunity for new team members to learn about the complexity and intricacies of the systems they are building.
- It provides review of incident response procedures and techniques that have worked well in minimizing incident impact.
- Just like open-source software, when post-mortem reports are going to be viewed by future peers, and not just archived, there is more motivation for producing a quality document.

RECURSION

Recursion in learning is the process of deepening the understanding of the topic over time. As data infrastructures and model deployment environment improve, new practices to mitigate, or even prevent, past incident types from happening again.

Post-mortems document a snapshot of the mitigation actions possible at the time of the incident. As we use past post-mortems to train new data scientists on the team, there is also the opportunity to reconsider what new knowledge, processes, or practices are now available to reduce the negative impact of similar situations, should they occur.

The practice of recursion is crucial for a culture that values learning from past failures, allowing each incident to pay forward in multiple ways. When the team can focus on the future benefits of a post-mortem, it can shift the team's attitude to a positive one, even in times of crisis.

In summary, reciprocation, recurrence, and recursion are three tools you can use for establishing a culture of institutionalized learning. These tools can shift an otherwise negative experience in the post-mortem process into a learning opportunity that the team will value for years to come.

Next you will have an opportunity to self-assess and identify development focus areas. Ready? Let's get right to it!

5.4   Self-assessment and development focus

Congratulations on working through the chapter on manager and staff data scientist virtues! This is an important milestone for becoming a people manager or a staff data scientist in DS.

The purpose of this virtues self-assessment is to help you internalize and practice the concepts by:

- Understanding your interests and leadership strengths
- Practicing one to two areas with the choose, practice, and review (CPR) process
- Developing a prioritize-practice-perform plan to go through more CPRs

Once you start doing this, you will have courageously taken the steps to practice strong ethics, build diligence in rigor, and maintain a positive attitude to drive your team's long-term effectiveness.

5.4.1   Understanding your interests and leadership strengths

Table 5.2 summarizes the virtues discussed in this chapter. The rightmost column is available for you to check off the areas you currently feel comfortable with quickly. There is no judgment, no right or wrong, nor are there any specific patterns to follow. Feel free to leave any or all rows blank.

If you are already aware of some of these aspects, this is a great way to build a narrative around your existing leadership strengths. If some aspects are not yet familiar, this is the opportunity for you to assess whether they can be of help in your daily work, starting today!

Table 5.2   Self-assessment areas for virtues of managers and staff data scientists

Capability areas/self-assessment (*italic items primarily apply to managers*)			?
Ethics	Growing the team with coaching, mentoring, and advising	Coaching by observing and providing feedback to clarify goals, focus on what's needed, and discover the best strategies to achieve the goals	
		Mentoring by imparting wisdom and sharing knowledge to focus on the team member's career growth	
		Advising by providing information and direction, which involves specific feedback about specific questions	
	Representing the team confidently in cross-functional discussions	Practicing strong opinions, weakly held to seek collaboration early and overcome common biases	
		Using storytelling in persuasive narratives and presentations	
	Contributing to and reciprocating on broader management duties	*Helping in interviews, promotions, and feedback of partner team members; participating in reviews for product roadmaps, infrastructure roadmaps, and business operations*	

Table 5.2   Self-assessment areas for virtues of managers and staff data scientists *(continued)*

Capability areas/self-assessment *(italic items primarily apply to managers)*			?
Rigor	Observing and mitigating anti-patterns in ML and DS systems	Glue code—Cleaning the wrapper to allow algorithm upgrades	
		Pipeline jungle—Documenting data lineage	
		Dead experimental code path—Managing the code life cycle	
		Under-documented data fields—Using types and invariants to automate error detection in data pipelines	
		Excessive use of multiple languages—Limiting languages or cross-training team members for maintainability	
		Dependencies on prototyping environment—Clearly accounting for tech debts to avoid execution stagnation	
	Learning effectively from incidents	Organizing the team to participate and schedule post-mortems	
		Coaching the team to avoid pitfalls, using the five-whys process	
	Driving clarity by distilling complex issues into concise narratives	Simplicity in definitions—Articulating 15-second definitions for technical terms, and respecting others in conversations	
		Simplicity in algorithms—Carefully examining the trade-offs between complexity and cost of operations	
		Simplicity in presentation—Crystallizing a storyline with no more than three main points	
Attitude	*Managing the maker's schedule versus the manager's schedule*	*Accommodating the maker's schedule and flow with techniques in stand-up and one-on-one scheduling, meeting-free days, offsites, self-serve infrastructures, and on-call processes*	
	Trusting the team members to execute	*Goal setting—Guiding team members to set their own goals*	
		Positive feedback—Providing timely, specific, encouragement	
		Negative feedback—Providing timely and specific feedback, triggering the feeling of responsibility for the action, then building back confidence with trust and encouragement for the person	
	Creating a culture of institutionalized learning	Reciprocation—Engaging in discussions in post-mortem meetings to dive deep into the root causes of mistakes made	
		Recurrence—Holding periodic reviews of past incidents to keep best practices top of mind	
		Recursion—Monitoring how incidents have been handled, and iteratively improving mitigation processes	

5.4.2   *Practicing with the CPR process*

Remember the tech lead virtues assessment in section 3.4? You can experiment with a similarly simple (CPR) process with two-week check-ins. For your self-review, you can use the project-based skill improvement template to help you structure your actions over the two weeks:

- *Skill/task*—Select a virtue to work on.
- *Date*—Select a date in the two-week period when you can apply the virtue.
- *People*—Write down the names of the people with whom you can apply the virtue, or write *self*.
- *Place*—Select the location or occasion at which you can apply the virtue (for example, your next team meeting or during the next incident post-mortem).
- *Review result*—How did you do compared to before? The same, better, or worse?

By holding yourself accountable for these steps in a self-review, you can start to exercise your strengths and shed light on your blind spots in the DS manager and staff data scientist virtues.

Summary

- *Ethics* for a manager or a staff data scientist include growing team members' capacities, representing the team in cross-functional discussions, and contributing to and reciprocating on broader management duties with peer and partner teams.
  - To grow team members' capacities, you can create a safe environment and provide coaching, mentoring, and advising where appropriate.
  - To represent the team confidently, practice strong opinions, weakly held to seek collaboration early, and use storytelling in persuasive narratives and presentations.
  - To contribute to and reciprocate on broader management duties, you can help in interviews, promotions, and feedback of partner team members and participate in reviews for product roadmaps, infrastructure roadmaps, and business operations.
- *Rigor* is the craftsmanship that observes and mitigates anti-patterns in ML and DS systems, learns effectively from incidents, drives clarity, and reduces complexity.
  - To observe and mitigate system anti-patterns, watch for and avoid excessive glue code, pipeline jungle, dead experimental code path, under-documented data fields, excessive use of multiple languages, and dependency on prototyping environment.
  - To learn effectively from incidents, organize the teams to participate in post-mortems and coach teams to avoid pitfalls in the five-whys process.
  - To drive clarity and reduce complexity, distill complex issues into concise narratives by simplifying definitions, algorithms, and presentations.

- *Attitude* is the mood a DS manager and staff data scientist nurtures in their team when managing the maker's schedule, trusting team members to execute, and creating a culture of learning.
  - To accommodate the maker's schedule and team members' flow time, a manager can be respectful in stand-up and one-on-one scheduling, constitute meeting-free days, organize offsites, create self-serve infrastructures, and institute on-call processes.
  - To build trust with the team in execution, guide team members to set their own goals, provide timely and specific positive feedback to encourage more positive behavior, and provide timely and specific negative feedback for their mistakes, then build back their confidence with encouragement.
  - To create a culture of institutionalized learning, practice reciprocation by discussing incidents in post-mortems, practice recurrence by periodically reviewing past incidents, and practice recursion by iterating to improve mitigation processes.

References

[1] P. Saffo. "Strong opinions weakly held." Saffo.com. https://www.saffo.com/02008/07/26/strong-opinions-weakly-held/

[2] Buster Benson, "Cognitive bias cheat sheet: Because thinking is hard," betterhumans, 2016. https://betterhumans.pub/cognitive-bias-cheat-sheet-55a472476b18

[3] D. Scully, "Hidden technical debt in machine learning systems," *28th Int. Conf. on Neural Information Processing Systems*, December 2015, pp. 2503–2511.

[4] F. Pedregosa, et al., "Scikit-learn: Machine learning in Python," *JMLR*, vol. 12, pp. 2825–2830, 2011.

[5] "Introducing Collibra Lineage." https://www.collibra.com/blog/introducing-collibra-lineage

[6] "Apache Airflow." https://github.com/apache/airflow

[7] "SEC charges knight capital with violations of market access rule." US Securities and Exchange Commission. https://www.sec.gov/news/press-release/2013-222

[8] "The $440 million software error at Knight Capital." Henrico Dolfing. https://www.henrico-dolfing.com/2019/06/project-failure-case–study-knight-capital.html

[9] O. Serrat, "The five whys technique," *Knowledge Solutions*. Singapore: Springer, 2017, doi: 10.1007/978-981-10-0983-9_32.

[10] "Netflix recommendations: Beyond the 5 stars." Netflix Technology Blog. https://netflix-techblog.com/netflix-recommendations-beyond-the-5-stars-part-1-55838468f429

[11] "I'd rather be writing principles." I'd Rather Be Writing. https://idratherbewriting.com/simplifying-complexity/macro-micro.html

[12] P. Graham. "Maker's Schedule, Manager's Schedule." PaulGraham.com. http://www.paul-graham.com/makersschedule.html

[13] K. Blanchard and S. Johnson, *The New One Minute Manager*. New York, NY, USA: William Morrow and Company, 2015.

[14] T. Hecht, *Aji: An IR#4 Business Philosophy*, The Aji Network Intellectual Properties, Inc., 2019.

[15] J. Lunney and S. Lueder. "Postmortem culture: Learning from failure." Google. https://landing.google.com/sre/sre-book/chapters/postmortem-culture/

Part 3

The director: Governing a function

With your superior integrity in managing projects and nuanced approaches in leading a productive team of data scientists, you are ready to take on greater responsibilities. You can lead a DS function with a team of teams, manage managers, and solve challenges you are not there to witness directly. You can also be on the individual contributor track as a principal data scientist, influencing partners of broader scopes and leading efforts of greater complexity.

Leading at the DS function level requires a different set of skills than leading projects or teams of individuals. You are responsible for producing more significant impact over a longer horizon of time, often across multiple quarters. What differentiates this role is the clarity in focus and prioritization required for projects with longer time horizons.

The clarity in focus and prioritization comes from a deep understanding of your company's business model. You can leverage this understanding to craft roadmaps to accomplish strategic business objectives, while avoiding management and technology pitfalls.

An effective roadmap deconstructs an ultimate goal into a step-by-step strategy for your team leaders to execute. The execution of these roadmaps requires an acute sense of emerging issues in the organization, both technical and people related. Only when the milestones are completed successfully can the ultimate business objectives be accomplished.

Efficient execution often requires a specific organization of teams for particular company initiatives at hand. Teams can be built and iteratively reorganized over time as you craft the function by managing its people, process, and platforms. To develop a resilient foundation for execution for the long term, you are also responsible for creating a robust hiring process for your talent pipelines and clear career paths for team members.

These strategies' success requires you to lead your DS teams at the function level for your company. In chapters 6 and 7, we dive into the capabilities and virtues you can demonstrate through discussions in technology, execution, expert domain knowledge, ethics, rigor, and attitude.

Capabilities for leading a function

This chapter covers

- Crafting technology roadmaps to deliver the right features at the right time
- Sponsoring and championing promising projects
- Delivering consistently by managing people, processes, and platforms
- Building a strong function with clear career paths and a robust hiring process
- Anticipating business needs and driving fundamental impacts

Your capabilities as a DS director or a principal data scientist are demonstrated by architecting roadmaps and championing technologies that can increase the DS function's impact. Also necessary for success are the consistent execution of roadmaps and the application of expert domain knowledge in anticipating and preparing for the upcoming needs of the business.

A roadmap is a strategic plan that describes the steps an organization needs to take to achieve stated outcomes and goals. They are valuable as a tool to clarify and align teams toward common goals. Crafting and communicating technology roadmaps is essential for aligning team members, partners, and executives on clear milestones. Technology roadmaps can include roadmaps for data, models, infrastructures, and processes. Sequencing the roadmap milestones according to the desired business outcomes and their technical dependencies allows the right things to be built for the right people at the right time. When DS projects emerge that align well with strategic technology direction but lack specific short-term benefits, it is your responsibility to champion them and work with partners to get them funded.

For the execution of roadmaps, the focus is on delivering business KPIs on budget and on time. This focus involves organizing and reorganizing teams to be as efficient as possible by maneuvering people, processes, and platforms on delivering the business KPIs. To increase the function's impact, you are responsible for growing existing team member capabilities and justifying additional headcount in critical areas. Most importantly, as the execution landscape changes over time, staying aligned with senior leadership through goal drifts and business pivots is essential for maximizing DS impact with the right set of priorities.

Domain knowledge is vital for anticipating, crafting, and driving critical business KPIs across product development stages. When the business requires specific intelligent components, such as personalization or anti-fraud capabilities, a DS director or principal data scientist with domain expertise can rapidly apply domain experience against urgent product features or business challenges. For example, when faced with difficult strategic decisions, such as reusing capabilities and creating dependency or replicating capabilities and duplicating maintenance costs, a deep understanding of the drivers of fundamental business models and the organization's strategic roadmap is required to weigh the necessary trade-offs.

As a DS director, while you can be removed from the day-to-day technical decisions, your primary responsibility is to build a DS function that can achieve the business goals of the executive team. This building process involves capabilities in technology, execution, and expert domain knowledge.

As a principal data scientist, you are responsible for the technical directions at the function level to craft the roadmaps that align the function and partner functions toward achieving the business goals of the executive team. Let's dive into this chapter to discuss the details.

6.1 Technology: Tools and skills

A strong DS function is led with clarity in focus and prioritization. The function doesn't have to be large. A nimble team can be highly impactful. For example, a team of six data scientists collaborating with three anti-fraud investigators over one year at Yiren Digital prevented US$30 million a year in fraud losses. The reasons behind the success of these high-impact DS teams can often be traced to three main technological capabilities of the DS director and the principal data scientists:

- Well-crafted technology roadmaps for DS
- A diligent focus on building the right thing for the right people at the right time
- Empowering promising projects by championing them to get partner buy-in

Clear technology roadmaps are essential for execution success. However, it can be challenging to create roadmaps that align the various product and functional partners, as every partner has its execution priorities. This challenge is especially prominent in large companies, where each functional team may have met their KPIs quarter to quarter, but the overall business objective is not accomplished.

The director and principal data scientist's responsibilities are to make sure technology roadmaps for data, models, infrastructure, and processes are clarified and aligned, such that the overall desired business outcome can be achieved by completing the step-by-step milestones. We discuss this in section 6.1.1.

Roadmaps can fall out of alignment for many reasons, such as a change of priority or new learning from results of controlled experiments. We must constantly be ready to adjust priorities and pivot business directions. A diligent focus on using experimentation to build the right thing for the right people at the right time can ensure the always-limited resources are focused on the most impactful projects at the time. This demonstrates the efficiency of the DS function and is discussed in section 6.1.2.

Sometimes, important DS projects that are not part of the existing roadmap emerge. To make things more complicated, some projects, while crucial for the long-term success of the business objective, lack short-term immediate business benefits. It is often difficult, if not impossible, to fit them into the scope of work. As a director or principal data scientist, it is your responsibility to champion these projects to ensure long-term investments are made in time to contribute to the overall business objectives. We will discuss this in section 6.1.3.

6.1.1 Crafting technology roadmaps

Remember that a *roadmap* is a strategic plan that describes the steps an organization needs to take to achieve stated outcomes and goals. They are valuable as a tool to clarify and align teams toward common goals.

One famous roadmap in the semiconductor industry is the International Technology Roadmap for Semiconductors (ITRS), which has driven the digital transformation and advancements in DS over the past 50 years. The roadmap establishes the directions of research and their timelines up to about 15 years into the future to synchronize efforts to tackle a wide range of technical feats, including system design processes, semiconductor materials, manufacturing chemicals and equipment, assembly, packaging, and testing of the semiconductor product. Its success is self-evident in the proliferation of digital electronics in our everyday lives, enabled by an increasingly complex ecosystem of semiconductor design and manufacturing processes to integrate tens of billions of transistors into a single chip. This roadmap ensures that the cost of computation is exponentially decreasing, so more complex algorithms can be applied to a broader range of data over time.

For DS, a well-crafted roadmap also has a similar synchronization power of aligning multiple teams and functions to collaborate and coordinate accomplishing an overall business objective. You may recall from chapter 1 that Stephen, a well-respected director, noticed that his team's morale dropped with a few regrettable attritions. That DS team was feeling the pain of a lack of a clear technology roadmap. Let's talk about what that means.

038

A well-crafted roadmap has the synchronization power of aligning multiple teams and functions to collaborate and coordinate accomplishing an overall business objective. Crafting roadmaps is an essential skill for data science function leaders.

A clear technology roadmap can be developed in five steps. The steps are illustrated in figure 6.1. We will dive into each step one by one.

Figure 6.1   Five steps for developing an effective technology roadmap

DEFINING BUSINESS OBJECTIVES

Business objectives are refinements of the company mission and vision for execution. They drive common goals that teams and functions align on to collaborate and coordinate. For a consumer-facing product that depends on users forming habits to use the product, improvements of daily active users (DAU) or weekly active users (WAU) can be a metric of success.

For a product serving small and medium-sized businesses (SMBs), a business objective can be driving an indispensable percentage of your customers' revenue streams. Some companies have successfully navigated this business objective. A few examples are Stripe for online payments, Square for offline payments, and OpenTable for online restaurant reservations.

For enterprise products, a business objective is to become their customers' de facto operating process. A few product examples include GitLab, Slack, Zoom, and Google Docs.

One common mistake is to define a business objective that is too narrow. An example is using real-time analytics for personalization. It is difficult to align on common goals across different teams and functions when a business objective is not relevant to others' priorities. The higher-level objective to drive cross-team alignment in this example could be to increase customer engagement with personalization being one approach and real-time analytics being one technology.

PREPARING AND RESEARCHING

To achieve higher-level business objectives, you must first understand the range of potential intermediate milestones by validating customer needs and technology paths. Validating customer needs involves identifying constraints and requirements for a successful path to implementation. You can play the role of a product manager for your roadmap, interview stakeholders, and synthesize intermediate milestones meaningful for your stakeholders.

For example, for a product with customer support hotlines, what are the constraints limiting the customer support team gaining customer trust? What are the needs of your company's customers, such that they can depend on your company's product for their important business processes?

While you may not have these answers, identifying a knowledgeable product partner with firsthand information on these questions can help you orient the intermediate milestones when you construct your roadmap. New technologies for DS capabilities are emerging every day. If you would like to leverage some technology component that is not yet tested in your specific usage scenario, at your specific scale, or by your specific team, you will need to validate the technology. You can conduct a *proof of concept* (PoC) as a preparation step before crafting a roadmap, or we can allocate one of the initial milestones for proving out the technology, so technology risks do not disrupt the roadmap at a later time. When deploying proven technologies, we can use prior deployment experiences to estimate the complexity and risks of incorporating the technologies in future roadmaps.

DESIGNING STRATEGIC STEPS

With clarity of the business objectives and preparations to understand customer requirements and available technologies, you are ready to develop roadmaps to guide your teams.

DS projects touch many technical and business areas. There are numerous types of roadmaps we can develop to advance business impact. Let's look at eight common types of roadmaps. If some of them are missing in your function, you can establish an initial one. If you have an initial roadmap implemented, there are opportunities to broaden or deepen its scope, as illustrated in figure 6.2.

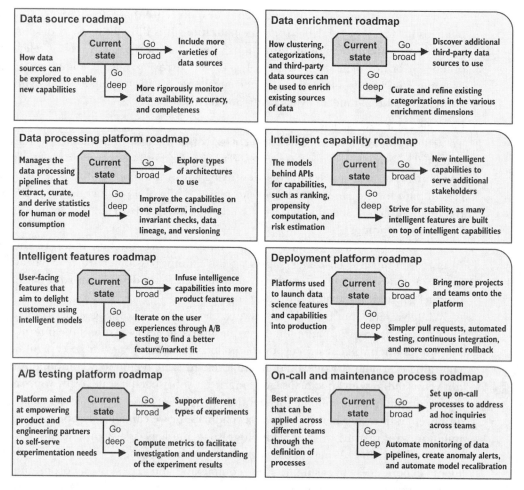

Figure 6.2   Eight areas for crafting roadmaps to advance business impact

Data source roadmaps

Data source roadmaps describe how new data sources can be explored to enable new capabilities and how existing data sources can be made more stable. There are many types of data sources in a company, such as marketing conversion data, sales transaction data, customer relationship data, and financial planning data.

In broadening the variety of data sources, online user behavior data can inform user engagement for companies with websites or apps. User-contributed content, such as reviews or posts, can also be studied to understand user interests and creation and consumption patterns for online platforms.

To dive deep into a data source that supports models in production, we can rigorously monitor data availability, accuracy, and completeness, as discussed in sections 2.2.2 and 3.2.2.

Data enrichment roadmaps

Data enrichment roadmaps describe how categorization, clustering, and third-party data references can be used to enrich existing sources of data. We can go broad and/or deep. To go broad, we can discover additional third-party data sources to use. To go deep, we can curate and refine existing categorizations in the various enrichment dimensions.

For example, credit card companies often attempt to understand users' spending habits by analyzing their credit card transaction history. You can derive the spending categories through a third-party merchant categorization code (MCC) table. But if we wanted to understand someone's cuisine preferences when dining out, we would need to either go broad to find alternative third-party APIs or go deep to use NLP to derive cuisine preference from the restaurant name or location information.

Data processing platform roadmaps

A *data processing platform* manages the data processing pipelines that extract, curate, and derive statistics for human or model consumption. To go broad on the types of architectures to use, you can go from manually kicked-off ad hoc processes to scheduled weekly or overnight processes to intraday, near-real-time micro-batch runs to a completely streamed event-based architecture. You can also incorporate graph databases to accelerate relationship lookups and assist in detecting indirect relationships between data entities.

To go deep to improve the capabilities on one platform, the platform can incorporate directed acyclic graph (DAG) dependencies with invariant checks between processing steps to verify data quality. Metadata on the data lineage and data versioning can also be stored and analyzed for bug tracking and data auditing.

Intelligent capability roadmaps

Intelligent capabilities are the models behind APIs for ranking, computing propensities, estimating risks, and so on. They drive intelligence features such as search, sales follow-up, marketing drip campaigns, and anti-fraud mechanisms.

A broader scope can include new types of intelligence capabilities to serve additional stakeholders. To go deep into existing intelligence capabilities, you can refine the models to produce higher precision and recalls.

Intelligence capability roadmaps should strive for stability, as many intelligent features can be built on top of the same intelligence capability. One example is how a purchase propensity estimation API can drive personalization, sales, marketing, and customer service features.

Intelligent feature roadmaps

Intelligent features are user-facing features that aim to delight customers. They are based on intelligent capabilities and focus on the specific manifestations that can create a product/market fit. For example, you can build intelligent features such as more precise marketing drip campaigns and sales follow-ups based on an intelligent capability computing personalized recommendations for next best actions (NBAs).

To broaden your scope, you can infuse intelligence capabilities into more product features. To deepen your investment in existing features, you can iterate on the user experiences through A/B testing to find a better feature/market fit and continue to monitor the effectiveness of features as potential primacy and novelty effects wear off.

Intelligence feature roadmaps should strive for nimbleness through iterations and pivots, as many features will not be effective as originally proposed. Two to five rounds of iterations can be reasonable milestones in a roadmap to prove a particular feature hypothesis.

Deployment platform roadmaps

Deployment platforms are used to launch DS features and capabilities. Some teams may share common deployment platforms with the software engineering team, while other teams may use notebook-based infrastructures to minimize the deployment barrier from development to deployment.

To broaden the reach of a deployment platform, you can bring more projects and teams onto the platform. To go deep, you can improve the deployment process, such as by employing simpler pull requests, automated testing, continuous integration, and more convenient rollback.

Deployment platform efficiency is an often-neglected aspect of DS teams. Improving it can have broad impact on the operating efficiency of all DS projects, which is especially important in large DS organizations.

A/B testing platform roadmaps

The capabilities of your *A/B testing platform* determine the velocity of innovation. An effective A/B testing platform can empower product and engineering partners to self-serve many experimentation needs. An ineffective one can become a bottleneck for feature launches. Progress on this roadmap can also involve buy-versus-build decisions and is not limited to your team's capacity.

To broaden the scope, A/B test infrastructures can support different types of experiments, such as experiments controlled by visits, users, advertisers, clusters of users in social networks, or split-budget tests for different treatments of advertising campaigns. To dive deep into a specific type of experiment, A/B test infrastructures can compute various metrics to facilitate the investigation and understanding of the experiment results. For mid- to long-term effects, A/B test infrastructures can provide hold-back monitoring as well as surrogate metrics to predict long-term benefits using short-term signals.

On-call and maintenance process roadmaps

As the DS function matures, best practices can be applied across different teams by defining processes. Processes related to on-call scheduling to maintain launched products are especially important, as maintenance obligations can build up over time.

To broaden the scope of on-call and maintenance processes, you can set up on-call processes to efficiently address ad hoc inquiries across teams and schedule model maintenance to ensure data drifts and changing product context do not hurt models' predictive performance. To dive deep into specific maintenance practices, you can create milestones to automate the monitoring of data pipelines, create anomaly alerts, and automate model configuration re-calibration procedures. Applying best practices in these processes can free up valuable DS resources to devote to more impactful new projects, while maintaining the anticipated impact from past projects.

By specifying the above strategic steps in the roadmaps, you are creating the potential for the DS function to deliver more business impact. This potential must then be prioritized by aligning with the priorities of your partners.

Those were quite a few types of roadmaps! If you are feeling a little disoriented, that's perfectly normal, and a breather may help before we align roadmaps.

ALIGNING ROADMAPS

We mentioned before that DS is a team sport. Many roadmaps require collaboration and coordination with business and engineering partners. Alignment with partners is a prerequisite to producing business impact. Specifically, alignment involves agreeing and committing to the key performance indicators, sequence, scope, and schedule of roadmap milestones.

KPIs

The *key performance indicators* (KPIs) are the definition of success. They should be necessary and sufficient for the ultimate business objectives. For example, in a recommendation system for a customer support center to improve resolution efficiency, the necessary condition is to meet a certain service level agreement (SLA) for recommendation latency. The sufficient condition is the capability to aggregate feedback in real-time to train better models. If the necessary condition is not satisfied, it will be difficult to deliver success for business partners. If a condition is sufficient but not necessary, it can be placed on the roadmap to mature at a future time.

Sequencing

Some milestones have dependencies on partners to complete certain tasks first. Other milestones require partners to work on a project with you at the same time. The order must be aligned and coordinated.

Scoping

A project may take on too much or too little scope. When a business partner is looking for a 10% boost on an already-mature model, unless there are major changes in the environment, such as new data sources becoming available, the boost expectation may be too large and unrealistic. If a project is too narrowly defined for a limited subset of the population, the scope can be too small to be worth the investment of cross-team collaboration. Even if the project is kicked off, it is likely to be deprioritized as soon as unexpected urgent issues arise.

Scheduling

Unless there are specific dates set for the expected completion date of the milestones, the roadmap is not yet aligned. Avoid vague dates, such as *tentatively this quarter* or *next quarter*. If there is no delivery date set, it will be challenging to keep the team and partners accountable for the alignment. When it is hard to determine a specific date for a milestone, writing in the last day of the quarter as the delivery date can often help contain any slippage to days or weeks rather than quarters.

TAKING RESPONSIBILITY FOR THE ULTIMATE BUSINESS RESULTS

As the roadmaps get executed, you may need to allocate additional time and resources for experimentation, iterations, handling integration risks of new components, and testing new capabilities.

When assessing whether to pursue a roadmap item, a simple question to ask yourself is: if it takes twice as long, would it still be worthwhile to do? If the answer is no, you should find roadmap milestones with a higher ROI to pursue.

As for Stephen from chapter 1, who is a well-respected director troubled by the dropping morale of the DS team, the ability to craft clear roadmaps described here can help. With clear roadmaps, Stephen can better communicate the innovation paths as well as the paths to pay off tech debt with his team. He can also better coordinate with partners to prioritize project milestones. This can boost team morale and help reduce future regrettable attritions.

6.1.2 Guiding the DS function to build the right features for the right people at the right time

A key responsibility of a DS director or a principal data scientist is to quantitatively guide the organization to build the right features for the right people at the right time. It involves validating product hypotheses using A/B tests and adapting project directions and prioritizing roadmap milestones based on the learning.

BUILDING THE RIGHT FEATURES

You may already know that A/B tests are controlled experiments where multiple versions of a feature are implemented and deployed to different randomized cohorts at the same time. Cohorts are controlled, such that the only difference between them is the specific feature under test. User response for the test cohort can be measured to infer the business impact when a feature is launched to all users.

The validation process assumes a null hypothesis that there is no difference between the different cohorts under test and collects evidence to reject the null hypothesis. This approach avoids confirmation biases, as discussed in section 3.2.1.

For example, your product partner may have a product hypothesis for email campaigns that inserting a user's first name in the subject line could increase the email open rate and improve response to the campaign. A controlled A/B test would select two disjointed, randomly selected cohorts for the series of email campaigns, where the only difference between the control and the treatment is the subject line.

When we observe the results of the campaign, we see a statistically significant increase in open rate compared to the control. We can then reject the null hypothesis and confirm the product hypothesis for the increase in open rate.

At the same time, we also observe a drop in response rate for users who have opened the emails. Some drop is expected when the open rate goes up, as the more engaging subject line can attract less-motivated users to open their emails, reducing the average response rate. In this case, we find no statistically significant increase in response rate per email sent across the treatment and control. Although the subject-line test was able to increase the open rate, it was not able to increase the response rate per email sent. By rigorously collecting and assessing evidence to validate product hypotheses, you can ensure that the team is building the right features.

BUILDING THE RIGHT FEATURES FOR THE RIGHT PEOPLE

Careful assessment of A/B test results can also help us identify whether we are building them *for the right people*. This can be accomplished by running experiments *globally*, across all users, and analyzing the results *locally*, over specific segments, to dissect whether there are specific cohorts of users a feature would be most beneficial for.

Continuing on the email campaign example above, we may identify cohorts of users that have different interaction frequencies with a product. By analyzing the response rate for WAU, infrequent users, and dormant users, we find that the WAU cohorts have a statistically significant improvement in response rate once the email is opened when a more personalized subject line is used. The effect is not significant in infrequent users and dormant users. Through deeper analysis of A/B test results, this observation is explained by the quality of personalization in the email content. More active users received more accurate personalization in their email content.

BUILDING THE RIGHT FEATURES AT THE RIGHT TIME

To build the right features at the right time, features should be prioritized, tested, and deployed to produce the most positive impact for customers. When past features' launches have clear documentation for A/B test results and encountered challenges, they can serve as useful references for resource estimation and project prioritization.

Reaching such maturity in product development takes time and resources. You can use the following four stages [1] to assess your current maturity levels, illustrated in figure 6.3:

1 *Crawl*—Build foundations for the practice of A/B testing, and demonstrate its feasibility.
2 *Walk*—Standardize metrics and pipelines for running experiments, and build trust.
3 *Run*—Perform A/B tests at scale, and evaluate all new features and changes.
4 *Fly*—Democratize A/B tests using tools for product and engineering.

In the crawl stage, the team can perform approximately 10 tests a year. For each increase in maturity level, the capacity can increase by four to five times, reaching around 50 tests per year at the walk level, around 250 tests per year at the run level, and over 1,000 tests per year at the fly level. Many companies, such as LinkedIn [2], have successfully built up a culture of experimentation that provides a wealth of reference cases to build the right features for the right people at the right time.

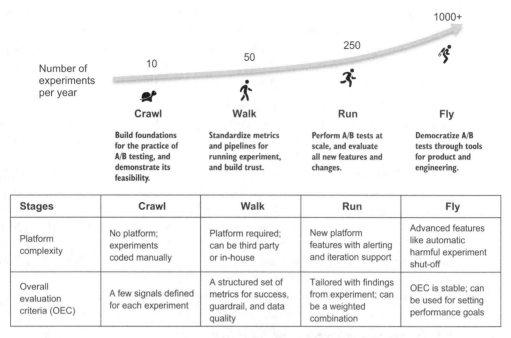

Figure 6.3   **The four stages of experiment evolution: crawl, walk, run, and fly [1]**

ARE THERE THAT MANY FEATURES TO LAUNCH AND TESTS TO RUN EACH YEAR?

Yes! Here are six dimensions where tests can lead to business impact:

- *Diversity of functions*—Each business function can have at least a couple of ongoing projects to test in a month. These functions include marketing channels/narratives, sales/growth methodologies, customer support, user experience, infrastructure performance, and in-app features.
- *Outside in*—Many tests can be developed as responses to observed customer behavior, interpretation of customer feedback, or detected competitors' actions.
- *Cross-functional brainstorming*—Some feature alternatives to test may come from collaborations with partner teams and the cross-pollination of ideas between team members with different areas of expertise, which may change user targeting, user conversion processes, and technology platforms.
- *Micro tweaks*—Tests can also come from incremental tweaks to improve the effectiveness of existing products, such as narratives, images, calls to action (CTAs), social proofs, surveys, order flows, designs, and offers.
- *Reassessing past A/B tests*—Institutional knowledge bases can be revisited and refreshed to see if past results still hold.
- *Feature ramps*—Tests may ramp and hold at different percentage levels to allow longer-term effects to be assessed.

This list can easily reach hundreds of concurrent tests, even for a company with a limited product portfolio. The bottleneck is often the maturity of the infrastructure, as you may expect, which determines the cost of running a test.

HOW CAN WE PRIORITIZE WHEN THERE ARE TOO MANY IDEAS?

Section 2.2.1 shared a framework for assessing risk, impact, confidence, and effort required for projects. Priorities are generally given to projects with high confidence, high impact, low risk, and low effort. High-risk and high-effort projects are often carefully selected such that only one or two of the highest-impact projects are undertaken at any time to maintain team focus.

You may assess that certain ideas or projects are well-aligned with the broader data strategy. These are the projects you can help champion. We discuss the best practices for championing projects in section 6.1.3.

6.1.3 Sponsoring and championing promising projects

DS projects can deliver outsized impact by executing on your DS roadmaps guided by the validated learnings from A/B test results. What else can a DS director or a principal data scientist do to guide these promising projects to success?

Many DS projects fail not because of their technical merits but because of the lack of trust in the coordination and communication between business functions, which leads to the project receiving a lack of attention and resources. Too often, as priorities change in collaborating teams, vital resources are shifted away, and projects languish.

Project failures caused by non-technical issues can hit the morale of a DS team especially hard. Remember Stephen from chapter 1 and the attrition on his team? The causes often look opaque, and the failures appear to be out of the project lead's control. Failures also create gaps in roadmaps and impede further progress toward an organization's ultimate business objectives.

As a director or a principal data scientist, you need to ensure that DS projects are sponsored and championed to minimize the risk of failure. Figure 6.4 illustrates these two roles.

Sponsor	**Champion**
A senior business leader with the authority to muster subject matter experts, headcounts, data, equipment, and funding toward a solution	A middle- to senior-level executive who is intimately familiar with the project's technical and business merit and also a business beneficiary of a successful project outcome
Responsibilities: • Articulate the project's problem statement. • Define the team's objectives. • Validate the business case in project charter. • Justify the ROI, priority, and urgency to executives. • Provide assessment and approval at launch, throughout project milestones, and to completion.	Responsibilities: • Get educated on the subject. • Create a consistent vision. • Prepare to sell the vision to others, then sell it. • Develop and maintain relationships. • Listen, ask for input, and deal with objections. • Be optimistic, hopeful, and patient!

Figure 6.4   Two essential roles for data science projects: sponsor and champion

A *sponsor* is responsible for articulating the project's problem statement, defining the team's objectives, and validating the business case in the project charter. The person is often a senior business leader with an important business objective and the authority to muster subject matter experts, headcounts, data, equipment, and funding toward a solution. They may not be aware of all the technical details, but will be responsible for evaluating whether the business objective has been achieved.

A *champion* is a mid- to senior-level executive who is intimately familiar with the project's technical and business merit and a business beneficiary of a successful project outcome. When a collaborating project partner team looks to adjust priorities and considers dropping the project, the champion must emerge as a strong advocate and negotiate with the partner team to reprioritize the project. When the project encounters stressful situations, the champion is there to encourage and inspire the team to keep moving forward.

039

A project sponsor may not be aware of all the technical details but has the authority to muster subject matter experts, headcounts, data, equipment, and funding toward a solution. The project champion is intimately familiar with a project's technical and business merit and is there to encourage and inspire the team to keep moving forward.

As a DS director, you may be the sponsor and the champion of some DS productivity projects. In most projects with goals to increase revenue or reduce cost, a sponsor is a business executive, and a champion is a product owner with profit and loss responsibilities. In some companies with simpler organizational structures, the sponsor and champion responsibilities may be held by the same business executive. When you or your team wants to work on a promising project, it is your responsibility to identify a motivated project sponsor and a committed project champion.

BEING A SPONSOR

You can be the sponsor of a project if you have the delegated authority of the CEO to execute a company-wide initiative with pools of resources and funding. Examples of DS-centric initiatives include taming transaction fraud risks in a fintech company or controlling abusive behaviors on a social gaming platform.

When working in a sponsor's role, you are responsible for articulating the project's problem statement, defining the team's objectives, and validating the business case in the project charter. It is up to you to justify the ROI, priority, and urgency of the project to the CEO, the finance department, and any other executives compared with all other projects in the company.

Your assessment and approval will be required at project launch, throughout its milestones, and to its completion. The project's success or failure will also reflect how well you can pick projects to deploy resources to with the goal of achieving the business objectives you are responsible for producing.

WORKING WITH A SPONSOR

When a DS project aims to improve the performance of a particular business line, the project sponsor is often a senior executive of the business line. You and your team are responsible for providing accurate information for articulating the project's problem statement, defining the team's objectives, and validating the business case in the project charter. When your project narrative aligns well with business needs, you will stand a better chance of identifying a motivated sponsor to provide the resources necessary to make the project successful.

BEING A CHAMPION

You can be the champion of a project if you are intimately familiar with the project's technical and business merits and are also a business beneficiary of a successful project outcome. As a director in data science, you can be a champion for projects such as data and modeling platform upgrades, and A/B testing infrastructure development and integration.

When working as a project champion, there are many areas in which you can prepare yourself for project success. Here are six top areas [3]:

- Getting educated on the subject
- Creating a consistent vision
- Preparing to sell the vision to others, then sell it
- Developing and maintaining relationships
- Listening, asking for input, and dealing with objections
- Being optimistic, hopeful, and patient

Getting educated on the subject

Being knowledgeable on a topic can generate trust with partner teams to keep the project top of mind when company priorities shift. It can also help with keeping the team members motivated and focused in stressful times.

Become knowledgeable on a topic by studying books, blogs, articles, and attending seminars and conferences. Case studies are especially helpful, as they provide experiences of real-world challenges, successes, and failures to anticipate in your project.

Creating a consistent vision

The project you are championing should be part of a broader vision for what you can do for others. A product-focused vision could be making customers' choices simple, timely, and personalized. A more technology-focused vision would be using valuable information to service individual and organizational needs. As illustrated in these examples, a vision should be concise and take no more than six to seven words to express. It should also be clear how the vision can deliver business value to others.

A consistent vision throughout the project builds identity and trust for you as the project champion. Team members can align with this vision by making detailed trade-offs in the course of your project.

Preparing to sell the vision to others and then sell it

For the project you are championing, you are responsible for preparing 30-second, 3-minute, 15-minute, and 30-minute presentations to deliver to the team and partners. The 30-second "elevator pitch" version is around 100–150 words in length and can be delivered in an elevator ride or on a walk to a meeting room. The 3-minute version is great for coffee or lunch discussions. The 15-minute and 30-minute versions are ideal for 30-minute and 60-minute meetings where you may be a part of a partner team's meeting agenda, leaving time for plenty of questions and feedback.

When delivering the vision, make sure to customize a portion of the presentation to your audience to highlight how your project can contribute to their work. Real-world examples are ideal for helping the audience make the connection. For example, if you are meeting with the growth team, describe how the project and your vision can lower customer acquisition costs, improve conversion, and simplify workflows. These business impacts can capture the attention of your audience and better align with their concerns. That said, unless explicitly delivered in the project, be careful not to set any unrealistic expectations and overpromise.

Developing and maintaining relationships

DS is a team sport. Most projects will require collaboration and coordination between multiple teams. You can work with your project sponsor to identify the right people to include in the project, acquire resources, and prioritize the project with partners for success.

The project kick-off meeting should include the project sponsor and all the partner team supervisors to formally communicate project-wide milestones. Senior executives can communicate a broader perspective on how initiatives can contribute to corporate goals. The kick-off meeting is also an opportunity for partner team supervisors to get to know each other and understand the implications of their milestones on others.

To champion the project successfully, it is important to catch emerging situations early. Set up one-on-one meetings with team members and partner team supervisors to get to know them on a personal level. When you notice prioritization shifts or delays happening, discuss and resolve them in a timely manner, as unresolved issues can ruin your relationships. When you see positive behaviors, call them out by formally thanking your partners personally via email. With their permission, you can also share with their supervisor.

One way to keep your project top of mind for partners is to regularly pitch the project. By using the 30-second version during a 5-minute conversation or the 3-minute version during a 30-minute lunch, you can nudge partners to stay focused on their milestones for your project without overwhelming the conversations with relationship building.

Listening, asking for input, and dealing with objections

If a partner agreed to meet about your project and listen to your presentation, that's great! It then becomes the time to listen and learn. You can grow your relationship by listening in an attempt to understand your partner's perspective. This includes how they feel and react and the key points that they are making.

If your partner asks questions, that's a sign that there is an active effort to deepen their understanding. Make sure you understand the questions, so you can answer openly and honestly.

If your partner rejects the idea and refuses to discuss the reasons, don't fight it. Smile and thank them for their time. This happens from time to time. It is best to leave on a good note and circle back another time. You can document the meeting and work with your manager on other routes to get alignments.

Being optimistic, hopeful, and patient

As a project champion, nobody will be more enthusiastic about the project than you are. The project partners rely on you to make sure nobody drops out of the project prematurely. The team members rely on you to motivate them when the project gets tough.

You may run into negative people with negative comments. Focus on the positive partnerships, and be patient in bringing people in the negative partnerships around over time. Be optimistic, hopeful, and patient when working through organizational or technical roadblocks. This is key to maintaining the energy you need to see the project through.

As a project champion, you are also responsible for ensuring that the project wins are articulated; communicating with all team members, project partners, the project sponsor, and their boss; and thanking each of them for their support in making the project happen. This can help you to receive sponsorship and support for future projects.

WORKING WITH A CHAMPION

For most projects where the main beneficiary is not DS but a business line, the champion for the DS project is a product person with profit and loss responsibilities in the business line. As a DS director or a principal data scientist, your role is to provide the necessary background technical information and business insights to the business line product champion to formulate the elevator pitch and presentations. You can also recommend roadmaps and alternatives to help your business line champion create and sell a compelling vision.

Shadowing the business line champion in some meetings can help get a first-hand feel for partner input and objections related to the project. When priorities shift, you can support the project champion by providing alternative scopes and paths to negotiate with project partners to adjust or reprioritize toward reaching the ultimate business objective.

ESSENTIAL ROLES FOR DS PROJECTS

Executive sponsors and champions are essential for a promising DS project to gain traction on the organization's roadmaps. A sponsor is responsible for validating the business case and mustering resources toward a solution. A champion is the top advocate of a project who is intimately familiar with the project's technical and business merit and is also a business beneficiary of a successful project outcome.

As the director, you can be a sponsor for DS-centric projects and the champion for DS infrastructure projects. Most of the time, you will be making sure your team identifies a sponsor and a champion for their project and that your team is supporting the project sponsors and champions to ensure DS project success. In Stephen's case, he can work to identify strong sponsors and champions for his projects, which can provide confidence for his team to get out of the vicious cycle of attrition, low morale, and other breakdowns.

6.2   *Execution: Best practices*

The execution challenges at the function level are most often related to delivering business objectives consistently—quarter after quarter, year after year. The solution involves building a DS function with strong teams, nimble and consistent processes, and robust platforms. With a successful and productive function behind you, you can focus on working with other function directors to support the executive-level initiatives.

This section discusses three aspects of function-level execution capabilities for the DS function:

- Delivering consistently by managing people, processes, and platforms
- Building a strong function with clear career paths and a robust hiring process
- Supporting executives in executing top company initiatives

Consistency in delivering DS results is challenging because successful DS projects often require collaboration with many partners. Priorities across partners must be aligned to deliver results. Many DS processes are unfamiliar for partners in different business lines and business functions, and the platforms required for doing efficient DS in most companies are often a work in progress. Unanticipated breakdowns and a lack of processes or platforms can cause unexpected project delays or failures. Section 6.2.1 shares best practices for working with people, processes, and platforms to consistently deliver results in both early-stage startups and mature companies.

Data scientists come from a diverse range of backgrounds and are challenging to hire and retain. Section 6.2.2 discusses two techniques to allow initiatives to be staffed more nimbly. One is to grow existing team members to take on more responsibilities by establishing and coaching them through clear DS career paths. A crystallized set of roles and responsibilities for team members at various levels can motivate them by providing specific developmental areas to stay focused on during career growth in your organization. The other technique is to build a robust and standardized hiring pipeline that can provide a continuous stream of candidates. Both techniques aim to staff the projects on your roadmaps faster and allow you to reach business objectives more quickly.

As a director, your main responsibility is to collaborate with your peer directors to support executive-level initiatives. As a principal data scientist, your main responsibility is to drive function-level initiatives. Section 6.2.3 introduces the first team concept to prioritize collaboration in delivering for your executive's initiatives, discusses the process of managing up to your executive, and maintains skip-level conversations to understand the intentions of your boss's boss.

6.2.1 *Delivering consistently by managing people, processes, and platforms*

As a DS director or principal data scientist, your success is demonstrated by your function's capability to deliver consistent results. Consistently delivering quarterly and annual objectives can be challenging, especially when you are immersed in trust building and relationship management within your teams and with various partners. As a director, when you are layers removed from the detailed technical decisions and business situations, you must be even more sensitive to pathological symptoms, such as team member attritions, project delays, and the occurrence of incidents, and diagnose the root cause of team issues.

While you can respond when team members quit, projects fail, or incidents occur, proactively detecting issues is essential to avert failures early. Let's look at the challenges through three lenses:

- People management
- Process management
- Platform management

PEOPLE MANAGEMENT

At the director level, it may be tempting to empower your manager to do their job and only step in if there are problems. While this is the eventual goal, empowerment of the team must be balanced with your responsibility for the company's bottom line and diagnosing and intervening to avert project failures early. Figure 6.5 illustrates techniques to manage people-related challenges to deliver results consistently.

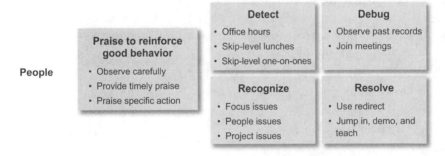

Figure 6.5 Five sets of techniques to manage people-related challenges to deliver results consistently

Section 5.3.2 explained how you can strike this balance by setting goals with your DS managers to align on the results and avoid micromanagement. It involves spending time with them at the beginning of a new project or a new set of responsibilities to clarify expectations, provide praise for what was done right, and deliver redirection to correct mistakes.

To praise what was done right, you can observe your team's actions and notice those indicative of thoughtfully taking on responsibilities and producing positive results. By taking care to praise the actions aligned with your vision for the DS organization, you can positively reinforce your vision and improve culture.

040

> To praise what was done right, you can observe your team's actions and notice those indicative of thoughtfully taking on responsibilities and producing positive results. By taking care to praise the actions aligned with your vision for the data science organization, you can positively reinforce your vision and improve culture.

One point worth noting is that when you thank a person for their positive contributions, it is important to focus on the action and not the person. Use phrases such as:

- "This project was done well because . . ." not "They were great on this project . . ."
- "This issue was handled beautifully because . . ." not "They were awesome in . . ."
- "This action set a good example . . ." not "They are role models for others to follow . . ."

When you praise the person, it can leave them vulnerable to self-doubt when they encounter difficulties later. For the rest of the team, if being successful sounds like an innate ability of some superstar team members, it's easy to lose motivation and stop trying.

Giving specific praise for the positive actions and approaches, such as careful planning, persistence in efforts, or a collaborative attitude, clarifies the processes others can follow to succeed. This book provides you with many narratives for specific praises you can use to describe positive actions.

To detect issues early and provide feedback for the DS managers in your team, in addition to your normal one-on-ones with your direct reports, you have the following three techniques at your disposal for broader visibilities into the function. Each has its own advantages and disadvantages:

- Office hours and an open-door policy
- Skip-level lunch
- Skip-level one-on-ones

Office hours and an open-door policy

This is the most scalable technique for collecting feedback from your team. It involves allocating time each week for anyone to schedule time with you to discuss their concerns one on one. While this approach sounds reasonable in principle, it makes three strong assumptions:

- Your team members can recognize emerging problems to describe them well.
- Your team members are brave enough to skip their managers to report a problem.
- Managers in your team are not preventing problems from getting escalated to you.

Because of these assumptions, you may miss many issues in their early stages because they are not escalated to you. Office hours can be one of the many techniques you use. But if it is the only technique you use, many issues can fester and explode later with symptoms such as team churn, project delays, and initiative failures.

Skip-level lunch

This technique is somewhat scalable. You can have a monthly lunch with skip-level team members to understand how the teams are doing. If three to five managers are reporting to you, you can reserve one lunch a week for this purpose. There are four techniques to consider for skip-level lunches to be successful:

- *Skip-level*—The team members' manager must not be present at the lunch.
- *Scheduling regularly*—Holding one doesn't generate the perception that something is wrong for your DS managers or their team.
- *Focusing on the positive*—Most people are not comfortable complaining about their managers in front of peers or their manager's manager.
- *Focusing on how you can help*—Whether it is explaining high-level company objectives, resolving partner collaboration challenges, or simplifying cumbersome processes or areas where more efficient tooling can improve team productivity, there are places where only your level of influence can make the team more successful.

An important function of team lunch is discovering places where projects are going well. You can highlight these successes across the broader team and help spread the best practices across the organization. This technique is similar to the "catching someone doing something right" management approach shared in section 5.3.2. Here are some specific questions [4] you can use in your skip-level meetings:

- What do you like best/worst about the project you are working on?
- Who on your team has been doing really well recently?
- What change do you think we could make to the product?
- Are there any opportunities you think we might be missing?
- How do you think the organization is doing overall? Is there anything we could change?
- Are there areas of the business strategy you don't understand?
- What's keeping you from doing your best work right now?
- How happy (or not) are you working at the company?
- What could we do to make working at the company more fun?

The focus on opportunities and potential can make the lunch more enjoyable. The discussions can shed light on gaps in communication, coordination, or execution that you can address immediately or choose to dive deeper into during skip-level one-on-ones. You can also look for signs of potential issues when people don't attend or when a usually vocal team member is quiet. These can be indications that there are topics team members may be more comfortable sharing on a one-on-one basis.

Skip-level one-on-ones

Through your skip-level lunch and other skip-level communications, you can identify topics and team members for one-on-ones. In a more intimate one-on-one setting, some more reserved or modest team members may feel more comfortable sharing their accomplishments, and other team members may open up better to discuss what's troubling them.

In these skip-level one-on-ones settings, you may be able to address the more intimate questions, such as:

- What do you like best/worst about your projects?
- Do you have any feedback about your manager or your project partners?
- How happy (or not) are you working at the company?
- How do you think the organization is doing overall? Is there anything we could change?
- Is there anything that may be keeping you from doing your best work right now?

Regarding skip-level feedback on their manager, it is vital to set the context that you are looking for their help to better develop their manager's career, who is also your direct report. It is a responsibility you have for your direct reports. Everyone has blind spots, and anything that can help their manager grow is appreciated.

Skip-level one-on-ones can be useful for diagnosing issues, but they are expensive in terms of time commitment. Even for a modest team of 30 people, holding one a day would take six weeks for one round. It is best to keep these on an ad hoc basis, so you can vary the frequency of skip-level one-on-ones based on changing needs.

RECOGNIZING, DEBUGGING, AND RESOLVING DYSFUNCTIONS OF THE ORGANIZATION

Office hours, skip-level lunch, and skip-level one-on-ones are the first steps in identifying organizational dysfunctions early. The symptoms you discover are often just fragments of situations shared from different perspectives. This requires you to form hypotheses about what could be wrong and collect information to validate or invalidate those hypotheses.

041

As a data science director, the symptoms of organizational dysfunctions you discover are often just fragments of situations shared from different perspectives. Diagnosing the situations require you to form hypotheses about what could be wrong and collect information to validate or invalidate those hypotheses.

Recognizing

The following is a list of common dysfunctions to help recognize and diagnose:

- Focus
  - A project had a scope reduction to meet the launch timeline about which the team did not feel good. Did the scope reduction involve features, technical quality, or both? Why are team members concerned? How was it decided and communicated?

- Team members are confused about how decisions are delegated. Is there a process for assigning decision-making responsibilities? How was it communicated?
- Team members are not clear about when projects are done. Is it done at code complete? The start of A/B testing? How were the responsibilities communicated?
- Team members are confused about why they are chosen to work on their project. How were the goals, roles, and responsibilities communicated?

- People
  - Rising members of the team are doing great work but feel neglected. Are there plans to coach them to take on leadership roles? Have plans been communicated?
  - Junior members feel overwhelmed. Has a project of too large a scope been delegated to a team member who was not ready for it?
  - A couple of team members were causing a lot of negativity on the team. How can you resolve the issue and communicate it?
  - Team meetings have not been very useful. Are company-wide initiatives shared? Have pass-down, partner initiatives, and team highlights been shared with the team?

- Project
  - A project is not getting the necessary support to be successful. Does the project champion lack domain knowledge or organizational level authority? Will we need to reconstitute the project with a new project champion?
  - A project is no longer a top priority for the business area. Has the focus of the company changed? Should we reprioritize, delay, or defer the project?
  - Team members are not getting the necessary milestone feedback, and partners are confused or surprised. Has there been a lack of follow-up with stakeholders for the project? Would reengaging partners with regular communication cadence help?
  - Team members are unclear about what is good enough, and the goal is not aligned between team members, their manager, and their partners. Is there a lack of concrete metrics for success? Were the available success metrics clearly communicated?

These team dysfunctions can help you form hypotheses about the root cause of your execution or performance issues. You still need to validate your hypotheses and debug them.

Debugging

Investigating potential team execution issues can be a data-informed process. You can either observe past records or observe team dynamics. Observing past records can be done without much team coordination overhead. This includes looking at past sprint completion records, incident reports, email threads, shared chat channels, project or code review comments, and vacation or sick day records.

From time to time, past records don't show any significant issues. You may need to join some team meetings to observe whether the team understands what their goals are. Are meetings effective? Are people enthusiastic about discussions? Do people like each other? Is there tension in relationships that needs to be resolved? There are significant advantages to being able to diagnose the issue firsthand. However, keep in mind that your presence may change the team's behavior. You may not be able to see the issues that are present when you are not there.

Resolving

The issues validated may be a blind spot for the DS manager in your team. Ultimately, it is the DS managers' responsibility to improve the output of their teams. A redirect that first points out the mistake, then reaffirms your trust in them may be enough. This is described in detail in section 5.3.2.

In some instances, when the issue involves a skills gap, you may need to jump in and help solve the issue. Make sure to explain to the struggling managers what was done. It can help them better navigate similar situations next time.

PROCESS MANAGEMENT

Processes are the best practices that can be transferred from person to person, team to team, and organization to organization. When observing the actions of your team and partner teams, you may notice positive and negative outcomes being generated through people's existing practices to reinforce or reconstitute. Managing processes involves executing and delegating existing processes and driving process changes. Figure 6.6 illustrates three techniques for delivering consistent results.

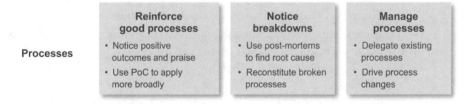

Figure 6.6   Three approaches for managing processes to deliver consistent results

Reinforcing good processes

As director or principal data scientist, you may notice positive, transferable practices that, when followed, can consistently produce good results. You can develop a process around these practices for ease of adoption, then designate champions to propagate them throughout the organization.

Best practices can be found in many areas of DS. Section 2.2.2 described nine common types of DS projects with opportunities to discover best practices in each:

- *Tracking specification definition and implementation*—Identify champions in engineering to drive tracking as an integral part of feature development to ensure the effectiveness of features will be accurately measurable at first launch.

- *Monitoring and rollout*—Features are ramped from less than 1% of the user base to all users through phases. The rollout is monitored, and all partner teams work proactively with DS to balance speed, quality, and risk factors in rollout [5].
- *Metrics definition and dashboarding*—Coordinate with business partners on metrics definitions that align with business objectives to evaluate feature trade-offs, especially when the objective function involves surrogate metrics that use short-term signals to predict long-term behavior.
- *Data insights and deep dives*—Deep dives involve gaining a deep understanding of the current product landscape, discovering gaps in features, and advising on establishing new feature roadmaps (see section 2.3.3).
- *Modeling and API development*—Best practices are abundant in feature engineering, model roadmap development, and expectation setting for partners. Examples include mapping scenarios to known optimization techniques (see section 2.1.1), vigilance in discovering patterns in data (see section 2.1.2), and evaluating the success of a solution (see section 2.1.3).
- *Data enrichment*—Choosing and implementing first-party and third-party data that can unveil new opportunities has many best practices related to discovery, evaluation, ROI estimation, deployment, and value realization. Being effective means enabling delightful user experiences without triggering reservations about data privacy.
- *Data consistency*—Best practices involve aligning on a standard metric definition and implementing the standard across business lines, so organization-wide resources can be more efficiently allocated.
- *Infrastructure improvements*—A clear infrastructure improvement adoption playbook can help manage partner expectations and maintain partner relationships in the always-difficult conversations to deploy infrastructure change.
- *Regulatory items*—Best practices involve complying with laws and regulations in your specific industry to reduce non-compliance risks.

When introducing new best practices to the team, one good approach is to use proof of concept projects to validate how well they work within your organization. Many external best practices have to be tweaked to best fit a particular team's needs.

Noticing breakdowns

When you notice breakdowns in projects and initiatives, going through the rigorous post-mortem process described in sections 3.3.2 and 5.2.2 can uncover the root causes and craft mitigation roadmaps to fundamentally address them. To summarize, a rigorous post-mortem includes producing a document with an incident summary, a detailed incident timeline, a root cause analysis using the five-whys methodology, resolution and recovery, and actions to mitigate future risks. This is the iterative nature of process improvements, such that the conditions for breakdowns are eliminated or mitigated.

In nascent organizations, processes may not yet have been defined. In more mature organizations, breakdowns may happen because existing processes are not followed. As a director or a principal data scientist, you have the responsibility and authority to define new processes or examine the root cause of why an existing process was not followed. Did the environment change, such that the existing process no longer made sense? Were there personnel changes on the team, such that the roles and responsibilities for enforcing the process were no longer clear? Based on your assessment, you may need to reconstitute the process or find new process champions to take responsibility for process execution.

Managing processes

There are eight steps in constituting and executing a process. While you don't have to complete each one yourself, you do need to coach your delegate on each step, so the processes can successfully deliver consistent results for your function:

1. *Identifying stakeholders*—These are the team members, partners, and executives involved to constitute the definition of success and the path to success for the process. Stakeholders for a process can take on different roles:
   - *Performer*—The team members who will be executing the process.
   - *Champion*—The person who will train and coach the performers, defend the process when making execution trade-offs, and document the process.
   - *Consultant*—The domain experts who advise on improvements of processes over time.
   - *Executive*—The person who evaluates the success of the process.
   - *Informed*—Team members, executives, partners, managers, and anybody who may be affected by the process. For smaller organizations, one person can take on multiple roles. An executive can also champion a process at the beginning, then delegate the champion role later on.

2. *Clarifying the current situation and breakdowns*—This clarifies the opportunity cost of not having a process, as sometimes illustrated by the output gap of teams with the process versus the teams without. The opportunity is to close the gap.

3. *Describe the proposed new process*—This is the step-by-step proposal of what the new process involves with clear definitions of the roles and responsibilities.

4. *Crafting the details and metrics of success with partner inputs*—Partner perspectives, preferences, and constraints are essential to design and craft into the process for ongoing success in execution, especially when steps in the process require commitments on timely responses or a sign-off from a partner team.

5. *Evangelizing the process with roadshows*—With buy-in from executors and executives, the process champion must inform all teams involved in the new process. This can be done via presentations in partner team meetings to evangelize the importance of following the process and galvanize support to execute the process.

6. *Championing the process change to get resources allocated*—With support from executives and team leaders, gain the resources for executing the process.

7 *Following the process and debugging compliance issues*—The champion has the responsibility to defend the process when execution trade-offs are being made, detect compliance challenges, observe team dynamics, anticipate potential breakdowns, and do whatever possible to keep the process in place.

8 *Communicating early wins and ongoing successes*—Communicate every win broadly to gather momentum for more teams to benefit from the process.

When your organization is growing rapidly, it is important for onboarding material to include existing processes and the reasons they were developed. When you have big wins from your processes, you can conduct roadshows to share your processes and establish an identity for yourself, preparing support for any future process improvement proposals.

To successfully drive process changes, you can promptly communicate the changes with clarity and authority. One powerful way is to start with one-on-one communication, coordinate a plan of record, announce the aligned plan of record, and solicit any questions or comments before moving forward. These steps are described in detail in section 3.1.2.

PLATFORM MANAGEMENT

To further democratize best practices or processes from your best people, you can build platforms to automate the processes, so more team members can effectively, consistently, and predictably produce quality results. Figure 6.7 illustrates two aspects of platform management, operationalizing best practices, and democratizing access to tools.

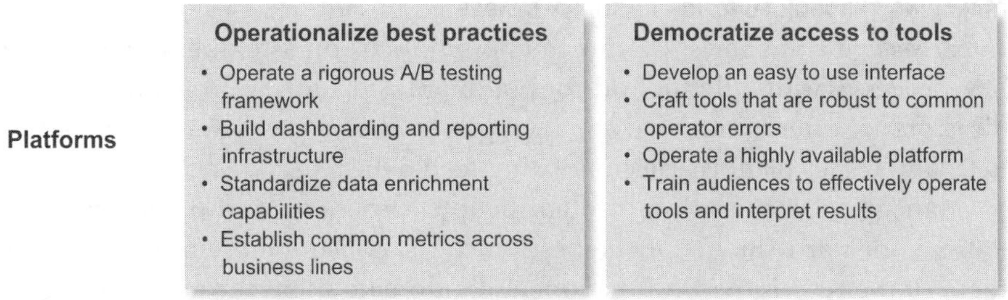

Platforms

Operationalize best practices
- Operate a rigorous A/B testing framework
- Build dashboarding and reporting infrastructure
- Standardize data enrichment capabilities
- Establish common metrics across business lines

Democratize access to tools
- Develop an easy to use interface
- Craft tools that are robust to common operator errors
- Operate a highly available platform
- Train audiences to effectively operate tools and interpret results

Figure 6.7 Two aspects of platform management to deliver results consistently

Best practices can be operationalized through four platforms highlighted in section 4.1.2. These are platforms that can allow DS functions to produce high-quality models and analyses consistently. They are:

- An A/B testing framework
- A dashboarding and reporting infrastructure
- Data enrichment capabilities
- Common metrics workflows

Successful platforms democratize best practices to be accessible by not just data scientists but also analysts, engineers, product managers, and executives. With a diverse audience, the platforms must be easy to use, robust against common operator errors, and highly available. Training needs to be tailored to the tool's audience segments to operate the platform properly and interpret the output correctly. Successes in deploying platforms include the popularity of third-party analytics platforms such as Tableau and Looker, third-party A/B testing platforms such as Optimizely and GrowingIO, and open source metrics workflow management platforms such as Airflow and Azkaban.

Platforms can also be built in-house. At Acorns, a neo-bank in the United States looking to serve everyday Americans by helping them build financial resilience, we had developed an interactive system in the app's news feed to effectively nudge customers to save more toward a better financial future. Highly personalized messages based on sound behavioral economic principles are created based on users' specific spending patterns to engage them on their own path to savings opportunities. Highly targeted messages are effective but have narrow reach, while less-targeted messages have broader reach but are often less effective. The challenge is to experiment with nudges that are the most engaging and cost-effective to maintain.

A nudge messaging platform was built to enable hundreds of variants to be developed, launched, and tested every year. The efficiency of the platform amortized the cost of launching any specific nudge and enabled highly targeted nudges to small audiences to be viable. This produced a portfolio of effective nudges that improved customer retention and avoided spamming most users with non-relevant nudges.

MANAGING THROUGH FUNCTION MATURITY STAGES

In early-stage companies, DS directors often focus on assembling the team, defining new processes with little support for building DS platforms. In mature companies, DS directors are often concerned about employee churn, processes being stale and out of date, and legacy platforms accumulating tech debts.

Managing DS execution through people, processes, and platforms allows you to notice your star team members' best practices, constitute them into processes, teach them to the rest of the DS function, and automate them through platforms to make them available to partners. This way, today's best outcome becomes tomorrow's standard for success. When managed successfully, these practices can shift company culture and allow the DS function to more consistently deliver quarterly and annual objectives for the organization.

042

Managing data science execution through people, processes, and platforms allows you to notice your star team members' best practices, constitute them into processes, teach them to the rest of the function, and automate them through platforms for partners. This way, today's best outcome becomes tomorrow's standard for success.

6.2.2 *Building a strong function with clear career maps and a robust hiring process*

Building a strong DS function is a primary responsibility of a DS director. Yet team development and talent acquisition are often mentioned as a side note in many quarterly plans and annual goals. There are two main challenges when building a strong DS function:

- Many DS team members have worked only in small teams in small organizations. Without exposure to complex organizational maneuvers, it is hard for them to develop the sensitivities to appreciate the skills required to take on senior leadership roles.
- Hiring is often an extra burden for DS team members. When they are tapped to interview candidates, the time for pre-interview preparation, conducting interviews, and post-interview sync-up is often not accounted for in sprint planning. It is not surprising that interviews at many companies feel disorganized.

We can address these two challenges with two sets of tools:

- To develop the careers of team members in DS, a clear set of opportunities, responsibilities, and success evaluation metrics is required. This book is structured in a way to help you clarify the career maps for your DS team members.
- To acquire the best DS talent, specific projects for talent acquisition can be constituted in your execution plan with time and resources allocated for clarifying hiring goals, sourcing candidates, training interviewers before the interview, providing guidelines for the interview, and conducting the post-interview discussion free of personal biases. These are all parts of a standardized interview process for DS.

DEVELOPING AND IMPLEMENTING A DS CAREER MAP

This book is dedicated to the career maps of data scientists. As a DS director, you can use a career map as a reference for your own career path. You can also use it to coach your team members to self-assess and self-improve their capabilities and virtues to perform at the tech lead, manager, and director level. While many career maps describe the minimum standards each data scientist should meet to be promoted, this book explains the aspirational goals for a data scientist to perform at their desired level of leadership.

Great leaders are not perfect data scientists. They leverage their team to compensate for their personal weak areas. In the end, it is the output of their team that speaks for the effectiveness of a leader.

043

Great leaders are not perfect data scientists. They leverage their team to compensate for their personal weak areas. In the end, it is the output of their team that speaks for the effectiveness of a leader.

To inspire your team members to become the best data scientists they can be, you can build and implement DS career maps that are most relevant to your organization by following the six steps illustrated in figure 6.8. Let's look at the six steps one by one.

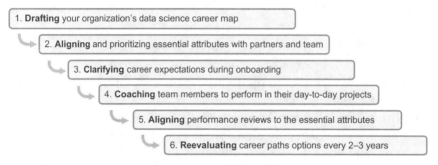

1. **Drafting** your organization's data science career map

2. **Aligning** and prioritizing essential attributes with partners and team

3. **Clarifying** career expectations during onboarding

4. **Coaching** team members to perform in their day-to-day projects

5. **Aligning** performance reviews to the essential attributes

6. **Reevaluating** career paths options every 2–3 years

Figure 6.8   The six steps of implementing a career map

Step 1: Drafting your organization's data science career map

The purpose of drafting a baseline career map is to clarify your priorities in building a function with the culture you see fit for the broader organization. It must be cohesive with the vision of the engineering, product, and operations culture in your particular industry. In a traditional industry, the DS function may be focused on optimizing existing processes or pioneering an experimentation culture. In a fast and continuously pivoting new industry, DS may be a force of stability in specifying and driving a synchronizing metric for the organization to make continued and focused progress.

The concepts introduced in this book provide a foundation for selecting the essential areas that match your organization's maturity. Each organization will require a set of essential attributes a leader must excel in and other optional, nice-to-have attributes. Smaller companies may emphasize ownership and autonomy in recognizing and solving issues that arise. Larger companies may emphasize working with clear roles and responsibilities and practicing influence on partner organizations' priorities. You have completed this step when you have clarity on the function's vision and the roles and responsibilities you would like to emphasize in your DS career map.

Step 2: Aligning and prioritizing essential attributes with partners and the team

The purpose of this step is to provide a voice for your partners and data scientists in what constitutes good performance at various levels of responsibility. You may need to seed the discussions and ask questions about what the team has seen as good practices in their previous and current roles. It's your responsibility to take these inputs and synthesize them into a coherent narrative for the DS career map. When you have provided partners and your team voices in clarifying their career milestones, they are more likely to align and own the paths for advancing to the next stages of their career.

Step 3: Clarifying career expectations during onboarding

As you grow your team, it is important to share the team's expectations with each new member. The milestones are intended to be stepping stones and not tripping stones.

They suggest opportunities to learn, practice, and demonstrate how to be more effective leaders.

Clarifying career expectations during onboarding can help new team members quickly ramp up through the maze of capability accumulation and desirable virtue formation in their new roles. They can move faster toward performing the best work of their careers in your team. Onboarding is discussed in more detail in section 10.3.5.

Step 4: Coaching team members to perform in their day-to-day projects

Nobody's perfect. When each new team member can assess their own strengths and gaps with the expectations at each level of leadership in mind, you can aid them in identifying sources of help in the organization.

Improving all areas in the career map can be overwhelming. What often works well is to pick two to three key essential attributes to focus on per quarter to learn, practice, and demonstrate the ability to perform at a specific level of leadership. You can delegate projects to team members to practice these attributes and coach them through the projects.

When you have succeeded in this coaching practice, your team members will be able to accumulate accomplishments over one to three years that clearly demonstrate their increased leadership abilities, so they can advance to the next stage of their career.

Step 5: Aligning performance reviews to the essential attributes

As you coach your team members, it is your responsibility to align their personal career development goals with their contributions to company initiatives through the projects they work on. This way, performance reviews can be synchronized with milestones in their career paths.

This alignment is not as challenging as some might think. For example, if you coach a team member on their rigor at the tech lead level, spearheading a practice to write simple invariant checks when launching a new data processing pipeline will do. These activities can be attached to one of many DS projects that require metrics or features to be calculated, and the learning can be documented and shared across multiple teams. When successful, such projects are great demonstrations of leadership that the team member can build on for the next stage of their career.

Step 6: Reevaluating every two to three years according to company maturity and needs

The function of data scientists and the industries they serve often move too fast for any specific set of career map milestones to stay constant for long. At the same time, the general areas of capabilities (i.e., technology, execution, and expert knowledge) and virtues (i.e., ethics, rigor, and attitude) tend to stay consistent and can withstand the test of time. You likely need to come back to this book and reevaluate the specific milestones for your DS career map every two to three years.

If your career map milestones become stale, they can become hurdles for high-performing star players to advance their careers in your organization. With the significant competition for DS leadership talent in the marketplace, you will run the risk of the regrettable attrition of star team members when they find more relevant career development paths elsewhere.

When you reevaluate the career map, make sure team members who are already close to achieving their promotions within the existing career map are not affected. You can quickly lose trust if you change evaluation criteria while a star team member is working toward their next career milestone.

With the above six steps as the life cycle of a DS career map, you can establish a clear path for data scientists in your organization to develop their capabilities and virtues over years of service in your organization.

BUILDING A ROBUST DS HIRING PROCESS

Talent acquisition management is one of the most important responsibilities for a function director. You are the subject matter expert for the function. Executives and team members look to you to set the bar for whom to invite to join the team.

DS talent acquisition is hard. Table 6.1 illustrates a typical candidate funnel in DS. A typical hiring goal of three data scientists in one quarter can take up to 270 hours to complete. This process takes around 0.5 headcounts of work across various functions involved, which is a significant use of resources.

Table 6.1   A talent acquisition funnel sample with a velocity of three hires a quarter

Talent acquisition funnel	# of candidates	Hours/candidate	Total hours	Stakeholders
1. Constituting project	—	—	3	Hiring manager
2. Defining hiring criteria	3	3	9	Hiring manager
3. Sourcing candidates	100–150	1/3	50	HR => scale
4. Conducting screening interview	30–50	1	50	DS team => scale
5. Conducting technical interview	15–20	5	100	DS team => scale
6. Conducting partner/executive interview	8–10	5	50	Partners => scale
7. Making offers	6	2	12	HR/hiring manager
8. Receiving an offer acceptance	3	2	6	Hiring manager
Total			**270**	

For a growth velocity of three data scientists in a quarter, you should expect to do three to four phone screens per week, one to two technical interviews per week, and one partner/executive interview per week to reach the hiring goal. Too often, we speak about the importance of building a high-quality team without aligning the team, partner, and executive expectations on the time commitments necessary to make that happen.

044

Too often, we speak about the importance of building a high-quality team without aligning expectations among the teams, partners, and executives on the time commitments necessary to make that happen.

Large companies have figured this out quite well. Function leaders can craft a standardized hiring process across their teams. The goal here is not to strip the manager of their hiring decisions and responsibilities but to free them from the details of the earlier hiring stages, so they can focus on making the most strategic hiring decisions at the end of the funnel.

Let's walk through each stage in the talent acquisition funnel and discuss how the most resource-intensive stages can scale when you are planning to hire more than one data scientist per month:

1   *Constituting a talent acquisition project*—To commit to specific hiring goals within a particular time window, you should constitute a hiring plan and communicate it with the stakeholders on your expectations for their commitment. For example, if you are looking to have a product partner in your interview panel, arrange for a cohort of two to three product managers you can reach out to for scheduling specific interviews every week. This planning process can also highlight the need to train multiple team members to handle the velocity of three to four screening interviews per week.

2   *Defining hiring criteria*—You should carefully craft the hiring criteria for each open headcount according to the current project needs and the essential areas established for a data scientist to succeed in your organization. Every candidate has a stronger and weaker set of capabilities and virtues. A good fit for a role will not compromise on the essential areas and will not unnecessarily require other areas to be as strong. Looking for the perfect candidate can often result in failing to hire good candidates quickly enough to accomplish the DS function's execution goals.

3   *Sourcing candidates*—This is the top of your candidate funnel, and actions here determine the quality of the pool of candidates you get to work with down the funnel. There are two types of candidates you can attract: active candidates and passive candidates.

Active candidates are candidates who are actively seeking new employment over your time window for an open position. With data scientists' tenure averaging around two years and hiring windows around one and a half months in normal market conditions, you will only be looking at around 1/12th of the total DS talent pool in your area. They can be reached with job postings on various job boards and job search websites. If you require candidates to be local, you will be constrained in the pool of candidates available in your geographic area.

Passive candidates are qualified candidates who are not actively interviewing for new positions. You can find their profiles on LinkedIn and reach out to see if they are open to new opportunities. When you contact passive candidates, the response rate may be low, as these candidates are less likely to move. Efficiency in this process is key to make it worthwhile. Between active and passive candidates, depending on the quality of hire and strength of the company's talent brand, you may need to identify 30–50 candidates at the sourcing stage to result in one hire.

One technique to scale this process is to organize data scientists and partners to mine their professional network for referrals. Assuming the organization has been careful in selecting its initial employees, the professional network of existing data scientists and partners from school, prior companies, and volunteer organizations, as well as their second-degree connections, are all potential candidates. Some teams even organize competitions with prizes to the team that refers to the most candidates (per member) who can pass the screening interview.

Candidates introduced through referrals generally have the best conversion rates into employees. Mining people's professional networks can significantly scale the sourcing process for your talent sourcing partners.

4 *Conducting screening interviews*—Depending on your talent brand and the candidate pool you can generate, screening interviews can take on one of two flavors: qualifying or selling. When you are in a well-known company with a strong talent brand or are a well-known DS leader in the industry, you can generate much interest in the positions you would like to fill. Requesting candidates to complete a set of case studies can help prioritize who to invite back for later rounds of interviews. These types of case studies usually involve a set of analysis or modeling tasks that should take no more than 3–8 hours, and candidates are asked to complete them at home over three to seven days.

When your talent brand is not as strong, requesting a take-home case study at the beginning may dissuade potentially strong candidates. The screening interview should be used to sell the opportunity at hand to nudge candidates toward the next interview stage and conduct a basic check on technical abilities to protect technical interviewers' time.

For scaling this stage, while you can have motivated team members to conduct the screening interviews, training is crucial to ensure the first touch of a candidate with the company leaves a good impression. Case study presentation interviews should focus on listening and qualifying questions. There should be a healthy amount of respect when candidates bring up ideas not anticipated in the standard solution. Selling and qualifying interviews should be conducted by as senior a team member as possible, so candidates can feel valued and motivated to learn more about the company in later rounds of interviews.

Conversion metrics between the screening and technical interviews should be kept judiciously to adjust the case studies' complexity. Regrettable attrition, where qualified candidates choose not to continue in the process, should also be tracked to adjust the amount of opportunity selling that's required in the interview process.

5 *Conducting technical interviews*—Technical interviews assess the candidates' strength in the essential areas selected from the technical capabilities, includ-

ing technology, execution, and expert domain knowledge, as discussed in this book. Committees are often set up to avoid personal blind spots and biases in the interview process.

Technical interviews are usually organized as a sequence of three to four interviews of 45–60 minutes in length. Each interview should cover one or two essential areas the team is hiring for. Care should be taken to have a consistent set of questions to ask every candidate to make sure the candidates' responses are comparable.

Before each interview, a quick 10- to 15-minute sync should be scheduled between all the interviewers to align on the position the team is hiring for and the particular essential area each interviewer is responsible for. As the process becomes more mature, this sync can happen asynchronously over emails or instant messages.

After each interview, there should be a 15-minute sync on each candidate's performance, where merits and red flags are discussed. The decision can then be made on whether the candidate can move on to the next stage of the interview.

To scale this stage, the evaluations from multiple interviewers on the same essential area should be aligned. This requires training the interviewer to take on standardized interview modules with consistent questions to ask and consistent points to assess. When evaluating the feedback, personal biases on whether the interviewer is a more lenient or harsh evaluator for a module should be taken into account to be as fair as possible for the candidate.

6 *Conducting partner/executive interviews*—This stage of the interview looks to assess a candidate's psychosocial virtues in ethics, rigor, and attitude, as discussed in this book. A committee of product, engineering partners, and at least one executive, such as yourself, should be involved. Having partners in the interview committee provides the candidates a sense of who they will be partnering with in their roles across different functions and provides your partners a say in who you hire.

Partner/executive interviews usually take place as a sequence of three to four interviews of 30–45 minutes in length. As in the technical interviews, each interview should cover one or two essential areas the team is hiring for with similar pre-interview and post-interview syncs to focus the interviews and standardize modules to keep the process consistent across candidates.

7 *Making offers*—Candidate experience in this part of the hiring process is crucial to not let all the efforts of the previous stages go to waste. Know the market rate for the level of candidate you are hiring for and align with your human resource partners to make a competitive offer where possible. For startup companies, be sure to help the candidate understand the potential of any equity components of the compensation.

Many savvy DS candidates will have done independent compensation research of their own and negotiate, so make sure to align internally to have some salary increase headroom in your offer strategy. This can avoid a long turnaround for receiving compensation increase approvals that might cause you to miss the candidate's decision time window for any competing offers.

Some less-savvy data scientists do not negotiate their compensation. Be sure to give them a reasonable level of compensation. When people find out they have lower-than-average compensation levels after joining, it will affect their attitude and motivation at work. By then, it can be a much more complicated situation to manage, as it can be much harder to justify a raise.

8   *Receiving an offer acceptance*—Congratulations! The candidate has accepted your offer. However, this is not the time to relax. Most offers have language regarding the offer's validity, pending reference checks. Reference checks serve two purposes: a sanity check on past experience and learning how best to work with the candidate once they come on board. To fulfill these two purposes, the hiring manager should personally conduct the reference checks.

Between offer acceptance and the prospective employee's first day, the hiring manager's responsibility is to stay in touch with the prospective employee at least once a week on topics such as equipment preferences, company news, and onboarding advice. There have been many instances where an existing employer made a counteroffer that your prospective employee can't refuse, and the hiring manager is not there to learn about it to organize a response.

As illustrated here, the purpose of this hiring process is to make DS hiring as robust and scalable as possible. It provides guard rails for removing bias and sets fundamental quality control to help hiring managers make the best hiring decisions possible. With these process recommendations in mind, you are on your way to building a robust DS function.

DEVELOPING FROM WITHIN, OR HIRING FROM OUTSIDE

Depending on the growth roadmap of your DS function, you can either develop DS leadership talent from within or hire leadership talent from outside. Developing leaders from within the organization has several advantages. An internal star player is familiar with the industry domain and organizational history and context. If they are well respected within the team, as long as they are willing to step out of their comfort zone and learn new leadership skills, they can become a great leader.

Developing internal leaders also has its limitations. Leadership skills take time to build, and there are typical caveats new leaders often fall into; those learning processes often happen at the expense of attrition risks within the team. Internally developed leaders, especially those who have joined the company fresh from school, may have limited exposure to best practices in the industry. Their understanding of business processes and leadership styles may be limited to what has been observed and learned from within one company.

Hiring leadership talent from outside has many advantages. When the organization is growing fast, external leadership talent can quickly fill the ranks to build out the organization. The experiences and best practices they bring in from across the industry can quickly up-level the team to more mature operating states.

Introducing outside leadership talent also carries many risks. The simple action of the candidate search can de-motivate internal star team members looking to be promoted into more senior leadership positions. A search can take months, especially when the talent needs time to conclude their current position. Even when the capabilities of the talent look to be a good match, the management style and cultural fit will often only manifest themselves on the job. Each mistake in hiring can be expensive for the organization when forced to manage the leader out.

How do you decide when to develop talent from within and when to hire from outside? One rule of thumb to use is execution velocity. When hiring and onboarding a DS leadership talent is likely to take two to three quarters, you can look at whether any existing team members have the potential to develop the necessary skills in six to nine months. When you don't have any team members who are capable and willing to grow into the management roles your organization needs within the next six to nine months, it's time to hire from outside.

When you have one high-potential team member in your organization, declaring the intent to develop them can be highly motivating. A roadmap should be established to coach them to build the necessary skills to step up, and projects should be crafted and delegated for them to build the leadership identity within the team and relationships of trust with partner teams.

When you are fortunate enough to have multiple high-potential team members in your organization capable and willing to step up within the next six to nine months, it is time to build more ambitious roadmaps. A more ambitious roadmap can provide more opportunities for your team members to unleash their potential. If they don't see the career growth path within your organization, there are plenty of DS opportunities elsewhere for them, and regrettable attrition becomes a real risk.

Stephen from chapter 1, the well-respected director troubled by the dropping morale of the DS team, can specify a clear career map and build a strong hiring pipeline to attract motivated team members to strive for the next stage of their career growth. Having examples of peers who have successfully advanced in their career in the team can boost team morale and help reduce future regrettable attrition.

6.2.3 *Supporting executives in top company initiatives*

Delivering results consistently and building a strong function are ways to support executives' ability to execute top company initiatives with DS. To effectively execute at the function level, here are two non-obvious capabilities for you to internalize:

- The concept of first team
- The ability to think two levels up

The concept and ability are meant to take you beyond the perspective of the DS function to interpret team interaction dynamics, and prioritize your time and your function's focus on the bigger picture.

A DS DIRECTOR'S FIRST TEAM

In his book *High Output Management* [6], Andy Grove describes the cultural value in a successful organization by stating, "the interest of the larger group to which an individual belongs takes precedence over the interest of the individual himself." This altruistic behavior is not limited to individual contributors and their teams.

Patrick Lencioni coined the term "first team" in his book *The Five Dysfunctions of a Team* [7]. At the function level, as illustrated in figure 6.9, the first team refers to the team of peers and directors reporting up to the same boss in an organization.

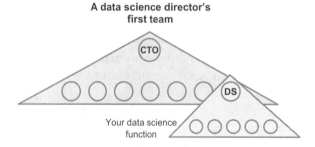

Figure 6.9   A data science director's first team

As an example, for a DS organization that reports up to the CTO, your first team includes your peer directors of data engineering, product development engineering, quality management engineering, site reliability engineering, technology research, enterprise security, and IT. Making this team the first team means the priorities of this team will trump any priorities of your DS organization.

Why is this not obvious? If we were survey DS directors on their number one priority, whether it is the team organized under the CTO or the team organized under themselves, the majority would choose the latter.

After all, this is the team that you, as a DS director, have nurtured day after day and depend on to produce DS accomplishments for the company. You have hired many of them personally, and you share their interest and expertise in DS. It is only natural for you to feel a duty, as their leader, to prioritize their interests.

As it turns out, at an organizational level, this can be dangerous. When each function prioritizes their own interest over their first team's priorities, Lencioni compares the situation to a United Nations or US Congress setting, where the directors will meet to lobby for their own constituents rather than looking out for the greater good.

The practice that creates successful organizations, as outlined by both Andy Grove and Patrick Lencioni, is that at every level of the organization, including yours, it must be made very clear that the priorities stay with what's right for the company or the organization over a leader's direct reports.

045

Your first team refers to the team of peers reporting up to your boss in an organization. A practice that creates successful organizations is for the priorities to stay with what's right for the company and your first team, which trump any priorities of your data science organization.

If this is the case, where does that leave the DS function that you have carefully nurtured? DS is a highly collaborative field. When you, as the function leader, do not coordinate well with your first team and align company or organizational priorities with partner functions, your team members suffer the most as they attempt to do their job without the support of partner team leaders.

As a principal data scientist, your first team is also your peers who share the same boss. Your responsibility is to work with your first team to address your boss's priorities. The first team concept not only empowers you and your peers to serve your boss's priorities better, but it also benefits the greater good of the company and allows your DS team members to have a clearer path to success.

THINKING TWO LEVELS UP

While this book talks about leadership, we are all followers first. In fact, as a DS director or a principal data scientist, you are a follower of your company's executives.

Section 6.2.1 discussed skip-level meetings as a management technique. You should expect to have conversations with your manager's manager as well. Depending on the size of the company or organization, this could be the chief technology officer, the CEO, or board members.

Executives value team members who consistently and effectively think two levels above their own. In DS, this means to consider not only the DS trade-offs but also the broader implications of intelligence capabilities on customer psychology, marketing narrative, talent brand, financial bottom line, market perception, legal implications, and social impact.

As an example, when fintech companies bring new features to their customers, they are continually balancing the ease of use of their products and protecting customers from financial fraud. However, fraudsters are always finding new ways to defraud companies. Machine learning models can be used to catch and deter fraud, but there is always fraud not caught in time, resulting in losses. These missed cases can then be used as training samples to improve anti-fraud models over time.

The thinking at the DS level is to improve the accuracy of the anti-fraud models. The thinking one level up is to monitor the impact of fraud losses on the unit economics and the profit margin, which determines the company operating strategy on the amount of fraud to tolerate for a given velocity of customer growth trajectory.

The thinking two levels up is the financial impact of fraud losses on the company's survival, given potential operating strategies. The CEO and the board would need to estimate how much funding to budget in fundraising, such that the company can have enough runway before the next set of milestones can be reached to receive increased valuation and capital infusion.

Thinking two levels up does not mean skipping over your boss to talk to your boss's boss. Instead, it means understanding your boss's boss's intentions to better support your boss to serve their first team.

046

Team members who can consistently and effectively think two levels above their own levels are valued in organizations. Thinking two levels up does not mean skipping over your boss to talk to your boss's boss. Instead, it means understanding your boss's boss's intentions to better support your boss to serve their first team.

How do you learn to think two levels up? Here are three things you can try:

- *Learning the priorities of your boss two levels up*—Listen carefully at company-wide communication meetings and understand the company priorities. Ask questions in skip-level one-on-ones with your boss's boss, and listen to their answers. Learn who they are, what they don't yet know that you can help them learn, and how they like to work. Answer their questions candidly as well, and relax and be yourself to let them see who you are.

- *Watching for the style and personality of your boss two levels up*—Some executives are more receptive in private than in public, some prefer to hash things out in the moment instead of revisiting discussions later, and some prefer verbal dialogues over a written argument. Some prefer short conversation more than long discussion. Some prefer a broad range of options to one top recommendation. Matching their style can make your recommendations more effective.

- *Helping them form opinions on issues of importance*—When discussing your ideas, avoid simply seeking their judgment. You are the DS subject matter expert. Directly seeking judgment puts them in a difficult situation of trying to figure out what questions to ask to evaluate a decision in front of you. If, for example, you believe the group has grown too risk-averse, begin a broader discussion about risk. Share examples of how the group has dealt with it in the past and then ask them about their experiences and ideas.

Most leaders understand the difficulty of speaking truth to power, yet they must depend on their teams for honest feedback. Look for opportunities to provide candid feedback on key aspects of their agenda. If there are challenges in implementing their initiatives in the current organizational environment, diplomatically bring the relevant dynamics to their attention, and share prior cases of how others were able to get around it.

With limited opportunities to interact with your boss's boss, you won't get it right every time. But as long as you are sensitive to their intentions and styles, you will improve your ability to manage up and make better recommendations over time.

6.3   *Expert knowledge: Deep domain understanding*

As part of senior management responsible for DS, your team members look to you for clarity in focus and prioritization within the function. Your boss and peers look to you for clarity in focus to use DS to contribute to executive business objectives. The clarity in focus comes from a clear understanding of the critical needs for business growth through:

- Anticipating business needs across stages of product development
- Responding to urgent issues with proven initial solutions
- Driving fundamental business impact in your industry

6.3.1   *Anticipating business needs across stages of product development*

Expert knowledge in product or service adoption cycles can help you understand and anticipate upcoming partner needs. You can propose and align DS roadmaps, adjust resources to hire, prepare processes, establish platforms, and minimize execution risks even before they emerge.

To assess the maturity of a product or feature, we reference Geoffrey Moore's technology adoption stages [8], illustrated in figure 6.10. You can anticipate DS capabilities that are commonly requested at each stage, proactively qualify the needs with partner teams, and coordinate and align roadmaps for your DS teams to follow.

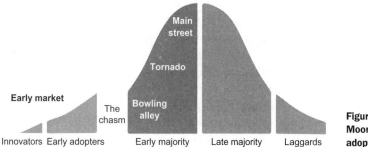

Figure 6.10   Geoffrey Moore's technology adoption stages [8]

The technology adoption cycle contains distinct stages. Table 6.2 illustrates the corresponding relevant DS projects in each adoption stage.

Table 6.2   Technology adoption cycle stages

Maturity stage	Customer type(s)	Common concerns	Relevant DS projects
Early market	Innovator	Finding product/market fit	Customer segmentation
	Early adopter		Feature engagement
Crossing the chasm	Early majority	Proving business wins	LTV prediction
			ROI estimation

Table 6.2 Technology adoption cycle stages *(continued)*

Maturity stage	Customer type(s)	Common concerns	Relevant DS projects
Bowling alley	Early majority	Leveraging wins in one segment for another	Customer awareness Customer acquisition Feature adoption
Tornado	Early majority	Managing operational efficiency in hyper-growth	Activation, revenue, and referral funnels
Main street	Late majority	Nurturing the existing captured market	Revenue and retention optimization Value-add feature adoption funnel Robust A/B test infrastructure
Mature market	Laggard	Investigating the next markets (e.g., exploring international markets)	Customer segmentation Potential acquisition due diligence

Early market

In early markets, the product gets adopted slowly by a few customers who love technology for technology's sake. These are the *innovators*. Then, the technology gets noticed and adopted by a larger portion of the market—a group of customers who are willing to overlook incompleteness in feature sets and bugs for the potential of the products and their massive opportunities down the road. These are the visionary *early adopters*.

The goal is to deliver measurable product-market fit with partners such as technical marketers, product managers, and engineering teams. Technical marketers would focus on segmenting the target market and discovering trends in customer behavior. Customer segmentation projects are key to understanding who the innovators and early adopters are and how to identify them across marketing channels.

Projects in partnership with product managers can include interpreting and prioritizing customer segments to target as well as designing experiments with testable hypotheses, which can inform business decisions to increase the company's bets in a segment or to pivot away. Early success cases in particular segments can become references for building trust with more customers.

Partnerships with engineering teams can include enumerating test conditions to ensure success metrics are available, correct, and complete. This allows user engagement to be accurately measured to detect bugs or bottlenecks that cause friction in the adoption process.

Crossing the chasm

When a product is *crossing the chasm*, it is maturing to attract the early majority customers who are pragmatic and want referenceable solutions to their existing problems. They only buy products that are fully baked. Strong references from the early adopters are key to demonstrate that adoption has low risk and high reward.

The goal is to deliver repeatable sales processes with marketing and sales teams. Partnership with marketing can focus on generating customer KPI interpretation and competitive positioning assessments, often using external data. Partnership with sales can focus on generating high-quality prospects within market segments, measuring the value created for customers and demonstrating proven business wins with ROI estimates that consider the *total cost of ownership* (TCO) for your customers as references.

Bowling alley

Having major wins and a strong foothold in one market segment is like having knocked down the front pin in a bowling game. At this point, a product enters the *bowling alley* stage. Its customers in this stage are the *early majority*, who will help specify and create the whole product. A company can leverage these definitive wins in one market segment to expand to adjacent segments, then iterate until they have a product acceptable to the entire market.

The goal is to deliver a whole product to a scalable target audience. Partners to look for include marketing, product, business operations, and engineering. DS can help the marketing team improve the reach in new market segments to improve awareness. It can also help improve targeting precision to increase the effectiveness of campaigns. Projects can include spend-to-conversion attribution, marketing channel efficiency optimization, and marketing spend optimization.

When partnering with the product team, the focus can be deep dives to improve the customer acquisition funnel stages to remove bottlenecks and prepare the product to scale efficiently. When partnering with business operations and engineering, investigations into how customers adopt specific features of the product can shed light on ways to accelerate adoption and reduce customer churn.

Tornado

With customer adoption ramping up, you enter the *tornado* stage. The organization has finished building the whole product and faces surging demand from its customers, the *early majority*. In this hyper-growth stage, the company needs to scale exponentially to keep up with the demand for its products and services. Prioritizing the use of limited resources to improve operating efficiency becomes central to the speed at which it can capture the marketplace.

The goal is to deliver scalable onboarding. Partners to work with include marketing, sales, and business operations. With marketing, you can grow the top of the funnel by diversifying channels to increase reach and optimize conversion effectiveness to reduce customer acquisition costs.

In partnership with sales, DS can prioritize prospects for the sales team with opportunity sizing. DS can also produce closing propensity estimation to focus the sales team on the most promising customers. In partnership with business operations, DS can help optimize customer activation when there are trial periods, shorten the paths to revenue with personalization and the power of defaults, and identify the most effective referrals for organic growth.

Main street

As the market matures and the product is proven in the market, growth becomes limited. Profit margins can still be high, and additional customers are part of the *late majority*. These customers need to be nurtured to avoid getting captured by competitors who provide lower margin alternatives. The goal at this stage is efficiency in creating and delivering *lifetime value* (LTV) for customers. Partners include marketing professionals, product managers, sales professionals, and engineering teams.

By partnering with marketing, you can focus on disruptor identification and competitive analysis to fend off challengers. Partnership with the product team can focus on retention optimization, LTV expansions, and creating platforms for +1 feature evolution like the Einstein AI platform from Salesforce. These plays can leverage the size of the business to out-innovate competitors and protect profit margin.

Partnerships with the sales teams can focus on renewal and upsell pipeline optimization for go-to-market (GTM) functions with dashboards and reports that can illustrate the customer values created. Partnerships with the engineering teams can focus on driving efficiency in fast A/B tests for incremental features to maintain and grow the pace of innovation.

Mature market

Some always-skeptical buyers are only interested in a product after everyone else has proven that the product works. The goal here is to identify and ride the next disruption. Partners for DS include technical marketers, product managers, and executives.

Partnerships with the technical marketer can focus on segmenting new target markets, discovering customer behavior trends, identifying disruptors, and performing competitive analysis. Partnerships with the product team can focus on prioritizing segments to target and identify disruptors and potential acquisition targets. Partnerships with the executives include conducting due diligence on potential acquisition targets to validate their technology capabilities.

At any point in time, there may be multiple product lines at different maturity stages in a company. Understanding the inherent needs for DS capabilities can allow you to discuss needs and priorities with partner teams proactively. After successfully anticipating future needs from partners, we can use the planning techniques introduced in Section 2.2.1 to prioritize needs by assessing risk, impact, confidence, effort, and aligning with data strategies.

Not all the capabilities need to be built in-house. There are many emerging third-party tools and data sources to accelerate your features' time to market. When business needs can be identified early, there can be enough time allocated to evaluate external tools before they are required in business operations.

In summary, expert knowledge in product or service adoption cycles can help you understand the upcoming needs of the product or the operating teams. By identifying the early market, crossing the chasm, bowling alley, tornado, main street, and mature market stages, you can anticipate, build, hire, or buy capabilities to meet your organization's growth needs.

6.3.2 Applying initial solutions rapidly to urgent issues

While there are projects that can be anticipated based on the product adoption cycle, there are also emerging challenges that must be responded to rapidly. Often, there is not enough time, resources, or historical data to explore a state-of-the-art solution. You are expected to leverage your domain expertise to put in place an initial solution along with a roadmap to a state of art solution, as time allows and the situation demands.

Initial solutions are often confused with proof of concept (PoC) projects, as discussed in section 3.2.3. The differences are contrasted in figure 6.11.

Initial solution	Situation	Proof of concept
Emergent challenges: Require quick, proven solutions	**Situation** How did the challenge emerge?	Planned projects; complex and risky
Low risk with maximized reuse: Something is better than nothing	**Confidence** What's the risk of failure?	Prove out the highest risk components first to remove project uncertainty
Aim for impact: Do 20% of the work for 80% of the return	**Impact** What should you optimize for?	Aim to remove risks; short-term impact is secondary
Reach as many users as possible to maximize the return	**Reach** Who will see the results?	Limited to a small audience to test out the new and often unproven ideas to reduce risk

Figure 6.11 Comparing and contrasting initial solution and proof of concept projects

While they are both starting points for more ambitious technology roadmaps, there are three key distinctions between initial solutions and PoC projects:

- *Confidence*—Initial solutions should be high confidence endeavors, reusing as many existing proven building blocks as possible. Their focus is based on the belief that something is better than nothing, and they can trade-off architecture elegance for speed to implementation. As explained in section 3.2.3, PoC projects have the purpose of exploring the feasibility of the portion of a project with the lowest confidence to remove uncertainty. Should the project fail as originally architected, we can find out as early as possible and pivot to an alternative solution.
- *Impact*—The impact of initial solutions should be as large as possible with respect to the effort used. Where possible, the goal is to do 20% of the work to get 80% of the return. PoC projects look to remove the highest risks of failure first, and the impact of the PoC is often a secondary consideration.

- *Reach*—Initial solutions would like to reach as many users as possible to provide a solution to the urgent issue. PoC is often limited to a small audience to test out the new and often unproven ideas before launching to a larger population.

Using these distinctions, let's look at two cases of initial solutions in the field of personal finance apps. One case is a frontend challenge in personal finance apps to increase user engagement. Another is a backend challenge to manage fraud when launching new fund transfer services.

047

Initial solutions are low-risk solutions that use 20% of the effort to get 80% of the impact, with a roadmap to refine the solution later and pay down tech debts. Initial solutions are often confused with proof of concept (PoC) projects, which are high-risk projects that prove out the components with highest risk first to remove project uncertainty.

CASE 1: INCREASING USER ENGAGEMENT

A wave of neo banks has emerged to serve customers of financial services with an online-only, and sometimes even a smartphone-only, platform. This model dramatically reduces the overhead of banking services and allows the neo banks to offer no-fee bank accounts to people without a minimum deposit or charging an average of hundreds of dollars of bank fees a year.

However, one major challenge remains. People's habitual interaction with banking services is, at best, a few times a year. One way neo banks are triggering more interactions from their customers is by providing money-saving offers from brands for purchases customers are already making. This generates a win–win situation where neo banks get the engagement they need to deliver value-added services, and customers get to save money as they spend. This challenge of increasing engagement can be mapped to a recommendation problem of using a customer's past purchasing behavior to personalize money-saving offers from brands.

To provide an initial solution for recommending brand offers, there are many solutions possible, including simple momentum-based linear models, as mentioned in section 2.1.2, as well as content-based filtering, matrix factorization, and deep learning-based approaches, as illustrated in figure 6.12.

Based on the criteria of high confidence and highest impact within a limited time, a simple momentum-based linear model can be a good choice. For commerce-related scenarios, brands that have patterns of repeated purchases are the most obvious ones to select first. You can apply the recency, frequency, and monetization model to select what purchases should be recommended first.

Some brands have purchases that are easily recognizable in bank transactions. These include department stores, grocery stores, convenience stores, and restaurant chains. You can identify recency factors, such as time since last purchase; frequency factors, such as the number of purchases made within the past three months; and

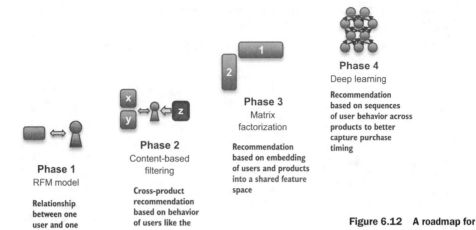

Phase 1
RFM model

Relationship
between one
user and one
product

Phase 2
Content-based
filtering

Cross-product
recommendation
based on behavior
of users like the
user

Phase 3
Matrix
factorization

Recommendation
based on embedding
of users and products
into a shared feature
space

Phase 4
Deep learning

Recommendation
based on sequences
of user behavior across
products to better
capture purchase
timing

Figure 6.12 A roadmap for
a recommendation engine

monetization factors, such as the dollar spend of each purchase to predict the likelihood of the purchase happening again in the next one to two weeks. The fundamental assumption is that if a brand is top of mind, an offer from that brand may be more relevant for the user.

By focusing the team on an initial solution that can be quickly developed and launched within six to eight weeks, you can improve the customer experience for a significant portion of the population. With the initial solution in place, you can assess when more significant investment for other options based on content-based filtering, matrix factorization, and deep learning is worthwhile to pursue.

CASE 2: MITIGATING FRAUD

As neo banks connect with existing financial institutions for money transfers, opportunities for fraud emerge. Fraud can happen during ACH bank transfers, mobile remote check deposits, or credit card or debit card swipes. It can come in the form of first-party fraud, where the account holder intentionally commits fraud, or third-party fraud, where someone other than the account holder commits fraud. Many frauds can occur early in a product's life cycle when there is little data for detecting fraud patterns. Organized third-party fraud at scale can cause severe losses, even to the point of disrupting cash flow and business operations.

In the absence of historical data, an initial solution can involve a set of rules based on common fraud techniques to formulate a scorecard. The purpose of such a scorecard is to highlight the obviously risky cases for further fraud investigation. In a scorecard, risk factors are identified based on prior expert domain knowledge, and weights are assigned to these risk factors. A threshold is chosen, such that each customer or transaction scoring above a threshold is deemed risky and worth investigating.

An initial solution based on a scorecard can take only one to two weeks to set up. Such a scorecard is a generative model. We can assess its performance through the precision and recall of the high-risk cases it highlights based on if fraud actually happened afterward.

Figure 6.13 illustrates the technology roadmap for anti-fraud solutions to flag potentially fraudulent transactions, starting with a simple scorecard and evolving to deep learning models based on engineered or learned features.

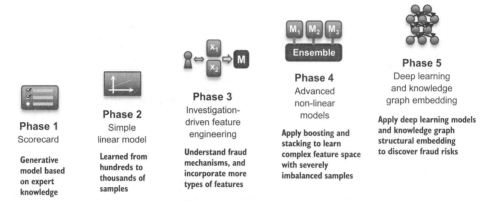

Figure 6.13   A roadmap for an anti-fraud solution

With a few hundred to a few thousand data points, the model can be updated to transaction-level fraud detection models learned from data (phase 2). As new fraud cases appear, the team can determine when to collaborate with fraud investigators to engineer more features (phase 3). There is also the opportunity to focus on upgrading to better models based on existing features and data (phase 4). If the fraud situation is severe and justifies the investment, deep learning and structural embeddings from knowledge graphs can be applied to extract otherwise hard-to-find fraud indicators.

To summarize, domain knowledge and insights can be crucial in quickly setting up initial solutions that can deliver immediate value without creating much tech debt for future solution roadmaps. In the two cases illustrated here, a team can deploy simple solutions within two weeks to two months and then iterate on the solution as more data becomes available. As illustrated in the above two case studies, when launching initial solutions, it is critical to also present the roadmap. The path forward to refine solutions at a later time can drive architectural trade-offs when the team implements initial solutions.

6.3.3   *Driving fundamental impacts with deep domain understanding*

Whether you are anticipating business needs based on the product adoption cycles or applying initial solutions to respond to urgent issues, projects and roadmaps should be aligned with making fundamental impacts in your industry.

What constitutes a fundamental impact? In consumer-facing and enterprise products and services alike, fundamental impacts ultimately contribute to customer acquisition and customer retention, which provides long-term business viability.

For acquisition, you are optimizing the customer acquisition process, so acquisition costs are lower than customer LTV. For retention, you are nurturing consumer habits or enterprises' dependence on your products or services to create customer value and then monetize it over time.

In contrast, efforts that do not generate fundamental impacts involve hacking vanity metrics, such as:

- *Buying traffic to increase monthly active user numbers or the number of downloads*—The focus should instead be on acquiring customers who are likely to convert.
- *Spamming users with irrelevant emails for engagement*—This may increase short-term engagement but can be detrimental to long-term engagement, as users are trained to ignore your emails or, worse, unsubscribe.
- *Temporarily diluting the overall delinquency rate by approving lots of new loans*—If the approval process is not improved, new loans will have similar delinquency rates.
- *Using hairlines in mobile ad images to trick users into tapping on an ad*—Taps may get a temporary boost, but users will be annoyed, and you may be kicked off ad networks.

As a case study, let's look at some examples of fundamental impacts for improving customer acquisition and customer retention with DS in the consumer-facing financial industry, as illustrated in figure 6.14.

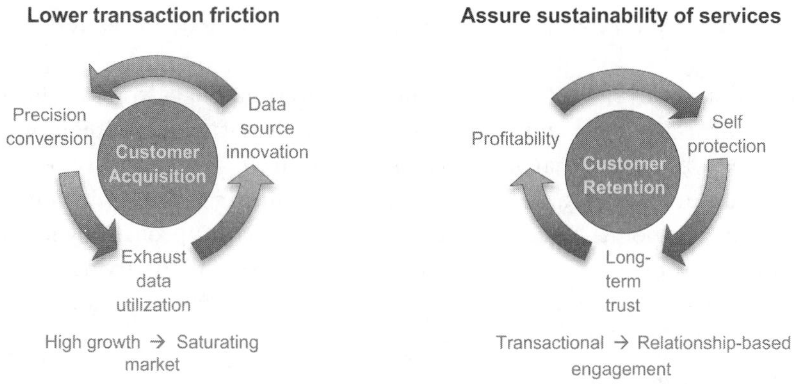

Lower transaction friction

Precision conversion · Customer Acquisition · Data source innovation · Exhaust data utilization

High growth → Saturating market

Assure sustainability of services

Profitability · Customer Retention · Self protection · Long-term trust

Transactional → Relationship-based engagement

Figure 6.14   Case study: Fundamental impacts for customer acquisition and retention

CUSTOMER ACQUISITION

As customers are increasingly engaging with financial institutions via mobile devices, effective internet-based customer acquisition playbooks are becoming crucial to financial services companies. The role of DS is to lower the transaction friction for customers by providing a better user experience when they are introduced to the service. Three areas of innovation opportunity include data-source innovation, precision conversion, and exhaust-data utilization.

Data-source innovation

Smartphone devices maintain a wealth of information, as a user carries them everywhere. They have a unique device identifier—a specific phone number. It records the IP addresses we have used, the locations we have been to, the account information we use to log into services, our contacts in our address books, as well as all the apps we have downloaded and are using.

People can choose to share some dimensions of data when sharing can benefit them. We often share our location data to find the nearest ATM and to automatically remove credit card anti-fraud restrictions when we travel out of the country. Some users share their contacts to select who in their network they can forward a promotion offer to. Others give access to photo albums to attach photos to deposit checks. For an emergency loan, we may share access to our banking portals to download historical financial records to prove we are creditworthy. DS can use information collected with the user's permission to simplify the registration and activation process and provide more personalized services aiming to lower the friction in customer acquisition.

Precision conversion

Precision conversion innovates on the availability of financial transaction streams. Streams of financial data are known to be predictive of impactful insights.

Neo banks such as Acorns, Chime, and Varo obtain users' authorization to connect to users' existing bank accounts to manage transfers between accounts and see ongoing transactions within those accounts. Interpretations of income levels and spending habits are used to help provide nudges for the users to set aside money for emergencies.

With a continuous view of the user's income and spend data, you can detect inflection points, or triggering events, in users' financial lives, such as graduation, moving, getting a new job, getting married, and having children. Financial service acquisition costs for insurance, brokerage, and retirement accounts can be significantly lowered at these inflection points. Even when the customers are not proactively looking for a new financial product, they can be more open-minded about trying one at these inflection points when presented with better alternatives. Detecting and using inflection points to lower conversion costs is a fundamental impact.

Exhaust-data utilization

In the internet customer acquisition funnel, not all users are suitable for a particular set of products and services a company offers. This is the case for many lending and insurance products. You can also observe this in consumer-facing freemium products by noting the large numbers of users who are signed up but are not active or contributing revenue. During the registration process, you have collected some information about these inactive users. This extra information that falls out of your customer acquisition funnel is called exhaust-data.

This exhaust-data can be valuable in many ways. When you have learned a significant amount of information about the users and determined you can't serve many of them at the moment, you can often make a grounded assessment about the most appropriate third-party partners to refer these users to.

If you can set up a referral process, the process can improve customer experience, as customers can benefit from the company's understanding of the industry. The process can also bring in referral income to offset customer acquisition costs, which can be reinvested into customer acquisition. The amortization of customer acquisition costs by monetizing exhaust-data is a fundamental business impact.

CUSTOMER RETENTION

Customer retention involves providing consistent product quality and ensuring service sustainability. Quality and sustainability can allow the organization to continue to serve customers well in the long run. Innovations in DS in the consumer-facing financial industry should aim for profitability, self-protection, and long-term trust building.

Profitability

The profitability of a financial product depends on managing costs. For example, in lending, accurately assessing credit risks and rigorously monitoring the modeling pipelines for changing market conditions is crucial to sustaining a lending product's profit margin.

There are seven directions where profitability for models in production can be maintained and improved on:

- *Identifying data sources*—To expand the customer base for which you can discern creditworthiness
- *Selecting data sources*—To reduce the cost of assessing a loan application
- *Mining for features*—To extract useful details from existing data sources
- *Assessing features and developing a feature portfolio*—To maintain and monitor a set of model features for effectiveness and stability
- *Managing incremental and imbalanced labels*—To incorporate new data from daily operations in a timely fashion and adjust for label imbalance
- *Developing a modeling strategy*—To balance modeling complexity and accuracy
- *Assessing results and generating decision explanation*—To provide mechanisms for fast feedback

With a rigorous modeling process, the application of AI can provide a foundation for a profitable financial lending model and contribute a fundamental impact.

Self protection

With a profitable financial business model, a consumer-facing financial company must also protect itself from fraud. Many transactions today are taking place on smart devices without face-to-face interaction between the transacting parties. This can make fraud rampant.

For example, in online lending, millions of dollars of loans could be approved in minutes and dispersed to fraudsters by mistake in a few hours with no hope of collecting repayment. Fraudsters have created complete playbooks for known vulnerabilities along with an entire black-market ecosystem to hide their traces. The role of DS here is to recommend and implement ways to increase the cost of fraud without interrupting the product experience of a non-fraudulent customer.

In one case, a FinGraphs knowledge graph [9] was created at Yiren Digital with 260 million nodes and one billion edges, based on user data. It was used to find rogue lending agents who are committing fraud and was able to stop the dispersion of $30 million dollars of fraudulent loans in a year.

In another case, a deep-learning anti-fraud model for credit card transactions created by Danske Bank [10] used a six-layer residual convolutional neural network to reduce the false-positive rate of fraud alert by 10–100×. DS innovations are ideal for implementing anti-fraud capabilities, and the losses saved go directly to improving profit, which fundamentally impacts a company's survival and growth.

Long-term trust-building

In the consumer-facing financial industry, customer service is an area many users value. Especially when there is a glitch in the technical systems or the network, being able to pick up the phone and call customer service is crucial for gaining confidence that your life savings is safe. Even a neo bank with a few million users may employ thousands of customer agents.

However, customer service is also susceptible to vishing calls, which are voice solicitations over the phone to extract information or data points about a user's account that can be used for a later attack. Hackers use social engineering techniques, such as fake stories about the situation and caller ID number-spoofing, to fool customer service agents into passing out sensitive information about a user.

> **NOTE**   Vishing is different from phishing. Phishing is the fraudulent practice of sending emails purporting to be from reputable companies in order to induce individuals to reveal personal information. Vishing calls are voice solicitations over the phone to extract information or data points about a user's account that can be used for a later attack.

Intelligent chatbot technologies, either in text or voice, can alleviate customer service agent workloads and prevent out-of-compliance human errors from leaking user information, which can fundamentally impact the trust between a consumer-facing financial company and its users.

In summary, focusing your teams on fundamental impacts is an important responsibility of a DS director. Fundamental impacts include the efficacy of customer acquisition and improving the economics of customer retention. This section provides six examples in the consumer-facing financial industry, some of which you may find applicable to your domain.

6.4   Self-assessment and development focus

Congratulations on working through the chapter on director and principal data scientist capabilities! This is an important milestone for leading the DS function.

The purpose of the capabilities self-assessment is to help you internalize and practice the concepts by:

- Understanding your interests and leadership strengths
- Practicing one to two areas with the choose, practice, and review (CPR) process
- Developing a prioritize-practice-perform plan to go through more CPRs

Once you start doing this, you will have courageously taken the steps to practice strong ethics, build diligence in rigor, and maintain a positive attitude to drive your team's long-term effectiveness.

6.4.1   Understanding your interests and leadership strengths

Table 6.3 summarizes the virtues discussed in this chapter. The rightmost column is available for you to check off the areas you currently feel comfortable with quickly. There is no judgment, no right or wrong, nor are there any specific patterns to follow. Feel free to leave any or all rows blank.

If you are already aware of some of these aspects, this is a great way to build a narrative around your existing leadership strengths. If some aspects are not yet familiar, this is the opportunity for you to assess whether they can be of help in your daily work, starting today!

Table 6.3   Self-assessment areas for virtues of directors and principal data scientists

Capability areas/self-assessment (italic items primarily apply to managers)			?
Technology	Crafting technology roadmaps to align teams	Coordinating and aligning teams by clarifying business objectives, validating customer needs and technology paths, developing intermediate milestones, aligning with partner roadmaps, and taking responsibility for the ultimate business results	
	Guiding function to build the right features for the right people at the right time	Validating product hypotheses to build the right things with A/B tests. Running A/B tests globally and assessing results locally to build features for the right people; prioritizing with validated learning from A/B tests to build features at the right time	
	Sponsoring and championing promising DS projects	Identifying or taking on project sponsor roles to articulate the project's problem statement, defining the objectives, and validating the business case in the project charter	
		Identifying or taking on project champion roles to be a strong advocate in project prioritizations and inspiring the team to move forward in stressful situations	

Table 6.3   Self-assessment areas for virtues of directors and principal data scientists *(continued)*

Capability areas/self-assessment (italic items primarily apply to managers)			?
Execution	Delivering consistently by managing people, processes, and platforms	Managing people by interacting with not just direct reports but also with the broader organization with office hours, skip-level lunches, and skip-level one-on-ones to recognize accomplishments and best practices and debug and resolve dysfunctions of the organization	
		Managing processes by promoting transferable best practices to ensure consistency of efforts across the teams, especially in fast-growing ones	
		Managing platforms to democratize capabilities for a broader audience by automating best practices	
	Building a strong function with clear career maps and a robust hiring process	*Retaining the best talent by crafting a clear set of opportunities, responsibilities, and success metrics for your team members, as described throughout this book*	
		Acquiring the best talent by constituting talent acquisition as a project in your execution plan with time and resources allocated for clarifying hiring goals, sourcing candidates, training and conducting interviews, and post-interview discussions	
	Supporting executives in top company initiatives	Prioritizing working with your first team (peers reporting up to your manager) to work on company initiatives	
		Thinking two levels up to bring better recommendations to your manager by broadening your perspectives to variables your boss's boss considers in decisions	
Expert knowledge	Anticipating business needs across stages of product development	Using product/service adoption cycles to anticipate the business needs to hire people, prepare processes, and establish platforms	
	Applying the initial solution rapidly against urgent issues	Leveraging domain expertise to deploy initial solutions for urgent issues along with a roadmap to a state-of-art solutions as time allows and the situation demands	
	Driving fundamental impact with deep domain understanding	Driving customer acquisition with data-source innovation, precision conversion, and exhaust-data utilization	
		Driving customer retention by creating and capturing customer value, protecting against fraud and abuse, and building long-term trust with customers	

6.4.2   *Practicing with the CPR process*

As with the tech lead capability assessment in section 2.4 and the manager capability assessment in section 4.4, you can experiment with a simple CPR process with two-week check-ins. For your self-review, you can use the project-based skill improvement template to help you structure your actions over the two weeks:

- *Skill/task*—Select a capability to work on.
- *Date*—Select a date in the two-week period when you can apply the capability.
- *People*—Write down the names of the people with whom you can apply the capability, or write *self*.
- *Place*—Select the location or occasion at which you can apply the capability (for example, in the next one-on-one with a team member or an alignment meeting with your engineering partner).
- *Review result*—How did you do compared to before? The same, better, or worse?

By holding yourself accountable for these steps in a self-review, you can start to exercise your strengths and shed light on your blind spots in the DS director and principal data scientist capabilities.

Summary

- *Technologies* for directors and principal data scientists include tools and practices to craft technology roadmaps, guide the function to build the right thing for the right people at the right time, and to sponsor and champion promising projects for success.
  - When crafting technology roadmaps, you can coordinate and align teams by clarifying business objectives, validating customer needs and technology paths, developing milestones, aligning with partner roadmaps, and taking responsibility for business results.
  - When guiding the function's focus, you can validate product hypotheses using A/B tests and adapt project directions and prioritizations to the learning.
  - When sponsoring promising projects, you can validate the business case and muster resources toward a solution. When championing promising projects, create and sell a consistent vision, build relationships, and motivate the team through difficult times.
- *Execution* capabilities for directors and principal data scientists include delivering consistent results by managing people, processes, and platforms; building a strong function with career mapping and hiring; and supporting executives in top company initiatives.
  - When delivering consistent results, you can notice star team members' best practices, constitute them into processes, and automate them through platforms, so today's best outcome becomes tomorrow's standard of success.
  - When building a strong function, you can draft a DS career map with concepts in this book and coach the team in day-to-day projects. You can also constitute hiring as talent acquisition projects to get commitments from partners and the team.
  - When supporting executives, use the first team concept to prioritize collaborations between peer directors and serve your boss's initiatives, and think two levels up to hold a broader perspective in recommendations that can help your boss resolve the concerns of your boss's boss.

- *Expert knowledge* for directors and principal data scientists can be demonstrated by anticipating business needs across product development stages, responding to urgent issues with proven initial solutions, and driving fundamental business impacts in your industry.
  - When anticipating business needs, you can refer to the common DS capabilities requested at each of the product adoption stages, proactively qualify the needs with partner teams, and coordinate and align roadmaps with your team.
  - When responding to urgent issues, put in place an initial solution with high confidence of success, maximum business impact, and broad customer reach, along with a roadmap to a state-of-the-art solution as time allows and the situation demands.
  - When driving fundamental business impact, improve customer acquisition and customer retention for long-term business viability with opportunities in data-source innovation, precision conversion, exhaust-data utilization, profitability, antifraud, and trust-building with customer service.

References

[1] A. Fabijan et al., "The evolution of continuous experimentation in software product development: From data to a data-driven organization at scale," *ICSE* '17, May 20–28, 2017. [Online]. Available: https://exp-platform.com/Documents/2017-05%20ICSE2017_EvolutionOfExP.pdf

[2] Y. Xu et al., "From infrastructure to culture: A/B testing challenges in large scale social networks," *KDD*, 2015.

[3] R. Seiner. "So you want to be a data champion?" The Data Administration Newsletter. https://tdan.com/so-you-want-to-be-a-data-champion/7193

[4] C. Fournier, *The Manager's Path*, Sebastopol, CA, USA: O'Reilly Media, 2017.

[5] Y. Xu et al., "SQR: Balancing speed, quality and risk in online experiments," *KDD* 2018, pp. 895–904.

[6] A. S. Grove, *High Output Management*, New York, NY, USA: Vintage Books, 1995.

[7] P. Lencioni, *The Five Dysfunctions of a Team: A Leadership Fable*, San Francisco, CA, USA: Jossey-Bass, 2002.

[8] G. Moore et al., "Crossing the Chasm: Marketing and Selling High-Tech Products to Mainstream Customers," *HarperBusiness*, 2006.

[9] T. Wang and J. Chong, "Is knowledge graph and community analysis useful in financial anti-fraud analysis?" O'Reilly, 2016. [Online]. Available: https://www.linkedin.com/in/jikechong/detail/treasury/position:679798820/

[10] R. Bodkin and N. Gulzar, "Fighting financial fraud at Danske Bank with artificial intelligence," in Artificial Intel. Conf., O'Reilly, New York, 2017. [Online]. Available: https://learning.oreilly.com/videos/oreilly-artificial-intelligence/9781491976289/9781491976289-video311819/

Virtues for leading a function

7

- Establishing project formalizations across your function
- Coaching as a social leader and organizing initiatives for team career growth
- Driving successful annual planning processes, while avoiding planning anti-patterns
- Securing commitments from partners and teams
- Recognizing diversity, practicing inclusion, and nurturing belonging within your function

As a director or principal data scientist, your virtues can shape the function's virtues. Your emphasis becomes the function's focus. Where you scrutinize, the function tends to develop competency. With the knowledge that your words, actions, and habits shape the culture of the DS function, what are some specific tools and practices that can provide you the necessary power and influence for directing your function?

Your ethics or standards of conduct are demonstrated in how you establish project formalizations across the function; how you coach your team with interpretations, narratives, and requests; and how you organize initiatives to provide career growth opportunities. Your rigor shows up in how you drive effective annual planning processes, avoid project planning execution anti-patterns, and secure commitments from partners and teams. Your compassionate attitude is felt in how you recognize and promote diversity, how you practice inclusion in decision-making, and how you nurture belonging in your function. Let's look into the dimensions of ethics, rigor, and attitude one by one.

7.1   Ethical standards of conduct

There are many challenges in governing the DS function. Projects often require long time horizons and significant investments to demonstrate business impact. Talent constantly get tapped by external competing opportunities and can change employers every few years. What is an ethical standard of conduct you can practice to maintain a productive function that also motivates team members?

For projects, you are in a position to anticipate and detect early symptoms of issues across projects to guide the function away from systematic failures. Establishing project formalization can help you increase your projects' success rates and improve the sense of accomplishment among your team members, so you can better retain your talent.

For your team, it can be increasingly difficult to lead by demonstrating what you would like done. Your leadership is more effective by sharing your interpretation of situations, your narratives for direction, and your requests for coordinated action. Your role becomes more of a coach to grow team members' capabilities.

You have limited hours in a week to guide projects and coach team members, so organizing opportunity paths for team members' career growth can be effective in providing scalable leadership opportunities. These opportunity paths also provide clarity for team members to understand their growth dimensions and recognize their accomplishments.

7.1.1   Establishing project formalizations across the function

Depending on the size of your function, you may have tens to hundreds of projects in progress each quarter. How do you keep track of the projects? How do you decide which projects to double down on or cancel when they inevitably encounter difficulties? What happens when each project meets its KPIs, but the overall business results are not produced?

As a function leader, you are best positioned to have visibility into systematic issues in your function. Not taking care of these systematic issues can lead to resources not being allocated to projects with the most impact. This can result in a loss of product competitiveness and, for startups, a loss of valuable cash flow runway.

048

Not detecting and acting on systematic issues across projects can lead to resources wasted from scope estimation biases in planning; integration challenges; and scheduling, communication, and stakeholder risks. The resource waste can result in loss of product competitiveness and, for startups, a loss of valuable cash flow runway.

One way to stay on top of your projects is to hire project managers to formalize the definition and management of those projects. Project managers can oversee, help train, and guide DS tech leads and managers to assist you in leading projects through their development process.

We introduced the structure of a project plan when discussing a tech lead's responsibilities in section 2.2.2. It involves clarifying the project motivation, definition, solution architecture, execution timeline, and risks. A tech lead is expected to take care of project-specific risks from new data sources, potential partner team reorganizations, new data-driven feature tracking, legacy product nuances, and solution architecture dependencies.

A director or a principal data scientist is expected to detect early symptoms of systemic issues that occur across projects, based on experience or observations. Figure 7.1 illustrates a list of five top systematic project issues for your reference, so you can guide the function away from systematic failures, including:

- Project scope estimation biases
- Project integration challenges
- Project scheduling risks
- Project communication risks
- Project stakeholder risks

Scope estimation biases

Scope estimation is an assessment of the time and resources required for a project.
- *Challenge*—Under/over estimation can defund a project. There is no one right answer, as people have different strengths and blind spots.
- *Solution*—Provide early and broad feedback; validate estimates at project end to calibrate for future estimation.

Integration challenges

Data science often provides one of many components that must be integrated together into a product.
- *Challenge*—Technical risks, team risks, and ambiguities abound.
- *Solution*—Systematically delegate risk handling to team members closest to the challenge. A function leader is responsible for clarifying role ambiguities.

Scheduling risks

Scheduling changes in one project may impact another project. Data science schedules are affected by changes outside the function.
- *Challenge*—Centralized function structures are more susceptible to scheduling risks.
- *Solution*—Use project management support, or try decentralized or federated team structures.

Communication risks

Projects are conducted across time zones, which can take a toll on team dynamics.
- *Challenge*—Insensitivities in meeting scheduling can make a remote team feel neglected.
- *Solution*—Draft and enforce operating principles to respect a remote team's working hours to build trusting working relationships.

Stakeholder risks

Data science projects may involve many collaborating stakeholders over long time horizons.
- *Challenge*—Stakeholder priorities may change and affect DS projects.
- *Solution*—Nurture relationships, monitor project priority changes, promptly influence reprioritization and realignment decisions, and pivot when changes become inevitable.

Figure 7.1 Five top systematic project issues to overcome in project formalization

- *Project scope estimation biases*—Project scope estimation is an essential step for prioritizing projects in the planning process. The estimation involves specifying feature scope and implementing a time horizon to reach specific business or product objectives. Overestimation or underestimation of project scope can be the difference between the project being prioritized or not. What's challenging is that there isn't one right answer.

  Different tech leads and managers have different experiences and strengths in anticipating and handling common challenges in DS, so it is reasonable for them to have different scope estimations for similar projects. Past experiences and personalities can also create blind spots in project scope estimation. For example, a seasoned tech lead with five years of experience developing enterprise products on desktop platforms may not be aware of all the nuances of working with a mobile-centric consumer product. After a series of successful projects, some may underestimate potential challenges ahead.

  As a function leader, you can establish practices in the planning process to reduce the variance of project scope estimation biases from person to person. Common techniques include:

  - Early feedback on scoping through office hours hosted by experienced tech leads
  - Broad feedback on scope in the project proposal review
  - Scope estimation validation at project completion to correct for biases

  These techniques can be managed systematically using project managers as part of the project formalization process to best create and use institutional knowledge within your organization for future project scope estimations.

- *Project integration challenges*—In large projects, DS often provides one of many components that must be integrated to create business value. Project integration is a challenging process with technical risks, team risks, and ambiguities. Each area of risk should be systematically delegated to the team member closest to the challenge.

  Technical risks are best addressed with the project tech lead. Team risks are best handled by the DS team managers, who are responsible for developing close working relationships with partners and resolving any immediate issues between individuals and groups. Ambiguities in a project specification can be resolved by the tech lead. Ambiguities within roles and responsibilities can be escalated to the managers or you, the function leader.

- *Project scheduling risks*—Project scheduling challenges are especially prominent in companies where the technical teams sit as a centralized pool of resources organized by functions. We discuss this type of organization in section 8.1.3, including consulting and centralized structures for the DS function where projects are planned across the entire function. Delays in one project can affect many other projects while waiting for team members to roll off the delayed project.

Having project management support is essential when operating in these organization structures, as DS project progress can be affected by unexpected delays outside the control of the function. There are also techniques to maintain function productivity. You can maintain a backlog of projects with few external dependencies, such as data source exploration or tech debt resolution, so your teams can make progress even when unexpected external scheduling delays block them from starting new projects.

The ultimate solution is to work with executives to reorganize the technical function into decentralized, center of excellence, or federated structures. As discussed in section 8.1.3, these structures designate dedicated resources toward product or business lines to prevent one project delay from affecting many other projects.

- *Project communication risks*—Many companies now include geographically diverse teams that collaborate on meaningful projects and initiatives. Coordinating time zone differences can take a toll on team dynamics. This is especially challenging for collaboration between team members on the US West Coast and the Indian subcontinent or between team members on the US East Coast and Southeast Asia. In these cases, a team in one location may be driving a project, and another team 12 hours away may be supporting the project. The workday does not overlap, and only one team is operating during regular business hours. Insensitivities in scheduling meetings can make the remote team feel neglected in the communication process and damage productive relationships.

To govern a function with these challenges, some operating principles can help create a productive work environment that respects the contributions of the geographically diverse teams:

  - *End-to-end involvement*—Teams in both locations should have visibility on the projects from end to end to minimize gaps in context and key decision considerations.
  - *End-stakeholder engagement*—Teams in both locations are invited to key meetings with end stakeholders to drive project ownership. This means setting up meetings with end stakeholders, at convenient times in their respective time zones, to engage the remote team in end-stakeholder challenges and feedback.
  - *Internal communication*—You can schedule project internal sync meetings with time zone differences in mind. The meeting times can alternate between more convenient early-morning or late-night time slots.
  - *Presentation of results*—Whoever works on the project should present the work to the end stakeholders to ensure effective delivery of insights and exposure for their accomplishments.

These operating principles can be constituted by the director and enforced by the tech lead, team managers, and project managers to build trusting working relationships. When possible, also build personal relationships between the teams across locations. Personal relationships can ameliorate project communication tensions when they arise, and prevent remote teams from losing motivation or burning out.

■ *Project stakeholder risks*—Stakeholders of DS projects are constantly reprioritizing and realigning their portfolio of projects. This is expected, as they anticipate and respond to internal and external changes in dynamic technical and business environments. DS projects are susceptible to stakeholder reprioritization and realignment because they can require long time horizons to succeed.

As a leader of the DS function, identifying projects with more stable stakeholders can reduce stakeholder risks. Your responsibilities include nurturing stakeholder relationships, monitoring the project's priority, and following the project's impact on stakeholders. When you identify the first signs of priority changes, you can promptly influence reprioritization, realignment decisions, and helping DS teams pivot when stakeholder-triggered changes become inevitable.

In summary, as part of the standard of conduct for efficiently governing a DS function, you need a set of best practices and support to implement them. The project formalization process is a best practice that can help you deploy resources more effectively over time. Bringing a project manager on board can give you the support you need for developing and managing projects and allow you to delegate the responsibilities to track and mitigate scope estimation biases, integration challenges, scheduling risks, and communication risks.

7.1.2 *Coaching as a social leader with interpretations, narratives, and requests*

To perform at the function level, you are expected to delegate as much as possible to your team, so you can focus on establishing technology roadmaps, championing promising projects, building teams, and supporting executives in implementing their DS vision. Your leadership practices also need to transition from individual leadership to social leadership [1]. Your actions will likely shift from advising and mentoring to coaching. What are the differences in these leadership practices and actions? Figure 7.2 illustrates the key differences.

Individual leaders lead through the demonstration of their capabilities when taking care of technical and people challenges. Their team members learn best practices by

Individual leader	Social leader
• *Typical roles*—Tech leads and team managers	• *Typical roles*—Directors and executives
• *Leadership approach*—Lead through demonstrations of their own capabilities to take care of technical and people challenges	• *Leadership approach*—Lead by offering interpretations of the situation, narratives for direction, and requests for coordinated action
Team members learn best practices by observing leaders' actions in: • Managing technical projects • Influencing partners • Upholding professional rigor and ethics	Team members look to the leader to: • Interpret the situation when external market shifts or internal technical incidents happen • Specifying goals and milestones with success criteria for the immediate next steps

Figure 7.2   The distinctions of an individual leader and social leader

observing their leaders' actions when managing technical projects, influencing partners, and upholding the profession's rigor and ethics. This is common when you are the tech lead or the manager, as you mentor and advise your team.

You may recall from section 5.1.1 that mentoring focuses on sharing your past experiences to help team members build skills. Advising focuses on how you can provide information and direction to solve team members' specific challenges.

As a director, you are often too far away from the specific technical challenges to be providing past experience or specific solutions. But you can still be an effective leader through coaching.

Social leaders lead by offering *interpretations of the situation, narratives for direction*, and *requests for coordinated action*. We usually find directors and principal data scientists performing at this level. When external market shifts or internal technical incidents happen, the team looks to you to interpret the situation. In business planning cycles and when responding to incidents, the team looks to you for goals and milestones with specific success criteria for the immediate next steps.

Team members choose to grant you the authority to constitute the rules, goals, and roadmap when they believe in your *interpretation of the situation* and *the narratives for direction* align with your *requests for their coordinated action*. How can you produce an interpretation, a narrative, and requests the team can rally around?

049

Individual leaders lead through the demonstration of their capabilities when taking care of technical and people challenges. Social leaders lead by offering interpretations of the situation, narratives for direction, and requests for coordinated action.

INTERPRETING THE SITUATION

You can first understand if and how situations may impact your organization, your partner's organization, and your technology roadmaps (see section 6.1.1 for crafting your technology roadmaps) in the short term and over the long term. Your responsibility is to first collect information on the impact from stakeholders, then synthesize the information to form your narrative for directions for your teams.

NARRATIVES FOR DIRECTION

When the new situation does not impact your roadmap, you can reaffirm to the team that they will stay the course. Reaffirmation is good for the stability of the team and can address their anxiety when facing ambiguities in a new situation.

When new situations trigger changes in your roadmap, take the time to realign new directions with stakeholders one by one to show respect for their perspectives. This diligence can help you build trust with the team when your narrative for direction is well-researched.

Not realigning in new directions with stakeholders first may result in a later reversal of narratives. This hurts the authority of all your future narratives, as the team will question whether your narratives may be reversed later.

REQUEST FOR COORDINATED ACTIONS

The *request for coordinated actions* is the most challenging component for a social leader. There are many details in a request. At the director level, you may not be aware of all the coordination details required for success. The common symptom of this failure mode is when the team achieves the KPIs you laid out, but the function fails to produce the desired business impact.

One technique to help in coordinating actions is using the GROW model [2]. The GROW model is an acronym of the names of its four stages: goal, reality, obstacles or options, and will or way forward. You may have used it when identifying your development focus areas, starting in chapter 3. The framework has been used successfully in organizations like Google and McKinsey to engage people, inspire performance, and maximize productivity. It can be highly effective for you to build trust and coordinate commitment as a social leader in DS. Table 7.1. illustrates the four stages of the GROW model and provides a set of questions to help set goals, assess reality, identify obstacles and options, and make commitments for the way forward.

Table 7.1   40 top coaching questions for reference when using the GROW model

Goal		
	1	What would you like to accomplish toward the business impact?
	2	What goals align with the technology roadmap?
	3	What does success look like?
	4	How do you measure success?
	5	Why are you hoping to achieve this goal?
	6	What would the benefits be if you achieved this goal?
Reality	1	Where are you now in relation to your goal?
	2	How would you describe what is being done today?
	3	What is working well right now?
	4	What has contributed to your success so far?
	5	What progress have you made so far?
	6	What do you think is stopping you?
	7	How could you turn this situation around this time?
	8	Do you know other people who have achieved your goal?
	9	If you asked ____, what would they say about the situation?
	10	On a scale of 1–10, how severe/serious/urgent is the situation?
Obstacles/options	1	What do you think you need to do next?
	2	What would happen if you did nothing?
	3	If anything was possible, what would you do?
	4	What could be your first step?
	5	What would happen if you did that?
	6	Whom do you know who has encountered a similar situation?
	7	Who else might be able to help?
	8	What has worked for you already? How could you do more of that?
	9	What is the most challenging part for you?
	10	What are the advantages and disadvantages of each option?
	11	How have you tackled a similar situation before?
	12	What could you do differently?

Table 7.1 40 top coaching questions for reference when using the GROW model *(continued)*

Will/way forward		
	1	What do you think you need to do right now?
	2	When are you going to start?
	3	How are you going to do that?
	4	How will you know that you were successful?
	5	Is there anything else you can do?
	6	On a scale of 1–10, what is the likelihood of your plan succeeding?
	7	What would it take to make it a 10?
	8	On a scale of 1–10, how committed/motivated are you to achieve your goal?
	9	What would it take to make it a 10?
	10	What roadblocks do you expect that require planning?
	11	Is there anything missing?
	12	What do you need from me or others to help you achieve this?

GOAL

In requesting coordinated actions, you can start by sharing your narratives for direction. This allows you to set up the context for discussion with your tech leads or DS managers about their goals. In section 5.3.2, we discussed techniques for setting up goals together with your direct report to encourage ownership of the goals. Coaching team members through the GROW model can train them to interpret and execute your direction narrative, empowering you to be a more effective *social leader.*

In coaching your team members to set goals, look for their passion and focus in the context of your direction narrative. Suppose your narrative for directions is to gain a deeper understanding of the customers, and you have a team member with passion and expertise in natural language processing (NLP). In that case, you can encourage the team member to recommend goals involving NLP to improve customer understanding.

To coach and provide feedback, you can choose to reinforce goals that align with your established technology roadmaps with additional resources. This reinforcement can be in the form of tools or data to help accelerate progress toward your technology roadmap milestones. For example, when working toward a deeper understanding of the customers, your team member may recommend a goal of using NLP to improve customer understanding. You can encourage the team member by providing additional data engineering resources to accelerate the collection and cleaning of more unstructured natural language data for training models.

To clarify the goals, you can coach your team members to establish SMART goals that are specific, measurable, attainable, relevant, and time bound. When team members are motivated to identify and specify the goals, there will be greater ownership to accomplish them.

REALITY

The *reality* stage involves an assessment of the current situation. Coaching a team member through the reality stage provides a shared understanding of the gap between the current reality and the goal.

The series of questions in table 7.1 provides an opportunity for the team member to reflect on the current situation. The reflection process can include assessing the current challenges, collecting perspectives from stakeholders, and benchmarking products or features. You can complement the results of the reflection with additional executive perspectives. The information aggregated here can be used to assess the severity and urgency of the challenges for better prioritization.

OBSTACLES/OPTIONS

The obstacles and options stage involves a conversation on what gaps and roadblocks we are likely to encounter when working toward the goals from the current reality. With a shared understanding of the gaps and roadblocks, you can coach team members to brainstorm ways to close the gap.

Your coaching here can focus on the breadth and depth of the options considered. For breadth, constraints in location, timing, and resources can be removed to generate a greater variety of options that can trigger more ideas. For depth, specifying the options' early steps and their consequences can help identify their advantages and disadvantages.

WILL/WAY FORWARD

In this stage, a team member generates a well-reasoned set of options with specific recommendations for the next steps. Coaching involves helping the team member assess their confidence and motivation in pursuing a specific course of action toward the goal. You are successful when the team member can create accountability milestones with structures for tracking progress.

The key to coaching with the GROW model is for your team members to learn over time to start with your narratives for direction, independently create goals, assess the situation, brainstorm options, and formulate a set of coordinated actions for your review. Over time, your coaching empowers your team members to mature to a state where they are not just escalating problems for you to resolve, but are also bringing complete solution plans with recommendations to discuss and review.

7.1.3   *Organizing initiatives to provide career growth opportunities*

While coaching is an effective approach for up-leveling your team members' capability over time, there are also more scalable techniques at your disposal that free you up for other strategic projects. More scalable techniques can empower team members to follow a path to grow technically and build a sense of belonging in the function. Figure 7.3 illustrates four examples.

Build identity as a subject matter expert	Build relationships and practice leadership
For team members with expertise in an area: Hold office hours and propagate best practices—a low-cost way to build identity in an organization	*For team members who want to manage*: Onboard new team members—a natural area where you can mentor teammates and build working relationships

Build business understanding	Build redundancy in responsibility
For team members who want more scope: Become the point of contact (PoC) for business lines—take on perspectives outside the domain of data science	*For team members who want to be promoted*: Conduct succession planning—take care of business continuity when you take on new responsibilities

Figure 7.3   Four career growth opportunities for your team members

The opportunities for empowering team members include:

- *Building identity as a subject matter expert*—Holding office hours and propagating best practices
- *Building relationships and practicing leadership*—Onboarding new team members
- *Building business understanding*—Becoming the point of contact (PoC) for business lines
- *Building redundancy in responsibility*—Planning for succession

Let's look into each opportunity one by one.

BUILDING AN IDENTITY AS A SUBJECT MATTER EXPERT: HOLDING OFFICE HOURS

When a team member has expertise in an area, you can encourage them to hold office hours to advise others on the topic. Examples of expertise include data source nuances, data processing pipelines, controlled experiment setups, causal analysis, and storytelling in presentations.

Holding office hours is a lightweight initiative that may take no more than one hour a week. Yet it is powerful in establishing your team members' identity as the team's subject matter experts and allowing them to gain exposure to a variety of team challenges.

Section 4.2.2 introduced the four key elements of setting up an efficient office hour:

- *Determine the purpose*—Starting with a clear purpose.
  - *Example*—The storytelling office hour helps peer data scientists turn their analyses into impact and build their brands as powerful communicators.
- *Define a format*—Setting aside one or two fixed 30-minute slots every week can minimize disruptions for the team member running the office hour.

- *Specify the topic*—To make the best use of a 30-minute session, provide a set of guidelines for the audience to come prepared with for the office hour.
- *Follow best-practices*—The purpose, format, and topic can be published on a wiki and announced over email to the intended audience.

Holding office hours is a significant milestone for an individual contributor to develop into a tech lead. The technique can work well, as it motivates the practice of leadership from a team member's area of strength. When an office hour is well-utilized, the up-leveling of expertise in the team can produce impact across many projects, which benefits the organization.

While it may be tempting to require project leads to attend office hours for technical review, it is best to keep office-hour attendance voluntary. Requiring project leads to attend office hours can turn an opportunity into a burden, bottlenecking project progress, damaging team dynamics, and missing the point in building the identity of the team members holding the office hours.

Instead, when office-hour sessions make some real impact, you can share their success with the team to evangelize their benefits. When they don't work as expected, you can collect feedback to iterate with the team members holding the office hours on alternative formats and topics that may work better for your organization and culture.

Building relationships and practicing leadership: Becoming an onboarding mentor

One opportunity to help technical team members build interpersonal relationships is to become a mentor in onboarding new team members. An *onboarding mentor* is a role with responsibilities outside the technical domain. The relative difference of tenure within an organization allows your technical team members to share familiar domain knowledge of the industry and organization, while focusing on practicing relationship building with new team members.

The ramp velocity of the new team members is an indicator of success, which you can calibrate to your organization's and industry's complexity. A fast ramp of new team members' productivity creates business value for the organization and can build trust for future working relationships within your teams.

To provide a smooth and fast ramp-up process, the mentor can leverage an onboarding document which can include:

- Company vision and mission
- Function practices and principles to live by
- Relevant product and feature roadmaps
- Product and engineering partners to build relationships with
- Access to IT tools and ways around the office
- Important meetings and their cadence

While the hiring manager is ultimately responsible for developing an onboarding project, the mentor can organize team members to update the onboarding document. The mentor can also recommend a schedule for the first days and weeks with an efficient path to gain hands-on experience on essential tools and processes, as well as help introduce the new member socially to partners and teams. At the end of the onboarding process, the mentor can also work with the new hire to reflect on what part of the onboarding process went well and what can be improved, producing a better template for future onboarding processes.

By mentoring new team members, your technical team members can develop an appreciation for leading team members and facilitating best practices in processes. The mentoring process is also an opportunity to improve the team member onboarding experience, accelerating the time from ramp to productivity for your teams.

BUILDING BUSINESS UNDERSTANDING: BECOMING THE POINT OF CONTACT

The DS function interacts with many stakeholders in an organization. Table 7.2 illustrates examples of these interactions at the business line level and across functions. As the function leader, you are ultimately responsible for these relationships. You can delegate some of these responsibilities to team members in the PoC role to facilitate their growth.

Table 7.2   Illustration of the delegation of responsibilities to PoCs

	Product 1 PoC: Andrea	Product 2 PoC: Brian	Product 3 PoC: Brian	Product 4 PoC: Christina
User experience **PoC: Diane**	Project A	Project D	—	
Algorithm APIs **PoC: Frank**	Project B		Project F	Project H
Data aggregation **PoC: Georgia**	—	Project E	—	
Financial **PoC: Yourself**	—	—	Project G	—
Legal **PoC: Yourself**	Project C	—	—	Project I

A DS PoC is the member of your team who is the first person a partner will contact for opportunities, issues, and requests related to DS. This arrangement helps your partner gain a clear interface with the DS function. A PoC's responsibilities include:

- Understanding partner challenges
- Aggregating DS capabilities that can resolve partner challenges
- Setting partner expectations on what is technically possible
- Working with the DS team to prioritize potential solutions
- Escalating requests to DS leadership
- Holding partner domain knowledge and concerns to advise on future DS initiatives and roadmaps

As a function leader, you can delegate these responsibilities to multiple PoCs, where each PoC is responsible for a non-overlapping partner. At the same time, one person can also take on the PoC role for multiple partners. For example, Brian is the PoC for both project 2 and project 3 in table 7.2. Taken to an extreme, if you are not delegating the PoC responsibilities, you are the PoC for all partners.

050

> As a data science director, if you are not delegating the point of contact (PoC) responsibilities, you are *the* PoC for all partners.

Holding the responsibility of a PoC allows a team member to understand business and external function concerns outside the immediate scope of DS. The role also provides opportunities to maintain relationships with non-data scientists, synthesize partner requests, influence DS peers, and escalate requests. These are valuable skills to develop toward becoming a tech lead who will be responsible not just for communication and coordination, but also for the success of specific projects.

BUILDING REDUNDANCY IN RESPONSIBILITY: SUCCESSION PLANNING

Succession planning is usually known as a process for identifying and developing new leaders who can replace old leaders when they leave. The process increases the availability of experienced and capable employees who are prepared to assume leadership roles as they become available.

What is not so obvious is that succession planning can be done for any role, not just for leadership roles. All three of the roles we discussed in this section—the office-hour host, the onboarding mentor, and the point of contact for partners—as well as the leadership roles in your function, can have succession plans.

051

> *Succession planning* is usually known as a process for identifying and developing new leaders who can replace existing leaders when they leave. What is not so obvious is that succession planning can be done for any role. Good succession planning can retain valuable institutional knowledge and best practices within the team.

As members of your team mature, they are destined to be promoted or move on to different projects with different responsibilities. The typical role transitions take a few weeks at best, and much of the institutional knowledge and best practices can be lost in the process.

Coaching your team members to have a succession plan for their current role encourages them to be mindful of the knowledge and best practices that make them and the function successful. Often, just the act of explicitly documenting the knowledge and best practices can reinforce what works well. It is part of the function-building process.

Developing junior team members to bridge skill gaps can be motivating for senior team members, as it empowers them to take on more responsibilities. The process of mentoring and teaching junior members is also a reinforcement of senior team members' accumulated learning. This way, succession becomes a continuous process rather than the weakest link in your path to building a successful function.

Organizing initiatives to provide career growth opportunities is an important part of building a successful function. Only when team members feel they have room to grow in your organization can you unleash the full potential of their productivity. Holding office hours, mentoring new team members as part of the onboarding process, becoming a point of contact to partner teams, and taking care of their own succession planning are initiatives for you to scale your function's productivity and build working relationships with your star team members.

7.2 Rigor in planning, higher standards

Rigor is the craftsmanship that creates trust for the DS function. One area that separates strong and rigorous function leaders from weak ones is their approach to annual planning. You may have experienced or observed extremes of the planning process where it is conducted bottom-up. There is often a lack of focus, and the function ends up chasing more priorities than the number of data scientists on the team. This lack of focus can result in important projects failing to get sufficient resources. At the other extreme, when a planning process is driven top-down, the resulting plan can demand unrealistic goals and alienate key players, as their perspectives and expertise are not taken into account.

The rigor in planning lies not in the amount of detail in the plan but in the focus of its direction and the flexibility it reserves for execution. We discuss the rigor in planning at the function leadership level, then discuss two components that call for more attention within the planning process.

052

> The rigor in planning lies not in the amount of detail in the plan but in the focus of its direction and the flexibility it reserves for execution.

One component is the rigor in recognizing anti-patterns in projects and acting quickly to resolve them. *Anti-patterns* are patterns of undesirable practices that will lead to failures in projects and loss of trust from executives, partners, and team members. We highlight three top anti-patterns in project planning, execution, and completion that plague many DS functions.

The other component is the rigor in gaining commitment from team members and partners for milestones in the plans. It is not enough to create a plan. Alignment to the plan involves the explicit commitment from all stakeholders with clear communication on what the stakeholders will be accountable for.

7.2.1 *Driving a successful annual planning process*

A successful and rigorous planning process achieves three goals: highlighting priorities, setting realistic goals, and leaving flexibility in execution. The best annual plan is not the most detailed. In DS, many of the issues, roadblocks, and insights are not yet known during the planning process. Anticipating them in planning means including flexibilities in a realistic delivery schedule, such that teams and partners can align on expectations.

When your company has more than 100 employees and the DS team has more than 10 members, the annual planning process can be daunting. It requires teamwork amongst executives, function leaders, partners, and team leads to explore the many potential paths forward, align on a single path, and specify the milestones along the way. If not careful, significant effort could be wasted on exploration and specification, and a significant amount of trust could be lost in the alignment process.

Planning best practices at LinkedIn, Airbnb, and Eventbrite [3] start with a clear declaration of roles:

- The executives' role:
  - Specify the high-level vision and strategy, which reduces wasted efforts from team members proposing plans outside the top priority area.
  - Collect feedback from the teams to integrate and prioritize projects, which makes the plan a coherent strategy.
- The team members' role:
  - Propose plans that align with the high-level vision and strategy.
  - Tweak and confirm the buy-in of the final plan before starting to execute.

To be more specific, planning can take four steps:

- *Context*—Leadership shares their top priorities with the teams.
- *Plan*—The teams respond with proposals.
- *Integration*—Leadership integrates the teams' proposals into a single plan.
- *Buy-in*—Highlight gaps and risks, commit to goals, and execute.

These steps are illustrated in figure 7.4. Let's look at these steps one by one.

STEP 1: CONTEXT

The context for planning is a concise overview of what leadership believes is the path to winning. This first step of the planning process includes two phases. The deliverable for the first phase includes:

- *Vision and mission*—The desired future position and its approach to getting there
- *Goals*—Specific results over a specific time horizon
- *Strategies*—The path to the goal within the time horizon

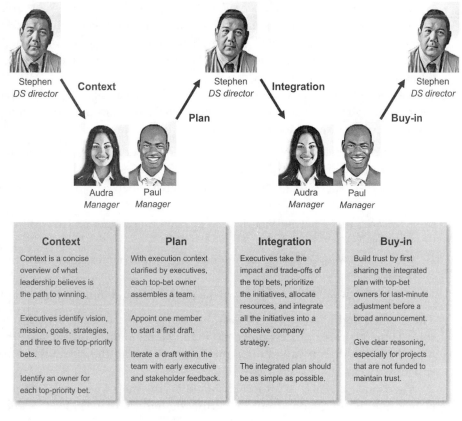

Figure 7.4   The four-step annual planning process [3]

- *Strategic pillars*—Three to five top priority bets, each including the following:
  - *Description*—What is the bet?
  - *Meaning*—What if we don't achieve it? What will success look like?
  - *Key initiatives*—Distinct track of work for achieving success.

As the function leader for DS, you can work with executive leadership to clarify these items if they are not yet clear. At times, the leadership team may be hesitant to commit to some of the details. It is still necessary for you to start with a written plan of record for your team, so your team can begin planning with as much context as possible.

Once the strategies for winning are determined and the top-bet priorities reflect the executives' thinking, you can work to understand the context behind the prioritization with rigor. This includes discerning what the executives believe to be true and what they think may be true. The team is encouraged to push back with well-articulated arguments and recommendations to the contrary if there are gaps in the executives' understanding.

A well-articulated set of *strategic pillars* should prioritize no more than three to five top bets. For example, the pillars for a maturing consumer-facing business may include improving engagement, building trust, and growing users in a new demographic. Any more bets may indicate that the executive team can't agree among themselves on what the priorities should be.

The second phase of executive context clarification can start once the top bets are clear. In this phase, you are identifying one individual (an owner) for each top bet to develop key initiatives, which include the following:

- *Description and strategy*—What is the course of action, and why should we take it? What is the sequence of steps?
- *Projects*—What are the various moving parts between functions to make it happen?
- *Timeline and impact*—What is the expected time horizon? How will success be measured?
- *Resource needs*—What are the engineering, infrastructure, and marketing spend needs?
- *Risks and dependencies*—What are the major risks and initial mitigation plans?

The top bets and initiatives don't need to align with the existing organization structure. As the planning process proceeds, the organization can restructure around the top bets rather than trying to force the bets to fit within the current organizational structure.

The owner assigned to a top bet should be the most knowledgeable person for elaborating the top bet and not necessarily the most senior DS leader reporting to you. The intent is to elaborate the top bets within the company vision/mission and goals, so project planning in the next step can be as focused as possible.

Once the two phases of the first step are complete, you can share the timeline for the next three steps with the broader team. The following steps are project planning, integration, and buy-in, and each step can take one to three weeks.

STEP 2: PLAN

In the second step of the annual planning process, each top-bet owner assembles a team and kicks project planning into gear with the executive contexts established in the first step. At this step, the contexts are suggestions and up for debate. If the team sees major challenges with the strategy or timeline, this is the time to provide alternative recommendations.

We discussed project-level planning in section 2.2.2. For annual planning, the project motivations follow from the top bets. The project definitions are the key initiatives. The teams' planning work primarily articulates the solution architecture, estimates the execution timeline (in engineering months or quarters), and brainstorms the project risks.

In this step, it is essential to validate whether the project definitions can help the company advance the big bets. You can do this by quantifying the potential ROI for partner functions, such as sales or customer service, and get their confirmation of whether the project goal can make a difference.

The plan owner can identify one team member to start the planning process with a rough first draft of the team plan, then iterate the draft with the team, while getting early feedback from executives. To keep the plan realistic, the team needs to make sure to check for buy-in for all stakeholders involved.

The plan proposal is ready to be submitted when it fits the executive context, has ambitious but achievable impact, and the required resources are clearly defined and well explained. The plan owner should also set the expectation with the team that no matter how polished the plan proposal is, there will be changes as you receive feedback from the executives.

In a well-run process, the plan owner has an opportunity to present the plan to the executives in person to address any potential gaps in the proposal. The in-person meeting can help the executives make an informed decision in the integration step of annual planning.

STEP 3: INTEGRATION

When the teams have assessed the impacts and risks of the top bets, it's time for the executive team to make some hard trade-offs. The purpose of the integration step is for the executive team to prioritize the initiatives, allocate resources, and integrate all the initiatives into a cohesive company strategy.

Important questions the executives will be asking themselves when making these hard decisions include:

- Are the most important projects prioritized and funded?
- Does each of the funded initiatives have a positive ROI?
- How confident are we that we have the right teams working on the right projects?
- How can we increase that confidence?
- Is the team being ambitious enough? Or too ambitious?
- Is the company doing too much?

The integrated plan should be as simple as possible. In execution, market drifts and new priorities frequently emerge. If the plan looks complicated at this stage, it will be overwhelming to execute later.

STEP 4: BUY-IN

The buy-in step is a key step that can build or break the trust between the executives and their team. The finalized plan is first shared with the top-bet owners and the planning team they have assembled. This is to make sure nothing critical is missing. You can build trust by getting their feedback and working in last-minute adjustments before the plan is shared company-wide. If you only give them a quick heads up without addressing their concerns, you may end up losing trust. The planning teams have spent long days putting together the details of the project plans and seeking alignment from partners. When their projects get cut without a clear narrative, or when they can no longer commit to goals with some resources missing, they may feel discouraged about working in another planning exercise in the future.

As part of the senior leadership team, make sure to avoid surprises in prioritization decisions, and share the reasoning behind the decisions as early as possible. Help the team understand where the decisions come from and get them excited about their next projects.

At the function lead level, you are going to be exposed to the company-wide annual planning process. Many of the practices and concerns in this process are also applicable for quarterly planning as well. With this four-step planning process as a reference, you can strive to craft a clear annual plan for your function before the year ends and set your function up for success in the new year.

7.2.2 *Avoiding project planning and execution anti-patterns*

Patterns in software engineering and DS are reusable solutions to commonly occurring problems. Anti-patterns are patterns of bad practices that will lead to failures in projects and result in a loss of trust from executives, partners, and team members.

There are many practices that well-meaning data scientists fall into that can cause project failures. A rigorous function leader should watch for these patterns and guide the team out of them as quickly as possible. We highlight three top anti-patterns [4], in project planning, execution, and completion, respectively, that plague many DS projects:

- *Project planning*—Death-by-planning pattern
- *Project execution*—Fire drill pattern
- *Project completion*—Throw-it-over-the-wall pattern

053

A rigorous function leader watches for anti-patterns in project planning, execution, and completion, such as the *death-by-planning* pattern, *fire drill* pattern, and *throw-it-over-the-wall* pattern, and guides the team out of these anti-patterns as quickly as possible.

PROJECT PLANNING: THE DEATH-BY-PLANNING PATTERN

In section 2.2.2, we introduced the process of project planning for tech leads. While planning is essential for aligning expectations on a project, a project can fail despite careful planning, the *death-by-planning* pattern. There are two failure modes to watch out for:

- A plan is developed and reviewed at the beginning of the project but not updated or tracked against execution. Many emerging issues in execution are not promptly communicated with stakeholders. Stakeholders are surprised when the deadline arrives and the project is not complete. This often happens in organizations when the focus is on controlling schedules rather than the delivery of results.
- A plan is overly complicated and shows an untrackable amount of details. There is a perception that everything is under control, while too much time is spent on planning rather than delivering results. When delays happen, too much time is spent updating the plan, which causes further delays and more replanning.

The causes for these failure modes come from a lack of a pragmatic, common-sense approach to planning, scheduling, and tracking. A project plan only needs to be as detailed as the milestones you can track.

As a solution, for DS projects, milestones at the granularity of 5 to 10 days (one sprint) are usually detailed enough, such that we can refine the details as part of sprint planning and assess our progress toward the goal on a weekly or per-sprint basis. Each milestone should have a set of verifiable deliverables and acceptance criteria, so we can be confident that we have reached them. Examples of such milestones and key deliverables can include:

- Architecture reviewed
- Model prototyped
- Unit test suite completed
- All P1 bugs fixed
- A/B test scheduled
- A/B test results analyzed
- Feature ramped

The purpose of planning is to increase the chance of success for projects by crafting their direction, scoping their deliverables, and anticipating their breakdowns. Project tracking provides early feedback for the team to respond and get the project back on track. Here are some well-defined states for tracking:

- *On track*—The team expects the project to complete as scheduled with no new risks.
- *Delivered*—The project is completed according to acceptance criteria and accepted by the sponsor or customer.
- *Early*—The project is ongoing and is expected to complete earlier than expected.
- *At risk*—The project encountered issues, and on-time delivery is still possible with catch-up work.
- *Late*—The project encountered issues, and delivery will be delayed to a new date without additional help.

The *on track* and *delivered* states are self-explanatory. To highlight a few of the other states, the *early* state is important to call out as a success for the delivery team. As a function leader, you will want to examine the reasons for finishing milestones early and not squander a teachable moment. Were there some best practices to share? Did some anticipated risk not happen? Was there some heroic effort by a highly productive team member? If planning was done in good faith, it is your responsibility to dispel the appearance of an intentional lowering of expectations (or sandbagging) in planning, such that future plans will not be unrealistically aggressive. If the expectations were intentionally lowered, you will need to talk with the tech lead about the danger of sandbagging, as promising projects can be canceled or deprioritized for low ROI.

When a project is *at risk*, the project is delayed compared to the plan's milestones, but there is still a path within the project lead's capabilities to getting it back on track to deliver on time. As a function leader, this is the time to show your appreciation for the heads-up from the project lead, reinforce the act of timely communication by offering support when required, and empower the tech lead to work out schedule risk. When tech leads can learn to manage projects through delays, it can free you up to lead more strategically.

When a project is *late*, the project has no path toward on-time delivery without adjusting the scope, the resources, the deadline, or all of the above. You can empower the tech lead to work with project stakeholders to propose options, so the project sponsor can select and approve the changes. You can support your tech lead by redirecting resources to accelerate project progress where possible, while clarifying the delay's impact on other affected projects and informing all stakeholders. The goal is to align on a new achievable scope or timeline, such that the project can be delivered. Your support can build trust between you and your team leads and pave the path for the DS function to better work together to deliver projects successfully.

PROJECT EXECUTION: THE FIRE DRILL PATTERN

The fire drill pattern occurs when a DS project is initiated but delayed because of design, data, pipeline, scheduling, or team politics. At the risk of being canceled, the team makes a desperate attempt to complete the project in a fraction of the time, compromising on scope and quality and creating mountains of tech debt in the process.

Some tech leads may actually be incentivized toward this pattern. In the normal course of the project, specifications and architecture go through rigorous reviews and iterations before being declared acceptable. In a fire drill scenario, the management team might accept any specification and architecture that can complete the project before the deadline. The urgency can make the job easier for tech leads to get through specification and architecture review at the risk of creating tech debts to be paid in the future. Rigorous DS cannot be performed in a fire drill scenario. Here are a few potential root causes for the fire drill scenario with solutions that can emerge from your leadership:

- *Analysis paralysis*—The team is stuck in a protracted period of analysis and planning, compressing the development schedule and leading to a fire drill scenario. There should be clear milestones for the completion of the analysis and planning phase of the project. As a function leader, you can guide the tech lead to place the project in the *at-risk* or *late* states, to call attention to the project for support in moving it out of the analysis and planning stages.
- *Schematics engineering*—The project is stuck in the architecture schematic phase and can't pass the review process. As a function leader, you can recognize this symptom and push the project into the prototyping phase to prove out any potential technical risks instead of discussing theoretical concerns on paper.
- *Volatile specifications*—Stakeholders cannot agree on some output details, and the project is stuck in the specification phase. As a function leader, you can guide the tech lead to architect an internal and external portion of the project such that the internal components can flexibly support variations of output format, while the stakeholders refine the specific external specifications by a later date.

PROJECT COMPLETION: THE THROW-IT-OVER-THE-WALL PATTERN

The *throw-it-over-the-wall* pattern can occur when products are developed by one team and are intended to be operated by another team. For DS projects, this can happen when a model developed by the DS team is maintained by the product engineering or site reliability engineering teams.

The throw-it-over-the-wall pattern happens when the model may be code complete but is not yet rigorously tested and is weakly documented. A lack of input drift and output anomaly monitoring also makes a model susceptible to unexpected behaviors in operations, leading to user experiences degradation.

This anti-pattern can have several potential root causes. We explore them here and discuss possible solutions:

- *The project plan was not comprehensive enough* to allocate time for testing, documentation, and monitoring input drifts and output anomalies. As a function leader, project proposals should be held to a high standard of completeness. The expectations for project completion should be aligned with the teams that will be operating the deliverables. It is your responsibility to introduce this standard of rigor for project planning.
- *Project scope was cut* because of delays in earlier phases, company priority changes, or resource constraints. As a function leader, you should set clear expectations of scope-cut impacts on tech debts. It may be a well-articulated trade-off to cut some scopes, but the payback plan for the created tech debt should also be articulated. If tech debt is not addressed in time, a project can produce significant disruptions in end-user experience over time.

- *Execution issues from an individual* could be the cause for the lack of testing, documentation, or monitoring in a project. As a function leader, you can investigate whether this is a symptom of a systematically weak onboarding process, a systematic lack of mentorship from senior tech leads, or an individual ability or motivation issue. If the issue has a systematic cause, processes can be improved to mitigate future occurrences. If it is an individual issue, it is best to understand the individual's deeper concerns before the lack of rigor affects the team and partners' morale.

As a function leader, reflecting on recurring root causes from project failures is an excellent way to collect and document these anti-patterns. The anti-patterns provide a wealth of institutional knowledge for detecting and correcting situations in the future.

7.2.3   *Securing commitments from partners and teams*

A commitment is a declaration of personal responsibility to produce a result or outcome. Team and partner alignment is a form of commitment that declares the parties have agreed to a common goal to deliver results through some process by a particular date. Securing commitments from partners and team members is key in project coordination and execution. However, ambiguities in language and understanding often get in the way.

Have you encountered situations where you thought a commitment was made, but the other parties had different interpretations? We can leverage rigorous commitment techniques to minimize these ambiguities.

A commitment to coordinate DS projects can take on different forms. As effective function leaders, you can first notice and observe the various forms of commitments, practice the rigor for producing clear commitments, and solicit clear commitments from others to successfully coordinate projects.

FORMS OF COMMITMENTS

Even simple commitments can have distinct components that, if missing, can reduce the effectiveness of your team. For example, when you commit to accepting a request from a partner, regardless of how vague the request is, being rigorous means that you will clarify the *condition of satisfaction* for delivering the results within a *specific time frame.* You should also *confirm the consequences of accepting* the request with a partner, including deprioritizing other projects with the partner, coordinating on input and reviews during the project, and expecting a better working relationship between the teams for future collaborations.

There are five forms of simple commitment [1] you can observe in the workplace: promises, requests, assertions, assessments, and constitutive declarations. As shown in table 7.3, each has distinct components that must be specified to make a commitment clear. When commitments are not clearly defined and delivered, you can lose trust with your teams and partners.

Table 7.3   Five forms of simple commitments and their components

Commitment	Components
Promise	A condition of satisfaction and a time frame for completion
Request	An ask for a specific promise and the consequences of accepting or declining
Assertion	A claim of truth or fact with references that can be cited upon request
Assessment	An interpretation or judgment with grounding and logical reasoning
Constitutive declaration	A declaration of purpose and boundaries

Let's look at each of the commitments in more detail in the context of the DS function:

- *Promises*—Promises are commitments to produce satisfactory results by a specific time. For example, you can promise a product manager that you will produce an analysis and a proposal with a recommendation for the next steps by Friday. In turn, a product engineering partner can also promise to track user behavior and provide the tracking data to you in a specific form to analyze by Wednesday.

  It is critical that a time frame is specified for a promise. We discuss a bit later how a promise to "get around to it" is not a commitment, as you cannot coordinate on actions following the completion of the promise.

- *Requests*—Requests are commitments to ask for specific promises from others, coupled with the willingness and ability to produce consequences for accepting and declining the request.

  Consequences may be natural or imposed. Natural consequences are situations that evolve naturally as a person accepts or declines your request. Situations can include the success of a company initiative if the request is accepted, or the trust and capabilities built through fulfilling a request for future collaborations. Imposed consequences are situations you can put on the person you are making a request to, including rewards or bonuses for successful execution or performance penalties for declining your request.

  As a function leader, you have the authority to produce positive and negative imposed consequences for team members in your function. When using imposed consequences, the consequence has to be significant enough for your request to be accepted. You also need to be willing to follow through with the imposed consequences. If you cannot follow through with the reward or penalty, your imposed consequences will carry little weight in the future.

  At the workplace, natural consequences are always preferred for making requests to team members and partners. This is because natural consequences remove the willingness and ability limitations in following through as compared to an imposed consequence. Natural consequences will fall into place should your team members or partners accept or decline your request. If you are struggling for ideas, think of the natural consequences to the organization, the individual, yourself, and your relationship with them.

For these reasons, clarifying consequences, especially significant natural consequences, to team members and partners themselves, can make your requests more powerful, which can increase the chance that your requests will be accepted and fulfilled.

- *Assertions*—Assertions are commitments to claims of truth and facts. They appear everywhere when we share results or make recommendations on the paths forward. As discussed in section 3.2.1, scientific rigor is the expectation from the rest of the organization for our work. Your professional reputation is at stake, so have references ready upon request.

  Similarly, when we hear assertions from partners or the marketplace, we should be aware of the underlying standard of rigor for these assertions, so we can leverage them with the appropriate level of confidence in our results and recommendations.

- *Assessments*—Assessments are commitments to interpretations or judgments. Data scientists use quantitative criteria to interpret situations through mathematically and logically rigorous approaches. The output of our analysis and predictive models are assessments of the past and the future. When we share assessments rigorously, we are not just sharing our interpretations or judgments, but we are also sharing both the grounding and the logical reasoning for them. This is also why explainable analysis and models are often required for making important decisions. When we receive assessments, we also have an opportunity to examine the grounding and logical reasoning behind them before accepting.

- *Constitutive declarations*—Constitutive declarations are commitments to ways of being, such as by constituting a professional identity, a project charter, or a team charter. For a data scientist's professional identity, the commitment is to rigorously produce trustworthy quantitative results with a positive business impact. Project charters commit to resolving customer pain points with specific deliverables. Team charters commit to clarifying team direction, while establishing boundaries. The rigor in working on projects and with partner teams is to understand their charters and work with the declared roles and responsibilities.

  In organizations using holacracy as a structure, fluency in constitutive declarations is required. In a *holacracy*, the culture promotes a hierarchy of self-managed units or *circles*, each with its own governing process, to constitute teams, define roles, make decisions, and evaluate performance. Companies such as Zappos have implemented this organizational structure successfully. Holacracy as an organizational structure is discussed in more detail in section 10.2.4.

When you make and accept commitments, your rigor as the DS function leader is to understand and clarify the components of these commitments with your teams and partners, so you can build long-term trust.

COMMITTING TO COMMITMENTS

With a commitment clarified, you can ask whether a team member or partner can commit. You may get an answer that sounds like this:

- "I'll try."
- "I can probably do that."
- "I'll do my best."

These responses often sound like commitments, but they are not. There are only three types of responses you can anticipate:

- A clear commitment includes what is committed to and over what time frame.
  - Example: "Yes, I promise to deliver the product deep dive by Friday."
- A renegotiation of the terms of the commitment with a proposal.
  - Example: "No, I will not commit to that, but I can commit to delivering it by next Friday."
- Decline to commit.
  - Example 1: "No, I will not commit—I'll try."
  - Example 2: "No, I cannot commit yet. I need clarification."
  - Example 3: "No, I cannot commit yet, but I'll get back to you by tomorrow."

The goal of seeking commitment is not to force your team member or partner to commit. It is an opportunity to understand whether they can commit, and if not, what are some reasons that they cannot commit.

In a commitment conversation, when your team member or partner has responded "yes" to a commitment, the rigorous practice is to summarize the terms of the commitment for a second confirmation. For example, you can check with, "Great. In summary, you are committing to delivering daily tracking data in the data warehouse by Wednesday. Is that right?" If your team member or partner responds with any hesitation, it's best to diagnose the potential risks and work to mitigate them right away rather than hoping that the data will show up Wednesday.

Finally, conclude the commitment conversation with a request for communication as early as possible if a commitment will not be fulfilled by the agreed-upon date. This can maximize the chance that the commitment can be carried out.

It is also good etiquette to send a follow-up note in writing, summarizing the commitment agreed to. When you are talking to partners who are team managers, they may be delegating the commitment to their team members. A written summary can minimize the chance that some components of the commitment get lost in the delegation.

As a function leader, your rigor can be demonstrated in situations as broad as company-wide annual planning or as narrow as securing commitments with an alignment conversation. These practices are essential tools for you to be effective in a senior-level leadership role. They are also great coaching topics for your team members, so they can be more effective in their work.

7.3   *Attitude of positivity*

Attitude is the mood with which you approach workplace situations. As the leader of a function, you oversee the team members as they work through failures with positivity and tenacity (section 3.3.1). You nurture a culture of institutionalized learning when projects succeed or fail (section 5.3.3). And you mentor new managers to adapt to the manager's schedule from the maker's schedule (section 5.3.1). Over time, these are the practices that you will be delegating and coaching your project and team leads to take on. What, then, are the attitude concerns for a director or a principal data scientist in leading the DS function?

Diversity in the team becomes more important as you grow your teams. As a quantitative discipline, we tend to simplify diversity into a question of gender ratio and racial makeup. While these ratios are important, they are lagging success indicators for diversity. To build a productive function, the implications of diversity go much deeper. Section 7.3.1 highlights the association and potential causations between diversity and productivity.

If diversity is compared to inviting someone to a party, *inclusion* can be compared to asking them to dance. In a professional setting, inclusion means listening to people's input, respecting their preferences, and actively soliciting their ideas. Section 7.3.2 discusses how contributions of ideas can be acknowledged and reinforced, and how team members can feel engaged in their work.

While diversity and inclusion are what you can do as a function leader, the true metric of success is when team members feel *belonging*, which requires deeper trust among team members that can only be nurtured over time. Belonging can be challenging to build and easy to break. Making it work can mean the difference between crushing tech debts and high talent churn, and a productive pool of data scientists with deep institutional knowledge. Section 7.3.3 discusses how belonging can be nurtured in your DS function for team members to bring their whole selves to contribute to the team.

054

If diversity is compared to inviting someone to a party, inclusion can be compared to asking them to dance, and belonging is when your guest feels comfortable dancing.

Diversity, inclusion, and belonging all contribute to the attitude of positivity in a DS function. They are not unique to DS. But given the broad range of impact a DS function can provide a company, there are unique opportunities you can capture. Let's dive into some of them.

7.3.1 Recognizing and promoting diversity within your team

Diversity speaks to ways people are alike and different. Diversity dimensions that people often discuss include race, gender, and ethnicity. There are actually many more dimensions of diversity, including some that are visible and some that are invisible. Figure 7.5 illustrates a partial list of the various dimensions of diversity, including many dimensions that transcend race, gender, and ethnicity and are invisible when you first meet or work with someone.

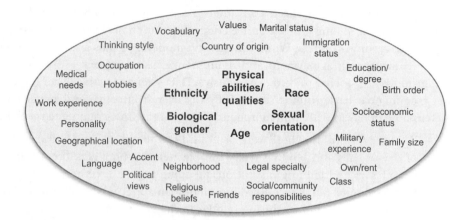

Figure 7.5 A partial list of the dimensions of diversity

Just like sampling in any high-dimensional space in DS, even when you have a team with few members, they can still represent diverse backgrounds across many of the dimensions shown in figure 7.5. This characteristic makes diversity an important topic for teams large and small.

As you recognize the diversity in your team, when team members feel safe to share their deeper experiences across multiple dimensions with team members, you will also find other benefits. Across the plethora of dimensions, the likelihood that team members can discover shared attributes in some dimensions increases dramatically. As a side note, this is also the statistical effect that led to the Bonferroni correction, where when multiple hypotheses are tested (in this case, when multiple dimensions are compared), the chance of observing a rare event or an accidentally matched dimension increases.

PROMOTING DIVERSITY IS MORE THAN A SOCIAL CAUSE

Promoting diversity is not just a social cause. It has real productivity and business implications. A DS team with diverse backgrounds can be more innovative in recognizing new business opportunities. One real-life case is from Ant Group, the internet finance arm of Alibaba, which is part of China's largest e-commerce portal. A customer DNA project extracted relationships between various types of customer purchasing behavior on a broad set of purchases on Alibaba's e-commerce websites. One of the many findings is that there is a close relationship between tight clothing purchases and smartphone screen repair purchases.

Arriving at this type of finding requires a DS team with a diverse set of backgrounds to recognize the hidden social concepts behind the data. Based on this finding, Ant Financial developed a smartphone screen-repair warranty product and marketed it to people who purchased tight-fitting clothing. The product has been getting good traction.

Another real-life case can be seen in the consumer lending industry. Many developing countries lack centralized consumer credit systems, so companies have been using cell phone billing history and e-commerce purchase histories to assess loan applicants' creditworthiness. While some credit modeling teams are focused on traditional features, such as payment and delinquency history, teams with more diverse backgrounds are looking to be more inclusive. Data scientists with call center analytics and e-commerce backgrounds successfully discovered effective and novel features, such as time of day for calls and merchandise return rate in e-commerce records:

- *Time of day for calls*—There were profound connections found between the time of day of calls and lending risk. Late payment reminders and collection calls from banks and lending institutions all come from call centers during regular business hours. Many recently delinquent loan applicants have resorted to turning off their cell phones during regular business hours and only using their cell phones on nights and weekends. A change in cell phone usage behavior can indicate financial stress that is observable much earlier than public legal records for delinquencies.

- *Merchant return rate*—There were also correlations found between merchant return rate and high delinquency rate. While the exact causal effect is not known, one can speculate about the moral hazards of taking advantage of generous return policies to the merchant's detriment and how that may indicate the likelihood of a borrower to repay a loan.

Identifying these features would not have been possible without a DS team with a diverse set of experiences. They are concrete evidence for you to consider to produce real business impact by building diverse DS teams.

TECHNIQUES FOR RECOGNIZING DIVERSITY

When approaching sensitive topics such as diversity, some team members may have strong opinions that have been formed over the years. Recent management research [5] suggests that an experiential learning environment in a group setting is best to illustrate common blind spots, share experiences, and allow questions to be asked about diversity.

Experiential learning is a process whereby knowledge is created through the transformation of experience in a group setting. Its effectiveness is second only to experiencing situations firsthand. Experiential learning creates a professional environment for recognizing diversity, allowing team members to cultivate their cultural awareness and take responsibility for sharing their perspectives.

These group sessions need to set ground rules to avoid off-the-cuff comments of particular attendees from damaging long-term working relationships within the team. You can reference a set of four ground rules for setting up a safe space:

- Equalize the space
- Check your assumptions at the door
- Retain the right to be human
- Have consensual dialogue

To *equalize the space,* the details discussed should be kept confidential. Confidentiality encourages a more impactful, open discussion on diversity. You can share experiences and lessons learned but not gossip or identify details about who said what. More vocal team members should hold back a little to allow others time to speak. Less vocal team members should try to speak up. When voicing disagreement, speak to the idea or the practice, rather than the person with a different opinion. Everyone's truth in the conversation is equally worthy of being true, so the team can honor multiple perspectives as you move through the diversity conversation.

To *check your assumptions at the door,* there should be no judgment on others for what they say and no disclaimers on what you have to say. Everyone speaks as an individual rather than as a representative of a group. Speak about your own perspective using "I" statements, such as "I feel X when you behave Y," to own your knowledge. In the diversity discussion, everyone should believe in the team's common intention to discuss and learn more about a complex topic.

To *retain the right to be human,* when a team member steps over the ground rules with an emotional comment, give them a break, as they might be having a bad day, but do point it out politely. When considering different perspectives, honor the diversity in backgrounds by highlighting the team members' origins in culture, race, class, gender, and so on. Acknowledge emotions in the discussions appropriately, as the topic of diversity may be more sensitive to some than others. If there is a comment that may be too sensitive for some, practice being the bigger person by giving forgiveness.

To *have consensual dialogues* in these sessions, practice active listening by focusing your attention with appropriate eye contact, checking your body language, and inquiring about and using team members' preferred pronouns. In a session, everyone is encouraged to take a risk and speak up, but everyone also has the right to pass. If someone is coerced to speak, it is likely they will not be sincere, which can provide bad data for the conversation. Every party in the conversation has an equal responsibility to speak up to find a solution if you bring up a problem, and to define the problem if you bring up a solution.

What is challenging for many DS practitioners is that, while science is based on objective observations, truth in social issues is subjective to the observers' background. Especially when it comes to how a narrative makes people feel, there is often more than one truth. As DS practitioners, we must embrace the concept of many truths when building relationships for diversity to flourish in the DS function.

With these ground rules, a diversity session can then focus on first understanding our own diversity attributes. One way is to write down and share how we identify ourselves across the dimensions listed in figure 7.1. We can then list our own top five dimensions and share them with the team. In this exercise, you are likely to discover many dimensions your teammates identify with that do not show up in your daily work. You may also discover dimensions where you share common attributes that were not apparent before. When we understand what our team members identify themselves with, we can start the discussion for inclusion.

TECHNIQUES FOR PROMOTING DIVERSITY

There are many best practices you can consider and pitfalls to avoid when promoting diversity. Recognizing the diversity that already exists in your function is the low-hanging fruit. Bringing in new team members with more diverse backgrounds can be more challenging.

In many successful, fast-growing DS functions, meeting hiring targets for growth is hard enough. Having diversity requirements is additional pressure on a hiring manager. Meeting diversity requirements is especially challenging for hiring managers, as they are often working with the candidate pipelines sourced by the HR team.

In turn, HR talent-sourcing teams are guided by their experience of successful hires and the machine-learned, search-ranking algorithms in the tools they use. The search-ranking tools are often trained to promote the types of candidates that have generated more interest in the past. So historical cultural biases for DS candidates persist and feed into themselves in many entrenched ways.

Adding in the social factor, when diverse candidates consider joining your function, they often look at your team's existing diversity. So the most challenging diversity hire on your team may be your first diversity hire.

What are some best practices that you can constitute as a function leader to make it fair for the stakeholders involved? You can consider a two-step process to benchmark and then drive change.

Benchmark

As a DS function leader, you can first articulate the expected number of diverse team members if there were no biases in your hiring practices. You can then estimate your company standing with respect to your peers. For example, if you are building a team of 12, should you target six male and six female data scientists?

In 2020, the male to female ratio across all data scientists in the US was about seven to three [6]. To check whether your team is an unbiased sample in the gender dimension, you can use a binomial distribution with $p = 0.3$, using the number of team members in your function. If you are within one standard deviation from the mean, you have a low probability of a systematic gender bias in your hiring process.

For example, if you are leading 12 other data scientists in your function, you should expect on average three to four female data scientists on the team if your team is a random sample of the US data scientist population. If you have a team with two or fewer females and eleven or more male members, you will be more than one standard deviation away from the mean gender ratio for data scientists in the US.

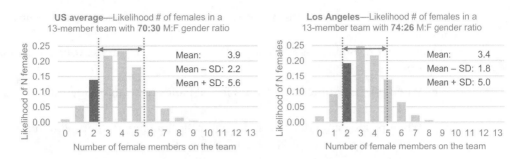

Figure 7.6   Benchmarking the male-to-female ratio for data science team diversity

For many companies, the candidate pool is limited to local candidates. You can also benchmark your current team composition with the local candidate pool available to you. Suppose your company is in Los Angeles, one of the largest metropolitan areas in the US. In that case, the female-to-male ratio for professionals with the data scientist title is 26% to 74% (see figure 7.6). Having two female data scientists on your 13-member team (you and your 12-member team) places you within one standard deviation of the mean for your local candidate pool. Companies with geographically distributed teams can leverage team diversity across multiple locations to improve the quality of business decisions.

Drive change

The diversity ratio is a result of a company's hiring and employee retention practices. If the current level of diversity is unacceptable, you can look at correcting potential biases in hiring or in the working environment. One place you can drive changes is at the top of the talent funnel.

First, open roles should be widely advertised, so everyone has an opportunity to apply. Second, in sourcing candidates, to counter any biases in searching and ranking of talent, you can require at least a certain ratio of diverse candidates interviewed before a hiring decision is made. The hiring decision can still be merit-based, and the hiring manager can be empowered to focus on matching the right talent with the right opportunity.

To fundamentally close the gender ratio gap in DS, we as a field can inspire people of diverse backgrounds to become part of the next generation of data scientists and DS leaders. We would like to invite everyone to come with us on this journey to improve the diversity of talent leading DS.

7.3.2   *Practicing inclusion in decision-making*

To create a safe and harmonious work environment for your function, it is not enough to just have members with diverse backgrounds on the team. You also need to acknowledge and welcome their different cultural backgrounds and treat everyone with respect.

The concept of inclusion can be more subtle than diversity, as there are no hard metrics to measure its success. We help highlight the challenges from a discussion and learning perspective to contrast the positive and negative situations and their natural consequences.

To reflect on your actions in leading the function, you can ask yourself the following questions:

- When selecting times and venues for all-hands or team outings, what messages am I sending?
- When picking attendees for meetings, calls, lunches, dinners, committees, and stretch assignments, who is or isn't included?
- In whom have I shown interest to guide career goals, projects, teams, and opportunities?
- In requesting feedback in meetings or in writing, who have I included or not included?
- If I solicited input and ultimately went in another direction, have I explained why I have not acted on others' ideas?

Biases, whether intentional or not, can create an appearance of non-inclusion. It is not enough to claim that one has no intentional biases. All of us grew up in some environment with certain assumptions that form some biases in our unconscious minds.

055

Biases, whether intentional or not, can create an appearance of non-inclusion. Watch out for potential biases when you select meeting or activity times, venues, or attendees, and who you show interest to guide for career goals, projects, teams, and opportunities.

For example, when you have a challenging project with opportunities for advancement that may require a short period of overtime, do you offer it to a single male or a mother of two young children who may be equally qualified? If you choose the single male, are you making decisions with the best intentions but systematically biasing your team members' career prospects?

Challenges in inclusion: Microaggressions

Many common challenges in inclusion come from *microaggressions*, the conscious or unconscious biases that float around the office and can hurt team members' feelings, make them feel not welcomed, or damage their long-term careers.

In the example above, if the team member who is a mother of two young children is repeatedly skipped over for opportunities, it is a form of microaggression and non-inclusion despite any best intentions. Biases can come from the stereotype that mothers of young children cannot simultaneously prioritize family and work responsibilities. A more effective approach is to offer the choice to the mother and include them in the decision process. There are many examples of women who can take care of family and work responsibilities simultaneously. And most of us don't hold similar biases for fathers of young children when considering giving them more responsibilities.

There are three types of microaggressions that can damage an inclusive culture: microassaults, microinsults, and microinvalidations.

Microassaults are conscious and intentional acts of discrimination. They often occur when comments are left anonymously, when telling offensive jokes among other like-minded colleagues, or when an individual becomes emotional and loses control. These are straightforward to recognize when you see them.

Microinsults are comments or actions that communicate insensitivity to a person's identity or heritage. The perpetrator is not usually consciously aware of the harmful nature of their behavior. Examples include: "That was quite a confidently presented set of results for an Asian data scientist"; "This model is pretty rigorous for an analyst"; or "You are the smartest blond data scientist around here." They can appear to be a compliment on the surface, but have a hidden insulting message.

Microinvalidations are comments or actions that ignore or dismiss the thoughts or feelings of a member of the underrepresented class. Examples include: a member of the minority being told that they are overly sensitive, which invalidates their emotions; Asian Americans repeatedly being asked where they are from, which implies that they are foreigners in their own country; teammates reminding their colleagues that they live in a post-racial society, invalidating their experiences of being treated differently.

All three types can shut down team member engagement, reinforce biases, and undermine your best efforts to provide a safe environment to include everyone in the team's decision-making process.

TECHNIQUES TO REDUCE BIASES

The first step in reducing your biases is to take an inventory of your own biases. Everyone has biases formed as part of their upbringing and their journey through life. Even Netflix VP of Inclusion Strategy Vernā Myers acknowledged her personal biases on a commercial flight: while she encountered turbulence in the air, she felt concerned about her safety as the captain onboard happened to be female. She noticed her biases, as she did not feel the least concerned on the return flight while encountering similar turbulence with a male captain onboard.

There are many bumpy and turbulent situations you may encounter at work. We instinctively lean on our personal biases when we are under stress, especially when responding to situations for the sake of our own survival.

As the function leader, you can start reducing your biases by first moving out of denial and acknowledging your own biases. You can notice what gets you excited in interviewing candidates, managing new employees, and selecting technology vendors. What do you focus on and ignore in a résumé? Who have you sponsored or mentored over the years?

To weaken your biases, slow down your decision processes by disengaging your intuitive thinking and engaging your analytical thinking. Remember to check how you are making any decisions important for your team members.

Building close relationships with a diverse set of team members across functions and backgrounds can also help weaken your biases. It can be uncomfortable at the beginning, as there are many unfamiliar topics, and the conversations can feel awkward and weird. It is important to get past the discomfort to form deeper bonds, so the relationships can push against any of your existing biases.

Biases and microaggressions can cause discomfort and stress in the workplace and result in team members' disengagement. To build an inclusive function, notice when these microaggressions arise, call them out, and make them teachable moments. Even over the holidays or during a team lunch, the inaction of not calling out biases and microaggressions can be interpreted as acceptances or even endorsements.

No one is perfect. When you have caused a microaggression, apologize sincerely, and move on. If someone else experienced a microaggression, make sure to also check on the offended person afterward to help them feel considered and included as a member of the team. Each team member should be encouraged to play their part in actively calling out biases and microaggressions to make sure your DS function has an inclusive environment.

7.3.3 *Nurture belonging to your function*

When you have recognized and promoted diversity in your team and practiced inclusion in decision-making, you can begin to nurture the feeling of belonging in your function. In a team with limited diversity, there can be many common attributes among team members to drive belonging. In a diverse team, driving belonging can be much more challenging.

Belonging can be driven proactively and reactively. In times of steady growth of the function, there are a set of techniques that you can use to proactively drive belonging in the team. In turbulent times, where external factors threaten the company's culture and the team, you are expected to react to the external factors appropriately.

These are no simple tasks! Let's dive into these two situations one by one.

DRIVING BELONGING PROACTIVELY

In normal times, here are three proactive approaches to drive belonging in your function:

- *Recognize dimensions of diversity*—As discussed in section 7.3.1, we can recognize different dimensions of diversity. With more than 30 dimensions listed in figure 7.5, statistically, there may be many dimensions in which team members share common attributes and interests that they may not have realized before. These shared attributes and interests can be topics of discussion that allow team members to feel they are working with real people with shared human experiences. The relationships that emerge from these understandings can provide social credit during the inevitable turbulent and stressful times in projects. When teammates can give each other the benefit of the doubt and look out for each other as one of their own, it can produce a feeling of belonging within the team.
- *Realize each other's strengths*—In section 4.2.1 on team execution, we discussed four levels of realization: realize your individual leadership strengths, realize your team's portfolio of leadership strengths, realize how individuals can complement one another, and realize how teammates with unique strengths can take on responsibilities to improve the team performance in a strength area.

In level 3 and level 4 of the realizations, when team members can see how their peers and the entire team are dependent on them for certain personal leadership strengths, it can be a powerful feeling to be accepted, valued, and needed in the team. This can increase the feeling of belonging among your team members.

- *Driving a culture of acknowledgment*—You can drive a culture of "catching your teammates doing something right." This technique was discussed as a management technique in section 5.3.2, but it can also be applied to the entire function. When team members learn to value and appreciate teammates' effort, it can encourage teammates to help each other more actively. The party receiving help can feel they are accepted by the team. The party providing help can feel their efforts are appreciated by the team.

  These positive actions can be reinforced with company thank you notes and company-sponsored gift programs. They can also play a part in documenting good behavior toward bonus points in promotion cases.

Beyond the feeling of belonging within the DS team, there is also the feeling of belonging within partner teams and the company's vision and mission. For the feeling of belonging with the partner teams, techniques such as recognizing the dimensions of diversity and driving a culture of acknowledgment can work well when you can organize team building across functions. At the beginning of mid- to large-size projects, a team-building opportunity can shed more light on the people behind the functions, so collaborations can be more relationship-based rather than just transactional.

You can connect each project at the time of kickoff to how it contributes to the company's vision and mission to reinforce project members' feelings of belonging. This connection can allow each team member to realize how their contributions increase the company's enterprise value and its ultimate success.

DRIVING BELONGING REACTIVELY

Turbulent times can arise unexpectedly. Situations such as the Black Lives Matter movement in the US, tensions in the Middle East, high volatility in the stock market, or a tight race in a presidential election are sensitive triggers for tension in a diverse team with members holding different perspectives.

Despite our best efforts in creating a safe environment that promotes inclusion and belonging, when we are bombarded with news on our connected devices all day long, emotions can leak into meetings, and social topics can inevitably come up.

How do you deal with disturbing external situations that affect a subset of the team much harder than others? In a team with diverse backgrounds, people may choose to stay silent or risk a heated debate that may have undesirable consequences.

Starting these conversations can be challenging, but staying silent has worse consequences. When you remain silent, your silence may be taken as a confirmation that certain diversity identities are ignored in the workplace, which is a form of microinvalidation, as discussed in section 7.3.2.

You may be tempted to reach out to team members who you believe are most affected by a news event to show your concern. But people can respond to external events differently and in unexpected ways.

For example, suppose you approach an African American team member regarding some disturbing news related to race and racism and not other team members. In some cases, the African American team member may feel singled out because of their race, and other team members who feel strongly about the news may feel not included. These actions can be taken as forms of microinsults, as discussed in section 7.3.2, despite your best intentions.

One way to get around this dilemma is to address the issue in a team setting and allocate time to discuss it in a private meeting. You can try saying, "Hey, team. I wanted to take a moment and address what's been going on in the headlines. I know it's hard to separate these things from work at times. I'm opening up an hour this afternoon for anyone to come and have a private meeting to talk." With this approach, you can be available for anyone who feels strongly about the topic without making assumptions about who to reach out to or who may or may not feel comfortable talking about it with you.

If you are still concerned about particular team members, you can also get an assessment in regular one-on-one meetings by saying, "You've expressed before how these events can be hard on you. How are you feeling today? On a scale of 1–10, with 1 being 'I just want to crawl in bed and shut off the world' and 10 being totally unaffected." Using a scale can help guide your team member to provide you with an assessment without having to articulate potentially personal feelings they may or may not be ready to share.

When team members do share what they think, you should be there to *listen*. Don't attempt to share a different perspective, correct small factual mistakes, or downplay the significance. You can make observations and repeat back what you heard and saw by saying something like, "There is a lot of emotion in your voice as you discuss the impact on you and your family"; "Your interpretation of the news event is different from some other team members but not all of them—I agree"; or "What do you need right now?" If you can hold these difficult conversations in coordination with your HR partners to help your team members feel heard and to recognize them for the diverse identities they own, you are well on your way to help them feel belonging in your function.

7.4   Self-assessment and development focus

Congratulations on working through the chapter on the director and principal data scientist virtues! This is an important milestone for leading the DS function.

The purpose of the virtues self-assessment is to help you internalize and practice the concepts by:

- Understanding your interests and leadership strengths
- Practicing one to two areas with the choose, practice, and review (CPR) process
- Developing a prioritize-practice-perform plan to go through more CPRs

Once you start doing this, you will have courageously taken the steps toward formalizing your project to avoid systemic issues, coaching team members as a social leader, organizing initiatives for team member career growth, driving successful planning processes for clarity in focus, and nurturing diversity, inclusion, and belonging in your function.

7.4.1   *Understanding your interests and leadership strengths*

Table 7.4 summarizes the virtues discussed in this chapter. The rightmost column is available for you to check off the areas you currently feel comfortable with quickly. There is no judgment, no right or wrong, nor are there any specific patterns to follow. Feel free to leave any or all rows blank.

If you are already aware of some of these aspects, this is a great way to build a narrative around your existing leadership strengths. If some aspects are not yet familiar, this is the opportunity for you to assess whether they can be of help in your daily work, starting today!

Table 7.4   Self-assessment areas for virtues of directors and principal data scientists

	Capability areas/self-assessment		?
Ethics	Establishing project formalizations across the function	Anticipating and detecting early symptoms of issues to guide the function away from systematic failures in areas such as project scope estimation biases, project integration challenges, project scheduling risks, project communication risks, and project stakeholder risks.	
	Coaching as a social leader with interpretations, narratives, and requests	Individual leaders lead through demonstrations of their own capabilities. Social leaders lead by offering interpretations of the situation, narratives for direction, and requests for coordinated action.	
		Coaching with the GROW model with four stages to set goals, assess reality, identify obstacles and options, and make commitments for the way forward.	
	Organizing initiatives to provide career growth opportunities	Setting up career growth paths for DS talent and helping them build identities as subject matter experts, mentor peers to build relationships and practice leadership, accumulate business domain expertise as a point of contact for business lines, and build redundancy in responsibilities for succession planning.	
Rigor	Driving successful annual planning processes	Planning with rigor to achieve three goals in four steps. The three goals are: highlight priorities, set realistic goals, and leave flexibility in execution. The four steps include context, plan, integration, and buy-in.	
	Avoiding project planning and execution anti-patterns	Anticipating, detecting, and mitigating anti-patterns that are bad practices that lead to project failures in project planning, execution, and completion.	
	Securing commitments from partners and teams	Distinguishing the five forms of commitments to practice making them yourself and to secure them from partners and teams.	
		Securing and following up on commitments with rigorous language and processes.	

Table 7.4   Self-assessment areas for virtues of directors and principal data scientists *(continued)*

Capability areas/self-assessment			?
Attitude	Recognizing and promoting diversity in your team	Recognizing diversity as the ways people are alike and different, with dimensions that transcend race, gender, and ethnicity, highlighting in group sessions to cultivate cultural awareness and take responsibility in sharing perspectives.	
		Promoting diversity involves benchmarking your team according to the diversity in your candidate pool, and driving change through the principle of equal opportunities by sourcing diverse candidates, while running a merit-based hiring process.	
	Practicing inclusion in decision-making	Acknowledging team member differences from differing cultural backgrounds and treating everyone with respect in meeting scheduling, team events, and career coaching.	
		Being aware of social biases within the team and reducing microaggressions, such as microassaults, microinsults, and microinvalidations.	
	Nurturing belonging in your function	Driving belonging proactively by recognizing dimensions of diversity, realizing each other's strengths, and driving a culture of acknowledgement.	
		Driving belonging reactively by acknowledging social tensions in group settings and offering opportunities to discuss sensitive topics and provide support in private settings.	

7.4.2   *Practicing with the CPR process*

As with the tech lead virtues assessment in section 3.4 and the team manager virtues assessment in section 5.4, you can experiment with a simple CPR process with two-week check-ins.

For your self-review, you can use the project-based skill improvement template to help you structure your actions over the two weeks:

- *Skill/task*—Select a virtue to work on.
- *Date*—Select a date in the two-week period when you can apply the virtue.
- *People*—Write down the names of the people with whom you can apply the virtue, or write *self*.
- *Place*—Select the location or occasion at which you can apply the virtue (for example, your next team meeting or during the next incident post-mortem).
- *Review result*—How did you do compared to before? The same, better, or worse?

By holding yourself accountable for these steps in a self-review, you can start to exercise your strengths and shed light on your blind spots in these virtues.

Summary

- *Ethics* for a director or a principal data scientist include the standard of conduct for establishing project formalization across the function, coaching team members as a social leader, and organizing initiatives to provide career growth opportunities.
  - To establish project formalization, you can anticipate and detect early symptoms of issues to guide the function away from systematic failures in project scoping, integration, scheduling, communications, and stakeholder commitments.
  - To coach team members as a social leader, you can offer interpretations of situations, narratives for direction, and requests for coordinated action.
  - To provide career growth paths, you can help team members build identity by holding office hours, practice leadership by onboarding new members, aggregate domain understanding by becoming business line PoCs, and build redundancy in responsibility by crafting succession plans for team members as they are promoted.
- *Rigor* for a director or a principal data scientist is driving higher standards for clarity in the direction and focus for your function through successful annual planning, avoiding planning and execution of anti-patterns, and securing commitments from partners and teams.
  - To drive successful annual planning processes in DS, you can highlight priorities, set realistic goals, and leave flexibility in execution. This can be accomplished in four steps: setting executive context, collecting team proposals, executive integration, and aligning buy-ins.
  - To avoid bad practices that lead to project failures, anticipate, detect, and mitigate anti-patterns in project planning, execution, and completion.
  - To secure commitments, distinguish the five forms of commitments and work with their components to secure and follow up with rigorous language and process.
- *Attitude* is the mood a director or a principal data scientist promotes in a DS function to recognize diversity, practice inclusion, and nurture belonging.
  - To recognize diversity, create a safe space for the group to share their deeper experiences and identities. To promote diversity, benchmark your team diversity with the local talent pool and drive changes when required.
  - To practice inclusion, reflect on your personal biases, learn about the types and harms of microaggressions, and be ready to call them out and take the lead to improve culture, maintain trust, and retain talent.
  - To nurture belonging, proactively recognize dimensions of diversity, realize each other's strengths, and drive a culture of acknowledgment. In emergent situations, react by acknowledging the sensitive issues publicly, and provide opportunities to discuss privately.

References

[1] T. Hecht, *Aji: An IR#4 Business Philosophy*, The Aji Network Intellectual Properties, Inc., 2019.

[2] G. Alexander, "Behavioural coaching—the GROW model," *Excellence in Coaching: The Industry Guide*, 2nd ed. J. Passmore, Ed. (London; Philadelphia): Kogan Page, pp. 83–93.

[3] L. Rachitsky and N. Gilbreth. "The secret to a great planning process—Lessons from Airbnb and Eventbrite." First Round Review. https://firstround.com/review/the-secret-to-a-great-planning-process-lessons-from-airbnb-and-eventbrite/

[4] W. H. Brown et al., *Anti Patterns: Refactoring Software, Architectures, and Projects in Crisis*, New York, NY: Wiley, 1998.

[5] D. Oliver, "Creating and maintaining a safe space in experiential learning," *Journal of Management Education*, vol. 39, no. 6, April 2015, doi: 10.1177/1052562915574724.

[6] "Global talent trends 2020," LinkedIn. [Online]. Available: https://business.linkedin.com/talent-solutions/recruiting-tips/global-talent-trends-2020

Part 4

The executive:
Inspiring an industry

Successful DS executives and distinguished data scientists exude influence beyond their companies. They do this by producing highly valued accomplishments to demonstrate DS's impact and inspire their industry. They operate with a sense of calm confidence with their executive presence, which leads to thoughtful and timely planning and actions, centered on bringing out the best from those in their organizations.

The executive leading DS may have a title such as chief data scientist, chief data officer, or VP of data. Sometimes, the DS team reports to the chief technology officer, chief financial officer, or chief risk officer. Individual contributor executives often have a title such as distinguished data scientist or DS fellow. Regardless of the reporting structure, a DS executive or a distinguished data scientist should be aware of an executive's attributes and practices to make the DS function successful.

The capabilities of an executive who is leading DS encompass responsibilities both inside and outside a company. This scope is broader than that of a director, which is primarily to govern the DS function within a company.

As internal focuses, a DS executive or a distinguished data scientist is responsible for the long-term viability of the company. This includes building multi-year business strategies, clarifying the DS mission, instilling a data-driven culture across functions, capturing emerging business opportunities to accomplish business objectives, and articulating business plans for new data-driven product lines.

As external focuses, they are responsible for clarifying the competitive differentiation of the business model among industry peers, building a strong talent brand and hiring pipeline, and learning best practices across industries. While both internal and external initiatives can be delegated, the champion and driver of these initiatives should be you, the DS executive.

To practice executive presence, you must channel your personal passion toward making a positive difference for others, exercise positive thinking patterns, maintain executive poise with effective emotional patterns, and project effective action patterns with the team.

Chapter 8 will introduce the capabilities of DS executive and a distinguished data scientist, discussing the internal and external responsibilities in technology, execution, and expert knowledge. Chapter 9 will elaborate on the executive virtues through discussions on the ethics, rigor, and attitude of practicing DS.

Capabilities for leading a company

8

This chapter covers

- Crafting technology roadmaps to align teams and to support executive initiatives
- Sponsoring and championing promising DS projects
- Delivering consistently by managing people, process, and platforms
- Building a strong function with clear career maps and a robust hiring process
- Anticipating business needs and applying initial solutions against urgent issues

Executives and distinguished data scientists leading DS operate with a different level of capability than directors. While directors and principal data scientists seek to bring clarity in focus and prioritization to the DS function, executive and distinguished data scientists are concerned about a company's overall business strategy and articulate how a company can be competitive within its industry.

As an executive or distinguished data scientist leading DS, in the technology dimension, you are responsible for architecting the long-term business strategy in data and creating and driving a data-driven culture in all aspects of the business process. Executives have the added responsibility to structure the DS organization according to its business needs.

For execution, you are responsible for infusing DS capabilities into the vision and mission; building a strong talent pool at the organization, function, and team level; and clarifying your own roles and priorities to the CEO and team members.

To use domain knowledge as an executive, you can articulate how to apply DS to differentiate your products and services among industry peers, recognize and capture emerging business opportunities, and articulate business plans for new data-driven products and services. With your capabilities in technology, execution, and expert knowledge, you can seek to inspire your industry by unleashing DS's full potential.

8.1   Technology: Tools and skills

As an executive or distinguished data scientist leading DS, you are a visionary subject matter expert with deep knowledge of technology trends. The company depends on you to craft a mid- to long-term business strategy and put it into practice. To do this, you will need to stay current with emerging technology, create a data-driven culture, and structure the DS organizations to fit your organization's business needs.

To craft the mid- to long-term business strategy, you can determine *what* technologies should be considered and *how* the technology stacks should be organized for DS to stay aligned with various functions in the company. To create a data-driven culture, all aspects of the DS function, including data engineering, modeling, and analytics, must mature concurrently. Otherwise, challenges in one aspect can bottleneck the overall progress.

To build an efficient DS function, you can structure it to fit the overall business organization. Trade-offs include communication overhead, development of deep domain insights, team member career development, and retention. With a business strategy supported by solid technologies, a data-driven culture, and a suitable structure for your organization, you are taking good care of the technology concerns as a DS executive.

8.1.1   Architecting one- to three-year business strategies and roadmaps in data

As a visionary subject matter expert in DS crafting business strategies to transform your industry, you are looking for the technologies that can fundamentally improve the way business is conducted. There are two aspects of technology you can focus on. One focus is on *what* specific technologies can transform business processes. Examples include stream processing, creating a data lakehouse, self-serve insights, data/ML ops automation, and global data governance.

The other is *how* technology components are organized and architected in stacks that allow efficient collaboration across functions to launch products and services.

Examples include resolving the tension between the stability and agility of data platforms and using middleware to introduce new intelligent capabilities.

Let's look at two case studies. One focuses on *what* technologies could be considered. Another focuses on *how* technology stacks could be organized.

CASE 1: TECHNOLOGY DISRUPTION FOR BUSINESS TRANSFORMATION

One area ripe for disruption is how data is organized, stored, and accessed, such that businesses can respond rapidly to events happening in the marketplace.

For the past half-century, data has been stored in databases to be accessed by analysts and data scientists to produce insights and predictions for human decision-making. The paradigm was to intelligently use data in various human-based business processes, such as marketing, sales, operations, and customer service, to acquire and serve customers for the business. As each business function's decision-making processes are automated into software business logic and DS models, this paradigm is shifting.

The new paradigm promotes the role of software to trigger actions, react, and respond to other software components directly. In this new paradigm, business processes become fundamentally algorithm-based decision processes with humans monitoring their activities.

For example, for a commercial bank operating a personal loan product, the business process is traditionally human-based. As shown in figure 8.1, marketing drives customer acquisition, the credit team assesses credit risk, the loan officers assess behavioral risk and make final decisions on whether to approve the loan, and the collections department works on collection maximization. A DS team can work with each department to create algorithms for marketing models, application models, behavioral models, and collection models.

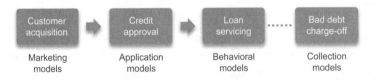

Figure 8.1 A typical loan application process with data science support

When effective algorithms are in place to automate each step of the personal loan process, the models can be triggered automatically by an incoming loan application or loan payments, allowing the entire process to complete within seconds to minutes rather than days.

The infrastructure that supports this new paradigm is *event streaming*. An event is a record of a performed action. Examples include user registrations, login attempts, loan applications, commerce transactions, deliveries, and payments. An event stream is a continually updated series of events that includes historical records and real-time situations.

Your overall data infrastructure can then be organized into a *two-speed architecture* with one that encompasses the traditional databases to provide a system of record and the other that is based on event streams to form a system of engagement. This two-speed architecture is illustrated in figure 8.2.

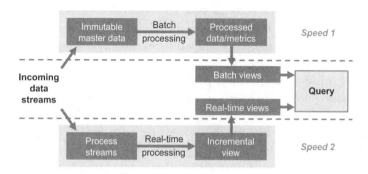

Figure 8.2   A data infrastructure with a two-speed architecture

Jay Kreps, co-founder and CEO of Confluent, describes event streaming as the central nervous system of modern enterprises. He envisions it as a way to connect the disparate decision-assisting DS capabilities into a system of decision-making processes connected by event streams. How does a system of decision-making processes connected by event streams evolve over time?

Adoption of event streaming often starts with one use case that enables a single, scalable, real-time feature. The initial usage can spread rapidly within a company to other applications, as an event stream can support multiple readers, or "subscribers," that process, react, or respond to it. Each reuse lowers the entry barrier for additional related use cases.

As you are working to establish the mid- to long-term business strategy, this virtuous cycle of adoption allows the first application to set up some critical data streams, which enable additional new applications to join the platform and gain access to those data streams. The new applications, in turn, bring with them their own streams, enriching the availability of real-time information in the system for making more real-time decisions.

By sequencing how streams enable applications and how applications bring in more streams, you can map out a technology roadmap that balances risks and rewards at each milestone to make investment feasible and worthwhile for your company.

CASE 2: HOW SHOULD TECHNOLOGY STACKS BE MANAGED?

As an executive or a distinguished data scientist, your responsibilities also include managing fundamental tensions in the data technology stack. Such tensions exist in both the maintenance of data/processes and the creation of new data-driven product features.

Maintenance of data and processes

In a data organization, we value stability in the data infrastructure, so data enrichments, models, analytics, and business logic can be built, iteratively improved, and maintained. Business lines, however, value agility, so they can iterate quickly on products, business logic, and predictive models to respond to market conditions, new customer insights, and new business initiatives. This tension is illustrated in figure 8.3.

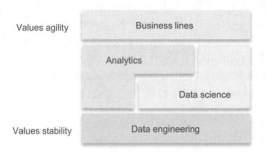

Values agility — Business lines — Analytics — Data science — Values stability — Data engineering

Figure 8.3 The fundamental tension for agility vs. stability in data organizations

The tension appears the sharpest in new product feature iterations where there can be disruptions to existing data ingestion and data reporting pipelines. Product changes can introduce serious side effects for the data pipelines and standardized metrics used to operate existing products.

056

Business lines value agility, and data engineering values stability. Data science and analytics are caught in the tension between these competing requirements.

For example, for a search feature in an application, a well-intentioned improvement may be introducing instant search. This feature allows the search engine to start showing search results as you are typing queries into a search bar—even before the search button is pressed. A version of this feature was the default search behavior on Google between 2010 and 2017.

While such an instant search feature can make search feel more responsive, it can also dramatically increase calls to the search API as partial search queries are submitted. The feature can also disrupt reporting metrics and the search relevance calibration pipelines. It is especially hard when you are conducting A/B tests, as the number of *search engine result page* (SERP) loads and the associated click-through rates between test and treatment are no longer indicative of the same user search behavior.

As a solution, careful planning and coordination on downstream data implications are required to avoid disruptions to critical operations metrics and relevance model calibrations. As a DS executive or a distinguished data scientist, you are responsible for ensuring data engineering teams are informed early in the new product/feature development processes. This can allow data engineering to anticipate potential challenges in maintaining the stability of the data infrastructure.

To protect the data infrastructure's stability and to accommodate agile product iterations, you can use tiered service-level agreements for data pipelines and models. Mature organizations maintain a set of executive-tier metrics and a set of production-tier models for company-wide initiatives. These top-tier metrics and models have clear data lineage, and data sources and pipelines involved require a higher level of planning and coordination. Then, there can be metrics specific to business lines and experimental models in lower tiers, such as tier 1 and tier 2, that can be more nimbly modified to accommodate fast product iterations with trade-offs for long-term reliability. You can develop your specific tiering system based on the service level agreement required for your products and the roles and responsibilities you have to maintain them. A sample metrics hierarchy is illustrated in figure 8.4. Similar ones can be constructed for models with tiers, such as production, shadow runs, and experimental betas.

Metric hierarchy

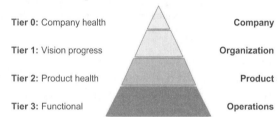

Tier 0: Company health — Company

Tier 1: Vision progress — Organization

Tier 2: Product health — Product

Tier 3: Functional — Operations

Figure 8.4   Tiered metrics provide clear trade-offs in agility and stability

In the tiered approach, metrics and models can be prototyped in lower tiers and promoted to higher tiers by improving the robustness of data sources and data pipelines. The ownership of the metrics can also shift from a product team to a centralized operations team that has on-call capabilities. When metrics and models are modified or updated, they can also shift from higher tiers to lower tiers with the understanding that they won't be as stable over a window of time.

Tiering can set expectations and provide DS leaders a process to make clear ROI trade-offs on supporting metrics and models, such that data infrastructures can be as agile or as stable as required.

Creation of new data-driven product features

Beyond maintenance and incremental iterations of features, we would also like to develop new intelligence features rapidly to adapt to customer insights. You can face similar trade-offs between stability and agility when developing new intelligence capabilities.

An intelligence capability can be a recommendation engine, an anti-fraud model, a churn reduction model, and so on. Using the recommendation engine as an example, you may get related requests, such as providing personalized recommendations for a mobile app, a website, email campaigns, and customer service upsells.

One option is to build a separate model for each of the requests for intelligence products. As you may remember from chapter 6, you are likely to face the challenging trade-off of serving additional stakeholders with more versions of similar models or refining the existing model for the current intelligent product. Section 6.1.1 covers this in more detail.

As an executive or distinguished data scientist, one approach to navigate this trade-off is to guide the organization to architect intelligent capabilities as *middleware*. In the recommendation engine example, the various requested scenarios can be parameterized calls to the same recommendation API. Parameters can include weights for individual preference for user propensity, weights for general popularity for diversity and coverage, or weights for the expected return to optimize revenue. You can also use filters to select mobile-optimized content for a smartphone app or check deep-link availability in recommendations for email campaigns.

This middleware approach allows product owners to adjust parameters and construct A/B tests to optimize user experience nimbly. Simultaneously, data scientists can focus on maintaining a stable model across changing market environments and drifting user behaviors over time.

You can apply the middleware architecture to many intelligent capabilities:

- For anti-fraud models, sensitivity and recall can be customizable to adapt to different use cases, such as automatic rejection or human investigation prioritization. You can also adjust weights for user risk factors and situational risk factors for various user vintages or customize lists of fraud attack vectors to include in the fraud model.

- For churn reduction models, you can parameterize seasonality, renewal cycles, and individual behavior factors to drive specific churn-reduction use cases.

As illustrated in figure 8.3, a stable set of models as middleware can also provide additional features and metrics for the analytics team to build new user segments and extract new data insights. It can broaden the DS team's impact, while focusing the team's resources on building stable intelligent capabilities.

Before you decide to apply the middleware architecture, be sure to understand the potentially diverse requirements up front and follow the scaling needs of various applications closely. Applications can demand differing levels of availability and reliability that may make a shared middleware architecture inefficient or impractical.

8.1.2 Delivering data-driven culture in all aspects of business processes

Culture governs how people will work when you, the DS executive or the distinguished data scientist, are not in the room. Transforming an organization to have a data-driven culture is no small task. You cannot simply install a culture overnight. There are many organizational muscles required, and you can build them in phases across the different aspects of DS.

As DS evolves, three aspects emerge. These include data engineering, modeling, and analytics. *Data engineering* focuses on strengthening trust in data through investments in infrastructure. *Modeling* focuses on infusing intelligence into business functions and user experiences. *Analytics* focuses on democratizing the use of data in an organization. Successful teams require a portfolio of these aspects of skill sets. Successful data scientists usually have a broad knowledge of all three aspects with strengths in a subset.

057

Culture governs how people will work when you, the data science executive or the distinguished data scientist, are not in the room. Culture is not built overnight. There are many organizational muscles to be built in phases across data engineering, modeling, and analytics.

When instilling a data-driven culture, it is helpful first to recognize the current maturity stages spanning data engineering, modeling, and analytics. With this recognition, you can articulate gaps, diagnose whether a lack of maturity in one aspect could be holding back progress in other aspects, and prioritize efforts to fill gaps and advance an organization. Let's look at the set of maturity levels for data engineering, modeling, and analytics capabilities in DS and work through some case studies on prioritizing efforts toward building a data-driven culture.

DATA ENGINEERING ASPECT OF DS

The data engineering aspect of DS can empower the business with trusted data for critical business decisions. The trust for data comes from the capabilities for aggregating, processing, and maintaining data safely and reliably.

Figure 8.5 illustrates five levels of maturity for data engineering, from collection to cultural. Here are some details:

1. *Collection*—Data from business transactions, user behavior, marketing campaigns, customer service data, experimentation data, and user-generated contents are aggregated from various sources and stored in their raw forms.

2. *ETL+storage*—Raw data is enriched, processed, and stored in forms optimized for usage. Data can be stored in structured, unstructured, and knowledge graph-based formats to support various retrieval patterns. Schemas are architected and articulated according to business needs.

3. *Governance*—Special attention is given to ensuring data quality with automated availability, correctness, and completeness checks. Data lineage is documented, maintained, and searchable. Data life cycles are developed to avoid the accumulation of data bloating a system and reducing its usage efficiency. Data consistency ensures a single source of truth for metrics for making important decisions.

4. *Streaming*—The architecting of a two-speed system with a layer for a traditional system of record and a new layer of system of engagement with event-based streaming capabilities, enabling real-time reporting and alerting and real-time intelligence in the user interface.

5. *Cultural*—A trusted event streaming foundation is in place to serve as a "central nervous system" to support real-time business decision processes. Processes and platforms for security and privacy are mature. Robust data pipelines are routinely developed and put in place by partner teams according to data engineering guidelines.

Data engineering-focused maturity stages

COLLECTION	ETL+STORAGRE	GOVERNANCE	STREAMING	CULTURAL
Logging, third-party APIs, experiment instrumentation, and user-generated contents	Transactions, ETL pipelines, structured, unstructured, and graph-based data storage	Data quality, data lineage, data life cycle, disaster recovery, and data consistency Manage tech debt, and maintain velocity Mature incident post-mortem	Fast ingest, real-time data enrichment, real-time reporting and alerting, real-time intelligence in UX	Trusted "central nervous system" platform Mature process and platform for security and privacy Routinely productionize robust data pipelines

Figure 8.5 Data engineering-focused maturity stages for data science

Many organizations are operating at the *ETL+Storage* stage, with the tech debts that have accumulated over time preventing them from succeeding in data governance. If you are struggling here, the tiering approach of metrics and models can help you improve your organization's maturity and focus efforts on the data governance of the most crucial metrics first. You can find more detail on this in Section 8.1.1.

If you assess that your organization has already reached the *governance* stage, congratulations! *Streaming* stage capabilities bring unique opportunities to engage your customers but also add another layer of complexity for metrics and models. Queries on databases that produce the metrics and model features for business decisions need to be reorganized to accommodate streaming data with new challenges for governing data quality and consistency. Feature stores and feature servers can address the complexity of two-speed architecture involving batch and real-time processing. We discuss them in more detail in section 10.1.4. Your organization only reaches the *cultural* stage when partner teams can efficiently coordinate with you to create new business opportunities with event streaming capabilities and maintain the velocity of innovation with the proper governance of the data assets.

MODELING ASPECT OF DS

The modeling aspect of DS infuses intelligence into business functions and user experiences. The predictive capabilities are focused on generating business results and making strategic impact.

Figure 8.6 illustrates five levels of maturity for modeling, from building ad hoc models to creating a culture of incorporating intelligence into business functions and user experiences. Here are some details about each stage to help you recognize the stage your organization is in:

1 *Ad hoc*—Opportunities for predictive capabilities are just being prototyped. There is no data infrastructure, so projects have to start from data sourcing and cleansing. Productivity is low, as much coordination is required to implement and deploy models in a product.

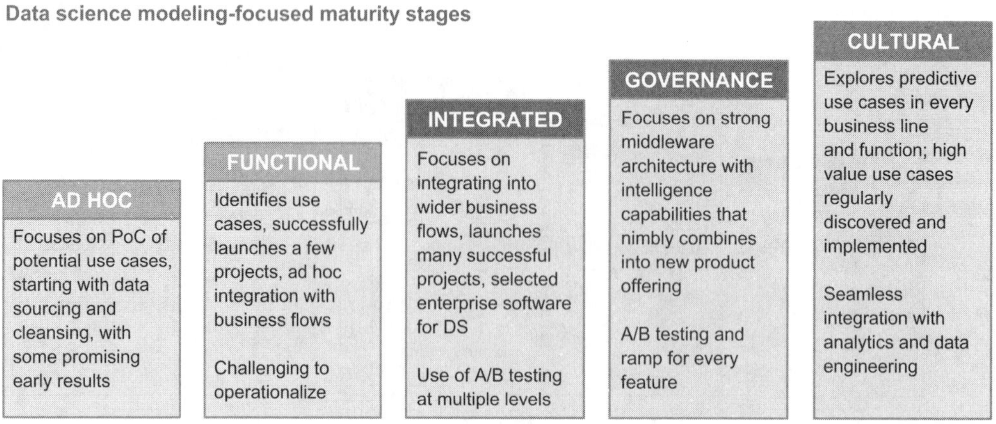

Data science modeling-focused maturity stages

Figure 8.6   Modeling-focused maturity stages for data science

2 *Functional*—A few use cases have been successfully launched with positive results. There are still challenges with the reliability of the solution and the efficiency in coordinating with business partners to launch new capabilities.

3 *Integrated*—There is an efficient process for coordinating with business partners to launch new predictive capabilities. Predictive capabilities are being deployed into a wide range of business functions and user experiences. A/B testing methodology is being used at multiple levels of products, including frontend UI and backend algorithms.

4 *Governance*—Predictive models are automatically calibrated, and inputs are being actively monitored for data drifts. Predictive capabilities are consolidated into middleware to serve a greater range of product scenarios nimbly. A/B test is being applied to every feature launch.

5 *Cultural*—Every business line and function is capturing opportunities in DS. Partner teams are regularly articulating and collaborating on new high-impact use cases. New capabilities seamlessly integrate with analytics and data engineering aspects of DS.

Many DS organizations are in the *ad hoc* and *functional* stages. Some organizations have matured into the *integrated* phase, where DS modeling and predictive projects are routinely launching into the business flow, producing a sizable impact on the fundamental business model. These stages are also discussed in section 2.3.3.

Many organizations struggle to achieve the *governance* phase, where the focus is on establishing the middleware architecture, as discussed in section 8.1.1, and automatically monitoring when existing models are no longer delivering the expected performance. You know that you have reached the *cultural* stage when partners are proposing new use cases and coordinating on prioritizing and launching features to capture significant business impact.

THE ANALYTICS ASPECT OF DS

The analytics aspect of DS advises business partners with data-driven best practices and recommendations. It builds its authority by demonstrating business insights and in-depth data understanding. Its ultimate aim is to democratize data usage in business decisions for data scientists, partners, and executives.

Figure 8.7 illustrates five maturity levels for modeling, from building ad hoc reporting to creating a culture of self-served data insights. Here are some details about each stage to help you recognize your organization's stage:

1 *Reporting*—Work is focused on answering ad hoc questions from business partners and providing monthly and quarterly reports and business forecasts. The team extracts insights by passively responding to business partner requests.

2 *Dashboarding*—Common requests are automated into dashboards that are periodically refreshed and actively pushed to business partners. There is strong coordination with data engineering teammates to govern data quality.

3 *Discovery*—Relevant metrics are being proactively crafted, and recommendations on products and processes are proactively proposed to business partners based on data insights, modeling, and deep domain understanding. There is strong coordination with modeling-focused teammates to improve the quality of recommendations.

4 *Governance*—Best practices for logging, instrumentation, and data interpretation are documented. Metrics and recommendations are followed through with product partners to realize the potential business impact. There is strong coordination with data engineering teammates to govern data quality.

5 *Cultural*—Every business line and function is making data-driven decisions. There is training on the concepts, process, and platform to promote self-serve data insights. The DS team is then focused on developing best practices and advising the rest of the organization.

Many analytics organizations are at the *dashboarding* stage of maturity, capable of actively pushing some reports out to the organization. However, the remaining ad hoc

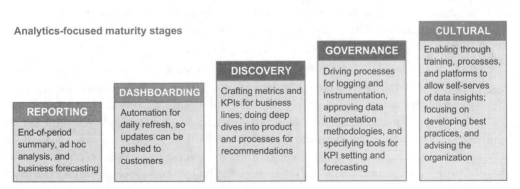

Analytics-focused maturity stages

REPORTING
End-of-period summary, ad hoc analysis, and business forecasting

DASHBOARDING
Automation for daily refresh, so updates can be pushed to customers

DISCOVERY
Crafting metrics and KPIs for business lines; doing deep dives into product and processes for recommendations

GOVERNANCE
Driving processes for logging and instrumentation, approving data interpretation methodologies, and specifying tools for KPI setting and forecasting

CULTURAL
Enabling through training, processes, and platforms to allow self-serves of data insights; focusing on developing best practices, and advising the organization

Figure 8.7   Analytics-focused maturity stages for data science

requests are taking up significant resources and preventing the organization from reaching the *discovery* stage, where the team can produce deeper insights for greater impact on the organization. Section 5.3.1 discussed using the on-call processes to lift the team out from the burden of excessive ad hoc requests, while efficiently prioritizing the most urgent and important requests to service.

To reach the *governance* stage, the team can recognize the best practices of the best people on the team and create processes to institutionalize best practices within the team, across teams, and across the organization. It also involves automating best practices into platforms to allow more team members to use best practices more efficiently. These are discussed in detail in section 6.2.1.

To reach the *cultural* stage, the team can focus on aligning and empowering the entire organization with training and support in producing and using analytical insights. The analytics-focused team can then use its analytics expertise to incorporate more advanced methodologies, such as causal inference to up-level the organization's ability to discern how actions, interventions, or treatments affect business outcomes to establish causation.

MATURING THE THREE ASPECTS CONCURRENTLY

Transforming an organization's culture into a data-driven one requires the data engineering, modeling, and analytics aspects of DS to mature concurrently. A deficiency in any of the aspects may bottleneck the transformation of the overall organization. Across all three aspects, the *governance* stage is an important stage to reach the *cultural* stage, where the teams are focused on developing best practices and advising the rest of the organization.

058

Transforming an organization's culture into a data-driven one requires the data engineering, modeling, and analytics aspects of data science to mature concurrently. A deficiency in any of the aspects may bottleneck the transformation of the overall organization.

With an overview of the maturity stages above, let's look at two case studies where the DS organization is blocked from advancing in maturity.

Case 1: Tech debt

- *Symptoms*—The team is efficient in producing reports, deep analysis, and models on historical data, but the business impact is low. While dashboards and metrics are being produced, the data is delayed by days at a time. New intelligent product features are being developed and launched. However, they are trained with stale data and are fragile in production. Data issues creep up every other week, which require data scientists to go into a war room to resolve. Over time, a large portion of the team is responding to maintenance issues instead of producing new analysis or new intelligent features.

- *Root cause*—Data infrastructure has accumulated tech debt over time to a size that has become unmanageable. With thousands of tables and no clear schema, owner, or lineage, it is hard to know what part of the infrastructure requires maintenance. The team is fighting to keep the infrastructure up and running every day with little time to think about how to fix the problem.
- *Interpretation*—The organization is bottlenecked by tech debts at the data engineering *ETL+storage* maturity stage. This blocks the analytics aspect from going beyond the *dashboarding* stage and prevents the modeling aspect from moving beyond the *integrated* stage.
- *Solution*—You can apply the tiering approach for metrics and models, as introduced in section 8.1.1. The approach can help you focus the limited resources on supporting the most impactful metrics and models. This focus involves coordinated efforts to improve data quality, data lineage, and data consistency on a small subset of metrics. You can then more realistically arrive at the reliability and trustworthiness of the data that partners expect.

With fewer breakdowns of critical metrics and model pipelines, you can unblock the analytics and modeling-focused team members to advance the organization to higher maturity levels.

Case 2: Uneven adoption of intelligence features

- *Symptoms*—The team has produced successful business impact with intelligent features for one business function but cannot gain traction in use cases for other business functions. Many attempts were made. Some experiments were developed and successfully improved one particular metric, but the solutions also caused other metrics to drop, making them not launchable.
- *Root cause*—Analytics capabilities lack depth in proposing metrics to measure business success. With no clear recommendations on metrics that align with the creation of customer value, models cannot target the right optimization goals to iterate toward launchable improvements.
- *Interpretation*—A lack of maturity in the analytics aspect's *discovery* stage is blocking further progress in the modeling aspect of DS. Deep domain insights are required in the analytic *discovery* stage to move the modeling efforts beyond the *functional* stage.
- *Solution*—Your team can develop a deep understanding of your business partner's fundamental concerns and the nuances in their KPI definition. These are described in section 4.3.1 and summarized in table 4.1. This deep understanding allows you to produce more balanced metrics as optimization goals, aligning the optimization of your intelligent features to business value for your customers. You can also benchmark and interpret external reference data to understand the optimization headroom, so you can choose the improvements that can unleash the most potential. This is discussed in section 4.3.2.

8.1.3   *Structuring innovative and productive data science organizations*

As a DS executive, you have the responsibility to structure the DS organizations to fit your company's business model. In this section, we specifically discuss the structure of the DS organization. The overall company structure, including functional, divisional, matrix types, and alternatives, such as holacracy, is discussed in section 10.2.

Depending on your company's maturity and overall business structure, there are many options to structure the DS organization. Accenture has proposed six types of organizational structures for a data function [1]. Each type has its advantages and disadvantages, which are summarized in table 8.1.

Table 8.1   Types of organizational structure and their advantages and disadvantages

Organizational structure	Description	Advantages	Disadvantages
Functional	Data scientists reporting to specific functions, such as technology, finance, or risk management	▪ A clear focus on a few functions ▪ Can build a deep understanding of the specific function over time	▪ Limited impact on overall company initiatives and contexts ▪ Challenges in rigorous interviews in hiring processes ▪ No DS manager to guide career growth and best practices
Decentralized	Data scientists distributed in business units and functions reporting to respective non-DS leaders	▪ Clear allocation of resources ▪ Flexible to address ad hoc requests ▪ Can build a deep understanding of the business unit or function	▪ Effort siloed with duplication, decentralized reporting, and a lack of standardization ▪ Low efficiency and no prioritization across functions/business units ▪ Challenges in rigorous interviews in hiring processes ▪ Career path management not clear; few improvements in best practices
Consulting	Data scientists centralized and consult on specific projects in an ad hoc manner for business unit or functions	▪ Fluid allocation of resources ▪ Can work well with small to medium DS projects ▪ DS leadership manages best practices and career growth	▪ Reliance on functional or product leads for requests ▪ Long-term projects, such as data quality improvements, are difficult to get funded ▪ Little investment in product building and decision-making
Centralized	Data scientists are centralized in one function and work on long-term projects based on enterprise-level prioritization	▪ Can work with function and business leads to prioritize ▪ Able to scale faster and fund fundamental work, such as improving data quality ▪ Good for career growth and best practices sharing	▪ Projects can lose touch with business lines over time ▪ High overhead of prioritization ▪ Some business lines or functions may receive intermittent DS resources, making feature development difficult

Table 8.1 Types of organizational structure and their advantages and disadvantages *(continued)*

Organizational structure	Description	Advantages	Disadvantages
Center of excellence	Data scientists are dedicated to business units and functions; activities are coordinated by a central entity	▪ Centralized coordination can coordinate joint initiatives ▪ The embedded team maintains domain knowledge ▪ Good for career growth and best practices sharing	▪ No centralized team is working on enterprise-level projects ▪ Expensive to maintain, as business lines and functions needs may vary over time, and teams may be understaffed or overstaffed
Federated	Most data scientists are dedicated to business units and functions; some are centralized and are strategically deployed to enterprise-wide initiatives	▪ Centralized team can prioritize company initiatives ▪ Embedded team maintains domain knowledge ▪ Good for career growth and best practices sharing	Project ownership between centralized and embedded teams may cause tension

How do you choose the most appropriate structure at various stages of a company? Let's look at how these structures arise in organizations and how to evolve them:

- *Functional structure*—Intelligent data use cases often emerge in a company with a visionary function leader hiring a couple of data scientists. This scenario leads naturally to the functional structure, where the data scientists are reporting to a business line or function lead. The functional structure allows a deep understanding of the function or business line to be developed over time. However, the scope of impact is limited to one part of the company and is bottlenecked by the business line or function leader's capability to hire the data scientist with the right skill set. It can also be a challenge to specify the right projects for the data scientists, guide their career growth, and improve on best practices. In this structure, the function leader can refer to the capabilities and virtues discussed in chapters 2 and 3 to hire and develop strong DS project leaders in their team.

- *Decentralized structure*—With some success in leveraging DS to produce business impact in one team, other teams may also start to hire data scientists. This scenario results in a decentralized structure, where different business lines and functions have their own distinct DS teams. While this structure provides each business line or function with dedicated resources, the siloed efforts can result in duplicate work, inconsistent metrics in reporting, and a lack of process standardization. Career paths for data scientists in decentralized structures are also not clear, which may increase churn risks. While business line or function leaders can hire or develop strong DS project leaders in their team according to the capabilities and virtues discussed in chapters 2 and 3, this does not fundamentally resolve the challenge of work duplication.

- *Consulting structure*—While many DS efforts evolve in a bottom-up approach, as described above, some companies also choose to deploy DS capabilities top-down by creating a centralized DS function that consults for various business lines and functions. This approach creates the consulting structure, where the DS capability is centralized and can be efficiently deployed to any business line or function. Best practices and career growth can be better managed with dedicated DS leadership.

  However, this structure relies heavily on functional or product leads for specifying requests. There is significant overhead on communicating business context in each project. There can be a long backlog of projects, and results may no longer be relevant when the projects eventually get prioritized. As a result, successful projects are often focused on answering specific questions with short- to mid-term wins. Long-term projects, such as data quality improvements, are difficult to get funded and prioritized.

- *Centralized structure*—With a strong DS leader who can work with function and business leads to prioritize and align initiatives, we can transform the DS organization into a centralized structure. In this structure, business lines and functions are served from a central team with resources available for enterprise-level initiatives and foundational work, such as improving data quality. A centralized team can also scale faster, share best practices, and provide clearer career growth opportunities for team members.

  However, as company-wide priorities shift, many business lines and functions may not get consistent support from a centralized organization to build up institutional knowledge for the long term. The overhead of prioritization for which business lines or functions get DS resources each quarter can be overwhelming. Without some form of dedicated resourcing, a centralized DS team can lose touch with domain-specific nuances when data scientists shift between business lines over time.

- *Center-of-excellence structure*—To address the shortcomings of the centralized structure, data scientists can be dedicated to business units and functions while a central entity coordinates their activities. This center-of-excellence structure allows the centralized coordination of joint initiatives, while business lines and functions get stable resources to create and maintain critical domain knowledge. Centralized coordination also provides opportunities for career growth and best practices sharing, which can improve talent retention.

  However, such a structure is expensive to maintain. DS needs in business lines and functions may vary over time with product or business cycles. Teams may be understaffed or overstaffed at any particular point in time. There are also no resources to work on enterprise-level initiatives.

- *Federated structure*—To allow more efficient use of DS resources, some data scientists can be dedicated to business units and functions, while others operate as a centralized team. This setup leads to the federated structure, where the data scientists dedicated to business units and functions can maintain domain knowledge. The centralized team can be strategically deployed to tackle enterprise-wide initiatives, improve shared technology stacks, or support specific business units and functions when required. This structure also provides opportunities for career growth and best practices sharing, which addresses talent retention.

When operating in the federated structure, a DS leader should be sensitive to situations where project ownership between centralized and embedded teams is ambiguous. When the centralized team is deployed to collaborate with an embedded team, there should be clear responsibilities and hand-off points to minimize confusion and tension.

EVOLUTION OF ORGANIZATIONAL STRUCTURE

For an early-stage company starting with one or two data scientists, the functional or distributed structure can work well. These structures provide a clear focus within specific business lines and functions to produce early wins and build momentum for additional investments in DS.

As more business lines or functions investigate opportunities to build up DS capabilities, reorganizing to a centralized structure can allow opportunities to be explored with resources to mature data foundations. With two to four business lines and fewer than 10 data scientists, prioritization overhead is still manageable.

As more business lines incorporate DS capabilities, planning and resource balancing across business lines can start incurring significant overhead. You can reorganize your team into a federated structure to lower prioritization overhead. The data scientist working with each business line and function can continue to focus on accumulating domain expertise. The centralized team can continue to refine the technology stack and back particular business lines and functions when required.

When a mature enterprise is incorporating DS into its product and business processes, a center-of-excellence structure can also work well. It can allow the data scientists to closely collaborate with business lines and functions to create proof of concept projects that demonstrate value while providing feedback on data infrastructure gaps and requirements to mature data capabilities.

Once proof of concept projects are successful and DS functions become accepted company-wide, reorganizing to a federated structure can improve the overall efficiency of DS and allow enterprise-level initiatives to be prioritized and executed.

ORGANIZING AND REORGANIZING FOR EFFICIENCY

As the DS executive, you also have the responsibility to structure the DS organization to fit your company's business model. Among the six organizational structures we share here, there is no one best organizational structure for everyone. Selecting an effective structure requires consideration of your organization's size and culture, your leadership style, the talent you have on your team, your ability to attract additional talent, and the culture you are looking to create around them.

As your DS function grows, reorganizing it into different structures can improve the DS function's efficiency. While you can overcome the disadvantages of any one structure with extra communication efforts, selecting an appropriate structure can simplify coordination, improve talent retention, and help the function scale more easily with available talent in the marketplace. For example, if you can only attract junior DS talent, a centralized structure can help you better control deliverable quality. If you can attract senior talent to your team, you can provide them with more leadership opportunities with a federated or distributed team structure.

8.2   *Execution: Best practices*

To drive execution in DS, a DS executive can infuse data and predictive intelligence capabilities into the company vision and mission, build a strong talent brand for the function, and review and communicate how the initiatives and teams are positioned to succeed over time. These are different responsibilities as compared to the director-level day-to-day concerns of delivering business objectives which are discussed in section 6.2.

Cross-functional coordination is crucial for the successful execution of many DS projects. Infusing data and predictive intelligence capability into your company's vision and mission can provide your DS teams with the executive mandate and influence to align priorities with partners in cross-functional coordination.

059

Infusing data and predictive intelligence capability into your company's vision and mission can provide your data science teams with the executive mandate and influence to align priorities with partners in cross-functional coordination.

In a successful company, there are often pressing demands for an expanding team of high-quality data scientists to perform a growing number of data-driven initiatives. Selecting locations to build up DS teams, crafting a stellar talent brand, and developing the talent already on your teams are crucial levers for attracting and retaining top talent.

At different phases of organization building, it is often helpful to reflect and communicate transparently with your peers and team the roles you are playing in a nimble team. You may be working as a strategist sometimes, as a mentor or consultant at other times, and still other times as a coordinator, which may be confusing to the team and partners who are not familiar with your responsibilities. These are all roles in which you can build trust with teams and partners through good and bad times. Let's now get into the details of how you can take good care of the execution concerns as a DS executive or a distinguished data scientist.

8.2.1 *Infusing data science capabilities into the vision and mission*

When companies grow beyond 100 to 200 people, it can be increasingly challenging for executives to communicate and align the company's direction with every employee. A crystallized vision and mission can guide team members on a path that can propel the company forward.

Section 2.3.1 discussed how DS tech leads could clarify their understanding of the company's vision and mission to understand the purpose of their project before diving in. This section discusses the crafting of this vision and mission at the executive level.

Vision is the desired future position of an organization. It is the dream, a team's true north, with the primary objective of inspiring and creating a shared sense of purpose throughout the company. A vision provides a sense of stability in times of change. For a startup in search of a repeatable and scalable business model, the DS executive often has to facilitate a difficult business pivot, which Eric Ries defines as "a change in strategy, without a change in vision" [2]. In a mature company, a DS executive has to notice, observe, and adapt to changes in the business environment through changing business strategies, while keeping the vision consistent.

Mission defines a company's business, its objectives, and its approach to reach those objectives. It is the overarching objective of the organization that should be measurable, achievable, and, ideally, inspirational. It should not be used synonymously with a vision statement. Every few years, as a company evolves and the business environment shifts, its mission statement needs to be redefined to adapt. How do you start infusing data and predictive intelligence capability into your company's vision and mission?

INFUSING DATA AND PREDICTIVE INTELLIGENCE CAPABILITY

Some companies you join or co-found don't yet have a company vision or mission crystallized. This is an opportunity to work with the executives to infuse data and intelligence capabilities into the company's vision and mission statements as they are being defined. Doing so provides the DS teams the mandate and influence to align with partners to drive crucial data-driven executive initiatives.

Stephanie Ray, VP of product at ProjectManager.com, shared eight traits for successful vision statements [3]:

- *Be concise.* A vision statement should be simple and easy to read, memorize, and repeat accurately.
- *Be clear.* Have one clear objective, so it is easier to focus on and achieve.
- *Have a time horizon.* Fix a point in the future when you will achieve the vision.
- *Make it future-oriented.* A vision is an objective of where the company plans to be in the future.
- *Be stable.* A vision is a long-term goal not affected by market or technological changes.

- *Be challenging*. A vision shouldn't be easily achieved, but it also should not be unrealistic and ignored.
- *Be abstract*. A vision should be general enough to capture interests and strategic direction.
- *Be inspiring*. A vision should rally the troops and be desirable as a goal for all involved.

A great mission statement defines a business so well that it can read like strategy. According to Chris Bart, professor of strategy and governance at McMaster University, there should be three components included in the mission statement [4]:

- *Key market*—The target audience
- *Contribution*—The product or service
- *Distinction*—What makes a product unique, or why you should buy it over another

Infusing data and intelligence capabilities in a company's vision and mission statement doesn't imply including data or intelligence capabilities in the text. While vision statements are often industry-specific, there are keywords to include in the vision and mission statements that can expand naturally to data and intelligence capabilities. Some example keywords are introduced in table 8.2. "Every," for example, implies some form of intelligent personalization. "Trust" implies a provider of reliable information, intelligent risk assessment, and protection against fraud.

Table 8.2   Sample keywords to incorporate into a company's vision and mission statements

Keyword	Examples
Every	*LinkedIn's vision*—Create economic opportunity for every member of the global workforce.
	Nike's vision—Bring inspiration and innovation to every athlete in the world.
Trust	*Ant Group (Alibaba's financial technology arm)'s vision*—To turn trust into wealth.
	Blue Cross Blue Shield of Michigan's mission—We commit to being our members' trusted partner by providing affordable, innovative products that improve their care and health.

What if your company already has vision and mission statements crystallized? If the vision and mission statements have components of the data or intelligence capabilities infused, congratulations! Your DS function is in good shape to use them to align with collaborating partners.

Suppose the company vision and mission statements do not yet have data or intelligence capabilities infused. In that case, you can align the DS capabilities with the company mission by creating a DS mission. A well-crafted DS mission brings three benefits:

- It brings the DS teams' everyday work closer to the company's mission, such that data scientists can more easily understand how they are contributing.

- It allows partners to better understand the importance of collaborating with DS through the DS mission to drive the company mission.
- It can attract talent by showcasing DS as a key stakeholder in the company's success. We discuss more in section 8.2.2.

For example, the mission of Acorns is: "With benevolence and courage, we look after the financial best interests of the up-and-coming, beginning with the empowering step of micro-investing." This mission was refined for the DS function to "Make Acorns for 'me' so that choices are simple, timely, and personalized." The refined DS mission focuses on personalizing the customers' financial choices, so customers can take advantage of Acorns' micro-investing opportunities.

BEST PRACTICES FOR CRAFTING THE VISION AND MISSION

The purpose of crafting the vision and mission of a company or a function is to clearly and concisely communicate executive direction. The team you assemble to craft the vision and mission should match this purpose.

When crafting the company vision and mission, the executive team should be present. Each team member can bring their perspective on the narrative and provide feedback on how different functions may interpret the company vision and mission.

The DS team can craft its own mission by refining its objectives and approaches from a subject matter perspective. It can inherit the company vision to provide a consistent desired future position for the company.

For crafting the DS mission, a selected set of eight to ten leaders in the DS team should be present. The function's mission statement can benefit from diverse perspectives, but too big a group makes active participation less effective.

One template for crafting the company vision and mission or the DS mission can involve a six-step process with the first three concentrated on one crafting session. This is illustrated in figure 8.8.

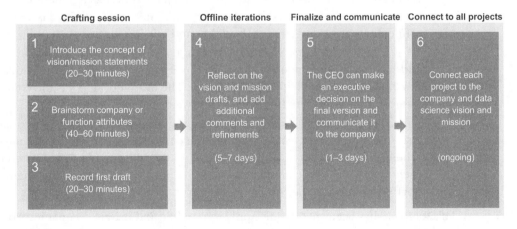

Figure 8.8 Six steps to craft the DS vision

The six steps are:

1 *Introduce the concept vision/mission statements* (20–30 min). You can share the definition of a vision and mission, with success criteria and examples, to guide the team to learn to assess what makes great vision and mission statements. You can use the material in this section of the book as a starting point. This step's output is a set of attributes for the final mission statement.

2 *Brainstorm company or function attributes* (40–60 min). Following a standard broaden-then-narrow-and-prioritize process of brainstorming, you can first broaden the concept horizon by allowing the team to generate keywords for the mission that cover at least:

   – The needs or the wants in the marketplace
   – What the business is doing for its customers
   – What the business is doing for its employees

   You can then cluster similar concepts together to form themes and broaden and deepen the themes. The team can then vote on the most important themes to focus on for the vision and mission. This is where the success criteria from step 1 can be used as selection criteria. The output of step 2 is a set of prioritized concepts and keywords that the vision and mission should consider.

3 *Record first draft* (20–30 min). The team can make attempts to produce first drafts of the vision and mission, discuss their thought process, and compare their drafts with the attributes the team has specified in step 1. The attempts are documented and shared within the team to review. The output of step 3 is a shared document with various drafts of the vision and mission statement.

4 *Follow up offline with iterations* (5–7 days). Over the next week, the team can reflect on the vision and mission drafts and add additional comments and refinements. You can collect additional feedback from selected members of the company who were not in the crafting session. The output of step 4 is additional refinements and comments of the vision and mission drafts.

5 *Finalize and communicate* (1–3 days). With additional refinements of the vision and mission drafts, the CEO can make an executive decision on the final version and communicate it to the company. The output of step 5 is the company-wide announcement of the vision and mission statements.

6 *Connect to every project the team prioritizes* (ongoing). Many neglect the ongoing assessment of how projects connect to the company and DS vision and mission. When projects are successfully connected to the mission and vision statements, each member of the company can more concisely understand how their daily work contributes to the company.

This template has been successfully applied in public and private companies. You can adjust and adapt it to your specific situation and organization as you see fit.

In summary, a well-crafted vision and mission of the company or the DS function can ground team members on how their daily execution is propelling the company forward. When the vision and mission are infused with data and predictive intelligence capabilities, they can provide the DS function with the mandate and influence to align with partners to drive important data-driven executive initiatives.

8.2.2 Building a strong talent pool in data science

With clear vision and mission statements crafted, the challenge remains to build a strong talent pool in DS to execute the vision according to the mission. A talent pool is the set of potential candidates for your organization. It is primarily constrained by the skill sets required and the location of your talent needs. It can also be constrained by the attractiveness of the company's mission and the compensation level the company can afford.

If you have open positions in DS in your organization, you likely have experienced the talent gap for practitioners in the DS field. It is likely that qualified talent for your team will have multiple offers. According to Andrew Flowers, an economist at Indeed Hiring Lab, from 2018 to 2019, job postings on Indeed for data scientists increased by 31%, while job searches increased by only 14% [5].

Catherine, the DS executive (from chapter 1, case 7), experienced this challenge in her work, where the team grew slower than the rest of the company, leaving the team bogged down with keeping-the-light-on projects, rather than spending time on strategic projects. The consequence was devastating. High-performing team members left the company to take on more strategic roles elsewhere.

How can you build a strong talent pool for your organization amidst an increasingly competitive talent marketplace? You can consider three levels of executive strategies: the organization level, the function level, and the team level. Figure 8.9 illustrates these three levels. Let's take a look at each of them.

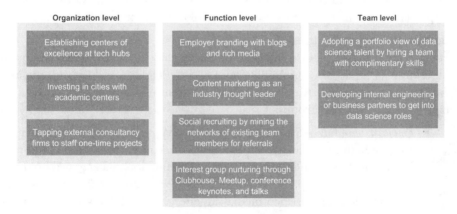

Figure 8.9   Three levels of executive strategy for building a strong talent pool

BUILDING AT THE ORGANIZATION LEVEL

For large organizations that can go where the talent is, there are locations around the world where the pools of DS talent are growing fast. You can consider two types of investments: establishing centers of excellence for DS at tech hubs and investing in academic centers to follow the talent.

For companies not located in tech hubs, the local talent pool can be limited. For example, Irvine is a vibrant city 40 miles (approximately 60 kilometers) south of Los Angeles, California. As of 2020, the reachable talent pool for data scientists in Irvine is limited to 200 to 300 data scientists, which is smaller than the DS function at a single company like PayPal.

Companies wishing to expand their DS talent pool can reference talent marketplace data, such as the LinkedIn talent insight tool, to assess the availability and competitiveness of the type of talent they would like to attract. As of 2020, top tech hubs in the US include San Francisco, New York City, and Boston; in India, they include Bangalore, Delhi, and Hyderabad; in China, they include Beijing, Shanghai, and Shenzhen; and in Europe, they include London and Paris.

For companies looking to capture the flow of future talent, consider investing in emerging talent centers where universities are adding and expanding artificial intelligence and data science programs today. These include cities such as Toronto, Montreal, Atlanta, and Pittsburgh. Smaller cities like Louisville, Kentucky, are also being tapped by companies like Microsoft for talent from the University of Louisville to work on artificial intelligence, DS, and the Internet of Things (IoT) [6]. Building dedicated outposts in talent hubs and investing in academic centers can be coordinated with other technology and product functions to amortize the overhead of starting a center.

To staff large-scale, one-time projects, you can tap external consultancy firms as a talent source. For frequently repeated processes across projects, you can invest in building tools to reduce the expertise required for data scientists to accomplish their responsibilities, which expands the talent pool from which you can hire.

BUILDING AT THE FUNCTION LEVEL

You can build a talent pool at the DS function level by using multiple techniques. With different techniques, you can build a pool of the broadest reach or with the most specific impact, including employer branding, content marketing, social recruiting, and tapping special interest groups:

- *Employer branding*—Crafting the company vision and mission to include data and predictive intelligence capability as core competencies is an important part of employer branding. It showcases the DS function as a key stakeholder for the success of the company. This is discussed in section 8.2.1. Telling this story through blogs or with rich media can energize candidates and align them with your vision and mission's unique brand positioning. You can make this narrative available on relevant content platforms, such as LinkedIn and Glassdoor. When candidates research your company, they will find the narrative and realize how impactful it can be to work on DS at your company.

- *Content marketing*—As a thought leader in your field and industry, content marketing is a more specific approach to building a DS talent pool. You can appear on podcasts, write technical blogs, or author books. Topics include introducing the types of initiatives you are working on to attract talent in your industry, or introducing the industry's particularities to DS talent looking to enter your industry.

Being interviewed on a podcast can be a quick way to reach an audience. Podcasts are typically 30 to 45 minutes in length and are often edited from an hour-long interview. Once they are published, they can be referred to in a company blog or linked to your LinkedIn profile, which can have marketing value for years to come. The challenge with podcasts is picking which podcast to get on. There are over 1.5 million podcasts worldwide with about 500 podcasts specifically on the topic of DS. Each podcast has influence over a specific audience who chooses to subscribe to it. And this audience may or may not be the one you are looking to reach to build your talent pool. You can find a podcast that carries the audience you seek by looking at categories, topics, host names, past guest lists, and reaching out with topics of interest to discuss on the hosts' podcast. For best practices on being a successful guest on a podcast, Tyler Basu has an excellent guide called "How to Get Interviewed on Top Podcasts in Your Industry" [7].

Technical blogs can be a great way to showcase the talent already on your DS teams. Companies such as Airbnb, Netflix, Google, and Stitch Fix all have DS cultures that emphasize giving back to the technical community by sharing learnings and even open-sourcing tools that can improve the productivity of practitioners in the field. When the topics are relevant and useful, the blogs can be great gateways for data scientists to learn more about your company, some of whom will choose to become part of your talent pool. However, when the topics are intentionally controversial, they can infringe on the ethical line and hurt your talent brand. Section 3.1.1 mentioned two cases: "Uberdata: The Ride of Glory" blog [8] from Uber, and the "We Experiment On Human Beings!" blog [9] from OkCupid. As a DS executive, it is your responsibility to clarify guidelines and review processes before blogs on sensitive topics are published.

060 Insensitive narratives in blogs can hurt a company's social identity. A data science executive is responsible for clarifying guidelines and review processes before data science blogs on sensitive topics are published.

Publishing technical books is yet another way to market a company's thought leadership in DS. DS leaders at companies such as LinkedIn, Google, Airbnb, Databricks, and Cloudera have published technical books with leading publishers on topics such as data architecture, experimentation, and open source tools. Having these authors on your team can be powerful in attracting talent who value learning from the top experts in their field.

- *Social recruiting*—Social recruiting leverages social connections to discover outstanding candidates to attract to your team. There are two main techniques to extend your social reach: through your entire team's social networks and through university affiliations.

  You can mine the team's social networks by inviting all employees at the company to post DS job openings on their social feeds as well as contacting past colleagues to look at opportunities with your team. This is discussed in section 6.2.2. Candidates introduced through referrals generally have the best conversion rates into employees.

  Many DS leaders are also active in alumni networks and even teach courses related to their fields in university programs. A university affiliation can provide a consistent source of fresh talent each year for internships and entry-level positions. As an example, the author Jike Chong's affiliation with the University of California–Berkeley allowed him to hire multiple interns from Berkeley for one summer. He was able to then hire the interns back as full-time employees. One of the interns even convinced a classmate to join full-time as well. They all became highly productive members of his team.

- *Interest group nurturing*—Talent with strong motivations to learn and grow are often active in industry interest groups. You can cultivate relationships with this part of the talent pool through Clubhouse, Meetup, conference keynotes, talks, and panel discussions.

  You can speak at, host, or even organize a meetup in your area, where talent in your industry or function aggregate and get to know each other. With a regular monthly meetup, you can quickly build a talent brand in the local area, so your company can be top of mind when talent decide to explore the next steps in their careers.

  Speaking at conferences is a great opportunity for your team members to build their identities in the industry. These opportunities can motivate rigor in your team members' work, and it can also attract talent who are motivated to do the best work of their careers at your company.

  One caveat of conference appearances is that, unless the appearances are consistent, it is difficult to keep your company top of mind. Inviting the audience to check out company blogs, podcasts, and books can make the impact more lasting.

Employer branding, content marketing, social recruiting, and interest groups can effectively broaden your reach and allow you to build deeper relationships with your talent pool. When talent and their friends consider the next steps in their careers, they may be more open to considering opportunities in your company and on your teams.

BUILDING AT THE TEAM LEVEL

It is often hard, if not impossible, to find talent that have just the right combination of experience to accomplish your business objectives. What can you do to increase the talent pool that can meet your business needs?

You can adopt a portfolio view of DS talent that takes the data scientists' potential into account. Rather than waiting three to four months to find a team of individual talent who have all the skills required, you may consider hiring a team of data scientists in one or two months with complementary skill sets. In this case, you are hiring for potential. You can create projects for them to cross-train each other in the skills required to get the job done. This portfolio view can significantly increase the talent pool you can assess with the caveat that you will need to effectively evaluate a candidate's potential in picking up missing skills on the job.

061

> You can adopt a portfolio view of data science talent that considers the data scientists' potential. You may hire a team of data scientists with complementary skill sets and create projects for them to cross-train each other in the skills required to get the job done.

Your talent pool is not only outside the company. There can be paths for current engineers and business partners to take DS courses and step into DS roles. Internal candidates can bring existing domain expertise and perspectives from different functions to enrich the composition of DS teams.

You can also use automation platforms to democratize DS best practices, such that data-driven decision-making can scale beyond a small team of highly specialized PhDs and reduce challenges in talent acquisition for recruiters and managers. This is discussed in Section 6.2.1.

BUILDING A STRONG TALENT POOL AS A PRIMARY RESPONSIBILITY

Building a strong talent pool in DS is a primary responsibility of the DS executive. You can tap talent pools at the organization level by opening new sites to recruit talent in tech hubs and academic centers. You can scale talent pools at the function level through employer branding, content marketing, social recruiting, and interest group nurturing. You can also expand the talent pool at the team level by taking a portfolio view of skill set requirements and developing automation platforms to democratize DS across functions. By tapping, scaling, and expanding your talent pools, you can prime your organization for growth.

When Catherine from chapter 1 can practice these techniques at the organization level, the function level, and the team level, she can start to build a strong talent pool for her organization.

8.2.3 *Clarifying your role as composer or conductor*

The execution of a data strategy is sometimes compared to a performing symphony. In a symphony, many parts are performed together to realize the composer's intent, as interpreted by the conductor. When a symphony is produced with precision and synchronization, even people not familiar with the production process can appreciate the result. When a piece is produced poorly, the result can be a painfully incoherent cacophony.

As a DS executive, you have various tools at your disposal to prepare to execute. You can specify the mid- to long-term business strategy in data, create and drive a data-driven culture in all aspects of the business process, and structure the DS organization according to business needs.

When executing the business strategy, you are aligning teams with the company's vision and mission and are preparing a pipeline of talent to bring on board to execute. What roles do you play in this process? How can you explain what you are doing to your boss, the CEO, your peers, and your team?

Companies often realize the need for an executive to lead DS when they have reached a bottleneck on producing or reproducing DS impact across the organization. Depending on the maturity stage of the company and the function, your role could look very different.

EARLY STAGE: THE COMPOSER ROLE

When a company does not yet have a coherent data strategy, the first role for a DS executive is similar to that of a composer in a symphony. In this role, you learn about the business initiatives and the cultural context. You also frame and align the data strategies across various partnering teams, such as product, DS, analytics, and engineering. This process is like composing a symphony by creating multiple movements in a sequence to express the themes or characters with melodies assigned to collaborating instrument sections, such as strings, woodwinds, brass, and percussion.

What happens when the composer role is not fulfilled? In making music, if the performers' expectations and objectives are not clear from the scores, the performers will start to improvise to try to achieve a good outcome. At times, if you are lucky, you might get some reasonable tunes. However, the performance quality will not be consistent, especially when performers with varied interpretations create melodies that together could sound incoherent.

In leading DS, if the expectations and objectives are not clear, collaborations among product, DS, analytics, and engineering are often improvised, up to a point, until ad hoc coordination no longer suffices. Incoherencies show up when data produced does not have the necessary properties to be used in metrics or models, metrics produced cannot drive decisions, and models created cannot drive intelligence features.

062

In leading data science, if the expectations and objectives are not clear, collaborations among product, data science, analytics, and engineering are often improvised, up to a point, until ad hoc coordination no longer suffices. Then, incoherencies start to show up everywhere.

When data projects are clearly articulated across data analytics, modeling, and data engineering, product, and engineering teams, you can anticipate steady progress in maturing a company's DS capabilities.

Maturing stage: The conductor role

At the age of 45, Benjamin Zander, a conductor for 20 years, suddenly realized that the conductor of an orchestra doesn't make a sound. They depend, for their power, on their ability to make other people powerful. As a DS executive, the expectation in execution is orchestrating partnering teams to produce powerful data and intelligence capabilities together while empowering each function to be successful in contributing to the business outcome.

There are many similar challenges between leading DS and performing a symphony, including perspective challenges, performance challenges, and conducting challenges:

- *Perspective challenges*—Each performer in an orchestra is seated in a particular section and will hear a different version of the symphony as it is performed. The partnering teams for each data initiative will have different perceptions of the project. As a DS executive, when you are aware of your data strategy's alternative perceptions, you can align teams and partners, so function and business-line bias will not derail the overall data strategy.

- *Performance challenges*—In a symphony, when one performer plays in a mismatched pitch, the rest can perceive it as very distracting. This can cause confusion, sowing self-doubt. Other performers may wonder, "Am I playing incorrectly? Should I adapt to the mismatched pitch for the sake of harmony in the group even if I know they are not playing correctly?"

   In DS projects, when internal issues arise and are not quickly resolved by the DS executive, mistrust and tension can build up between partnering teams, which destroys the collaboration.

   Like a conductor resolving the situation in a symphony, by perceiving the issue, making eye contact, and "tipping the baton" at the offending team member, you can prevent any tensions from building up between teams and resolve issues to maintain trust. Section 6.2.1 discussed the techniques of skip-level lunches and one-on-ones that you can use to perceive any subtle tensions building up, diagnose the root causes, and even them out before they destroy trust within the teams.

- *Conducting challenges*—In a symphony, when a conductor focuses only on the music, and not the musicians, the musicians can be left feeling disconnected, as the conductor is conducting solely for their personal enjoyment.

   In DS projects, when the DS executive cares only about the technical accomplishments and business results, and not about the team's development, team members can feel disenfranchised.

Effective conductors conduct for the passion and spark in each musician's eyes, empowering them to give the best performance of their lives. Effective executives in DS lead to grow the function's capabilities and nurture the teams' professional accomplishments, so the company can build up maturity to continuously produce industry-inspiring results.

063   Executives in data science often lead to grow the function's capabilities and nurture the teams' professional accomplishments, so the company can build up maturity to produce industry-inspiring results.

In summary, you can use the analogy of the composer versus the conductor to explain the role you are taking on for different data strategies and at various stages of function maturity so your CEO, peers, and teams can understand and support your actions.

8.3   *Expert knowledge: Deep domain understanding*

Expert knowledge empowers executives leading DS and distinguished data scientists to go beyond technical leadership and begin creating innovations that can inspire an industry. The deep understanding of an industry domain allows companies to break through traditional industry limitations with DS to transform customer experiences and unleash new economic potential.

We have previously witnessed how industries have been transformed with technology. E-commerce transformed the retail industry. The rideshare model has transformed the transportation industry. The short-term home rental model has transformed the hospitality industry. One-on-one online learning and tutoring services are transforming the education industry. The common thread that drove these transformations' success is the aggregation of users in a two-sided marketplace and the creation of key algorithms to generate trust to facilitate transactions. Similar transformations based on data and algorithms continue today, rippling through industries such as retail banking, digital health, home care, and the logistics industry.

Capturing these new opportunities requires deep expert knowledge in industry pain points, viable long-term business models, and focused DS execution. There are three common tools available to executives and distinguished data scientists transforming industries:

- Identifying differentiation and competitiveness among industry peers
- Guiding the business through pivots
- Articulating business plans for new data-driven services or products

Let's explore these tools one by one.

8.3.1   *Identifying differentiation and competitiveness among industry peers*

Inspiring an industry with DS requires more than catchy positioning with buzz words thrown into marketing campaigns. The DS executive or the distinguished data scientist is responsible for creating real value that can differentiate their company's services from its competitors. There are six main dimensions illustrated in figure 8.10 in which you can use DS to generate differentiation, depending on your industry landscape.

Figure 8.10   Six dimensions to use DS to differentiate your product

The six dimensions include:

1. *Product differentiation*—Differentiation in key features through intelligence-driven business models and data aggregation frameworks to create virtuous cycles of growth. This type of differentiation can have a limited lifetime, as advantages can be copied by competitors over time.

2. *Service differentiation*—Differentiation in delivery, unboxing, customer service, ease of setup, consistency, and timing of services that can make a product or service sticky to the customer.

3. *Distribution differentiation*—Differentiation in availability and access to products and services when a user needs them, which is especially important in fragmented markets.

4. *Relationship differentiation*—Differentiation through deep customer understanding and engagement.

5. *Reputation differentiation*—Differentiation through consistent actions toward a brand that resonates with the target customer.

6. *Price differentiation*—Differentiation on the price offered, which can be simplified for ease of understanding or made more nuanced to specific segments of customers to capture more value.

Depending on the industry, your opportunity to drive value for your company and inspire your industry can be different. Let's look at two case studies: one in consumer lending and one in health care.

CASE 1: CONSUMER LENDING WITHOUT A CENTRALIZED CREDIT-REPORTING AGENCY

Many countries do not have mature financial systems with individual credit scores that can be used for personal lending. At the same time, personal loans can unleash purchasing power, increase productivity, and accelerate a country's economic development.

With increased smartphone adoption globally in the early 2010s, the younger generation is spending an increasing amount of time on mobile platforms. These activities have created a rich pool of online behavioral traces that, when shared, can be used to assess an individual's creditworthiness without the need for credit scores from a centralized credit-reporting agency.

Product differentiation

In China, Yiren Digital is one of the pioneers in capturing this opportunity to offer an online lending product with loan sizes as large as a person's annual income. In an environment where there is a lack of unsecured personal loan products offered by the banking industry, Yiren Digital started providing loans based on application information submitted from a mobile device without a credit score pull from a centralized credit reporting agency. The lending product depends heavily on data modeling techniques to make approval decisions consistently across the organization with lending volumes eventually reaching billions of US dollars a year.

Service differentiation

As the industry evolved and competitors followed and caught up with the product innovation, Yiren Digital continued its innovations in service quality. The company refined its data sources for its main lending product to include only those that can be downloaded and verified from reliable third-party portals. The approval processes became fully algorithmic. The data aggregation, the credit assessment, and the loan approval processes can complete within a few minutes. This is a 1,000× improvement in application efficiency as compared to the industry norm of taking days to approve a loan. With same-day transfers, funds can reach customers' accounts in a few hours. Customers are often under financial pressure when they apply for a loan. Rapid approval and fast fund release became a significant differentiation in services in the consumer lending industry. This differentiation became a strong engine for growth for Yiren Digital toward its IPO in 2015.

Price differentiation

As the industry adopted these fast loan approval service frameworks, Yiren Digital shifted its differentiation to price. With historical loan performance aggregated over time, it charged four levels of interest rates for customers with varying credit risk levels. For customers assessed to have lower credit risks, Yiren Digital can offer loans with a lower interest rate than the competition. For customers assessed to have higher levels of credit risk, Yiren Digital can better determine who it can approve with an economically-viable interest rate.

For years, Yiren Digital has inspired consumer lending in China through three phases of development, including product differentiation, service differentiation, and price differentiation. The industry is not standing still. As a DS executive or a distinguished data scientist, you have to constantly reassess the industry landscape and prepare for the next phase of differentiation within your industry.

CASE 2: APPLIED HEALTH SIGNALS

In the health care industry, there is a convergence of three trends: digital health, big data, and precision health. Digital health sensors, such as wearables, smartphones, connected glucometers, and connected blood-pressure sensors, can now generate data streams that can be analyzed in real time to identify individual-level risks and generate recommendations for interventions.

While the vision is grand, consumers are often left overwhelmed by the vast amount of health information available. Most consumers do not have the necessary medical knowledge to interpret and act on the information. When digital health device companies attempt to interpret the data streams, they often work with a narrow scope of signals from specific devices without a full picture of the consumer's health profile and medical history. This lack of visibility of the bigger picture limits the appropriateness and relevance of any health recommendations.

Livongo is an applied health signal company that challenges industry limitations to provide improved health outcomes through a differentiated AI+AI product framework that stands for aggregate, interpret, apply, and iterate:

- *Aggregate*—Livongo aggregates its inputs from Livongo devices, services, and third-party sources. Device information includes cellular-enabled blood glucose meters, blood pressure monitoring systems, and digital scales for real-time readings. Service inputs include human interactions, such as Livongo coaches. Third-party sources include medical claims and pharmacy claims.

  By owning the signal streams from Livongo devices and partnering with self-insured employers, health plans, and pharmacy benefit managers, Livongo differentiates itself from other digital condition management companies by having its own proprietary signals and comprehensive health contexts to trigger timely medical action to prevent more costly interventions.

- *Interpret*—To interpret the aggregated health signals, Livongo has a proprietary set of processes for dimensionalizing, combining, mapping, and interpreting signals for each customer, and they build relevant health care messages by considering customers' medical conditions and their cross-condition clinical requirements.

  Compared to consumer tech companies, Livongo differentiates itself with its integrated team of data scientists, behavior specialists, and clinicians working on interpreting signals to deliver deep insights on prompting optimal behaviors for better end-user health outcomes.

- *Apply*—To apply the interpreted health situation, Livongo triggers end-user actions through device notifications on blood glucose meters, blood pressure cuffs, and digital scales, as well as live coaching sessions, voice calls, pharmacist transfers, care team connections, and provider doctor connections.

  Compared to big data analytics companies serving the health care industry, Livongo differentiates itself through its direct-to-customer connections, where its actionable recommendations can directly engage with the end users.

- *Iterate*—To continuously optimize the data aggregation processes, the interpretations of data streams, and the effectiveness of the action recommendations to improve long-term health outcomes, a feedback loop must exist to assess its progress.

  Livongo differentiates itself from other telehealth providers by focusing on patients living with chronic conditions, rather than acute conditions, such that the long-term relationships with its users can allow its aggregate, interpret, and apply practices to be measured and improved on in time.

With AI+AI, Livongo pioneered the applied health signals industry category. Its comprehensive intelligence-focused product architecture and business model can be inspirational not only to companies in the health care industry. Other industries such as financial wellness may also find it applicable.

Catherine, the chief data scientist for a growth-stage company from chapter 1, can work on identifying the differentiation of her company among industry peers to better sell candidates on joining her team. When she can build up her team to match the growing needs for DS in her company, her team can better balance maintenance projects and strategic projects in their work.

8.3.2   *Guiding business through pivots when required*

As a DS executive or a distinguished data scientist, you are responsible for guiding the business through its ups and downs with the power of DS. We discussed the director-level concerns of anticipating business needs across product development stages in section 6.3.1. In this section, we discuss the recognition and execution of business pivots.

Pivots are changes in business strategy without a change in vision [2]. They are necessary when a business encounters growth bottlenecks that prevent it from continuing to be successful. The bottleneck may be imposed externally as in the market shifts that occurred during the global COVID-19 pandemic in 2020 and 2021. Or, it may be an intrinsic recognition that a business needs to expand beyond the current book of business to reach new customers serving new marketplace needs.

As an example, let's look at the financial wellness company Acorns. It has a subscription-based business model for financial investments that allows anyone to start investing a few dollars at a time (micro-investing) into the stock market. Its service removes the barriers of starting the process of wealth accumulation so everyone can benefit from growth compounding. Its vision is to be the "good bank" that looks out for customers' best financial interests. It charges customers only one dollar a month to maintain an investment account with no additional management fees (as of 2019) for up to a million dollars in assets under management.

Micro-investing has some critical bottlenecks in its business model. While the micro-investing capability allows investors to set up regular automated small contributions into the investment account, the *set and forget* nature of the feature becomes a disadvantage when investors grow less engaged with the process, withdraw their investment after a while, and then leave the service. The average lifetime for an investor is measured in years.

In 2017, to improve customer retention, Acorns executed a zoom-out pivot to incorporate tax-advantaged investing and started offering individual retirement accounts (IRAs). Through this zoom-out pivot, the original investment product becomes just one of the two features in the new Acorns platform. Users can make investments through a brokerage account or a tax-advantaged account.

Investors who have retirement accounts have a much lower churn rate, which increases a user's lifetime on the platform from years to decades. This pivot increases the user LTV, which helps justify acquiring more users at a higher customer acquisition cost. In this pivot, DS pays significant attention to understanding the churn rate and users' LTV for those opening a tax-advantaged investment account.

In 2018, Acorns executed an engine-of-growth pivot by developing a debit card product that can increase the average customer revenue by 10×. This pivot expands Acorns' product horizon from investing to directly managing user transactions, where the transaction interchange fees can become a significant revenue source. In this pivot, DS was key to understanding the pivot's impact, catching transaction fraud, and facilitating monthly transfers of funds onto the debit card, so the product generated interchange fees, as designed.

Other than the zoom-out pivot and the engine-of-growth pivot, there are also many other types of pivots you may consider when crafting business strategy hypotheses for the next stage of your company's growth. One cautionary point to keep in mind is that business strategy pivots are hypotheses waiting to be proven or disproven by building experiments, testing with customers, and synthesizing the learning. While we often read about successful pivots, many pivots are unsuccessful. You may need more than one pivot to sustain growth and achieve success, and not pivoting under challenging situations could mean going out of business.

Let's examine an example. One of the most common triggers of pivots is business growth challenges. In one business, the pace of growth has slowed. Acquisition cost is trending higher, and the conversion metrics are not improving. As you observe the unit economics deteriorate, what can you do? Figure 8.11 and the following list illustrate three potential pivots given three hypotheses:

- *Hypothesis A*—The product is exhausting the current channels' reach and needs to adopt new channels to reach more customers.

  Potential pivot A—Use the *channel pivot* to deliver the same solution through a different sales or distribution channel with greater effectiveness. For example, can products sold through consulting and professional services firms be simplified to be sold in a software-as-a-service (SaaS) format to reach more customers? Is display ad the only format you have used, or have you tried using video, podcasts, or other formats to reach your customers?

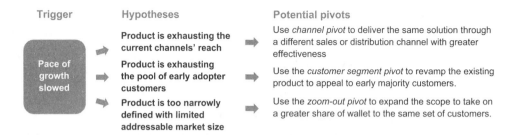

Figure 8.11 Same challenge with different hypothesis, leading to different pivots

There may be a subset of existing channels that performs better than others. If DS and marketing can understand why these channels work better, there can be a joint effort to experiment, assess, and redesign the marketing channel portfolio.

- *Hypothesis B*—The product is exhausting the pool of *early adopter customers* and needs a revamp to onboard *early majority customers* with higher usability requirements.

  Potential pivot B—Use the *customer segment pivot* to revamp the existing product to appeal to early majority customers. In a customer segment pivot, you are changing the target customers of your product or service. This can be a major endeavor that involves redesigning customer acquisition, engagement, retention, and the monetization process for the same product. You can benchmark KPIs such as customer acquisition cost and funnel conversion rate before the pivot, so you can assess the success of the pivot afterward.

  NOTE   *Early adopter customers* are those who are willing to overlook incompleteness in feature sets and bugs for the potential of the products and their massive opportunities down the road. Section 6.3.1 discussed them in the context of the technology adoption cycle. *Early majority customers* are those who are pragmatic and want solutions to their existing problems and only buy products that are fully baked.

- *Hypothesis C*—The product is too narrowly defined with the limited addressable market size. It needs to expand in scope and create more value to sustain growth.

  Potential pivot C—Use the *zoom-out pivot* to expand the scope to take on a greater share of wallet to the same set of customers. In this pivot, the whole product becomes a single feature of a much larger product. In the Acorns example, its investment product was expanded to include retirement investments, college savings, and commercial banking services.

  When working with the *zoom-out pivot* to tackle growth challenges, you are looking to use the product that has a lower customer acquisition cost to attract customers, build customer trust with the brand, and upsell customers to features with a higher customer acquisition cost.

As illustrated above, for the same symptom of slowing business growth, the potential pivot also changes. Hypothesis A assumes only the customer acquisition channels need to pivot, and the customer segment and the product stay the same. In hypothesis B, the customer segment needs to pivot, while the main product features stay the same. In hypothesis C, the product portfolio needs to pivot, while the customer segment stays the same.

Successfully identifying triggers, carefully diagnosing root causes with hypotheses, and effectively executing pivots can place a company on a new growth path to transform and inspire an industry. You can explore additional research [10] for more nuanced examinations of types of triggers and pivots that may apply to your specific challenges.

064

Successfully identifying triggers, carefully diagnosing root causes with hypotheses, and effectively executing pivots can place a company on a new growth path to transform and inspire an industry.

8.3.3 *Articulating business plans for new products and services*

As you drive innovation with DS, the purpose of crafting business plans and articulating profit and loss (P&L) is to focus the always-limited resources on products and services that can produce the most enterprise value. This is an essential skill when working with the CEO, the board of directors, and potential investors during fundraising.

While many DS executives and distinguished data scientists are crafting the data-driven strategies within the company business plan, some are developing new product lines, and others are going further as part of an emerging trend in DS executive leadership to shift toward a product-centric operating model [11].

Table 8.3 provides a side-by-side comparison of a business plan and a project plan. When crafting data-driven strategies within the company business plan, you are

Table 8.3 Comparison of a business plan and a project plan

Business plan	Project plan

■ Mission statement
  – Industry/customer pain points
    to resolve
■ Product or service
  – Description
  – Differentiation
■ Market
  – Market to enter
  – Competitors
  – Positioning
  – Market share to secure
  – Marketing narrative
■ Management team
  – Experience and prior successes
■ SWOT analysis
■ Financials
  – Cash flow statement
  – Revenue projections
	■ Project motivation
	  – Background: customers, challenges, stakeholders
	  – Strategic goal alignment: company initiative it
	    serves, impact scale, value
	■ Problem definition
	  – Outputs and inputs specification
	  – Metrics of project success
	■ Solution architecture
	  – Technology choices
	  – Feature and modeling strategy
	  – Configurations, tracking, and testing
	■ Execution timeline
	  – Phases of execution
	  – Synchronization cadence
	  – A/B test scheduling
	■ Risks to anticipate
	  – Data and technology risks
	  – Organizational alignment risks

developing a series of DS projects as strategies with a sequence of KPIs as success milestones. When developing independent product lines, you are setting up specific business models with teams that can continue to evolve to serve specific industry pain points. When shifting to a product-centric operating model, you are setting up new business lines with new organizations to serve new customers.

Project planning is a key skill for any DS leader. This is discussed in section 2.2.2. To start building business plans at the executive level, here are some key differences between a business plan and a project plan:

- *Time horizon*—Business plans describe the construction of repeatable and scalable business processes and organizations; project plans have finite start and end dates.
- *Goals*—Business plans speak to the P&L impact over years of operations; project plans have goals with KPIs to accomplish that may or may not be financial.
- *Markets*—Business plans describe markets to enter to acquire and retain customers; project plans define the customers and stakeholders to serve and to collaborate with.
- *Risks*—Business plans outline a broad range of market, people, product, and financial challenges; project plans outline a much narrower set of data, technology, and organizational risks.

In a *project-centric* operating model, the emphasis is on defining new products and new markets. Existing data science teams, existing HR and finance functions, and shared engineering and product personnel are often used to resource the new product areas.

In the *product-centric* operating model, the team is independently responsible for its P&L. Although some see it as an accounting nuance, such accounting can allow the team to own dedicated engineering and product resources and move more nimbly to demonstrate value with DS-focused endeavors beyond what is achievable as a technical service function in a company with shared resources.

As an executive driving a product-centric operating model, there are three key criteria essential for your success. Gahl Berkooz, vice president of data, data monetization, and venture acceleration at ZF Group, summarizes them as: organizational readiness, entrepreneurial skill set, and mature customers, illustrated in figure 8.12 and in the following list:

- *Organizational readiness*—When product lines have distributed P&L responsibilities, a new DS product can properly realize and account for the value it is creating.
- *Entrepreneurial skill set*—Building a successful DS product requires skill sets in customer discovery, product/market fit validation, and organization building. These are different skill sets than what is required for a successful DS function leader.
- *Mature customers*—Mature customers have a clear articulation of critical strategic pain points within their industries. A DS product that solves a well-defined pain point can provide significant ROI.

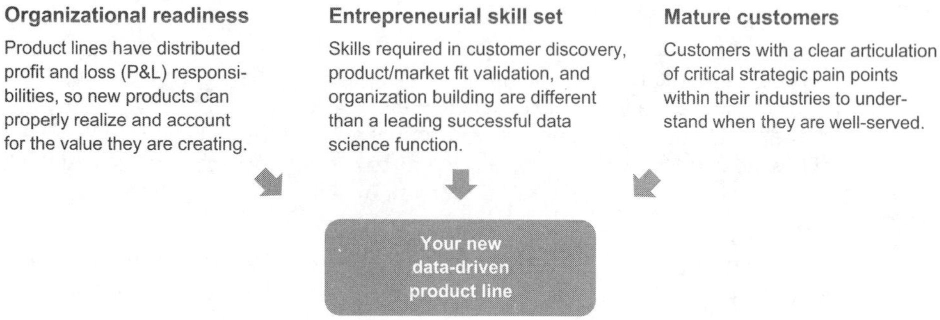

Organizational readiness

Product lines have distributed profit and loss (P&L) responsibilities, so new products can properly realize and account for the value they are creating.

Entrepreneurial skill set

Skills required in customer discovery, product/market fit validation, and organization building are different than a leading successful data science function.

Mature customers

Customers with a clear articulation of critical strategic pain points within their industries to understand when they are well-served.

Your new data-driven product line

Figure 8.12 Three components of readiness for starting a new business line

When these conditions are in place in your organization, you have an opportunity to unleash your in-depth expert knowledge of the domain and apply the entrepreneurial methodologies toward building a new product. The case study in the next sidebar is one example of a DS organization with a product-centric operating model.

065

There are three essential conditions for launching a data-driven product: organizational readiness, entrepreneurial skill set, and mature customers. When these conditions are in place, you have an opportunity to unleash a successful new product.

Case study: ZF group—Enrichment of existing products with data products

ZF Group is one of the world's largest automotive part suppliers with almost 150,000 employees in 230 locations in 40 countries. Gahl Berkooz, the vice president of data monetization and venture acceleration, drives initiatives to create new business lines by enriching intelligence capabilities in traditional automotive parts.

One of these initiatives involves the ball joints, which are spherical bearings used to attach the wheels responsible for steering on virtually every automobile made. The intelligence comes from an integrated Hall effect sensor in the ball joint that can measure ball joint angle data for traditional applications such as height-leveling, which adjusts headlight angles for better illumination of the road ahead. This data can also be repurposed for load monitoring, road condition monitoring, and predictive maintenance.

Monitoring the load of a car can help detect risks in vehicle stability, anticipate difficulties in steering, and maintain safe stop distances. Alerting on overloading can prevent risks in tires overheating, increased wear, and premature tire blow-out. Monitoring the road conditions can allow the rerouting of transportation fleets to use safer routes where possible. The signals collected can be used for predictive maintenance, where the driving conditions data predict what parts are most likely to fail early.

> **(continued)**
> Applying a predictive fleet maintenance methodology based on this sensor's data, a $7 automotive part can help a fleet save $400 per vehicle over 2.5 years. This increases the competitiveness of ZF Group's automotive parts and creates a new book of business based on data monitoring for ZF Group and automotive manufacturers.

Inspiring an industry is no simple task. A product-centric operating model provides more execution freedom for the DS executive in exchange for the P&L responsibility and more scrutiny on the enterprise value created. As a DS executive, shifting to this model places more pressure on demonstrating the value created and captured.

As illustrated in the ZF Group case study, to build a viable business, demonstrating the value created by measuring the potential savings is only a starting point. Questions remain on how the additional features will be sold to the automotive manufacturers, how the fleet owners will assess the features, and how the savings will be captured and distributed. These are the concerns to work out, so that the value created will be captured as profits on the balance sheet.

8.4   Self-assessment and development focus

Congratulations on working through the chapter on executive and distinguished data scientist capabilities! This is an important milestone for leading a company through DS.

The purpose of the capabilities self-assessment is to help you internalize and practice the concepts by:

- Understanding your interests and leadership strengths
- Practicing one to two areas with the choose, practice, and review (CPR) process
- Developing a prioritize-practice-perform plan to go through more CPRs

Once you start doing this, you will have courageously taken the steps to structure innovative organizations, nurture effective cultures, and craft competitive differentiation, while gaining clarity for the paths forward.

8.4.1   Understanding your interests and leadership strengths

Table 8.4 summarizes the capability areas discussed in this chapter. The rightmost column is available for you to check off the areas you currently feel comfortable with quickly. There is no judgment, no right or wrong, nor are there any specific patterns to follow. Feel free to leave any or all rows blank.

If you are already aware of some of these aspects, this is a great way to build a narrative around your existing leadership strengths. If some aspects are not yet familiar, this is the opportunity for you to assess whether they can be of help in your daily work, starting today!

Table 8.4 Self-assessment areas for capabilities of executives and distinguished data scientists

Capability areas/self-assessment (italic items primarily apply to managers)			?
Technology	Architecting one-to three-year business strategies and roadmaps in data	Crafting business strategies to transform your industry by looking at what technology to use and how technology stacks can fundamentally improve the way business is conducted	
	Delivering a data-driven culture in all aspects of the business process	Transforming an organization to have a data-driven culture with the data engineering, modeling, and analytics aspects of DS maturing concurrently	
		Articulating potential deficiencies in aspects of DS maturity that may be bottlenecking the overall organization's transformation	
	Structuring innovative and productive DS organizations	Structuring DS organizations to fit your organization's business model, its size and culture, your leadership style, the talent you have on the team, and the available talent pool in your geographical area	
		Restructuring DS organizations over time to improve efficiencies as the company grows by simplifying coordination, improving talent retention, and scaling the teams with available talent you can hire	
Execution	*Infusing DS capabilities into the vision and mission*	*Crafting and infusing data and predictive intelligence capabilities into the company's vision and mission, such that DS has the mandate and influence to align partners to drive executive-level initiatives*	
		Crafting the DS function's mission statement to refine its objective and approach from a subject matter perspective for your teams	
	Building a strong DS talent pool	*At the organizational level, evaluating geographic locations to capture qualified talent for team growth*	
		At the function level, driving employer branding, content marketing, social recruiting, and interest-group nurturing to attract talent	
		At the team level, cross-training talent within the organization to increase the capacity for DS to produce business impact	
	Clarifying your role as composer or conductor	*Setting clear expectations of your approach in executing your role as a DS executive to the CEO, your peers, and your team, whether by composing a coherent data strategy or conducting collaboration and alignment to execute the strategy*	

Table 8.4 Self-assessment areas for capabilities of executives and distinguished data scientists (continued)

Capability areas/self-assessment (italic items primarily apply to managers)			?
Expert knowledge	Identifying differentiation and competitiveness among industry peers	Identifying opportunities to substantively differentiate your business with product, service, distribution, relationship, reputation, and pricing strategies to create enterprise value	
	Guiding business through pivots when required	Diagnosing issues by clarifying hypotheses and executing pivots effectively to guide the business to sustain growth	
	Articulating business plans for new products and services	*Crafting business plans and articulating profit and loss for constructing repeatable and scalable business processes and organizations*	
		Readying the three key criteria in launching new products and services, P&L accounting, entrepreneurial skill set, and mature customer needs, then executing the business plan	

8.4.2 Practicing with the CPR process

As with the tech lead capability assessment in section 2.4, manager capability assessment in section 4.4, and director capability assessment in section 6.4, you can experiment with a simple CPR process with two-week check-ins.

For your self-review, you can use the project-based skill improvement template to help you structure your actions over the two weeks:

- *Skill/task*—Select a capability to work on.
- *Date*—Select a date in the two-week period when you can apply the capability.
- *People*—Write down the names of the people with whom you can apply the capability, or write *self*.
- *Place*—Select the location or occasion at which you can apply the capability (for example, in the next one-on-one with your team member or the alignment meeting with your engineering partner).
- *Review result*—How did you do compared to before? The same, better, or worse?

By holding yourself accountable for these steps in a self-review, you can start to exercise your strengths and shed light on your blind spots in the DS executive and distinguished data scientist capabilities.

Summary

- *Technologies* for executives and distinguished data scientists include tools and practices to architect long-term business strategies and roadmaps, deliver data-driven culture in all aspects of business processes, and structure productive DS organizations.

– When architecting strategies and roadmaps, you can look at what technology to use and how technology stacks can fundamentally improve the way business is conducted.

– When creating and driving a data-driven culture, you can guide data engineering, modeling, and data analytics aspects of DS to mature concurrently, articulating and mitigating aspects that may bottleneck progress of the overall organization.

– When structuring organizations, you can choose a structure that best fits your organization's business model, its size and culture, your leadership style, the existing talent on the team, and the talent pool available to you.

- *Execution* capabilities for executives include infusing DS capabilities into the vision and mission, building a strong talent pool, and clarifying your role as a composer or conductor.

  – Infusing DS capabilities into the vision and mission will empower your team to use the company mandate to influence and align partners. Clarifying the DS mission can also refine the company objective and approach for your team.

  – When building a strong talent pool, you can evaluate geographic locations for talent pools; drive employer branding, content marketing, and social recruiting to attract talent; and facilitate the cross-training of current teams to increase productivity.

  – When clarifying your role, you can set clear expectations on your approach to the CEO, your peers, and your team to compose a coherent data strategy or conduct collaboration and alignment to execute existing strategies.

- *Expert knowledge* for executives and distinguished data scientists include identifying differentiation and competitiveness among industry peers, guiding business through pivots when required, and articulating business plans for new products or services.

  – When identifying differentiation, you can explore six dimensions, including product, service, distribution, relationship, reputation, and pricing—with DS techniques to match your customers' needs better than any industry peers.

  – When guiding the business through pivots, you are changing the business strategy without changing the vision by clarifying the pivot hypothesis, then executing the pivot toward sustained business growth.

  – When articulating new products or services, you can craft business plans for repeatable and scalable business processes and organizations, and ready the three components for launch: P&L accounting, entrepreneurial skill set, and mature customer needs.

References

[1] "Building an Analytics-Driven Organization: Organizing, Governing, Sourcing, and Growing Analytics Capabilities in CPG," Accenture, June 19, 2013. [Online]. Available: https://www.accenture.com/us-en/~/media/Accenture/Conversion-Assets/DotCom/Documents/Global/PDF/Industries_2/Accenture-Building-Analytics-Driven-Organization.pdf

[2] E. Ries, *The Lean Startup: How Today's Entrepreneurs Use Continuous Innovation to Create Radically Successful Businesses.* New York, NY, USA: Currency.

[3] Stephanie Ray. "A Guide to Writing the Perfect Vision Statement (with Examples)," projectmanager.com, May 16, 2018. https://www.projectmanager.com/blog/guide-writing-perfect-vision-statement-examples

[4] Bart, Christopher K., "Sex, Lies and Mission Statements." *Business Horizons,* pp. 9–18, November-December 1997, https://ssrn.com/abstract=716542

[5] A. Flowers. "Data scientist: A hot job that pays well." Indeed Hiring Lab. https://www.hiringlab.org/2019/01/17/data-scientist-job-outlook/

[6] C. Brahm. "Solving the advanced analytics talent problem." MIT Sloan Management Review. https://sloanreview.mit.edu/article/solving-the-advanced-analytics-talent-problem/

[7] T. Basu. "How to get interviewed on top podcasts in your industry (complete guide)." Thinkific. https://www.thinkific.com/blog/how-to-get-interviewed-on-top-podcasts

[8] "Uberdata: The ride of glory." Ride of Glory. https://rideofglory.wordpress.com

[9] C. Rudder. "We experiment on human beings!" OkTrends. https://www.gwern.net/docs/psychology/okcupid/weexperimentonhumanbeings.html

[10] S. S. Bajwa et al., "Failures to be celebrated: An analysis of major pivots of software startups," *Empir Software Eng,* vol. 22, p. 2373, 2017. https://doi.org/10.1007/s10664-016-9458-0

[11] "Gartner research board identifies the chief data officer 4.0." Gartner. https://www.gartner.com/en/newsroom/press-releases/2019-07-30-gartner-research-board-identifies-the-chief-data-officer-4point0

Virtues for leading a company

This chapter covers

- Practicing responsible machine learning with ethical principles
- Ensuring the trust and safety of customers and taking social responsibility for decisions
- Creating a productive and harmonious workplace, while focusing on enterprise value
- Demonstrating executive presence and establishing an identity of industry leadership
- Learning and adopting best practices across industries

The virtues of a successful DS executive can inspire how an industry uses data to produce business impact. So can the virtues of a distinguished data scientist. When you are raising the bar for privacy and ethical practices, you are building trust with your customers and crafting a corporate identity. When you are aligning partners and team members, you are building trust with your peers. When you are demonstrating executive presence, you are communicating a passion for making a positive difference for your company and your industry.

This chapter discusses the ethics, rigor, and attitude of DS executives and distinguished data scientists. Ethics provide the references for how you can use data responsibly to improve business outcomes, while ensuring customers' trust and safety and taking social responsibility for decisions made with DS. Rigor is the diligence with which you create a productive and harmonious work environment for your partners and team members, improve your technical and business decisions' speed and quality, and focus on increasing enterprise value. Attitude is the energy patterns you demonstrate to convey executive presence, establish a leadership identity within your industry, and learn and adopt best practices across different industries.

Together, ethics, rigor, and attitude are the virtues of the DS practice. The ones discussed in this chapter can help you, the DS executive or the distinguished data scientist, inspire an industry.

9.1   *Ethical standards of conduct*

The ethical practices for DS executives cover a broad scope of issues focused on the long-term viability of a company's business practices and its role in society. We discuss it at three levels: principles of responsible machine learning (ML) technologies, trust and safety of customers, and societal responsibilities.

Responsible ML initiatives focus on following applicable laws and abiding by guiding principles in ethical concerns. They cover a range of considerations, including transparency, robustness, accountability, fairness, and human oversight of the machine learning technologies developed and deployed into operations.

The data for many machine learning scenarios comes from aggregating user-generated content, such as articles, reviews, pictures, videos, or livestreams. In these scenarios, if customers feel unsafe on a platform, the ecosystem collapses. Customers can be individuals or enterprises and must be kept safe from abusive behaviors, such as account takeover, fraud, and unfair practices.

Finally, users expect social media and social networking platforms to uphold the freedom of speech. The platforms have incentives to build a vibrant user community by deploying content moderation to keep out misleading, fraudulent, obscene, threatening, hateful, defamatory, discriminatory, or illegal content. Many boundaries are challenging to determine, even among scholars, intelligence officials, and journalists. Let's examine these ethical concerns at the executive level.

9.1.1   *Practicing responsible machine learning based on ethical principles*

Responsible machine learning (ML) aims to unlock the full power of ML, while minimizing its risks through frameworks that ensure the ethical and conscious development of projects across industries. To practice responsible ML, we first must comply with applicable laws and regulations in the geographical area in which we operate. Numerous laws and regulations are being proposed and implemented around the world. One example is the *General Data Protection Regulation* (GDPR) [1], a regulation in European

Union law for data protection and privacy, adopted by the European Parliament in 2016 and first enforced in 2018. Another example is the California Consumer Privacy Act (CCPA) [2], signed into law in California in 2018 and first enforced in 2020.

However, laws are not always up to speed with the pace of technological advancements. At times, they can be out of step with ethical norms or may not be well suited to address new possibilities enabled by new technologies.

Over the past decade, there have been deep reflections in the industry on ethical norms accepted by the public. In 2019, the European Commission published a report titled *Ethical Guidelines for Trustworthy AI* [3], which includes a set of principles and potential questions that you can use for assessing your own compliance. They are summarized in the following sidebar.

Seven ethical principles of trustworthy AI, as defined by the European Commission

1. Human agency and oversight

AI systems should support human autonomy and decision-making. They should not negatively affect people's fundamental rights and freedom. By agency, we need to preserve the users' ability to make autonomous informed decisions regarding AI systems. By oversight, humans should be able to ensure that an AI system does not undermine human autonomy or cause other adverse effects.

2. Technical robustness and safety

AI systems need to be resilient and secure. They need to be safe with fallback plans in case something goes wrong. Automated decisions should be accurate, reliable, and reproducible.

3. Privacy and data governance

Besides respecting privacy and governing data, the quality and integrity of data and the legitimate access to data must also be ensured.

4. Transparency

The data set used for training and testing should be traceable. The technical process and the final decision should be explainable. Systems and decisions made by AI should be clearly communicated as automated processes and decisions.

5. Diversity, non-discrimination, and fairness

Automated decisions should avoid unfair biases, especially when they can lead to unintended, direct or indirect prejudice and discrimination. A direct-to-consumer capability should be accessible to all people, regardless of age, gender, abilities, or characteristics. Stakeholders affected throughout an AI system's life cycle should be consulted and informed.

6. Societal and environmental well-being

AI systems should benefit all human beings, including future generations. They must ensure sustainability and environmental friendliness with minimal negative social impact for the society and democracy.

(continued)

7. Accountability

Algorithms, data, and design processes should be auditable, and audit reports should be generally available. Potential negative effects should be identified, assessed, documented, and minimized. Trade-offs should be addressed rationally and methodologically. When an unjust adverse impact occurs, mechanisms and parties to contact for redress should be clear.

The scope of these guidelines may look overwhelming. Fortunately, since their definition, an industry of regulation compliance technology companies has begun to emerge to help businesses adopt industry best practices in producing responsible machine learning. To inspire your business partners to work with the DS function to practice responsible ML, it is your executive level responsibility to ensure that the teams and processes are set up properly according to the guard rails described in the ethical principles.

For *human agency and oversight*, strong collaborations with product and operations teams are essential for developing business processes with human-in-the-loop or human-monitored operations right from the start. For example, for insurance payouts, human-in-the-loop operations would mean that an adjuster studied the information gathered, damages claimed, and payout recommended to make the final decision on the insurance payout. In a human-monitored operation, an algorithm makes the insurance payout decision. A member of the adjuster team will monitor payout statistics for anomalies and selectively audit cases to ensure the algorithms perform as expected.

For *technical robustness and safety*, collaborations with engineering teams, especially with site-reliability engineers and information security engineering, are important to prepare fallback plans and assess system behavior when it comes under attack. For example, if an important data source comes under attack, and the algorithm can no longer provide reliable output, a plan B should already be established to ensure business continuity.

For *privacy and governance*, basic processes include implementing strict role-based and time-limited access control for databases and desensitizing data by hashing or removing personally identifiable information (PII), where possible. More advanced techniques, such as differential privacy, can allow repeated queries of a data system without the possibility to reverse engineer sensitive personal information.

For *transparency*, you can document the collection and processing of data sets used for training and testing. The processing of data can introduce profound biases through data nuances, especially when dealing with missing fields. Methods of testing and characterizing the algorithm outcome within the business context should also be traceable.

The decisions from advanced algorithms, such as *deep neural networks* (DNN) and *gradient boosted trees* (GBT), are notoriously hard to explain, as a decision can depend on hundreds, if not thousands, of inputs in complex nonlinear relationships. Luckily, approaches such as LIME [4] and SHAP [5] are able to provide transparency by identifying top features for specific model outputs with implementations available in open source libraries.

Transparency is not complete without clear communication to the stakeholders in an intelligible way. For example, if an article was recommended, it should be shown with the reason that triggered the recommendation. Such explanations can help reduce the risk of confusion for decisions coming from an AI system.

For *diversity, non-discrimination and fairness*, the foundational challenge starts with the collection of data sets and continues through the use of historical choices and engagement signals that may have inherent human biases embedded. For example, if male job candidates for an engineering position are hired or viewed more often, an algorithm may be trained to rank them higher, above more qualified female candidates. Such situations can lead to disparate treatment for similarly qualified candidates and lead to disparate impact where male candidates may get more attention from recruiters.

This class of fairness issues in machine learning is group fairness, which asks: which groups of individuals are at risk for experiencing harm? They are being addressed by innovations and tools such as Microsoft's Fairlearn, IBM's AI Fairness 360, and the LinkedIn Fairness Toolkit (LiFT).

> **NOTE** Fairlearn is a Python package from Microsoft to assess and improve the fairness of machine learning models (https://github.com/fairlearn/fairlearn). IBM AI Fairness 360 is a comprehensive set of fairness metrics for data sets and machine learning models, explanations for these metrics, and algorithms to mitigate bias in data sets and models (https://github.com/Trusted-AI/AIF360). The LinkedIn fairness toolkit (LiFT) is a Scala/Spark library that enables the measurement of fairness in large-scale machine learning workflows (https://github.com/linkedin/LiFT).

Considerations for *societal and environmental well-being* are important for larger companies with significant influence. The energy use in data centers can have significant carbon footprints, contributing to global warming. There are numerous ways for companies to offset their energy usage by purchasing or investing in renewable energy. When a company has considerable reach in people's everyday lives in social media, e-commerce, or finances, there are significant responsibilities to keep out misleading, fraudulent, obscene, threatening, hateful, defamatory, discriminatory, or illegal influences, while upholding the freedom of speech. This is addressed in more detail in section 9.1.3.

For *accountability*, it is important to set a reasonable expectation with product partners and customers that there is always a risk of negative impact for any machine learning system. Statistical algorithms can make mistakes. What is important is to have the ability to audit the case and have adequate mechanisms to correct issues when they happen.

These considerations can be addressed in phases as technologies mature. An awareness of them can help avoid having a technology roadmap head down a dangerous path. When they are not addressed immediately, they can be noted as technical debt. When these ethics tech debts are not addressed and accumulate, they can cause disruptions in utilizing the machine learning capabilities or, worse, cause lasting negative social impact.

9.1.2 *Ensuring the trust and safety of customers*

The trust and safety of customers is essential for the long-term viability of a company. Only when customers feel the value of the products or services is worth the risk of transacting will they begin to transact with the company. Trust and safety can be discussed separately for direct-to-consumer companies and business-to-business companies. Let's look at the direct-to-consumer scenario first.

DIRECT-TO-CONSUMER SCENARIOS

For direct-to-consumer companies, there are three levels of trust, including physical safety, financial safety, and psychological trust and safety. These levels are illustrated in figure 9.1. Your role is to be sensitive to these levels of trust and work to inspire industries with DS techniques to increase their customers' trust and safety.

Hierarchy of safety for consumer-facing businesses

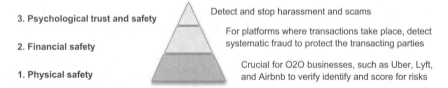

3. Psychological trust and safety — Detect and stop harassment and scams

2. Financial safety — For platforms where transactions take place, detect systematic fraud to protect the transacting parties

1. Physical safety — Crucial for O2O businesses, such as Uber, Lyft, and Airbnb to verify identify and score for risks

Figure 9.1   Three levels of safety for consumer-facing businesses

Physical safety

Trust starts with the feeling of safety when transacting with a company. *Online to offline (O2O)* direct-to-consumer brands, such as Uber, Lyft, and Airbnb, produce transactions online and deliver the services offline. Transacting on these two-sided marketplaces requires immense amounts of trust for customers' physical safety.

Before smartphones were common, you would be strongly advised not to let strangers into your house or vehicle. You would also hesitate to get a ride in a stranger's car or stay overnight in a stranger's house in a foreign country. Today, most people would not hesitate to use Uber or Lyft for rideshares or give rides as drivers. Almost 3 million people became Airbnb hosts worldwide in 2020, and over 500 million people have stayed with Airbnb.

Behind these successes is the rigorous identity verification processes. For example, all Lyft drivers must pass a series of background checks [6] for criminal records before giving a ride. All Airbnb reservations are scored for risk [7] across hundreds of signals before they are confirmed. These verifications are not just one-time checks, but continuous checks are made on flagged suspicious activities, such as identified fake accounts and potential *account takeovers* (ATO).

DS can facilitate these trust-building processes by experimenting and selecting the most effective and least disruptive form of acquiring identity verification and maximizing conversion in acquiring the identity verification. It can also play an instrumental role in scanning for fake accounts and detecting potential ATOs, so the offline delivery of services can be as safe as possible.

Financial safety

Many consumer-facing companies process payments. They sometimes receive payments as the first party, and at other times, they serve as a third party responsible for clearing transactions between parties. To increase financial safety, the top priority is to protect your customers' private information, encrypt them at rest, such that if your servers are compromised, the most sensitive financial information can be safe from hackers.

When a company serves as the trusted third party to clear transactions, it can take on additional responsibilities to protect its customers' interests. Continuing the example from the shared economy scenario, for P2P services such as Uber, Lyft, and Airbnb, transactions are routed through online platforms. This centralizes the maintenance of sensitive financial information, so the transacting parties don't have to request them from each other for every transaction. If an Uber driver did not deliver a ride or an Airbnb host did not provide a stay, the platform can withhold payment and refund the Uber rider or the Airbnb guest.

The platform also has an opportunity to detect systematic fraud by looking for patterns and mechanisms of past fraud cases. For example, if a set of financial information is involved in fraud, you can use a knowledge graph to examine and invalidate any related transactions. Any accounts involved in fraud can be frozen to prevent additional financial risks.

Psychological trust and safety

For companies with user-generated content, protecting users from psychological abuse is vital for generating a vibrant online community. Examples of platforms with user-generated content include online multiplayer games with chat rooms, social networks, media sharing sites, and online review sites. Abuses such as harassment, bullying, and scams must be handled to maintain users' trust and allow them to feel safe while using these platforms.

Harassment is the process of sending messages to cause psychological harm to a victim. Bullying is the repeated harassment from a bully to a victim. With many reported suicides [8] from cyberbullying, the threat to user safety is real. A victim has limited defense options. The victim can delete a direct harassment message; however, this requires the victim to have read the message, which may have already inflicted psychological harm. The victim cannot delete broadcasted messages directly and would rely on a moderator to remove the message.

Scams can be harder to detect. The actual act of scamming may happen outside the visibility of a specific online community, so it can be hard to evaluate whether a particular message is a scam. Scams are often reported long after they are committed, as it takes time for the victim to realize they have been scammed. Many victims may even be too embarrassed to report a scam.

As a DS executive or a distinguished data scientist, you can invest in algorithms and infrastructure to detect and mark harassment, bullying, and scam messages automatically. An algorithm can look for patterns of abuse in the messages, the sender, and the recipient's history. An infrastructure can block, mark for review, or pass through messages, depending on the assessed risk level for the recipient.

066

When serving individual consumers, a company must maintain physical, financial, and psychological levels of trust and safety. An industry can thrive in the long term only when customers feel the value of the products or services is worth the risk of transacting with a company. Data science can help minimize these risks in transactions.

BUSINESS-TO-BUSINESS SCENARIO

To win the trust and safety of enterprise consumers, a *software-as-a-service* (SaaS) solution needs to prove to customers that the data shared will directly benefit the customer, have no negative effect on usage or operations, and will not compromise or leak any business intelligence or metrics.

SaaS is a business model to deliver centrally hosted software licensed on a subscription basis. The approach is well-adopted within the business community and has many efficiencies. Recently, with the proliferation of in-depth analysis capabilities, new players are emerging to take multi-tenant hosting to new levels by offering some enterprise data to be aggregated in exchange for advanced features and benchmarking capabilities. These possibilities also bring with them some ethical considerations.

Software-as-a-service offerings have five primary advantages over traditional downloaded and installed software:

- *Fast ramp to value*—No installation and configurations required. A login could be all you need. The software often codifies best practices that you can start using right away.
- *Lower costs*—Software is often hosted in a multi-tenant environment with an economy of scale.
- *Scalability and integration*—There is no need to buy additional servers. If usage goes up, the hosted environment can often expand automatically.
- *Easy upgrades*—Standardized hosting means fewer issues in upgrades, and upgrades are handled by the SaaS provider.
- *Easy to use*—Easy to test and buy the software.

The traditional SaaS agreements often have terms on customer data that explicitly assign ownership of all customer data to the customers. They explicitly prohibit any use of the data by the provider for any purpose.

In the era of advanced analytics and machine learning, the traditional SaaS agreement permits limited analytics capabilities to be based on data from a single customer. This prevents significant value from being exploited across customers to benefit everyone on the SaaS offerings. New SaaS solutions are emerging to break through these challenges by granting the hosts of SaaS solutions specific limited access to the customer data to develop novel features that could not otherwise be possible.

Features that can benefit from limited access to customer data in SaaS solutions include:

- *Optimization and customization of user interfaces*—This includes the placement of menus and functions, messaging, and workflows presented in the SaaS solution. Usage behavior data across customers can provide more significant signals to improve usability much more quickly.
- *Relevance ranking algorithms*—This includes the relevance of content recommended in news feeds and in search functions within the SaaS solution. The feedback across many customers can provide faster feedback to train relevance algorithms.
- *Attribution of conversion*—When multiple touches can be attributed to converting a user to a new capability, how do we credit the different touches? Manually-labeled data can be sparse. But if sparse data is aggregated, we can be more informed about traffic source attribution.
- *Matching of entities*—Entities such as companies and contacts can be challenging to identify and canonicalize in large databases. Contact affiliation and business entity properties need to be constantly updated. With data aggregated across multiple customers, entity-matching capabilities can get more timely feedback for improving entity-matching accuracy.

For customers to opt in to these data-sharing agreements to enable data-driven optimization opportunities, the SaaS solution needs to *prove* to customers that the data shared:

- Will directly benefit the customer
- Will have no negative effect on the usage or the operations of the SaaS solution
- Will not compromise or leak any business intelligence or metrics

Holding a high bar for these ethical principles is essential for business customers to have enough trust for the SaaS solution to opt in to data sharing, enabling the long-term accumulation of capabilities and competitive advantages for the SaaS platform.

067

To win the trust and safety of enterprise consumers, a SaaS solution needs to prove to customers that the data shared will directly benefit the customer, have no negative effect on usage or operations, and will not compromise or leak any business intelligence or metrics.

In summary, the trust and safety of customers are essential for the long-term viability of a business. For a direct-to-consumer business, DS capabilities can address the customers' physical safety, financial safety, and psychological trust and safety. For a business-to-business solution, opportunities to enable limited data sharing can accelerate the pace of innovation, as long as ethical principles are clarified and observed.

9.1.3   *Taking social responsibility for decisions*

With great power comes great responsibility. DS is now driving decisions in domains, such as finance, employment, and social media, which affect billions of people and can impact their lives for years to come.

Taking social responsibility is hard in DS. Models are great at learning historical patterns, but making decisions based on historical patterns can also amplify historical human biases. Human biases are often embedded in training data. Identifying what's *fair* in decision-making goes beyond quantitative analysis.

068

Models are great at learning historical patterns, but making decisions based on historical patterns can also amplify historical human biases. Identifying what's *fair* in decision-making goes beyond quantitative analysis.

Fairness has many definitions [9], [10], including individual fairness, group fairness, predictive rate parity, equalized odds, equal opportunity, equal outcomes, and counterfactual fairness. These are all credible attempts at determining fairness in different contexts and may conflict with each other.

As a DS executive or a distinguished data scientist, you have the responsibility to recognize the complexity behind the concept of fairness within your social and business contexts. Let's look at examples in finance, employment, and social media to highlight the ongoing challenges with fairness and their side effects.

EXAMPLE 1: FINANCIAL FAIRNESS

The challenges in financial fairness can be exemplified by the nuances in approval decisions of loans [11]. Biases in loan approval can disadvantage whole communities by eliminating critical investments that allow people to increase their productivity by living closer to work, acquiring equipment, paying for education and training, or handling temporary cash liquidity gaps. Without these loans, people may be forced to take a hit on productivity or forgo opportunities to improve their overall financial standing and delay their ability to accumulate wealth.

Historically, biases in lending decisions have led to the stagnation and marginalization of whole communities [12]. How can we make credit decisions fairer and, at the same time, protect the interest of the lenders who want to lend only to creditworthy customers?

Unsecured consumer lending data in multiple cultures has shown that male borrowers are more likely to default on loans than female borrowers. At the same time, the loan application pool also overwhelmingly consists of male borrowers. Is this caused by data bias or the bias for males to take more risks?

The United States passed the Equal Credit Opportunity Act (ECOA) [12] in 1974 to make it illegal for creditors to discriminate based on race, sex, age, national origin, marital status, or because one receives public assistance. However, even when gender is not considered in assessing creditworthiness, women's average credit score is consistently lower than men's average score in the US. How could this be?

It turns out that a significant component of assessing creditworthiness is the *revolving credit utilization ratio*, which is the percentage of your credit limit you are using on a month-to-month basis. Because of the gender wage gap, women earn less than men on average, and the credit limit is closely related to one's income. Lower income leads to a lower credit limit. Even when the balances women carry are comparable to men's, as a ratio of the available credit limit, their revolving credit utilization ratio is higher, leading to a lower average credit score.

The historical wage gap does not just span genders. It is also present across races and ethnicities. So, despite the government's best efforts to remove discrimination in financial lending, historical biases in the economic environment can still propagate through many other dimensions.

As an executive in a company or a distinguished data scientist, the top priority is to first comply with the regulation. When there is a perceived business opportunity for female consumers, product design and marketing can appeal to a particular segment of customers. However, the credit approval process must follow the *fairness through unawareness* principle, which states that gender must not be a factor in approving a credit card or setting a credit limit for your customers. To more fundamentally address the historical wage gap, let's look at employment opportunity fairness next.

EXAMPLE 2: EMPLOYMENT OPPORTUNITY FAIRNESS

When sourcing talent for hard-to-fill roles, recruiters are increasingly dependent on searches in résumé databases and online profiles from companies such as LinkedIn or Indeed to find potential candidates to qualify for their hiring pipelines. LinkedIn and Indeed aggregate millions of jobs so that job seekers only have to search in one place to find all the opportunities available to them. They also attract job seekers to generate online profiles and upload résumés so that recruiters can find them when new opportunities come up.

Websites use recruiter engagement behavior as feedback to improve the relevance of the talent sourcing experience. Signals are collected as recruiters interact with talent sourcing search results. These signals help ranking algorithms understand what kind of profile and résumé summaries can better attract recruiters' attention. This approach, however, often reinforces existing human biases in gender, ethnicity, and race, which can perpetuate discrimination against specific groups.

As you look to improve employment opportunity fairness, how do you determine what metrics to optimize? Using the male-to-female ratio as an example, what would be considered fair? Here are three approaches to consider:

- *Fairness through unawareness*—No gender feature is directly used in ranking. This approach is the status quo in most environments. However, strong evidence suggests that historical human biases exist in hiring practices [13]. While the approach may be easier to validate and govern, it cannot effectively remove human biases in the search ranking of potential candidates.
- *Demographic parity*—An equal number of male and female candidates are included in the result. Search results can be ranked and partitioned by gender. The results can then be reconstructed to ensure there is a one-to-one ratio of male and female candidates on the top page. This approach is simple to implement, but the gender ratios for the talent pool in various professions are not one-to-one. One may argue that the gender with majority representation will be disadvantaged in top search results.
- *Equal opportunity*—The ratio of male to female candidates appearing at the top of the search result is proportional to the ratios in the talent pool with matching skill sets. Top search results will contain a set of candidates with gender ratios matching the talent pool. This approach introduces a representative set of gender-balanced candidates in the top results, while respecting the gender ratios within various professions. This approach has been adopted by industry leaders, such as LinkedIn [14].

As you can see, different notions of fairness are applicable in situations that can make career-changing differences to individuals, and the specific context has to be considered when selecting an approach. To identify the definition of fairness that is most apt for your scenario, refer to a survey [15] on this topic by Ninareh Mehrabi, et al.

EXAMPLE 3: SOCIAL MEDIA FAIRNESS

Social media platforms, such as Facebook, Twitter, YouTube, and LinkedIn, are increasingly influential in people's everyday lives. As of August 2018, around two-thirds (68%) of Americans get their news from social media [16].

The First Amendment of the US Constitution guarantees freedom of expression by prohibiting Congress from restricting the press's or individuals' rights to speak freely. Some bad actors can also abuse this freedom by disseminating harmful content that is misleading, obscene, threatening, hateful, defamatory, or discriminatory.

Moderation of content has become an important topic in the social media industry. In the 2016 US presidential election campaign, the top 20 fake news stories received more shares than the top 20 real news stories [17]. If these harmful contents are not detected and moderated early, they can have severe and long-lasting implications on democracy, the economy, and geopolitical stability.

As a DS executive or a distinguished data scientist, how do you walk the fine line of taking on social responsibility while not stifling the freedom of expression? There are many forms of moderation:

- *Manual moderation*—Editors moderate every message before they appear online.
- *Post-moderation*—Messages appear online first and are placed in a queue for editors to review.
- *Reactive moderation*—Users can report abuses. Only reported abuses are reviewed.
- *Distributed moderation*—Users vote content up or down to self-moderate.
- *Automated moderation*—Algorithms are used to detect and remove messages in violation of content policy.

Manual moderation and *post-moderation* can effectively enforce content policies and are frequently used for paid content such as advertisements. However, they are less scalable and not suitable for user-generated content. *Reactive moderation* and *distributed moderation* are highly scalable. However, they only fix problems that have already negatively impacted your audience. *Automated moderation* is still nascent with detection methodologies spanning knowledge-based, style-based, propagation-based, and source-based approaches [18]. While they can quickly react to potential abuses, they can also produce high-profile false positives [19] and are still a topic of research. Moderation systems in production today on social media platforms are often hybrid systems that include multiple forms of moderation with automated algorithms taking into account user feedback and editor choices.

There are many challenges with these content moderation systems. As with any machine learning system, moderation algorithms can make mistakes. If they are too gentle in moderating content, they can leave abusive content to propagate and harm more users. If they are too harsh on moderation, they increase the number of false positives in moderation actions, which can stifle legitimate voices [20].

On the legal front, since 1996, section 230 of the Communications Decency Act has protected internet companies like Facebook, YouTube, and Twitter from liability for content created by their users. It permits internet companies to moderate their sites without being on the hook legally for the content they host. However, the political tide is turning to revisit these policies.

The role of machine learning in content moderation will reflect your ethical stand on the issues. The balance between protecting the freedom of expression and protecting users from misleading, obscene, threatening, hateful, defamatory, or discriminatory information without censoring sensitive topics of discussion will become increasingly crucial for exercising your company's social responsibilities.

9.2 Rigor in leading, higher standards

As a DS executive or a distinguished data scientist, you define the DS culture at your company. This process involves the rigor of creating a productive and harmonious work environment for DS, accelerating the speed and increasing the quality of decisions, and driving breakthroughs that can increase enterprise value and inspire an industry.

There are many challenges in incorporating a nascent DS function into a company. Depending on your executive leaders' background, DS may or may not be equally valued across the organization. Some executives may prefer to hire dedicated internal analyst teams to maintain control over their data, leading to data silos within functions and business units. Some may go to another extreme to provide full data access, then anticipate that any unresolved data problem is a DS problem. A productive and harmonious work environment can be challenging to create. We discuss this in section 9.2.1.

As an executive, you are also expected to make rigorous decisions with speed and conviction. With a DS background, it is in our nature to be analytical. Many may find it challenging at times to be decisive. Yet being indecisive can cause you to miss opportunities and can cast doubt on executives' leadership capabilities. Making decisions with conviction provides consistency for the team, so the team can pursue long-term objectives that move it toward its vision. Being able to make hard calls rigorously based on limited information with velocity is an essential skill of a DS executive. We discuss this in section 9.2.2.

To inspire an industry, innovations can come from within or outside the corporate boundary. There are various standards to drive the rigor of internal innovations. These include filing patents as part of an intellectual property strategy, developing open source software that can be shared with and maintained by the developer community, or publishing results and methodologies written up as papers for the scientific community. For innovations outside your company, technologies can be licensed, and teams and companies can be acquired. With careful technical diligence, outside innovations can accelerate the growth of your company's enterprise value and inspire your industry. We discuss this in section 9.2.3. Let's dive in!

9.2.1   *Creating a productive and harmonious work environment*

Whether you are leading DS in a large or small company, garnering executive support for DS initiatives is crucial for creating a productive and harmonious work environment for your teams. Many of the challenges and pressures DS teams feel are best resolved at the executive level.

When executives across functions are aligned, they create a productive and harmonious environment for their teams to collaborate and execute. When the executives are not aligned, they leave their teams to struggle through execution with no effective escalation paths. The situation can be a recipe for a contentious and stressful work environment for all teams. What are some common challenges to proper alignment between you and your peer executives?

069

When the executives are not aligned, they leave their teams to struggle through execution with no effective escalation paths. The situation can be a recipe for a contentious and stressful work environment for all teams.

There are two main root causes for misalignment: lack of trust and lack of understanding. These are illustrated in figure 9.2. Lack of trust can show up as resistance to data collection or rejection of insights created. Lack of understanding can show up as treating DS functions as table and report generators or having an unrealistic expectation of the scope of DS. Let's discuss how to recognize and address these issues.

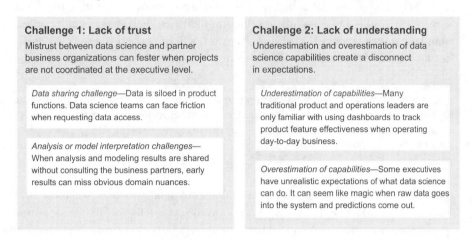

Challenge 1: Lack of trust
Mistrust between data science and partner business organizations can fester when projects are not coordinated at the executive level.

Data sharing challenge—Data is siloed in product functions. Data science teams can face friction when requesting data access.

Analysis or model interpretation challenges—When analysis and modeling results are shared without consulting the business partners, early results can miss obvious domain nuances.

Challenge 2: Lack of understanding
Underestimation and overestimation of data science capabilities create a disconnect in expectations.

Underestimation of capabilities—Many traditional product and operations leaders are only familiar with using dashboards to track product feature effectiveness when operating day-to-day business.

Overestimation of capabilities—Some executives have unrealistic expectations of what data science can do. It can seem like magic when raw data goes into the system and predictions come out.

Figure 9.2 Two causes for misalignment in the data science work environment

LACK OF TRUST

Mistrust between DS and partner business organizations can fester when projects are not coordinated at the executive level. This can lead to barriers in sharing data, interpreting analysis, or modeling results.

Data sharing challenges

In many companies, production data is recorded in the product and analyzed to make crucial business decisions. This data is often specified by product managers, collected by engineers, processed by analysts, and used to guide business operations. In nascent DS functions, when requesting data access, it is natural for the data owner to question how the data will be used.

From the DS perspective, projects are often proposed by first stating existing gaps, then highlighting how DS work could significantly improve business outcomes. When projects are proposed unilaterally by DS, the narrative could be seen as a criticism of the business partner's existing work with an attempt to take all the credit on improvements produced. This narrative angle breeds mistrust between teams, complicates getting access to additional data, and reduces the chance that business partners will accept and deploy the final solution.

Care should be taken to work with business partners to propose these projects together as equal partners. This type of narrative can better align motivations between the executives and the collaborating team.

Analysis or model interpretation challenges

In more mature organizations, when production data is already aggregated in data lakes and data warehouses, shared by their data owners, there are still many data nuances to be understood. Section 2.3.2 speaks to examples of these nuances in web sessions, geolocations, and financial transactions.

When analysis and modeling results are shared without consulting the business partners, early results can miss obvious domain nuances, such as seasonality or biases from standard business practices. Business partners will not take the results seriously, no matter how precise the analyses or models are, if domain nuances are not considered.

070

> Early analysis and modeling results can miss obvious domain nuances when shared without consulting the business partners first. Business partners will not take the results seriously, no matter how precise the analyses or models are, if domain nuances are not considered.

For example, if you work with personal spend data, you may see most transactions dated on Mondays or Tuesdays. But common sense tells you that people make more purchases over the weekend. What's happening? It turns out that credit card and debit card purchases made over the weekend are pending until they clear fraud checks at the card network before posting at the card-issuing bank on Mondays or Tuesdays. Historical records for financial transactions usually record just the cleared and posted transactions, while consumer user experiences are triggered by their spending in real time. When analysis or modeling does not take the transaction posting date nuance into account, it will be hard for business partners to trust any recommendations based on biased or flawed assumptions.

How do you build trust with peer executives? One powerful approach is understanding their pain points and selecting ones for which you can quickly produce business value. This is best done when you are new to an organization or a role and are meeting your new peers to understand their top priorities. Alignment starts with helping them with their major pain points and delivering real business value.

As you establish trust, you can select friendly executives for your early wins. These should not be the most ambitious endeavors but the low-risk quick wins that can build up your momentum of success to gain your peers' trust. With their trust, you can invest in bigger projects with them for major wins. In the early stages of building trust, avoid peers who may be skeptical of your work, as you will need all the goodwill you can get in building your momentum of success.

When securing early wins, be transparent and communicate what you are doing, as other executives may not be familiar with the iterative nature of DS efforts. Closely partner with the business throughout the project definition, execution, and evaluation process to avoid having your project get off track and become irrelevant. When you communicate results, make sure the success is presented as collaborations between business partners and DS. Avoid popular media's sensationalized narrative of *historically mismanaged operating states saved by a clever DS model*, which can quickly destroy relationships with business partners.

071

> When you communicate results, make sure the success is presented as collaborations between business partners and data science. Avoid popular media's sensationalized *narrative of historically mismanaged operating states saved by a clever data science model*, which can quickly destroy relationships with business partners.

What is most important for an executive, but is rarely talked about, is the importance of a powerful ally in the organization that can be a "lighting-rod" [21]. Every organization has histories that got it to where it is. When you are new to an organization, it is important to learn as much as possible about the organization's history. But you will inevitably step into some sensitive situations. To keep trust building on track, you will need a powerful figure in the organization as a "lighting-rod" to absorb any attacks when they come your way. Examples of powerful figures in the organization can be your projects' sponsors, champions, or the CEO.

LACK OF UNDERSTANDING

Once you have the trust of your peer executives in delivering business results, it is time to set the appropriate levels of expectation. Common challenges include the underestimation and overestimation of the capabilities of DS.

Underestimation of capabilities

Many traditional product and operations leaders are familiar with using dashboards of metrics to measure product feature effectiveness and to operate the business from day to day. While dashboard creation is an important part of the DS responsibilities, it is only one out of nine types of common DS projects, as illustrated in section 2.2.2. Other responsibilities include tracking specification definition, feature monitoring and rollout, data insights and deep dives, modeling and API development, data enrichment, data consistency, infrastructure improvements, and regulatory compliance. When your peer executives understand the breadth and depth of what DS can do to address their pain points, you can expand the horizon of possible alignments in which DS can be used to address business needs.

Overestimation of capabilities

Some executives have unrealistic expectations of what DS can do. To them, it can seem like magic that raw data goes into the DS systems, and out come predictions of the future. It is your responsibility to help your peer executives understand the opportunities and limitations of today's technology.

Exercises such as articulating roadmaps with necessary milestones can help executives articulate what is possible in what time frame. Then, there can be meaningful discussions about prioritization and trade-offs.

At the same time, many companies struggle with data quality challenges. Some executives may feel that a DS function should own all unresolved data issues. As the DS executive, there should be a clear articulation of the scope of the function. The focus should be on solving high-priority business challenges with timeboxed efforts on ad hoc data issues.

Formats such as weekly office hours can be suitable for addressing and deferring some unresolved data problems. Section 4.2.2 discusses the best practices for setting up office hours in more depth.

When a lack of trust and lack of understanding are addressed at the executive level, it creates a productive and harmonious environment from the top down. Even when conflicts appear in a specific project, with *clean escalation*, the conflicts can be quickly resolved in the context of the aligned goals.

> **NOTE**   Clean escalation is the process of bringing a misalignment to a higher level of management together with the misaligned parties, while highlighting a precise description of the misalignment, the negative impact of indecision, what has been agreed upon, and what information is missing to reach a commitment. Section 4.2.3 describes this in more detail.

9.2.2   *Accelerating the speed and increasing the quality of decisions*

A DS executive is expected to have the decisiveness of an executive and the deliberateness of a data scientist. Without decisiveness, you can miss opportunities and invite doubts to your executive leadership capabilities. Without deliberateness in the rigorous application of DS techniques, you can lose your DS teams' respect.

Decisiveness and deliberateness may seem contradictory. Yet, with a few simple techniques and assessments, you can successfully navigate this balance. If you have the right leaders reporting to you in your organization, only the most challenging decisions remain when they are escalated to you.

The positive impact of moving forward with a decision drives the urgency of a situation. For a decision to be worth an executive's time, it needs to have a significant upside compared to the trajectory of the status quo. What gives pause to decision-makers is the potential negative impact of making a wrong choice.

To be decisive and deliberate, you can use the decision tree illustrated in figure 9.3.

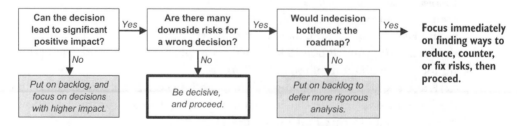

Figure 9.3   Decision-making process for being decisive and deliberate as a data science executive

ARE THERE MANY DOWNSIDE RISKS FOR A WRONG DECISION?

If the impact of a wrong decision is low, you can be decisive, accept the risk, and move forward. But how do you know if the impact of a wrong decision is low?

In section 2.2.1, we discussed the RICE technique for quantifying a project's reach, impact, confidence, and effort. A similar process can be used here with the added opportunity to limit the reach, impact, and effort of a potentially bad decision, while increasing the confidence of a good decision. Let's look at impact assessment for feature launches and changes in people, processes, and platforms.

For the go or no-go business decisions of feature launches, the challenges lie in how much to invest in an experimentation platform to more systematically evaluate launches. With an experimentation platform, features can be exposed to a limited user base to assess feature impact with minimal efforts for coordinating launches and rollbacks. This way, you can gain confidence in the features before launching to the full user base.

To limit impact, you can work with peer executives on a loss budget dedicated to experimentation. For example, the executive team can align on a loss budget of 3% of engagement or revenue. For a new feature with a 20% revenue loss risk, as long as you limit the feature exposure to no more than 15% of the user base, you can decisively proceed to test. You can be even more aggressive on the user base exposed to a new feature if there is frequent monitoring of experimentation results, such that you can stop a feature with unexpected large negative impact early and limit the losses.

For more complex decisions that involve changes in people, processes, and platforms, you can first decide to pilot the changes in a small number of teams/clients to limit the reach and potential negative impact. You can then iterate and improve the change process before driving the change more broadly across all teams or clients.

072

> For complex decisions that involve changes in people, processes, and platforms, you can decide to first pilot the changes in a small number of teams/clients to limit the reach and potential negative impact, then iterate and improve the change process before driving the change more broadly across all teams or clients.

When piloting a change is not possible, you can increase the confidence of your decisions by laying out proof of concept (PoC) milestones to build out the riskiest parts of a project first. As described in Section 3.2.3, this approach can detect insurmountable issues early, providing time and opportunity to pivot efforts through alternative paths to meet the ultimate objective.

WOULD INDECISION BOTTLENECK THE ROADMAP?

So far, we have discussed the assessment and the limiting of risks when moving forward with a decision. What about the opportunity cost of not moving forward?

Opportunity costs are much more difficult to assess, as they include all the things you are giving up on by not moving forward with a decision. With a clear set of roadmaps, as articulated in section 6.1.1, you can map a delay of some existing milestones to understand the impact of the delay on all later milestones.

For example, making the data-driven process more efficient in your company may require a reorganization of the DS team from a distributed structure to a federated structure. This is a change where most data scientists are dedicated to business units and functions, and some are centralized and are strategically deployed to enterprise-wide initiatives.

The decision of whether to reorganize is up to the DS executive. What would be the impact of delaying the decision? Without a centralized component of a DS team strategically deployed to enterprise-wide initiatives, data sourcing efforts can be duplicated across business units, leading to a fragmentation of metrics and creating data consistency tech debts in the data enrichment roadmap.

With few resources to improve the centralized data processing platform, each team is going through inefficient workflows, limiting the total potential impact of the function. With significantly more time spent on data processing, there is less time spent innovating intelligent capabilities and intelligent features to improve business metrics.

When there are great positive impacts for a good decision, large negative impacts for a wrong decision, and a high cost of indecision, it's time to focus on finding ways to reduce, counter, or fix the risk to move forward. Like interest compounding in finance, a delayed decision that holds up roadmap items can significantly reduce the overall returns of data scientists' efforts. Most of the project impact occurs after a successful launch and may require many iterations of optimizations to be effective. Recognizing the impact of a delayed decision can help you prioritize the deliberation of hard decisions.

HOW WOULD YOU HOLISTICALLY ASSESS THE SITUATION?

Generating a holistic assessment of risks and opportunity costs requires information you may not have at your fingertips. Calling large meetings to collect information can slow you down. Not consulting others can cause you to make the wrong decision. What are some best practices you can consider?

You can cultivate a close circle of advisors in both technical and business domains to validate and expand your understanding of the risks for a wrong decision and opportunity costs for indecision. To be decisive and deliberate, you can give the team a voice but not a vote. When you listen and solicit their input for important decisions, it shows that you are deliberate and respect their perspectives. After you make a decision, you can share clear decision reasoning based on the perspectives you have heard. The reasoning is crucial to help the team proceed with conviction in your decision.

One way to gather the teams' input is to have unstructured meetings to challenge your tentative decision and share new data and perspectives. In these meetings, care should be taken not to give the perception of democracy, as a consensus-driven process can be slow and may result in a least-bad compromise.

Once you have made a decision, own it and communicate it in writing. Putting decisions in writing can help the team refer to them and learn how you make trade-offs. Over time, the team can learn to apply your decision logic and rigor in their daily decisions.

When summarizing the decisive and deliberate process, focus on the decisions that can generate a significant positive impact. If there aren't many downside risks, be decisive and proceed. If the cost of being wrong is high, assess whether indecision will delay roadmap milestones. If the delay could be significant, focus on finding ways to reduce, counter, or fix the risk. If the delay is not significant, create a backlog to defer more rigorous analysis until a later time.

9.2.3 Focusing on increasing enterprise value

While DS projects can directly impact business operations, you can generate more significant enterprise value through rigor by generating innovations internally or acquiring innovations from outside the corporate boundary. The internal innovation standards and techniques for introducing external innovation are illustrated in figure 9.4.

Internal and external innovations to increase enterprise value

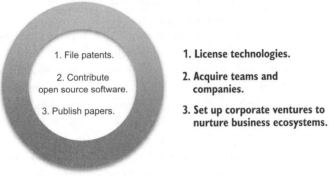

1. File patents.

2. Contribute open source software.

3. Publish papers.

1. **License technologies.**

2. **Acquire teams and companies.**

3. **Set up corporate ventures to nurture business ecosystems.**

Internal innovation **External innovation**

Figure 9.4   Techniques for aggregating innovations to increase enterprise value

There are three common standards to drive the rigor of internal innovations. These include filing patents as part of an intellectual property strategy, developing open source software that can be shared with and maintained by the developer community, or publishing results and methodologies written up as papers for the scientific community.

For innovations outside your company, you can license technologies, acquire teams and companies, and set up corporate ventures to nurture business ecosystems. With careful technical diligence, outside innovations can effectively accelerate the growth of your company's enterprise value. Let's look at them one by one.

INTERNAL INNOVATION STANDARDS

A rigorous internal innovation standard allows your team members to aspire to levels of craftsmanship for their projects beyond the bare minimum required to get the job done at the moment. It will enable the work product to stand the test of time and continue to deliver enterprise value long after a particular code base or result is deprecated.

Patenting requires the innovations to be rigorously documented by patent attorneys and reviewed by patent examiners. When a patent is granted, you have a government-endorsed monopoly to recoup your innovation investment over a limited time period in exchange for sharing your innovation with the world for others to improve upon. The patent system helps society build on innovations faster.

Open-sourcing projects requires the implementations to be clean and robust, such that they can be shared, reviewed, maintained, and used by a community of developers. Contributing to open source software can increase the rigor with which your team approaches software development, build your talent brand for attracting top talent, and amortize development and maintenance costs for your software infrastructure.

The publication of the methodologies and results allows the fundamental theory and reasoning behind the innovation to go through rigorous peer review to advance the world's scientific understanding. These are indicators of the rigor of work conducted in your organization. Let's look at these standards one by one.

Patenting as part of an intellectual property strategy

If your company or team is pioneering technology in a new business area or innovating technologies and systems in an existing business area, you can consider patenting your innovation. A patent publicly announces your innovation in exchange for government protection for a broad class of products and services, allowing your company to enjoy an exclusive right to commercialize the innovation over a time period.

Aside from using the innovation in your products or services to directly generate revenue, patenting your innovation also allows it to be licensed for a fee, used as leverage in cross-licensing with industry partners, or defended against competitors encroaching in your business domains. With the various opportunities patents create, a patented innovation can increase your enterprise value beyond its revenue through business operations.

What qualifies an innovation to be patentable? The two most important requirements are that the innovation must be *novel* and *non-obvious* at the filing date. This means that there is no such innovation prior to your filing date, and it is not a natural next step that anyone in the field could have implemented.

In satisfying these requirements, significant documentation is necessary to scope the claim of novelty and non-obviousness through prior art searches and detailed descriptions of the innovation.

What constitutes an intellectual property strategy? Some criteria are discussed here:

- *Identify your business goals.* Are you protecting your business's core technology? Or increasing revenue streams through licensing? Are you offensively looking to block specific competitors from a field of use? Or are you defensively reducing the risk of being sued by competitors? Different goals will lead to different patent portfolio strategies.
- *Produce a list of patentable ideas.* This is a list of ideas with a brief description for each idea, documenting your employees' company-related innovations. It can be used to establish your company's ownership over its IP.
- *Prioritize the list of ideas.* You can prioritize with questions such as: Which of these ideas are best aligned with your business goals? Which ideas are most likely to be patentable? Which ideas are competitors most likely pursuing? If a competitor infringes your patent, would you be able to find out easily? Are you planning to disclose any ideas outside the company soon?
- *Set a budget and a schedule.* Writing a defensible patent and filing it can require a significant amount of resources, both in legal fees and in the efforts of your data scientists. You can potentially file provisional applications first to lock in the priority date in the US, which involves lower filing fees and fewer formalities. You can then follow up with a non-provisional application within 12 months, which can mature into an issued patent.

With the promise of granted patents, you can motivate your data scientists to produce higher quality, patentable work and allow their innovations to generate greater enterprise value for the company.

NOTE Trade secrets and copyright can also be part of an intellectual property strategy to generate enterprise value. You can consult your legal department on how your company sees the opportunities here.

073 By constituting a patent strategy for your company in data science, you can motivate your data scientists to produce higher quality, patentable work and allow their innovations to generate greater enterprise value.

Open-sourcing projects

Open-sourcing projects is an approach to the design, development, and distribution of software, offering practical accessibility to a software's source code. For many software developers, founding and contributing to an open source project is a distinction that demonstrates their technical leadership and an opportunity to resolve key technical challenges in their domain with worldwide impact.

The proprietary code developed within a company is often seen and reviewed by only a few technical peers. When a project is open-sourced, the code could be seen and critiqued by thousands of peer developers. For a company where the teams aspire to produce software that they feel proud to open-source, developers often produce work with much more rigor than is used for a typical internal solution.

The rigor in creating highly scalable and extensible codebases can produce sustainable enterprise value. Further, companies known to support open source projects can attract top software engineering talent. The aggregation of top talent further attracts employees who want to work with and learn from them.

074

> Founding and contributing to an open source project builds an identity of technical leadership for your team members and your organization. The prospect of open-sourcing their work can help you attract top talent and motivate them to create scalable and extensible codebases with sustainable enterprise value.

When your team has developed an innovative software solution to a specific pressing technical challenge at hand, you can use the following two questions to assess whether it has the potential to become an open source project:

- Is the technical challenge a *common challenge* that many in the industry may face?
- Is the solution a *marginal solution* that does not disclose the core "secret sauce" of the business?

For an open source project to thrive, a community of developers should rally around a common technical challenge. Table 9.1 illustrates some examples of common technical challenges in DS. When there is a common enough and significant enough technical challenge, you can develop a solution with best practices and inspire the community to work together on evolving the solution.

Table 9.1   Examples of common technical challenges resolved by open-source software

Common technical challenges	Sample open-source software
Distributed computation on commodity hardware	Hadoop, Spark
Working with real-time event streams	Kafka
Computations on large graphs	Neo4j
Management of data processing pipelines	Airflow
Continuous integration of software projects	Jenkins, Hudson

For your company to feel comfortable opening up the source code of the software it has developed, it must not compromise its key competitive advantage. For example, Google is not likely to open-source its key search algorithm, but it does open-source its machine learning algorithm library TensorFlow. Airbnb is not likely to share its algorithm for personalization, but it does open-source its data processing pipeline management tool Airflow.

When your open source solution for an important industry challenge gains adoption, it is the ultimate proof that you have created an industry-leading innovation. It also demonstrates that you have created a work environment for top talent to aggregate to generate sustained growth for your company's enterprise value.

Publishing results and methodologies in the scientific community

Like open-sourcing software, publishing your results and methodologies in the scientific community is also proof that you are aggregating talent that can generate sustained growth for your company's enterprise value.

Publishing in top conferences and journals often means that your solution is *novel, interesting,* and *useful.* Rigor is demonstrated in the efforts to understand the deeper reasons for the advantages of your results peer-reviewed by domain experts. It is not surprising that published results are sometimes accompanied by open source code. You should determine whether to publish with the same two questions: whether the challenge is common and whether the solution infringes on the company's core "secret sauce."

EXTERNAL INNOVATIONS FOR DRIVING ENTERPRISE VALUE

In the pursuit of building intelligent products and services, many roadmaps can be accelerated by introducing external innovations. We see examples of opportunities in the plethora of resources available to purchase, including third-party data sources, data processing tools and services, and computing resources. There are three common levels of acquisition of external innovations:

- Licensing of data and technologies
- Acquiring companies and teams
- Nurturing a business ecosystem with a corporate venture

When an external innovation is a marginal practice that can accelerate your roadmaps, you can consider licensing the data or technology. When it is a key part of your company's vision, you may consider acquiring controlling ownership of the company or the team. When you are looking to nurture an external innovation that aligns with your corporate strategy, you may invest in them and include them as a part of your business ecosystem. With careful technical diligence, outside innovations can effectively accelerate the growth of your company's enterprise value. Let's look at the rigor involved in considering them one by one.

Data and technology licensing

Third-party data sources, data processing tools, and enrichment service vendors can greatly accelerate the pace of innovation in building intelligent products and services. To effectively license data and technology with rigor, there are four main elements to consider:

- *Alignment with your strategic roadmap*—The data and technology should be considered in the context of goals you would like to achieve, so you can assess the willingness to pay to make it a worthwhile investment. If it is too expensive to license, or the licensing terms prevent you from achieving your goals, you should walk away.
- *Technology compatibility*—The data, tools, or resources acquired through licensing should integrate well with existing infrastructures. If technical diligence shows that the technologies have incompatibilities that will be too costly to bridge, licensing may not be worthwhile.
- *Monitoring capability*—You can use internal analysis and reporting to monitor the contribution of the licensed innovation toward business value. This monitoring is crucial, especially for subscription-based licensing, as your customer segment may shift, and data quality or technology suitability may change over time. These situations may change the ROI for continued investment in licensing.
- *Team reward system*—To counter the "not invented here" bias, you can take care to align the performance of data scientists to the business impact produced rather than the lines of code written. This alignment is crucial for external innovations to take root in your organization.

Company acquisitions

When an external innovation is driven by another company with a product roadmap and business model that can contribute a new product line to your company, you can look to acquire the company. The rigor in such an acquisition is the due diligence process, which aims to work through dozens of concerns, including financial, technical, business, roadmap, team, regulatory compliance, and legal areas, to illuminate the opportunities and risks of acquisition.

As a DS executive or a distinguished data scientist, you can be called on to perform technical due diligence. The primary purpose of the technical due diligence is to ensure:

- The claims made by the team in the areas of technology are accurate.
- The team is technically credible and competent.
- The organization is capable of executing on its current roadmap.
- The technical strengths, weaknesses, and risks of the company are understood.

To conduct technical due diligence in the area of DS, here is a list of ten items to investigate:

- The main business challenges the innovation is solving for
- The success and maturity of solutions toward resolving the business challenges
- The architectures and infrastructures used to build and deploy solutions
- The maintainability, scalability, and defensibility of the solutions over time
- The customer experience and impact of your solutions
- The team's credibility and capability

- The team structure and interactions with partners
- The business challenge discovery and solution-crafting process
- Historical (18 months) and forward-looking (18 months) roadmaps
- External dependencies on talent pipelines, third-party data, and tool providers

With rigor in your technical due diligence, you can minimize the risk of failures in acquiring teams and companies at an early stage of their development by accelerating your product roadmaps and driving enterprise value.

Nurturing a business ecosystem with a corporate venture

When your company is innovating in providing a technology platform, such as the in-home voice-activated automation platform (Amazon's Alexa) or the micro-investment feature as a service (Acorns), creating an ecosystem of developers on the platform can facilitate an aggregation of value for your company and increase its enterprise value.

In building a successful corporate venture capital function with rigor, the following four main considerations should be clarified:

- *Objective*—You may want to clarify whether your investment objective is purely strategic. The goal can be to create and develop an ecosystem for your technology platform. An example of ventures with this type of objective is Amazon's Alexa Fund [22], created to fuel in-home smart speaker-based voice technology innovations. The challenge is balancing financial return considerations with the strategy of seeding innovation and developing an ecosystem in the investment decisions. If your objective is to be strategic, your success metrics need to capture the latent strategic benefits in their portfolio rather than focusing exclusively on the strength of financial returns.
- *Outlook*—To nurture an ecosystem of innovation by supporting companies with strategic early-stage investments, the time horizon of returns can be longer than an average venture capital firm that exclusively focuses on financial returns. It would be important to align these expectations up-front, such that the venture efforts are not affected by company restructuring across macroeconomic cycles.
- *Roles and obligations*—Corporate ventures fulfill specific roles by betting on innovative directions with leverage, as investments are often syndicated across multiple investors. Your company's core competencies are best developed with in-house R&D teams. For peripheral and ecosystem innovations, syndicated investments increase the leverage on capital invested, while still allowing for financial gains. These roles should be clarified such that funds for corporate ventures are not seen as sacrificing resources for in-house development. There should be a complementary relationship between in-house R&D efforts and corporate venture efforts.
- *Organization*—A corporate venture could be organized as a team under a company's finance or corporate strategy function. Or it could pattern itself as an independent venture capital firm. If it is organized as a corporate function where each investment requires board approval, it will greatly limit the competitiveness

in providing timely funding for the entrepreneurs and their innovations. When your corporate venture effort is organized as a venture capital firm, it risks losing the strategic focus to align itself with the evolving corporate innovation narrative. When you can closely align with the company strategically and have the autonomy to make investment decisions with velocity, you can maximally capture external innovations to drive enterprise value.

As a DS executive or a distinguished data scientist, you have at your disposal the tools to license external data to enrich your capabilities, acquire companies to accelerate your roadmaps, and invest in companies to make bets and drive innovations in the ecosystem. You can leverage these available external innovations to increase your company's enterprise value.

9.3   *Attitude of positivity*

DS is a nascent field with many opportunities to transform industries. Your executive attitude toward leading these innovations can be critical to inspire your industry. Your attitude can show up at three levels: the individual, the function, and the industry level.

At the individual level, your attitude is the executive presence that empowers you to stand out in a crowd, get heard, and leave people wanting to learn more from you. The techniques are no different than executive presence for other disciplines, but the implications are greater. Your confidence can garner trust for your strategies and plans from those unfamiliar with DS. Your individual executive presence is what we discuss in section 9.3.1.

At the function level, your attitude and focus allow you to establish an identity of leadership in specific strategic areas of excellence within the industry, so you can attract and retain the most promising talent to fuel your engine of innovation.

At the industry level, a humble and open attitude allows you to stay hungry to learn best practices from a broad range of related industries, then experiment and adopt selected practices that can transform your industry.

With the individual, function, and industry level attitudes, you can focus your energy on inspiring and transforming an industry. Let's dive in.

9.3.1   *Demonstrating executive presence*

Executive presence [23] is an attribute that an audience assigns to an effective and inspiring leader. It is observed in the executive's effective thinking patterns, effective emotional patterns, and effective action patterns. Many people mistake the trait as something that comes naturally to individuals who are highly charismatic or outgoing. But, in fact, it can be systematically developed through a passion for making a positive difference for others and practiced through techniques for high-presence thinking, emotion management, and both verbal and non-verbal actions.

075 Executive presence is an attribute that an audience assigns to an effective and inspiring leader. Executive presence is observed in the executive's effective thinking patterns, emotional patterns, and action patterns.

THE FOUNDATION: YOUR PASSION

A *passion* is a source of personal inspiration that is bigger than personal self-interest. When your executive presence is centered on a passion for making a positive difference for others, your passion can ground you during times of stress, pressure, and uncertainty, allowing you to draw strength from it to guide your perspectives, poise, and actions.

076 When your executive presence is centered on a passion for making a positive difference for others, your passion can ground you during times of stress, pressure, and uncertainty, allowing you to draw strength from it to guide your perspectives, poise, and actions.

So how do you form your passion statement? There are two potential approaches: inside-out and outside-in. For *inside-out*, you can look first to a social cause or a core value you are passionate about, then connect it to an identity you would like to build professionally. Examples of social causes can include equal economic opportunities, health care availability, or freedom of speech. Examples of core values can include compassion, integrity, decisiveness, or rigor. You can then identify the social causes or core values that manifest in your company's vision and mission and connect them into a passion, such that you can authentically ground yourself in it.

For example, Jike Chong's core values include rigor and trustworthiness. In his role as the chief data scientist at Yiren Digital, the first peer-to-peer lending platform in China to go public on the New York Stock Exchange (NYSE:YRD), a focus for DS is to use data to quantify loan applicants' trustworthiness for repaying their loans. Jike connected his core values into a passion to "unleash opportunities for people to leverage their trustworthiness to improve their lives."

As an alternative, you can also start outside and interpret your company's mission or vision statements in a way that aligns with your personal values to form your passion. For example, at Acorns, the financial wellness platform, the mission is to "look after the financial best interests of the up-and-coming, beginning with the empowering step of micro-investing." Connecting with Jike's core values of rigor and trustworthiness in the domain of DS, his passion is crystallized as "helping each customer make the best financial decisions, big and small, in all aspects of their financial lives."

Your passion can evolve, so don't stress about not having a perfect one. You should, however, have one at all times. For example, our passion for writing this book is to "inspire data practitioners to do the best work of their careers and maximize their potential to make a more significant positive impact on the world with data science!" You can even write down multiple alternatives and pick one that can get you up and energized each morning.

When you have it, make sure it describes how you are making a positive difference for others. This is essential for guiding your perspectives, poise, and actions to exhibit high executive presence in thinking, emotion managing, and acting.

EFFECTIVE THINKING PATTERNS

As an executive or a distinguished data scientist, you are expected to take a broader perspective, beyond personal, project, team, or function concerns, to encompass concerns across the entire business and your industry. This expectation requires you to consider a wider horizon of future possibilities in terms of time, resources, and the energy necessary to accomplish your goals.

For example, when reviewing a predictive capability to improve people's financial wellness by nudging people to save more and spend less, you are assessing more than the objectives and key results (OKR) completion, the prediction accuracy, the best practices, or the roadmap progress. You are reviewing the algorithm's impact on people's financial lives and what it means for their families. In the financial services example, you are expected to ask questions such as: Is the algorithm designed responsibly to nudge the right segment of users? Are people saving too little or too much money? Is the money saved allocated to the right financial instruments for their life stage? What are the psychological effects of people starting to save and invest for their future? Does it meaningfully improve people's financial resilience in an economic downturn?

We consider three domains of thinking patterns: *self, others,* and *action-focuses.* The high-presence thinking patterns are described and contrasted against low-presence thinking patterns in table 9.2. The high-presence thinking patterns are not exclusive to executives. We discussed some of them in earlier chapters of this book.

Table 9.2   Areas of high executive presence thinking patterns summarized by John Ullman [23]

Domains	Low-presence thinking	High-presence thinking	Interpretations
Self	Worry about what could go wrong.	Focus on options within your control.	Be aware of and mitigate the risks and anti-patterns with action (sections 2.2.2, 3.2.3, and 7.2.2). Worry only leads to indecision.
	Have too much self-doubt and fear of rejection.	Focus on what I can do to help others.	Empower yourself with your passion for making a positive difference for others.
	I need to be right.	I need to be effective.	Be open to being wrong sometimes, then learn from your mistakes.

Table 9.2 Areas of high executive presence thinking patterns summarized by John Ullman [23] *(continued)*

Domains	Low-presence thinking	High-presence thinking	Interpretations
Others	Focus on people's faults.	Look for the strengths in imperfect people.	Identify and turn people's best qualities into actions, and build teams with complementary strengths to shore up success (section 4.2.1).
	People are either for me or against me.	Treat people with respect and dignity even if they are against me.	How you treat people says more about you than about them. Today's adversary can become tomorrow's ally.
	Take things personally.	Take things purposefully.	Explore perspectives and check assumptions for attacks and calibrate your responses.
	Focus only on people who are here and now.	Be mindful of all stakeholders.	Advocate for all stakeholders' perspectives. To maintain the loyalty of people who are here and now, be loyal to those who are absent.
	Listen to people on my terms.	Listen to people on their terms.	Notice what people are saying and not saying. Understand their drive, motivation, and needs.
Action-Focuses	Focus exclusively on getting results (unaware of damages on relationship and reputation).	Focus on getting results that also strengthen relationships and reputation.	Inspire trust, loyalty, and confidence in others through every interaction. Listen more. Ask what people around you need, tell them how much you value them, and give them credit.
	Focus on what's urgent.	Focus on what matters the most.	Do not mistake the urgent for the important. Stay on track, on purpose, and on the top priorities.
	Focus on showing what I know.	Focus on bringing out the best that everyone here knows, including me.	Be open to what you don't know, and bring out the best insights from the team.

By training yourself to adopt high-presence thinking patterns, you are gaining awareness of yourself, your team, and all stakeholders in a decision. You will find yourself synthesizing others' perspectives into your executive decision, then inspiring them to deliver their best with focus, strengthening relationships and reputations in the process.

EFFECTIVE EMOTIONAL PATTERNS

Your emotions can be contagious to your audience. The initial dominant emotion can change the course of an entire interaction. With the right emotions, you can inspire your audience with your high-presence thinking patterns. However, your effective thinking patterns could also be derailed by highly stressful situations that trigger negative emotional reactions. When you react to situations with too much anger or appear emotionally disconnected, your response can undermine your leadership identity. Effective leaders with effective emotional patterns can channel their emotions in stressful situations to further their executive presence.

What are effective emotional patterns? To manage your emotions in executive presence situations, begin with the emotional end in mind. What emotional response are you looking to generate in your audience? Be proactive in leading the audience not just with words but also with emotions.

When you are looking to inspire your audience on an initiative, draw from your passion for making a positive difference for others by doing two things. First, *identify* how you feel when you are at your best. You may feel proud, purposeful, appreciated, accomplished, confident, or motivated. Remember this as your emotional goal. Then, before a presentation or a meeting, connect the situation with your passion for making a positive difference for others, and combine it with your emotional goal in a simple statement.

For example, our passion for writing this book is to "inspire data practitioners to do the best work of their careers." How we feel when we are at our best is *purposeful*. A simple statement can be: "It is a privilege for me to play a part in inspiring you to do the best work of your career."

By making this simple statement, you can start emotionally strong. And because it draws on your long-held passion, the statement is authentic for you and your audience.

What happens in stressful situations? When you are making progress on your passion for making a positive difference for others, you are at your best emotional state. When stressful situations appear in meetings, discussions, and incidents, you can be knocked out of your best emotional state. It is easy to be distracted, frustrated, and get into a low emotional state by dwelling on what happened. As an executive or a distinguished data scientist, when you lose your composure, it can quickly affect the team, the function, and the company.

While it is human to be derailed from your best emotional state, effective executives have a two-step technique to get back on track:

1 *Recognize how you feel*—We all have situations that cause us to lose our composure. It may be an irresponsible accusation about our work's rigor or a lack of coordination that resulted in wasted effort. The situations can leave us feeling exposed, disrespected, angry, frustrated, stuck, or isolated. You can feel the intensity of this emotion. We are only human.

2 *Redirect the emotion with intensity*—Instead of dwelling in the negativity, you can redirect it, along with its intensity, with an "and" phrase to get back toward your best emotional state. For example, if you feel frustrated and isolated because a lack of coordination resulting in wasted efforts, feel that frustration, and say to yourself: "I feel frustrated, and I am determined to improve the process, such that I am consulted and informed in the future." You can then redirect your intense frustration to improving the process.

EFFECTIVE ACTION PATTERNS

When employing high-presence thought and emotional patterns, you also need to project your thoughts and emotions with a strong delivery to gain an executive presence. A strong delivery includes verbal and non-verbal action patterns. In many contexts, non-verbal action patterns, such as postures and facial expressions, can be perceived as 75% to 80% of the message delivered [24].

There are seven domains of non-verbal communication techniques you can practice for body language and tone of voice. These are summarized in table 9.3.

Table 9.3 Non-verbal communication action patterns

Domains	Low-presence actions	High-presence actions	Notes
Posture	Slouching, being agitated, or standing rigidly	Standing up straight or sitting upright	Taking a confident posture two minutes before your presentation can make you feel more confident.
Movement and gesture	Moving erratically, with stiff or jerky motions and robotic gestures	Moving with purposeful, smooth, and fluid motions and gestures	When gestures are in sync with the points you are making, they are more effective for communication.
Facial expression	Making extreme expressions that contort your face	Showing emotions consistent with your purpose	Show a smile when appropriate. Extreme expressions make you look out of control or immature.
Eye contact	Failing to maintain appropriate eye contact	Connecting with people with an appropriate degree of eye contact	Depending on culture, the degree of eye contact can vary, but some is required to connect with people.
Appearance	Dressing in ways that distract attention	Dressing to add to your credibility without raising questions or doubts	Be appropriately dressed and well-groomed. You may meet someone important between meetings.
Aligning pitch, pace, and tone	Ending sentences with a rising pitch, speaking too quickly or slowly, speaking in a monotone voice	Ending sentences with a descending pitch with varied pace and pauses, and matching tone to the situation	Vary your speaking pace and pauses, which will add to your points of emphasis, and use a descending pitch to convey confidence.
Speaking with volume	Speaking too softly	Speaking loud enough for all your listeners to hear	Use the fullness of your voice to convey your confidence.

These non-verbal action patterns set the context in which your audience interprets your verbal actions. You can practice eight areas of verbal communication techniques for what you say to convey executive presence. These are illustrated in table 9.4.

These are the domains you can use to practice your executive presence. You can make a round of self-assessment, then check with a close friend or colleague to understand how you are practicing executive presence from an audience perspective. Pick one or two areas to work on over the next few weeks. The goal is for the high-presence verbal and non-verbal actions to become habits over time.

Table 9.4   Verbal communication action patterns

Domains	Low-presence actions	High-presence actions	Notes
Speak decisively.	Come across as vacant or wishy-washy.	Express a clear point of view.	Speak at the beginning and end to make a solid first or last impression.
Back it up.	Make empty claims without proof.	Support viewpoints with solid reasons and facts.	Prepare ahead of time for objections, concerns, and counterarguments.
Respond when challenged.	Take challenges personally, respond defensively, or go silent.	Be ready to respond, be clear, and be on-point in your response.	Respond purposefully with an awareness of all stakeholders' perspectives.
If wrong, admit it with strength.	Pretend you are right, or cringe and over-apologize.	Thank the person who points it out, then move on.	Acknowledge the correction. You are going for the truth, not self-interest.
Stay on course.	Go off on tangents or become distracted from your goals.	Stay on topic with what matters the most.	Getting distracted is a symptom of weak perspectives; being confused or being forgetful also hurts your presence.
Keep it simple.	Use technical language that limits your audiences.	Use simple language to reach diverse audiences.	If your narrative is not simple enough, you may be stereotyped as being just another subject matter expert.
Be concise.	Be long-winded.	Leave people wanting to hear more from you.	Speak confidently, then sit down and listen to others.
Engage others with kudos and questions.	Take sole credit for joint work; display no interest in others' work.	Give credit where it's due; ask thoughtful questions.	Be a champion of valuable contributions. Give others the space to speak, and encourage diverse viewpoints. Ask the right questions in respectful ways.

9.3.2   *Establishing team identity of industry leadership*

While you can practice executive presence to establish personal identity, it is also important to develop an identity of leadership for your company within your industry. Industry-wide recognition allows your team to feel proud of their accomplishments, reduce regrettable employee churn, and attract additional talent to your organization.

Your function's leadership identity can be established around product features, its organizational structure, a set of technologies it pioneers, or a social responsibility that it promotes. Figure 9.5 illustrates these four areas.

The process of establishing an identity takes more than technical excellence. It also involves leveraging general media, social media, technical publications, and latching onto social narratives, while avoiding certain pitfalls. Let's look at some success cases in establishing industry leadership and cautions against specific potential pitfalls.

TECHNOLOGY PLATFORM LEADERSHIP

If your company has developed industry-leading technical capabilities that can fundamentally transform the efficiency of doing business, it could be something that you can build an identity around. You can then leverage this identity to attract valuable talent to further your advantages in these business areas for enterprise value growth.

One example of a technology platform is a rigorous platform for running controlled online experiments. The team can quantitatively assess the benefit of user interfaces and algorithms before launch, such that only product improvements launch to the full population of users. Section 3.2.1 highlighted experimentation as the first of five principles of scientific rigor.

As a case study, the experimentation team at the Microsoft Bing search engine, led by Ron Kohavi, has successfully built an identity of industry leadership in running controlled experiments through technologies and best practices shared through research publications, blogs, and books. Its methodologies are implemented at top-tier technology companies with many companies running over 10,000 experiments a year to rigorously guide incremental improvements in product development. Some of these experiments are shared in tech blogs and papers.

While sharing learning in conferences and tech blogs can be an effective way to attract talent, you should set up experiments ethically. One misstep is shared in section 3.1.1, where one series of experiments at OkCupid profoundly impacted customers' emotional well-being.

The OkCupid experiment involved enrolling pairs of customers who are looking for partners to date on the OkCupid platform. An algorithm predicted 30%, 60%, or 90% compatibility matching scores. To test for the algorithm's effectiveness for each group, the app told a third of them that they were 30% matches, a third of them that they were 60% matches, and a third of them were 90% matches. This way, two-thirds of the population were intentionally shown a matching percentage that was not accurate.

While this type of experiment has technical merits, it crosses the line from trying out new features to being an experiment of deception or a power-of-suggestion experiment that focuses on behavioral experimentation on the relationships between people. As an executive or a distinguished data scientist, how do you avoid this kind of pitfall? As described in section 3.1.1, you can clearly communicate the three ethical principles to your team:

1 *Respect for persons*—Treat customers with respect. Provide transparency, truthfulness, and voluntariness (choice and consent) when conducting experiments.

2 *Beneficence*—Protect people from harm, and minimize risks and maximize benefits.

3 *Justice*—Ensure that participants are not exploited and that there is a fair balance of risks and benefits.

You can delegate a team member with good knowledge of potential ethical sensitivities to review experiments before they are set up and before publishing results to avoid potential pitfalls in building a leadership identity.

SOCIAL RESPONSIBILITY LEADERSHIP

Your team can seek to develop industry leadership in narratives on important social issues. In DS, important social issues include user privacy, AI transparency, and fairness in AI. For example, because AI algorithms are trained on human-generated data, many social and sampling biases are being trained into these algorithms [28].

Microsoft, Google, Facebook, and LinkedIn have all set up teams to address these socially sensitive challenges. For example, LinkedIn open-sourced their LinkedIn Fairness Toolkit (LiFT) [29] in 2020. LiFT was developed as part of its effort to monitor algorithm biases in machine learning algorithms. LiFT can be deployed in training and scoring workflows to measure biases in training data, evaluate different fairness metrics, and detect statistically significant performance differences across different subgroups. It can also be used for ad hoc fairness analysis or as part of a large-scale A/B testing system. In addition, LiFT has been effectively used to monitor gender biases of AI algorithms for recruiting.

While these efforts have earned the sponsoring company social goodwill, there are also pitfalls when key research results highlight important gaps in companies' current practices. Because the research is on socially sensitive topics, when incidents such as the departure of key researchers under unusual circumstances happens [30], it also becomes newsworthy and calls into question a company's true commitment to the social cause.

As a DS executive or a distinguished data scientist, when establishing an identity in socially sensitive causes, you must take care to align the company's interests with the social challenges, such that the identity you build has a positive impact on the company, and the message can withstand media scrutiny.

077 When establishing an identity in socially sensitive causes, take care to align the company's interests with the social challenges, such that the identity you build has a positive impact on the company, and the message can withstand media scrutiny.

Catherine, the chief data scientist from chapter 1, case 7, can establish her leadership identity around the product features, the organizational structure, a set of technologies the company pioneers, or a social responsibility that it promotes. She can leverage general media, social media, technical publications, and latching onto social narratives to attract talent to join her team. As her team grows with the same velocity as the rest of the company, there can be more balance between maintenance projects and strategic projects in their work.

9.3.3 *Learning and adopting best practices across different industries*

To lead an industry, the humility to learn and adopt best practices from other industries is required. A DS executive or a distinguished data scientist can build a broad perspective across multiple industries to draw inspiration from them. These practices can solve specific industry-wide challenges and improve industry practices. Let's look at a few case studies to highlight the importance of learning across industries.

CASE 1: BUILDING GOOD FINANCIAL HABITS

The personal finance industry has a big challenge. Everyone understands that it is a good financial habit to save money for a rainy day. But between the temptation of buying something that you can enjoy now and putting that money away for some unspecified future financial challenge, instant gratification usually wins.

Some have proposed saving for a more specific goal, like a dream vacation or the car they have always wanted. But when emergencies such as a car problem or a health issue come up, the carefully saved funds can get repurposed. After a few rounds of failed attempts, people tend to be discouraged.

The personal finance industry is stuck between a rock and a hard place. If savings goals are not specific, people opt for instant gratification. If saving goals are too specific and can't be reached, people get discouraged. How can we help people build financial resilience, save more money, and feel great about it?

Let's take a look at a similar challenge in the health wellness industry. The industry is also struggling with how to get people to build good exercise habits. Compared to watching your favorite show in the comfort of your couch, each physical exercise session can be tiring, especially after a long day at work. For many people, physical exercise is often neglected, leading to many societal-level health crises.

Katherine Milkman and her team introduced a concept called *temptation bundling* in 2013 [31]. It is a commitment to yourself to only do something you want along with something you need. In this case, something you want can be watching your favorite show, which provides instant gratification. Something that you need can be doing physical exercise, which has short-term pain but long-term health benefits.

In a peer-reviewed experiment with subjects bundling the joy of listening to their favorite audiobooks in the gym, researcher Katherine Milkman measured a 51% improvement in gym visit frequency compared to a control group without temptation bundling. How can this be used in the financial wellness field?

We can also use technology to bundle pleasurable spending with an investment in one's financial future. At Acorns, a micro-investment app that looks after the financial best interests of the up-and-coming generation, we have developed a technology to detect pleasurable spends, such as Netflix subscriptions or a night out at the movies, and bundle them with a matching investment in one's financial future.

This feature avoids the apparent trade-off of giving up instant gratification for long-term improvements, and avoids having too specific a goal with the discouragement of not reaching them. With this feature, every investment for the long term also feels good at the moment.

This feature was not easy to build. The instant gratification spends that act as the trigger for investment have to be carefully chosen and accurately detected. The investment amount needs to be something that is not too little to make an impact and not too much to cause hesitation at the decision point of whether to set up such bundling.

What is most encouraging is that, while the effect of temptation bundling tends to wear off for health wellness after six months, temptation bundling in personal finance can last quite a bit longer. As long as the user is still making the pleasurable spend and has not intentionally removed the bundling, the investment toward their long-term spend will continue.

With careful iteration and rigorous A/B testing, one can achieve more than 50% engagement by applying *temptation bundling* from health wellness to personal finance. This engagement level was achieved in a field where in-app message engagement often gets below a 10% CTR, making it a significant win for improving customer retention and customer lifetime value in the personal finance industry.

CASE 2: MAKING BUSINESS DECISIONS WITH A HIERARCHY OF EVIDENCE

As a DS executive or a distinguished data scientist, you often make difficult business decisions with limited information. In many situations, you may be caught between two extremes.

At one extreme, you are using online controlled A/B tests with randomized cohorts to evaluate the effectiveness of features, user experiences, and algorithm variations. While this is rigorous and effective, the scope of business decisions with this level of information is often limited. Success metrics for the results of experiments need to be immediately measurable metrics. To set up experiments, the up-front costs to implement multiple versions of the product at deployment quality need to be lower than the negative impact of a wrong decision.

At the other extreme, you may have to make executive decisions for product directions and technology initiatives that require a large amount of resource commitment up-front, where you cannot afford to produce multiple implementations. Examples include product focus decisions, architecture commitments, and build-versus-buy decisions. There is often only anecdotal data or evidence from case studies or expert opinions.

Are these extremes the only options? What are some alternative approaches for data-informed decision-making that we can learn from other industries or fields?

One place where important life-and-death decisions are made on a daily basis is the medical field. Over the 30 years between the 1960s and 1990s, the medical field went through a paradigm shift in clinical research [32]. The practice of evidence-based medicine went from the fringes to the mainstream.

Evidence-based medicine is the integration of individual clinical expertise with the best available external clinical evidence from systematic research. It leverages external clinical evidence to inform decisions and uses individual clinical expertise to assess whether a particular piece of external clinical evidence applies to a patient at hand. For example, when clinicians practicing evidence-based medicine see a patient who has experienced a seizure, they may use their individual clinical expertise to come to a diagnosis, leverage external clinical evidence from systematic research to inform the prognosis, and finally, discuss the potential treatment options with the patient.

You may see the striking similarities to making executive decisions. Similar to a diagnosis, an executive or a distinguished data scientist can be responsible for identifying gaps between where a product or organization should be and where it is today. There can then be the risk prognosis if nothing is done and an assessment of the ROI for intervening with a solution to improve the situation. Finally, similar to discussing the treatment with the patient, an executive needs to gain alignment with partner teams on the specific solution paths forward.

During the diagnosis, prognosis, and aligning of treatment plans, relevant data and evidence can all be admitted to informing decisions. What are the ranges of admissible evidence to inform evidence-based medical decisions? The Centre for Evidence-Based Medicine at the University of Oxford established a hierarchy of five levels of likely best evidence [33], where level 1 is most rigorous (table 9.5).

Table 9.5   A hierarchy of likely best evidence for evidence-based medicine [33]

Levels of evidence	Explanations	Adopted practices
1 Systematic review	An exhaustive summary of current evidence relevant to a question to inform decisions	Repeated experiments or retrospective review
2 Randomized controlled trials	Use of randomization to control confounding variables' influence in collecting evidence to answer a question and inform a decision	A/B tests to validate or invalidate hypotheses
3 Cohort studies	The observation of a cohort of subjects over time to understand the impact or risk to answer a question and inform a decision	Observational studies
4 Case series	Documented evidence in specific past scenarios and outcomes to inform a decision	Anecdotal cases to form hypotheses to be tested
5 Mechanistic reasoning	Speculations based on fundamental principles to inform a decision	Hypotheses to be tested

DS teams are routinely conducting A/B tests and forming hypotheses with inspirations from anecdotal cases and mechanistic reasoning. We can learn from the medical domain that systematic reviews that clearly validate a hypothesis can provide a solid grounding for critical decisions. This can be a prospective review of repeated randomized control trials over time [34], or a retrospective review of past experiments to validate methodologies' effectiveness.

Sometimes, randomized controlled trials are unethical to perform. For example, if you are studying the effects of smoking, you cannot ethically randomly subject people to the effects of smoking. If you are studying the effects of incomplete components in a job description on the success of hiring, you cannot ethically randomly hide sections from companies' job postings online.

Observational study techniques [35] can be introduced to DS teams to allow decision-makers to draw conclusions from existing data, while controlling for various confounding factors. There are three types of observational studies: cohort studies, cross-sectional studies, and case-control studies. *Cohort studies* can be used to study causes and infer future likelihoods. *Cross-sectional studies* can discern correlations but not the cause and effect. *Case-controlled studies* look for potential predictors and can inspire hypotheses to be tested with cohorts prospectively. As a DS executive or a distinguished data scientist, you can learn from the medical domain to acquire a more comprehensive toolkit across all evidence levels to better leverage your data assets for business decision-making.

9.4 *Self-assessment and development focus*

Congratulations on working through the chapter on executive and distinguished data scientist virtues! This is a critical milestone for leading in DS. The purpose of these virtues self-assessment is to help you internalize and practice the concepts by:

- Understanding your interests and leadership strengths
- Practicing one to two areas with the choose, practice, and review (CPR) process
- Developing a prioritize-practice-perform plan to go through more CPRs

Once you start doing this, you will have courageously taken the steps toward practicing responsible machine learning with ethical principles, ensuring customers' trust and safety, and taking social responsibility for decisions. You will also be creating a productive and harmonious workplace while focusing on enterprise value, demonstrating executive presence, establishing an identity of industry leadership, and learning and adopting best practices across industries.

9.4.1 *Understanding your interests and leadership strengths*

Table 9.6 summarizes the virtues discussed in this chapter. The rightmost column is available for you to check off the areas you currently feel comfortable with quickly. There is no judgment, no right or wrong, nor are there any specific patterns to follow. Feel free to leave any or all rows blank.

Table 9.6   Self-assessment areas for virtues of executive and distinguished data scientists

Virtue areas/self-assessment (italic items primarily apply to managers)			?
Ethics	Practicing responsible machine learning with ethical principles	Practicing responsible ML by complying with applicable laws and regulations and following ethical guidelines to unlock the full power of ML, while minimizing its ethical risks	
	Ensuring the trust and safety of customers	For B2C products and services, ensuring customers' physical, financial, and psychological trust and safety to build the long-term viability of a company	
		For B2B SaaS products and services, ensuring data usage directly benefits the customer, does not negatively affect feature usage, and does not compromise or leak any business intelligence	
	Taking social responsibility for decisions	Recognizing the complexity behind the concept of fairness within your social and business context, and crafting and implementing a standard of social fairness, referencing commonly-accepted principles for your organization	

Table 9.6 Self-assessment areas for virtues of executive and distinguished data scientists *(continued)*

Virtue areas/self-assessment (italic items primarily apply to managers)			?
Rigor	Creating a productive and harmonious work environment	Aligning executives with trust and understanding to resolve challenges such as resistance to data collection, rejection of insights created, and unrealistic expectations of scope to create a productive and harmonious environment for data scientists	
	Improving the speed and quality of decisions	*Being decisive and deliberate by rapidly qualifying the downside risk of a wrong decision and assessing the negative consequences of further deliberation to move as quickly as possible*	
	Focusing on increasing enterprise value	Driving internal innovations by filing patents, initiating and contributing to open source software, and publishing results and methodologies as scientific papers	
		Introducing external innovations by licensing data and technologies, acquiring companies and teams, and nurturing business ecosystems with corporate ventures	
Attitude	Demonstrating executive presence	Inspiring others with a passion for making a positive difference, and training yourself to practice effective thinking patterns, effective emotional patterns, and effective action patterns	
	Establishing team identity of industry leadership	Developing an industry-wide identity through product feature leadership, organizational structure leadership, technology platform leadership, or social responsibility leadership	
	Being open to learn and adopt best practices across industries	Being open to draw inspiration from other industries to solve business and technical challenges in your industry	

If you are already aware of some of these aspects, this is a great way to build a narrative around your existing leadership strengths. If some aspects are not yet familiar, this is the opportunity for you to assess whether they can be of help in your daily work, starting today!

9.4.2 Practicing with the CPR process

As with the virtues assessment for tech leads, team managers, and directors, you can experiment with a simple CPR process with two-week check-ins. For your self-review, you can use the project-based skill improvement template to help you structure your actions over the two weeks:

- *Skill/task*—Select a virtue to work on.
- *Date*—Select a date in the two-week period when you can apply the virtue.
- People—Write down the names of the people with whom you can apply the virtue, or write *self*.

- *Place*—Select the location or occasion at which you can apply the virtue (for example, in your next team meeting or during the next incident post-mortem).
- *Review result*—How did you do compared to before? The same, better, or worse?

By holding yourself accountable for these steps in a self-review, you can start to exercise your strengths and shed light on your blind spots in the DS executive and distinguished data scientist virtues.

Summary

- *Ethics* for executives and distinguished data scientists includes practicing responsible machine learning with ethical principles, ensuring customers' trust and safety when using its products and services, and taking social responsibility for business decisions.
  - When practicing responsible machine learning, you can first comply with applicable laws and regulations, then follow ethical guidelines where laws are not yet mature to unlock the full power of data and machine learning, while minimizing its ethical risks.
  - When ensuring customers' trust and safety, you can take care of customers' physical, financial, and psychological safety when using your products and services and ensure the data usage directly benefits your customers.
  - When taking social responsibility, you can recognize the complexity behind the concept of fairness within your social and business context, then craft and implement a standard of social fairness for your organization.
- *Rigor* for executives and distinguished data scientists includes creating a productive and harmonious work environment for partners and team members, improving the speed and quality of decisions, and increasing enterprise value.
  - When creating a productive and harmonious work environment, you can align peer executives through trust and understanding to resolve challenges, such as resistance to data collection, rejection of insights, and unrealistic expectations.
  - When improving the speed and quality of decisions, you can rapidly qualify the downside risk of a wrong decision and assess the negative consequences of further deliberation to move as quickly as possible.
  - When focusing on delivering enterprise value, you can drive internal innovations through filing patents, contributing to open source software, and publishing papers. You can also introduce external innovations through technology licensing, acquiring companies and teams, and running corporate ventures.
- *Attitude* for executives and distinguished data scientists includes demonstrating executive presence, establishing team identity of industry leadership, and being open to learn and adopt best practices across industries.

- When demonstrating executive presence, you can inspire others with a passion for making a positive difference and train yourself to practice effective thinking, emotional, and action patterns.
- When establishing team identity of industry leadership, you can develop product feature leadership, organizational structure leadership, technology platform leadership, or social responsibility leadership to inspire your industry.
- When learning and adopting best practices across industries, you can take the effort to learn about challenges in other industries and draw inspiration from their solutions to solve business and technical challenges within your industry.

References

[1] *Regulation (EU) 2016/679 of the European Parliament and of the Council of 27 April 2016 on the protection of natural persons with regard to the processing of personal data and on the free movement of such data, and repealing Directive 95/46/EC (General Data Protection Regulation).* https://eur-lex.europa.eu/eli/reg/2016/679/oj

[2] *California Consumer Privacy Act (CCPA).* https://oag.ca.gov/privacy/ccpa

[3] High-level Expert Group on Artificial Intelligence, "Ethics Guidelines for Trustworthy AI," European Commision. https://digital-strategy.ec.europa.eu/en/library/ethics-guidelines-trustworthy-ai

[4] Marco Tulio Ribeiro, Sameer Singh and Carlos Guestrin, "Local Interpretable Model-Agnostic Explanations (LIME): An Introduction. A technique to explain the predictions of any machine learning classifier." August 12, 2016. https://www.oreilly.com/content/introduction-to-local-interpretable-model-agnostic-explanations-lime/

[5] Scott M. Lundberg, Su-In Lee, "A Unified Approach to Interpreting Model Predictions," 31st Conference on Neural Information Processing Systems (NIPS 2017), Long Beach, CA, USA. https://proceedings.neurips.cc/paper/2017/file/8a20a8621978632d76c43dfd28b67767-Paper.pdf

[6] "Lyft's commitment to safety." Lyft Blog. https://www.lyft.com/blog/posts/lyfts-commitment-to-safety

[7] "Your safety is our priority." Airbnb. https://www.airbnb.com/trust

[8] Sameer Hinduja & Justin W. Patchin. "Connecting Adolescent Suicide to the Severity of Bullying and Cyberbullying," *Journal of School Violence*, 2018. doi: http://dx.doi.org/10.1080/15388220.2018.1492417.

[9] Ninareh Mehrabi et al. "A survey on bias and fairness in machine learning." Cornell University. https://arxiv.org/abs/1908.09635v2

[10] I. Perisic. "Fairness in AI: An intent and impact perspective." LinkedIn. https://www.linkedin.com/pulse/fairness-ai-intent-impact-perspective-igor-perisic/

[11] N. Vigdor. "Apple card investigated after gender discrimination complaints." *New York Times.* https://www.nytimes.com/2019/11/10/business/Apple-credit-card-investigation.html

[12] *Equal Credit Opportunity Act.* Federal Trade Commission. LAW: 15 U.S.C. §§ 1691-1691f. https://www.ftc.gov/enforcement/statutes/equal-credit-opportunity-act

[13] C. Goldin and C. Rouse, "Orchestrating impartiality: The impact of 'blind' auditions on female musicians," *American Economic Review*, vol. 90, no. 4, pp. 715–741, Sep. 2000. [Online]. Available: https://www.aeaweb.org/articles?id=10.1257/aer.90.4.715

[14] S. C. Geyik and K. Kenthapadi. "Building representative talent search at LinkedIn." LinkedIn Engineering. https://engineering.linkedin.com/blog/2018/10/building-representative-talent-search-at-linkedin

[15] N. Mehrabi, et al. "A survey on bias and fairness in machine learning." Cornell University. https://arxiv.org/abs/1908.09635

[16] E. Shearer and K. E. Matsa. "News use across social media platforms 2018." Pew Research Center. https://www.journalism.org/2018/09/10/news-use-across-social-media-platforms-2018/

[17] C. Silverman. "This analysis shows how viral fake election news stories outperformed real news on Facebook." BuzzFeed News. https://www.buzzfeednews.com/article/craigsilverman/viral-fake-election-news-outperformed-real-news-on-facebook

[18] X. Zhou and R. Zafarani. "A survey of fake news: Fundamental theories, detection methods, and opportunities." Cornell University. https://arxiv.org/pdf/1812.00315.pdf

[19] K. Klonick. "Inside the making of Facebook's supreme court." *The New Yorker.* https://www.newyorker.com/tech/annals-of-technology/inside-the-making-of-facebooks-supreme-court

[20] A. M. Martin. "Black LinkedIn is thriving: Does LinkedIn have a problem with that?" *New York Times.* https://www.nytimes.com/2020/10/08/business/black-linkedin.html

[21] "The most difficult thing in data science: Politics." rDisorder. https://www.rdisorder.eu/2017/09/13/most-difficult-thing-data-science-politics/

[22] "The Alexa fund." Alexa. https://developer.amazon.com/en-US/alexa/alexa-startups/alexa-fund

[23] J. Ullman. "Developing executive presence." LinkedIn Learning. https://www.linkedin.com/learning/developing-executive-presence

[24] A. Mehrabian, *Silent messages: Implicit communication of emotions and attitudes,* Belmont, CA, USA: Wadsworth Publishing, 1980.

[25] A. Narayanan and V. Shmatikov. "How to break anonymity of the Netflix Prize dataset." Cornell University. https://arxiv.org/abs/cs/0610105

[26] A. Narayanan et al., "Link Prediction by De-anonymization: How We Won the Kaggle Social Network Challenge," The International Joint Conference on Neural Networks, 2011. [Online]. Available: https://ieeexplore.ieee.org/document/6033446

[27] C. Dwork, "Differential privacy: A survey of results," TAMC, 2008

[28] J. Buolamwini and T. Gebru, "Gender shades: Intersectional accuracy disparities in commercial gender classification," Conf on Fairness, Accountability, and Transparency, 2018. [Online]. Available: http://proceedings.mlr.press/v81/buolamwini18a/buolamwini18a.pdf

[29] S. Vasudevan. "Addressing bias in large-scale AI applications: The LinkedIn Fairness Toolkit." https://engineering.linkedin.com/blog/2020/lift-addressing-bias-in-large-scale-ai-applications

[30] K. Hao. "We read the paper that forced Timnit Gebru out of Google: Here's what it says," *MIT Technology Review.* https://www.technologyreview.com/2020/12/04/1013294/google-ai-ethics-research-paper-forced-out-timnit-gebru/

[31] K. L. Milkman, J. A. Minson, and K. G. M. Volpp, "Holding the hunger games hostage at the gym: An evaluation of temptation bundling," *Management Science,* November 6, 2013. [Online]. https://doi.org/10.1287/mnsc.2013.1784

[32] Evidence-Based Medicine Working Group. "Evidence-based medicine: A new approach to teaching the practice of medicine." *JAMA* vol. 268, pp. 2420–2425, 1992.

[33] J. Howick et al. "The 2011 Oxford CEBM evidence levels of evidence (introductory document)." Oxford Centre for Evidence-Based Medicine. http://www.cebm.net/index.aspx?o=5653

[34] R. Kohavi, D. Tang, and Y. Xu, "Trustworthy online controlled experiments: A practical guide to A/B testing," Cambridge, UK: Cambridge University Press, 2020.

[35] I. Bojinov, A. Chen, and M. Liu. "The importance of being causal." HDSR, July 30, 2020. https://hdsr.mitpress.mit.edu/pub/wjhth9tr

Part 5

The LOOP and the future

As a high-performing DS practitioner, you are gifted in your analytical rigor. What if you can apply it to your career? Can you better unleash your potential? Where would you apply your analytical rigor to advance your career with confidence?

You may look in the *LOOP*, comprising the four areas of landscape, organization, opportunity, and practice. These areas form a loop, as you can revisit one area a month for new interpretations in your environment to assess what more you can do for your career.

Understanding the technology *landscape* can help you capture the next wave of opportunities that are transforming your industry. An appreciation of the evolution of the human *organization* behind your projects and initiatives can help you better navigate the operating dynamics of the teams and functions. An evaluation of the *opportunities* available to you with a robust onboarding plan can help you take on new responsibilities with confidence. Keeping abreast of the set of *practices* available in DS can help you recognize the skill sets you can hire and the career directions you can select.

Leading in DS is challenging, as it involves a broad skill set that can take time to internalize. This skill set is shaped by the unique challenges of working with data and coordinating executives, teams, and partners to make DS efforts successful.

We summarize the *why*, *what*, and *how* of leading in DS, so you can reference them at various stages of your career. We will also look ahead in time with some speculation on how the field may evolve in the roles, capabilities, and responsibilities to anticipate.

Chapter 10 provides a starting point to rigorously look at your environment through the lens of landscape, organization, opportunity, and practice, or the LOOP. Chapter 11 summarizes the deeper motivations behind DS leadership and speculates on trends that can fundamentally shape the field going forward.

Landscape, organization, opportunity, and practice

10

This chapter covers

- Monitoring the technology landscape for new architectures and best practices
- Navigating different organizational structures and analyzing the benefits and pitfalls of each one
- Evaluating career opportunities at industry, company, team, and role level
- Establishing a powerful and focused plan for onboarding into a new role
- Articulating practices to hire for and defining career directions for the next role

What are overarching perspectives that can empower you to accelerate your career more confidently? Let's take a look at the *landscape, organization, opportunity,* and *practice* (LOOP) areas to amplify how you can use DS to produce outsized impact:

- *Landscape*—When building intelligent systems to drive significant business impact, understanding the technology *landscape* can help you capture the next wave of opportunities transforming various industries.

- *Organization*—When developing intelligent capabilities, you need an appreciation for the evolution of the human *organization* behind the efforts. This evolution determines the structure of functions and teams, and their operating dynamics.

- *Opportunity*—With an understanding of the landscape and organization, you can review what factors are most important to you at the particular stage of your career and evaluate the industries, companies, teams, and roles for the *opportunities* available to you, then capture the opportunities and craft a robust onboarding plan.

- *Practice*—As a set of *practices* in DS, you can recognize the skill sets you can hire for your team, as well as the career directions you can pursue yourself.

You can revisit this LOOP as often as every few quarters. Finding new interpretations in your environment can help assess what more you can do for your career. Let's get started!

10.1   *The landscape*

The technology, platforms, and architectures to enable business impact in DS have matured significantly. Over the past decade, the field started with technologists from diverse backgrounds building business use cases from existing technologies. As best practices emerged, companies commercialized them and created new technology platforms. These technology platforms then enabled new architectures to empower more teams and businesses to unleash the value in data. Figure 10.1 illustrates the dynamics of this ever-shifting technology landscape.

Figure 10.1   The ever-shifting data science technology landscape

The practice started with data scientists writing scripts to process data already available in enterprises. Over time, more nuanced technologies were created to handle a *variety* of data sources, ingested and transformed with *velocity*, and stored in large *volumes* to create *value* for the business through historical analysis and predictive insights. Best practices in working with the variety, velocity, volume, and value of data have been further codified into platforms to manage metadata to increase data *visibility* and ensure data quality and integrity to improve data *veracity*, and secure data against *vulnerabilities*.

These 7Vs [1] of working with modern data architectures [2] are summarized in figure 10.2. Your specific use cases will likely only require a subset of the components in this architecture. More components may become relevant and useful as your systems evolve and mature.

Technologies used in DS have evolved to improve how data is stored, processed, managed, and used. Let's see how five trends may be impacting your work:

- *Data storage*—Data lakehouse
- *Data processing*—Stream processing
- *Data access*—Self-serve insights
- *Model deployment*—Data/ML ops automation
- *Data governance*—Feature store and data catalog

Variety	Velocity		Volume	Value		
Sources	**Ingestion**	**Transformation**	**Storage**	**Historical**	**Predictive**	**Output**
Business transactions	Batch processing	Data wrangling	Data warehouse	Ad hoc query engine		Dashboards
Customer profiles	Stream processing	ETL / ELT	Data lake	Real-time analytics		Anomaly alerts
Events from interactions	Change data capture	Steam processing	Graph database	DS and ML libraries		Microservice APIs
User-generated content		Data enrichment	File systems	DS and ML platforms		App frameworks
Third-party APIs				Feature store	Feature server	
System logs				Experiment tracking	ML frameworks	
					DL frameworks	
...				Model tuning	Model registry	
Metadata management						*Visibility*
Data quality and integrity						*Veracity*
Data security and privacy						*Vulnerability*

Figure 10.2   A unified data infrastructure architecture in 2020

10.1.1   Data lakehouse

Data lakehouse is a data management paradigm that addresses the limitations of other data management systems. Since the 1980s, computing technologies applied to business operations have involved collecting structured data with carefully crafted schemas and storing them into centralized databases called *data warehouses*. These data warehouses then serve the business's everyday analytics and reporting needs.

With the explosive growth of the variety, volume, and velocity of data in the 2010s, the speed of crafting schemas for new data sources became a bottleneck for getting data into the data warehouse. Even when data was entered into the data warehouse, DS and machine learning projects often required alternative approaches to extract insights from raw data. As people started saving copies of the raw data, the *data lake* was born. Data lakes enabled data scientists to collect data first, then work out the most appropriate schema and move the data from the data lake into the data warehouse later.

The additional processing step from raw data in the data lake to the data warehouse provided flexibility in schema development. It also meant that critical data is stored twice—once in the data lake and once in the data warehouse. Data in these locations needs to be consistent, and any data governance efforts will need to be applied in multiple locations.

The data lakehouse brings together the best attributes of data warehouses and data lakes. It provides the data structures and data governance features of the data warehouse and uses low-cost storage like the data lakes. Users can incrementally improve the quality of data in their lakehouse until it is ready for consumption. Analytics applications can directly connect to the lakehouse, eliminating the data consistency issues between the data lake and data warehouse. Early examples of the data lakehouse include the Databricks platform, Azure Synapse Analytics, Google BigQuery, and Amazon Redshift Spectrum. As you lead analytics projects and machine learning models, you can look for patterns of inefficiencies in your infrastructure and assess whether a data lakehouse can reduce your data governance overhead and accelerate your progress.

10.1.2 Stream processing

Stream processing is an event-based paradigm of computing that is becoming businesses' central nervous system [3]. Traditional computing is centered on databases and assumes that human operators create, update, and delete records in these databases.

As more business decisions, such as inventory management, marketing, pricing, and shipment routing, are automated through intelligent algorithms, business processes can be more streamlined to allow software agents to interact and respond to events in real time.

In many real-world business use cases, one event can trigger a variety of reactions. Using the sale of a box of cereal in a supermarket as an example, the event of a sale can impact pricing, reporting, operations, inventory management, shipments, and purchasing. In a streaming system, the sale can be an event broadcasted in a streaming system, and relevant impacted software agents can monitor such events and decide whether to trigger additional actions.

This type of event-based paradigm allows disparate software-driven business functions to react at the speed of software in real time or near real time, which can significantly increase the efficiency of the business. In the simple retail example, near real-time response can increase inventory turnover, while providing the same quality of service with lower inventory.

Streaming paradigms require different ways to process and manage metrics and features for analytics and predictive modeling projects. They are also more sensitive to processing latency. Streams can also coexist well with traditional databases in a two-speed architecture. This was discussed in case 1 in section 8.1.1. As you lead DS efforts to create specific intelligent software-defined business processes, you may think about how your intelligent business processes can eventually become part of the central nervous system for an emerging software-defined company.

10.1.3 Self-serve insight

Self-serve insight is the democratization of data insight creation for business decision-makers through processes and platforms based on the best practices of data analysts and data scientists. When business decision-makers look to data to guide the development and operations of the business, there are common use cases and ad hoc requests. Common use cases can be addressed with data dashboards. An analytics team is often on call to serve any ad hoc requests. Two criteria are crucial for successfully fulfilling these requests:

- *Trust*—The analysis provided is accurate and can be interpreted in the proper context.
- *Timeliness*—The analysis is completed in time for the business decision.

When the DS team fulfills the request, trust in the results is ensured by the expertise of the data scientists. Timeliness can be a challenge because of the always-limited resources for serving requests.

The self-serve approach uses technology platforms to resolve the timeliness issue by allowing business decision-makers to access insights independent of the DS teams. However, processes must be in place to ensure the accuracy of the conclusions from the self-served insights to maintain trust in the data.

Figure 10.3 illustrates the amount of technology required to provide self-serve insights with data at different stages of maturity. Dashboards are commonly used when use cases have been clarified.

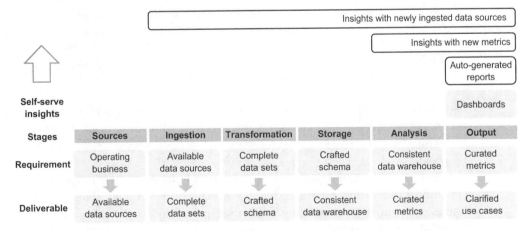

Figure 10.3 A spectrum of self-serve insights capabilities

When optimizing data and reporting in sales contexts, reports or presentations can be auto-generated through standardized templates for presentation. An example of this is Project Merlin at LinkedIn, where the DS team automatically generated sales decks from data.

If some metrics are not yet developed, off-the-shelf analytics platforms have drag-and-drop capabilities to allow new metrics to be explored and developed by business decision-makers on data from the data warehouse without learning querying languages. When data sources are not yet in the data warehouse, existing data integration vendors, like funnel.io and Domo, can ingest domain-specific data sources, such as marketing tools, with predesigned schema and metrics and output into BI tools, such as Tableau or Looker, without coding. Many of the intermediate ingestion and transformation steps have been automated as part of the integration, facilitating a seamless process to introduce new data sources for discovering insights.

As you lead DS efforts in democratizing data access with self-serve insights, a crucial trade-off to manage is accuracy versus efficiency. You are responsible for maintaining trust in data through data governance policies to prevent business partners from reaching inconsistent conclusions. The self-serving of insights is worthwhile only when the efficiency of producing insights increases without getting bottlenecked by any validation or approval process.

10.1.4 *Data and ML operations automation*

Data and machine learning operations automation (DataOps) is a set of practices and platforms for delivering DS and machine learning capabilities scalably and reliably from development to production [4], [5]. They are essential disciplines to ensure that the initial investment in the DS and machine learning models continue to deliver the anticipated business value over a model's lifetime.

078

Data and machine learning operations automation is a set of essential practices and platforms to ensure the initial investment in the data science and machine learning analyses and models continue to deliver the anticipated business value over their lifetime.

Many early data/ML flows are launched on an ad hoc basis with one-off efforts in preparing feature pipelines, data and model serving, and monitoring for data issues. Launching models in production this way can be a costly process, reducing the ROI of DS projects.

Figure 10.2 illustrated the main components of mature data/ML ops as part of the DS and ML platforms, including feature stores with versioning, feature servers, ML frameworks, experiment tracking, model registries, and model calibration processes. Data/ML ops also include data anomaly monitoring and model API serving as infrastructures for feature outputs. For example, you can develop a financial fraud detection model with a set of features based on an algorithm trained on historical and real-time data. To deploy the model responsibly, best practices in data/ML ops include:

- Maintaining and monitoring incoming data quality and output quality
- Maintaining separate development, integration, and production environments
- Version controlling data processing steps with branches and merges
- Version controlling features across data processing steps
- Virtualizing/dockerizing deployments for scalability and avoiding system dependencies
- Maintaining a cadence for recalibrating model parameters

When you lead DS to operationalize data and machine learning pipelines, your responsibility includes architecting DS and ML platforms to be scalable and robust in production.

Fortunately, there is a spectrum of solutions you can consider. You can develop proprietary internal solutions for your specific needs. Or you can leverage open source projects, such as Feast or Hopsworks, for your feature store or MLRun for ML experiment tracking. You can also consider a fully featured product, such as Tecton, which was built by the team that developed Michelangelo, the feature store used at Uber.

10.1.5 *Data governance*

Data governance encompasses the people, processes, and technology platforms required to assess, manage, use, improve, monitor, maintain, and protect organizational information. Data governance involves more than just the authentication of users for sensitive data sets. It covers a broad scope of concerns, including managing the data architecture, data quality, metadata, data security, data operations, reference and master data, and document and contents. Figure 10.4 illustrates the responsibilities for data governance.

Data governance

Data architecture management

Data warehousing and business intelligence management

Data quality management	Metadata management
Data security management	Data operations management
Reference and master data management	Document and contents management

Data catalog:
A data catalog can maintain a unified view of all data sets with a data glossary for discovery, metadata for data lineage tracking, privacy sensitivity labels for regulation compliance, analytics on data quality, and a data checkout process to authorize data access.

Figure 10.4 Governing data with the help of a data catalog

Early data governance efforts are centered on classifications of data sets into public, proprietary, confidential, sensitive, and personal categories. Data access is then managed across classifications for security and regulation compliance purposes with manual steps gating the approval process.

Through the democratization of data insights, the number of metrics and reports in an organization can increase rapidly. This increase creates pressure for data set classification and access approval. It also increases the likelihood of multiple versions of similar metrics becoming duplicated across different business functions and units. The duplication of metrics can result in confusion, loss of trust, and incoherence in business decisions. How do you resolve the explosion of responsibilities?

You can use a data catalog platform to maintain a unified view of all data sets. A data catalog maintains a curated data glossary for the metrics in use. With a data catalog, you can constitute a process to keep definitions coherent. Your data catalog and glossary can minimize confusion and improve trust in your organization's data assets.

079

The duplication of metrics can result in confusion, loss of trust, and incoherence in business decisions. A data catalog and glossary can minimize confusion and improve your organization's confidence in its data assets.

A data catalog can include additional metadata describing the data lineage; the sensitivity of the data concerning privacy; and the availability, correctness, completeness, and robustness characteristics of data. Data lineage describes the dependencies between data sets. You can use it to better assess impact when data sources fail and better trace data output issues through the data dependency chains. Privacy sensitivity information can support GDPR and CCPA compliance requirements and help automate regulation-compliant and security-compliant data access administration.

Creating a data catalog can be time consuming. Luckily, advanced data governance systems can automatically interpret metadata from the data pipelines and their execution logs in production. Some human curation is still required to label ambiguous fields that may contain personally identifiable information. Examples include search query histories, which may contain searches for oneself, and financial transaction descriptions, which may include paycheck transactions with the account holder's name.

For data scientists looking to gain access to data, the data catalog naturally lends to a shopping and checkout paradigm. One can browse the catalog for the data sources to use, place them in a shopping cart, and request access through a checkout process, and the data delivery process can include an auditable approval process transparent to the data requester.

As you lead the data governance process, you can develop an internal data catalog. Your effort can leverage open source tools, such as Amundsen, or consider vendors with enterprise solutions, such as Informatica, Collibra, and Alation, to help manage the data, the people, and the processes for data governance.

10.1.6 *Periodic review for major architecture trends*

In this section, we discussed five major architecture trends in DS, including:

- *Data storage*—ML and analytics use cases are converging in the data lakehouse.
- *Data processing*—Stream processing is emerging as the central nervous system for business processes with automated decision-making.
- *Data access*—Analytics are being democratized with self-serve insights.
- *Model deployment*—Data/ML ops and automation are streamlining intelligent capability deployment.
- *Data governance*—Data governance is curating data as an asset for enterprise growth rather than as a regulation compliance liability.

Every few quarters, it is worth exploring how the technology landscape has changed. DS is a fast-moving field where some new best practices are being invented and implemented every day. These new best practices are being incorporated into new technology platforms, which allow new architectures to be crafted to enable new DS capabilities to drive business impact. Staying on top of industry best practices and the latest architecture are key skill sets for an effective DS leader.

080

Data science is a fast-moving field where some new best practices are being invented and implemented every day. Staying on top of industry best practices and the latest architecture is essential for an effective data science leader.

10.2 *The organization*

Organizations are built to integrate individual efforts to accomplish goals more quickly and efficiently. To produce business impact as a DS leader, an awareness of how your company or organization is structured can help you clarify your roles, specify your responsibilities, identify partners, and craft team structure to better integrate individual efforts in a repeatable and scalable process to deliver business value.

DS is a nascent field that is still experimenting with best practices for producing business impact. As a DS leader, how can you think more fundamentally as you devise effective ways to integrate DS efforts into your organization?

Let's look at three traditional organizational structures, functional, divisional, and matrix structures, and one alternative organizational structure, called the *holacracy* structure, which is modeled after biological organisms with self-managing hierarchical units, such as cells, organs, and living creatures. These are illustrated in figure 10.5.

Functional organizational structure

The executive team is organized by function, which allows responsibilities to be separated by expertise. Functions integrate their efforts into products and services at the executive level.

Top-down approach—A CEO-initiated top-down appointment of a centralized data science function can drive tight cross-function collaborations for business impact.

Bottom-up approach—Data science efforts can start under disparate functional areas. Variations in methodologies, the duplication of efforts, and stunted professional growth are major challenges.

Divisional organizational structure

The divisional structure allows each division to be self-sufficient in resources and autonomously plan and execute initiatives with limited dependence on other divisions. It comes with unique opportunities.

Cross-divisional platforms and services—Best practices in one division can be distilled into a technology platform to be introduced in adjacent divisions with independent adoption authorities.

Creation of new division—Data science use cases can also enable new business lines. New divisions can be created with the support necessary to operate a new profit and loss business line.

Matrix organizational structure

The matrix structure has both functional and divisional leadership for projects. This allows functional expertise to develop over time and encourages strong coordination between functions within a division.

Authority confusion—When priorities do not align between the function and division leaders, who makes the final decision?

Resource planning—How should you balance resources for functional and divisional projects and initiatives?

Resource stability—How should you prioritize when multiple divisions simultaneously require data science functional expertise?

Implementing change—When a function leader pushes best practices within its function, the change needs to be coordinated with each divisional leader.

Alternative organizational structure

Holacracy is a management structure that promotes a hierarchy of self-managed units or circles, each with its own governing process to constitute teams, define roles, make decisions, and evaluate performance.

Adaptability over reliability—Holacracy works well when adaptability is more important than reliability.

Requires more management—All team members need to be well versed in self-defining roles, making decisions, and self-evaluating performance.

Reliability challenge—Mature data science projects require cross-functional integration and governance, which is hard to maintain in a holacracy.

Member fluidity—Team members move in and out of projects fluidly, maintaining the momentum for long-term data science projects is a challenge.

Figure 10.5   Four major organizational structures in which to operate data science

Let's discuss how DS can operate within these organizational structures and contrast them through the perspectives of the division of labor, integration mechanisms, distribution of decision-making authority, and setting and sustaining organizational boundaries.

10.2.1 *Functional organizational structure*

Many companies are organized in a functional structure. You can recognize this structure in the composition of the executive team, which has members with functional subject matter expertise, such as chief technology officer, chief marketing officer, chief operating officer, chief product officer, and chief financial officer. This structure is common in companies with a single product line operating in a single geographic location and is sometimes used in large companies like Apple with many product lines.

The functional structure allows responsibilities to be separated by expertise. Business value is created by integrating the efforts of different functions into products and services at the executive level. The priorities are determined as a company, and resources and plans are distributed to the functions. Each function has the authority to choose the tactics used to execute the company-wide strategy within its function domain.

When a data scientist is a member of a non-data function, they are often in supporting roles with unclear career growth paths. When companies commit to building a data function, professional growth paths for data scientists can become clearer.

There are two ways DS gets introduced in companies with functional structures: top-down or bottom-up. In the top-down approach, the CEO appoints a senior DS leader to build a function. In the bottom-up approach, various function leaders start experimenting with DS capabilities in specific projects, then expand the successful cases across multiple projects and functions.

TOP-DOWN APPROACH

A CEO-initiated top-down approach can work well when there is a clear expectation of what DS can do for a company. It signals strong executive support for driving DS initiatives, which requires tight cross-function collaborations for business impact. A DS leader who can succeed in this environment has three strengths:

- Strong ability to rapidly acquire domain knowledge to identify and prioritize use cases across the company
- Strong relationship-building capabilities to influence peer function executives to collaborate on projects
- Strong ability to attract talent to build a function

When the executive goal is not clear or the DS leader lacks some of these strengths, there are common failure modes to watch out for. The top three include:

- *Data infrastructure not yet mature enough to support effective DS initiatives*—A CEO can hire a DS leader prematurely [6], without the data infrastructure and business cases available for them to be successful. Mitigating actions include hiring a consultant or part-time chief data officer (CDO) to advise on clarifying the DS directions and hiring a few entry-level data scientists to conduct proof of concept projects before setting up an entire function.
- *Becoming isolated from the real business cases in partner functions*—A DS function can be self-absorbed in building proof of concept projects that are not meeting business needs or adapting to business changes. Mitigating actions include identifying and producing quick wins and staying close to business needs first before committing to larger infrastructural projects.

- *Becoming an executive consulting branch for investigating ad hoc business questions*—Priorities are focused on the urgent, immediate concerns rather than the strategically essential bets. Mitigating actions include identifying strategic business opportunities, crafting roadmaps, and aligning priorities with the rest of the executive team for early wins that put the company on a more strategic path.

In the top-down approach, it is crucial for the DS leader to prioritize and focus on a few specific early wins. Too often, DS leaders with academic research backgrounds start many projects to hedge against some of them not working out. This results in projects failing not because of a lack of potential but because of a lack of resources or attention dedicated to each project.

BOTTOM-UP APPROACH

In a functional organizational structure, DS efforts can start under any functional area. An effort that starts under the technology function in the engineering group may be called ML engineering. When an effort starts under marketing, it may focus on customer segmentation or conversion. Under finance, it may focus on margin optimization or sales forecasting. Under the operating function, it may focus on growth hacking, logistics optimization, customer service intelligence, or pricing optimization.

In these bottom-up approaches, DS use cases are first explored within a particular function. Successes in one function's use cases can motivate other functions to start exploring DS capabilities in their respective functions. While this approach allows DS efforts to stay close to business needs, it also creates multiple challenges:

- *Duplications of efforts and variations in methodologies across functions*—DS efforts can be duplicated across functions. Different business decisions can result from incoherent metrics calculated from the same underlying data.
- *Limited professional growth*—Data scientists across different functions often report to managers who are not data scientists. Professional growth for data scientists can be limiting, leading to attrition and loss of institutional knowledge.

One technique to mitigate these challenges in a company is to promote DS to be an independent function at the executive level, led by a chief data scientist or a chief data officer. This structure allows expertise to be built up within the DS function, where best practices can be institutionalized across functions to increase DS efficiency over time. It also allows work performance to be evaluated by peer data scientists and DS managers who can recognize the effort and impact for the business.

Looking into the future, as more CEOs recognize the strategic importance of the data function, it is likely to be as standard as a technology function in business organizations. This book is written anticipating this scenario, where more data leadership talent will be required to take on executive leadership roles in the marketplace.

As companies grow in size, communication becomes more costly. Coordination between large functions can be overwhelming for function leaders, as they must maintain good visibility into their own functions and keep abreast of their partner functions' priorities and roadmaps when making decisions. That is when a divisional organizational structure can help. Ready to dive in? Let's go!

10.2.2 *Divisional organizational structure*

The divisional structure allows the organization to be partitioned by product, geography, or market segment. Each partition is self-sufficient in resources and can autonomously plan and execute its business initiatives with limited dependence on other divisions.

Another way to understand the difference is that the functional structure is organized by the different *input* expertise required to create the product or service, and the divisional structure is organized by the *output* products or segments of customers that the products and services target.

In terms of division of labor, divisional structures allow each division to focus on serving its own cohorts of customers with profit and loss responsibilities for its own division. Authority of roadmaps, goals, and resource allocation are delegated to the divisions for more efficient decision-making. The integration of individual efforts happens at the division level with limited coordination across divisions. This structure works well for stable business models serving relatively static customer segments. Examples of static customer segments include consumer versus enterprise segments, and geographically distributed segments.

As a DS leader, being aware of these structures is important to set the appropriate expectations for cross-division collaboration and coordination. Unless there is a specific urgent initiative from the CEO's office for coordination, cross-divisional DS initiatives can face significant resistance.

081

The divisional organizational structure allows each division to be self-sufficient in resources so it can plan and execute its business initiatives independently. However, cross-divisional data science initiatives can face significant resistance unless the CEO's office has a specific urgent initiative for coordination.

While career growth for most data scientists often stays within a division, significant opportunities exist for strong DS leaders in companies with divisional organizational structures. Successful use cases within a division, such as recommendation platforms, anti-fraud capabilities, and cost-saving/revenue-generating best practices can be distilled and shared across divisions. These capabilities, practices and platforms can create value in two ways:

1 *Cross-divisional platforms and services*—Best practices in one division can be distilled into a technology platform to be introduced in adjacent divisions. Since each division has its adoption authority and owns its profit and loss accounting, early adopters can provide quantitative feedback for the benefits of adoption. The successes can form strong business cases for corporate-wide adoption, especially in large corporations with hundreds of divisions. Each division can be a customer for your best practices and platforms.

2 *Creation of a new division*—DS use cases can also enable new business lines. Customer referral services can be developed from product recommendation systems; risk scoring services can be developed from fraud detection techniques; and cost-reducing predictive maintenance services can be developed from predictions of parts fatigue and system failures. The divisional organizational structure allows new divisions to be created with the multi-functional support necessary to operate a new profit and loss business line. This is discussed in more detail in section 8.3.3.

While the divisional organizational structure can streamline decision-making within a division, functions such as IT or HR may be more efficient when centralized across divisions. There are also situations where customers can demand a coherent engagement experience across the product division. This is where a hybrid or matrix organizational structure can help, and we will be getting into it next. Now may be a good time to take a breather and let the functional and divisional organization structures sections sink in.

10.2.3 *Matrix organizational structure*

The *matrix structure*, or hybrid structure, seeks to avoid the limitations for both functional and divisional structures by closely coordinating within a function and across divisions. A team member working on a project who reports to a functional leader and a divisional leader, often with one as a direct-line manager, responsible for performance and promotions, and another as a dotted-line manager, responsible for advising and consulting. This structure allows functional expertise to develop within an organization and allows strong coordination between functions to occur efficiently within a division.

This structure can be ideal for DS. With DS as one of the functions, the DS leader can build deep technical knowledge and best practices and institutionalize them within the function. The functional focus increases the efficiency of the function. At the same time, the DS team can recognize opportunities and realize impacts within each division. The divisional focus improves the responsiveness to particular business challenges in various divisions.

082

The matrix structure seeks to avoid the limitations for both functional and divisional structures by closely coordinating across functions and divisions. It is ideal for data science, where the team can build deep domain and technical knowledge, craft best practices, and institutionalize them within the function and across divisions. But it does come with significant communication overhead.

However, the matrix structure has its challenges as well. There are four main challenges to watch out for, but they can be overcome with management techniques. The four main challenges are authority confusion, resource planning, resource stability, and change management, as discussed in the following list:

- *Authority confusion*—With direct-line reports and dotted-line reports, there can be authority confusion when priorities do not align between the function and division leaders. This confusion often occurs when limited resources must be dedicated to either improving efficiency by developing function best practices or expanding the capabilities within a product division. Such situations often happen not during times of crisis, when all leaders are aligned in the fight for survival, but in times of resource-constrained growth, when there are multiple paths to success with each favored by different leaders.

  One technique to counter this type of confusion is strong executive leadership, where the company can rally around one or two clear key performance indicators (KPIs). The executive focus can be used to arbitrate and prioritize between the various paths forward.

  Other prioritization techniques include favoring product-focused approaches for early-stage projects to nimbly iterate toward product/market fit or favoring function-focused approaches for late-stage projects to craft efficient executions to increase revenue and profitability.

- *Resource planning*—During each 3- to 12-month planning cycle, with the dual reporting matrix structure, a DS leader has to determine how to balance the funding of functional and divisional projects and initiatives.

  Most DS projects are essential for both the DS function's roadmap and the various divisions' roadmaps. For example, a recommendation engine project can be part of the DS function roadmap to build user understanding for better user segmentation. It can also be part of a business division's roadmap to increase product engagement and improve user retention and LTV.

  However, other projects, such as updates to A/B testing capabilities, model deployment methodologies, and data consistency and governance projects, may have little immediate impact for specific divisions but are highly strategic and important for the DS function to serve across multiple divisions.

  In a matrix structure, how would you determine which functional and divisional projects and initiatives to fund? One common approach is to reserve 10–30% of capacity for function initiatives as a tax for paying down tech debts and investing in future efficiencies, while devoting most of the capacity to advancing the divisions' roadmaps. A high-level agreement between the executives minimizes the pressure on individual data scientists to find a balance between competing interests.

  Another approach for fast-growing DS functions is focusing the current team members on advancing the divisions' roadmaps, specifying projects to pay down functional tech debt, and documenting opportunities for future efficiencies along the way. New DS team members can focus their onboarding projects on executing DS function initiatives before they are delegated projects for a specific division. This approach can provide a gentler onboarding for new DS team members and allow them to take on their later divisional responsibilities with some functional perspective.

- *Resource stability*—In a company with a matrix structure, multiple divisions can simultaneously require DS functional expertise. Often, the common practice in prioritization is to dedicate a stable number of resources to the larger and more mature divisions, then staff the emerging needs to early-stage divisions as resources are available. This practice can result in the emerging projects getting intermittent resource assignments from different team members. While this approach might work for completing software development projects, it can be detrimental for DS projects.

  DS projects have significant contexts learned over time for performing deep-dive analysis, crafting realistic roadmaps, or building predictive solutions. When a different data scientist is assigned from quarter to quarter for early-stage divisions, the project ramp-up overhead makes these assignments highly inefficient.

  One approach to overcome this issue is to dedicate point-of-contacts to early-stage divisions as well as mature divisions. When one early-stage division cannot be assigned a full team member's time, you can dedicate a partial resource to the division to allow the same team member to be the point of contact for multiple early-stage divisions' projects. For a mature division, as long as someone on the team retains its institutional knowledge, there can be more flexibility for other team members to move between divisions when resources need to be reallocated or when a team member is looking to broaden their experience across divisions.

  By having a dedicated point of contact, you can maintain the DS context for early-stage and mature divisions. You can also have the flexibility to shift resources between divisions when the situation demands it.

- *Implementing change*—When a function leader is looking to push out best practices within a function, it will inevitably affect processes across several divisions. In a functional organizational structure, the function has the authority to push out the best practices directly. In a matrix organizational structure, the function leader needs to work with each divisional leader to push out its best practices.

  While this process provides checks and balances to make sure the changes introduced by new best practices do not significantly disadvantage some divisions, it can dramatically slow down progress for implementing necessary changes to remove existing tech debts and prepare systems to scale.

  As a DS leader, one technique to implement change in a matrix structure is to find the initial one or two divisions to spearhead the change, prove the value of the change, then obtain sponsorship with the CEO to support and drive the change top-down into each of the divisions. To implement the change, you can leverage the 10–30% capacity reserved for implementing function-level initiatives during resource planning, so the resources are secured to complete the change.

Alright, that was a lot on the hybrid or matrix structure. Get ready, as next we will be discussing alternative structures where *management* looks a bit different.

10.2.4 *Alternative organizational structure*

The functional, divisional, and matrix structures are all traditional management structures within which you can integrate DS efforts to produce enterprise value. In these structures, management is responsible for crafting strategic roadmaps, constituting teams, defining roles, making decisions, and evaluating performance. In the age of distributed computing and user-generated content, can management's role also be distributed and democratized?

Holacracy is a management structure that promotes a hierarchy of self-managed units or circles, each with its own governing process to constitute teams, define roles, make decisions, and evaluate performance. This structure can be highly adaptable in responding to emerging needs in the marketplace, where circles are constituted to tackle business needs and dissolved when goals have been reached or are no longer relevant.

One successful example is Zappos, the online shoe and clothing store. When Zappos implemented holacracy, its 150 departmental units evolved into 500 circles. Each circle is a basic component of the organization, constituted with purpose, and roles are collectively specified and assigned to circle members to accomplish the work. Each employee can be part of multiple circles. In Zappo's case, the 500 circles were formed by 1,500 employees on projects, functions, and segments [7].

Holacracy can sound chaotic for those who have not experienced it firsthand. The process is actually more orderly than many imagine. Each circle goes through a rigorous constitution process, and its purpose must be clear enough to attract team members to join the circle to take on its roles. To prevent everyone from only joining the cool-sounding project and ignoring the mundane tasks, there are systems for executives to award points to circles by determining the business value of the circle's work. The points can be used for individuals to recruit individuals into roles.

As a DS leader, working in a holacracy can be both rewarding and challenging. DS projects involving exploration and prototyping tend to be the cool projects that attract individuals with engineering and product backgrounds. The maintenance and iteration of models can be neglected, causing DS tech debts to accumulate over time.

083

Holacracy is a management structure that promotes a hierarchy of self-managed units called circles. Working in a holacracy can be both rewarding and challenging. Exploration and prototyping projects tend to attract resources, while the maintenance and iteration of models tend to be neglected.

Holacracy organizational structure can work well for businesses where adaptability is more important than reliability. The process actually requires more management, as all team members need to be well versed in self-defining roles, making decisions, and self-evaluating performance. Success depends on:

- Mature team members who are well-trained in the holacracy process
- Deep understanding of the full life cycle of projects to anticipate resource needs
- Ability to clearly define roles and responsibilities
- Strong project management tool support for constituting, identifying, and joining projects
- Strong domain knowledge to provide performance feedback with tracking support

A holacracy structure can work well in the early stages of opportunity exploration and proof of concept work. These early projects have limited scopes, often with immediate demonstrable early wins.

As DS projects mature, cross-functional integration and governance become critical in setting up company-wide best practices and platforms. For projects to be successful, team members who understand the institutional nuances and system pitfalls need to stay with the project over multiple iterations, often without immediate short-term results. In a holacracy structure, when team members move in and out of projects fluidly, maintaining the momentum for maturing DS projects poses a significant challenge.

Once the DS practices and platforms mature, a holacracy structure can again work well to incrementally optimize subcomponents of well-architected processes and systems over time with demonstrable system-wide short-term benefits. If you are managing a DS team under a holacracy structure, there are a few techniques that can help:

- Constituting circles with long-term goals and clear key results for project phases can help retain team members with institutional knowledge of the data and domain nuances.
- Maintaining documentation with reproducible, transferable, and discoverable results, such that efforts can resume after team members churn or take a leave for other projects. Section 2.2.3 discussed this in more detail.
- Identifying executive sponsorship to attract cross-functional team members for important integration and governance projects to overcome the coordination hurdle of advancing DS maturity levels. Section 6.1.3 talks more about securing executive sponsors.

You have now seen the four major organizational structures in which to operate DS. Let us summarize the opportunities and challenges within them.

10.2.5 *Managing for opportunities and challenges in various structures*

The role of the DS function is to contribute its technical expertise and business insights, so they can be integrated into the product and services in the greater organization. Different organizational structures bring with them unique opportunities and challenges. We discussed four organizational structures: functional, divisional, matrix, and holacracy structures.

In the functional structure, DS is one of many functions. While there is significant opportunity for building expertise within the function, a data science leader should be careful to avoid losing touch with business needs.

In the divisional structure, an organization is partitioned by product, geography, or market segment, where the DS function is distributed to each division. This structure is great for fast-paced division-level decisions. A DS leader should watch out for duplicated efforts between divisions.

In the matrix structure, the DS teams report to a function head and a divisional head simultaneously. This structure enhances coordination across functions and divisions but comes at the cost of potential role confusion and can require a higher communication overhead.

In the holacracy structure with a hierarchy of self-managed units, or circles, where data scientists are distributed to projects, the opportunity is optimal for PoC exploration. However, projects need to be managed closely for securing maintenance resources and payment of tech debts. With an appreciation for the opportunities and challenges for data science to thrive in these organizational structures, you can adapt your focus and manage for the systematic pitfalls these structures bring.

10.3 The opportunity

As a leader in DS, you are fortunate to be in one of the fastest-growing professions today. When evaluating your next career move, you can review the factors that are most important to you at your particular career stage and assess potential industries, companies, teams, and roles of an opportunity.

A significant component of your leadership capability comes from the deep industry expertise you can develop on the job; hence, selecting an industry to go into is a critical decision for DS leaders. You can consider the size and growth rate of the different industries and their intensity of demand for DS talent. Above all, you should investigate what industry you personally feel passionate about, so you can maintain a positive attitude despite the inevitable project failures and workplace breakdowns.

DS is used at companies of all maturity stages, from early-stage startups to hundred-year-old enterprises. The applications of DS can shift based on a company's maturity stage. The choice of maturity level of company you join can affect how you build a repertoire of leadership capabilities and identity.

Leadership is practiced in team settings, so it is essential to evaluate the team you are joining. Considerations include the hiring manager's maturity, infrastructure maturity, and practice maturity.

To understand the responsibilities of a particular DS role, refer to the capabilities and virtues in this book. These capabilities and virtues can help you identify the needs of a specific industry, company, and team. They can also help you craft a narrative of your strengths that can best qualify you for an existing role or a new role you can propose.

Once you are selected to take on a role, you also need to be responsible for your own onboarding. Let's discuss the industry, company, team, and role-level considerations to evaluate the opportunities for the next stage of your career, as well as some effective onboarding strategies once you decide to pursue an opportunity.

10.3.1 Assessing an industry

You can apply DS to a broad range of industries. When evaluating an industry to enter, consider that large industries will have the most job opportunities, while fast-growing industries will create many leadership opportunities over time. For data scientists with appropriate experience levels, industries with the highest demand for data scientists are likely to pay a premium in compensation. Figure 10.6 illustrates some important considerations when selecting an industry.

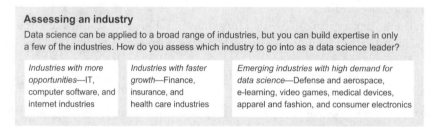

Assessing an industry

Data science can be applied to a broad range of industries, but you can build expertise in only a few of the industries. How do you assess which industry to go into as a data science leader?

Industries with more opportunities—IT, computer software, and internet industries	Industries with faster growth—Finance, insurance, and health care industries	Emerging industries with high demand for data science—Defense and aerospace, e-learning, video games, medical devices, apparel and fashion, and consumer electronics

Figure 10.6   **Three perspectives for assessing an industry to pursue**

The contribution of DS to the economy is still in its infancy as of 2021. According to LinkedIn Talent Solutions data, the discipline has found the most traction in *IT, computer software, and internet* industries. These three industries together employ 42% of the professionals with the data scientist job title in the US. The 42% number is not surprising, as these industries are at the forefront of computing technology adoption. They are closest to all the computing servers generating and storing the data responsible for delivering business impact. However, according to United States Bureau of Economic Analysis data, the *data processing, internet publishing, and other information services* industry together only make up 1.4% of the private sector GDP in the United States [8].

On the other hand, DS is rapidly gaining traction in two other areas that are much more significant to the economy. In the United States, the *finance and insurance* industries contribute 9.4% of the private-sector GDP, and the *health care* industry contributes 7.1% of the private sector GDP.

In the US, the *financial services, banking, and insurance* industries currently employ 12% of today's data scientists, and the demand is increasing faster than in the IT, computer software, and internet industries. The *health care, biotech, pharmaceuticals, and health/wellness/fitness* industries currently employ 10% of today's data scientists with an even higher growth rate.

If you are looking for leadership opportunities in DS in 2021, you can find the most opportunities in the IT, computer software, and internet industries. Many leadership opportunities will be created in the financial services, banking, insurance, healthcare, biotech, pharmaceuticals, and health/wellness/fitness industries in the coming years.

There are also many smaller, high-growth industries with high demand for data scientists. These include defense and aerospace, e-learning, video games, medical devices, apparel and fashion, and consumer electronics.

When selecting an industry to pursue, it should be one that you are passionate about. It can take two to five years to build up expert knowledge in an industry, including data nuances, organizational structural barriers, and regulatory stumbling blocks. You may encounter many failures and frustrations working with industry limitations. Being in an industry that you are passionate about will allow you to persist further on your path to become a leader in DS.

10.3.2 Assessing a company

Tens of thousands of companies worldwide have data scientists on their staff, and more are starting to hire. Picking a good employer can be the difference between a career-launching pedestal and valuable time lost to ad hoc busywork. What should you be looking for in a prospective employer?

You can look at companies based on their maturity stages and their standing within their industry. This perspective is illustrated in figure 10.7.

Assessing a company

Picking a good employer can mean the difference between a career-launching pedestal and valuable time lost to ad hoc busywork. What should you be looking for in a prospective employer?

Company maturity—*Early-stage* startups are iterating on product/market fit; *growth-stage* companies are looking to scale operations for existing products while developing new product lines; and *mature-stage* companies are focusing on revenue optimization, retention, and feature adoption.	*Company standing within industry*—A company in the industry leadership position is considered the *gorilla* of its industry. The contenders for the leadership position are described as the *chimps*, and they can take the leadership position when the leader stumbles. The smaller companies are called the *monkeys* of the industry.

Figure 10.7 Two angles to explore when assessing a company to join

Company maturity stages include early stage, growth stage, and mature stage. The maturity stage largely determines the types of DS projects required and the types of leaders required to lead them. In technology industries, companies compete to be the de facto standard for a technology or market category. Many industries eventually mature to having one company in the leadership position with a few contenders and many smaller players. The standing of a company in its industry can determine the resources available and the focus of its DS activities.

COMPANY MATURITY

Early-stage startups iterate on product/market fit. There may not be much internal first-party data to work with. You can use government and private third-party data sources to understand early customer segments and evaluate early indicators in the buyer journey, onboarding, and product engagement. Companies in this stage are often pre-revenue or have limited revenue from early customers. Venture-backed companies will often have a seed round or series A funding.

Growth-stage companies have found the product/market fit for their offerings. For venture-backed companies, this corresponds to companies with series B or later rounds of funding. These companies have onboarded multiple customers and are expanding their customer base. They have often reached $50 million to more than $1 billion in enterprise valuation and are looking to scale operations for existing products, while developing new product lines and expanding to more geographies to serve additional customer segments.

Growth stage is the stage when many companies start hiring DS leaders. As detailed in section 6.3.1, a company in the growth stage accumulates first-party data to understand the LTV of its customers; estimates the ROI for strategic projects; helps marketing increase customer awareness; optimizes channels for customer acquisition; analyzes the velocity of new feature adoption; and optimizes for activation, revenue, and referral funnels. With the variety of possible value-adding DS capabilities, there is significant room for a DS team to produce business impact.

You can identify these high-growth companies in the United States by referencing the Wealthfront [9] career-launching companies. See if there are any in an industry you are passionate about and in a geographical location of your interest.

Mature-stage companies can be private or public. They often have scalable and repeatable business models with stable customers and predictable recurring revenue streams. In mature companies, DS efforts can focus on revenue optimization, retention, and feature adoption. One particularly impactful effort is to operate a robust A/B test infrastructure with high precision to measure incremental improvement in key metrics. In a mature business with broad reach, even marginal improvements of 0.5% in key metrics can significantly impact revenue.

Many mature companies are pioneers in using DS capabilities and have built up large teams to serve their business needs. Apple, Amazon, Airbnb, Google, Facebook, Microsoft (which owns LinkedIn), Netflix, and Uber are the well-known mature companies in the internet space. Many may not realize that Capital One, JPMorgan Chase, and Wells Fargo in the financial industry all have over 100 data scientists on their teams. In the health care space, Aetna and UnitedHealth Group also have over 100 data scientists on their teams.

In the United States, the top 100 employers of data scientists (as ranked by their DS team size) have teams with 50 to more than 1,000 members. These 100 employers together employ 30% of the practicing DS workforce [10]. If you are looking to manage a large team of data scientists, these companies provide good opportunities.

For a balanced list of top companies to consider for DS practitioners, you can explore three factors: employer brand, team maturity, and team growth (section 10.3.3). Gradient Flow, a popular blog managed by Ben Lorica, ex-chief data scientist of O'Reilly Media, aggregated data from LinkedIn, Glassdoor, and Forbes Best Places to provide the top places to work for early-career and mature data scientists, as well as mid-to-senior level data science leaders [11].

A COMPANY'S STANDING WITHIN THEIR INDUSTRY

In technology industries, companies compete to be the de facto standard for a technology or market category. In *The Gorilla Game* [12], Geoffrey Moore described the company in an industry leadership position as the gorilla of the industry. Examples in the US market include Google in search and AWS in cloud services. The few contenders for the leadership position are described as chimps. Examples include Microsoft Bing in search and Microsoft Azure in cloud services. There are also many smaller players, which are referred to as the monkeys. Examples include DuckDuckGo in search and IBM Cloud in cloud services. The standing of a company in an industry can determine the resources available and the focus of their DS activities.

As you assess a company's standing within their industry, you can often use available data from analyst reports to determine its customer reach, enterprise valuation, or market share. A company reaches gorilla status by finding the product/market fit first and then executing rigorously on its advantage to grow its customer base. DS is critical in providing quantitative feedback in the product iterations toward product/ market fit and in the subsequent growth stage to optimize their efficiency in capturing market share.

When a company achieves gorilla status, there are many benefits. Herd mentality in the marketplace allows the company to charge more and secure higher profit margins, enabling the company to reinvest profits into their business at a more rapid pace. DS can be a beneficiary in this virtuous cycle, allowing it to be well funded and work to increase the company's competitive advantages.

Companies with chimp status are close behind the industry leader but have to justify in every deal why the customer should choose them over the industry leader. When the industry leader stumbles, there is a real chance for the chimp-status company to emerge as the industry leader. DS efforts can be strategic in creating the intelligent features that can help differentiate a company from the industry leader.

Companies with monkey status in an industry often over-promise features and undercut the competition on pricing to compete with the gorilla and chimps of the industry. They are inherently disadvantaged from the industry positioning perspective, and DS investments are often limited. A DS leadership role can be challenging because of the limited scale of investment available. On the other hand, the role may also offer a broader scope of responsibilities than in a larger company with gorilla or chimp status in the industry.

As you examine a next-play opportunity, it's worthwhile to understand the company's standing within its industry and have a realistic expectation of the outcomes. If you can work with a gorilla-status company in a fast-growth industry, you can anticipate significant growth in your team. If you are entering a chimp-status player, you can expect the intense need to create industry differentiation to get ahead. If you are joining a monkey-status player, you can look for a broader scope of responsibilities but may have relatively limited resources available.

084

As you examine a next-play opportunity, it's worthwhile to understand the company's standing within its industry to have a realistic expectation of the outcomes. Industry leaders, challengers, and small players offer different opportunities for career development.

10.3.3 Assessing the team

Assessing the team involves examining multiple dimensions, including the hiring manager's maturity, infrastructure maturity, and practice maturity (figure 10.8). Understanding these team properties can better prepare you to set appropriate expectations for the opportunity.

Assessing the team

Data science can be applied to a broad range of industries, but you can build expertise in a only few of the industries. How do you assess which industry to go into as a data science leader?

Hiring manager's maturity— Your manager's maturity stage can determine the amount of support you will receive for your work.	*Infrastructure maturity—* Maturity of the infrastructure determines the velocity of innovation in doing data science.	*Practice maturity—*The rigor with which your team and their partners practice data science is vital for execution efficiency.

Figure 10.8   Three areas to examine when assessing the team you would like to join

---

HIRING MANAGER'S MATURITY

When you are hired into a new role, your manager is the most important person you will work with. Your responsibility is to align with what's critical for the company, as delegated by your manager. You will be working with the scopes and priorities defined by your manager to the standards set by your manager.

085

When you are hired into a new role, your manager is the most important person you will work with. Your responsibility is to align with what's critical for the company, as delegated by your manager. You will work with the scopes and priorities defined by your manager to the standards set by your manager.

Your manager could be at different stages of their career. These stages of development include establishment, advancement, maintenance, and withdrawal:

- *Establishment*—If your hiring manager was recently promoted to their current position, they could be in the establishment stage. As detailed in chapters 2–9, capabilities and virtues for new leadership roles can be learned and practiced. You may anticipate times when directions need to be adjusted as your manager navigates their new responsibilities. Your hiring manager will appreciate your support in producing early wins as they establish credibility in the organization.

- *Advancement*—If your hiring manager has been successful in their current role for multiple quarters, they could be in the advancement stage. They are now comfortably practicing the capability and virtues at their leadership level. As their teams execute at high velocity, it can be a great opportunity to produce accomplishments. Your hiring manager will appreciate it if you can be a source of help to propose and provide feedback for large-scale initiatives to drive a greater impact on the organization.

- *Maintenance*—If your hiring manager has been successful in their role for many years, they could be at the maintenance stage. They have developed a stable set of attributes and have continued to receive promotions, new responsibilities, and increased identity. It can be incredibly rewarding to work with a manager at this stage, as they have both the experience and the energy to serve as a mentor for your professional growth. Your hiring manager will appreciate it when you present yourself as coachable and demonstrate growth when working with them.

- *Withdrawal*—If your hiring manager is running a declining team, they could be at the withdrawal stage of their career. You need to observe if they have developed apathy toward their job and have resorted to trying not to make fireable offenses. One indicator is recent attrition on the team, indicating the waning confidence of existing team members in the manager. You should be careful about joining such a team.

INFRASTRUCTURE MATURITY

Infrastructure for data and experimentation can significantly accelerate the velocity of innovation in DS. Infrastructures at different maturity stages require a leader to have different skill sets to be successful. Section 8.1.2 discussed some stages to consider, including data collection, ETL+storage, data governance, and model governance. Table 10.1 provides the specific questions for a checklist you can use to make the assessments. You can use the rightmost column as a checkbox.

Table 10.1 A checklist for infrastructure maturity in DS

Stages	Questions for your checklist	?
Data collection	Is the variety of data captured?	
	Are data sources complete for analysis?	
	Is data being captured for experimentation?	
ETL+ storage	Is there a data lake to capture the data collected?	
	Are schemas architected according to business needs in the data warehouse?	
	Is streaming capability being supported?	
Data governance	Are quality checks for availability, correctness, and completeness automated?	
	Is data lineage documented, maintained, and available in a searchable form?	
	Is there governance on the data life cycle to maintain access efficiency?	

Table 10.1   A checklist for infrastructure maturity in DS *(continued)*

Stages	Questions for your checklist	?
Model governance	Are model versions being documented and tracked?	
	Are features consistent between the training and production environment?	
	Are there automated integration and deployment capabilities for models?	

Each of these questions can draw out details on whether the infrastructure is mature enough for DS to produce business impact. As an example, for data collection, suppose you were to assess whether user engagement on a website has been captured correctly for performing analysis. It is not enough to capture just the clicks/taps on a piece of content, but you will also need to know how many times a web page or a web element has been viewed. Capturing the views can be more nuanced than many expect, as some content on a page can require scrolling or expansion to be visible. Content is often loaded with a web page but not seen by a user until specific user actions are performed. Proper data capture requires the page load, user impressions, and clicks/taps to be captured rigorously across platforms and products, which requires some diligence and maturity.

Some DS leaders thrive in not-so-mature infrastructure stages and don't mind wrangling data into an analyzable form. Others may require more mature infrastructures to be available in order to be effective. With an understanding of infrastructure maturity and your strengths, you can decide if an opportunity works for you.

PRACTICE MATURITY

Practice maturity describes the rigor with which the DS team and their partners practice DS. Maturity in practices is vital for team efficiency and can be challenging to develop. Section 8.1.2 describes, from an executive perspective, a roadmap to nurturing a data-driven culture in an organization. When evaluating an opportunity, you can assess three perspectives: data engineering practices, data analysis practices, and data modeling practices. Table 10.2 lists some industry best practices to look for. You can use the rightmost column as a checkbox.

Table 10.2   A checklist for practice maturity in DS

Perspectives	Questions for your checklist	?
Data engineering practices	Is there a robust data engineering foundation with an acceptable quality of service?	
	Are best practices for data security and privacy enforced?	
	Are robust data pipelines routinely developed and launched into production by partner teams according to data engineering guidelines?	
Data analysis practices	Are best practices for logging, instrumentation, and data interpretation followed?	
	Is an A/B test being applied to every product change?	
	Are all business lines and functions making data-driven decisions through self-service of data insights according to data analytics guidelines?	

Table 10.2 A checklist for practice maturity in DS *(continued)*

Perspectives	Questions for your checklist	?
Data modeling practices	Are features consistent between and monitored across development and production environments?	
	Are models versioned and deployed as middleware to serve a diversity of products?	
	Are partner teams regularly articulating and collaborating on new high-impact use cases?	

Most companies are not at these levels of maturity yet. You can assess the team's willingness and executive support to head in these directions. It is your responsibility as a leader in DS to establish a path and lead the team in building an efficient data-driven organization.

10.3.4 Assessing the role

As you assess opportunities for your career development, an understanding of the company's mission, priorities, and success criteria over 3–12 months can help you focus and align your goals and succeed in a new role. This is illustrated in figure 10.9.

Assessing the role

Understanding the company's mission, priorities, and success criteria over 3–12 months can help you focus and align your goals and succeed in a new role.

Company mission—Knowing the underpinning narratives of a company can help you assess if you are passionate about a role at a company and how easy it will be to attract talent.

Priorities and success criteria—Can you assess whether expectations are real? What does success look like? What are the negative consequences if goals are not achieved?

Figure 10.9 Two areas to examine when assessing the role you would like to take on

COMPANY MISSION

A company's mission defines its business, its objectives, and its approach to reach those objectives. You can find it shared on company career pages and news releases and discussed in company blogs. Understanding the underpinning narratives of a company can help you assess whether you can be passionate about a role at the company. If you are a DS executive, part of your responsibility is to infuse DS capabilities into a company's mission.

When you evaluate an opportunity as a DS leader, you can observe in the interview process whether cross-functional partners are aligned with the company's mission. This alignment is crucial for your projects and initiatives to be prioritized by your cross-functional partners among their competing responsibilities.

COMPANY PRIORITIES AND SUCCESS CRITERIA

The company's mission provides a general direction for the company. At each stage of a company's growth, company-level initiatives drive top priorities in the planning process. These priorities come with goals to achieve over specific time horizons that you will be responsible for executing, so it is crucial to assess three key questions:

1   How realistic are those expectations?
2   What would success look like?
3   What are the negative consequences if they are not achieved?

You can synthesize your assessments of the industry, the company, and the team to evaluate how realistic your hiring manager's expectations are.

This independent evaluation of priorities and expectations is crucial for your success in considering a new role. The potential impact of DS can sometimes be over-hyped in popular media. If expectations from executives and hiring managers are too high and not realistic, you can be set up for failure before you even start. There are four levels of confidence various data applications can provide, including recommendations and ranking, assistance, automation, and autonomous agents. Section 2.1.3 describes them in more detail. You can refer to these levels to determine what success could look like with your hiring manager.

Besides understanding what success looks like, you should also understand the negative consequences if goals are not achieved. The more severe the negative consequence, the more crucial it is to achieve the goals. Negative consequences, especially the natural ones that are direct implications of failure, can be very helpful in motivating your team, and cross-functional teams prioritize work to achieve their goals. They can also be helpful for you in understanding the constraints of the situations and avoiding potential pitfalls when executing on the priorities. Section 7.2.3 discussed communicating consequences in more detail.

CRAFTING A NEW ROLE

In some cases, when you are passionate about joining a company or a team, and the company values your skills and experience, they may create a role for you. When you understand the industry, the company, the team, and the priorities, you may have enough information to present a role description as your offer for the company.

You can discuss the dimensions of the technology roadmaps and the data-driven cultural maturity roadmaps to take responsibility for and work with the company to iterate on realistic success criteria to justify a new role. When you can start making your own offers of help to companies and organizations, you can be a much more powerful leader for producing business impact.

10.3.5 *Onboarding into a new role*

As a leader in DS, you are taking on significant responsibilities for projects, teams, functions, and companies. 95% of the companies that hire data scientists have teams with fewer than 10 members. Onboarding processes are often elementary, if not missing, especially for DS leaders. To own a successful onboarding, DS leaders often have to map out their own onboarding processes. But where do you start?

When joining a new company or taking on new responsibilities within the same company, you often have a period to build your leadership identity. For junior leadership positions, it may be 30 days. For more senior leadership positions, the window could be 90 days.

Onboarding is demanding. There are long checklists [13] available for DS individual contributors. For DS leaders at different levels, your onboarding focus can be drastically different.

086

> For data science leaders, onboarding processes are often elementary, if not missing. To own a successful onboarding, data science leaders often have to map out their own onboarding processes. You can reference autonomy, mastery, and purpose as the three key areas to work on with your manager.

You can reference *autonomy, mastery,* and *purpose* as the three key areas to work on with your manager and team to ramp up toward performing your best [14]:

- *Autonomy*—Autonomy is our desire to be self-directed. For DS leaders, this involves making decisions in a broader context with considerations for your team, across partners, and within your first team. When your decision overlooks these contexts, it can be overruled by your manager through unpleasant escalations or result in project failures, which can hurt your autonomy in the long run.
- *Mastery*—Mastery is our desire to acquire better skills. For DS leaders, these skills include your ability to navigate the technologies used for DS to make business impact, as well as the relationships required to drive technical and personnel decisions.
- *Purpose*—Purpose is our desire to do something meaningful and important. For DS leaders, it's your responsibility to internalize the company vision, mission, and line of business (LOB) strategic directions to focus your team's work on the most meaningful and important items for the company.

How do these areas look at each stage of DS leadership?

TECH LEAD ONBOARDING

New DS tech leads are often promoted or hired for a particular reason. There is usually a clear set of projects and responsibilities defined. Be sure to understand the scope of your responsibilities, the resources available to you, and the partners you are expected to work with, so you can exercise your *autonomy* within those constraints.

The tech lead role will also have its *purpose* articulated. In the first week of your onboarding process, you can learn about the company vision and mission, the company-wide strategic priorities, and how your team's work connects to the strategic priorities.

A large part of your onboarding focus is on *mastery*. There are two components of mastery for a DS tech lead:

- Navigating the technology landscape
- Building relationships with business and functional partners

087

Tech lead onboarding can focus on two components of mastery: navigating the technology landscape and building relationships with business and functional partners.

New to the company

If you are joining a new company, you may face a steep learning curve for the technology landscape and partner relationships. Your technology onboarding process is more than getting the equipment and productivity tool logins. As a tech lead, your onboarding involves an assessment of the available infrastructure and architecture, the points of fragility, and existing tech debts in the backlog.

Many teams have onboarding notes on equipment and account setup processes. You can identify buddies who can help you locate and get started on the existing processes, infrastructures, and roadmaps. To understand the points of fragility in the infrastructure, you can also seek out incident reports of past system failures, which can quickly illuminate tech debts in the system.

To build relationships with teammates and business partners, you can work with your manager to identify early-win projects. These projects can help you establish an identity within the team. Relationship building and early wins are discussed in more detail below. Once you are familiar with the technology landscape and risks, you can be more confident in navigating the relationships with team members, business partners, and your manager.

Promotions

If you are promoted within the same company, you may already be familiar with the technology stack. The focus can then be on building relationships with business and functional partners from your new position, where you have more capacity to offer help and your partners have new expectations from you and the team.

One way to build the relationship is to work with partners and your team members to secure early wins that matter to your boss and partners. This involves working with your boss and partners to choose and complete projects over a few weeks to demonstrate business value. These early wins allow partners to build confidence in you and your teammates' ability to deliver, which is a critical factor in future project prioritization assessments.

You can use three criteria to assess whether a project is a good candidate for an early win:

- The project has a clearly defined scope.
- There is a significant measurable business impact that the team and partners care about.
- The project can be completed within a few weeks with available resources.

Examples of early-win projects include automating a business process to improve business productivity, producing data insights and deep dives, and designing the definition of a metric for business operations.

Other small-scale projects may not have clear short-term business impact by themselves. These include things like tracking specification definition and data enrichment, which have to be integrated into other projects to demonstrate business value. Projects such as building new models and API from scratch and ensuring data consistency may require significant cross-functional alignment between product and engineering. They can be easier to pursue when you have a few early wins secured. It's your responsibility to work with your manager to ensure your first project is set up right for a good onboarding into your new tech lead role.

MANAGER ONBOARDING

As a DS manager, you are the face of the company for your team members. It is critical to gain a clear interpretation of your team's *purpose* as constituted by the executives. At the same time, your role is beyond leadership in technology and relationships. You are responsible for the productivity of your team. While the tech lead onboarding is focused on *mastery*, your team manager level onboarding is focused on *autonomy*.

Autonomy for a manager means making effective projects and personnel decisions for your team to move with velocity. Ironically, gaining autonomy does not mean making decisions by yourself in a vacuum but rather by tapping a broad network of help that can incorporate the concerns from your team, across your partners, and within your *first team*. Figure 10.10 illustrates the main project and people responsibilities of a manager.

Project responsibilities

Planning:	Communications:	Resource management:
• Setting direction/defining success	• Addressing team conflicts	• Budgeting/cost control
• Achieving results	• Managing process changes	• Planning and prioritization
• Delegating work assignments	• Managing organizational change	• Allocating resources
• Planning headcounts		• Ensuring legal compliance

People responsibilities

Employment:	Team operations:	Team building:
• Recruiting and hiring	• Holding weekly one-on-ones	• Leading team meetings
• Setting compensation	• Coaching/mentoring	• EVS action planning
• Retaining employees	• Training and development of team	• Organizing and attending offsites and summits
• Assisting with immigration cases	• Maintaining motivation and morale	• Fostering an inclusive and diverse environment
• Onboarding and integration	• Giving rewards and recognition	
• Handling transitions associated with exiting employees	• Managing performance	
	• Calibrating talent	
	• Implementing disciplinary acctions	

Career development:
• Self-development as a manager
• Succession planning

Figure 10.10   Project and people responsibilities for a DS manager

NOTE   Your first team consists of peers reporting to your manager, who should be working together to solve your manager's challenges. See section 6.2.3 for details.

088

Manager onboarding can focus on *autonomy*. Ironically, gaining autonomy does not mean making decisions by yourself but rather by gaining the ability to tap into a broad network of help to incorporate the concerns from your team, your partners, and your peers in your decisions.

There are four main areas of concern for autonomy in project decisions:

- *Business orientation*—As a manager interacting with partners and your first team, it is not enough to understand your specific part of the business, but you will also need to understand the concerns of the whole business. This understanding allows you to think beyond the financials, product, and strategy to include concerns for branding, sales, and talent pipelines for making people and technology decisions.
- *Stakeholder connection*—DS is a team sport. Identifying key stakeholders in projects and developing cross-functional relationships early is crucial to understand and mitigate project risks when assessing project viability.
- *Expectation alignment*—Business moves fast. Regardless of how well you think your initiatives align with the business, check and realign frequently, as situations and priorities may have shifted.
- *Culture adaptation*—In a new role, depending on whether the culture is authority-driven, process-focus, consensus-oriented, relationship-driven, or something else, you may need to adjust your style to fit the culture. Adjustment is crucial for success in DS, as you may need to adapt and bridge partner functions with different subcultures.

During onboarding, you can work with your manager to collect and synthesize information about these four areas of concern from your team, across your partners, and within your first team. This learning can help you develop your approach to planning, communication, and resource management responsibilities with autonomy.

When managers change, it is often a stressful time for team members and partners. Star players may start thinking about leaving, and partners may shift their priorities to pause support for some collaborations. To gain autonomy in personnel decisions, you can work with your manager to identify a list of key team members and partners to meet. Reviewing your team members' past performance reviews allows you to understand their strengths in order to discuss their career goals. Deeply understanding prior commitments between your team and partners will enable you to maintain trust between teams that have been built up over time. You can identify buddies with long tenures to share historical accomplishments and commitments as contexts for your personnel decisions. As you make personnel decisions, your manager can help you identify the HR partners who will work with you on the processes and obligations for fulfilling many of the employment, team operations, and team-building responsibilities.

DIRECTOR ONBOARDING

As you become a senior-level leader, you are entrusted with more autonomy from the start. Your onboarding focuses on clarifying the *purpose* of your function by setting the success criteria and standards.

Criteria is a set of basic requirements for a team to fulfill its responsibilities. It is sometimes called *table stake*, the minimum requirement for your team to be recognized as a function. A standard is a set of requirements that can deliver a level of customer satisfaction. For example, a hotel at the four-star standard should have luxury bedding, quality towels, and a fitness center.

In DS, the function's *purpose* can be synthesized from the diagnosis of your inherited situation. Table 10.3 shows an example of a diagnosis framework in DS. For each responsibility area for your function, you can specify the criteria, or table-stake requirements, to be productive. You can specify the *platinum* standard as a stretch target, so your teams reach higher in each of their projects. You can also craft a vision for each responsibility area to align roadmaps with partners and set long-term goals.

089

Director onboarding can focus on purpose. For each responsibility area for your function, you can specify the criteria, or table-stake requirements, to be productive. You can set the platinum standard as a stretch target, so your teams reach higher in each of their projects. And you can also craft a vision for each responsibility area to align roadmaps with partners and set long-term goals.

Table 10.3 Sample diagnosis of DS standard of operations

Area	Criteria (table stake)	Platinum standard	Vision
Objectives and key results (OKR) planning	Transparency in prioritization and trade-offs, while building relationships and trust	Thought partnership that anticipates product roadmaps	DS becomes an integral part of all product planning processes.
Empowering data-driven launches			
Tracking	Detecting issues and partners to prioritize resolving tracking issues in a timely manner	■ *People*—A tiger team as cross-functional data champions ■ *Process*—End-to-end management to ensure tracking quality ■ *Platform*—Enhanced monitoring system	Engineering considers tracking to be as important as developing features.
A/B testing	Performing A/B tests for product launches with clear hypotheses	Rigorously following experiment guideline to balance speed, quality, and risk [15]	All partner teams proactively work with DS on defining A/B tests and discussing results.
Optimizing with insights			
Establishing new metrics	■ Clear use case and assumption ■ Rigor in articulation and definition	Driving business value by defining metrics with urgency	Product/engineering/ AI begin initiatives with quantifiable metrics as part of the charter.

Table 10.3   Sample diagnosis of DS standard of operations *(continued)*

Area	Criteria (table stake)	Platinum standard	Vision
Analysis/deep-dives/state of the union reports	Providing insights as soon as metrics are available	Delivering insights to drive the product roadmap	Data-first product roadmap creation.
Solidifying measurements and foundation			
Tracking health	Awareness of data sets and tiering of criticalness to business	▪ Publishing data assets and documentation to empower partner self-help ▪ Providing office hours to support official readouts	Business partners can find, query, and interpret data independently.
Data pipeline health	Maintaining data availability and backfilling when required—no partner reminders required	▪ Using up-to-date data sources ▪ Using up-to-date programming languages ▪ Monitoring, alerting, investigating, and resolving upstream data availability issues before customers are aware of them	Meet 99.9% SLA for all flows. Resolve all upstream data availability issues within 24 hours.
Metric consistency	Maintaining consistency of executive-facing metrics across organizations	Partners trust and operate confidently with all executive-facing metrics	Partners come to DS for the source of truth in defining success.

During your second 30 days of onboarding, you can work with your boss to align criteria and standards for your function, assess the gaps, and craft roadmaps for areas to address. You can then focus your manager's attention on the costs and benefits of what you can accomplish with different sets of resources they provide.

Once you align on the direction with your boss, you can communicate your new vision with the teams through offsites or all-hands, so the teams can clarify interpretations, craft plans, and make commitments toward satisfying the criteria, reaching for the platinum standard and working toward the ultimate vision.

In the third 30 days, you can look to demonstrate initial traction for early wins. These early wins can help you build an identity for effective execution. With early wins, you can also start exploring more ambitious moves, such as restructuring teams, optimizing processes, and building platforms, to execute against your aligned vision for your function.

EXECUTIVE ONBOARDING

At the executive level, your company is looking to you to guide it forward. The executive responsibilities are less structured, and you are expected to own your onboarding process. The focus of an executive onboarding process is to negotiate success and achieve early wins, both internal and external to your company.

A successful onboarding starts with staying in sync with your boss, who may be the CEO. Communicating often and aiming for early wins are key to building trust with your boss. This includes setting expectations up front for a 90-day onboarding process.

You can reserve the first 30 days for a listening tour that aims to deliver a detailed assessment and plan, then align the goals and actions in the second 30 days, and use the third 30 days to execute early wins.

As Deborah Liu, CEO of Ancestry, shared [16], "Leaders are not hired to have all of the answers, rather they are sought out because they can facilitate the company finding the answers together."

090

> "Leaders are not hired to have all of the answers, rather they are sought out because they can facilitate the company finding the answers together."—Deborah Liu

The detailed assessment can include your learnings about the past, present, and future. For the past, this consists of the organization's performance, root causes for good and bad outcomes, and a history of changes that have taken place.

For the present, you can learn about the vision and strategies currently in place and the capabilities of your teams and partners. You can also observe key processes, learn about culturally or politically sensitive subjects to avoid, and early wins that are important for the team, partners, and your boss.

For the future, you can learn about the challenges and opportunities on the roadmap, barriers you are likely to encounter, resources you are likely to require, and cultural elements you can embody and amplify. At the end of the 30 days, you can share your learnings with your boss and request any resources necessary to align and execute your early wins in the next 60 days.

What's an efficient process for this learning process? Andrew Bosworth, VP of Facebook Reality Labs, suggests starting with four simple steps [17] to discuss in one-on-one settings:

1 Ask your boss, peers, partners, and team members to tell you everything they think you should know. Take copious notes. Stop them only to ask about things you don't understand.
2 Ask about the biggest challenges the team has right now.
3 Ask who else you should talk to. Write down every name they give you.
4 Repeat the above process for every name you're given. Don't stop until there are no new names.

This process can give you an overwhelming set of information. Be sure to review the information as you collect it to catch the common threads. By week one, you can start the outline of a *state of the union document*, which reflects what you have heard. By week two, you can refine areas of this document with commentaries and quotes. By week three, you can start soliciting feedback from key people for crucial contexts. By week four, you can add your final thoughts and share.

By sharing your state of the union document, you are communicating to your teams what's working, what's not working, and your recommendations for the next 60 days and beyond. It is important to coordinate with your boss for the necessary resources to get started on your recommendations with early wins achievable in your first 90 days.

A few common blind spots in the executive onboarding process include:

- *Neglecting external stakeholders and only focusing on your teams.* An executive has responsibilities both internal and external to the company. It would serve the executive well to understand the perspectives of the customers, distributors, suppliers, and analysts, so the recommendations will not create external breakdowns.

- *Neglecting to close the loop with people who have shared their perspectives.* It's not enough for you to listen in your listening tour. You also need to make people feel that they have been heard. When sharing what's working and what's not working, you can use quotes from your listening tour to back up your observations and recommendations.

- *Neglecting to set clear expectations about where your priorities are.* You can lose credibility when people share their perspectives, and they do not see a change in a few months. When you clearly communicate your focus and early milestones, stakeholders can see the progress and momentum and trust you to get to their concerns soon.

During your second 30 days, you can focus on communicating your new vision for DS and aligning the organization with this vision. Techniques such as offsites can be effective for clarifying interpretations, crafting plans, and making commitments toward realizing the new vision. You know you have succeeded in alignment when there is a clear set of metrics or goals that the team commits to with a clear timeline.

Over your third 30 days, you can focus your teams on fine tuning priorities and unblocking teams as they start making progress toward the new vision. By the end of the third 30 days, you know you have succeeded when you can share steps taken on the roadmap. If you can drive early wins, that can be even more powerful for building your identity.

SAMPLE ONBOARDING TIMELINES

To summarize, the DS onboarding process is demanding. At various leadership levels, the focus of your onboarding process may look quite different. Table 10.4 illustrates the focus areas for each type of leadership role described in this book.

For a tech lead, the onboarding focus is *mastery*, as the function's vision and mission are often already clarified, and team and project charters are already specified. You are looking to become productive in execution as quickly as possible.

For a manager, the onboarding focus is *autonomy*, as the function's vision and mission are often already clarified, and the team's charter is already specified. You are

Table 10.4 Sample DS onboarding timeline (with book section references)

Roles	First 30 days	Second 30 days	Third 30 days
Tech lead	• Clarifying responsibilities, scope, partners, and available resources • Focusing on *Mastery* • Navigating the technology landscape • Building relationships with business and functional partners	• Producing early wins • Learning domain data nuances (2.3.2) • Navigating organizational structures (2.3.3) • Taking responsibility for enterprise value (3.2.3)	• Continuing to perform your best in your new role
Manager	• Creating a clear interpretation of team purpose as constituted by executives • Focusing on *Autonomy* • Business orientation • Stakeholder connection • Expectation alignment • Culture adaptations	• Aligning early wins • Assessing team, influencing partners, and managing up (4.2) • Leveraging HR partner for people management	• Producing early wins • Building a network of technical advisers, culture interpreters, and political counselors
Director	• Going on a listening tour to assess and learn from the teams • Focusing on *Purpose* • Diagnosing the status of projects and teams • Identifying table-stake standards • Setting a platinum standard for stretch goals • Crafting a vision to align roadmaps	• Communicating your vision for projects and processes • Organizing offsites • Negotiating success • Requesting resources for early wins • Specifying metrics or goals • Sharing learnings	• Demonstrating traction with early wins • Building an identity for effective execution • Structuring teams, optimizing processes, and building platforms that align with the vision
Executive	• Going on a listening tour to assess and learn from the teams • Sharing a state of the union document • Assessing the past, present, and the future • Sharing what's working and what's not • Providing a direction forward for internal and external stakeholders	• Communicating your new vision in DS, and aligning the organization with the vision • Aligning teams and influencing partners to adopt the new vision • Organizing offsites • Specifying metrics or goals • Sharing learnings	• Focusing teams on updated priorities and unblocking teams in their progress • Demonstrating progress • Progressing on long-term execution and roadmaps • Driving metrics and goals • Sharing learnings

looking to build the technical and relationship contexts as soon as possible to make critical decisions about projects and people.

For a director, the onboarding focus is *purpose*, as your company is depending on you to set new visions for projects, teams, and processes. You are looking to provide directions for the function based on your vision, while crafting and executing the roadmaps toward your vision.

For an executive, your responsibilities include infusing the DS perspective into the company vision and aligning it with internal and external stakeholders. You will then align your teams and guide their progress toward that vision.

10.4   *The practice*

As a DS leader, your goal is to amplify your impact with DS by leading a project, a team, a function, or an industry. Throughout this book, we discuss the practices you can personally develop to create business impact. As you build your team, you can also hire talent to satisfy critical needs. What are some practices that new team members can bring in when you hire them? Once you have built out a robust function, what are some emerging career development directions for yourself at the leadership level? In this section, let's look at the existing and emerging practices you can hire into your team and emerging leadership roles for current DS leaders.

10.4.1   *Skill sets you can hire into your team*

As the DS field evolves, skill sets are emerging to tackle specific business needs. When you can recognize these specific business needs, you can acquire talent with particular skills and promote cross-training between team members to amplify your teams' strengths in executing best practices in these areas.

What are some of these practice areas? Figure 10.11 maps the expert practice areas in the context of the data architecture pipeline. Not surprisingly, many of the skills are associated with the data architecture pipeline's output stage, where they are closest to providing business impact. It is worth noting, however, that your team's efficiency is highly dependent on your DS platforms, tools, and data architecture. Let's go into each of these practice areas to understand what they are and when you need them.

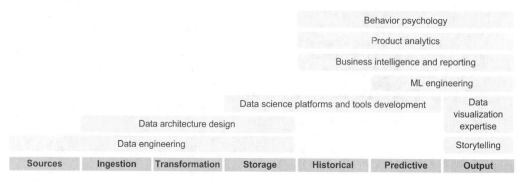

Figure 10.11   Skill sets you can hire into your team

BEHAVIORAL PSYCHOLOGY

Behavioral psychology is a theory of learning based on the idea that all behaviors are acquired through conditioning. It has been successfully applied in solutions for health wellness, financial wellness, and mental wellness. The goal is often to condition behaviors that enable users to better experience the value of the product, service, and policies.

You know you need some behavioral psychology expertise on your team when you are looking to modify people's behavior to better engage with your product or services. For example, Livongo uses behavioral psychology principles to improve medication compliance and outcomes for people with chronic conditions. Acorns uses behavioral psychology principles to help people form savings habits to put away more money and become more financially resilient to financial emergencies. Companies such as Google and Walmart have set up teams in the behavioral sciences to improve how people use their products and services.

When you are looking to guide people to make good health, financial, or other behavioral decisions, the behavioral psychology practice can be extremely helpful to formulate default choices, craft rewards, and avoid pitfalls. Some organizations have found it especially helpful to involve behavioral psychologists in early product design processes. They also rely on behavior psychologists to design randomized trial experiments and evaluation metrics to measure the effectiveness of various approaches. Products are then positioned to condition users along the "happy" usage paths that allow them to get value from the product and services more quickly. A successful data scientist with a behavioral psychology skill set can convert interests in the behavioral sciences into impactful projects, quantify the effect and magnitude of the wins with convincing experiments, and generate buy-in throughout the organization.

091

A successful data scientist with a behavioral psychology skill set can convert interests in the behavioral sciences into impactful projects, quantify the effect and magnitude of the wins with convincing experiments, and generate buy-in across the organization.

PRODUCT ANALYSIS

Product analysis is the process of quantitatively understanding a product's performance and making improvement recommendations. A successful data scientist practices product analysis by working closely with product managers, user researchers, and designers to deeply understand the user journey, define the key metrics to measure success, and propose new product features that advance the success metrics.

A data scientist specializing in product analysis can assess *which* metrics are important to measure by leveraging their deep understanding of the product domain, vision, and roadmaps. For example, when assessing the quality of a search feature, the CTR of the search result must be augmented with the destination dwell time to determine the quality of the search results and filter out clickbait. For fraud risk assessment, it is not enough to focus on the catch rate (or the recall) of fraud cases but also the precision of any fraud indicator, which determines the false positive rate and the cost of investigating fraud alerts.

Product analysts are also experts in *how* to measure. They are deeply in tune with the meanings and limitations of data sources. Measurements such as CTR need to filter for bot traffic if you are looking to determine human user behavior instead of crawlers from search engines and data aggregators. Geoposition data in the form of longitude and latitude from mobile devices has varying levels of precision, depending on the technology used, such as IP-based, cell tower-triangulated, WiFi-triangulated, or GPS locations.

When you hire a data scientist with product analysis expertise, you can assess their domain knowledge and their ability to build models or conduct analysis to recommend product features aligned with the company's strategic vision. This knowledge and skill is key to producing business impact.

BUSINESS INTELLIGENCE AND REPORTING

Business intelligence and reporting is a skill set that focuses on serving the analytic and reporting needs of non-product functions, including marketing, sales, finance, and customer service. Data scientists with this skill set work closely with function leaders to create tools to visualize, report, and forecast metrics important for function and company health.

Data scientists with business intelligence and reporting skills understand the fundamental concerns of the business functions they work with and are excellent at translating vague business questions into specific analysis with available data. When they are successful and have the trust of the business function, they will receive many requests, often beyond what can be answered within the available time. Triage and prioritization skills are essential for focusing their time on the highest-impact work.

When you hire a data scientist with business intelligence and reporting skills, you can assess their function area knowledge and ability to prioritize requests, develop self-serve processes, train function partners on interpreting results, and propose new high-impact analyses for their business functions that are aligned with the overall business strategy.

ML ENGINEERING

ML engineering focuses on producing scalable machine learning model implementations that can be deployed in production. Data scientists with this expert practice usually have a computer science background with experience collaborating in large software projects. They are sensitive to the testability and maintainability of the solutions they produce and can make implementation choices that balance the overall cost of operating an ML model with model performance.

Good data scientists with ML engineering expertise can frame vague product requirements into machine learnable formulations, articulate success metrics and model features, set up A/B testing capabilities to measure successes, write engineering implementation specifications and acceptance criteria, coordinate with software engineering teams in integration and testing, and set up invariants and alerts for the effective operation of the ML models they produce.

When you hire a data scientist with ML engineering expertise, you can assess their ability to write production-quality code while working with ambiguous specifications. They can also work with data engineers to produce robust data pipelines and design backoff solutions with site reliability engineering to prepare for scenarios when data processing or model inference infrastructures inevitably fail.

DS PLATFORM AND TOOL DEVELOPMENT

When the DS team reaches a certain size, small improvements in platforms and tools can create significant leverage in team productivity. Examples of platforms and tools include A/B test infrastructures for evaluating feature success, feature stores to centralize feature production and maintenance, and model serialization infrastructures to deploy machine learning models into production.

A successful data scientist with specialized skills for platform and tool development can recognize the common bottlenecks in DS projects and propose and prioritize which bottlenecks should be addressed first with the least investment to generate the most significant returns.

When you hire a data scientist with platform and tool development expertise, you can assess their capabilities in focusing on the most impactful practice, process, and infrastructure improvements. You can also assess their ability to drive changes that can improve team productivity.

DATA VISUALIZATION

Data scientists with expertise in *data visualization* focus on using the most impactful visualization to communicate the implications of data. Popular examples of powerful visualization include motion charts that use time-lapse bubbles to look at complex four-dimensional relationships over time. Other examples include Apple Watch's daily exercise goals, which are illustrated as concentric rings of various colors to be "closed" as the goals are accomplished.

> **NOTE** The motion chart was made popular by Hans Rosling (1948–2017), Swedish physician, academic, public speaker, and founder of Trendalyzer software, to animate data compiled by the UN and the World Bank (https://www.gapminder.org/fw/world-health-chart). Google acquired Trendalyzer software in 2007 and made it freely available as a Google Gadget for public statistics (https://developers.google.com/chart/interactive/docs/gallery/motionchart).

Successful data scientists with specialized skills for data visualization are focused on communicating critical results from analysis through carefully selected chart types and meaningfully exposed trends to make their message intuitive and memorable. They use no-coding tools like Tableau, scripting tools like Python and R libraries, public APIs like Google Gadgets for data visualization, and serious visualization coding tools like D3.js to realize their visualizations.

When you hire a data scientist with data visualization expertise, you can assess their curiosity for the data in your application domain, their enthusiasm for understanding audience biases and preferences, and their rigor in testing the suitability of visualizations with different data sets to ensure that visualizations work well for multiple distributions of customer data.

092

A successful data scientist with data visualization expertise is curious about the data in your application domain, enthusiastic about understanding audience biases and preferences, and rigorous in testing the suitability of visualizations with different data sets.

STORYTELLING

Data scientists with expertise in *storytelling* are skilled at providing context to an analysis or model, so the audience can connect to the deeper implications of the results. The skill set involves understanding their audience's needs, delivering actionable recommendations, and presenting them with a clear structure.

Successful data scientists with storytelling expertise can leverage powerful data visualization with crafted narratives that can clarify the impact of their results within a context directly relevant to their audience. Their skill set applies not only to presenting results. Storytelling is crucial in the planning process to develop mock *press releases* for when the project is successful, clarify project focus, assess project impact, and attract sponsors and champions.

When you hire a data scientist with storytelling expertise, you can look at their use of impactful visualizations, listen to the narrative of their past projects, and observe the structure of their story. Their skill level should be evident in the complexity of cross-functional projects and how they can navigate audience needs and simplify their messages to get the story across.

093

A successful data scientist with storytelling expertise can clarify audience needs, and use impactful visualizations, compelling narratives, and clear story structure to get messages across in complex cross-functional projects.

DATA ARCHITECTURE DESIGN

Data scientists with expertise in *data architecture design* can significantly impact data model development for new lines of business and data model upgrades for existing businesses. The data architecture [18] defines the data standards used in an organization. They include formal data names, comprehensive data definitions, effective data structures, precise data integrity rules, and robust data documentation. The standards are often expressed as a set of specifications that define data requirements and guide the integration and control of data assets.

Successful data scientists with data architecture expertise can provide a standard common business vocabulary for the domain, express strategic data requirements from stakeholders, and outline high-level integrated designs for the data architecture. They can align the data architecture closely with the business model and data use cases, which can produce far-reaching impacts on data analysis and data pipeline implementations.

When you hire a data scientist with data architecture expertise, you can look for their curiosity in understanding business and DS use cases and experience in the full data life cycle from definition to sourcing, maintenance, and deprecation. They should also be familiar with planning for data technology, data integration, and definition and maintenance of enterprise taxonomies, namespaces, and metadata.

DATA ENGINEERING

Data scientists with expertise in data engineering can design, implement, deploy, and maintain data solutions to meet company needs. Their responsibilities start with sourcing data and include ingesting, transforming, and storing data in the data lake, data warehouse, or data lakehouse.

Successful data scientists with data engineering expertise are proficient technically and can understand business drivers, translate them into data requirements, and comply with policies and regulations. The organization depends on them to protect data quality through data pipeline deployment and operation, data governance through data catalog and lineage management, while balancing implementation trade-offs for master data, reference data, and data streams.

When you hire a data scientist with data engineering expertise, you can look for their sensitivity to business needs, their diligence to implementation details, and their ability to leverage data incidents to improve the overall robustness of the data ecosystem over time. They should be able to build and maintain the environment and infrastructure to support DS and analytics needs and improve and tune the systems to increase the team's efficiency.

10.4.2 Emerging career directions for DS leaders

Being a DS leader, you already have a unique set of capabilities across DS technologies, execution skills, and expert domain knowledge. You are also collaborating with product, engineering, and design to create enterprise value. Depending on your strengths and interests, you can consider four major career development directions in data, product, business, and engineering. These are illustrated in figure 10.12. Let's discuss them one at a time.

Data direction
Increasing responsibilities in setting vision, roadmaps, and data function management

Product direction
Scaling data-driven products as a product manager and developing new products or services

Business direction
Operating and growing a line of business with responsibilities to make business decisions

Engineering direction
Architecting, developing, testing, deploying, and maintaining engineered intelligent systems

You as a leader in data science

Figure 10.12 Four career directions for data science leaders

THE DATA DIRECTION

Career progress in the data direction can include titles such as project lead, team manager, head of the DS function, or data executive.

The data direction is extensively discussed from chapters 2–9 of this book. As one industry veteran described, good managers often have an overdeveloped sense of responsibility. Career progression is about driving a more significant impact on the business, rather than an urge to manage or control.

This book provides a learning path for partnership alignment, people management, crafting of roadmaps, and techniques to inspire and lead an industry. There are specific skills to be proficient at for each level of responsibility.

To serve at executive levels in this data direction, many companies seek chief data officers (CDOs) with responsibilities for DS, data analytics, and data governance.

The data analytics mandate is often to partner with product managers in using data to make business decisions. This mandate includes working on ad hoc deep dives for exploring business directions, specifying and tracking success metrics for new products and features, maintaining dashboards for business operations, deploying analytics platforms, and setting up training to democratize data insights.

The data governance mandate is often defined as making data a company asset. As the aggregation and use of data become more strategic for organizations, data can be both an asset and a liability. When data resources are correctly cataloged, managed, and efficiently accessible, they can be assets. When data resources are not governed effectively, non-compliance with regulations, such as GDPR and CCPA, can carry hefty fines.

The paths to the role of CDO can be fulfilling for DS leaders to expand their current scope of responsibilities to produce more significant business impact in their organizations.

THE PRODUCT DIRECTION

Career progress in the product direction can include titles such as data product manager or product line owner.

Many DS project leaders are already taking on data product design responsibilities for their teams. These responsibilities include specifying and delivering internal-facing metrics dashboards, cost-saving predictive intelligence for existing business processes, and even intelligent external-facing user experiences.

Individuals with DS training have an advantage in understanding the entire intelligence capability life cycle. These capabilities often require strategic considerations to continuously collect signals to calibrate and adapt predictive capabilities to market conditions. The tight feedback loops in calibration and adaptation may not be evident for product managers unfamiliar with data products.

To be successful as a data product manager or a product line owner, you need deep knowledge in the following four domains:

1 *Your customers*—Know your customers' issues, pains, and desires, and know how they think.
2 *Your data*—Quantitatively understand how customers are doing.

3 *Your business*—Understand and operate with the constraints of your stakeholders.

4 *Your market and industry*—Understand key technology trends and competitions.

As a DS leader, you already get exposure to your data and your business. The skills to focus on developing involve a deeper understanding of your customers, your market, and your industry. This knowledge can help you set a long-term vision and strategy for your company's product roadmap and communicate them to your stakeholders.

Career development directions for DS leaders can also include taking on a business unit's profit and loss responsibilities. This can happen in two scenarios:

1 Monetizing a set of data capabilities as a product line, with examples such as:

  a Netflix leverages its understanding of user preference to cast its original movies and series.

  b ZF Group is looking to monetize its automotive ball joint sensor data, which was traditionally used in height-leveling to adjust for headlight angles. The data can also be used for load monitoring, road condition monitoring, and predictive fleet maintenance requirements.

2 Taking a set of best practices and building a software platform and business around it, with examples such as:

  a Confluent is a company that leveraged the Kafka data streaming infrastructure developed at LinkedIn to build a fully managed enterprise stream processing platform.

  b Tecton, the feature store, was created by the team that developed Michelangelo, the feature store used at Uber, to enable companies to acquire state-of-the-art feature management capabilities for robust machine learning pipelines.

With today's many technology-driven companies, the product direction can get you closest to founding or leading a company.

THE BUSINESS DIRECTION

Career progress in the business direction can include titles such as director of growth, operations manager, or supply chain management.

As a DS leader, you may already be heavily involved in the operations of your product, tracking and interpreting critical aspects of the state of business. Through deep-dive analysis into conversion fall-offs and feature gaps, you may have already produced recommendations for product improvements. If you enjoy this process, what are some next steps in your career to take on more responsibilities and produce more impact?

You may consider roles such as director of growth, operations manager, or supply chain manager. These are roles at the intersection of product, sales, and data. In these roles, rather than making recommendations, you will be responsible for making the business decisions.

Your in-depth understanding of the data is an advantage in these roles. You will need to develop:

1 A deep understanding of your customers
2 A clear north star metric
3 An ability to craft a roadmap and establish a cadence for growth or operations

Like the product managers, you will need to know your customers' issues, pains, desires, and how they think to make operations decisions quickly. A clear north star metric can help you align functional teams toward common operations goals. A roadmap and an operational cadence allow efforts to be synchronized.

When you have an overarching perspective on these three areas, as the team encounters issues, your partners in engineering, product, and DS will look to you for perspectives that they may not have from within their respective domains.

The roles of director of growth, operations manager, or supply chain manager are well suited for quantitatively focused DS leaders with business operations ambitions. If you have strengths and interest in these areas, you can optimize and scale lines of business with existing foundational product/market fit to produce significant business impact.

THE ENGINEERING DIRECTION

Career progress in the engineering direction can include titles such as data engineering manager, ML manager, or ML ops manager.

As more intelligent capabilities are deployed in production, rigorous engineering processes are becoming essential for robust user experiences. For the engineering-focused DS leaders, there is extensive growth potential in the engineering direction.

Data engineering managers are responsible for orchestrating the flow of data through ingesting, processing, storing, and serving data in an organization. ML managers are responsible for specifying, implementing, launching, and recalibrating intelligent capabilities. ML operations managers are responsible for monitoring and maintaining incoming data quality and model output quality, version-controlling data and models, and optimizing launch processes.

As a DS leader, you have a firm foundation in the scientific approach and a good understanding of statistics. With experience specifying DS projects, you also have a broad understanding of business and products. You have distinct advantages in architecting and specifying ML systems to be deployed at scale. If you enjoy the process of building intelligent software features and launching them into production, the engineering direction can be a good direction to consider.

A caveat to note is that engineering functions generally spend most of their time implementing and maintaining mission-critical technologies in production. There is often less time spent on exploring and prototyping data use cases. If your aspirations include the full range of exploration and deployment responsibilities, you can look for leadership roles in organizations where you have ML engineers dedicated to your DS projects.

So there you have it—the four career growth directions for DS leaders. They include the data direction, where your responsibilities can grow in scope up to the chief data scientist or chief data officer; the product direction, where you can develop product roadmaps and take on profit-and-loss responsibilities; the business direction, where you can drive growth in a business or operate an entire business line; and the technology direction, where you can head up engineering teams to develop and optimize data and ML features and pipelines to enable a streamlined model development and productization process. Refer to these directions every few quarters to reexamine your area of interest and passion for the next stage of your career.

10.5 Reviewing the LOOP

Congratulations on working through this chapter on landscape, organization, opportunity, and practice (LOOP)! We hope this chapter can provide you with an overall industry perspective that can empower you to seek out your next play and accelerate your career. A LOOP review includes the following four items:

- *Technology landscape*—New tools or paradigms becoming available
- *Human organization*—How your teams are structured or restructured
- *Career opportunities*—The industry, company, team, role, and onboarding
- *Professional practices*—Skill sets to hire for, and your own career directions

These four items are provided to help you broaden your perspective when facing bottlenecks in your career development. You can revisit one LOOP area each month or every few quarters. Once you start doing this, you will have taken courageous steps toward forming new interpretations in your environment to assess what you can do for your career.

Table 10.5 summarizes the areas discussed in this chapter. The last column on the right is available for you to check off the areas you may already have thought deeply about. There is no judgment and no right or wrong. Feel free to leave any or all rows blank.

Table 10.5   Self-assessment areas for landscape, organization, opportunity, and practice

LOOP areas/self-assessment			?
Landscape	Monitoring the technology landscape for new architectures and best practices	<ul><li>*Data storage*—ML and analytics use cases are converging toward the data lakehouse.</li><li>*Data processing*—Stream processing is emerging as the central nervous system for business processes with automated decision-making.</li><li>*Data access*—Analytics with self-serve insights are becoming democratized.</li><li>*Model deployment*—Intelligent capability deployments are being streamlined with data/ML ops and automation.</li><li>*Data governance*—Data governance is curating data as an asset for enterprise growth rather than a regulation compliance liability.</li></ul>	

Table 10.5 Self-assessment areas for landscape, organization, opportunity, and practice *(continued)*

		LOOP areas/self-assessment	?
Organization	Navigating different organizational structures, each with its benefits and pitfalls	<ul><li>*Functional*—DS is one of many functions. Great for building expertise within the function, but can lose touch with business needs if not careful.</li><li>*Divisional*—Company is partitioned by product, geography, or market segment, where DS is distributed to each division. Great for fast-paced division-level decisions but can duplicate efforts between divisions.</li><li>*Matrix*—DS teams are reporting to a function head and a divisional head simultaneously. Structure enhances coordination across functions and divisions but has a higher communication overhead.</li><li>*Holacracy*—Promotes a hierarchy of self-managed units, or circles, where data scientists are distributed to projects. The structure is great for PoC exploration but needs to manage maintenance resources and payment of tech debts.</li></ul>	
Opportunity	Industry assessment	<ul><li>The top three industries employing data scientists are IT and software, finance, and healthcare. Industries with fast-growing DS needs include defense and space, e-learning, video games, and consumer electronics.</li></ul>	
	Company assessment	<ul><li>Company maturity is a dominating factor in the type of data and projects you can complete as a DS leader. A company's standing within its industry can determine its chance for a successful outcome.</li></ul>	
	Team assessment	<ul><li>Hiring manager maturity is a determining factor in your success. Look for patterns of advancement, not withdrawal.</li><li>Infrastructure maturity determines the reliability and velocity you can produce results.</li><li>Practice maturity determines the amount of coaching required to help the team be more productive.</li></ul>	
	Role assessment	<ul><li>Company mission, priorities, and success criteria are critical contexts for clearly defining your role with your manager.</li></ul>	
	Establish a powerful and focused 90-day plan for a new role	<ul><li>Ramp up in autonomy, mastery, and purpose in 90 days. – *Tech lead*—Focus on *mastery* to produce early wins – *Manager*—Focus on gaining *autonomy* in decisions – *Director*—Focus on clarifying *purpose* for the function – *Executive*—Listen, craft vision, align, and drive roadmaps</li></ul>	

Table 10.5 Self-assessment areas for landscape, organization, opportunity, and practice *(continued)*

LOOP areas/self-assessment		?
Practice	Skill sets you can hire for	■ More refined skill sets are emerging within DS. Depending on the project, you can hire or develop these diverse areas of expertise to meet business needs.	
	Career directions for DS leaders	■ *Data direction*—Increasing responsibilities in management ■ *Product direction*—Scaling data-driven products as a product manager and developing new products or services ■ *Business direction*—Operating and growing a line of business with responsibilities to make business decisions ■ *Engineering direction*—Architecting, developing, testing, deploying, and maintaining engineered intelligent systems	

Summary

- *Landscape* for technologies in DS has been changing quickly as new best practices are crystallized into new platforms, creating new architectures and enabling new best practices.
- *Organization* structures need to be carefully navigated when constituting a DS organization, as each structure has its benefits and pitfalls.
  - In a functional company structure, DS is one of many functions. It is great for building expertise within the function but loses touch with business needs.
  - In a divisional structure, DS is distributed to each division. It is great for fast-paced division-level decisions but can lead to duplicate efforts across divisions.
  - In a matrix structure, DS teams report to a function head and divisional head simultaneously, enhancing coordination across functions and divisions but creating higher communication overhead.
  - In a holacracy structure, data scientists are distributed to project circles. This is great for PoC exploration, but you need to stay vigilant about paying off tech debts.
- *Opportunities* to further your career can be assessed at the industry, company, team, and role level. A carefully crafted 90-day onboarding plan can powerfully launch you into a new role.
  - An industry assessment informs the growing importance of DS in your industry.
  - A company assessment evaluates a company's maturity and its standing in its industry.
  - A team assessment involves evaluating the hiring manager, the infrastructure, and existing practices. The hiring manager maturity determines the support you can expect for your success. The infrastructure maturity determines the reliability and velocity possible for producing results. The practice

maturity determines the amount of coaching required for the team to be productive.

– A role assessment includes understanding the mission, priority, and success criteria for defining your role with your manager.

– A 90-day onboarding plan can help you focus on ramping up in autonomy, mastery, and purpose, depending on the level of your DS leadership role.

■ *Practices* are the skill sets you can hire into your DS team and the career directions for you, the DS leader, as you grow.

– The skill sets you can hire into your team can tackle specific business needs. You can recognize these skill sets, acquire them for particular projects, and cross-train team members to amplify your team's strengths in these skill sets.

– As a DS leader, management, product, operations, and engineering are top directions you can grow into to increase your impact professionally.

References

[1] P. K. Illa. "Modern unified data architecture." Towards Data Science. https://towardsdata-science.com/modern-unified-data-architecture-38182304afcc

[2] M. Bornstein, M. Casado, and J. Li. "Emerging architectures for modern data infrastructure." Andreessen Horowitz. https://a16z.com/2020/10/15/the-emerging-architectures-for-modern-data-infrastructure/

[3] J. Kreps. "Every company is becoming software." https://www.confluent.io/blog/every-company-is-becoming-software/

[4] DataKitchen. "DataOps is NOT Just DevOps for Data." https://medium.com/data-ops/dataops-is-not-just-devops-for-data-6e03083157b7

[5] C. Breuel. "ML ops: Machine learning as an engineering discipline." https://towardsdata-science.com/ml-ops-machine-learning-as-an-engineering-discipline-b86ca4874a3f

[6] M. Rogati. "How not to hire your first data scientist." https://medium.com/hackernoon/how-not-to-hire-your-first-data-scientist-34f0f56f81ae

[7] E. Bernstein et al. "Beyond the holacracy hype: The overwrought claims and actual promise of the next generation of self-managed teams." *Harvard Business Review*. https://hbr.org/2016/07/beyond-the-holacracy-hype

[8] "United States Bureau of Economic Analysis, 2019 data." Dec. 22, 2020. [Online]. https://apps.bea.gov/industry/Release/XLS/GDPxInd/GrossOutput.xlsx

[9] "Career-launching companies list." Wealthfront. https://blog.wealthfront.com/career-launching-companies-list/

[10] "Global talent trends 2020." LinkedIn. [Online]. https://business.linkedin.com/talent-solutions/recruiting-tips/global-talent-trends-2020

[11] J. Chong, B. Lorica, Y. Chang, "Top Places to Work for Data Scientists: We identify organizations that will help you develop your career in data science." Gradient Flow. https://gradientflow.com/top-places-to-work-for-data-scientists/

[12] G. Moore, P. Johnson, and T. Kippola, *The Gorilla Game: Picking Winners in High Technology.* New York, NY, USA: Harper Business, 1999.

[13] L. Cohen and M. Storey. "Onboarding to a DS team." Medium. https://medium.com/data-science-at-microsoft/onboarding-to-a-data-science-team-2b735dae464

[14] D. Pink, *Drive: The Surprising Truth About What Motivates Us.* New York, NY, USA: Riverhead Books, 2009.

[15] Y. Xu, W. Duan, and S. Huang, "SQR: Balancing speed, quality and risk in online experiments," *KDD*, 2018.

[16] D. Liu. "A guide for onboarding into a new role: Six simple lessons to help you get started." https://debliu.substack.com/p/a-guide-for-onboarding-into-a-new

[17] A. Bosworth. "A Career Cold Start Algorithm." https://boz.com/articles/career-cold-start

[18] M. Mosley et al., *The DAMA Guide to the Data Management Book of Knowledge.* Basking Ridge, NJ, USA: Technics Publications, 2009.

Leading in data science and a future outlook

This chapter covers

- Clarifying four reasons why leading in DS is increasingly important
- Summarizing what we can learn when building a career
- Mastering how to practice leading in DS
- Anticipating future roles, capabilities, and responsibilities in building trust and pursuing a career

As human beings, we understand our world through what we see with our eyes, with what we detect with machines, and with reasoning, deduction, and hypotheses that can be tested against reality. DS helps us drive a quantitative understanding of the world around us through reasoning, deduction, and hypotheses that can be tested against reality. It provides a data lens with which we interpret and anticipate the ways the world works. This book aggregates the top capabilities and virtues for successfully leading efforts in DS for the purpose of better understanding and influencing our world.

094 Data science provides a data lens with which we can interpret and anticipate the ways the world works. It drives a quantitative understanding through reasoning, deduction, and hypotheses that can be tested against reality.

Leading in DS is challenging, as it involves a broad skill set that can take time to internalize. This skill set is shaped by the unique challenges of working with data and coordinating with executives, teams, and partners to make DS efforts successful.

In this final chapter, we summarize the *why*, *what*, and *how* of leading in DS, so you can reference these at various stages of your career. We also speculate about how the field may evolve in the future.

11.1 The why, what, and how of leading in DS

We have covered much ground in this book by sharing practical guidance on leading in DS. Let's step back to consider *why* learning to lead in DS is becoming increasingly important. *What* can be a framework to organize the skills necessary for leading in data science? And *how* do we put the framework into practice?

By answering these questions, you can be more purposeful in understanding the drivers behind DS leadership roles. You can recognize areas you already have strengths in, identify others' strengths, and discover potential blind spots. With these recognitions and discoveries, you can develop and strengthen your capabilities and virtues to become a better DS leader.

11.1.1 Why is learning to lead in DS increasingly important?

Why is learning to lead in DS important? As illustrated in figure 11.1, we see four main reasons:

- DS is one of the fastest-growing fields with a high demand for leaders.
- It has a unique set of challenges that make it unlike software engineering or consulting.
- Requirements are often vaguely defined, as the quality of results is hard to predict.
- Projects require broad cross-functional collaboration to produce business impact.

Figure 11.1 Four reasons why learning to lead in data science is increasingly important.

Fast growth

The number of data scientists is growing at 37% annually [1], which is creating a strong demand for DS leaders. Early traction at companies where DS projects are making a business impact is fueling this growth. 67% of companies in one survey are looking to expand their DS functions and scale their business impact [2].

As the data science field continues to be one of the highest-compensated professions [3], more talent is moving into the field. However, demand for talent is still increasing faster than the supply. Talent retention is a common challenge in the DS function.

The average tenure of a data scientist is two years. If you can create an environment for your data scientists to grow professionally, you can retain their institutional knowledge within the team for longer, and make your team significantly more efficient.

Unique challenges

DS projects operate differently from typical software engineering or consulting projects, which provide unique challenges for DS leaders. Three top differences include project team size, project uncertainty, and demonstration of value:

- *Project team size*—Typical DS projects involve 1–2 data scientists compared to 3–10 engineers collaborating to deliver an engineering goal.
- *Project uncertainty*—Data-dependent risks must be handled on top of engineering risks toward project success.
- *Project value*—Success is demonstrated through feature and recommendation deployment in production with impact quantified with A/B tests. Feature completion (as in engineering deliverables) or recommendation delivery (as in consulting milestones) are not enough for success.

These differences call for adjustments to the management of projects through a combination of agile and waterfall methodologies (discussed in section 2.2.2), the structuring of teams (discussed in section 8.1.3), and the crafting of opportunities for team member career development to maximize the retention of top talent (discussed in section 7.1.3).

Vague requirements

Interpreting business needs can be challenging for new DS leaders. Many business and function partners are not yet familiar with all the capabilities DS can bring and provide requests that may be a suboptimal framing of the problem. The responsibility is on the DS leader to ask the question behind the question to validate and refine the partner request, propose and align roadmaps, and prioritize projects rigorously, so DS projects are scoped realistically and efforts are used efficiently. This responsibility is discussed in more detail in section 2.2.1.

Broad collaboration

Nearly all successful DS projects require a team effort. Product and software engineering partners collaborate to track important events, features, and actions. Data engineering partners collaborate to create the data pipeline to load and store the data into data lakes. Data scientists collaborate to cleanse and transform the data to build data warehouses and efficiently visualize the data for insights. Where possible, data scientists are also building intelligent algorithms to anticipate and influence the future. Product and software engineering partners then collaborate to act on the insights or intelligent algorithms to improve the product or service.

DS leadership must craft and align roadmaps, identify sponsors and champions, and develop talent and partner trust to ensure the success of DS projects. The fast growth, unique challenges, vague requirements, and broad collaborations make DS leadership an essential role in a business's strategic growth.

11.1.2 What is a framework for leading in DS?

Leadership is about amplifying your capability to produce a more significant impact than can be achieved individually. It involves building an identity of *trust* with those around you, so you can influence, nurture, direct, and inspire them to produce impact.

Your identity is a characterization of you by others. This characterization allows people around you to anticipate how you think and act in various situations. You can build an identity of trustworthiness so that others are more willing to be influenced, nurtured, directed, and inspired by you.

095

> Your identity is a characterization of you by others. You can build an identity of trustworthiness so that others are more willing to be influenced, nurtured, directed, and inspired by you.

What is *trust*? We can interpret trust in three components [4]: competence, sincerity, and reliability (figure 11.2).

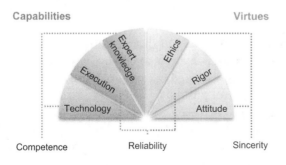

Three components of trust

Figure 11.2 The three components of trust: competence, reliability, and sincerity

Competence is the ability to produce an accomplishment. We discuss it in the *technology* and *expert knowledge* dimensions. The *technology* dimension describes the tools and frameworks in DS that you can use to lead more effectively. The *expert knowledge* dimension describes the domain knowledge in your specific industry to clarify project alignment to organizational vision and mission, account for data source nuances, and navigate structural challenges in the organization.

Sincerity is the virtue of building long-term relationships, while accomplishing your goals. We discuss it in the *ethics* and *attitude* dimensions. The *ethics* dimension involves the standards of conduct at work that enable you to avoid unnecessary and self-inflicted breakdowns. The *attitude* dimension speaks to the moods with which you approach workplace situations.

Reliability is the ability to produce accomplishments despite challenges and disruption. We discuss it in the *execution* and *rigor* dimensions. The execution dimension describes the practices required to fulfill leadership obligations. The *rigor* dimension describes the craftsmanship that allows your customers to believe the results you produce.

Competence, sincerity, and reliability are the three components necessary for generating an identity of trustworthiness for you. What if one of the three components is missing?

When you focus on competence and sincerity and neglect reliability, you can produce results and have the sincerity to align with partners to deliver but lack the skills to manage risks and overcome obstacles. You will be unlikely to consistently produce positive business impact.

When you focus on competence and reliability and neglect sincerity, you can be capable and reliable in delivering results, but lack the motivation or the positive attitude to align goals and build relationships in the process. In this case, you could be delivering DS results that are misaligned with what the business needs.

When you focus on sincerity and reliability and neglect competence, you can align goals, manage risks, and remove obstacles to do the job but lack the technical or domain knowledge to complete the project. In this case, the projects you undertake are still unlikely to succeed.

Building an identity of trustworthiness with all three components is essential for successfully leading DS. At different stages of your career, you have options to do different things. We summarize the topics discussed in this book for DS tech leads, managers, directors, and executives in figure 11.3.

What about the perspective of the experienced data scientist on the individual contributor career track? Figure 11.4 illustrates the areas discussed in this book relevant to the staff data scientist, principal data scientist, and distinguished data scientist. The areas that primarily apply to managers have been shaded and italicized. More than 80% of the topics discussed are relevant for an experienced data scientist on the individual contributor career track.

		Tech lead	Team manager	Function director	Company executive
Capabilities	**Technology**	**Framing** the problem to maximize business impact **Discovering** patterns in data **Setting** expectations for success	*Delegating projects effectively* **Managing** for consistency across models and projects **Making** build-versus-buy recommendations	**Crafting** technology roadmaps **Guiding** function to build the right things for the right people at the right time **Sponsoring and championing** promising projects	**Architecting** one- to three-year business strategies and roadmaps in data **Delivering** data-driven culture in all aspects of business processes *Structuring innovative and productive data science organizations*
	Execution	**Specifying and prioritizing** projects from vague requirements **Planning and managing** projects **Striking** a balance between trade-offs	*Building powerful teams under your supervision* **Influencing** partner teams to increase impact **Managing up** to your manager	**Delivering** consistently by managing people, processes, and platforms *Building a strong function with a clear career maps and a robust hiring process* **Supporting** executives in top company initiatives	*Infusing data science capabilities into vision and mission* *Building a strong talent pool in data science* *Clarifying your role as composer or conductor*
	Expert knowledge	**Clarifying** business context of opportunities **Accounting** for domain data source nuances **Navigating** the organizational structure	**Broadening** knowledge to multiple technical and business domains **Understanding** the fundamental domain opportunities **Assessing** ROI for prioritization, despite missing data	**Anticipating** business needs across product development stages **Applying** initial solutions rapidly against urgent issues **Driving** fundamental impact with deep domain understanding	**Identifying** differentiation and competitiveness among industry peers **Guiding** business through pivots when required *Articulating business plans for new products and services*
Virtues	**Ethics**	**Operating** in customers' best interest **Adapting** to business priorities in dynamic environments **Imparting** knowledge confidently	**Growing** the team with coaching, mentoring, and advising **Representing** data science confidently in cross-functional discussions *Contributing to and reciprocating on broader management duties*	**Establishing** project formalizations across the function **Coaching** as a social leader with interpretations, narratives, and requests **Organizing** initiatives to provide career growth opportunities	**Practicing** responsible machine learning based on ethical principles **Ensuring** the trust and safety of customers **Making** socially responsible decisions
	Rigor	**Getting clarity** on the fundamentals of scientific rigor **Monitoring** for anomalies in data and in deployment **Taking responsibility** for enterprise value	**Observing and mitigating** anti-patterns in ML and DS systems **Learning** effectively from incidents **Driving clarity** by distilling complex issues into concise narratives	**Driving** successful annual planning process **Avoiding** project planning and execution anti-patterns **Securing** commitments from partners and teams	**Creating** a productive and harmonious work environment *Accelerating the speed and increasing the quality of decisions* **Focusing** on increasing enterprise value
	Attitude	**Exhibiting** positivity and tenacity to work through failures **Being curious and collaborative** in incident response **Respecting** diverse perspectives in lateral collaborations	*Managing the maker's schedule versus the manager's schedule* *Trusting the team members to execute* **Creating** a culture of institutionalized learning	**Recognizing and promoting** diversity in your team **Practicing** inclusion in decision making **Nurturing** belonging to your function	**Demonstrating** executive presence **Establishing** team identity in industry leadership **Learning and adopting** best practices across different industries

Figure 11.3 An overview of concepts discussed for data science leadership

		Tech lead	Staff data scientist	Principal data scientist	Distinguished data scientist
Capabilities	Technology	**Framing** the problem to maximize business impact **Discovering** patterns in data **Setting** expectations for success	*Delegating projects effectively* **Managing** for consistency across models and projects **Making** build-versus-buy recommendations	**Crafting** technology roadmaps **Guiding** function to build the right things for the right people at the right time **Sponsoring and championing** promising projects	**Architecting** one- to three-year business strategies and roadmaps in data **Delivering** data-driven culture in all aspects of business processes *Structuring innovative and productive data science organizations*
	Execution	**Specifying and prioritizing** projects from vague requirements **Planning and managing** projects **Striking** a balance between trade-offs	*Building powerful teams under your supervision* **Influencing** partner teams to increase impact **Managing up** to your manager	**Delivering** consistently by managing *people*, processes, and platforms *Building a strong function with a clear career maps and a robust hiring process* **Supporting** executives in top company initiatives	*Infusing data science capabilities into vision and mission* **Building** a strong talent pool in data science *Clarifying your role as composer or conductor*
	Expert knowledge	**Clarifying** business context of opportunities **Accounting** for domain data source nuances **Navigating** the organizational structure	**Broadening** knowledge to multiple technical and business domains **Understanding** the fundamental domain opportunities **Assessing** ROI for prioritization, despite missing data	**Anticipating** business needs across product development stages **Applying** initial solutions rapidly against urgent issues **Driving** fundamental impact with deep domain understanding	**Identifying** differentiation and competitiveness among industry peers **Guiding** business through pivots when required *Articulating business plans for new products and services*
Virtues	Ethics	**Operating** in customers' best interest **Adapting** to business priorities in dynamic environments **Imparting** knowledge confidently	**Growing** the team with coaching, mentoring, and advising **Representing** data science confidently in cross-functional discussions *Contributing to and reciprocating on broader management duties*	**Establishing** project formalizations across the function **Coaching** as a social leader with interpretations, narratives, and requests **Organizing** initiatives to provide career growth opportunities	**Practicing** responsible machine learning based on ethical principles **Ensuring** the trust and safety of customers **Making** socially responsible decisions
	Rigor	**Getting clarity** on the fundamentals of scientific rigor **Monitoring** for anomalies in data and in deployment **Taking responsibility** for enterprise value	**Observing and mitigating** anti-patterns in ML and DS systems **Learning** effectively from incidents **Driving clarity** by distilling complex issues into concise narratives	**Driving** successful annual planning process **Avoiding** project planning and execution anti-patterns **Securing** commitments from partners and teams	**Creating** a productive and harmonious work environment *Accelerating the speed and increasing the quality of decisions* **Focusing** on increasing enterprise value
	Attitude	**Exhibiting** positivity and tenacity to work through failures **Being curious and collaborative** in incident response **Respecting** diverse perspectives in lateral collaborations	*Managing the maker's schedule versus the manager's schedule* *Trusting the team members to execute* **Creating** a culture of institutionalized learning	**Recognizing and promoting** diversity in your team **Practicing** inclusion in decision making **Nurturing** belonging to your function	**Demonstrating** executive presence **Establishing** team identity in industry leadership **Learning and adopting** best practices across different industries

Figure 11.4 An overview of concepts discussed for experienced data science individual contributors

Where did this framework for leading in DS come from? Pursuing an ambitious career has been part of human history for thousands of years. DS as a profession is one of many careers that have emerged over the past decade. To lead a successful career, we refer to ideas from ancient Chinese and Greek philosophers, including Confucius (551–479 BC) and Aristotle (384–322 BC) and have interpreted them for the DS field.

One core concept from Confucianist teachings [5] focuses on the career moves a person can make toward a harmonious world. Applied to practicing DS, it speaks to inspiring your industry with innovations you produce. There are eight steps toward inspiring an industry:

1   Discover the operating principles. （格物）
2   Be disciplined in getting to the heart of the truth. （致知）
3   Be principled in the standard of conduct. （诚意）
4   Maintain moods of positivity, curiosity, tenacity, and respect. （正心）
5   Cultivate one's leadership skills. （修身）
6   Nurture a team. （齐家）
7   Direct a function. （治国）
8   Inspire an industry. （平天下）

This book maps the first four steps of the Confucianist teachings to the TEE-ERA fan as the foundation necessary to lead in DS. These four steps focus on expanding our knowledge and cultivating our *selves*. They are central to each of the next four career development steps—from leading projects to leading teams, functions, and industries. These concepts are illustrated in figure 11.5.

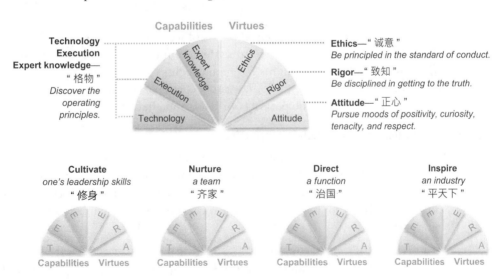

Figure 11.5   Confucianism concepts used in data science career development

Confucianism teaches that all people are capable of learning, and that failure is not a result of a lack of ability but a lack of effort. This book shares this belief and is organized as a practical field guide for your reference at different stages of your career.

096

Confucianism teaches that all people are capable of learning, and that failure is not a result of a lack of ability but a lack of effort. This book shares this belief and is organized as a practical field guide for your reference at different stages of your career.

Why do we call soft, psychosocial skills virtues? Aristotle's teachings from 2,500 years ago include a concept called *eudaimonia* (εὐδαιμονία), which is a sort of happiness and well-being worth seeking or having as part of one's career. For a person to be *eudaimon*, they need to have *virtues,* which are the necessary character traits that enable them to obtain happiness and well-being.

We see *ethics, rigor,* and *attitude* as the necessary virtues toward producing long-term positive business and social impacts. These virtues are skills that can be learned over time through practice to become habits and characters of effective DS leaders.

097

We see ethics, rigor, and attitude as the necessary skills in data science for producing long-term positive business and social impacts. We call these skills *virtues* that can be learned over time through practice to become habits and characters of effective data science leaders.

The book identifies the top practical pearls of wisdom at various career stages. It provides case studies with leadership strengths to emulate and potential blind spots for you to check on. It also highlights 101 gem insights for easy consumption and sharing. By practicing them in your work, they can become part of your identity of trustworthiness and eventually become part of your habit and character.

11.1.3　*How to use the framework in practice?*

Each chapter of this book provides a checklist of learning points for your self-assessment to help you clarify your development focus. To best use the book, we recommend a four-step process to help build your confidence, discover your blind spots, recognize resources available to you around your organization, and practice your learning:

  1　*Find your strengths.* You can use the *self-assessment* and *development focus* sections at the end of each chapter (section 4 of chapters 2–9) to recognize your leadership strength areas. This practice provides you with a narrative to build a trustworthy identity, set examples for others, and produce career accomplishments.

2 *Identify your opportunities.* Some areas described in this book may be blind spots for you. These are opportunities where you can recognize, learn, and adopt new practices. When you practice these new learnings in real-world situations, they can become effective habits and even part of your positive identity.

3 *Leverage your environment.* In most situations, your role is within a much larger organization, where there are resources you can leverage within your team or across teams and functions to amplify your strengths. Understanding who to make requests to, what requests to make, and how to make them are essential leadership skills.

4 *Put learning into practice.* With clear goals identified in the first three steps, the fourth step is to line up a roadmap and put the learning into practice one concept at a time. As with sprint planning, you can specify a one- to three-week cadence, to set goals and schedule a time to check back and evaluate progress.

There can be many concepts to learn and practice at each stage of career development. As long as you are working on something each week, you will make concrete progress on your career development.

11.2 The future outlook

DS is the quantitative approach with which we understand the past, assess the present, and anticipate the future. Without a doubt, it is a function that will continue to be essential for creating value for companies and organizations in the future. But how is the field going to evolve, and what can you do to prepare for it?

There are three trends that DS leaders can anticipate to better chart their careers:

- *Role*—Emergence of data product managers
- *Capability*—Availability of function-specific data solutions
- *Responsibility*—Instilling trust in data

Let's dive in one by one.

11.2.1 The role: The emergence of data product managers

The creation of data and intelligence-driven products often require innovations. Many of these products and features just did not exist before. They are invented by product managers working closely with data scientists based on deep empathy for customer pains, data strategies that can amplify their advantages over time, and robust business models that can capture the value created.

098

Data and intelligence-driven products are invented by product managers working closely with data scientists based on deep empathy for customer pains, data strategies that can amplify their advantages over time, and robust business models that can capture the value created.

Product managers are essential partners for data scientists in the process of exploring product/market fit. Yet only a small fraction of product managers currently have a DS background. The scarcity of data product manager talent is a significant bottleneck for companies looking to develop data and intelligence-driven products and features.

What's the difference between a data product manager and a product manager? A data product manager understands data strategy, data source intricacies, and data/model life cycles. This is on top of understanding software technologies, user experience, and business concerns required for all software product managers. With the extra knowledge in data products, data product managers can design and scope modeling and API projects and better define tracking specifications and success metrics.

In 2021, DS leaders often are called on to bridge the data and product knowledge gap. Indeed, many successful data-driven products today are developed through tight collaborations between product managers and data scientists. This is often because many software product managers do not yet have the statistics and ML background necessary to understand the capabilities, risks, and scopes of data-driven products.

In these collaborations, data scientists often take the recommender role and rely on product managers to make the final call on product directions before implementing them. The product managers are leading the process of defining useful, feasible, and valuable products [6] while balancing customer and business needs, working with executives to get resources, and making critical business and product decisions.

A source of frustration for many data scientists is when intelligence capabilities and DS methodologies are introduced in products as an afterthought. DS often gets involved only at the end of a product development cycle as product and engineering teams look to measure the success of a feature. It's no wonder that some data scientists are motivated to transition into product management, looking to take on the decision-maker role for product directions.

The situation is improving. Many data scientists with deep technical backgrounds are learning from their product manager partners and acquiring skill sets that help them to become powerful data product leaders. Many product managers are acquiring DS skill sets to understand the data product life cycles better. With the emergence of product managers with deep DS knowledge, the roles and responsibilities to successfully build data-driven products and features are shifting.

For the DS leaders who aspire to the product management role, they should know that there are skills they already have as data scientists, shared skills that overlap with product management, and new product management skills they need to develop. These skills are illustrated in figure 11.6. Let's first highlight the shared responsibilities between DS leaders and data product managers and then discuss the new skill sets required to succeed as a data product manager. We will then examine the implications of the emerging data product management role for data scientists and their organizations.

Data product management

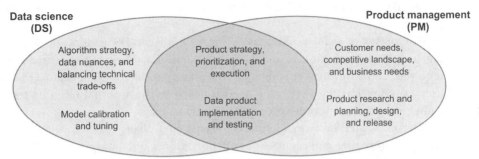

Figure 11.6 The data product manager's skill set combines the data science and PM skill sets

SHARED RESPONSIBILITIES AND NEW SKILLS

Product strategy, prioritization, and execution are the three main responsibilities of product leaders [7]. Adam Nash, former president and CEO of Wealthfront, articulated two product strategy questions a great product leader can clarify:

1 What game are we playing?
2 How do we keep score?

Getting these two questions right can quickly align a cross-functional team to focus in the same direction and make trade-offs in executing the most impactful projects. DS leaders already have the skills to define a data product's vision, quantify the value provided to the customer, and establish a company's differentiation from its competitors.

The prioritization challenges often emerge from a surplus of good ideas. As a result, brutal prioritization can distinguish successful companies with clarity on what to execute first. DS leaders already have tools such as RICE, which uses reach, impact, confidence, and efforts to prioritize projects. However, balancing broader concerns about customer needs, the competitive landscape, and business needs are new skills to acquire. For execution, making time/benefit trade-offs, using analytics to understand product performance, and measuring success are strong skills of a DS leader.

Product managers have essential skills to oversee the product life cycle with steps in research and planning, design, implementation and testing, and release [8]. DS leaders will need to develop these skills to work with or become product managers.

Products and features start with *research and planning*, which determine what to build next. The ideas can be classified into three buckets: metrics movers, customer requests, and customer delights [9]. Metrics movers are the company-focused features, customer requests are features customers are actively requesting, and customer delights are features customers haven't asked for but would delight them to have. Being able to drive a portfolio of features from these buckets with executive and engineering alignment is a crucial set of skills to acquire.

The *design* step involves specifying the user experience and defining the features and functions of a product. Crafting the goals, use cases, requirements, wireframes, and describing all possible feature states, while taking care of accessibility and security can be daunting for a DS leader. These are new skills to acquire to become a data product manager.

The *implement and test* steps may be more familiar to DS leaders and include defining technical specifications and acceptance criteria, clarifying specifications where required, and adjusting schedules when a feature is delayed. For features focused on user experience, DS leaders may need to learn to run internal usability tests before launching online experiments to identify bugs to fix.

The *release* step involves a launch checklist, identifying teams to support the product, and preparing emergency shut-off procedures for data pipeline or production issues. These are often new skills that DS leaders will need to develop.

IMPLICATIONS FOR DS LEADERS

When more data product managers become available, a DS leader can focus more on the people, processes, and platforms of running a DS function. This focus is centered on ensuring the trustworthiness of data analysis and predictions and empower the company to be more data driven in its decision processes.

With more data product managers, product knowledge will still be essential for DS leaders when seeking alignment in cross-functional collaborations. We may start seeing data product managers inviting the DS perspective earlier in the product development process, strategically setting up project phases based on available data, and planning with adequate anticipation of data risks in project scheduling.

IMPLICATIONS FOR THE DS FIELD

This emergence of DS product managers is likely to be gradual for two reasons. There is still a scarcity of data scientists, and only a limited number of them are interested in developing into product managers. More professionals are working in product management, but the technical foundation of DS is deep and can take significant effort for one to learn.

One likely short-term solution is to create a technical data product manager role modeled after the technical product managers for software projects. In some companies, the product development role is split between the product managers and technical product managers (TPM), where the more business-oriented product manager focuses on research, planning, and release. In contrast, the more technically-oriented TPM focuses on design, implementation, and testing.

The split product management roles can be a formal approach to bridge the data product manager talent gap in the short term. Many DS leaders are currently stepping up to fill this gap in the absence of a formal technical data product manager role. As companies and teams grow, the data product manager role can provide a more precise set of responsibilities for tackling strategic projects.

Going forward, the role of the data product manager will be increasingly important. Many products can be transformed through data-driven innovations, and many function-specific data solutions are being defined and deployed by data product managers.

11.2.2 *The capability: The availability of function-specific data solutions*

DS capabilities have broad applications across many functions in a company. When successful, a DS team will receive requests from all lines of business and functions to assess how quantitative techniques can help.

For any business, there are areas of core competencies and areas of marginal practices. As an example, for an SaaS enterprise software company, intelligent features in its product offering are core competencies. Marketing conversion, sales analytics, and financial forecasting are marginal practices.

Some DS leaders choose to focus on collecting low-hanging fruit in the marginal practices first at the expense of developing more intelligent core competencies. Others choose to focus on developing the core competencies of the business and neglect the marginal practices.

In an environment where there is a lack of mature third-party function-specific data solutions available, the focus on collecting low-hanging fruit first makes sense. A DS leader can quickly produce early wins in improving operations in marginal practices and leverage the trust built up for deeper cross-function collaborations.

As more function-specific data solutions become available, identifying and integrating third-party data solutions can produce value faster than internally developed solutions. With the DS resources freed up, placing bets in a company's core competencies can have higher returns over the long term.

Fortunately, a generation of DS best practices are emerging to serve marginal practices. These best practices for marginal functions are being crystallized into independent data product offerings.

> **NOTE** This proliferation of data product offerings is partly enabled by the data product managers we discussed in section 11.2.1, who are taking the entrepreneurial steps to build new companies by crystallizing function-specific best practices in tools tailored for specific marginal practices in companies.

Let's look at two examples—one for the marketing function and one for the sales function. These two examples have different characteristics, but both attempt to cover the entire data stack, from data aggregation to final insights, in a domain narrow enough to be meaningful.

MARKETING-SPECIFIC DATA SOLUTIONS

Providing data insight in marketing is challenging. The metrics involved are not complex, but aggregating data from the diverse advertising platforms is a marketing department pain point. While the top advertising platforms, such as Google Ads, Bing, and Facebook Ads, may provide the volume of leads, they are often priced at a premium. You may use an affiliate network or drive engagement with email marketing campaigns. Each may have a different portal for their platform-specific data. Even a mid-size company may experiment with 20–50 advertising platforms at a time.

Pulling data from each of the platforms can be repetitive busywork for reporting purposes. Other than manually exporting reports, each platform can have different conventions for field names that must be normalized. For example, your advertising spend on Twitter is reported as "spend," on Facebook it is "amount spent," and on Google Ads it is "cost."

Even with the data collected and normalized, there are still the challenges of attributing revenue to advertising spend and computing return on advertising spend (ROAS) metrics across time periods and currencies. These challenges make it difficult to keep up-to-date reports on marketing performance, often resulting in non-optimal marketing budget allocation or over/under spending each month. While such challenges can be daunting for any company to solve for a marginal practice like marketing, they can be excellent challenges for an independent technology company to focus on.

Funnel.io is one such company. It provides a platform to centralize advertising data from hundreds of sources, enabling automated export and download as frequently as on an hourly basis, and automatically normalizes data fields such as the marketing spend across platforms. It can then attribute advertising cost with sales data for specific industry verticals such as e-commerce and group campaigns across multiple platforms, and then present the insights on data dashboards.

In essence, it is an integrated solution that solves data ingestion, transformation, load, and some analysis processes. It even has some elementary dashboarding capabilities. The automatic normalization allows you to have a single source of truth for your marketing data with no coding required. Most importantly, you can export the cleansed data into the data warehouse of your choice. Your analysts and data scientists can use the exported data to perform additional analysis and processing, so you don't have to load sensitive information into the Funnel.io platform.

A timely assessment of marketing spends can be highly valuable for high-growth companies with millions of dollars of advertising spend each month. It can be well worth the cost of integrating such a marketing-specific data solution.

SALES-SPECIFIC DATA SOLUTION

Enterprise field sales is an area that can produce a high business impact. The process can be complex, especially for products and services with over US$100,000 of revenue per customer per year. A deal can require multi-month sales processes from lead qualification to closing.

Companies commonly use customer relationship management (CRM) software to track these processes. Aggregating deal status from the CRM to produce a dashboard is not complex from a technology perspective. The challenging part is ensuring that sales professionals are promptly updating the deal statuses in the CRM systems.

Sales leaders must have an up-to-date understanding of the sales pipeline and any risks that could prevent them from accomplishing quarterly sales goals. Revenue predictability is especially important for public companies that value delivering on earnings guidance. Sales leaders often resort to one-on-one calls with each salesperson to assess the closing likelihood of each deal to understand the team's standing within the quarter. This can be a painful process for everyone involved.

So why are sales professionals not updating the CRM in a timely fashion? Many of them are under tremendous pressure to make their sales numbers. Updating CRM entries manually for internal reporting is often a secondary concern. The laborious time spent in CRM data entry cuts into the time needed for selling. The resulting incompleteness of data in CRMs makes applying data-driven solutions for sales forecasting extremely difficult.

Fortunately, AI and machine learning-enabled *automatic activity capturing* can help mitigate the manual data entry bottleneck. A new breed of companies is emerging to log sales interactions from calendars and emails into the CRM automatically. Examples of these companies include Salesforce (Einstein Activity Capture), People.ai, Groove, and Zero Keyboard.

The main innovation is in the ingestion of new data sources, such as sales professionals' calendars and emails. The extract, transform, and load processes for these new data sources involve entity recognition and matching to extract structured interactions from unstructured data between sales representatives and prospects. You can then perform analytics on the captured activities in a structured form to more reliably predict revenue outlook toward quarterly goals. When the sales team subscribes to a particular sales methodology, data from activity capturing can provide indicators for reaching specific milestones in the sales process and can even be used for sales coaching.

Activity capturing is an example of AI and ML techniques to mitigate the manual data collection bottleneck. Solutions such as Salesforce Einstein Activity Capture and People.ai handle the entire data pipeline to provide the current state, future outlook, and potential coaching to prescribe and guide behavior in the domain of sales. Such techniques are not limited to sales processes. They can also be effective for the hiring process, where closing means bringing talent onboard.

FUNCTION-SPECIFIC SOLUTION EVALUATION

As function-specific DS products and services emerge as third party solutions, they can provide intelligence capabilities for companies' marginal practices with economies of scale that cannot be easily duplicated in individual companies.

From a company's perspective, there are several factors to consider when selecting a solution, including time to deploy, process changes, and solution extensibility. This is illustrated in figure 11.7 and the following list.

Time to deploy	Process change	Solution extensibility
Time from contract signing to full deployment. The faster the process, the less friction and risk to adopt a function-specific data solution.	The smaller the process change from stakeholders required, the faster the time-to-value. For full benefit of the solution, some process change can occur over time.	The solution should enable the exporting of data to allow for additional processing to happen external to the solution.

Figure 11.7   Three evaluation criteria for function-specific data solutions

- *Time-to-deploy*—The time to deploy is often measured from contract signing to making the DS solution available to users. For marketing-specific data solutions, the data sources originate from outside the enterprise. Their aggregation through user authentication does not involve any engineering efforts.

  In contrast, the data sources for sales-specific solutions originate from within the enterprise and can include access to people's email accounts and calendars. That requires a higher degree of trust and significantly more engineering effort to integrate. The friction in the adoption process can limit the velocity of a company's growth. At the same time, deep integration also has the benefit of making a solution less easily displaced once a customer chooses to deploy them.

- *Process changes*—To deploy the function-specific data solution, any required process change for the stakeholders can become friction for adoption. For the above marketing-specific solution, no behavior change is required to deploy the solution. The always-up-to-date marketing reports can drive further marketing channel optimization in the stakeholder's own time frame.

  For a sales-specific solution enabled by activity capturing, no behavior change is necessary from the sales professionals. There would be a learning process for sales managers to understand how to interpret and use the captured activities for sales improvements. When captured activities are presented through a sales framework such as BANT [10] or MEDDIC [11], the technology change can be rolled out as part of a process change in the organization.

- *Solution extensibility*—One concern for using a third-party, function-specific data solution is that your functions become standardized with little room for differentiation among industry competitors. That's when industry best practices in data solutions become the new industry standards.

  Data solution vendors can counter this concern by allowing data to be exported to data warehouses for further processing and enrichment. For example, Funnel.io enables the aggregated, normalized, attributed, and transformed data to be exported out to a data warehouse. Your analysts and data scientists can then process the exported data with other data sources to produce deeper cross-functional insights.

099 Third party function-specific data science products and services can provide intelligence capabilities for companies' marginal practices with economies of scale that cannot be easily duplicated in individual companies. You can evaluate their time to deploy, process changes required, and solution extensibility before adoption.

Function-specific solutions can be evaluated based on the time-to-deploy, process-change, and extensibility characteristics to allow best practices to be adopted across the industry. This trend empowers companies to focus DS resources on core products and services to increase their innovation velocity.

11.2.3 *The responsibility: Instilling trust in data*

In a future where product managers are intimately familiar with data strategy, and function-specific data solutions are readily available for marginal functions, what become the core responsibilities of the DS function?

We anticipate that the DS function will take on two main responsibilities. One is to build the data-driven capabilities in a company's core product to drive customers' trust in the company. The other is to maintain the trust and integrity of data usage in the organization. Figure 11.8 illustrates these two responsibilities.

Building the core product	**Maintaining trust and integrity of data**
Working with executives and product managers to focus data science capabilities toward improving the key benefits that customers can experience when using the company's product.	Maintaining a single source of truth for important metrics across third-party data solutions will be increasingly important. Key decisions must be made when selecting and integrating these solutions.

Figure 11.8   The two main responsibilities of DS: Core product and maintaining trust

BUILDING THE DATA-DRIVEN CAPABILITIES FOR A COMPANY'S CORE PRODUCT

The core product is a concept that describes the benefit a customer derives from using a company's product. It is a concept in contrast to the actual product and the augmented product. For example, the core product of a car is a mode of transportation that can quickly and safely take you from point A to point B. The actual product is the physical car with properties such as the mode of propulsion, size, trim, and price. The augmented products for a car include payment options, warranty, insurance, and maintenance packages. For the DS leader, building data-driven capabilities for the core product means working with executives and product managers to focus the aggregation, processing, analysis, and prediction capabilities toward improving the key benefits that customers can experience.

Continuing the automotive example, Tesla has more than one million cars on the road and has accumulated more than three billion miles of autonomously driven miles as of 2020. The company is well-known for its ability to log, store, and aggregate vast amounts of road conditions from its cars to help improve its autonomous driving algorithms. For low-frequency events, like detecting heavily occluded stop signs, Tesla is able to leverage its cars on the road to aggregate examples to train its algorithms. This involves labeling and actively learning from the aggregated examples and using the examples in the test set to qualify newer versions of its algorithms. The ability to improve its autonomous driving algorithms directly improves Tesla's core product, which is how it can quickly and safely take passengers from point A to point B. This type of data strategy is what DS leaders are responsible for in order to improve the company's core product over time.

In another example, in the financial services industry, the core product can be defined as the process of building a relationship that can expand to customers' different areas of financial needs. SoFi is a fintech company that was founded with a business model to refinance student loans. Once it has built a relationship with customers who have successfully completed their education and are gainfully employed, it expands services to provide mortgages, personal loans, and car loans; and, later, to wealth management, insurance, checking accounts, and debit cards to serve customers' everyday financial needs.

We anticipate that DS will be increasingly applied to companies' core product areas, so choosing an industry domain early and accumulating domain knowledge will be crucial for DS leaders to be competitive in the future.

100   Data science will be increasingly applied to companies' core product areas, so choosing an industry domain early and accumulating domain knowledge will be crucial for data science leaders to be competitive in the future.

MAINTAINING THE TRUST AND INTEGRITY OF DATA USAGE IN THE ORGANIZATION

In a future where there is an increasing number of function-specific data solutions for marginal practices, selecting and integrating the right solutions can accelerate your company's growth velocity. Integrating function-specific data solutions affects more than your technical architecture. They have real implications on the people, processes, and platforms for the whole company.

Selecting and integrating a third-party data solution means the DS organization can serve more data needs with a smaller team. Function-specific data solutions often crystallize industry best practices into a data platform for the functions they target, including marketing, sales, customer services, human resources, and finance. Many function-specific dashboards and predictive models are readily available on these platforms and can be directly used by the function partner.

Does this make DS involvement redundant in these functions? We believe the opposite is true. There is likely more DS involvement for maintaining a single source of truth for important metrics across third-party data solutions.

101   Integrating function-specific data solutions is likely to require more data science involvement for maintaining a single source of truth for important metrics across multiple third-party data solutions and internal data infrastructures.

When you have multiple third-party data solutions integrated, you will need to determine and manage a single source of truth for business-critical data and metrics. The third-party data solutions can overlap in their offerings. Having a single metric show up with different values in different tools invites confusion and breaks partner trust. Data catalogs, peer-reviewed data pipelines, version-controlled feature stores, and data flow scripts are essential processes for maintaining a single source of truth for key metrics. When third-party data solutions produce unexpected results, data scientists need to diagnose the failures and implement mitigating solutions.

As operations within a function become efficient with the function-specific data solutions, cross-functional insights become more critical. Examples of cross-functional insights include calibrating the return on advertising spend (ROAS) across marketing channels, or estimating support cost associated with different sales channels and customer types. These are critical executive insights that require smooth coordination between functions. With the pressure on maintaining the trust and integrity of data usage, we anticipate DS leadership positions will become increasingly important in the future.

Summary

- *Why?* DS is a fast-growing field, with unique challenges different from software engineering and consulting. DS often deals with vague requirements and data uncertainties, and it requires cross-functional collaboration to produce impact.
- *What?* Success depends on building trust with competence, sincerity, and reliability. There are opportunities to cultivate leadership skills, nurture teams, direct functions, and inspire industries.
- *How?* To grow your career, you can find your strengths, build your confidence, identify your opportunities, and discover your blind spots; leverage your manager, team, and partners; and practice your learnings so they become habits and part of your character.
- *The future outlook* speculates on the trends in the role, capability, and responsibility of DS in organizations going forward.
- *Role*—With the emergence of data product managers taking more responsibilities for the feasibility, usability, and value of the data initiatives, DS leaders will likely focus more on the design, implementation, and testing of data products.
- *Capability*—As more function-specific data solutions become available, they capture and democratize industry best practices to serve marginal business functions. These solutions will allow internal DS teams to focus on the core product.
- *Responsibilities*—DS priorities will focus on delivering intelligence in the core product across the entire data life cycle, maintaining a single source of truth for metrics across the function-specific data solutions, and providing cross-functional insights.

References

[1] "2020 emerging jobs report." LinkedIn. https://business.linkedin.com/content/dam/me/business/en-us/talent-solutions/emerging-jobs-report/Emerging_Jobs_Report_U.S._FINAL.pdf

[2] J. DuBois. "The data scientist shortage in 2020." https://quanthub.com/data-scientist-shortage-2020/

[3] "2020 Salaries and Demographic Trends for Data Scientists & Analytics Pros." Burtch Works. https://www.burtchworks.com/2020/08/26/2020-salaries-and-demographic-trends-for-data-scientists-analytics-pros/

[4] T. Hecht, *Aji: An IR#4 Business Philosophy*, The Aji Network Intellectual Properties, Inc., 2019.

[5] Zengzi, "DaXue (大学) - The great learning." Chinese Text Project. https://ctext.org/liji/da-xue/ens

[6] M. Cagan, *Inspired: How to Create Tech Products Customers Love*, 2nd ed., New York, NY, USA: Wiley, 2017.

[7] A. Nash. "Be a great product leader." Psychohistory. https://adamnash.blog/2011/12/16/be-a-great-product-leader

[8] G. L. McDowell and J. Bavaro, *Cracking the PM Interview: How to Land a Product Manager Job in Technology*, CareerCup, 2013.

[9] A. Nash. "Guide to product planning: Three feature buckets," Psychohistory. https://adamnash.blog/2009/07/22/guide-to-product-planning-three-feature-buckets/

[10] "BANT opportunity identification criteria." IBM. https://www-2000.ibm.com/partnerworld/flashmovies/html_bp_013113/html_bp_013113/bant_opportunity_identification_criteria.html

[11] "About MEDDICC." Meddicc. https://meddicc.com/page/about/

epilogue

The field of data science is evolving quickly! Yet the fundamentals for developing a career have existed for thousands of years. In writing this book about progressing careers in data science, we reflect that leading in data science means much more than wielding the technology as a hammer searching for nails. It is also not just about getting promoted to the next rung of the corporate ladder. Leading in data science involves the compassion to feel the pains of our stakeholders, including managers, teams, partners, and customers, with the willingness and readiness to act to relieve such pains through data science.

To be compassionate, the priority is to listen. As Epictetus (50–135 AD), the Greek philosopher, said, "We have two ears and one mouth so that we can listen twice as much as we speak." We hope you can use the concepts from this book to better listen and comprehend stakeholders' pains, and use your superpower in data science to address those challenges.

Time is of the essence. In 2021, the average life expectancy in the developed world is around 80 years. Counted in days, that is just under 30,000 in a lifetime. If you were to start your first full-time job at 22 years old, you would already be 8,000 days into your 30,000 days' journey on this Earth. Our goal in writing this book is to help you accelerate your career growth through the next 100 to 1,000 days, so you can effectively get to where you want to be in your career sooner.

We want to thank you for spending some of your precious time reading this book. We have spent quite a few of our 30,000 days writing to share our experience in leading data science with you. We sincerely hope that these frameworks, techniques, and examples can help you boost your career growth, and there will be more time to pursue your passion.

It has been a privilege for us to play a part in inspiring you to do the best work of your career and in maximizing your potential to make a significant positive impact in the world with data science. If you found the book useful, please share your learning on social media. We would love to hear from you!

index